Public Speaking
in a Diverse Society

Media Edition

Patricia Kearney
California State University, Long Beach

Timothy G. Plax
California State University, Long Beach

THOMSON

Australia · Canada · Mexico · Singapore · Spain · United Kingdom · United State

THOMSON
™

Public Speaking
Kearney / Plax

Custom Editor:
Robert Tessman

Sr. Project Coordinator:
K.A. Espy

Cover Design:
Krista Pierson

Project Development Editor:
Nathan Anderson

Pre-Media Services Supervisor:
Dan Plofchan

Cover Image:

Marketing Coordinators:
Lindsay Annett and Sara Mercurio

Rights and Permissions Specialist:
Kalina Hintz

Compositor:
Thomson Corp.

Production/Manufacturing Supervisor:
Donna M. Brown

Senior Prepress Specialist:
Kim Fry

Printer:
BR Printers

For permission to use material from this text or product, contact us by:
Tel (800) 730-2214
Fax (800) 730 2215
www.thomsonrights.com

Public Peaking / Kearney / Plax – Third Edition
ISBN 0-759-35778-1

In memory of Gail A. Sorensen—
special friend and colleague who happened to care about students

And for our parents and daughter, Kerry.

●

For even the most successful business executives, political leaders, and entertainers, the process of giving a speech can be a frightening and humbling experience. As speech communication teachers and researchers, we have spent our professional lives trying to understand the complexities involved in standing up before an audience and saying "a few words." Over the years, we have worked with thousands of individuals, teaching them how to prepare and deliver a speech. We've also spent a great deal of effort researching and writing about this process. One of the most important observations we've made is that for speakers to be effective, they must learn how to manage their fears and anxieties about speaking. In this book, we tell students how to do that. We have also learned that speakers today must be able to adapt to culturally diverse audiences. Unless they can speak to people who are different from themselves, they are likely to be ineffective with contemporary audiences. More than anything else, these observations led us to develop our own approach to teaching public speaking.

Our approach is unique in the way it teaches students to be more inclusive in their public communication. We believe our approach is suited to the very real needs and concerns of our students today. No other text, in our opinion, offers a fuller appreciation and understanding of the critical issues facing speakers in today's culturally diverse society.

OUR MAJOR GOALS

We had two main objectives in writing this book. Our first was to present the most important principles and skills of public speaking in a clear and readable manner. Our second was to frame this discussion of public speaking within a multicultural perspective. With these goals in mind, we hope to help students become more effective public speakers in a culturally diverse environment.

Goal 1: To Teach Principles and Skills of Public Speaking

To achieve our first goal, we present a practical, research-based discussion of the process of public speaking. We take the position that public speaking is a lot like normal conversation. Effective speakers are those who appear natural and spontaneous—even though public speaking is generally more formal, planned, and organized than other communication exchanges. Good speakers also regard the audience as more than a remote collection of faces; instead, they are able to relate to audience members one-on-one, as unique individuals. Our discussion of public speaking is framed around our communication-based model of public speaking, which includes the source (speaker), message (speech), channel (face-to-face or via media), receivers (audience), feedback (audience response), and context (time, place, and occasion).

For each part of the speech process—from audience analysis to speech delivery—we provide students with the theoretical background they need to understand the basis for the practical strategies we advise. Building on this theoretical foundation, we include a wealth of strategies and exercises to help students develop their public speaking skills and become more effective and confident speakers. Skills-related information is found both in the text and in special highlighted boxes (see the section titled "Pedagogical Features and Learning Aids").

Goal 2: To Teach Public Speaking from a Multicultural Perspective

Our second goal was more challenging. Giving serious consideration to cultural diversity in a public speaking text represents a new approach to the teaching of this subject. Although most residents of the United States participate in mainstream American culture, each of us brings a unique cultural background to our communication exchanges. These cultural divisions can create special challenges for public speakers who want to communicate accurately and effectively.

Many students of public speaking are taught that what works for a speaker or audience that is predominantly white and Anglo will be similarly effective for all speakers and audiences. We know from both our review of the intercultural research and our own experiences as speech communication teachers and researchers that this is not true. Speakers and audiences interact in different ways depending on their unique cultural backgrounds, and to assume that all speakers and audiences should act and respond in the same ways ignores our rich cultural mix. To ignore or give only token attention to the impact of cultural diversity on public speaking is to be ineffective as a public speaker.

The title of this book, *Public Speaking in a Diverse Society*, reflects our commitment to move beyond a generic approach to the teaching of public speaking to one that reflects the cultural diversity of the United States. This attention to cultural diversity has been an integral part of our approach from the start, and it pervades the entire text. Cultural diversity is also treated in a separate chapter (Chapter 3). We consider the impact of cultural diversity in each step of the speech preparation process, including the selection of speech topics, organizational structures, types of evidence, and logical or emotional appeals. We examine how cultural background affects the speaker's level of communication apprehension, use of body language—including eye contact and gestures—and use of words and phrases,

repetition, and other rhetorical devices that affect delivery. And we consider how audience expectations and responses may be tied to cultural affiliation.

In looking at the effects of cultural diversity on public speaking, we focus on co-cultural groups living in the United States; we do not deal with international communication. We limit our discussion of cultural diversity to the six largest ethnic co-cultures in the United States—Euroamerican, African American, Latino, Asian American, Native American, and Middle Eastern American. We also consider gender co-cultures—females and males—which are embedded in all other co-cultures. The communication styles of these eight co-cultures are described in detail in Chapter 3, and they provide a basis for much of the discussion and many of the examples in other chapters. When appropriate, and where relevant research is available, the impact of other cultural affiliations on public speaking is also described, including those based on sexual orientation, age, and geographic region. Our discussion of the communication styles of co-cultural groups is based on research done on these groups and, where little research is available, on our own extension of studies on international communication patterns.

We would like to stress that *this book is intended first and foremost as a text on public speaking*. It is not a book about cultural pluralism, political correctness, ethnocentrism, or intercultural communication. That's not to say that we do not consider these important issues in our discussions of public speaking. But we do not intend to be sidetracked with personal, social, or political agendas. We want to teach students to recognize cultural diversity and respond or adapt appropriately and sensitively when preparing and delivering public presentations. Culture, then, becomes important to our teaching of public speaking when it makes a difference in how speakers speak and how audience members respond.

CHANGES TO THE MEDIA EDITION

Based on the feedback from many instructors who used the first edition, we have incorporated a number of changes into this edition that we believe strengthen the book.

- **Refined coverage of culture:** The cultural coverage (especially in Chapter 3) has been refined to teach students to recognize and adapt to cultural differences in communication without stereotyping.
- **Expanded coverage of persuasion:** The coverage of persuasive speaking has been significantly

expanded with the addition of Chapter 13, "Generating Arguments." This new chapter includes material on deductive and inductive reasoning, the Toulmin model, common patterns of reasoning, and strategies for evaluating the soundness of arguments.

- **Streamlined organization:** The first-edition chapters on speaker self-presentation and ethics are combined into a single chapter in this edition. Chapter 5, "Being a Credible and Ethical Speaker," includes coverage of the process of self-presentation, methods for establishing speaker credibility, and the ethical obligations of public speakers.

- **New coverage of the Internet:** Chapter 8, "Selecting and Researching Your Topic," now includes coverage of how to use the World Wide Web to research speech topics. Guidelines for how to evaluate information from the Internet are also presented.

- **New material on presentation software:** Chapter 17, "Using Visual Aids," has been expanded to include information on how to use computers and PowerPoint and other presentation software programs to create visual aids and enhance presentations.

- **New examples and speeches:** New examples and sample student speeches are included throughout this edition.

CONTENT AND ORGANIZATION

Public Speaking in a Diverse Society is divided into five parts. The three chapters in Part I, "A Multicultural Approach to Public Speaking," lay the foundation for understanding the process of public speaking. In this part, we set forth our communication-based model of public speaking, which includes a focus on the impact of cultural diversity; we provide an overview of the steps involved in preparing a basic speech; and we conclude with a discussion of the influence of culture on public speaking.

Part II, "A Focus on the Speaker," contains two chapters designed to help students cope with communication apprehension and build confidence as speakers, boost their credibility with audiences, and make informed decisions about their ethical obligations as speakers.

In Part III, "A Focus on the Audience," we devote one chapter to analyzing and adapting to diverse audiences and another chapter to listening. The latter chapter focuses on those listening responsibilities that speakers and audience members share.

Part IV, "Preparing the Text of Your Speech," discusses the nuts and bolts of selecting and researching a speech topic, organizing and outlining a speech, and crafting motivating introductions and conclusions. Separate chapters are devoted to the preparation of two common but important speech types: speeches to inform and speeches to persuade. For both speech types, we give serious attention to the rules and strategies that will increase audience learning and understanding, as well as effect attitude and/or behavior change. A new chapter extends this section by looking at how arguments and evidence can be used, strengthened, and evaluated.

In Part V, "A Focus on Speech Delivery," we offer strategies to help students make every word and gesture in their speeches count. We encourage students to develop their own unique rhetorical style. We provide guidelines for using visual aids effectively. And, to conclude the text, we look at a variety of special occasion speeches and group presentations that students are likely to encounter during their personal and professional lives.

We don't want to describe each chapter in detail here, but there are several we would like to highlight:

- Chapter 3, "The Influence of Culture on Public Speaking," describes the ways in which culture influences communication in general and public speaking in particular. Eight unique co-cultural styles of speaking are discussed in detail. Students learn not only how culture influences communication but also why understanding these influences contributes to more effective public speaking.

- Chapter 4, "Developing Confidence: Coping with Your Fears About Public Speaking," gives students a variety of strategies for dealing with public speaking anxiety. It describes how cultural background can affect communication apprehension and offers advice on how English as a second language (ESL) speakers can overcome their anxiety about speaking before a group.

- Chapter 5, "Being a Credible and Ethical Speaker," provides students with a framework for establishing their credibility as speakers and for making ethical decisions about speaking publicly. It shows students how to communicate, both verbally and nonverbally, to be perceived as credible, ethical speakers.

- Chapter 9, "Organizing and Outlining Your Speech," presents the more typical linear organizational speech patterns (topical, problem-solution, cause and effect, spatial, and chronological), but it also introduces configural ways of organizing a speech (web, narrative, multiple perspectives, and problem–no solution). Sample outlines and speech abstracts help students become familiar with both linear and configural structures.

- Chapter 13, "Generating Arguments," includes coverage of deductive and inductive reasoning, the Toulmin model, and common patterns of reasoning (by example, by analogy, by cause, by sign, and by authority). Common errors in reasoning and strategies for evaluating the soundness of arguments are also discussed.

- Chapter 16, "Developing Your Own Rhetorical Style," describes personal rhetorical styles suited to public speaking and encourages students to develop their own particular style of speaking. Masculine and feminine speaking styles are given special attention.

PEDAGOGICAL FEATURES AND LEARNING AIDS

Public Speaking in a Diverse Society contains a variety of features designed to attract and hold students' attention and highlight important principles and skills. Four types of boxes are included:

- **Speaking Out** boxes showcase interviews with students and professionals. The interviewees talk about how they've dealt successfully with different public speaking challenges and offer advice to novice speakers. Many of the interviewees describe how their cultural background has affected their style of communication and their public speaking experiences.

- **Building Your Skills** boxes present practical tips and strategies that allow students to easily apply what they've learned in the text to their own speeches. Examples include strategies for reducing communication apprehension, adapting to different audiences, and increasing listening effectiveness.

- **Assessing Yourself** boxes help students evaluate their knowledge about effective public speaking, pinpoint their strengths and weaknesses as speakers and audience members, and gain insight into their individual styles of communicating. These activities include evaluating one's level of communication apprehension, assessing personal ethics and values, and determining whether one's style of communicating promotes verbal and nonverbal immediacy.

- **A Closer Look** boxes highlight examples and topics of special interest. These boxes examine such issues as plagiarism, leading questions, and patterns of faulty reasoning.

Additional features are designed to facilitate teaching and learning:

- **Learning objectives** open each chapter, providing students with a quick preview of the most important points.

- **Chapter summaries** provide students with a concise review and a way to make sure that they have grasped the most important concepts.

- **Questions for Critical Thinking and Review** give students the opportunity to develop their critical thinking skills and to delve more deeply into some of the issues raised in the chapter.

Patricia Kearney

If anyone had told me 20 years ago that I would be researching, teaching, and writing a book on public speaking, I would have said, "No way! Not! No how!" I remember my first public speaking course in college: I was so scared, so nervous, I don't know how I managed to get through the course. And yet, because of my overwhelming fear, I wanted to learn more about how to manage communication apprehension. Over the years I've been able to successfully do that—and to teach others how to manage their fears about communicating as well. I wish I knew then what I know now. Because of my own early experiences with communication apprehension, I am probably more empathetic with beginning student speakers. No one need remain a victim of his or her fears. There is much an individual can do to become an effective, confident speaker.

Pat Kearney graduated with her doctorate (Ed.D.) from West Virginia University, having worked with Jim McCroskey. She has done considerable research in communication apprehension, but she is best known for her research on teacher power and student resistance in the classroom, and more recently, faculty/student mentoring. She has published over 50 research articles and 3 books and presented over 60 conference papers. Pat is currently Professor of Communication Studies at California State University, Long Beach, and Director of the Teaching Associates in that department. She teaches and directs over 1,000 students each semester in public speaking and interpersonal communication.

Timothy G. Plax

When I was 16, I worked part-time selling shoes. I discovered I was pretty good at it. Meeting people for the first time and carrying on extended conversations with them seemed very natural to me. A few years later, I was asked to give my first speech in a required course at El Camino Community College. That experience didn't seem quite so natural! Apparently, the formality of the public speaking situation changed the way I talked. I began to wonder why I could so easily communicate one-on-one, but found speaking more difficult in front of a large group. I didn't realize it at the time, but eventually I discovered that this was a significant issue in the study of communication. After 25 years as a speech communication researcher, I have much to say about what those differences are. Public speaking is a highly complex activity; however, with effort, understanding, and a lot of practice, anyone can learn to appear "natural" when speaking before a large group.

Tim Plax graduated with a Ph.D. in Speech Communication from the University of Southern California, where he worked with Ken Sereno and Ed Bodaken. He has done extensive research in the areas of persuasion and organizational communication, but he is best known for his programmatic research in instructional communication. He has published over 70 research articles and 3 books and presented more than 90 conference papers. For six years Tim served as internal consultant for The Rockwell International Corporation. Currently, he is Professor of Communication Studies at California State University, Long Beach, and regularly teaches courses in persuasion, public speaking, and organizational communication.

CONTENTS

CHAPTER **TWELVE**

Speaking to Persuade   209

CHAPTER **THIRTEEN**

Generating Arguments   231

CHAPTER **SEVENTEEN**

Using Visual Aids 293

CHAPTER **EIGHTEEN**

Special Occasion Speeches and Group Presentations 309

Public Speaking in a Diverse Society

Chapter 1

A Contemporary Approach to Public Speaking

For effective public speakers, the payoffs are extraordinary. When good public speakers take to the stage, everybody listens. It is the good speakers who get hired and promoted, admired and honored, elected and respected. Today, effective public speaking is a requirement for success in virtually every field. No politician could command a following without being able to speak eloquently before the camera. No ambassador could represent his country's position accurately without careful attention to his message. No business executive could negotiate a large contract without presenting her proposal effectively. And no religious leader could inspire a congregation without thoughtfully preparing and rehearsing the sermon. Anyone wanting to succeed professionally has to learn to speak informatively, persuasively, and, often, humorously.

You need not be a politician, ambassador, executive, or religious leader, however, to require effective public speaking skills. Consider some of the following, more common circumstances:

Learning Objectives

After reading this chapter, you should be able to do the following:

1. Identify the components of a communication-based model of public speaking.

2. Discuss how public speaking is a lot like planned conversation.

3. Recognize the extent to which culture influences public speaking.

4. Recognize the need to be culturally sensitive as a speaker and as an audience member.

5. Critically analyze and evaluate information that you present or hear.

- As a course requirement, you are assigned to present a portion of your group's project to the rest of the class. Your grade depends on how well you organize and present the group's ideas. The speakers before you have been dull and boring. Now it's your turn, and you want to impress both the teacher and your peers with your speech.
- Your friends have urged you to run for class treasurer. Unfortunately, even this office requires that you give a campaign speech. You are very nervous about having to do that, but you want to win this election.
- A close relative has died, and you want to say a few words at the memorial service. Never having done this before, you're not sure how to begin or what to say. But it's important that you show respect for the family and maintain your composure.
- Your daughter wants to join a local social club. Unfortunately, this club excludes certain groups from membership, including persons of color, gays, Catholics, and Jews. For the next public meeting of this group, you've decided to voice your objections in a way that won't alienate the members, but instead will persuade them to change club policies.

You will face many situations during your life that will require you to speak before all kinds of audiences and for all kinds of reasons. How effective you are will depend on your skills as a public speaker. Good public speakers aren't born; they're made. Many people have learned how to successfully inform, persuade, and entertain audiences. You can, too.

Public speaking is both a remarkable communication activity and a highly complex process. Those self-help books that promise to transform readers into great public speakers in three easy steps oversimplify the involved process of preparing and delivering an organized, interesting presentation—a process requiring that a wide range of questions be asked and answered: What topic do I choose? What is my audience like? What do they want from me? What is my purpose or function? What should I wear? Where will the event be held? Should I use the podium? Should I write out my speech word for word, or should I speak from brief notes? Do I need references? What kind of testimonials or statistics do I use? Will I need visual aids? What kind? How many? How do I start my speech? How should I end it?

As if those aren't enough questions to overwhelm the beginning speaker, consider the fact that most public speakers worry a great deal over their stage fright. Fear about standing in front of an audience begins long before the actual speech event, often as soon as a speaker discovers he or she will be speaking. In fact, few students enroll in a public speaking class without experiencing some degree of reluctance or trepidation: What if my topic is boring? What if no one laughs at my jokes? Or what if the audience laughs at *me*? What if myaudience becomes angry or hostile? Or worse, what if they become bored and walk out? What if they disagree with my ideas? What if they ask questions I can't answer? What if I forget my second main point? Or worse, what if I get stuck and forget the entire rest of my speech? These and other questions pose seemingly insurmountable problems that only add to the complexities of speech preparation and presentation.

This text will help you confront and reduce your fears about speaking before a group. At the same time, it will provide you with the essential principles and skills to help you become an effective speaker. Meeting those objectives is no simple task. Fortunately, rhetorical and empirical researchers in communication have discovered a great deal about effective public speaking, including such things as how to grab and hold your audience's attention, increase your credibility, influence an audience that holds an opposing viewpoint, and even orchestrate applause. The text presents concrete strategies for achieving these goals, as well as the information you need to successfully navigate each step in the complex process of preparing and presenting speeches.

Although these kinds of skills are important for anyone who wishes to be a good public speaker, even more information and thoughtfulness are needed to be a truly effective speaker in a culturally diverse society. In the past, speech experts tended to assume that the same communication style—essentially one that worked for white, Anglo (Euroamerican) speakers and audiences—was equally effective with all types of audiences. Today we know this isn't true. Intercultural communication research has shown that what is appropriate for one cultural group does not necessarily generalize to others. In our culturally diverse society, effective public speakers must be knowledgeable about different groups of people, sensitive to a variety of communication issues and styles, and capable of adapting to all kinds of audiences. Anyone wishing to become a good public speaker must be able to communicate with culturally diverse audiences. By the same token, anyone wishing to make sense of the pressing issues of our time must be able to listen to and understand the messages presented by culturally diverse speakers.

PUBLIC SPEAKING AS EXTENDED CONVERSATION

Historically, public speaking has been studied apart from communication, as if it were so different from normal, everyday interactions that it could not, or perhaps should not, be guided by some of the same principles. In fact, to refer to public speaking as "extended conversation" is a recent innovation in the thinking and teaching of public speaking. This section compares everyday conversations with more formal public speaking events to provide insight into the process of speaking to an audience. By looking at some of the basics of communication, you will learn how to transform some of your own daily interactions into polished presentations.

What Is Communication?

Defining communication is no simple task. In fact, the nature of communication has long been debated. Ancient proverbs from the Masai, the writings of Confucius, and the work of early Greek scholars like Plato and Aristotle, to name only a few, reveal a deep interest in how personal meanings for the world outside people's minds are acquired through the use of speech and language, how words or symbols are used to represent reality, and how people are influenced by communication exchanges. In more recent times, social scientists have tried to identify the essential features of the human communication process.

Human communication is defined as a process by which sources use verbal and nonverbal symbols to transmit messages to receivers in such a way that similar meanings are constructed and understood by one another. At first glance, this definition may seem hopelessly complicated, yet it is little more than a list of factors involved in how people communicate with each other.

But what elements does the list contain? Communication is a **process**—that is, a series of stages in which something undergoes transformation at each step. In communication, a person serving as a **source** transforms her thoughts and ideas, or her **meanings**, into **messages** by selecting appropriate words and gestures (verbal and nonverbal symbols). This process, known as **encoding**, requires that the source choose words and gestures that will translate into her intended meanings accurately and efficiently.

The **transmission** of messages occurs through space and time via numerous **channels**, including sight and sound, or various media, such as radio, TV, computer, and telephone. The **receiver** then sees or hears these messages and transforms them back into his own symbolic understanding of the thoughts and ideas (meanings). This transformation process is known as **decoding**. Presumably, both the source and receiver encode and decode similar meanings.

Finally, the roles of source and receiver switch as the original receiver encodes and transmits messages back to the original source (now acting as the receiver). This process, called **feedback**, lets the original source know whether the message was decoded accurately. Framing the entire communication process is the **context**—the time, occasion, and place of the interaction. Like all the other factors involved in the process, context influences how meaning is shared or understood.

Communication as Transaction This linear model of communication is very helpful in understanding the process, but it does not provide a complete picture of communication. In a typical conversation, people take turns encoding and decoding so rapidly that it is difficult to determine who is the source and who is the receiver at any given point. Most of our communication exchanges occur simultaneously, so we often act as sources and receivers at the same time. This process of simultaneous encoding and decoding is called **transaction**.

How do we manage to do this? Most communication transactions involve both verbal and nonverbal symbols. **Verbal symbols** are the conventional utterances we call words. Words help us share our meanings with others. **Nonverbal symbols**—including gestures, actions, objects, sounds, time, and space—arouse meanings in others as well. Whenever we communicate with others, we rely on both verbal and nonverbal symbols. During the middle of an utterance, for example, the so-called receiver may frown, wrinkle his forehead, and cock his head upward and to the side. (Now who is the

source?) These nonverbal cues may be decoded to mean that he is confused and fails to understand what is being said. (Now who is the receiver?) If the source concludes that the other person is perplexed, she may attempt to modify her message to help the individual better understand her intent. (Who is encoding now?).

As you can see, designating one person as a source and the other as a receiver becomes problematic because communication is primarily transactional. But the problems associated with the labels of source and receiver become a little less confusing in the special context of public speaking, in which, for the most part, the speaker is considered the source and the audience the receiver.

Achieving Accurate Communication We have all had experiences when we just couldn't get our message across to someone. To achieve completely accurate communication, all the source's intended meanings must match the receiver's decoded meanings. This does not happen, primarily because meanings are entirely subjective. They occur only in our heads, where no one but we can experience them. Even when confronted with the exact same event, no two people will perceive it or reconstruct it exactly the same way. Suppose, for example, that you and a friend are both watching television when, suddenly, your program is interrupted by a special announcement. The surgeon general of the United States delivers a short presentation on a proposal to make cigarette smoking illegal. Shortly afterwards, another friend enters the room and asks what the presentation was about. You tell your version, and then your friend tells hers. To what extent will those eye- and ear-witness accounts be similar or different? Ideally, the two versions will overlap a great deal, yet they will surely vary, because people selectively attend to, perceive, and remember distinctly different things. In this example, a number of factors might contribute to this lack of overlap or congruence—say, an individual's prior history with smoking, his or her success or failure at trying to quit, or even his or her bout with lung cancer!

To confuse matters still further, individuals encode and decode messages differently as well. The words you use to verbally symbolize and transmit your meanings to someone can interfere with communication. These symbols are usually selected deliberately, but poor word choice can distort rather than clarify. For example, using the term "man" to refer to all people implies a lesser, exclusionary status for women, and using the racial label "Negro," rather than "African American," carries distorting connotations that are unacceptable today. Even nonverbal symbols can confuse or distort the intended meanings. For example, a simple wink from a speaker, intending to belie or contradict what was just said, can be missed (or misunderstood).

These and other factors all contribute to inaccuracies in communication—making it extremely difficult to get any message across. It's a small wonder that we are able to exchange meanings with each other as effectively as we do! Luckily, we can get by with limited accuracy; that is, although communication transactions rarely are completely accurate, they are usually accurate enough for practical purposes.

A Communication-Based Model of Public Speaking

Public speaking is a special kind of communication event and is generally more formal, planned, and organized than most other communication exchanges. It is, nevertheless, a form of communication. The elements that make up the communication process also function in the context of public speaking. All the elements involved in communication take on meaning in the public speaking context as well.

The Source Within the context of public speaking, the source is easily recognizable; she is the one standing in front of the group, encoding a preplanned message, and transmitting it verbally and nonverbally to the audience. But in keeping with the transactional nature of communication, the source also acts as a receiver by picking up cues from the audience: What are they doing? What are they thinking? What are they feeling? An effective speaker must ask and answer these questions, thereby also acting as receiver.

But to the audience, the speaker serves the role of the source. As the source, she brings her own unique cultural background and experiences that influence how she communicates. Part II focuses on you as the source. We discuss how to handle your communication apprehension before a large group (Chapter 4) and how to make a good first impression, establish your credibility, and ensure that your speech is both ethical and culturally sensitive (Chapter 5).

The Message Basically, the message is what the source says to the audience. The source must encode messages carefully and strategically in order to inform and influence the audience. Part IV focuses on how to prepare the text of your speech. Unlike all other communication contexts, public speaking requires careful planning of the message. Selecting and researching your topic is only the beginning (Chapter 8). Next, you must carefully organize your message so that it makes sense to you and your audience (Chapter 9) and then prepare a credible, captivating introduction and a memorable conclusion (Chapter 10). We also offer specific, practical strategies that you can use to both inform (Chapter 11) and persuade diverse audiences (Chapters 12 and 13).

Encoding requires more than preparing a message inside your head. Encoding also relies on verbal and nonverbal abilities to communicate meanings to others. Consequently, Part V focuses on your speech delivery skills. We discuss ways to polish your presentation by selecting just the right words and phrases that will help the audience warm up to you and to your ideas (Chapter 14). Next, we examine how to use nonverbal gestures, eye contact, and other body movements to capture audience attention (Chapter 15). Because every speaker is special, we also help you discover your own unique rhetorical style (Chapter 16) and show you how to use visual aids to enhance your overall presentation (Chapter 17). The bulk of this text, then, focuses on the message. Clearly, there is much to learn about encoding a message.

The Channel The channel is the way the message is transmitted through space and time. Most public speaking events are face-to-face; that is, the message is conveyed through sight and sound. The audience can both see the nonverbal message and hear the verbal message delivered by the source. Some public speaking events rely on additional transmitters to extend or amplify the voice and visual cues. No doubt you have heard and seen speeches transmitted via a microphone, television camera, or radio waves. Even then, the speaker typically has an immediate audience whose presence is visible to him. The channel plays an important role in how the message is delivered and received.

The Receivers Receivers are the people for whom the message is intended; they are the listeners or audience members who receive and decode your messages. Because all audiences are different, one of a public speaker's first tasks is to identify and learn about the audience. Delivering the same canned speech to one audience after another doesn't work very well, simply because each audience member brings different expectations, beliefs, attitudes, and values—depending in large part on his or her own unique set of experiences and cultural background. Ask any comedian who has tried to deliver the same joke on the same day in exactly the same way to two different audiences. One audience may laugh so hard the tears start to flow; the other

Audience feedback lets the speaker know how well he or she is doing. A good audience signals to the speaker that they like what they hear. Given favorable feedback, the speaker is likely to feel comfortable and successful.

may merely grin or even groan. And then, of course, there are major individual differences within each audience: some members of the same audience will love the joke; others just won't get it! Thus, in Part III, we help you recognize and adapt to differences both within and between different audiences (Chapter 6).

Feedback Even though the definition of communication does not explicitly use the word "feedback," no model of communication or public speaking would be complete without recognizing its importance. Feedback completes the communication process by having the receiver return a message to the source. In this stage of the process, the audience actually takes on the role of the source, supplying critical information to the speaker. In formal public speaking contexts, feedback generally takes the form of nonverbal messages, such as smiling, snoring, clapping, or rolling eyes in disbelief. However, feedback can also be verbal—as it generally is in normal conversations. Receivers interrupt, ask questions, extend what was just said, and so on. But in public speaking events, verbal feedback is usually more limited. Audience members may raise their hands and ask questions; some may occasionally shout out a response.

Nothing causes public speakers quite so much fear as the audience itself. While much of that fear may be irrational, some of it may be grounded in reality. After all, from a speaker's point of view, there are two general types of audiences: good ones and bad ones. Good audiences can make you feel comfortable and successful; bad audiences will make you wish you hadn't agreed to give the speech in the first place. Chapter 7 focuses on developing effective listening skills; it also emphasizes the responsibility of the audience to give the speaker the opportunity to be heard and understood.

Context Framing the entire communication process is the situation itself—or the time, occasion, and place of the transaction. Communication always takes place within some sort of context. An everyday conversation could occur at the kitchen table, in the bedroom, or in someone's office. Public speaking events typically take place in more formal and spacious surroundings, such as a large room or auditorium with a stage and podium in front or even a school cafeteria, gymnasium, church, or outdoor park.

Context also refers to the time of day and the conditions of the room or environment: Does the speech occur first thing in the morning or at the end of the workday? Is the room unduly hot or cold? Are the chairs comfortable and available to everyone? Context further refers to the occasion or circumstances surrounding the event: Is the occasion a funeral or a wedding celebration? Is the event an awards ceremony or a commencement exercise? All these details play a major role as you select your topic, plan what you have to say, and plot how you will deliver your speech. Because the context frames your entire presentation, you will need to recognize and then adjust your speech to accommodate time, place, and occasion. Chapter 18 provides a variety of specialized speeches suitable for all kinds of occasions.

Culture Another factor that influences every aspect of the public speaking process is the cultural backgrounds or identities of the speaker and the audience members. Cultural background affects the way a speaker perceives the audience, encodes and transmits her message, and decodes feedback from audience members. It also affects how audience members perceive the speaker, receive and decode her message, and provide feedback. Many of the complexities and dynamics of a public speaking encounter are a direct result of the mingling of different meanings and communication styles among members of different cultural groups. Chapter 3 examines how culture affects communication and, more directly, public speaking.

As mentioned previously, public speaking is a special kind of communication event. But it would be a mistake to view public speaking as so different from how we normally converse with one another. As the communication-based model of public speaking shows, public speaking is really conversation on a much larger scale. The next section emphasizes those features of public speaking that parallel ordinary interpersonal transactions.

PUBLIC SPEAKING AS PLANNED CONVERSATION

Public speaking is a lot more like normal conversation than you might think. Effective public speakers can make their presentations seem easy, natural, and spontaneous. Of course, giving a speech is none of the above. Public speaking isn't a simple matter of conversing freely and openly with an audience; however, the more you can make it appear as if you are casually interacting, face-to-face and one-on-one, with the audience, the more successful your efforts will be. Let's examine, then, the characteristics of public speaking that resemble your everyday interpersonal conversations.

Relating One-on-One

A normal conversation is often between two people, yet even when the number of individuals increases to three or more, the exchange is generally considered to be one-on-one. That is, the participants in the conversation tend to personalize their interactions by carefully considering the "audience" when choosing which topics to bring up, what information to reveal (or conceal), and what words to use. A conversation with a friend is likely to be quite different from a conversation with a parent, employer, or significant other. Some computer on-line services and software programs recognize the need to personalize our interactions with one another by offering standard greeting cards that users can individualize by entering their own special messages.

You can personalize your own "conversation" with an audience of a hundred or more by thinking about your audience as more than a remote collection of faces. By recognizing various audience members as individuals, you can begin to relate to them as unique persons. This approach is jokingly referred to as the "Mister Rogers method" of public speaking. On his television show for young children, Mister Rogers speaks directly to the camera and simulates an intensely personal relationship with each viewer. The child quickly becomes convinced that Mister Rogers exists on television just for him or her. This is a very good style for speaking before any audience—each and every individual should feel a personal relationship with you. Once that happens, you can begin to successfully inform, influence, or entertain your audience.

Communicating Face-to-Face

Except for the telephone and other computerized methods of communication, interpersonal exchanges generally occur face-to-face. Physical proximity has the important benefit of contributing to accurate and efficient communication. When we communicate face-to-face, feedback is easily accessible. We are able to recognize both obvious and subtle verbal and nonverbal cues that tell us whether we're being understood as intended: eyebrows that suddenly go up, the hint of a frown, eyes that glaze over, tears that begin to form, or a jaw that tightens or relaxes. In our everyday conversations, such subtle and obvious reactions are immediate, frequent, and perceptible— and they are not available in other communication contexts, like television or letters. Face-to-face interactions allow us to adapt to each other's concerns, follow up with questions and comments, try to explain our position another way, pause to let the other person talk, and, simply put, interact flexibly and competently with one another.

Fortunately, many public speaking situations also involve face-to-face interactions. When you can actually see audience members react to your presentation, you can readily adapt to their confusion, frustration, boredom, curiosity, or concerns. An accomplished speaker can anticipate audience reaction even before the actual presentation and adapt his speech accordingly. For example, if a speaker expects the audience to have trouble understanding a particular point, he can include an additional example or extend the explanation. Even when delivered via mediated channels, such as television, radio, or print, the speech may be more effective if the speaker imagines the presence of a large audience.

Novice speakers often assume that all revisions of a speech come before the actual presentation itself; that is, once a speech is written and rehearsed, that version is what gets delivered. But experienced public speakers, relying on audience reaction, continue to make changes during their actual presentation. Suppose you are giving a speech on your views on environmental cleanup and your audience unexpectedly begins to groan in disagreement or disgust. You have two options: (1) Ignore the audience, plow ahead, and finish your speech as planned; or (2) respond to audience feedback by recognizing and responding to their concerns. Obviously, option 2 is a better choice. Effective speakers take advantage of the feedback provided by face-to-face communication.

Planning for Spontaneity

Interpersonal conversations are nearly always spontaneous and unplanned. When we talk with friends or relatives, we seldom lay out a strategy or organize what we are going to say beforehand. We may have some general purpose in mind or some idea of what we want to talk about, but we usually do not plan the entire event. There are exceptions, of course. For example, when we are in anxiety-producing situations or feel we have a lot at stake (like during a job interview or a marital conflict), we may imagine our interactions with others beforehand to help us figure out what to say and how to say it.[1]

Few situations are more anxiety-producing than giving a speech. But rehearsing your actual performance before the event can help you create an impression of spontaneity. Your goal is to come across as relaxed, casual, and natural before the group, as if you do this sort of thing every day. Audiences expect speakers to look poised and in control, to have done their homework ahead of time, and to know what they're doing. In short, audiences expect speakers to have something to say and to say it with confidence. Planning to be spontaneous may sound like a contradiction, but that's exactly what you will need to do to appear natural and relaxed before an audience.

Comparing the process of public speaking with everyday conversations should take some of the mystique out of public speaking and, at the same time, reduce some of your apprehensions about speaking before a large group. As you begin to give speeches, you will have the opportunity to extend your conversational skills to include presentational speaking. With time and practice, you will learn to speak with confidence before an audience.

COMMUNICATING IN A CULTURALLY DIVERSE SOCIETY

This text's approach to public speaking recognizes that the United States is a culturally diverse society. Because of this, speakers need to consider the impact of cultural diversity in their choice of topics, in their use of or preferences for certain kinds of evidence, in their selection of organizational structure, in their choice of logical or emotional appeals—in all the decisions and choices that affect each and every step of the speech preparation process. Speakers must consider the impact of cultural diversity in their use of eye contact, gestures, words and phrases, repetition, and other rhetorical devices that affect delivery. Speakers must also consider audience expectations and responses that may be tied to cultural affiliation. To ignore or to pay only lip service to the impact of cultural diversity on how speakers need to package and present their ideas to U.S. audiences today is to remain ineffective as a public speaker. This section defines culture, discusses the vast mix of cultures in the United States, and acknowledges the inherent need to interact competently with one another. (Refer to the box "Interview with a Student: Naomi Rodriguez," which focuses on the relationship between cultural diversity and communication.)

What Is Culture?

Culture is a term introduced by anthropologist Edward B. Tylor in 1871. Tylor wrote, "Culture . . . is that complex whole which includes knowledge, belief, art, law, morals, custom, and any other habits acquired by man [and woman] as a member of society."[2] Tylor's rather broad definition of culture is still appropriate today. Perhaps the key to understanding the nature of culture

Interview with a Student

Naomi Rodriquez

Naomi Rodriguez is a senior majoring in communication studies and is the current president of the student body at California State University, Long Beach. She was the former president of Delta Sigma Chi, a co-ed Latino fraternity, and spent some time in Washington, DC, as an intern for the Federal Communications Commission.

Given your political and social involvement in campus affairs, you must find yourself giving a lot of speeches. Do you ever get nervous?

I'm always a little nervous before I speak before a large audience. Who isn't? But I enjoy public speaking. I get a rush from it—especially when I'm talking about something I really feel a passion for. If I'm going to speak to our student body about an issue I feel strongly about, it's like "Aw, get me up there! I want to speak!" I think that has a lot to do with my cultural upbringing. My mom (Latina) did everything she did with passion—whether it was to cook, to clean, to work, or to go to school. She's a very passionate woman, and so am I. Some people actually accuse us of being emotional. That's not it. Emotional speakers, in my opinion, react. Passionate speakers are thoughtful. When I'm being passionate, I've thought about something over a period of time and I've learned to value it, to care deeply.

Do you believe your culture has influenced your public speaking style in a positive way?

Definitely. Sometimes when I'm really trying to reach my audience, to connect with them, to get them to listen to me, I start to accent things. I hit my hand like that (fist into hand), my voice becomes louder, and the tone gets higher. Sometimes I use rhyme, too. And I like pauses. Pauses do a lot. They make the audience think about what I'm saying—it's connection time. I can almost hear them thinking, "She just said that. Oh, okay. Yeah, I feel her, I hear her." Making that connection is very important to me. When I speak, I become very physical. I like to use my hands. I use a lot of hand and arm gestures. I don't like speaking from behind a desk or using a podium. I have to connect. I can't always physically reach out and touch the audience, but I like to walk through the audience and talk to them.

You're an excellent speaker, Naomi. What advice would you give to students interested in learning how to speak before a large group as easily and as professionally as you do?

Everyone always assumes that because I speak well and come across as so relaxed, it's something that just comes naturally to me. Not true. I work at it. My speech classes have helped me tremendously. And I practice. I practice to this day. I even practice short, sixty-second presentations in front of the mirror. I don't care how good you are, you have to practice. Jesse Jackson practices, I guarantee you! I look myself in the mirror and I practice.

---

is to emphasize the difference between a *society* (a number of people carrying on a common life) and its *culture* (what they collectively produce and practice). In other words, a **culture** is not a group of people; rather, it is the things they use, the beliefs they share, and the **norms,** or the distinctive rules or patterns of behavior, they follow.

Culture is an umbrella term—a very broad and inclusive concept covering different types of cultures. Two categories of culture fit under that umbrella in the United States. The first is the **mainstream culture** (or general culture), which brings a certain uniformity to the ways of life of people living in a diverse society. The second is the **co-culture,** which refers to the specialized or unique ways of life that characterize an enormous number of groups within our society that are distinguished by such factors as **race** or **ethnicity,** gender, age, and profession.

Mainstream Culture To the extent that people in a society share a more or less similar material culture and live together within a common set of major social institutions—even though there may be many diverse groups among them—they participate in a mainstream culture. This basic culture enables all of us to coexist within a larger, single society and to communicate with one another in relatively predictable ways. It holds society together in a functioning system regardless of the birthplace of our parents or grandparents, the color of our skin, or the first or second language we speak.

In a diverse society, mainstream culture consists of the most common language, the basic social institutions (schools, hospitals, police and fire departments, and so on), the material artifacts and technologies in use, and the values to which most people subscribe. For example, almost all of us living in the U.S. mainstream culture obey the nation's laws, rely on automobiles for transportation, buy things in supermarkets and shopping malls with U.S. currency, watch TV, live in homes furnished with tables and chairs, and so on. Most of us also value children, condemn crime, wear clothing, and generally live out our lives in and around the major social institutions of our society.

Co-Culture The second and equally important category of culture is the co-culture. In referring to specialized cultures, the term "co-culture" has generally replaced the more traditional "subculture," because the prefix "sub" implies inferiority. The term "co-culture" avoids such negative connotations.[3] Co-cultures illustrate unique or specialized ways of thinking and speaking that characterize people in particular racial and ethnic groups, religious organizations, social classes, regions of the country, occupations, and so on; examples include Latinos, Muslims, the very wealthy, vegetarians, midwesterners, lesbians, men, first-year college students, factory workers, marines, and prison inmates. Somewhat distinctive patterns of beliefs, attitudes, and norms for behavior set each co-culture apart from others in society.

In a diverse society, people normally identify with a number of different co-cultures, all of which affect how they think, feel, and behave. An individual might identify herself as an Asian American (one co-culture), a woman (a second co-culture), an attorney (a third co-culture), a Buddhist (a fourth co-culture), and a Republican (a fifth co-culture). Perhaps she also classifies herself as a nonsmoker, belongs to Jenny Craig, and plays in a softball league. The amount of influence an individual's affiliation with the mainstream culture or a particular co-culture has on that person depends on a number of factors. For example, "being a woman" may not be one of your more dominant identities for most of your interactions with others; however, being a woman may be an important part of who you are when discussing affirmative action programs or maternity leave. Similarly, your identity as a U.S. citizen may not be especially salient—until your country goes to war!

For some people, **assimilation** into the general way of life in the United States is fairly thorough; others retain distinct identities in our multicultural society. Importantly, the mainstream culture and all the various co-cultural groups represented in the United States are not completely separate entities—they do interact and overlap. When disparate cultures come in contact with one another, some assimilation and accommodation are inevitable. Consequently, we borrow from or imitate one another, enjoy one another's holidays and foods, adopt one another's specific words and phrases,

and adjust to one another's customs and traditions. The result is a whole mix and match of diversity coming together.[4] Things that were originally unique to one co-culture may, over time, become part of the ever-evolving mainstream culture.

Recognizing and Managing Our Diversity

Our cultural diversity is greater than that of any other nation in history. No other nation can boast of the special contributions made by each of its many co-cultures. We are at heart a nation of diversity, and though we often fall short of our ideals, we strive for justice, equality, and harmony among all people. But because of that diversity, there is an inclination toward conflict and misunderstanding.

As Table 1-1 shows, when we examine the variety of groups based on ethnicity or national origin represented in the United States today, we see an interesting collage of cultural diversity. A summary of current census data and projections reveals that in the early twenty-first century, ethnic and racial minority groups will outnumber so-called whites in some major cities and regions across the country for the first time in our history. In cities across the country—including Miami, Detroit, New York, Washington, Baltimore, Chicago, Laredo, Gary, Atlanta, San Antonio, Houston, and Memphis—**minority majorities** are emerging; that is, the combined population of such groups as African Americans, Native Americans, Pacific Islanders, Latinos, and Asian Americans is greater than the Euroamerican population.[5] In California, Hawaii, New Mexico, and the District of Columbia, Euroamericans currently make up 50 percent or less of the total population; by 2015, Latinos are expected to outnumber Euroamericans in California.[6] In the nation as a whole, the proportion of the population that is Euroamerican is expected to decline from about 72 percent in 2000 to about 53 percent in 2050.[7]

How does the United States cope with the diversity of its population? Initially, the nation was committed to a **melting pot policy**, in which the schools were used to transform the children of immigrants from "foreigners" to "Americans" as soon as possible. In the early twentieth century, the national goal was to eradicate the differences between people and thereby eliminate language, social, political, and economic problems. Over the years, however, the melting pot policy has been strongly criticized for not respecting people's ways of life. Furthermore, it often produced severe problems for immigrant families—especially between children, who assimilated

TABLE I-I   U.S. POPULATION BY ANCESTRY OR ETHNIC ORIGIN

THE 1990 CENSUS OF THE UNITED STATES ASKED PEOPLE TO STATE THEIR ANCESTRY OR ETHNIC ORIGIN.
THE GROUPS WITH THE LARGEST NUMBER OF RESPONSES WITHIN EACH GENERAL GEOGRAPHICAL AREA ARE LISTED.

WESTERN EUROPE

GERMAN	57,947,374
IRISH	38,735,539
ENGLISH	32,651,788
ITALIAN	14,664,550
FRENCH	10,320,935
DUTCH	6,227,089
SCOTCH-IRISH	5,617,773
SCOTTISH	5,393,581
SWEDISH	4,680,863
NORWEGIAN	3,869,395
WELSH	2,033,893
DANISH	1,634,669
PORTUGUESE	1,153,351
BRITISH	1,119,154
GREEK	1,110,373
SWISS	1,045,495

EASTERN EUROPE AND FORMER SOVIET UNION

POLISH	9,366,106
RUSSIAN	2,952,987
SLOVAK	1,882,897
HUNGARIAN	1,582,302
CZECH	1,296,411
LITHUANIAN	811,865
UKRAINIAN	740,803
CROATIAN	544,270
ROMANIAN	365,544

WEST INDIES

JAMAICAN	435,024
HAITIAN	289,521

NORTH AMERICA AND THE PACIFIC

AMERICAN INDIAN	8,708,220
FRENCH CANADIAN	2,167,127
ACADIAN/CAJUN	668,271
CANADIAN	549,990
HAWAIIAN	256,081

CENTRAL AND SOUTH AMERICA AND SPAIN

MEXICAN	11,586,983
SPANISH/HISPANIC	3,137,263
PUERTO RICAN	1,955,323
CUBAN	859,739
DOMINICAN	505,690
SALVADORAN	499,153
SPANIARD	360,935
COLOMBIAN	351,717
GUATEMALAN	241,559
ECUADORIAN	197,374

AFRICA

AFRICAN AMERICAN	23,777,098
AFRICAN	245,845

ASIA

CHINESE	1,505,245
FILIPINO	1,450,512
JAPANESE	1,004,645
KOREAN	836,987
ASIAN INDIAN	570,322
VIETNAMESE	535,825
TAIWANESE	192,973
LAOTIAN	146,930
CAMBODIAN	134,955
THAI	112,117
HMONG	84,823

MIDDLE EAST

LEBANESE	394,180
ARMENIAN	308,096
IRANIAN	235,521
SYRIAN	129,606
TURKISH	83,850
ISRAELI	81,677
EGYPTIAN	78,574

SOURCE: U.S. Bureau of the Census. (1992). *1990 Census of Population Supplementary Reports, Detailed Ancestry Groups for States*. Washington, DC: U.S. Government Printing Office.

rapidly, and their parents, who retained their culture of origin.

Most importantly, the melting pot policy has been criticized for its majority-superiority stance. Any culture outside the majority—the **minority**—was expected to assimilate or conform to the majority. A quick look at the number of members in each ethnic group in the United States reveals that the majority represents primarily Euroamerican cultures. Whereas the word "majority" was intended to refer to actual numbers, it has since assumed other connotations, including dominant, superior, and powerful. In comparison with the majority culture then, all other so-called minority "subcultures" were regarded as somehow less significant, less dominant, and less important. This tendency toward **ethnocentrism**—when individuals regard themselves and their way of life as superior to others[8]—persists still today. To examine your own attitudes toward other cultures, take a few minutes to complete the questionnaire in the box "Are You Ethnocentric?"

In spite of this attempt to build a common mainstream culture, the melting pot policy failed to completely eradicate cultural differences among people. In communities across the United States, people whose ancestors came from one "old country" or another continue to keep alive many of the traditions and feelings of identity that the policy was intended to remove. Even people who are several generations removed from their immigrant ancestors still feel the influences of their cultural roots.

Today our nation embraces a policy of **cultural pluralism**, which aims to tolerate and accept differences, maintain a strong sense of diversity, and, at the same time, keep a unified nation committed to similar democratic ideals. Within the context of cultural pluralism, we recognize that although we remain diverse, U.S. citizens of all backgrounds share a mainstream culture that enables us to carry on our day-to-day activities and relate to one another in fairly predictable ways. Thus, complete assimilation is no longer needed, nor is it particularly desirable.

Regardless of how long they or their ancestors have been living in the United States, most U.S. citizens are proud to be "American." When faced with outside threats or aggression, they are typically extremely patriotic. To some degree, pride, loyalty, and patriotism toward a country or culture are beneficial; but in the extreme, such beliefs can be detrimental, particularly when they are used to exclude or dominate others' valued cultural orientations. Our sense of cultural pride can also lead us to believe that our way of life is somehow better than or superior to

all others. Cultural pluralism depends on **cultural inclusion**—a commitment to acknowledge, respect, and, when possible, adapt to others who may think, feel, and behave differently from ourselves. In contrast, **cultural exclusion** ignores our inherent diversity and imposes a singular view of the world—one right way to think and act.

Cultural Exclusion in Public Speaking

The traditional approach to public speaking has been to instruct and evaluate speakers based on the communication norms of the mainstream culture, which is most closely related to the white, Anglo (or Euroamerican) co-culture. According to this approach, what works for Anglo speakers should also work for all other co-cultural groups represented in our society. But this is simply not true. Moreover, there is no universal agreement among people of different co-cultures regarding what constitutes ideal ways to speak and listen. If we described and prescribed the "right" way to give a speech based solely on Euroamerican communication norms, we would be guilty of ethnocentrism. And we would be less than optimal public speakers.

Cultural exclusion in everyday interactions takes many forms. A bias toward standard American English is one of the most obvious instances of cultural exclusion. Researchers tell us, for example, that talking with someone who uses a dialect or accent different from the so-called standard often leads us to critically or negatively evaluate that speaker's intelligence, financial and social status, and overall general likelihood of success.[9] Indeed, we have all interacted with someone whom we perceived to "talk funny." And yet how funny or different our talk seems depends entirely on our audience. A speaker born and raised in Beckley, West Virginia, would not be considered by his neighbors to have an accent; however, if he were to interact with folks from Fargo, North Dakota, he might be accused of talking very differently.

Characterizing speech patterns that deviate from the norm as somehow substandard is a form of cultural exclusion. Another example of cultural exclusion in public speaking is the traditional emphasis on using statistics and other so-called objective, or hard, evidence to support what a speaker has to say. Although this approach is consistent with the communication norms of many Euroamericans (particularly male Euroamericans), the use of statistical evidence is not as meaningful to members of other co-cultures. For example, many Latinos and African Americans are more likely to prefer other types of evidence, including

Are You Ethnocentric?

Instructions

All of us hold stereotypes about one group or another. This questionnaire is designed to assess some of your stereotypes about your own and others' membership in particular co-cultures. Complete these five steps in order:

1. Think of one co-culture of which you are a member (for example, female, Muslim, student, or Latina)—but only select one.

2. Think of another co-culture to which you don't belong (for example, male, Jewish, professor, Middle Eastern American)—but again, only select one.

3. In the column labeled "My Co-Culture," check five descriptive adjectives you think apply to your group.

4. In the column labeled "Another Co-Culture," check five descriptive adjectives you think apply to that group.

5. Go back through the list of descriptive adjectives and rate each adjective you selected in terms of how favorable a quality you think it is: (5) very favorable, (4) moderately favorable, (3) neither favorable nor unfavorable, (2) moderately unfavorable, or (1) very unfavorable. Put these ratings in the column labeled "Favorableness Ratings."

My Co-Culture	Another Co-Culture	Descriptive Adjectives	Favorableness Ratings
——	——	Intelligent	——
——	——	Materialistic	——
——	——	Ambitious	——
——	——	Industrious	——
——	——	Deceitful	——
——	——	Conservative	——
——	——	Practical	——
——	——	Shrewd	——
——	——	Arrogant	——
——	——	Aggressive	——
——	——	Sophisticated	——

My Co-Culture	Another Co-Culture	Descriptive Adjectives	Favorableness Ratings
——	——	Conceited	——
——	——	Neat	——
——	——	Alert	——
——	——	Impulsive	——
——	——	Stubborn	——
——	——	Conventional	——
——	——	Progressive	——
——	——	Sly	——
——	——	Tradition loving	——
——	——	Pleasure loving	——

Calculating Your Score

The adjectives you checked reflect the stereotypes you hold about your own and another co-cultural group. Add the numbers for the two groups separately and enter the two scores below. Each score should range from a low of 5 to a high of 25. The higher the score, the more favorable the stereotype.

My co-culture = ——   Another co-culture = ——

Compare your two scores, and consider what they say about your own degree of ethnocentrism. In what ways are you ethnocentric? To what extent do you think your stereotypes about another person's culture are real or grounded in truth? Do you think your stereotypes about your own co-culture generally reflect the way everyone really is who belongs to that group? Why or why not? Are stereotypes ever favorable? Why do you think so? Can so-called favorable stereotypes ever be a problem for members in that group? Why?

SOURCE: Adapted from Gudykunst, W. B. (1991). *Bridging differences: Effective intergroup communication* (p. 75). Newbury Park, CA: Sage.

personal testimonials, vivid descriptions of events, and stories grounded in emotional appeals (see Chapter 3). Disregarding this variability is ethnocentric and ignores the potential advantages of adapting the message to the intended audience. There are many ways to make

your presentations more culturally inclusive and, thus, more effective.

However, it is also important not to overlook the mainstream, more Euroamerican style of public speaking. Euroamericans constitute more than 70 percent of the U.S. population; they are the largest ethnic co-culture in the United States. The chances are very good that even if you are not a Euroamerican yourself, a significant number of your audience members will be. In addition, many assimilated U.S. citizens will expect public speakers to assume a Euroamerican stance in their speech presentations. Two studies examined intercultural influences on one particular type of public speaking—the teaching or lecture situation. In both studies, researchers found that regardless of cultural affiliation, college students appreciated teachers significantly more who engaged in those verbal and nonverbal behaviors that reflect primarily Euroamerican practices and recommendations.[10] Mass media have exposed people in the United States to a singular, Euroamerican way of public speaking, and that is the style of speaking that many people expect and prefer.

Cultural Inclusion: The Contemporary Approach

To be an effective public speaker in a diverse society, you must approach public speaking in a way that emphasizes cultural inclusion—the inclusion of all primary cultural groups that live together and interact with one another. Because audience members in U.S. society are likely to be culturally mixed and represent cultures other than your own, you need to recognize, respect, and make an effort to adapt to how others communicate.

The first step toward being a culturally inclusive public speaker is to recognize that people in your audience may be both similar to and different from you. It may seem obvious, for example, that some members of your audience are male and some are female, yet the fact that there are women in the audience will make a huge difference if you plan to give a speech on women's reproductive rights. Without recognizing that the women in your audience are likely to have strong feelings on this topic, you may find that the strategies you've chosen to persuade undermine rather than enhance your intended purpose.

Like gender differences, ethnic diversity can also play an important role in how speakers talk and how audiences respond. Consider, for instance, an Asian American company manager who was put in the rather uncomfortable position of having to brief his Euroamerican employees about upcoming layoffs. He spent a lot of time praising the employees, telling them all how valuable they were to the company, and expressing his sincere sorrow at seeing them all go. The employees were confused and frustrated: If they were such fine workers, why were they being let go? But any-

one familiar with the norms of many Asian cultures can understand the speaker's strategy. Many Asian cultures value sensitivity to others and face-saving.[11] Rather than tell the employees that their productivity had dropped or that they lacked new and essential skills, the manager wanted to assure them that they could leave the company with honor, dignity, and pride. By recognizing the influence of culture on this particular speaker's approach, audience members would have been more likely to understand the intended message and perhaps appreciate the manager's attempts to save them from feelings of humiliation or disgrace.

Once you recognize the diversity of your audience, the next step in being a culturally inclusive speaker is to demonstrate respect for that diversity by adapting your presentation in appropriate ways. Begin by carefully choosing what you say and how you say it so as not to alienate or offend anyone. For example, an audience of senior citizens will be offended if you refer to the elderly as "old" or "ancient." Similarly, you will want to adapt your language to accommodate the labels others prefer to apply to themselves: "feminists" as opposed to "femi-nazis," "gays" as opposed to "homos," "challenged" as opposed to "crippled," and so on. Other ways you can adapt your presentations to diverse audiences are discussed in subsequent chapters; they include the types of evidence you choose and the way you organize and present your speech.

Speakers are not the only ones who need to adapt, however. Audience members also share the responsibility for successful public speaking. They, too, must often adapt to give a speaker every chance to be heard and appreciated. An audience member may need to overlook certain aspects of a speaker's message to understand the speaker's position. Consider the popular radio talk-show hosts Rush Limbaugh and Howard Stern, both of whom make a living regularly offending listeners nationwide. Whether you believe either has anything worthwhile to say, you are obligated as an audience member to first give them a fair and complete hearing before you make up your mind.

This book presents a variety of options available to you as a public speaker to help you adapt to the co-cultural differences of the diverse audiences you are likely to meet. The goal is to help you become more culturally sensitive and inclusive as a public speaker. Some of the proposed recommendations will also be helpful in making you a more sensitive audience member.

Before the chapter concludes, we should touch on one more element crucial to successful public speaking—critical thinking.

PUBLIC SPEAKING AND CRITICAL THINKING

Thinking critically is essential to your roles as presentational speaker and potential audience member. **Critical thinking** is the careful, deliberate process people use to determine whether a particular conclusion or claim should be accepted or rejected.[12] Thinking critically involves a lot of skills, including the ability to listen carefully, to generate and evaluate arguments, to look for errors in reasoning or logic, and to distinguish between fact and opinion. In your role as critical public speaker, then, you should be committed to selecting and presenting only the best evidence available—that is, accurate, relevant, and up-to-date information. You should be willing to challenge audience members to learn new information, to consider arguments that may conflict with their views, and to reexamine traditional ways of doing things. And, most importantly for your role as a critical public speaker, you must be committed to argue reasonably, logically, and ethically—all while respecting individual differences in opinion, values, and behavior.

As an audience member, you must also learn to listen actively and openly, giving the speaker every opportunity to present her perspective. Perhaps the greatest challenge is to listen with an open mind (and heart) to a speaker whom you may not agree with or like very much. Thinking critically means being open to ideas even when they conflict with what you believe. Having listened attentively and with an open mind, you must critically evaluate what you have heard. That is, you must weigh both the evidence and sources of evidence, judge the merits of what was said, and decide if the reasons and evidence actually support the speaker's claim. (The box "Characteristics of Critical Thinkers"

summarizes some of the most important attitudes and behaviors of effective critical thinkers.)

Because critical thinking is central to your roles as a public speaker and an audience member, this and subsequent chapters conclude with questions designed to stimulate critical thinking. Carefully consider each question and your response in an effort to expand your capabilities as a critical thinker.

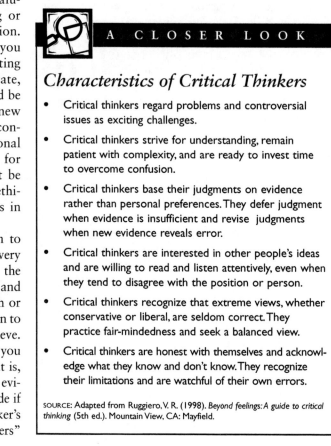

A CLOSER LOOK

Characteristics of Critical Thinkers

- Critical thinkers regard problems and controversial issues as exciting challenges.

- Critical thinkers strive for understanding, remain patient with complexity, and are ready to invest time to overcome confusion.

- Critical thinkers base their judgments on evidence rather than personal preferences. They defer judgment when evidence is insufficient and revise judgments when new evidence reveals error.

- Critical thinkers are interested in other people's ideas and are willing to read and listen attentively, even when they tend to disagree with the position or person.

- Critical thinkers recognize that extreme views, whether conservative or liberal, are seldom correct. They practice fair-mindedness and seek a balanced view.

- Critical thinkers are honest with themselves and acknowledge what they know and don't know. They recognize their limitations and are watchful of their own errors.

SOURCE: Adapted from Ruggiero, V. R. (1998). *Beyond feelings: A guide to critical thinking* (5th ed.). Mountain View, CA: Mayfield.

CHAPTER REVIEW

- Public speaking is a special kind of communication event. Communication is a process by which sources encode verbal and nonverbal messages that they transmit to receivers for decoding; in turn, receivers feed back encoded messages to the original sources. Most of our interactions are transactional, with sources and receivers encoding and decoding messages simultaneously.

- Although public speaking is generally more formal, planned, and organized than most other communication transactions, it can still be examined from

a communication perspective. The seven components of the communication process are the source (speaker), message (actual speech), channel (face-to-face or mediated), receivers (audience), feedback (audience response), context (time, place, and occasion), and culture (speaker and audience identities).

- A communication-based model of public speaking reveals that public speaking is really conversation on a much larger scale. The characteristics that resemble elements of normal conversation include the speaker's abilities to relate one-on-one with the audience, to communicate face-to-face in an effort to receive and adapt to audience feedback, and to plan ahead to at least appear to be spontaneous, natural, and relaxed.

- Culture plays a significant role in how speakers and audiences relate. The co-cultural diversity of the United States is greater than that of any other nation in history. Initially, our nation tried to cope with cultural diversity by adopting a melting pot policy of assimilation. Today our nation follows a policy of cultural pluralism, which respects differences among people. The contemporary approach to public speaking is intended to be culturally inclusive rather than exclusive.

- Essential to your effectiveness as a public speaker or audience member is your ability to critically present (or listen to) and evaluate information. Critical public speakers are committed to present only the best available evidence; to argue reasonably, logically, and ethically; and to provide information or claims that may conflict with what the audience already believes to be true. Critical listeners must be willing to suspend judgment, listen actively, and evaluate information, sources, and arguments.

QUESTIONS FOR CRITICAL THINKING & REVIEW

1. Audience members generally appreciate a presenter with a conversational style of speaking. Are there circumstances or conditions in which this style might be inappropriate? What are they?

2. Does audience feedback increase or decrease public speaking fears and anxieties? If given a choice, will you want your audience to provide you with feedback? Why or why not?

3. A well-known leader of the Ku Klux Klan will be coming to campus to give a speech on white supremacy. Would you attend? If required to attend, would you listen? Why or why not?

NOTES

1. Edwards, R., Honeycutt, J. M., & Zagacki, K. S. (1988). Imagined interaction as an element of social cognition. *Western Journal of Speech Communication, 52*, 23–45.
2. Tylor, E. B. (1871/1981). *Primitive culture, researches into the development of mythology, philosophy, religion, art and custom* (p. 1). London: Murray.
3. Samovar, L. A., & Porter, R. E. (1995). *Communication between cultures* (2nd ed.) (p. 60). Belmont, CA: Wadsworth.
4. Dasenbrock, R. W. (1992). The multicultural West. In P. Aufderheide (Ed.), *Beyond PC: Toward a politics of understanding* (pp. 201–211). St. Paul, MN: Graywolf Press.
5. Lustig, M. W., & Koester, J. (1993). *Intercultural competence: Interpersonal communication across cultures* (p. 9). New York: HarperCollins.
6. U.S. Bureau of the Census. (1996). *Population projections for states by age, sex, race, and Hispanic origin: 1995 to 2025*. Washington, DC: Author. Online. Available: http://www.census.gov/population/projections/state/ stpjrace.txt.
7. U.S. Bureau of the Census. (1996). *Population projections of the United States by age, sex, race, and Hispanic origin: 1995 to 2025* (P25-1130). Washington, DC: Author.
8. Sumner, W. G. (1906). *Folkways* (pp. 28–30). Boston: Ginn.
9. Bradford, A., Farrar, D., & Bradford, G. (1974). Evaluation reactions of college students to dialect differences in the English of Mexican-Americans. *Language and Speech, 17*, 255–270; Jensen, M., & Rosenfeld, L. B. (1974). Influence of mode of presentation, ethnicity, and social class on teachers' evaluations of students. *Journal of Educational Psychology, 66*, 540–547; Richmond, V. P., & McCroskey, J. C. (1995). *Nonverbal behavior in interpersonal relations* (pp. 101–107). Needham Heights, MA: Allyn & Bacon.
10. Powell, R. G., & Harville, B. (1990). The effects of teacher immediacy and clarity on instructional outcomes: An intercultural assessment. *Communication Education, 39*, 369–379; Sanders, J. A., & Wiseman, R. L. (1990). The effects of verbal and nonverbal teacher immediacy on perceived cognitive, affective, and behavioral learning in the multicultural classroom. *Communication Education, 39*, 341–353.
11. Ting-Toomey, S. (1988). Intercultural conflict styles: A face-negotiation theory. In Y. Kim & W. B. Gudykunst (Eds.), *Theories in intercultural communication* (pp. 213–235). Newbury Park, CA: Sage.
12. Moore, B. N., & Parker, R. (1998). *Critical thinking* (5th ed.) (p. 4). Mountain View, CA: Mayfield.

Chapter 2

GETTING STARTED: YOUR FIRST SPEECH

He looks up from his seat with a start; he has just heard his name being called: "Enrique? You're next." He drags himself from his chair and, head down, heart pounding, he trudges toward the front of the room. "I'm next," he thinks, "and I'm doomed. Why can't this be over?"

Enrique has given speeches before—in high school and at work. But this is his first formal presentation before a group of his college peers and speech communication teacher. As if that weren't enough to make him apprehensive, Enrique feels especially nervous because it's only the second week of the public speaking course and already the teacher is having everyone stand up and speak in front of the group. And Enrique spent so much time looking for something interesting to talk about that he ran out of time trying to put his presentation together.

This chapter is designed to help you avoid some of the problems Enrique faced. It provides a quick preview of how to put together a simple speech, the kind of speech you might be asked to give during your first or second week of class. Communication teachers realize that good speakers must engage in rehearsal and practice right away. In some ways, learning how to give a speech is like learning how to ride a bicycle. Before you could ride a bicycle easily, you had to gain motor skills with the help of training wheels. As you practiced, riding became easier and more natural until, one day, you could say, "Look, Ma. No hands!" With practice, you learned to ride with grace and style. Similarly, before you can stand up and give an effective public presentation, you need to acquire the necessary skills. With practice and effort, you will reach the "no hands" stage of public speaking, when you will be able to do it easily, naturally, and effectively.

Your communication teacher likely will get you involved in public speaking experiences early on. This might include giving a simple self-introduction, introducing someone else from your class, identifying your favorite movie or food, revealing your most embarrassing moment (besides giving this speech!), revealing what irritates you the most about people, or choosing some other personal topic that does not require a lot of preparation or library research. Whatever the assignment, your first speech is likely to be brief, informative, and simple. Communication instructors try to make these early speaking experiences sufficiently easy to help build and reinforce your confidence in your ability to stand up and address a large group. With practice, you might even begin to look forward to, or at least not avoid, public speaking events.

To help you get started speaking before a group, this chapter provides a straightforward discussion of the steps involved in putting together a simple, bare-bones speech. Because this chapter is so basic, it covers only the fundamentals; subsequent chapters will help you further develop and refine your preparation and presentational skills. However, if you need and want more in-depth information as you read along, turn to the specific chapters referenced throughout the discussion.

Learning Objectives

After reading this chapter, you should be able to do the following:

1. Differentiate the four goals or functions of speeches.

2. Identify the advantages and disadvantages associated with each of the four modes of speech delivery.

3. List the steps involved in preparing a speech for public presentation.

4. Deliver a speech extemporaneously.

COMMON GOALS OR FUNCTIONS OF SPEECHES

One of the first tasks in preparing your speech is to consider what effect you want to have on your audience members. Do you intend to inform them of the issues? Do you hope to persuade them to change their minds about something? Do you want to entertain them? Or perhaps you have an entirely different purpose in mind, such as accepting an award, giving thanks, offering praise and congratulations, or introducing the next speaker. Having a clear goal from the start is crucial, because the purpose of your speech will influence what type of evidence, organization, and presentational style will be most effective and appropriate. Figure 2-1 summarizes the common goals or functions of speeches.

Informing Others

The goal of an **informative speech** is to teach, to impart knowledge, or to change audience members' factual beliefs in some way. Perhaps you hope to extend what they already know about a topic, help them think about an issue in a new way, or teach them something about an entirely new subject. To inform your audience members, you need to provide them with accurate details and clear facts about your subject. Moreover, you must be credible; the audience must be willing to buy into what you have to offer. (Chapter 5 offers strategies to help you do this.)

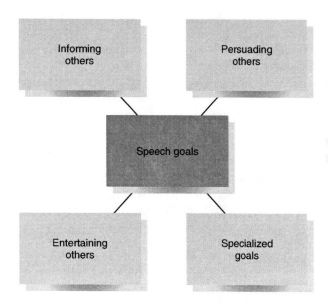

Figure 2-1 Common goals or functions of speeches. Every speech falls into one of four general categories based on its overall primary goal.

Consequently, your task is twofold: (1) You need to make sure your points are understood, and (2) you must inspire your audience to have confidence in what you have to say. (For a closer look at how to put together an informative speech, see Chapter 11.)

Persuading Others

The goal in a **persuasive speech** is not simple to achieve. After all, people generally resist attempts to influence their beliefs or change their ideas. Nevertheless, many occasions require that you do exactly that. Persuasion typically involves conveying messages designed to change opinions, attitudes, beliefs, or even behavior. Speaking to persuade requires that you take a position on an issue and advocate a cause, policy, product, or idea. You may want to sell the latest CD stereo system, convince audience members to support farm relief programs, encourage them to join a bowling league, or advocate that all U.S. citizens read and speak English. Whatever the topic, your purpose is to get people to feel, think, or behave differently as a consequence of your speech. (See Chapters 12 and 13 for details on how to effectively persuade diverse audiences.)

Entertaining Others

An **entertaining speech** is one of the more difficult presentations to prepare. Although speaking situations rarely call for this kind of speech, many effective informative, persuasive, and specialized speeches demand that the speaker amuse or at least create positive feelings to some degree. But when the overriding purpose is to entertain the audience, to make them laugh, you have your work cut out for you. You can amuse people by telling humorous anecdotes or jokes, and you can also entertain them by describing an exciting adventure, place, or story. Whatever your approach, you need to make sure that someone other than your close friends finds your talk entertaining, too. Furthermore, your humor must be tasteful and appropriate for the occasion and the audience. (Chapter 18 discusses how to design an entertaining speech, and Chapter 16 examines how to develop a humorous style of speaking.)

Specialized Goals

Even though most speeches are designed to entertain, inform, or persuade, occasionally you will need to prepare a speech for a distinctive event, such as a funeral, wedding, convocation, or awards ceremony. Most often, a **specialized speech** is short and to the point. For example, the audience expects the speaker to deliver a brief toast or thank the group in some way and then sit down. (Chapter 18 discusses specialized speeches in more detail, including introductions, welcomes, awards, tributes (eulogy or toast), and readings. To assess what you know about public speaking, take a few minutes to complete the survey in the box "What Do You Know about Public Speaking?"

MODES OF SPEECH DELIVERY

Once you decide on your goal—to entertain, inform, persuade, or pursue some other specialized function—you have to determine your mode of delivery. As Figure 2-2 shows, you have four basic options: manuscript, memorized, impromptu, and extemporaneous. Which mode you select depends largely on the occasion, the topic, and the speaker.

Manuscript Delivery: Reading from a Prepared Text

With **manuscript delivery**, you write the entire speech out beforehand and simply read the speech aloud to the audience. This delivery mode is the most attractive to novice speakers because of the security it provides: When reading from a prepared text, you are unlikely to

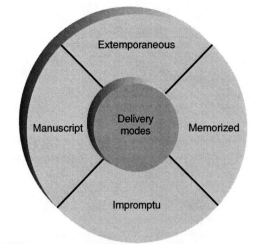

Figure 2-2 Modes of speech delivery. Each of the four basic modes of speech delivery has unique advantages and disadvantages. The type and context of the speech determine which mode is the best choice. For most situations, exemporaneous delivery is recommended.

overlook any major point, to be at a loss for words, or to struggle for just the right phrase. The manuscript mode has the advantage of enhancing your ability to be

---

What Do You Know about Public Speaking?

Instructions

This survey measures your background knowledge about public speaking. For each statement, mark "T" for true or "F" for false. No maybes are permitted!

___ 1. You should always use the podium if one is available.

___ 2. You should select a topic that you know will interest your audience—even if you don't happen to know a lot about the subject yet.

___ 3. Professional speakers never memorize their speeches; doing so limits their fluency.

___ 4. The first step involved in preparing a speech is to select your topic.

___ 5. Extemporaneous speeches are the most difficult to deliver.

___ 6. Compared to all other modes of delivery, audiences most prefer the impromptu form of delivery.

___ 7. Some speech topics should be avoided simply because they are inherently boring.

___ 8. Before you rehearse your speech, you need to write it out word for word.

___ 9. You should apologize to the audience for any mistakes you make during your speech.

___ 10. You should conclude your speech by thanking the audience for their time and patience.

Calculating Your Score

Your score should be easy to calculate; all the answers should be marked false. If you have a perfect score, then you have a basic understanding of what is involved in planning and presenting a speech. You should do well on your early presentations in this course. Undoubtedly, subsequent chapters will help you become even more competent in your presentational skills. If you answered any questions incorrectly, then this chapter was meant for you. Continue reading; you will find some very useful suggestions to help you in preparing and delivering your first speech.

accurate, precise, and convincing; you can place facts and figures throughout the text for easy reference. Without the text, it is difficult to recall specific numbers, exact dates, and precise statistics. Imagine a mayor giving a speech on civil rights to a group of African Americans and saying, "Martin Luther King's birthday is sometime in January," or a Defense Department budget expert saying, "Expenditures for the coming fiscal year are somewhere in the billions of dollars." Manuscript delivery also allows for easy access to the complete speech text for publication or other purposes.

However, a number of drawbacks are associated with the manuscript mode. First, reading from a manuscript makes it very difficult to simulate a natural, normal conversation between speaker and audience. Even experienced speakers read aloud in a way that differs from normal speech. Many people read in a kind of singsong pattern, which can quickly bore audiences. Second, trying to read word for word from a text makes it very difficult to look at the audience. In fact, when speakers do notice the people out front, they are likely to be startled and lose their place. Third, when a speaker is clutching a manuscript, attempts to gesture or move away from the podium are inhibited and awkward. Finally, a prepared text limits your ability to adapt to the audience even if feedback is abundant.

Manuscript delivery is like a train on a track. It goes along a fixed path; as a result, opportunities for change or deviation are limited or nonexistent. Planned spontaneity cannot be maintained, and relating one-on-one, assessing audience feedback, and adapting to the audience rarely take place.

Memorized Delivery: Reciting the Text from Memory

Memorized delivery is the second most attractive method for novice speakers. It's also the most difficult, and most experts warn against its use. The memorized mode requires that you write out the speech beforehand and practice it repeatedly until you commit the entire text to memory. The advantages of this approach

Reading a speech from a prepared text, called manuscript speaking, gives speakers the security that they will not forget any major points. However, it can limit speakers' ability to adapt to the audience and speak conversationally.

are the same as those associated with manuscript delivery. In addition, memorized delivery allows you to use gestures, to look at the audience, and to move around rather than remain tied to the podium.

The big disadvantage to the memorized mode is that it's hard to do well. Even if you deliver your speech perfectly at home in front of the mirror, your memory may fail you in front of an actual audience (a constant source of anxiety for inexperienced speakers). If you were to forget part of your speech, the only way to get back on track might be to start from the beginning—a clear signal to the audience that the speech was memorized, and an embarrassing moment for you.

As with manuscript reading, a speech recited from memory often comes across as rhythmic and monotonous. Anxious to get through the speech, speakers tend to rattle their lines off so fast that many audience members are not able to follow. And finally, the memorized mode does not allow the speaker to interpret or respond to audience feedback. A confused look from an audience member, a ripple of laughter, or a shudder of disgust may be overlooked in the interest of simply getting through the speech without interruption.

One appropriate use of the memorized mode is by professional speakers such as politicians, some management consultants, and evangelists, who repeatedly perform standardized addresses. For them, it is extremely efficient to commit speeches to memory, from which they can be summoned as the occasion demands. These professional speakers can then concentrate on developing a fluent, polished delivery; practice using gestures and varying vocal cues; and rehearse appropriate pauses for applause, laughter, or tears. They may even memorize quotable or applaudable phrases that predictably invite audiences to respond.

Impromptu Delivery: Speaking Off-the-Cuff

Impromptu delivery requires little or no lead time or formal preparation. This method of speaking is what we use in our everyday interactions with others. But impromptu speaking is dreaded by many people in other contexts. For example, students may fear being called upon in class, and employees may be uneasy when asked to give a briefing or provide instructions to others on the job. Despite the practice we get in impromptu speaking in everyday conversation, many of us may become inarticulate and suffer from an acute case of self-consciousness when suddenly called on to speak before a group. Clearly, the luxury of having sufficient time to prepare a well-organized presentation far outweighs whatever benefits may be associated with impromptu speaking.

With practice, impromptu speakers can come across as knowledgeable and thoughtful about a variety of subjects. Everyone admires individuals who can speak confidently and smoothly when suddenly called on or, as the saying goes, "think on their feet." Without warning, your boss may ask you to explain a proposal, defend your absence, or justify the purchase of new software at a monthly staff meeting. Being able to quickly organize your thoughts and deliver your ideas in a coherent manner can only enhance your credibility.

Extemporaneous Delivery: Speaking from Notes or an Outline

Extemporaneous delivery is the most common and highly recommended mode of speech delivery. With this mode, you rely on a well-organized, well-rehearsed speech outline rather than a complete text. Instead of writing out the entire speech or reciting it verbatim, you use only an outline or notes that highlight the major points and important but hard-to-remember dates, figures, and other specifics. A speech rehearsed and delivered from an outline will differ slightly every time you deliver it—examples may change, word usage and sentence structure will differ, and major and minor points may be shortened or extended. Nevertheless, the speech will cover the same points in the same sequence and incorporate the same essential meanings.

Because the speech is not memorized or read, extemporaneous delivery allows for a far less formal style. You can gesture frequently, elicit and maintain eye contact with audience members, and move freely around the stage or even among the audience. Speaking from an outline empowers you to adapt flexibly to audience feedback: Should I spend more time on this point? (The audience seems interested!) Should I skim over the next part? (The audience seems to know all about it already.) The extemporaneous mode allows you to ask and answer these types of questions and adapt your speech accordingly. With an outline nearby, you can spontaneously deviate from your plan and then easily return to the next point.

Audiences also prefer the extemporaneous approach; they like speakers who appear to speak naturally and spontaneously and yet are sufficiently prepared to know where they are going and where they have been with their talk. And extemporaneous delivery allows you to approximate the conversational style of speaking—spontaneous, face-to-face, and one-on-one—that serves as the basis for the model of public speaking presented in Chapter 1. You can accommodate, adapt, and adjust to individual audience members as your speech progresses.

The extemporaneous mode does have some disadvantages. It is easier to make slips of the tongue, deviate from proper grammar, and fumble for words or phrases. In addition, there is no prepared text available to the press, so that "quotable quotes" may be overlooked and information distorted. Nevertheless, the advantages of the extemporaneous mode far outweigh any of these potential drawbacks, and it is this mode that you will rely on through much of your public speaking course and in many public speaking situations in your future.

STEPS IN PREPARING YOUR FIRST PRESENTATION

Once you have selected a goal for your first speech and chosen an appropriate mode of delivery, you are ready to begin preparing your presentation. What follows is a brief overview of the speech-preparation process: (1) Analyze your audience, (2) select your topic, (3) research your subject, (4) organize and outline your presentation, and (5) rehearse your speech. Subsequent chapters discuss each of these steps in greater detail. (For some additional advice on giving your first speech, refer to the box "Interview with a Student: Co Tang.")

Analyze Your Audience

Most inexperienced speakers mistakenly choose a topic before considering the audience. The audience is central to all decisions that relate to preparing and delivering a speech, particularly when you consider the co-cultural diversity likely to be represented in any given audience. **Audience analysis** involves the systematic gathering of information about your intended audience: Who are these people? Why are they here?

SPEAKING OUT

Interview with a Student

Co Tang

Co Tang, 19, is a first-year student majoring in speech communication at California State University, Long Beach. Born in Vietnam, Co has lived in the United States for most of his life.

Now that you've finished a college course in public speaking, what advice would you give students who will be giving their very first speech?

Definitely look at the way the teacher intends to grade your speech so you can get a feeling of what the teacher wants. When giving a speech, the planning stages of your speech are vital. Select a topic that you can make interesting and delightful for your audience. Definitely read the book. Don't go up there in front of the class without reading the book. You should know what the professor knows. Think about what you read. Spend a lot of time on it. Rehearse the speech in front of your friends. Practice it aloud. Ask them to point out your nervous mannerisms. Move around. Use a lot of gestures. Don't use the podium. Don't stand behind the podium and hang onto it for your life!

Can you tell when someone hasn't practiced their speech beforehand? How can you tell?

I can always tell when someone hasn't spent a lot of time preparing for their speech. If they're looking down a lot and if they're, like, delaying four or five seconds and they have to look down to find out where they are or can't think of anything to say even

after they look down—that's when I can tell when people haven't prepared a lot for a speech.

Did you actually rehearse your own speeches in front of your friends?

I did. I did a lot. Usually three times. I'd practice it in front of my friends the night before. And then I'd do it again just before class. My friends pointed out to me all my little antics. I would pull back my shoulder, crumple a piece of paper. They would always point it out to me. That was very helpful.

In spite of the advice we give, some novice speakers still think that the best way for them to prepare for a presentation is to memorize their speech. In the course you just completed, we saw students try to do that over and over again. Have you ever memorized a speech yourself?

I memorized a speech for a business banquet that I attended last month. The speech was only a couple of minutes long. The speech seemed to go fairly well, but I was not able to express my emotional feelings. Memorizing the speech seemed to make it dull and not alive. Memorizing or reading a speech seems very boring and difficult to get the audience's attention. Speaking freely to an audience is the best approach for me. I like to pretend that I'm speaking to my friends, and I just allow the words to come naturally. My recommendation? Avoid reading or memorizing your speech!

What are they interested in? Of course, your audience in this course is a captive one, so you already know why they are here. The following specific questions are designed to help you determine who your audience members are and what they are interested in:

- How many men and how many women are there in my audience? Is the audience mostly male, mostly female, or evenly mixed?
- How old are the audience members? What is their approximate average age? Are most of them over 25 or under 21?
- Are most of them married, single, or divorced?
- Do they have children?
- What are the different ethnic backgrounds represented in this group?
- What other primary co-cultural affiliations are represented in this group?
- Where do these people live? At home with their parents, in their own apartments, or on campus in the dorms?

After you have answered these questions, you should be able to form a general impression of your particular audience. For example, you should have an idea of whether they know (or care to know) the difference between a good cabernet wine and a merlot; or whether they might be interested in employment opportunities, pension plans, or deferred tax annuities; or whether they prefer Leon Russell or Ani DiFranco. In other words, try to come up with an impression of who you think these people really are, what they are like, what they might be interested in, and so on. Obviously, your audience profile could be wrong, but at least you tried to ground them in some general information you happen to know about them. (Chapters 3 and 6 provide more information about audiences and how to analyze them.)

Select Your Topic

Selecting a topic is often the most difficult step in preparing a speech. Like Enrique in the example that opens this

A speaker must carefully consider the makeup of the audience when preparing and delivering a speech. Understanding who will be in the audience and what they are interested in is critical to a speaker's effectiveness. Which audience characteristics do you think would be most important to consider in this speaker's audience?

chapter, you may find yourself wasting far too much time searching for a topic—rather than actually preparing the content of your speech. Selecting a topic is important, but it is not nearly as important as what you have to say about it. Often, speakers reject topic ideas before they give them a chance; too quickly, they assume that this topic or that one is unbearably dull. But, as discussed in Chapter 8, topics are not inherently boring; it's what people do with them that makes them so dull. We've all witnessed speeches, movies, or television productions that promised to be entertaining and compelling—only to find ourselves wishing we were somewhere else! By the same token, we know of speakers, comedians, and actors who can transform the most ordinary tale into something fresh and exciting. Speakers, not topics, make for fascinating presentations.

Your task, then, is easier than you thought. Consider two important issues in your selection of a topic: (1) what subject areas might interest your particular audience, and (2) what you already know that might fit one or more of those interests. Based on your audience analysis, you can begin to brainstorm some themes you

---

A CLOSER LOOK

Suggested Speech Topics

Dating	Fear of spiders	Rosh Hashanah
Tattoos	Co-cultural slang (such as CB slang or rap)	Respect for the elderly
Term limitations in Congress		Rosa Parks
Women bodybuilders	When teasing has gone too far	Ash Wednesday
Social Security	Accepting compliments	Boxing
Grading practices in college	Relationship openers, or pickup lines	Do we need a vice president?
Teacher evaluations	Small talk	Boring dates
Cohabitation before marriage	Telephone answering machine courtesy	Embarrassing moments
Practicing safe sex	White lies	Favorite movie genre
Car pool lanes	Raising the minimum wage	Protecting the opossum
Student loans	Choosing the right pool cue	Diet pills
Rap music	Meditation	Altruism
Immigration	Daily multiple vitamins	Keeping a promise
Credit cards	Power food	Guilt works
Traveling by bus	Soul food	Intuition
Living in the East (or South or West or North)	Manners	Rational argument
	Ethics	Punctuality
Preserving our deserts	Cheating	Planning a wedding
The gnatcatcher (or other bird of interest)	Nannies	Criteria for best friends
	Car insurance rates	Decaffeinated drinks
Romantic dialogue	Writing song lyrics	Double-bind situations
Fifty ways to leave your lover	Killer bees	Talking on the phone too long
Self-disclosure: men versus women	Greenpeace	Unfair fighting techniques
Physical attraction: the eye of the beholder	Animal rights	Changing your last name when you marry
	Pet peeves	
Cats or dogs	Daylight saving time	

think would appeal to your audience. Don't discard any topic at this point; just let your mind wander from one topic to another. (Refer to the box "Suggested Speech Topics" to help you think up some topic ideas of your own.) Once you've finished your list, review each topic and select issues you already know something about. Familiar subject areas are a lot easier to talk about and are more likely to be interesting to you.

Now you will need to narrow the topic so that you can cover it in the time allotted. Suppose you only have three to five minutes to give your first class presentation. That is hardly enough time to say everything you know about, say, computers. Even though that time may seem like an eternity once you get in front of the group, it is less than it takes for most of us to make a phone call just to say hello. Computers as a topic is far too general to be presented in a short speech, but it can be narrowed to very specific issues. For example, you could talk about the advantages of one word processing system over another, or you could delineate the problems associated with using computer clones, or you could visualize what the future holds for computer-driven households. The list of possible topics will seem limitless when you try to narrow and specify a topic suitable to both the audience and yourself.

Research Your Subject

Evidence often makes the difference in whether your audience will believe you and accept your point of view. Evidence should help you define, clarify, illustrate, and support your position. There are two ways to research a subject: (1) Rely on your own personal experience with the topic, and (2) rely on what the experts know. Both research methods will provide the evidence you need to help prove or support your position.

Remember, it is important to select a topic that is already familiar to you. If you have had some direct experience with the subject matter, you can rely on yourself as an important source of information. Suppose you know a lot about the benefits of wearing a helmet when riding a motorcycle. What are your own subjective experiences associated with that topic? List those benefits, or even develop a story that illustrates your own personal experience. You may have had a relative injured in a motorcycle accident, or you may have had a near miss yourself.

Next, consult the experts. You can interview physicians or other hospital personnel; you can consult the library in search of congressional arguments in favor of (or opposed to) legislation requiring helmets; and you can find newspaper or magazine accounts of individuals who have suffered head injuries from motorcycle accidents. Find information that will help you explain why it is important that everyone wear a helmet while riding a motorcycle. Facts, statistics, testimonials, personal stories, examples, credible quotes—all assist you in convincing your audience. Because your audience is likely to be diverse, try to vary the kinds of evidence you employ in the speech. Once again, this text will have more to say about finding supporting materials to use in your speeches—including criteria for selecting just the right evidence to use—in Chapters 8 and 13. In the meantime, rely on yourself, current events (reported in newspapers and magazines or on TV), and the library for researching most topics.

Organize and Outline Your Presentation

Outlining your presentation is simply a technique to help you organize your speech. It helps to answer the question, What comes first, second, and third? Outlining helps to make sense of the speech both for you, as speaker, and for your audience. Some outlines are detailed and written in complete sentences; others consist of brief phrases. Like the other steps involved in preparing your first presentation, the principles associated with organizing and outlining, as well as audience co-cultural preferences for different kinds of organizational patterns or schemes, will be examined in greater detail in Chapter 9.

Except for the most sophisticated presentations, all formal speeches are organized around the same basic format: an introduction, a body, and a conclusion. The introduction captures the audience's attention and provides a preview of what will follow. The body describes the main ideas and reveals the supporting evidence for those ideas. The conclusion summarizes the main ideas and ends with some kind of memorable statement. Or, to put it another way, first you tell them what you're going to tell them; then you tell them; and finally, you tell them what you just told them!

Begin organizing your speech by stating both your specific purpose and your central thesis. Stating your **specific purpose** helps you stay focused on your goal by precisely laying out what you want to accomplish with your speech—what you want your audience to know, to believe, or to do after listening to your speech. The next step is to lay out your central thesis. Your **thesis statement** should be a concise, one-sentence summary of the core of your message or argument, the most essential points of your speech. Consider the following examples:

Topic: Motorcycle helmets

Specific Purpose: To persuade my audience to support legislation requiring motorcyclists to wear helmets

Thesis Statement: Motorcyclists who refuse to wear helmets are likely to wind up injured, paralyzed, or dead.

Topic: Potbellied pigs

Specific Purpose: To inform my audience about the benefits of having a potbellied pig as a house pet

Thesis Statement: Potbellied pigs are clean, affectionate, and highly intelligent.

Next, assemble the body of the presentation. List your two to four main ideas (any more than that and your speech will probably be too long). Then, for each of the main ideas, insert supporting materials, including examples, illustrations, facts, quotations, and so on—all as subpoints. After you have "filled in" the body of the speech, you are ready to write the introduction and conclusion. Both the preview and the summary should recap the two to four main ideas identified in the body. Finally, you need to devise an attention-gaining device to begin your speech and a captivating way to leave your audience in the conclusion. (Chapter 10 discusses in greater detail how to begin and end your speech.)

Include all relevant references at the end of your outline so that you can respond to spontaneous audience questions, should any be asked. (For a variety of sample speech outlines, see Chapters 9, 11, and 12. For a summary of these guidelines for organizing and outlining a speech, see the box "Basic Format for Speech Outlines.")

Rehearse Your Speech

After organizing your speech in outline form, you can begin to rehearse your presentation right from the outline. Don't write out your speech word for word. Remember: Your method of presentation should be extemporaneous and conversational. With outline in hand, begin to speak in front of a mirror, to an empty couch, or to a blank wall. Practice giving eye contact, smile when appropriate, try looking (or acting) comfortable and confident, and speak with enthusiasm. Mark Twain captured the importance of this kind of rehearsal when he declared,

> [The] best and most telling speech is not the actual impromptu one, but the counterfeit of it; . . . that speech is most worth listening to which has been carefully prepared in private and tried on a plaster cast, or an empty chair, or any other appreciative object that will keep quiet until the speaker has got his delivery limbered up so that they will seem impromptu to an audience.
>
> MARK TWAIN, "On Speech-Making Reform"

A CLOSER LOOK

Basic Format for Speech Outlines

Purpose statement: A precise statement of what the speaker wants to accomplish with the speech—what the audience should know, believe, or do after listening to the speech

Central thesis: A summary of the central message or argument of the speech

Introduction

Attention-gaining strategy or opening line

Preview of the main points of the speech (I, II, and III)

Body

I. Main point 1

    A. Supporting material

    B. Supporting material

II. Main point 2

    A. Supporting material

    B. Supporting material

III. Main point 3

    A. Supporting material

    B. Supporting material

Conclusion

Summary of main points (I, II, and III)

Memorable closing statement

References

If possible, tape-record or videotape your practice sessions. After each rehearsal, play back your tape and make any adjustments you need in your next run-through. Try not to be too critical of your first few trials; after all, there is a world of difference between thinking about a speech and actually talking one through. Eventually, you will need to put your outline on notecards; you may even feel secure enough to put only key words or main points on the cards.

After five or six trials, you are now ready for a pilot audience. Ask a friend or two, roommate, spouse, or parent to sit in on your rehearsal. With an actual audience, even if it's only one individual, you will find that you must make adjustments once again. Confronting individuals face-to-face, one-on-one requires that you

Preparing Your First Speech

1. *Analyze your audience.* Gather information about your intended audience, and form a general impression of members: Who are they? Why are they here? What are they interested in?

2. *Select and narrow your topic.* Select a subject that you are familiar with and that you think will interest your audience. Narrow your topic to something that you can cover easily in the time allotted for your speech.

3. *Research your topic.* Gather a variety of evidence—facts, statistics, personal stories, examples, and so on—to define, clarify, illustrate, and support your position. Use evidence from experts and from your own experiences.

4. *Organize and outline your presentation.* Specify your purpose and lay out your central thesis—the core of your message or argument. The speech itself should begin with an introduction that captures the audience's attention and previews the main points of the speech. The body of the speech should contain two to four main ideas, each supported by evidence. The conclusion of the speech should recap the main ideas and finish with a captivating ending. Your outline should conclude with a reference list.

5. *Rehearse your speech.* Practice your speech extemporaneously from an outline or notes. Record your practice sessions if possible. After a few trials, rehearse in front of a pilot audience.

6. *Deliver your speech!*

notice and adapt to their feedback. As a sensitive, effective speaker, you will want to change your speech to accommodate your audience. (Chapters 14, 15, and 16 focus on delivery and presentational style.)

After rehearsing and readjusting your speech presentation, you are ready to face your official audience. Keep in mind that you are likely to change your speech again to adapt to this particular audience—and you should. You will change some of your nonverbal gestures, the precise verbal expressions you practiced, and even some of the emphasis you give to one point or another. That's okay; you're supposed to.

If you follow each of these five preparatory steps, you will probably find that some of your anxieties about facing an audience have diminished. (The box "Preparing Your First Speech" summarizes these steps.) That doesn't mean you won't still feel nervous, but it does mean that you will have done everything you possibly could to ensure that your early speaking experience is successful. This chapter ends with an introductory speech by student Jenner McNeil. Her presentation should give you some idea of what an early speaking experience entails.

SEE WHAT YOU THINK: A STUDENT'S FIRST SPEECH

For her first major speech, Jenner McNeil, a communication major at Santa Barbara City College,

decided to speak on strategies for becoming involved in a social, athletic, or professional group. She selected a topic that she knew a lot about, because she had taken a class in group communication; consequently, she could speak informatively and credibly on the subject. After analyzing her audience, she determined that not many students had completed the course in group communication and may not have had the same ability to make new friends in a group of strangers. Her speech was a success; audience members could relate to the feelings of loneliness she described in her introduction because many of them were new college students away from home for the first time.

Afterward, the instructor complimented Jenner on her extemporaneous style. Jenner really came across as if she were having a conversation with her audience. Sometimes, however, the tone of that conversation became a little too informal, as when Jenner slipped in the occasional "like" and "you know?" Her teacher also recommended that she slow down her rate of speech and try to control her use of gestures. Still, Jenner's instructor and audience appreciated her friendly and informal speaking style, and her teacher praised the logical structure of the speech. Jenner received an A on her first speech.

S P E E C H

You're Only a Stranger Once

Jenner McNeil, Santa Barbara City College

Imagine moving to a new city where you don't know *anybody*. Imagine the feeling of being in your apartment *all by yourself* and realizing that for the first time in your life, you are truly alone in your corner of the world. No one to call . . . no one to see a movie with . . . no one to go out for a beer with . . . just plain no one. What would you do?

One way to overcome loneliness and make fast friends is to join a club or group. I know that sounds like a lot of work—especially if you are uncomfortable meeting new people—but once you find the right group of people and brush up on your conversation skills, it's easy! I learned about becoming involved when I took a small group communication class last semester, and it's really changed my outlook on making new friends. In fact, this summer I joined a sand volleyball league all by myself! I met new male and female friends and have become a better volleyball player, too. Today I'd like to talk about how to decide what group is right for you, and some ways to turn strangers into friends.

How do you find a group that suits you? Think about things like the group's goals and activities. Ask yourself, why does it exist? What do they do in this group? Decide whether you'd have fun with this group, doing what it does, and whether you agree with what the group is all about. If you think about joining a snowboarding club, you better like the snow! Personally, I like the sun and sand, so I think the volleyball league was a better choice for me!

Then look at the members of the group. Look for groups made up of people that seem to be similar to you or who have qualities that you admire. Things to consider are the ages of the members, how many males and females there are, what their occupations are, and whether or not they are students. Do these people seem like you'd enjoy spending time with them? They don't always have to be people just like you, either; sometimes it's fun to meet different kinds of people.

Once you've joined a group that seems right for you, it's time to start making some friends. Think of this public speaking class as a group you've joined. Wouldn't you be more comfortable right now if you had a friend? So, after class, make some small talk with someone in the group. It's not so hard; remember, everyone probably feels as nervous as you do. Exchange phone numbers. Maybe you and your new friend could practice your speeches for each other. As you get to know people in the group, suggest talking on the phone or getting together socially. The more you talk and hang out, the better you'll get to know one another.

Title: Jenner's title is intriguing; it reflects the thrust of her speech and, at the same time, compels the audience to listen.

Introduction: *Jenner gains the audience's attention right away with a scenario members could either relate to from personal experience or be sympathetic to. Not many of us would like to be alone in a new city with absolutely no friends.*

After introducing her topic and relating a personal example, Jenner previews her two main points.

Body: *Jenner begins her first point by asking a thought-provoking question and ends with a personal anecdote that got a laugh from her classmates at this beachfront college.*

Jenner uses the transition "then" to move to the second subpoint of her first main point.

In her second main point, Jenner makes an interesting, relevant comparison between her topic and the public speaking class she's taking. She makes concrete suggestions to the audience that apply to members' experiences in this class. Her delivery style and spirited personality are effective at making the audience believe that it really is easy to engage in small talk with strangers.

In conclusion, before I took a class in group communication, I was uncomfortable about joining a group of strangers. That class opened my eyes, and now I think that my ability to meet someone and quickly get to know them is one of my greatest strengths! It just took some practice. Getting involved in a group has benefitted me a great deal. I now know the real meaning of the old saying "You're only a stranger once."

Conclusion: Jenner signals the end of her speech clearly, and she ends with a memorable statement. However, strong as it was, her conclusion lacks a summary statement of her main points.

CHAPTER REVIEW

- Your first assignment will likely be a brief, informative, and fairly simple speech. Early speaking experiences are designed to build and reinforce your confidence in talking before an audience.

- Before you begin to prepare your speech, you should consider what effect you want to have on your audience. Do you want to entertain, inform, persuade, or achieve some other specialized goal?

- You should also consider the four basic modes of speech delivery. Manuscript delivery and memorized delivery offer the advantages of communicating accurately and precisely, yet both modes can pose problems of spontaneity and flexibility. Impromptu delivery is in some ways the most difficult mode, yet speakers who can think on their feet are highly regarded. Most speakers are trained in extemporaneous delivery, in which they rehearse and deliver a speech from brief notes or an outline. The extemporaneous mode has the unique advantage of approximating extended conversation.

- You should begin preparing for your first speech by analyzing your audience members and developing an overall profile of their backgrounds and interests. Second, select a topic and narrow it down to fit the time constraints for your presentation. Your topic should interest your audience and represent something you already know about. Third, research your topic or gather information about the subject, relying on yourself and expert sources for that information. Fourth, outline or organize your speech by specifying an introduction, the major points and subpoints that make up the body, and the conclusion. Fifth, rehearse your speech extemporaneously from the outline or abbreviated notes.

QUESTIONS FOR CRITICAL THINKING & REVIEW

1. Do you admire those who can deliver an impromptu speech effectively and apparently with ease? What other kinds of speakers do you admire? Why?

2. Do you think a preference for an extemporaneous mode of speaking is influenced by culture? In other words, what co-cultural group might appreciate an extemporaneous mode more than another?

3. Are you or do you anticipate having trouble selecting a topic for your speeches? In general, why do you think people have such trouble? What tips can you borrow from this chapter to help you in your topic search?

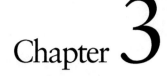

Chapter 3

THE INFLUENCE OF CULTURE ON PUBLIC SPEAKING

Learning Objectives

After reading this chapter, you should be able to do the following:

1. Demonstrate why culture and communication are inseparable.

2. Describe the four basic cultural features that make a difference in how people communicate.

3. Understand that speaking style preference is a function, in part, of a person's co-cultural background.

4. Characterize the speaking styles of individuals representing particular ethnic and gender co-cultures in the United States.

Most people in the audience really liked his speech. They laughed along as Jernay told one outlandish story after another about growing up with his grandparents in West Virginia. He claimed to have lived "so far up the holler, you had to pipe in sunshine!" And he regaled them with tall tales of turtle races, sweet potato pie, and sandlot baseball. The more they laughed, the more incredible his childhood stories became. But Jernay did not intend simply to entertain; each story was punctuated with one simple refrain: "But Grandpa can no longer recall." A victim of Alzheimer's disease, Jernay's grandfather no longer shares those memories with him. After some explanation of the disease—its causes, symptoms, and prognosis—Jernay concluded his presentation by bringing the message back home. "One day very soon," Jernay exclaimed, "Grandpa will no longer remember me." Afterwards, the audience gave Jernay spontaneous and meaningful applause.

Unfortunately, not everyone thought his presentation was so great. Some in the audience privately accused Jernay of being untruthful. (One individual was fairly certain that Jernay had grown up with his parents somewhere in the Midwest—he only visited his grandparents in West Virginia during summer vacations!) They claimed he misrepresented the facts just to tell a good story. (How could anyone believe that people sat around all day long watching and waiting for turtles to crawl some distance?) Moreover, they faulted him for being overly emotional and highly manipulative. (Even if his grandfather does have Alzheimer's, why didn't he just stick to the medical facts and statistics? And was that single tear falling from his eye at the end of his speech for real?)

Rhetorical critic Patricia Sullivan believes that many people are uninformed when analyzing the speech patterns typical of ethnic co-cultures other than their own.[1] For example, she argues, in the African American tradition, relying on personal stories and testimonials is a compelling way to make the issues relevant and meaningful to the audience. And in that same tradition, storytellers or performers are allowed some deviation from the "truth"; speakers are supposed to improvise to make the story relevant, interesting, and captivating to their audiences. These were some of the strategies used by Jernay, who is African American.

Critics' culturally shortsighted reactions to Jernay's speech and to other speakers with different co-cultural affiliations can be unjust and ethnocentric. These uninformed evaluations are important to discuss, however, because they force us to consider the significance of culture as it applies to public speaking. Examining such reactions can help us understand more fully what the term "culture" really means within the context of public speaking. These reactions also illustrate how powerfully culture influences both speakers and audiences.

Although much research has examined the influence of culture on communication in general, virtually no research has examined the specific relationship between culture and public speaking. This book aims to extend existing research and thinking to include public speaking as well. This chapter examines the relationship between culture and communication more generally and then focuses on the unique styles of communicating that reflect each of the major U.S. ethnic and gender co-cultures. Understanding why and how different co-cultures communicate will help you to better adapt your own public speaking message and style to meet the needs and expectations of your co-culturally diverse audiences.

THE INFLUENCE OF CULTURE ON COMMUNICATION

Culture and communication are inseparable. Anthropologist Edward T. Hall argues that culture is communication and that communication is culture.[2] He explains that how we communicate, what we believe, what we say, what language system we use, and which gestures we employ are all functions of the culture we acquire. How we speak and relate nonverbally to others is learned from the culture in which we grow up. And how we dress; how we use time; what fragrances we savor, and what smells we abhor; what distances we maintain when interacting with others; when, where, and with whom we maintain eye contact—all are dictated, to a large extent, by the culture of our particular society or group.

At the same time, the way we communicate says a lot about the particular culture we represent. Communication style speaks volumes about a person's co-culture. For example, Chinese Americans tend to be indirect and to understate their own accomplishments and successes.[3] Euroamericans, by contrast, learn to be assertive and to show pride in what they can do.[4] Nonverbally, some Latinos and African Americans might associate direct and prolonged eye contact with status and power—to look steadily at someone of higher status is a sign of disrespect.[5] It is not difficult to understand, then, that communication and culture are inseparable.

Understanding Intercultural Communication

The increasing awareness that cultural and co-cultural backgrounds are central to understanding communication has been coupled with dramatic economic, political, and social needs to communicate internationally. These urgent factors have led researchers to try to discover those factors that make a difference in our efforts to communicate accurately and efficiently with others.

Probably the single most striking lesson learned so far is that simply knowing another culture's language is not equivalent to understanding that culture. In fact, effective communication requires much more than learning how to speak, say, Spanish or Russian. It requires an understanding and appreciation of the co-cultures that permeate the interaction. Some foreign visitors who are quite competent English speakers (some understand English grammar better than native speakers) may nevertheless violate co-cultural norms. For example, they may invade another person's space or arrive late for a dinner engagement. Similarly, many U.S. citizens traveling abroad have earned the reputation of being "ugly Americans" because they did not recognize, accommodate, or respect the rules of other cultures. For example, they may blunder when they jump too quickly to a first-name basis with the English or French, ignore the strict dietary rules of a devout Hindu, or heartily slap a Taiwanese businessperson on the back.[6] Similar problems occur right here in the United States when people violate one another's co-cultural norms.

But exactly what does intercultural communication mean? **Intercultural communication** refers to an exchange of messages that takes place when people of different co-cultures communicate under conditions in which their co-cultural backgrounds influence or change the process in some significant way. In other words, to classify a transaction as "intercultural communication," it must take place "between people whose cultural [or co-cultural] perceptions and symbol systems are distinct enough to alter the communication event."[7] Take a few minutes now to complete the survey in the box "What Are Your Perceptions of Co-Cultural Communication Styles?" When you're done reading the entire chapter, complete the survey again.

Identifying Cultural Features That Make a Difference

The need to get along with people of all co-cultures within our own society, to accept them fully, and to be able to communicate with them accurately has never been more important. We all live within the mainstream U.S. culture. But if we think about our own gender, profession, and family history for a moment, most of us can clearly identify with several distinctive co-cultures—all of which influence in some fashion how we communicate with others.

What Are Your Perceptions of Co-Cultural Communication Styles?

Instructions

This survey contains statements designed to assess your feelings about and perceptions of people from your own and other U.S. co-cultures. Complete this survey twice: (1) *before* you read the rest of the chapter and (2) *after* you've read the entire chapter. Indicate the extent to which each of the following statements reflects your own beliefs, attitudes, and perceptions by marking "T" for mostly true or "F" for mostly false.

——— 1. Intensity characterizes the speaking styles of both African American and Latino co-cultures.

——— 2. Male speech is more absolute, directive, and authoritative than female speech.

——— 3. Compared to African Americans, Asian Americans often seem quiet and withdrawn.

——— 4. Compared to Latinos, Euroamericans are much more expressive in their verbal and nonverbal communication.

——— 5. Latino businesspeople like to get down to business immediately and become annoyed when Euroamericans engage in small talk.

——— 6. Women's communication behavior is rated as more attractive overall than men's.

——— 7. Asian Americans are more likely to value conformity and collaboration in their dealings with others, whereas Euroamericans are more likely to be competitive and independent.

——— 8. Japanese Americans are more likely to maintain eye contact and be facially expressive than Latinos.

——— 9. Native Americans communicate more like Asian Americans than Middle Eastern Americans.

——— 10. Maintaining direct eye contact is often a sign of hostility and aggression for Native Americans.

——— 11. Men usually talk louder than women.

——— 12. Taking personal credit for doing well in school or in sports is more typical of Native Americans than it is of African Americans.

——— 13. When trying to make a case, Middle Eastern Americans are more likely to discuss the future benefits of a plan than to show why it has worked in the past.

——— 14. More than any other co-cultural group, Middle Eastern Americans value public discourse.

——— 15. Middle Eastern Americans care more about *what* is said than *how* it is said.

——— 16. When talking with others, women typically use more arm and hand gestures than men.

——— 17. In conversations, men smile more often than women.

——— 18. When communicating with others, Euroamericans tend to be more sensitive and responsive than their Asian American counterparts.

——— 19. Eye contact is a *universal* sign of respect and attentiveness.

——— 20. For the most part, women talk more than men.

——— 21. Compared to the Native American, the African American communication style is more expressive and colorful.

——— 22. Whereas Asian Americans tend to be more subtle in their expressions, Latinos appear flamboyant and dramatic.

——— 23. Compared to Asian Americans, Euroamericans tend to be more assertive.

——— 24. Native American schoolchildren are extremely competitive and typically strive to be the best.

——— 25. Latino speakers enjoy telling a good story.

——— 26. African Americans tend to hide or mask their emotions when they communicate.

Interpreting the Results

If you've completed the survey for the first time, read the entire chapter before completing it again. If you've already read the entire chapter, check your second set of responses against your first. How culturally aware were you before you read the chapter? How culturally aware are you now? Do some of these differences and similarities surprise you? How well do you think you fit with the stereotypical portrayals presented here? How accurate do you think these stereotypes are? Why do you think it's important to learn about these characteristics—knowing that not all members of any given co-culture actually exhibit these qualities?

In this way, we all bring something different to our multicultural society, and thus to the public speaking situations in which we participate. What we bring from our specialized co-cultures are different (and sometimes opposing) values or ways of viewing the world that can impact how we communicate with one another. Researchers have found four cultural features that make a difference in how we relate with one another: (1) individualism and collectivism, (2) high and low context, (3) high and low power distance, and (4) masculinity and femininity. Each cultural feature represents a value or worldview continuum. No cultural group or individual actually embodies the extreme ends of these continua, but a particular co-culture may prefer one value orientation over its opposite.

Individualism and Collectivism The first cultural feature that seems to make a difference in how we communicate relates to whether a particular culture views the world from an individualistic or a collectivistic orientation. A culture with an orientation toward **individualism** places a high value on people who can speak or stand up for themselves and not have to depend on others beyond their immediate family. People who view the world this way like to think of themselves as rugged individualists who can stand alone and take care of themselves. They work hard to remain emotionally independent of any particular social, organizational, or institutional affiliation. Individualists emphasize the "I" when they speak, not the "we." They promote individual initiative and achievement, and they believe they have the right to their own property and opinions.[8]

At the other extreme of this value continuum is **collectivism**, characterized by close-knit, familylike groups of people who clearly define themselves as part of a particular in-group and others as part of the out-group. Members of the in-group (relatives, clans, organizations) are required to take care of one another in virtually every situation and context. In-group membership means not competing with others in the in-group—collaboration and respect are required. In exchange for loyalty, the group offers support, care, and protection. Collectivists emphasize the "we" when speaking, not the "I."

Figure 3-1 illustrates where 40 countries lie along the individualism–collectivism continuum. Later in the chapter, we'll look at where U.S. co-cultures lie along this continuum.

Highly individualistic countries

United States	164
Australia	160
Great Britain	156
Canada	120
Netherlands	120
New Zealand	116
Italy	104
Belgium	100
Denmark	96
France	84
Sweden	84
Ireland	80
Norway	76
Switzerland	72
Germany	68
South Africa	60
Finland	52
Austria	20
Israel	16
Spain	04
India	−08
Argentina	−16
Japan	−16
Iran	−36
Brazil	−48
Turkey	−52
Greece	−60
Philippines	−72
Mexico	−80
Portugal	−92
Yugoslavia	−92
Hong Kong	−100
Chile	−108
Singapore	−120
Thailand	−120
Taiwan	−132
Peru	−136
Pakistan	−144
Colombia	−148
Venezuela	−152

Highly collectivistic countries

Figure 3-1 Ratings of 40 countries on the individualism–collectivism continuum. A positive score near the top of the scale indicates an individualistic preference; a negative score near the bottom of the scale indicates a collectivistic preference. (Ratings are in standardized scores, with decimal point omitted.) SOURCE: *Lustig, M. W., & Koester, J. (1993). Intercultural competence: Interpersonal communication across cultures. New York: HarperCollins. Adapted from Hofstede, G. (1984). Cultural consequences: International differences in work-related values (p. 315). Beverly Hills, CA: Sage.*

High and Low Context A second cultural feature that influences how people from different cultures relate to one another is context.[9] **Context** has to do with whether what is communicated is inherent in the setting and simply understood by the people involved (high context) or whether the bulk of information must be communicated overtly through the spoken exchange of messages (low context).

Low-context individuals tend to be verbally explicit, precise, and accurate. They do not assume that others will be able to figure out what they mean without a lot of help. Interaction with a computer is an example of low-context communication: For your instruction or command to be understood by the computer, you must place every letter, every space in precisely the right order and sequence. Just as in interacting with a computer, people communicating in a low-context culture have trouble understanding each other unless they are as explicit and clear as possible. In a public speaking situation, a low-context speaker is likely to provide a lot of facts, figures, statistics, and other background information that tell the audience what to think and how to interpret the data.

High-context cultural groups are more verbally implicit. They tend to be more indirect and subtle, and they rely more on nonverbal cues when communicating with each other. The interactions of two people who have been married a long time represent a simple example of high-context communication. Over the years, they have come to know each other so well that they can complete each other's sentences; they can anticipate how the other will respond in any given situation; and they no longer feel a pressing need to talk in order to understand each other.

In other words, people in high-context cultures rely more on what is *not* said than on what is actually said in the explicit message. They look for meaning from the physical setting itself or from the implied demands of the situation. As a result, they often talk in "verbal shorthand."[10] Recognizing that not everything needs to be spelled out to the audience, high-context public speakers rely more on metaphor, innuendo, and implication. Rather than tell an audience how to think and what to do, high-context speakers merely suggest or offer alternatives. Figure 3-2 illustrates where a number of world cultures fall along the context continuum.[11]

High and Low Power Distance
How cultures distribute power, rank, and status among their members—their power-distance preference—is a third cultural feature that influences the way people communicate with one another. Some cultures allow for, encourage, and even legislate as much equal status, rank, and power among individuals as possible; other cultures greatly value status differences and social hierarchies.

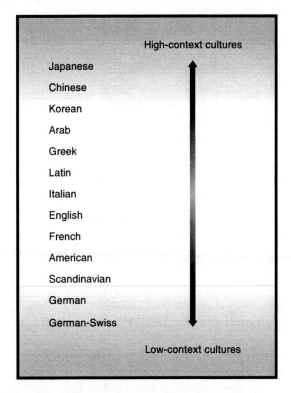

Figure 3-2 Cultures arranged along the context continuum. Selected world cultures can be arranged on a continuum based on the role context plays in typical communication behavior in each culture. SOURCE: *Adapted from Samovar, L.A., & Porter, J. M. (1995). Communication between cultures (2nd ed.). Belmont, CA: Wadsworth.*

Mainstream U.S. citizens value equality as a way of life; no one is inherently superior or inferior to anyone else. They believe they can speak to virtually whomever they want about almost any topic, in practically any style of delivery, and in any public or private situation, without having to consider a person's power, rank, or status. U.S. citizens can call in to radio and TV talk shows and direct questions to, say, the president or other prominent elected officials. Such interactions would be unheard of in other parts of the world.

Other cultures place a high value on social status, birth order, and occupational or political rankings. In these high power-distance cultures, people tend to have less access to and direct communication with individuals of higher status. They tend to accept the actions of high-ranking individuals, often without question or justification. Vietnamese American children, for instance, are expected to obey their parents without question or debate;[12] by contrast, African American children are often rewarded for being assertive and challenging their parents' points of view.[13] Your own co-culture's view toward power and status may similarly influence how willing or reluctant you are to do any of the following:

- Disagree with a teacher during class (even when you know the teacher is wrong)
- Ask questions in class
- Interrupt your boss at work
- Call your instructor by his first name
- Question your boss's evaluation of your performance
- Report your boss to a higher authority when you feel she has done something unethical or illegal
- File a grievance at work
- Marry someone your parents disapprove of
- Drop by your professor's office just to say hello

In public speaking situations, speakers who value power or status differences are likely to be formal and distant with their audiences. Similarly, high power-distance audiences may show respect by agreeing politely (at least in public), avoiding confrontation, and listening quietly. Low power-distance speakers, or those who value equality, tend to come across as accessible, approachable, and unassuming. Low power-distance audiences consider it their right to question the speaker and show how they really feel. Figure 3-3 arranges 40 countries on the power-distance continuum.[14]

Masculinity and Femininity
The fourth cultural feature is the extent to which cultures are traditionally more masculine or more feminine in their orientation. **Masculinity** in this regard refers to the degree to which a culture values and encourages assertiveness—sometimes illustrated as achievement, success, ambition, and competitiveness. **Femininity**, on the other hand, has to do with a culture's preference for nurturance—often defined as friendliness, affection, compassion, and general social support.[15]

For more masculine-oriented cultures, gender roles are clearly differentiated; males are supposed to be aggressive, and females passive. Personal achievement and competitiveness are highly valued in masculine cultures; relational concerns are secondary. Winning is more important than how one plays the game. Ambition is a highly desirable personal quality, as is being a good provider for the family.

Feminine-oriented cultures de-emphasize strictly held role definitions. Gender roles are more flexible, and equality between the sexes is likely. In feminine cultures, social and personal relationships are highly valued. More than achieving, winning, or accomplishing some instrumental goal, getting along, cooperating, and collaborating are more likely to be recognized and rewarded. Being a good person and showing sympathy and concern for others are culturally valued qualities.

		High power-distance countries
Philippines	210	
Mexico	145	
Venezuela	145	
India	125	
Yugoslavia	120	
Singapore	110	
Brazil	85	
France	80	
Hong Kong	80	
Colombia	75	
Turkey	70	
Belgium	65	
Peru	60	
Thailand	60	
Chile	55	
Portugal	55	
Greece	40	
Iran	30	
Taiwan	30	
Spain	25	
Pakistan	15	
Japan	10	
Italy	−10	
Argentina	−15	
South Africa	−15	
United States	−60	
Canada	−65	
Netherlands	−70	
Australia	−80	
Germany	−85	
Great Britain	−85	
Switzerland	−90	
Finland	−95	
Norway	−105	
Sweden	−105	
Ireland	−120	
New Zealand	−150	
Denmark	−170	
Israel	−195	
Austria	−205	Low power-distance countries

Figure 3-3 Ratings of 40 countries on the power-distance dimension. A positive score near the top of the scale indicates a high power-distance preference; a negative score near the bottom of the scale indicates a low power-distance preference. (Ratings are in standardized scores, with decimal point omitted.) SOURCE: Lustig, M. W., & Koester, J. (1993). Intercultural competence: Interpersonal communication across cultures. New York: HarperCollins. Adapted from Hofstede, G. (1984). Cultural consequences: International differences in work-related values (p. 315). Beverly Hills, CA: Sage.

		Highly masculine countries
Japan	225	
Austria	145	
Venezuela	115	
Italy	100	
Switzerland	100	
Mexico	95	
Ireland	90	
Germany	80	
Great Britain	80	
Colombia	70	
Philippines	70	
South Africa	65	
United States	60	
Australia	55	
New Zealand	40	
Greece	35	
Hong Kong	35	
Argentina	30	
India	30	
Belgium	20	
Canada	10	
Pakistan	00	
Brazil	–05	
Singapore	–10	
Israel	–15	
Taiwan	–25	
Turkey	–25	
France	–35	
Iran	–35	
Peru	–40	
Spain	–40	
Thailand	–80	
Portugal	–95	
Chile	–110	
Finland	–120	
Yugoslavia	–145	
Denmark	–170	
Netherlands	–180	
Norway	–210	
Sweden	–225	Highly feminine countries

Figure 3-4 Ratings of 40 countries on the masculinity–femininity dimension. A positive score near the top of the scale indicates a highly masculine orientation; a negative score near the bottom of the scale indicates a highly feminine orientation. (Ratings are in standardized scores, with decimal point omitted.) SOURCE: Lustig, M.W., & Koester, J. (1993). *Intercultural competence: Interpersonal communication across cultures. New York: HarperCollins. Adapted from Hofstede, G. (1984). Cultural consequences: International differences in work-related values (p. 315). Beverly Hills, CA: Sage.*

Within the context of public speaking, speakers in the **masculine style** are likely to emphasize their credibility and expertise on a topic, to prefer objective data, and to come across as forceful and direct. Speakers in the **feminine style** strive to connect with their audience by building rapport and empathy, to

seek audience support for their views, and to appeal to others' feelings and personal experiences. Figure 3-4 illustrates how masculinity and femininity preferences are distributed across 40 countries.[16]

CO-CULTURALLY UNIQUE STYLES OF SPEAKING

Each of the four cultural features just discussed influences how we communicate with people from our own co-cultural background and how we react to others whose co-cultural backgrounds differ from our own. When we understand *why* other people communicate or behave as they do, we can begin to accept and understand our own pluralistic society. The specific co-cultures examined in this section in most cases serve as the groups discussed throughout the rest of this book. Figure 3-5 summarizes the value orientations of these major U.S. ethnic and gender co-cultures.

Although people in the United States take pride in their individual co-cultural identities, they acknowledge the importance of all cultural groups. Part of becoming an effective public speaker, then, is to acquire enough information about other people's co-cultures to be able to communicate your respect and adapt to those differences when making public presentations.

Before turning to the discussion of the basic communication styles of particular U.S. co-cultures, note the following three considerations. First, we must *never* assume that just because someone belongs to a given co-culture, he or she will necessarily exhibit all of its characteristics. In other words, the danger in identifying patterns of unique co-cultural characteristics is the very human tendency to stereotype all individuals affiliated with that co-culture. For example, just because Cuban Americans *as a group* value social contact with friends and family more than with others, we cannot assume that *all* Cuban Americans share this value. Because there is diversity within groups, we must be open to exceptions and individual variations at all times.

Second, the following co-cultural characterizations are based on limited available research. Much of the intercultural communication research focuses on international groups rather than U.S. co-cultures. This research gives us important insight into the various ancestral roots of many co-cultural groups, but it fails to consider the degree of assimilation that results when co-cultures coexist and regularly interact. And because this research is designed to look for similarities within and differences between groups, it also fails to consider all the diversity that persists

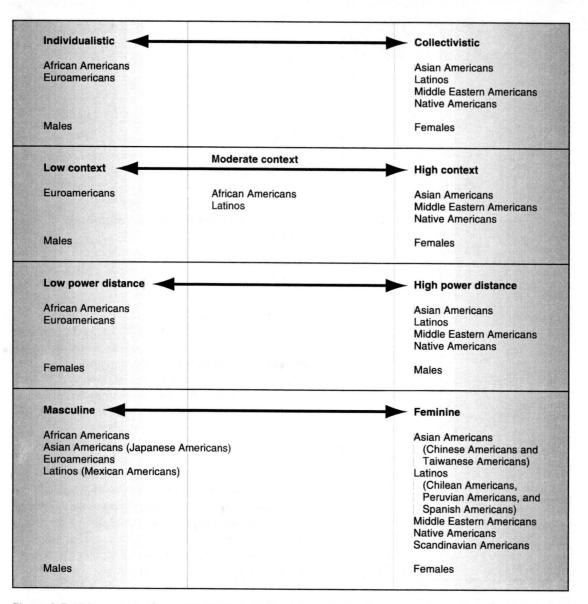

Figure 3-5 Value orientations of U.S. ethnic and gender co-cultures. Each of the ethnic and gender co-cultures described in this chapter can be placed on continua representing the four different cultural features. An individual's ethnic and gender co-cultures may differ in their orientations. The amount of influence a particular orientation has depends on the individual and the context: In some situations, ethnic background may be the dominant factor influencing communication style; in others, gender or another co-cultural identity may be the more important factor.

among members within each co-culture. As a result, the following co-cultural characterizations should be viewed as mere guidelines for the decisions we must make in relating effectively with one another.

Third, we need to keep in mind our almost inescapable tendency to be ethnocentric. When examining the unique characteristics of each co-culture, we need to suspend judgment and recall the principle of cultural relativity: We all do things differently. What

works for another group is all right—even if it's different from our own way.

To illustrate how even sophisticated people can be surprisingly ethnocentric, one of the authors of this text had the following experience. Pat Kearney comes from a small farming community in the Midwest that actively promotes hunting for game birds, rabbits, and, occasionally, deer. Currently, she lives in a very urban environment in Southern California. Her family continues to send as special delicacies the pheasants and wild rabbits they have hunted themselves. On one very special occasion, Pat invited her city friends to a dinner of baked rabbit. Much to her dismay, they refused to eat the "little bunnies" that had been hunted down, terrorized, and murdered!

The point is, we are in for some surprises when we spend time with people from different co-cultural backgrounds. To prevent problems from arising, we must recognize that we are all ethnocentric to some degree and inclined to judge people by our own co-cultural standards. We should also remember that our goal is to communicate accurately and efficiently with others who are not like us. Consequently, we need to suspend judgment and instead try to understand why other groups of people behave as they do.

What are the principal co-cultures in the United States? As indicated in Chapter 1, the people grouped under the heading Euroamericans make up the largest group in the United States. African Americans make up the second-largest group, followed closely in number by Latinos and Latinas. Based on ethnic or national origin, Asian Americans are the fourth-largest group, followed by Native Americans (including Eskimos and Aleuts). Middle Eastern Americans constitute the sixth-largest group. The final pair of co-cultures examined in this section overlap all the ethnic co-cultures just listed: females and males.

Euroamericans

This text uses the term "Euroamerican" to refer to individuals residing in the United States whose common cultural heritage is primarily European; other labels that are sometimes used include "European American," "white," and "Anglo."[17] Although Euroamericans are a large, diverse, and frequently misrepresented group of people, they tend to illustrate a number of unique communication patterns that distinguish them from other co-cultures. But note that the Euroamerican co-culture consists of a heterogeneous group including the Irish, French, Polish, Germans, English, Russians, and Scandinavians. And don't forget that within each of these groups are co-cultures represented by profession, sexual orientation, political preference, region, religion, and so on. Even so, some commonalities exist across most individuals who identify themselves most clearly with the Euroamerican co-culture.

So what distinguishes Euroamerican communicators from other co-cultural communicators in the United States? To begin with, Euroamericans tend to avoid disclosing much personal information. Although this tendency may be more descriptive of male than female Euroamericans, it is often illustrated in conversations between strangers, casual acquaintances, or business associates. That is, when Euroamericans first meet someone, they normally engage in a period of "small talk" about uneventful or unimportant issues such as the weather, a TV program, or a type of automobile. They avoid discussions about more substantive topics such as financial matters, religion, politics, and sexual behavior.[18]

The nature of communication exchanges between Euroamericans also distinguishes them from other co-cultures. Euroamericans tend not to speak with each other for a very long time, and their public presentations are generally short. There is little formalized ceremony or ritual in exchanges between Euroamericans. Because they value equity, Euroamericans are careful to take turns when they talk, and they tend to be impatient with people who talk too much or too long.[19] They also tend to avoid arguing when they communicate publicly, because this is considered rude. When Euroamericans do argue in public, they strive to remain noticeably calm, objective, and unemotional or rational.[20]

Euroamericans also tend not to get too involved with each other when they communicate. Again, this is probably more true of Euroamerican males than females. And Euroamericans tend to avoid close involvement with a lot of different people, reserving their involvement for a few close friends and family. When they do communicate with each other, they often want to know what the objective of the conversation is and how long it will take.[21]

In terms of the cultural features discussed previously, Euroamericans rank high in individualism, low in context and power distance, and high in masculinity. Based on these features, then, it is possible to assume that Euroamericans (particularly males) are highly ambitious and competitive and appreciate assertive, outspoken communication behavior. Euroamericans generally value individual versus group achievement, believe in equality, and minimize status differences. They also rely more on explicit than implicit information when they communicate; that is, they rely more on verbal than nonverbal messages. This overwhelming preference for verbal communication is revealed in their preoccupation with facts and evidence as opposed to emotional appeals. They tend to distrust people who overemotionalize an argument or a message.[22] Composure is a sign of credibility; loss of control or extreme displays of emotion are considered signs of weakness.

In sum, many Euroamerican speakers and listeners can be characterized as individualistic or self-oriented, unemotional, rational, objective, primarily verbal (as opposed to nonverbal), direct, exact, nondisclosive, and uninvolved. If you happen to be Euroamerican yourself, you can probably find exceptions to this picture of the so-called typical Euroamerican (especially if you're female!). You might claim, for instance, that Euroamericans are not really uninvolved and distant; they're just careful not to disclose too much too soon to people they hardly know.

As with all co-cultures, not every Euroamerican fits this description. It is important to again stress that we must be open to exceptions and individual variations in people who identify themselves with a particular co-culture. However, it is also important to note that each of us is typically the last to know what we are like as communicators—especially as we appear to other co-cultural groups. So, even though these characterizations may seem overly simplistic, keep in mind that people do tend to perceive others in such terms. (See the box "Defining People by Categories," which discusses whether such classifications help or hinder communication.)

African Americans

African Americans represent the second-largest ethnic co-culture in the United States. The designation "African American" acknowledges the influence of the African culture on people in the United States of African heritage. Although it has become more popular, the term "African American" is not accepted by the entire membership of this co-culture.[23] A significant number of African Americans still refer to themselves as "blacks" or as "Afro-Americans."[24]

Like all other co-cultures, African Americans are sufficiently unique in their speaking behavior to be distinguished from other co-cultures. The African American style of speaking tends to be intense, expressive, distinctive, forceful, and openly emotional.[25] How people connect and share with each other—how they use wit, humor, intelligence, touch, and other characteristics—is of primary importance to this group.[26]

African American audiences are also known to employ "call–response patterns" as positive feedback to public speakers. (Call–response patterns—in which audience members actively respond to a speaker with such phrases as "I hear you" and "Damn straight!"—are described in more detail in Chapter 6.) African American audience members let speakers know that

they are actively listening and giving their approval and support.[27]

African Americans tend to be highly individualistic, more moderate in context, low in power distance, and high in masculinity. In other words, as a group, they value competition and personal distinctiveness, trust their emotions and feelings but also appreciate the power of the spoken word, and tend to be highly intense and assertive. African Americans tend to use personal testimonies when arguing a point, and they have a keen sense of justice.[28] More generally, the style of speaking and communicating of a large number of African Americans can be characterized as active, expressive, colorful, emotional, often humorous, more nonverbal (as opposed to verbal), distinctive, stylized, open, demonstrative, and, overall, positive in outlook.[29]

Again, do not assume that all African Americans are likely to communicate in these ways—or at all times. Like the Euroamerican co-culture described previously and other co-cultural groups that follow, the African American co-culture comprises all kinds of people who think and behave in very different ways.

Latinos and Latinas

The third-largest ethnic co-culture in the United States is made up of people whose surname or cultural identity can be traced through their family background to Spain or a Spanish-speaking Latin American country.[30] A number of designations are used to identify people in this co-cultural category. Researchers Ron Lustig and Jolene Koester effectively distinguish among them:

> Hispanic *derives from the prevalent use of the Spanish language, but many shy away from this term because it tends to homogenize all groups of people who have Spanish surnames and who use the Spanish language.* Chicano (or Chicana) *refers to the "multiple-heritage experience of Mexicans in the United States" and speaks to a political and social consciousness of the Mexican American. Specific terms such as* Mexican American *or* Cuban American *are preferred by those who wish to acknowledge their cultural roots in a particular national heritage while simultaneously emphasizing their pride in being U.S. Americans. Finally,* Latino (or Latina) *is a cultural and linguistic term. As Juan Gonzales, Jr., suggests,* Latino *includes "all groups in the Americas that share the Spanish language, culture and traditions."*[31]

Taking the lead from Lustig and Koester, this text refers to this group of people as "Latinos" or "Latinos and Latinas."

Like the African American co-culture, Latinos are very expressive when they speak. To the Latino, a person's manner of expression is often more important than what the person says. Socializing and being friendly are very important to typical Latinos.[32] Arguing or disagreeing in public is considered rude and disrespectful; instead, Latinos prefer to appear agreeable and courteous.[33] They like to talk, visit, and establish an amiable, cheerful climate or speaking environment. These characteristic communication styles may (and often do) frustrate traditional Euroamerican businesspeople, who are often preoccupied with time; that is, they want their Latina or Latino associates to get down to business. For Latinos, however, showing concern for one another and chatting to show that they care are precursors to doing business. Demonstrating diplomacy, tact, and respect for one another is essential.

In the context of public speaking, Latino speakers are highly expressive, compelling, and intense. Like African Americans, they enjoy telling a good story, often relying on metaphors or parables. More important than the story itself, however, is the telling of it—the use of graphic, vivid speech expressions. As audience members, Latinos tend to be responsive and agreeable. They are unlikely to challenge a speaker publicly even when they think she or he is wrong; instead, they prefer to show respect.

In terms of worldview orientation, Latinos are collectivistic, moderate in context, and very high in power distance. Some Latino co-cultures are highly masculine in orientation (Mexican American); others are more feminine (Chilean American, Peruvian American, Spanish American). Latinos prefer relating with in-groups, and they are very loyal to family and friends. Moreover, they value conformity, obedience, and respect for authority. Latinos are a "contact culture"; that is, they stand closer to one another and engage in more physical contact than others might find comfortable. Even though the stereotypical perceptions of male "machismo" have not been fully documented, traditional gender roles are strongly encouraged. Males are expected to fill the roles of husband, father, and provider and be responsible and brave; females are expected to be protected, stay closer to home, and nurture and support their families.[34]

Latino communication can be characterized as amiable, expressive, dramatic, flamboyant, elegant, emotional, friendly, cheerful, and extroverted. But, again, remember that these characterizations are merely guidelines for the decisions we must make in our attempts to relate effectively with one another.

Asian Americans

"Asian American" is a broad term that includes a number of very different co-cultures. These unique co-cultures consist of people whose ancestral and cultural roots are in China, Japan, Korea, Singapore, Thailand, Vietnam, the Philippines, and other Asian and Pacific Rim countries. In spite of this diversity, research shows that Asian Americans tend to share certain communication patterns that differ from those of other U.S. co-cultures.

More than any other cultural feature, collectivism dominates the worldview of Asian American co-cultures.[35] First-generation Asian Americans—more so than more assimilated Asian Americans—are likely to value collaboration, conformity, loyalty, and acceptance of or acquiescence or even deference to authority. Power, rank, and status differentials are valued and highly respected. These cultural values contrast sharply with the dominant values of the African American and Euroamerican co-cultures.

Many Asian Americans may hesitate to voice their opinions or express what they truly think simply because it is customary to show deference to persons of authority, higher status, or greater age.[36] Moreover, Asian Americans as a group tend to be more sensitive to the feelings of others and thus unwilling to directly challenge a person's beliefs or attitudes or give unsolicited advice. Instead, they may be more likely to disagree or offer advice in some indirect and highly tactful manner.[37]

As members of a high-context culture, Asian Americans tend to mask their emotions when they communicate. Many Asian Americans are restrained in their nonverbal behavior and will not engage in direct eye contact, nod, smile, or gesture when talking or listening. An example will illustrate how confusion can result when Euroamericans and Asian Americans interact. One sensitive student of intercultural communication related the following incident: While at work, he observed his Euroamerican supervisor becoming increasingly frustrated with an Asian American employee. The problem arose when the supervisor was explaining to the employee how to proceed on a particular job. Instead of looking directly at the supervisor and occasionally providing some nonverbal feedback (a nod, a smile, or an "uh-huh"), she continued to look down and away, waiting respectfully for the supervisor to finish his "lecture." The supervisor misinterpreted her response, believing she was inattentive or resistant to his suggestions. If the student hadn't interfered and explained to the supervisor the co-cultural communication norms his coworker was bringing to the encounter from her community, she might have lost her job.

Family honor is another important part of the Asian American collectivistic orientation.[38] One's personal achievements bring honor to the entire family; one's failures bring shame and dishonor. Evidence of this orientation can sometimes be seen in the classroom. Students of Asian American co-cultures work hard to achieve high grades—not just for their own self-satisfaction but, importantly, for the honor of the family.[39] To fail a course can mean letting one's family down or even bringing disgrace. In the Euroamerican co-culture, by contrast, the individualist is likely to take (and be granted) personal credit for her or his successes and at the same time be forced to take responsibility for personal failures.

Within the context of public speaking, we might expect Asian American speakers to be much less flamboyant and outgoing than either Latinos or African Americans. Compared to all other co-cultures discussed so far, Asian American speakers are likely to be restrained in both their manner and words. They do not typically engage in assertive behavior or self-disclosure. Their style is simple and reserved, with little or no dramatic, illustrative facial expressions or gestures. They tend to be more indirect in their approach, preferring that audience members provide their own interpretations and draw their own conclusions. As an audience, Asian Americans can be counted on to be quietly reserved, polite, tactful, and pleasant. Consistent with collectivistic, high-context cultures, they are unlikely to ask questions or publicly challenge a speaker's point of view.[40]

In review, Asian Americans are highly collectivistic and high in both power distance and context, yet they are not easily classified on the masculinity–femininity continuum. Japanese Americans tend to be high in masculinity (assertive, ambitious, achievement oriented), but some other Asian American co-cultures tend to be less so. In general, Asian Americans can be characterized as understated, deferential, quiet and somewhat withdrawn, courteous, inexpressive, harmonious, and sincere—and always respectful.

Native Americans

Ambiguity surrounds both what constitutes membership and what is the most appropriate label to use when talking about this co-cultural group. We've chosen to use the term "Native American" because "it connotes both the heritage of the original inhabitants of this continent and the group's status as U.S. citizens."[41]

Native Americans, like the other co-cultures described in this chapter, represent a number of tribes, nations, pueblos, and unique individuals that are not easily categorized or characterized. Though diverse, Native Americans exhibit a number of identifiable co-cultural patterns. As in the Asian American co-culture, collectivism is highly valued;

cooperation, harmony, and getting along are the norms when interacting with one another. Unless personal competition benefits the entire group and the situation is clearly defined as competitive (as in an athletic event), competitiveness is considered an undesirable characteristic.[42] Among the Pueblo nations, such as the Zuni of New Mexico, the traditional culture restricts anyone who tries to outdo others by striving for personal power or success.[43] This restriction on competition can pose significant problems for Native Americans who attempt to assimilate into other co-cultures.

Given the high-context nature of their co-culture, Native Americans also avoid sustained and direct eye contact when speaking. Both the Hopi and Navajo define direct eye contact as offensive. In fact, staring can be interpreted as a form of aggression.[44] Moreover, the Hopi tend to be restrained in their nonverbal facial expressiveness; their communication exchanges tend to be more implicit than explicit. Compared to other moderate- or low-context co-cultures (such as Latinos, Euroamericans, and African Americans), Native Americans are observably less dramatic and animated in the way they normally communicate with others.[45]

Although their nonverbal behaviors may not seem expressive to those outside their co-culture, these cues are a vital means for relating. Historically, Native Americans have taken pride in passing on their traditions and customs through oral myths, legends, and stories. "One can learn much by 'listening' to what Native Americans are expressing through body language, eye movements, silence, and tone of voice."[46]

Native Americans can be characterized as a high-context co-culture. Thus, as speakers and listeners, they tend to be indirect, quiet, understated, inexpressive, nonassertive, and even somewhat withdrawn. Also, because they are collectivistic, Native Americans are group- and family oriented, noncompetitive (except under special circumstances), publicly agreeable (privately, they may disagree), and cooperative. In terms of power-distance orientation, Native Americans respect elders: With age comes experience, and with experience comes knowledge.[47] As a group, they also believe in harmony and balance with nature and in showing respect for all living things. And finally, Native Americans can be characterized as more feminine in their value orientation. The family is of utmost importance, and interpersonal relationships are more valued than personal success or ambition. Native Americans also tend to be wary of material wealth and the accumulation of material possessions.[48]

In the context of public speaking, we might expect Native American speakers to express themselves much like Asian American speakers. Their nonverbal gestures and body movements are likely to be restrained or subdued. They appreciate telling a good story, relying heavily on myths and legends that have been passed down through the generations. (See the box "Interview with a Student: Jesse Castner" for more information on the role of stories.) They are likely to suggest rather than insist on a particular way of thinking or behaving. As an audience, Native Americans often appear agreeable and accommodating. Saving face, or maintaining the dignity of self and others, is important to them. They "are keenly sensitive to being singled out for public disapproval, laughter, or ostracism."[49] Consequently, Native American audiences are likely to be publicly polite and receptive to speakers—whether or not members agree with or like the speaker.

Middle Eastern Americans

Middle Eastern Americans form another ethnic co-culture that has substantial representation in the United States. People from Egypt, Israel, Lebanon, Jordan, Armenia, Iran, Iraq, Syria, and other Middle Eastern countries have long made the United States their home. Despite their assimilation into mainstream society, they maintain many traditional aspects of their cultural identity, and some of their behaviors differ noticeably from the social and cultural practices of other U.S. co-cultures.

Like Native Americans, Middle Eastern Americans have a predominantly oral culture. For centuries in the Middle East, people relied on tribal storytellers to serve as the record keepers of significant events, recording history and passing it on orally generation after generation.[50] Today in the Middle East, this oral tradition continues, but the storytellers are now called poets. Poetry is an essential part of contemporary Middle Eastern culture. Poets often interpret political and social events; thus, poets influence what opinions people hold and how they respond to events.[51] Poets are held in very high esteem in Middle Eastern countries.[52]

The oral tradition of the Middle East has influenced the way people from this part of the world define public discourse more generally. Middle Easterners view public speaking as a highly valued activity. Much of their public discourse relies heavily

Interview with a Student

Jesse Castner

Jesse Castner, 19, is a freshman at California State University, Long Beach, majoring in biology. Born in Laramie, Wyoming, Jesse is a Navajo Indian.

We make the claim that when compared to Latinos, Euroamericans, and African Americans, Native Americans are observably less dramatic and animated in the way they communicate. Is that your experience?

I feel this claim is very accurate. As a child, I was raised with communication values that directed my own communication style to be fairly unemotional and less animated. Both my grandparents and my mother communicated in a stoic manner with very little eye contact. I believe that for members of my co-culture, this stoic, serious communication style gives credibility and respect to the speaker. Sometimes I have to catch myself; I find myself avoiding eye contact; so I force myself to look. I know I've had to teach myself to be different. When I try to talk serious, my voice becomes monotone. I have to talk myself out of that.

We also claim that Native Americans appreciate telling a good story, relying heavily on myths and legends that have been passed down through generations. Do you find this to be the case?

In my experience, Native Americans use legends extensively in order to teach lessons and values or explain the world we live in to the children. A lot of our stories come out of the story of creation. It's one big story with everything fitting into it, how things

came to be. Like bears in the creation story. If you've ever seen bear prints, their feet are kind of crooked; their toes are pointed inward. In the creation story, all the night animals have to hide when the sun comes up. They're supposed to hide during the day. But one night all the animals were playing cards or dice or some kind of game, and the sun started coming up. Seeing the sun come up on the horizon, the bear had to put on his shoes real fast and he got them mixed up; he didn't make it and ended up putting them on the wrong foot. The sun got him! That's why the bear's feet stick out today.

What function or purpose do myths and legends (stories) serve in public speaking?

Myths and legends are really examples to learn from and to base life on. They tell us why things are the way they are and how they came to be. Most of them include an underlying meaning or lesson for life. Traditional legends are almost the sole means to pass on traditional culture for Native Americans. They are very important because they hold our cultural groups together and set us apart from all others. They also form the foundation for our traditional beliefs.

I personally try to use a lot of stories to help me relate better to people and to try to include them. I think stories are a lot more interesting than just a lot of arguments and facts. I enjoy telling stories, and I'd rather others told me stories, too. It's more inclusive.

on religious references; it is not unusual for Muslims to quote extensively from the Koran, or Jews from the Torah.[53] Their style of speaking is highly emotional, and they rely heavily on the rhythm of language and the sounds of words as they compose their messages. Both the content and the logical presentation of ideas in a speech are secondary.[54] Middle Eastern Americans often use dramatic gestures, oaths, exaggeration, and repetition to emphasize their messages.[55]

Middle Eastern Americans are less likely than Euroamericans to believe that the future can be controlled. Because they tend to be more retrospective than prospective about life, what happened in the past concerns them more than what will happen in

the future; thus, Middle Eastern Americans view speaking primarily as a way of relating rather than controlling. Speaking eloquently holds particular appeal to them. They might speak publicly to express formal generosity to someone or to maintain their cultural pride, honor, and personal self-respect.[56]

Like African Americans and Latinos, then, Middle Eastern Americans tend to be dramatic, demonstrative speakers. They frequently speak to evoke an emotional effect as opposed to communicating a specific message. Middle Eastern Americans prefer a high-context speaking style; they imply or suggest, expecting others to know or understand what they mean. Their arguments rely more on subjective, personal experience than on objective data. Middle Eastern Americans also tend to be collectivistic, somewhat high in power distance, and marginally feminine in their value orientations. Middle Eastern Americans are very sensitive to others' perceptions of them. As a proud group of people, they make every effort to be perceived positively in all social and political situations.[57]

Females and Males

No matter what co-culture we belong to—ethnic or otherwise—we all identify with a particular gender. That is, we are either male or female. Being either male or female means that we hold unique worldviews that relate directly to our biological sex. Whatever the conditions during childhood and adolescence, both females and males are genetically programmed and socialized throughout life to think and behave in

particular ways. If you are a male, you have been encouraged in a variety of ways to act the way males in society are supposed to act; the same is true for females. When males and females don't behave in gender-appropriate ways, they encounter negative reactions. Growing up as a male implies being part of the male co-culture, and growing up as a female means being a member of the female co-culture. How does membership in a particular gender co-culture affect how we communicate?

The same four cultural features that significantly influence how people from different ethnic co-cultures communicate can help us understand how females and males communicate. Across U.S. co-cultures, certain tendencies define women's value orientations as they differ from men's. Obviously, these value orientations are influenced by each individual's ethnic or ancestral co-cultural affiliation, as well as by other factors. Even so, when compared to men, women tend to be collectivistic, high context,

Females and males are socializd early in life to communicate in particular ways. As a result, women learn to be more sensitive and indirect in the way they communicate, and men learn to be more controlling and assertive.

low power, and feminine in their orientation. As a result, we might expect women to place a high priority on personal relationships, particularly family and friends.

Providing support, showing compassion, and nurturing others are important personal and social qualities for many women. To achieve symmetry or equality, "women often match experiences"[58] to show others, "I felt that way, too," or, "The same thing happened to me." Moreover, because they value being polite to, showing respect for, and acting courteous toward others, they "avoid criticizing, outdoing, or putting others down."[59] Women also tend to be more sensitive and indirect in their communication transactions. By contrast, men tend to be more individualistic, low context, high power, and masculine. Consequently, we might expect them to prioritize individual success and achievements, appreciate competition, assert themselves and challenge others, and control or dominate interactions.

To some extent, research findings support the influence of such value preferences.[60] Women's speech is perceived as being deferential and polite; men's speech is perceived as being forceful and assertive. Women use more qualifiers than men: "maybe," "perhaps," and "This may be trivial to ask, but . . ." Women further rely on verbal fillers during silent, awkward moments: "okay," "well," "sure," and "you know." Women also use tag questions two to three times more often than men: "It's a beautiful day, *isn't it?*" And women are more likely to insert intensifiers into their speech; instead of saying, "That's pretty," women are more likely to say, "That's so pretty."

Nonverbally, women use more facial expressions than men, and they initiate and return smiles more often (even when they're not happy). They also rely on more eye contact to communicate. Men tend to talk in a louder voice than women, at a lower pitch, and with less tonal variation. Men also use more sweeping hand and arm gestures when they speak, tap their feet more than women, and take up more physical space. While men usually sit with their legs apart and seem to expand when they sit on a chair, women hold their knees together and seem to contract.[61]

One of the myths that is often perpetuated between the sexes is that women talk more than men. Contrary to popular belief, no single study supports that claim.[62] In fact, there appears to be no difference between how much females and males talk; however, consistent with our characterizations of male speech, in most contexts (but particularly so in male–female conversations), males are more likely to decide what is talked about and for how long! And, when men talk, they tend to be more absolute, directive, and authoritative than women.[63]

These differences between male and female speech styles have led some researchers to label men's talk as "powerful" and women's talk as "powerless."[64] Unfortunately, such nonegalitarian labels can have devastating effects on women in politics, at work, at home, and in virtually any social context. For example, research indicates that women speakers who use numerous intensifiers, qualifiers, verbal fillers, and tag questions are often perceived negatively—by both men and women.[65] Listeners tend to interpret such verbal cues as indicators of uncertainty, a lack of knowledge (or intelligence), and a limited ability to influence others. Alternatively, others suggest that such tentative female speech reflects women's desire to create equality and invite others to participate in conversation.[66] (Consistent with the latter interpretation, how might the different co-cultural groups we've identified in this chapter perceive female speech? Do you think Native Americans might interpret female speech patterns differently than Euroamericans? How about Asian Americans and Middle Eastern Americans? In other words, how does co-cultural affiliation influence how women's and men's speech styles are perceived?)

What is disturbing is the research finding that women are negatively perceived when they use such verbal cues but that men, when they use the same tag questions and qualifiers, are often perceived as polite and receiver oriented.[67] At the same time, however, women's speaking behavior is also rated as more attractive, polite, and closer to the ideal than men's.[68] Although the female communication style is preferred, a double standard is applied when it is used by women; that is, women are less likely to be attributed with authority, credibility, and control.

In terms of public speaking, your own co-cultural background directs what you are probably going to be like both as a speaker and an audience member. As this chapter shows, particular co-cultures define effective public speaking in very different ways. Whatever your own co-cultural affiliations, remember that each person represents a number of co-cultures and that it is your responsibility to acquire enough information about others' co-cultural backgrounds to be able to communicate respect and adapt to those differences.

CHAPTER REVIEW

- Culture and communication are inseparable. How we communicate, what we believe, what we say, what language choices we make, what gestures we employ—all are a function of the culture we acquire. Knowing how to speak another language is not equivalent to understanding another culture; we must also learn the other culture's ways of behaving in and viewing the world. When we don't recognize, accommodate, or respect the rules of other people's cultures, we violate co-cultural norms and expectations.

- Intercultural communication takes place when individuals' co-cultural perspectives are distinct enough to make a difference in the communication exchange. Researchers have identified at least four cultural features that influence how different cultures communicate: individualism and collectivism, high and low context, high and low power distance, and masculinity and femininity.

- Because culture influences communication and because so many different co-cultures are represented in the United States, communication exchange between co-cultures becomes a challenge. Of particular inportance are the co-cultural orientations and communication styles of the six largest U.S. ethnic co-cultures—Euroamericans, African Americans, Latinos and Latinas, Asian Americans, Native Americans, and Middle Eastern Americans—as well as the communication styles of women and men, two co-cultures that cut across all ethnic co-cultures.

QUESTIONS FOR CRITICAL THINKING & REVIEW

1. Collectivistic cultures place a high value on the family. Does that mean that individualistic co-cultures do not? How do these two orientations compare in terms of the value placed on the family?

2. Individualistic co-cultures place a high value on individual initiative and achievement. Does that mean that collectivistic co-cultures do not and that in collectivistic co-cultures individuals do not compete and try to get ahead? What are the differences between the two value orientations?

3. Of all the different co-cultural speaking styles that are characterized in this chapter, which speaking style do you most prefer? Least prefer? Why? Are your preferences rooted in your own co-cultural background?

4. Of all the different co-cultural speaking styles that are characterized in this chapter, which style do you think is best suited for public speaking? For one-on-one interpersonal conversations? For sales demonstrations? For funeral eulogies? What characteristic(s) of each style influenced your selections?

NOTES

1. Sullivan, P. A. (1993). Signification and African-American rhetoric: A case study of Jesse Jackson's "Common ground and common sense" speech. *Communication Quarterly, 41,* 1–15.

2. Hall, E. T. (1959). *The silent language* (p. 37). New York: Doubleday.

3. Locke, D. C. (1992). *Increasing multicultural understanding: A comprehensive model* (pp. 91–93). Newbury Park, CA: Sage.

4. Samovar, L. A., & Porter, R. E. (1995). *Communication between cultures* (2nd ed.) (pp. 80–81). Belmont, CA: Wadsworth; Lanier, A. R. (1988). *Living in the*

U.S.A. (4th ed.) (pp. 22–27). Yarmouth, ME: Intercultural Press.

5. Samovar & Porter, 1995, pp. 194–195.
6. Axtell, R. E. (1990). *Do's and taboos of hosting international visitors* (pp. 6–7). New York: Wiley.
7. Samovar & Porter, 1995, p. 58.
8. Samovar & Porter, 1995.
9. Hall, E. T. (1976). *Beyond culture.* New York: Anchor Books/Doubleday.
10. Lustig, M. W., & Koester, J. (1993). *Intercultural competence: Interpersonal communication across cultures* (p. 133). New York: HarperCollins.
11. Samovar & Porter, 1995, p. 104.
12. Locke, 1992.
13. Hecht, M. L., Collier, M. J., & Ribeau, S. A. (1993). *African American communication: Ethnic identity and cultural interpretation.* Newbury Park, CA: Sage.
14. Hofstede, G. (1984). *Cultural consequences: International differences in work-related values.* Beverly Hills, CA: Sage.
15. Dodd, C. H. (1991). *Dynamics of intercultural communication* (3rd ed.) (pp. 73–74). Dubuque, IA: Brown; Hofstede, 1984, pp. 189–191.
16. Hofstede, 1984.
17. Cyrus, V. (1993). *Experiencing race, class, and gender in the United States* (p. 12). Mountain View, CA: Mayfield.
18. Althen, G. (1988). *American ways: A guide for foreigners in the United States* (pp. 22–23). Yarmouth, ME: International Press.
19. Althen, 1998, pp. 21–29.
20. Althen, 1998, pp. 23–25.
21. Althen, 1998, pp. 25–26.
22. Althen, 1998, pp. 27–28.
23. Hecht et al., 1993, p. 74.
24. Lustig & Koester, 1993, p. 21.
25. Kochman, T. (1981). *Black and white styles in conflict.* Chicago: University of Chicago Press.
26. Hecht et al., 1993.
27. Hecht et al., 1993, pp. 102–103; Kochman, 1981, pp. 111–113.
28. Locke, 1992, p. 26.
29. Hecht et al., 1993.
30. Marin, G., & Marin, B. V. (1991). *Research with Hispanic population* (p. 1). Newbury Park, CA: Sage.
31. Lustig & Koester, 1993, p. 21.
32. Collier, M. J. (1988). A comparison of conversations among and between domestic cultural groups: How intra- and intercultural competencies vary. *Communication Quarterly, 36,* 122–144.
33. Locke, 1992, pp. 140–141.
34. Marin & Marin, 1991; Locke, 1992.
35. Gudykunst, W. B. (1991). *Bridging differences: Effective intergroup communication* (pp. 45–49). Newbury Park, CA: Sage; Hofstede, 1984; Hofstede, G., & Bond, J. (1984). Hofstede's culture dimensions. *Journal of Cross-Cultural Psychology, 15,* 417–433.

36. Locke, 1992.
37. Ting-Toomey, S. (1988). Intercultural conflict styles: A face-negotiation theory. In Y. Y. Kim & W. B. Gudykunst (Eds.), *Theories of intercultural communication* (pp. 213–235). Newbury Park, CA: Sage.
38. Locke, 1992.
39. Locke, 1992.
40. Ting-Toomey, 1988.
41. Locke, 1992, pp. 46–47.
42. Bennett, C. I. (1990). *Comprehensive multicultural education* (2nd ed.) (pp. 164–165). Boston, MA: Allyn & Bacon.
43. DeFleur, M. L., D'Antonio, W. V., & DeFleur, L. B. (1981). *Sociology: Human society* (3rd ed.) (p. 92). Glenview, IL: Scott, Foresman.
44. Samovar & Porter, 1995, p. 195.
45. Samovar & Porter, 1995, p. 193.
46. Locke, 1992, p. 50.
47. Locke, 1992.
48. Locke, 1992.
49. Dutton, B. P. (1983). *American Indians of the Southwest* (p. 13). Albuquerque: University of New Mexico Press.
50. Hamod, H. S. (1963). Arab and Moslem rhetorical theory. *Central States Speech Journal, 14,* 97–102.
51. Almaney, A. J., & Alwan, A. J. (1982). *Communicating with the Arabs: A handbook for the business executive.* Prospect Heights, IL: Waveland Press.
52. Anderson, J. W. (1991). A comparison of Arab and American conceptions of "effective" persuasion. In L. A. Samovar & R. E. Porter (Eds.), *Intercultural communication: A reader* (6th ed.) (pp. 96–106). Belmont, CA: Wadsworth.
53. Anderson, 1991, p. 98.
54. Anderson, 1991.
55. Nydell, M. K. (1987). *Understanding Arabs: A guide for Westerners.* Yarmouth, ME: Intercultural Press.
56. Nydell, 1987.
57. Condon, J. C., & Yousef, F. S. (1975). *An introduction to intercultural communication* (pp. 159–162). New York: Macmillan.
58. Wood, J. T. (1994). *Gendered lives: Communication, gender, and culture* (p. 141). Belmont, CA: Wadsworth.
59. Wood, 1994, p. 140.
60. For a review of that research, see Canary, D. J., & Emmers-Sommer, T. M. (1997). *Sex and gender differences in personal relationships.* New York: Guilford Press; Ivy, D. K., & Backlund, P. (1994). *Exploring gender speak: Personal effectiveness in gender communication.* New York: McGraw-Hill; Pearson, J. C., West, R. L., & Turner, L. H. (1995). *Gender and communication* (3rd ed.). Dubuque, IA: Brown; and Wood, 1994.
61. Pearson et al., 1995; Wood, 1994.
62. See, for example, Canary & Emmers-Sommer, 1997; and Pearson et al., 1995, pp. 130–131.
63. Pearson et al., 1995, pp. 130–134; Wood, 1994.

64. Lakoff, R. (1973). *Language and woman's place. Language in Society, 2*, 45–80; Lakoff, R. (1975). *Language and women's place.* New York: Harper & Row.

65. Bradley, P. H. (1981). The folk-linguistics of women's speech: An empirical examination. *Communication Monographs, 48*, 73–90.

66. Wood, 1994, p. 143.

67. Bradley, 1981.

68. Mulac, A., & Lundell, T. L. (1986). Linguistic contributors to the gender-linked language effect. *Journal of Language and Social Psychology, 5*, 81–101.

Chapter 4

DEVELOPING CONFIDENCE: COPING WITH YOUR FEARS ABOUT PUBLIC SPEAKING

Learning Objectives

After reading this chapter, you should be able to do the following:

1. Understand that stage fright, or public speaking anxiety, is normal.

2. Differentiate among apprehensive people, situations, and cultural groups.

3. Identify situational causes of public speaking anxiety.

4. Demonstrate three ways individuals can reduce their communication apprehension.

5. List and practice specific strategies to reduce your own public speaking anxiety.

Kimmi sat outside the paneled boardroom waiting for her turn to make her presentation. Having just been promoted to assistant manager of the transportation department, she knew she had a lot riding on the report she was about to make. In her previous job, she had never been asked to make a presentation to the board of directors, and frankly, she was very nervous. Being a first-generation Vietnamese American with English as her second language, Kimmi felt especially apprehensive about speaking fluently before the board. If she blew this speech, her career might well be over before it really got started.

Kimmi's anxiety had been growing over the past few weeks, ever since her boss had first informed her about the presentation. Kimmi spent nights and weekends outlining and preparing her speech. To avoid mistakes, she also rehearsed her speech, more than ten times, nearly boring her husband, Minh, to death in the process.

In spite of all these preparations, Kimmi began to panic as she sat waiting. She felt a hard knot in the pit of her stomach; her hands were trembling; and her mouth was dry. She wanted to bite her fingernails. She heard laughter coming from the boardroom. Oh no, she thought, are they laughing at me? The very thought made her feel nauseated. Why did she ever consent to do this? In college, she bailed out of a public speaking course because she had always dreaded the idea of getting up and talking in front of a group. Now she wished fervently that she had mastered her anxieties and completed the course after all!

To some extent, we have all had Kimmi's experience. Even polished and accomplished public speakers never quite get over a sense of nervousness and anxiety about making a presentation in front of a bunch of strangers. These feelings are common and unavoidable; in fact, they are the primary factors that interfere with public speaking performances.

Note that it was not that Kimmi lacked the necessary skills. She had a well-organized speech prepared; she knew her subject well; and she actually spoke English quite fluently (better than most native speakers, teachers had often remarked). But contrary to popular opinion, research reveals that public speaking performance has little to do with speech preparation and fluency skills.[1] All the skills training in the world may or may not increase your effectiveness as a speaker. Furthermore, contrary to popular wisdom, practice does not always make perfect. Performing time and again may help some speakers, but many others actually get worse. This is especially true for those speakers who, after repeated public speaking failures, learn to expect failure.

The bottom line is a speaker's emotional state—which has little to do with skills. In fact, over 200 separate studies reveal that a person's ability to perform well while speaking in front of a group is closely related to a condition called communication apprehension.[2] That condition, its causes and consequences, and ways to cope with it are the main topics of this chapter.

COMMUNICATION APPREHENSION AS A COMMON REACTION

Although this book focuses on public speaking, all of us have felt anxious about communicating in other kinds of settings as well. For example, we might feel extremely uncomfortable when we interact with people we don't know very well, engage in small talk, handle conflict, justify ourselves in an employment interview, work in a small group, give a briefing, or simply participate in class discussions. All such situations can provoke anxiety. Defined very simply, **communication apprehension** refers to fear or anxiety associated with either real or anticipated communication encounters.[3]

Note that communication apprehension does not have to coincide with the actual speaking encounter; it can occur simply in anticipation of having to speak. Take yourself, for example. Your grade in your public speaking course will depend, in part, on your ability to present a speech. Just knowing that you will have to talk before an audience may trigger enough anxiety to inhibit your ability to ask or answer questions. Similarly, anticipating the social demands of, say, a dinner party at your boss's home may stimulate communication apprehension long before you arrive. In other words, anxiety about communicating is a condition that can occur either prior to or during any particular encounter.

Some specialists regard communication apprehension as a special kind of shyness.[4] **Shyness**, like communication apprehension, is characterized by a general avoidance of or reluctance to engage in social interactions.[5] Whereas communication apprehension is rooted in people's fears about communicating, the reasons for people's shyness can vary greatly. Some shy people may lack communication skills; they may not know what to say, how to engage others in talk, or how to keep a conversation going. Others may have the necessary skills to communicate effectively

Communication apprehension refers to the fear or anxiety speakers feel when they face either real or anticipated communication encounters. Communication apprehension can occur in a variety of settings. For example, anticipating giving a presentation in an upcoming class may activate communication apprehension and give rise to thoughtful concentration.

but prefer being unobtrusive or reflective and, thus, be unwilling to communicate.

Certainly, not all shy individuals experience communication apprehension. Looking at the population as a whole, about 40 percent report being shy,[6] but only a little over 20 percent experience significant communication apprehension.[7] Therefore, about half of the people who are shy appear to be content to avoid interaction with others. The remainder, however, are probably shy because of some degree of fear about communicating. This is especially likely among those who lack communication skills. For example, an individual who is not good at small talk would probably be anxious about attending a large cocktail party. Another person, unskilled at speaking eloquently in front of a crowd, might become fearful if asked to say some words at a friend's wedding. Then there is the individual who would rather spend Friday night alone watching a movie than ask someone out on a date. Because of limited experience, these individuals may become even more shy or reticent as time goes on. Others dread communicating not because of any skill deficiency, but simply because they are afraid of the act itself. Even thinking about it ahead of time evokes fear. People who are afraid to communicate may actually avoid interaction, even when it's in their own best interest. For example, an employee may be unlikely to approach his boss to ask for a raise, although he knows he deserves more money. A student may avoid answering a professor's question in class, even when she knows the answer. In both instances, such communicators may know how to perform the required behavior—that is, they are capable of uttering the words necessary to request the raise or respond to the professor's questions—but their emotional reactions prevent them from doing so.

To understand further the nature of communication apprehension, we need to differentiate between three different categories of people in which this condition is present: (1) people who are nearly always apprehensive about relating to others, (2) people who have been in certain situations that have incited fears about communicating, and (3) people who belong to traditionally defined apprehensive cultural groups.

Apprehensive People

Apprehensive people fear communicating with almost anyone in any kind of situation. Jim McCroskey, who is best known for his research in communication apprehension, labels this type of more or less stable and predictable fear **traitlike communication apprehension**.[8] A **trait** is a relatively stable and predictable pattern of behavior that becomes characteristic of an individual's personality. There are literally thousands of traits with common labels—such as "stingy," "happy-go-lucky," "sweet," or "creative"—that describe observable features of a person's behavior over time. Similarly, individuals can acquire traits of being highly apprehensive about communicating across situations over time. To assess your own level of traitlike communication apprehension, take a few minutes to complete the survey in the box "How Much Communication Apprehension Do You Feel?"

Personality traits are not rigid. That is, individuals characterized by a particular trait may or may not exhibit the behavior in every instance. For example, a jovial person may not be good-humored in every circumstance. The same is true of an individual with a high communication apprehension trait. Much depends on the context and the other person (or people) involved. Individuals who are high in communication apprehension report little or no anxiety in the context of interacting with their best friends or with family. They may even be comfortable communicating with a specific professor or employer. Thus, they can talk freely without anxiety under some circumstances. Overall, however, persons high in the apprehension trait exhibit generalized avoidance toward most communication situations at most times.[9]

At the other extreme are people who actively seek out others and talk easily—and sometimes endlessly! Some talk so much that it's hard to get a word in edgewise. We would classify such individuals as very low in the apprehension trait. In our society, being low in communication apprehension can have great advantages—as long as it is not too low. For the most part, we tend to approve of individuals who can give a good interview, stand comfortably in front of a crowd and entertain, or meet new acquaintances with finesse and charm. In contrast to chronically high apprehensives who avoid communication encounters, those low in the trait seek them out. For example, a person low in communication apprehension will look forward to attending a party where he or she may not know anyone; an individual high in this trait would dread such a situation.

Research reveals that persons with little fear of communication tend to talk more, date a wider

How Much Communication Apprehension Do You Feel?

Instructions

This survey, officially entitled "Personal Report of Communication Apprehension–24" (PRCA-24), is composed of 24 statements concerning your feelings about communicating with other people. Enter the appropriate number in the space provided to indicate the degree to which each statement applies to you: (1) strongly agree, (2) agree, (3) are undecided, (4) disagree, or (5) strongly disagree. There are no right or wrong answers. Do not be concerned that many of the statements are similar to others. Simply record your first impression.

___ 1. I dislike participating in group discussions.

___ 2. Generally, I am comfortable while participating in a group discussion.

___ 3. I am tense and nervous while participating in group discussions.

___ 4. I like to get involved in group discussions.

___ 5. Engaging in a group discussion with new people makes me tense and nervous.

___ 6. I am calm and relaxed while participating in group discussions.

___ 7. Generally, I am nervous when I have to participate in a meeting.

___ 8. Usually I am calm and relaxed while participating in meetings.

___ 9. I am very calm and relaxed when I am called upon to express an opinion at a meeting.

___ 10. I am afraid to express myself at meetings.

___ 11. Communicating at meetings usually makes me uncomfortable.

___ 12. I am very relaxed when answering questions at a meeting.

___ 13. While participating in a conversation with a new acquaintance, I feel very nervous.

___ 14. I have no fear of speaking up in conversation.

___ 15. Ordinarily I am very tense and nervous in conversations.

___ 16. Ordinarily I am very calm and relaxed in conversations.

___ 17. While conversing with a new acquaintance, I feel very relaxed.

___ 18. I'm afraid to speak up in conversations.

___ 19. I have no fear of giving a speech.

___ 20. Certain parts of my body feel very tense and rigid while giving a speech.

___ 21. I feel relaxed while giving a speech.

___ 22. My thoughts become confused and jumbled when I am giving a speech.

___ 23. I face the prospect of giving a speech with confidence.

___ 24. While giving a speech, I get so nervous I forget facts I really know.

Calculating Your Score

The PRCA-24 allows you to compute both an overall communication apprehension score and four different subscores that measure your apprehension toward four familiar communication contexts: groups, meetings, dyads (interpersonal conversations), and public speaking situations.

1. Group = 18 + scores for items 2, 4, and 6; – scores for items 1, 3, and 5. Your group score = ___

2. Meeting = 18 + scores for items 8, 9, and 12; – scores for items 7, 10, and 11. Your meeting score = ___

3. Dyadic = 18 + scores for items 14, 16, and 17; – scores for items 13, 15, and 18. Your dyadic score = ___

4. Public = 18 + scores for items 19, 21, and 23; – scores for items 20, 22, and 24. Your public speaking score = ___

5. Overall Communication Apprehension (CA) = the sum of your subscores: Group + Meeting + Dyadic + Public. Your total CA score = ___

Interpreting Your Score

The possible range of scores is 24 to 120. (If your overall CA score does not fall within that range, you have made a computational error.) High CAs (scores higher than 83) are characterized as low talkers, shy, withdrawn, fearful, tense, and nervous. Low CAs (scores lower than 55) talk a lot, seem to enjoy the company of others, are friendly and sociable, and occasionally communicate even when others would rather

How Much Communication Apprehension
Do You Feel? (Continued)

they didn't. Moderate CAs (scores between 55 and 83) are considered more "normal." They know there are times when they should talk and times when they should not. Moderates are apprehensive during important job interviews but feel little or no tension when talking to friends or acquaintances.

By examining only your subscore on public speaking anxiety, you can determine just how fearful you may be about the prospect of giving a speech any time soon. Scores on each of the four contexts (group, meeting, dyadic, public) can range between 6 and 30. Any score above 18 reveals some degree of anxiety. And if your score is above 18 for the public speaking context, you experience stage fright, just like most people.[1]

Note

1. Richmond, V. P., & McCroskey, J. C. (1995). *Communication: Apprehension, avoidance, and effectiveness* (4th ed.). Scottsdale, AZ: Gorsuch Scarisbrick.

SOURCE: McCroskey, J. C. (1982). *Introduction to rhetorical communication* (4th ed.). Englewood Cliffs, NJ: Prentice-Hall.

variety of individuals, choose occupations that demand more social contact, communicate more assertively, and engage in more self-disclosure. By contrast, apprehensive individuals tend to be withdrawn, engage in steady dating (versus "playing the field"), select careers that allow them to work apart from others, agree with the opinions of others (rather than express independence), and avoid revealing much information about themselves.[10]

While individuals who are high or low in communication apprehension represent the ends of the continuum, most people can be categorized as moderately apprehensive. In other words, most people have some fear of communicating. About 20 percent of the population falls at the high end of the continuum, and roughly the same percentage is at the low end. This means that the remaining 60 percent—the majority—is somewhere in between.[11] These people typically experience apprehension only in certain situations. For example, most people experience some level of apprehension in situations in which their behavior is being evaluated. When people recognize that what they say and how they say it will make a difference in how some significant person (such as a prospective employer) views them, it is entirely normal for them to feel some anxiety or fear. Furthermore, it is highly likely that everyone experiences some fear before or during any kind of presentation. If a speaker is ill prepared or believes that the audience will be hostile, that fear probably will (and should) increase.

Apprehensive Situations

It is the rare individual who has not at one time or another temporarily experienced communication apprehension—this holds true even for low apprehensives. But the situations that trigger communication apprehension vary greatly from person to person. Some people feel anxious whenever they talk into a tape recorder or leave a message on an answering machine; suddenly, they can think of nothing intelligent to say. For others, particular individuals trigger their apprehension, such as a person conducting a job interview or a friend's parents. Take your pulse when you approach your boss for a raise, meet your future in-laws, ask someone special for a first date, or sign for a telegram. Sometimes there are good and logical reasons for concern. For example, if your boss suddenly calls on you in a staff meeting to explain why your department has exceeded its budget, your adrenaline will undoubtedly flow! Other times, however, people may feel distress even when the situation does not warrant it. Imagine, for instance, that your speech communication professor tells you that no grades will be assigned for your first speech assignment. There should be no real reason to feel apprehensive then, right? After all, it won't matter if you do well or not; it's just a practice session, right? Unfortunately, many people would still feel apprehensive.

When people's apprehension becomes temporarily provoked (even for low or moderate apprehensives), they are likely to respond just like high

Interview with a Student

Kim Lim

Kim Lim, 18, describes herself as Chinese–Cambodian American. Born in Cambodia, Kim has lived in the United States most of her life. Fluent in both Chinese and Cambodian, Kim is also quite fluent in English. At home, she speaks mostly Cambodian; at California State University, Long Beach, she's majoring in English. As a schoolchild, Kim tells us, she dreaded being called on in class; she would hide behind her desk and shiver whenever she thought she might have to speak. She recalls a particular event when she was so apprehensive in front of the class that she broke down in tears and ran from the room. Apparently, her childhood classmates were unsympathetic to her early attempts to speak English.

Do you think your fears about public speaking are about the same as everyone else's, or do you think you are more apprehensive than others?

I think I am more apprehensive than most people, and that has a lot to do with my culture. Being an Asian female, I was taught to be very passive and to look down. Asian women are taught to communicate differently than Asian men. All my life I've been told that I have to be passive, that I can't do this, I can't do that, and that I can't argue. In my culture, I was taught to give the utmost respect to my elders. I was told what to do—no questions about it. So, I would never dream of arguing with them. Because I was taught to be so passive, it terrifies me when I am asked to speak in front of a group—especially if that group consists of elders.

Now when I give a speech, I have to break with my tradition. When I am in front of an audience, I have to catch myself. I look away, and I tend not to give eye contact. Very few Asian women want to give eye contact. It's hard to break with all that I have been taught at home.

Do you think the fact that English is not your first language has any impact on your apprehension about speaking before a group?

Yes. When I speak in front of a group, even though I'm told that I am very fluent in English, I always think that

I'm speaking incorrectly or that I am going to "sting in people's ears" when I don't speak correctly. No matter how much I practice the English language, I know that I have not perfected it. Since my English is always being tested, my fear rises.

Add to that the fact that in Chinese and Cambodian (especially Cambodian), if you don't have the proper sentence structure, you're criticized for it. And so, you always have to have very polite mannerisms, and you always have to be correct in your sentence structure. If you don't, they say you are ignorant or that you're not very knowledgeable or intelligent. They judge you by the way you speak.

After taking this class in public speaking, do you find you are less apprehensive about speaking before a group? What advice would you give to other speakers who share your fears?

This class has given me a lot more confidence. When I entered the class, I was scared to death of my first speech because I was scared that everyone was going to throw things at me or laugh. But as soon as I got up there, everything came back to me, everything I knew came out. If you pick a topic that you know a lot about, then you don't have to do as much research and so you are more confident of that information. You know you can't go wrong. Because you have had that experience yourself, you are more confident and relaxed simply because you know it.

I advise people to pick subjects that they know by heart. Pick subjects that they are passionate about. Select topics that are of interest to them. Also, try to make things spontaneous, and try to be calm and relaxed and be confident in yourself. Remember: Fear is your biggest enemy. Don't let it overpower you. Whether you do bad or good, you did it, and that's what counts. Just be confident that you will do fine, and I assure you, you'll do better than you thought you would.

---

apprehensives—they will avoid apprehension-producing situations. Thus, like apprehensive people, they become avoiders, or they become incapacitated—unable to send or receive messages adequately. They might forget what they were planning to say, stammer in embarrassment, or clam up just when they need to perform their best.

Apprehensive Cultural Groups

Given the inherent relationship between communication and culture discussed in Chapter 3, it should come as no surprise that culture also influences individuals' general avoidance of communication or their level of apprehension. A number of studies report that internationally, culture has a profound impact on people's communication apprehension.[12] When compared to the norms in the United States and elsewhere, for instance, Japanese and Micronesians are significantly more apprehensive about communicating. Even though Swedes, Australians, and Chinese are generally more withdrawn and potentially less willing to communicate, their apprehension levels are similar to U.S. norms. By contrast, Puerto Ricans, Koreans, Filipinos, and Middle Easterners are much less apprehensive than Americans. (Importantly, the research defining U.S. "norms" is heavily influenced by Euroamericans—not because other cultural groups were systematically excluded from study, but because Euroamericans outnumbered all other groups sampled.)

In the United States, we can assume further that our own co-cultural affiliations affect our apprehension about communicating. Although there is very little research investigating this relationship, what research there is supports that conclusion. Nevertheless, it is important to note that any given member of a particular co-culture may or may not conform to the findings reported below. After all, that research is based on norms across large numbers of people, not specific individuals. (Refer to the box "Interview with a Student: Kim Lim" for a description of how co-cultural background influenced one student's level of public speaking anxiety and her overall communication style.)

One study shows that African American students report slightly lower levels of communication apprehension when compared to overall U.S. norms (that is, primarily Euroamerican norms). When surveyed about their fears of public speaking, African Americans report being significantly less anxious about giving a speech than Euroamericans—but they still experience some degree of apprehension.[13] In contrast, both Native American (specifically, Navajo, Hopi, Zuni, and Havasupai) and Asian American (primarily Chinese and Japanese American) students report higher levels of apprehension than Euroamericans.[14] Similarly, Hawaiian Americans indicate higher levels of communication apprehension.[15] Because Latinos value the spoken word, we would expect them to have lower levels of apprehension. And, consistent with the international cross-cultural research, we could predict that Middle Eastern Americans and Korean Americans experience lower apprehension as well.

Other research reveals that people from the southern regions of the United States tend to be more apprehensive than those from northern states.[16]

Individuals reared in rural areas are more likely to develop higher levels of communication apprehension than those from metropolitan communities.[17] The research reveals no consistent, meaningful differences between females and males in their levels of apprehension.[18] However, males and females who engage in more "feminine" behaviors (submissive, nurturing, emotional) tend to report higher levels of communication apprehension than females and males who tend to be more "masculine" (powerful, dominant, task oriented) in their approach.[19]

This overview of culture and communication apprehension may seem incomplete; after all, a number of co-cultures haven't been mentioned. That's because there is no other research available at this time. And, yet, what is known has important implications for public speaking.

CAUSES OF PUBLIC SPEAKING ANXIETY

Public speaking is the most anxiety-producing communication event you are likely to encounter. The anxiety associated with public speaking is known as **stage fright**. Of all situations—whether talking in groups, committees, or one-on-one—speaking before an audience ranks highest in people's fears. This finding is true for Euroamericans, African Americans, Swedes, Australians, Micronesians, and any and all other cultural groups examined to date. It is true for almost everyone, including individuals who regard themselves as being low, moderate, or high in traitlike communication apprehension. It is even true for professional speakers, writers, leaders, and entertainers, including Clint Eastwood, Michael Jackson, Janet Jackson, David Letterman, Barbra Streisand, James Taylor, Gloria Steinem, Harrison Ford, Colin Powell, Kevin Costner, and Barbara Bush.

What is it about public speaking that causes us to become so apprehensive? Researchers have identified a number of situational and psychological factors that can heighten our apprehension and affect our ability to communicate effectively.[20] Although each of these factors can influence our apprehension in a variety of contexts, the following discussion focuses on how these factors relate to our anxieties specifically in the context of public speaking.

Feeling Conspicuous and Inspected

Any context in which you are singled out, with the attention of an audience directly on you, can be a source of intense communication anxiety. More than any other aspect of a public speaking situation, conspicuousness—the belief that all eyes are riveted on you, scrutinizing everything you say and do—can induce a heightened sense of communication apprehension. It is difficult to communicate with an audience knowing that each and every member is attending to you and to you alone. Rather than focus on your presentation, you may wish that you were someplace else or that everyone would just go away.

Facing an Unfamiliar or Dissimilar Audience

It is always easier to talk to people you know and like than to those who are unfamiliar to you. Striking up a conversation with strangers is anxiety producing. What do you say to people you don't know? In many public speaking encounters, you will be faced with large numbers of people you don't know. Will they like you? Will they be open to what you have to offer? Will they help you do a good job, or will they not care?

Likewise, people who hold attitudes different from your own may make you anxious. Imagine seeing a longtime childhood friend who dropped out of high school and resents college students as snobs and smart alecks. Or imagine advocating your position on abortion before a group that strongly holds the opposite viewpoint.

Audiences who are culturally different from you may also create some anxiety. What if your audience consists primarily of Cuban Americans from Florida and you are a Navajo from Arizona? What if your audience is made up of African Americans from East Los Angeles and you are Korean American? Whether the cultural differences are real does not matter; what matters is whether you and your audience perceive them to be. Finding common ground to communicate constructively with either audience may be a challenge.

Confronting a Novel or Formal Speaking Situation

Because most people have not had a lot of experience speaking before a group, the novelty of the situation causes them to be apprehensive simply because they haven't had a lot of practice. Without practice or experience, you begin to feel uncertain: What am I supposed to do? How do I begin? Uncertainty creates worry. Formality can induce uncertainty and apprehension as well. And public speaking events tend to be the most formal communication situation you will ever experience. It's very difficult to behave casually and look relaxed when you're standing at a podium or sitting at a table, behind a microphone, looking out at dozens or hundreds of people.

Feeling Subordinate to Your Audience

Certain kinds of situations define for individuals their status and rank. Many of those situations underscore for people their own lower status compared to others. For example, attending a dinner party at your boss's home may serve to remind you of where you fit into the power structure—making you self-conscious about your behavior in the presence of those who can control your destiny. Communication apprehension is sure to follow! Often, when you are asked to speak before a large group, your status is defined as being higher than that of the audience. Even so, you may feel your high status is undeserved or questionable. Once again, communication apprehension is sure to rear its ugly head, making it difficult for you to communicate.

Undergoing Evaluation

Being "checked out" or evaluated by audiences is almost certain to bring on communication anxiety. In public speaking situations in which you know that, say, your boss or your speech communication professor is in the audience, you become immediately anxious. After all, you know they are appraising you on the basis of your oral performance. Even though you may do well without their scrutiny, the idea that you're being assessed heightens your apprehension about what to say or do. Students often report that when they practice their speeches at home, they experience no problems. But as soon as they see the professor with the grade book or critique form, they get nervous, forget their best lines, and generally perform poorly.

Remembering Repeated Failures

Memories of previous failures in identical or similar situations are a common source of apprehension. For instance, if you have asked someone for a date and been repeatedly turned down, trying another time might be distressing, to say the least. You may recall your prior efforts to give a speech as miserable experiences. In fact, you may have failed in those past attempts. But even if the audience applauded and the teacher told you that you did fine, your own anxieties about the event may have distorted those responses. So, instead of taking those reactions at face value, you conclude that the audience was merely being polite and sensitive. No wonder people feel nervous and reluctant about standing up and delivering a speech one more time.

Relying on English as a Second Language: A Special Problem

Your communication apprehension may be especially high when speaking before an audience whose primary language is different from your own. If your native language is English, you only have to travel to another country to discover how difficult it is to communicate with others—even when you think you already know their language. Normally talkative U.S. Americans often become withdrawn and reticent when they try to interact abroad. Similarly, English-as-a-second-language (ESL) speakers may become anxious and reluctant to engage in interactions with native English speakers, even when they apparently speak English very well. (For a description of how one ESL student found his level of apprehension affected, see the box "Interview with a Student: Layth Alashquar.") Research reveals that individuals who are normally not apprehensive communicating in their own language often become highly anxious when they switch to English.[21] Often, that anxiety is derived from the unrealistic expectation that spoken English should somehow be "perfect." In actuality, audiences are very appreciative of speakers' attempts to communicate in a second language and are much

SPEAKING OUT

Interview with a Student

Layth Alashquar

Layth Alashquar, 17, is a first-year student at California State University, Long Beach, majoring in biology. Layth is a recent immigrant from Jordan. His first language is Arabic, but he's been studying and practicing English most of his life. Even though he speaks English very well, Layth experiences some apprehension about speaking this second language to a U.S. audience. He still thinks in Arabic and translates into English when speaking. Sometimes, he claims, the translations don't work. Moreover, the speaking style of his culture makes it difficult to translate. Layth tells us that in his culture, it is highly appropriate to be very complimentary when speaking to another, using a lot of descriptors that flatter and praise. For instance, in Jordan, it's not at all unusual to tell a woman that she is "beautiful like a bird." "But here," he says, "nobody speaks like that. If I say something like that here, it sounds weird."

Do you think that the fact that English is not your first language has any impact on your apprehension about speaking before a group?

Yes, it does. When I go up there and I try to speak, they [the audience] know English better than me. Sometimes I know they are going to laugh at me because I make up or form a wrong statement. Or sometimes I might talk about something and they would understand it in a different way. After all, it's a totally different culture here. I know some things about American culture, but I really haven't studied it well.

Do you think your fears about speaking are about the same as everyone else's, or do you think you are more apprehensive than others?

I think I am more apprehensive than everybody in this class.

Than everybody in this class? Why do you say that?

Yes. First of all, I've been here only three years in the United States. And, I haven't got American friends my age. I talk Arabic at home. And most of my friends are Arab, so I talk Arabic with them, too.

After taking this class, do you find you are less apprehensive about speaking before a large group?

Yes, I do feel less apprehensive after taking this class. For my first speech, I was very apprehensive. Same for my second speech. But my last major presentation went better. When I first got up there, I was very apprehensive, but in seconds, it just went away. I became very comfortable, just like talking to my friends. For me, all I need is some practice speaking in front of a group. Students who are like me should make sure that they read the chapters in the book. Then, make sure you follow the criteria sheets [that your teacher provides]. Then, rehearse it at least four times before giving the final speech.

more likely to make a special effort to listen attentively when they do.

Having a regional accent or dialect can also make speakers feel apprehensive. We often judge and are judged by others based on how we talk. For example, people from the Midwest seem to talk through their nose, which may be perceived negatively by listeners from other geographic areas. The same can be true of those with a Texas drawl or the speech patterns characteristic of the deep South: Unfortunately, such speakers are often judged to be lazy or ignorant.[22] The same is true for African American speakers who switch both codes and style from Standard American English (sounding "white") to Black English (sounding "black").[23]

There is absolutely no relationship between accent or dialect and level of intelligence. It is a serious mistake to make any assumptions about other people's intelligence or personality traits on the basis of how differently they pronounce words. Nevertheless, our own apprehension level may be intensified knowing that our accent or dialect sounds strange to an audience.

In overview, most of us can readily identify with a number of sources of communication distress. We have all been in circumstances that provoked some degree of temporary or transitory apprehension. Clearly, the anxieties associated with the experience of speaking before a group are easy to understand and explain. However, the problem becomes more complex when we attempt to identify more deep-seated, long-term causes of communication apprehension that influence our anxieties about public speaking.

Individuals who are generally high in communication apprehension—that is, those whose apprehensions have become a part of their personality traits—perceive their environment differently than those who seldom experience anxiety. They tend to distort their interpretations of the situational factors discussed previously. For example, high trait apprehensives may perceive a public speaking situation to be even more formal or novel than it really is. They may feel even more conspicuous or different from the audience than they should. They may convince themselves that everyone in the audience noticed when they made a mistake and laughed at them. Even when we try to tell them otherwise, they don't buy it. Unfortunately, those with high trait apprehension engage in so much self-monitoring that they distort reality or the way other people interpret them and the situation.

DEALING WITH COMMUNICATION APPREHENSION

The good news is that none of us has to go through life avoiding or worrying endlessly about events that require us to communicate. We can learn to control our apprehensions. In particular, we can cope with stage fright and even modify a communication apprehension trait. That is not to say there is some easy way to transform someone who is chronically high in apprehension into a low-apprehensive individual. Nevertheless, plenty of evidence indicates that even those who are truly anxious can be moved to a moderate level, at which their apprehensions can be managed, so that they can communicate with others effectively in both public and private settings.[24]

Reducing Your Fears

Three methods have been touted as potential cures for communication anxieties: systematic desensitization, cognitive restructuring, and skills training. Although many other techniques have merit—such as hypnosis, group counseling, and psychoanalysis—they can be very costly and are not as effective. Today, most colleges and universities offer at least two of the three techniques discussed in this section as part of public speaking training. See if any of these techniques is available to you, and consider whether it seems suitable to your needs.

Systematic Desensitization Systematic desensitization, known commonly as SD, has the highest success rate of treatment programs for communication apprehension.[25] Developed in the early 1950s, SD is a form of treatment for many kinds of fears, including communication apprehension and fear of flying, heights, driving, and so on.

In the mid-1960s, research began on the effects of SD on public speaking anxiety. Experimenters repeatedly found that SD significantly reduced students' fears about communicating. In 1972, an SD program for students was initiated at Illinois State University. The program included published guidelines that others have used to initiate similar treatment programs at universities and high schools across the country.[26]

Systematic desensitization focuses on the physical responses to apprehension. We all become tense and tighten our muscles when we are anxious; it is an involuntary response. If we have reason to be fearful, our bodies automatically react to prepare for action—whether or not physical action is required to deal with

Communication apprehension is often high for speakers communicating to audiences whose primary language is different from their own. People who are not normally apprehensive when talking in their native language, like these ESL students, can become highly nervous when they must switch to English. Even so, audiences appreciate speakers who attempt to communicate in a second language.

the source of the anxiety. Systematic desensitization works on the principle that if an alternative response—muscle relaxation—can be substituted for tension and stress, people can learn to cope with anxiety-producing situations, including communication situations.

So, the big message of SD is *relax*! "Well," you say, "that's easier said than done. How can anyone ease back and relax when they have a speech to perform?" The fact is, it can't be done without learning how to do it. In SD programs, individuals are actually taught how to relax. They learn to tense and then relax each of their muscles and to control their breathing so that, on cue, they can "let go" as they exhale. As muscles relax, the rest of the body gets the message to ease up on the tension. With practice, the trainee can induce this relaxation quickly and easily. In this treatment program, then, the trainee becomes conscious of physical tensions, from whatever source, and practices methods of releasing that tension on command.

The next phase of SD introduces the anxiety-producing conditions the training is all about. In the case of communication apprehension, students are exposed gradually to a sequence of communication situations, as shown in Figure 4-1. At first, situations are presented that arouse relatively little apprehension. For example, while in a relaxed state, subjects are asked to imagine themselves talking on the telephone to their best friend. Next, to increase the level of potential stress, they may be asked to visualize themselves working on a group project or going on a blind date. In the later stages of the program, subjects are asked to visualize situations that would have produced a lot of stress before the therapy began, such as presenting a speech or being interviewed on television. By the time they get to this level, they have developed their relaxation techniques to a point at which they can handle the situation. Over time, individuals learn to associate relaxation, not tension, with the increasing demands of each successive communication situation.

```
                                    High apprehension

Giving a speech

Participating in a
class discussion

Standing in front of
the class without
talking

Asking a question
during class

Working on a group
project

Talking with an
instructor

Talking with a friend

                                    Low apprehension
```

Figure 4-1 Sequence of communication situations for systematic desensitization. In systematic desensitization, the individual learns to associate relaxation, not tension, with increasingly stressful speaking situations.

In addition to its proven success rate, SD is also cost-effective. Each session lasts about an hour, and the entire program runs only about five to seven sessions. Research shows that if students are exposed to SD at the same time they are enrolled in public speaking classes at which they learn specific skills, they are more likely to finish the course, perform competently, and report feeling less apprehensive about communicating.

Cognitive Restructuring
An interesting alternative to SD is **cognitive restructuring**. Whereas SD focuses on muscle tension—the physiological effects of our apprehension—cognitive restructuring centers on our thought processes. It examines an individual's interpretations of the anxiety-producing situation itself. Again, this is a general therapy system and is not restricted to communication anxieties. Nevertheless, it can be used to reduce temporary or chronic communication apprehension.

Proponents of this method argue that people label certain situations inappropriately and that they often evaluate events as being more negative than they actually are.[27] These negative evaluations are based primarily on specific irrational beliefs that underlie

a lot of their emotions. Three irrational beliefs that individuals commonly entertain can be summed up in the following statements:

"Everyone must love me all the time or I am a bad person."

"I must be competent or successful in all situations or I am a bad person."

"When life is not the way I want, it is awful and upsetting."

Cognitive restructuring focuses on changing these kinds of beliefs. The role of the therapist is to help individuals understand the basis for their anxieties. When irrational beliefs are exposed, the therapist challenges them, questioning each and arguing logically against them all. Then the therapist offers rational alternatives to replace the discredited beliefs. Troublesome beliefs are thus restructured or displaced, and new convictions are established.

When cognitive restructuring is applied to communication apprehension, four major steps are involved. Here, we will focus on the communication situation that apprehensive people find particularly lethal—public speaking. In the "introduction," the basic principles involved in cognitive restructuring are explained. The trainer (or therapist) explains that apprehension toward public speaking is learned and that anything that has been learned can be unlearned and replaced with new ideas and behavior. Apprehension can be reduced significantly when individuals become aware of the irrational beliefs or negative thoughts they hold about public speaking.

The first step requires that trainees identify negative self-statements that inhibit their speaking performances. These negative self-statements consist of derogatory remarks that anxious people often make (to themselves) about the situation or their activities in that situation. Trainees are asked to consider three separate occasions on which they might make those silent negative statements—before, during, and after the speech. The first column of Figure 4-2 lists some sample negative self-statements. Do you recognize any that you might use? What are others you may have said to yourself?

In the second step, each of these statements is analyzed for errors in logic. The second column in Figure 4-2 lists some sample logic errors that undermine or disable each negative self-statement identified. Cognitive restructuring aims to show individuals that they have been rehearsing an entire monologue of irrational negative self-statements that typically form the

1. IDENTIFY NEGATIVE SELF-STATEMENTS	2. IDENTIFY ERRORS IN LOGIC	3. LEARN NEW COPING STATEMENTS
Before the speech ➤		
My topic is so boring. Why did I pick it?	Topics aren't inherently boring. I will make this one interesting.	I chose my topic carefully. People in my audience will be interested in it.
I know I'll forget my second major point.	I have a notecard with all my major points listed.	I've rehearsed my speech, and I will be using notecards. I'll remember all my main points.
I know I'll forget my second major point.	People generally like me; they'll like what I have to say, too.	My audience will love me—and they'll love my speech, too.
During the speech ➤		
I can see that no one likes what I'm saying.	I'm overgeneralizing; of course someone will like what I'm saying.	Most of my audience is interested; they appreciate what I'm saying.
My hands are all sweaty. Everyone can see how nervous I am.	Sure they're sweating, but no one will even notice.	I am a little nervous; no one seems to notice it but me.
They don't think I'm funny. I'm doomed!	Not everyone will die of laughter, but I'm sure I can get most of them to smile.	Nearly everyone in the audience laughed or grinned when I delivered that funny line.
After the speech ➤		
I blew it.	I did it, didn't I? I gave my speech.	I did a good job. I did a great job!
I can't do it again.	Of course I can do it again. That's why I'm taking this course—to learn how to give a speech.	I'm looking forward to my next speech so I can do an even better job.
I was even worse than I thought I would be.	The truth is, I'm never as bad as I imagine I'm going to be. I didn't throw up; I didn't fall down; and I'm still alive.	I did very well—better than I expected.

Figure 4-2 Steps in cognitive restructuring. This process requires that you rethink your beliefs about public speaking and learn to cope with your fears and anxieties.

basis for a kind of self-fulfilling prophecy: Believing that they are failing, they wind up doing so. It is no wonder their attempts at public speaking have been so frightening and frustrating up to this point.

In the third step, trainees learn a new set of coping statements to communicate to themselves. The therapist helps them generate these alternative statements and substitute them for the negative ones. Once again, the coping statements are generated for use before, during, and after the communication event. (The third column in Figure 4-2 lists some sample coping statements.) The trainer encourages everyone to replace his or her entire repertoire of negative expectancies and evaluations with positive, self-directed statements. Rather than emphasizing the negative aspects of their performances, trainees learn to attend to the positives.

Finally, individuals practice the new coping statements. The trainer points out that given the number of years the trainees have been rehearsing negative self-statements, they should not realistically expect to replace them immediately with positive ones. Old habits are hard to break. A whole new tool kit of coping statements has to be developed, memorized, and made available for immediate recall when the occasion demands. Eventually, these coping statements become automatic and help the individual reduce communication anxieties. This kind of automatic behavior is common in such physical tasks as driving, typing, reading, and playing tennis, in which, over time, we learned not to monitor every move we make. Our responses to communication situations can also be reduced to this level by appropriate cognitive restructuring.

Like SD, cognitive restructuring has a record of success in dealing with communication apprehension. The emphasis of the treatment program, however, should be on learning and practicing the coping statements themselves, not on understanding the underlying principles. Mere insight into the negative self-statements is insufficient and can even serve to increase anxieties simply by focusing excessive attention on the problem rather than the solution.

Skills Training The third and final method of reducing communication apprehension that we will consider differs sharply from the other treatment techniques. Rather than assuming our apprehensions lead to problems in communicating successfully with others, **skills training** reverses the causal sequence. That is, proponents of the technique argue that people's skills limitations in communicating influence their apprehension levels, that a primary cause of communication anxiety is a deficit in skills. Gerald Phillips, the leading spokesperson for this mode of treatment, reasons that some people develop apprehensions partly because they find themselves inept in communication situations.[28] In other words, they have a good reason for feeling anxious: They just don't know how to communicate effectively. Once they learn how to perform successfully, their apprehensions will be reduced. Thus, training programs based on these assumptions are designed to teach appropriate and effective communication skills.

When skills training is used to reduce individuals' public speaking anxieties, the usual approach is to expose speakers first to lectures, readings, and discussions of important public speaking concepts and principles. This exposure is usually followed by some form of rehearsal or performance of the principles studied. Speakers are encouraged to practice their new communication behaviors in front of an audience. Practice is seen as the key to success.

Early in this chapter, we maintained that practice does not always make perfect, yet the skills training method holds that it does. Undoubtedly, skills training can help speakers develop effective techniques and strategies for communicating in various settings. However, the degree to which it specifically reduces apprehension is debatable, because the research evidence on the effects of skills training on apprehension remains equivocal. In many instances, with specific training, amateur speakers have learned the requisite communication skills to become effective—and, thus, less anxious—public speakers.[29] If your own anxiety about public speaking stems from not knowing how to prepare and deliver a speech, skills training should help reduce your apprehension a great deal.

Nevertheless, there are people who have learned the necessary public speaking skills but whose apprehension continues to interfere with their ability to give a talk. The source of their apprehension, then, is not a deficit in skills, but some other anxiety-producing cause. In other words, sometimes skills training reduces apprehension, and sometimes it doesn't. Compared to SD and cognitive restructuring, skills training alone is probably a less effective approach to reducing apprehension. A recent evaluation of all of these methods reveals that a combination of all three is more effective than any single treatment.[30]

Managing Your Stage Fright

Stage fright is a common reaction that most of us experience every time we are faced with the prospect of giving a speech. Given the circumstances of public speaking, there is good reason for feeling apprehensive. After all, public speaking requires that we perform before an unfamiliar audience in a formal setting. Speaking before a group makes us feel conspicuous in such a way that everyone seems to be evaluating us. Many of us are not usually apprehensive in most other communication situations but find it difficult to face an audience in a public speaking situation. Consider, then, the chronically apprehensive person who is truly agonizing over the experience!

The chronically apprehensive will do almost anything to avoid speaking before an audience. When given the option, students high in communication apprehension will not enroll in anything remotely resembling a public speaking class. Because some universities require such classes, seriously apprehensive students may enroll, drop the class, and enroll again. Sometimes they do not muster the courage to enroll or to finish the class until the last semester of their last year in college! In fact, there are students who have never graduated simply because they were unable to complete that one required course.

In contrast, easy talkers typically enjoy public speaking courses and, despite experiencing mild and normal stage fright, learn to perform quite well. For such individuals, and indeed for those who are moderately apprehensive, stage fright can be controlled. By practicing skills, they learn to channel their apprehension in productive ways. Specifically, a certain amount of stage fright generates motivation—enough so that those who are low or even moderate in general communication apprehension can excel onstage.

Contrary to what you might think, you should not try to rid yourself completely of stage fright. Like certain kinds of unpleasant medicine, in limited doses, stage fright is often a necessary condition for expert performances. Unfortunately, many novice speakers, along with the chronically apprehensive, fail to manage their stage fright productively. Rather than using their anxiety to motivate themselves, they allow it to inhibit their abilities. They don't act on their fears, but rather give in to them. As a result, they cannot perform competently. What follow are some suggestions that should help you manage your stage fright sufficiently to motivate you to prepare and present your speech with confidence.

Select a Familiar Topic

As simple and obvious as this advice may seem, it turns out that highly apprehensive speakers rarely select a topic that is familiar to them.[31] As a result, they must spend considerable preparation time learning about the subject—at the expense of organizing and rehearsing the speech itself. It stands to reason that the less you know about a topic, the more you have to worry about what you will say. If you knew nothing about, say, the latest economic summit, the benefits of whole life insurance, or the persuasive effects of two-sided messages, your anxieties would surely increase if you were assigned to speak on one of those topics. Fortunately, for most of your speeches, you will either be assigned a general topic or allowed to pick your own. When given the option, be sure to select a topic that you already know something about.

Focus on the Audience.

Highly anxious speakers approach the presentation differently from those moderate or low in anxiety. Highly anxious speakers are likely to focus considerably more attention on themselves than on the audience or other environmental factors associated with the event.[32] Their concerns center on questions like, What happens if I forget something? Can I start over? What should I do if I don't know the answer to a question posed by an audience member? They also seem to be more concerned with evaluation: How will I be graded? What happens if my speech is too short? In contrast, low-anxiety speakers indicate greater concern for the speech environment. They ask questions like, How big is the room? Will there be a podium and microphone?

Speakers who are unusually apprehensive about getting up to speak often cling to the security of their notecards and research materials to the very last minute. Such failures to effectively manage communication apprehension can inhibit a speaker's abilities and often result in incompetent performances.

Interestingly, novice speakers do not seem to be all that concerned with the audience. John Daly, an expert in communication apprehension, and his colleagues asked students enrolled in a public speaking course what their primary concerns were in giving a speech.[33] Of the top 20 concerns, only 4 were directed at the audience: Will the people in the audience ask questions? How much do the people in the room know about my speech topic? Why are people listening to the speech? How many people will be in the audience? Importantly, an audience-centered approach to public speaking is likely to remove some of your most basic fears. Instead of worrying about how you look, how you sound, and how you feel, focus on whether the audience will care about and understand what you have to say. Approach your presentation not so much as a practiced performance, but as an extended conversation with your audience. Of course, this "conversation" is likely to benefit if you've planned and researched what you want to say.

Overprepare The surest way to reduce your fears about giving a speech is to do your homework. The only way you can really feel comfortable presenting a speech is to know what you are talking about—how to start your speech, where you're going, and how to end it. Actually, one of the benefits of having some degree of stage fright is that it propels you into doing just that. Spend time planning, researching, and organizing your presentation—right down to the last example or dramatic conclusion. When you have your outline in order, spend time rehearsing, revising, rehearsing, revising again, and then rehearsing some more. Even though practice doesn't always make perfect, it can certainly make you feel more confident about what you're going to say.

Visualize a Positive Experience More recent research on public speaking anxiety reveals that highly anxious speakers tend to focus on the negatives of their performances. For instance, communication researchers Melanie and Steve Booth-Butterfield asked students enrolled in public speaking classes to write down what they were thinking and feeling while they were giving a speech in class.[34] Highly anxious speakers were more likely to recall negative thoughts and feelings:

"I panicked."

"I'm sure the audience wasn't interested in my topic."

"I never do well at public speeches."

"My mouth was dry, and my heart was hammering through my chest."

By contrast, low-anxious speakers recalled more positive thoughts and feelings:

"I felt confident."

"I thought the speech seemed worth at least a B."

"I looked at the timer's cards and was in good shape."

"I could tell the audience liked what I was saying."

After reading both lists, you might begin to see some relationship between these recollections and the negative and positive statements listed in Figure 4-2. That is, anxious speakers engage in more negative self-statements and view the public speaking event as a threatening experience to avoid. They become hypersensitive to their own physical symptoms and get bogged down in all that possibly can go wrong. Restructuring those thoughts to include more positive self-statements can alleviate some, if not most, of that anxiety.

Accentuating the positive can be further enhanced through **visualization**. Visualization techniques are used by professional and amateur athletes to improve their performances. Basically, visualization requires that you sit back, relax, and "see" yourself being successful—from start to finish. When the technique is applied to public speaking, speakers are told to visualize the actual day on which they will be giving the speech, starting with getting up in the morning and selecting just the right clothes to wear. Speakers mentally walk themselves through the entire day leading up to the speech, the actual speech event itself, and, finally, the end of the presentation. Throughout the visualization process, speakers are urged to think of only positive outcomes. Speech communication scholars Joe Ayres and Tim Hopf tell us of one successful visualization exercise their students employed to reduce speech anxieties. Following is an excerpt from that visualization script:

> Now see yourself presenting your talk. You are really quite brilliant and have all the finesse of a polished, professional speaker. You are also aware that your audience is giving head nods, smiles, and other positive responses, conveying the message that you are truly "on target." The introduction of the speech goes the way you planned. In fact, it works better than you had expected. . . . When your final utterance is concluded, you have the feeling that it could not have gone better. . . . You now see yourself fielding audience questions with brilliance, confidence, and energy equal to what you exhibited in the presentation itself. You see yourself receiving the congratulations of your classmates.[35]

By highlighting and then visualizing a positive experience, you should be able to approach your next public speaking event with less anxiety and a lot more confidence.

There are a number of other ways to help you manage your public speaking fears, but most of that advice is fairly obvious and probably easier said than done—or is based on remedies that haven't yet been empirically verified. (Refer to the box "Reducing Your Public Speaking Anxiety" for other common strategies you might want to try.) In any case, see what works for you, and then use it.

CHAPTER REVIEW

- A person's ability to speak competently before a group requires learning not only the appropriate communication skills but also ways to reduce or manage apprehensions about public speaking. Communication apprehension can be the nature of (1) apprehensive people, who, regardless of the situation, almost always feel anxious about relating to others; (2) apprehensive situations that incite fears about communicating; and (3) apprehensive cultural groups.

- One communication context stands out as the most anxiety producing: public speaking. Seven factors contribute to that anxiety: (1) feeling conspicuous in front of a group, (2) facing an unfamiliar or dissimilar audience, (3) confronting a novel or formal speaking situation, (4) feeling subordinate to the audience, (5) being evaluated by the audience, (6) focusing on past failures, and (7) speaking English as a second language or using regional accents and dialects.

- A number of treatment programs are available to help people reduce their communication apprehension, including systematic desensitization (SD), cognitive restructuring, and skills training.

- Other strategies to help manage stage fright include selecting a familiar topic, focusing attention on the audience, overpreparing, and visualizing yourself speaking successfully before a group.

QUESTIONS FOR CRITICAL THINKING & REVIEW

1. In general, people high in communication apprehension seem to be at a disadvantage when it comes to others' perceptions of their competence, leadership abilities, and social attractiveness. Why do you suppose others perceive them that way? How might you caution someone with negative perceptions of people high in communication apprehension?

2. To what extent do you think your own co-cultural background influences your level of communication apprehension?

3. Research reveals that African Americans report less apprehension about giving a speech than many other U.S. co-cultural groups. What aspects of the value orientation or communication style of the African American co-culture might contribute to this lack of apprehension?

4. Research reveals that Asian Americans report significantly higher levels of apprehension about giving a speech than other U.S. co-cultural groups. What aspects of the value orientation or communication style of the Asian American co-culture might contribute to this apprehension?

5. One way to reduce your fears about public speaking is to overprepare, yet too much preparation can actually increase apprehension. Why do you think this is true?

NOTES

1. Allen, M., Hunter, J. E., & Donahue, W. A. (1989). Meta-analysis of self-report data on the effectiveness of public speaking anxiety treatment techniques. *Communication Education, 38,* 54–76.
2. McCroskey, J. C. (1982b). Oral communication apprehension: A reconceptualization. In M. Burgoon (Ed.), *Communication yearbook 6* (pp. 136–170). Beverly Hills, CA: Sage; McCroskey, J. C. (1984). The communication apprehension perspective. In J. A. Daly & J. C. McCroskey (Eds.), *Avoiding communication: Shyness, reticence, and communication apprehension* (pp. 13–38). Beverly Hills, CA: Sage.
3. McCroskey, J. C. (1977). Oral communication apprehension: A summary of recent theory and research. *Human Communication Research, 4,* 78–96; McCroskey, J. C. (1982a). *Introduction to rhetorical communication* (4th ed.). Englewood Cliffs, NJ: Prentice-Hall; McCroskey, 1984.
4. McCroskey, J. C., & Richmond, V. P. (1996). *Fundamentals of human communication: An interpersonal perspective* (pp. 55–65). Englewood Cliffs, NJ: Prentice-Hall.
5. Pilkonis, P., Heape, C., & Klein, R. H. (1980). Treating shyness and other relationship difficulties in psychiatric outpatients. *Communication Education, 29,* 250–255.
6. Zimbardo, P. G. (1977). *Shyness: What it is, what to do about it.* Reading, MA: Addison-Wesley.
7. Richmond, V. P., & McCroskey, J. C. (1995a). *Communication: Apprehension, avoidance, and effectiveness* (4th ed.) (p. 35). Scottsdale, AZ: Gorsuch Scarisbrick.
8. McCroskey, 1984, pp. 14–22; McCroskey et al., 1986, pp. 70–71.
9. McCroskey, 1982b; Richmond & McCroskey, 1995a, pp. 43–44.
10. McCroskey, 1982b; Payne, S. K., & Richmond, V. P. (1984). A bibliography of related research and theory. In J. A. Daly & J. C. McCroskey (Eds.), *Avoiding communication: Shyness, reticence, and communication apprehension* (pp. 247–294). Beverly Hills, CA: Sage; Richmond, V. P.

(1984). Implications of quietness: Some facts and speculations. In J. A. Daly & J. C. McCroskey (Eds.), *Avoiding communication: Shyness, reticence, and communication apprehension* (pp. 145–156). Beverly Hills, CA: Sage.

11. McCroskey & Richmond, 1996, p. 71.

12. Klopf, D. W., & Cambra, R. E. (1979). Communication apprehension among college students in America, Australia, Japan, and Korea. *The Journal of Psychology, 102,* 27–31; Klopf, D. W., & Cambra, R. E. (1980). Apprehension about speaking among college students in the People's Republic of China. *Psychological Reports, 46,* 1194; McCroskey, J. C., & Richmond, V. P. (1990). Willingness to communicate: Differing cultural perspectives. *The Southern Communication Journal, 56,* 72–77; Watson, A. K., Monroe, E. E., & Atterstrom, H. (1989). Comparison of communication apprehension across cultures: American and Swedish children. *Communication Quarterly, 37,* 67–75.

13. Ralston, S. M., Ambler, R., & Scudder, J. N. (1991). Reconsidering the impact of racial differences in the college public speaking classroom on minority student communication anxiety. *Communication Reports, 4,* 43–50.

14. Núñez, S. L. (1992, October). *Addressing communication apprehension in the multicultural public speaking classroom.* Paper presented at the Communication and Cultural Diversity in American Institutions Conference, Fullerton, CA.

15. Klopf, D. W. (1984). Cross cultural apprehension research: A summary of Pacific Basin studies. In J. A. Daly & J. C. McCroskey (Eds.), *Avoiding communication: Shyness, reticence, and communication apprehension* (pp. 157–169). Beverly Hills, CA: Sage.

16. Andersen, P. A., Lustig, M. W., & Andersen, J. F. (1990). Changes in latitude, changes in attitude: The relationship between climate and interpersonal communication predispositions. *Communication Quarterly, 38,* 291–311.

17. McCroskey, J. C., & Richmond, V. P. (1978). Community size as a predictor of development of communication apprehension: Replication and extension. *Communication Education, 27,* 212–219. Richmond, V. P., & Robertson, D. L. (1977, February). *Communication apprehension: Community size as a causative agent.* Paper presented at the annual convention of the Western Communication Association, Phoenix, AZ.

18. For a review, see Booth-Butterfield, M., & Booth-Butterfield, S. (1992). *Communication apprehension and avoidance in the classroom.* Edina, MN: Burgess; Richmond & McCroskey, 1995a.

19. Greenblatt, L., Hasenauer, J. E., & Freimuth, V. S. (1980). Psychological sex type and androgyny in the study of communication variables: Self-disclosure and communication apprehension. *Human Communication Research, 6,* 117–129.

20. Buss, A. H. (1980). *Self-consciousness and social anxiety.* San Francisco: Freeman; McCroskey et al., 1986, pp. 56–58.

21. McCroskey, J. C., Fayer, J. M., & Richmond, V. P. (1985). Don't speak to me in English: Communication apprehension in Puerto Rico. *Communication Quarterly, 33,* 185–192.

22. Richmond, V. P., & McCroskey, J. C. (1995). *Nonverbal behavior in interpersonal relations* (3rd ed.). Boston: Allyn & Bacon.

23. Hecht, M. L., Collier, M. J., & Ribeau, S. A. (1993). *African American communication: Ethnic identity and cultural interpretation* (pp. 84–95). Newbury Park, CA: Sage.

24. For an overview of that research, see Allen et al., 1989.

25. Friedrich, G., & Goss, B. (1984). Systematic desensitization. In J. A. Daly & J. C. McCroskey (Eds.), *Avoiding communication: Shyness, reticence, and communication apprehension* (pp. 173–187). Beverly Hills, CA: Sage.

26. McCroskey, J. C. (1972). The implementation of a large-scale program of systematic desensitization for communication apprehension. *Speech Teacher, 21,* 255–264.

27. Fremouw, W. J. (1984). Cognitive-behavioral therapies for modification of communication apprehension. In J. A. Daly & J. C. McCroskey (Eds.), *Avoiding communication: Shyness, reticence, and communication apprehension* (p. 210). Beverly Hills, CA: Sage; Fremouw, W. J., & Scott, M. D. (1979). Cognitive restructuring: An alternative method for the treatment of communication apprehension. *Communication Education, 28,* 129–133.

28. Phillips, G. M. (1977). Rhetoritherapy versus the medical model: Dealing with reticence. *Communication Education, 26,* 34–43. See also Kelly, L. (1984). Social skills training as a mode of treatment for social communication problems. In J. A. Daly & J. C. McCroskey (Eds.), *Avoiding communication: Shyness, reticence, and communication apprehension* (pp. 189–207). Beverly Hills, CA: Sage.

29. Kelly, 1984.

30. Allen et al., 1989.

31. Daly, J. A., Vangelisti, A. L., Neel, H. L., & Cavanaugh, P. D. (1989). Pre-performance concerns associated with public speaking anxiety. *Communication Quarterly, 37,* 39–53.

32. Daly et al., 1989.

33. Daly et al., 1989.

34. Booth-Butterfield, M., & Booth-Butterfield, S. (1990). The mediating role of cognition in the experience of state anxiety. *The Southern Communication Journal, 56,* 35–48.

35. Ayres, J., & Hopf, T. S. (1989). Visualization: Is it more than extra-attention? *Communication Education, 38,* 1–5.

Chapter 5

BEING A CREDIBLE AND ETHICAL SPEAKER

Learning Objectives

After reading this chapter, you should be able to do the following:

1. Demonstrate the power of first impressions.

2. List and differentiate among the five dimensions of speaker credibility.

3. Show how you can increase audience perceptions of your own credibility as a public speaker.

4. Identify ways public speakers are obliged to be ethical.

5. Demonstrate how speakers make decisions about behaving ethically when faced with ethical dilemmas.

6. Identify common justifications that people give when deciding to lie.

For her first speech assignment in class, Colby was asked to introduce herself by identifying a particular co-culture to which she belonged. Although she could have chosen to talk about the fact that she was a Texan, white, Christian, and single, she chose her co-cultural identity as a lesbian. She suspected her audience would be astonished—at least initially. She also knew that her disclosure might offend, frighten, or alienate some audience members. Even so, she wanted to have the opportunity to represent her co-culture in the same way that, say, Latinos, African Americans, and Native Americans would portray theirs—as reasonable, tenable, legitimate, and deserving respect. Her challenge, then, was to develop a strategy that would help her come across to her audience as credible, thoughtful, and sincere.

On the morning of her speech, Colby selected an outfit that made her feel comfortable, attractive, and feminine. She wore her long hair down, applied some light makeup, and then, giving herself a satisfied look in the mirror, declared, "Now *that* ought to dispel the fiction that all lesbians look like or would rather be men!" Then she rehearsed her speech aloud one more time.

Two hours later, Colby looked out at her audience and gave a warm smile. She opened with a story about a little girl who always felt different, excluded, and alienated from other little girls. She recounted how she felt unusual and unique, but not in that special way that others admire; instead, she felt peculiar and estranged. She talked about how those feelings and perceptions continued through her adolescence and stayed with her as a young adult. "Today that young woman better understands those feelings and is learning to accept her identity as different or distinctive from others," she contended. "I know who I am and I accept who I am. I am a lesbian."

Before she launched into the rest of her speech, Colby stopped. She gave a long look at the audience. Slowly, she smiled and shrugged. "If I startled you, imagine how *I* must feel! Whether you think I'm foolish or courageous to share my identity as a lesbian with you," she continued, "please understand my compulsion to be perfectly honest with you." With that plea, Colby showed real character and demonstrated trust in her audience to listen to and respect what she had to say. Knowing that audience members might be looking for ways that showed she was somehow different from them, somehow alien, Colby focused instead on all the ways she felt she was similar to them. She talked about the fact that she was a student who hated studying probably as much as everyone else, enjoyed Quentin Tarantino movies, worried about her career choices, preferred chocolate to vanilla ice cream, and liked being around both women and men. Next, she pointed out familiar, talented, and remarkable women who are also gay, including Martina Navratilova, Ellen DeGeneres, and k. d. lang. Throughout her presentation, Colby appeared fluent, confident, and relaxed. She came across as natural, expressive, and friendly. In the end, Colby may not have convinced everyone to accept her as a lesbian, but she went a long way toward eliciting their respect.

Colby's experience at influencing how others perceived her represents a common challenge faced by all public speakers who address audiences for the first time. Most public speakers are haunted by doubts about whether the audience will like them, appreciate what they have to say, find them credible and intelligent, and so on. What a speaker does and says leaves lasting impressions on the audience. How a speaker speaks, dresses, moves, and interacts with the audience sends messages about what kind of person she or he is—messages audience members quickly construct into impressions about what they think the speaker is "really like."

The impression an audience forms of a speaker is critical to the success of the presentation. If you are to achieve your goal in giving a speech, your audience must perceive you as being credible, ethical, knowledgeable, and worth listening to. Toward that end, this chapter focuses on three critical questions: (1) What can you do to influence the impression you make on your audience? (2) What are your ethical obligations as a public speaker? and (3) What specifically can you do, verbally and nonverbally, to be perceived as a credible, ethical speaker?

THE POWER OF FIRST IMPRESSIONS

Research has shown that people tend to form impressions quickly, on the basis of very limited information, and that these early impressions are difficult to change. Recognizing how audience members form early impressions can help you plan and manage what type of impression you will make.

The Process of Selective Perception

Selective perception plays a critical role in how people form impressions of others. **Perception** refers to the process of making sense of or attaching meaning to some aspect of reality that has been apprehended by the senses. Of course, not all people perceive or make sense of reality the same way; instead, they engage in some sort of **selective perception** process, choosing, selecting, and distorting all that they take in and assign meaning to. Research shows that people need to selectively perceive only a small number of characteristics or traits to size up one another but that they use this limited information to form fairly elaborate impressions of one another.[1] Particularly important are so-called **salient characteristics,** central traits that serve as a dominant attribute around which people construct a pattern of initial impressions.

First impressions can be compelling. People form impressions of one another quickly and based on limited information. How you look when you get up to speak dictates a large part of an audience's lasting impression of you.

As a public speaker, it may not comfort you to know that audience members will scrutinize certain of your behaviors, selectively perceived as salient characteristics, and then use these to make first (and often lasting) impressions of you. And your discomfort may increase when you realize that audience members will use those characteristics to interpret who they think you really are, evaluate what you have to say, and predict how you will act in the future. Although you cannot control the process of selective perception, you should recognize that it occurs and make any possible adjustments to present yourself in the best possible light.

The identification and evaluation of salient characteristics is an individual process that is closely tied to the **stereotypes** people hold toward certain characteristics of the speaker and to the co-cultural affiliations of audience members. The most obvious potential salient characteristics of public speakers are observable indicators, including mannerisms, speech patterns (including regional accents and dialects), gender, dress, hair color and length, jewelry, body size and shape, and other prominent and noticeable features. Obviously, we all wonder what our individual salient indicators are and what personality traits others will project onto us on the basis of what they see. Will the image others have of us represent who we are, or will it be grossly distorted and unfair?

The Impact of Stereotypes

Impressions formed from observable indicators are often stereotypical, based on ethnocentric or chauvinistic biases. Time and again, audience members form potentially inaccurate, prejudicial impressions based solely on a speaker's co-cultural identity or physical appearance. When that happens, it is extremely difficult, if not impossible, for speakers to strategically plan and manage their self-presentations. After all, how can we reasonably deny or change our sex, skin color, or accent? (And even if we could, would we want to?) One study, for instance, suggests that men are more likely to be perceived as credible speakers, at least initially.[2] Additionally, when speakers in this experiment, both males and females, were made up to look attractive, they were perceived as significantly more persuasive than when the same speakers were made to look unattractive; yet when comparisons were made between the unattractive female and male speakers, audience members found the unattractive males to be more credible. Other research confirms sex-based stereotypes: Male speakers are often rated higher in competence and dynamism, while female speakers are perceived higher in trust and attitude similarity.[3]

Body shape also appears to influence how people perceive others. In one study, participants were shown silhouettes of three body types: endomorphs (heavy, round, oval), mesomorphs (athletic, firm, muscular), and ectomorphs (thin, tall, slight). Without knowing anything else, subjects rated the unidentified silhouettes on a number of personal characteristics. For the most part, endomorphs were judged to be warmhearted, talkative, and lazy; mesomorphs were perceived as being adventurous, masculine, mature, and self-reliant; and ectomorphs were rated as tense, ambitious, suspicious, and stubborn.[4] This study was conducted over 30 years ago. Do you think those same results might still be obtained today? What other attributes might be assigned to those body types? How might co-cultural affiliation influence those selective perceptions?

Height is another observable indicator that affects first impressions. It may be no accident that a majority of top executives at Fortune 500 companies are over six feet tall. For many Americans, being tall is associated with credibility, success, status, and power; being short is not.

Skin color and ethnicity also affect how we are judged. Our country has a long history of responding with prejudice to many groups, including African Americans, Latinos, Asian Americans, Jewish Americans, Native Americans, and many others. Although often overlooked, prejudices are leveled against (or in favor of) Euroamericans as well. Similarly, men who engage in behaviors considered feminine or who openly identify themselves as gay can expect stereotypical responses from most audiences. The same is likely for women who employ characteristically masculine behaviors or who identify themselves as lesbian.

Although the responsibility for managing a positive first impression rests primarily on the speaker, audiences, too, must consider carefully the bases for the impressions they form of the speaker. Stereotypical impressions can form quickly, and those impressions are often based on some rather spurious, yet observable, speaker characteristics—impressions that are extremely difficult for a speaker to alter. Once formed, impressions tend to persist. But you can actively manage the first impressions you make on your audience.

The Process of Self-Presentation

The self refers to the pattern of beliefs, meanings, and understandings concerning our own nature and worth as a human being that each of us has developed through communication with others. When you interact with others, you present information about your inner nature to them—by what you say, how you act, how you dress, and so on. In the chapter opening, Colby carefully revealed several things about her self—by her clothes, by her hairstyle and makeup, by her subtle nonverbal behaviors, and by her self-disclosures. Similar to the model of public speaking described in Chapter 1, this presentation of self involves encoding and sending verbal and nonverbal messages to others about what kind of person you are. It works both ways, of course: You form impressions of others as they present themselves initially to you. This process of self-presentation is a universal and inescapable aspect of human behavior.

The messages you communicate about yourself may be deliberate or completely unintentional. Other people may evaluate you much differently than you wish or intend. Nevertheless, it is certainly possible, as Colby did, to plan a communication strategy and transmit verbal and nonverbal messages that are deliberately designed to create a particular set of impressions. Effective speaker self-presentation, or what sociologist Erving Goffman referred to as **impression management,**[5] is a critical skill on which personal, social, and professional success can depend.

How can you determine the best way to make a good first impression? Although no single way of presenting yourself to an audience will be effective in all contexts, there are some strategies that can help. Such strategies are designed to limit the display of salient characteristics the audience is likely to perceive negatively and to emphasize those salient characteristics that are likely to elicit a positive first impression. Two key salient characteristics for public speakers are credibility and ethics: To make a positive first impression, your audience must perceive you as being both credible and ethical.

The tools of speaker self-presentation are easy to identify. They consist of different aspects of nonverbal communication (including your clothing, gestures, posture, and demeanor) and verbal communication (the content and style of what you say and how you say it). Let's begin by examining those verbal and nonverbal strategies that will help to increase audience perceptions of your credibility.

ESTABLISHING SPEAKER CREDIBILITY

Perhaps no salient characteristic is more crucial to making a positive impression on an audience than speaker credibility. Audience members tend to believe and be influenced by public speakers whom they view as credible.[6] Speaker **credibility** refers to the degree to which the audience feels that a speaker is believable and trustworthy and that his or her messages are truthful. The degree to which a speaker is deemed credible varies from situation to situation and from one audience member to another. To one person, a speaker may seem to be a completely reliable source of information whose conclusions can be trusted; to another, the same speaker may seem sleazy and untrustworthy. One of the key challenges of speaker self-presentation is to be perceived as highly credible by a majority of audience members.

Speaker credibility can be enhanced (or significantly diminished) in a variety of ways. As Figure 5-1 shows, five major factors have been identified as the basis of speaker credibility: competence, trustworthiness, composure, sociability, and extroversion. Each of these is a dimension of the relationship a speaker must establish with an audience to make a

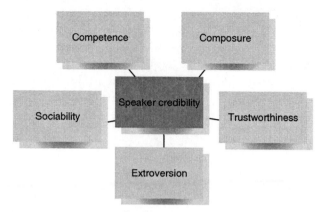

Figure 5-1 The five major dimensions of speaker credibility. Which dimension of credibility is most important for public speaking?

positive impression.[7] (The box "Establishing Your Credibility" lists specific strategies you can use to boost your credibility with your audience.)

Demonstrate Competence

The most important dimension of credibility for public speaking is perceived **competence**. Put simply, audience members demand that the speaker know more about the topic than they do. Speaker competence has little to do with intelligence; instead, it refers to how much valid information the speaker is perceived to command about the issue under discussion.

The first prerequisite for being perceived as competent is to research and study your subject. When you speak before an audience, you must have valid knowledge to offer. This means you need to obtain the available and relevant information on your topic.

Information is critical, but it is not the only factor influencing whether an audience perceives you as being competent; *how* you present that information is also important. Even if you know quite a bit about the subject of your presentation, you can still be perceived as incompetent. Some speakers create misperceptions from their own performance. For example, in an effort to make the material interesting and themselves entertaining or likable, speakers may make the material seem too easy. That is, they may simplify the information to the point of distortion and fail to address some of the more difficult yet substantive issues.

One of the text's authors, Pat Kearney, recalls an early teaching experience. Students in her introductory interpersonal communication course complained that the course content seemed "obvious" and that it was

Establishing Your Credibility

Because audience members tend to believe and be influenced by speakers they perceive as credible, it's important to manage yourself in such a way that your audience will perceive you to be competent, trustworthy, composed, sociable, and extroverted.

Demonstrate Competence

- Know what you're talking about. Research your subject thoroughly.

- Use precise language. When talking about something technical or difficult, don't be afraid to use the appropriate technical jargon. Just be sure to explain it clearly.

- Include oral footnotes. Reference your sources. Show the audience that experts agree with you.

- Admit your ignorance. When you don't know the answer to a question, don't try to sidestep or stonewall. Tell them you don't know—but you will find out!

- Look competent. Dress the part. Dress to look confident, well prepared, and knowledgeable.

- Arrange a validating introduction. Find someone to introduce you, someone who will disclose your expert credentials and impress the audience.

Generate Trust

- Be open and sincere. Don't be afraid to tell the truth.

- Be consistently honest and sincere. Don't fake an answer. Don't lie. Don't evade.

- Tell the audience your reason(s) for avoiding the question if you are asked an embarrassing question and would rather not disclose the truth.

Exhibit Composure

- Maintain a sense of confidence and composure— particularly during stressful moments. Don't let hecklers make you visibly angry.

- Appear self-assured by coming to the presentation well prepared. Know your material and rehearse your presentation often.

- Avoid slang words and phrases like "you know." Rather than try to fill pauses, simply remain silent.

- Avoid the use of adaptors. Keep nervous gestures and mannerisms to a minimum.

- Most of all, *practice* looking relaxed and confident.

Communicate Sociability

- Be friendly and pleasant.

- Rely on nonverbal immediacy behaviors, such as adopting a relaxed posture, smiling warmly, and making frequent eye contact.

- Learn audience members' names and use them.

- Say something nice about the audience, the location, the culture, or the event. Act *interested* in your audience.

Display Extroversion

- Walk up to people in the audience. Approach and be approachable.

- Make eye contact with each audience member.

- Expand your arm and hand gestures—enlarge your whole being.

- Show enthusiasm, energy, and dynamism. Smile!

- Keep talking.

---

all just "common sense." Pat inferred from those comments that she had somehow communicated the wrong impression; in her attempts to make the material both interesting and relatively easy to understand, she may have failed to alert students to the inherent complexities and problems associated with relationship management.

The next day, she came to class prepared to try another approach. She wrote on the board a common truism about relationships: "To know her is to love her." After some discussion in support of that claim, she wrote another truism about relationships that seemed to contradict the former: "Familiarity breeds contempt." Then she asked the class which adage was correct. Resolving the apparent conflict between the two statements helped her students recognize that common sense was not all that reliable. What seemed obvious or true in one moment was easily disputed by another so-called truism. After that, Pat often began her lectures with class discussions about other inaccuracies associated with commonsense relational advice. Presenting the information in this manner contributed to the students' perceptions that she was a highly credible speaker.

Speakers can use a number of different tactics to increase the likelihood that audience members will perceive them as being competent. They might use jargon, include oral footnotes, admit their ignorance (on occasion), *look* competent, and arrange a validating introduction.

Use Precise Language

To be seen as a competent speaker, use **jargon**—technical or special terminology characteristic of a particular subject area—but use it sparingly. When defining something that may be somewhat technical or difficult to understand, use the appropriate jargon, but be sure to explain it clearly. For example, speech communication experts often talk of the importance of establishing homophily with others. A good way to present such a term would be to use the technical phrase "principle of homophily" and to include a clear definition: "Homophily simply refers to attitude similarity, or how similar you and your audience perceive yourselves to be." Using redundancy when defining new terms can help further clarify their meaning: "How much people are alike—how much homophily they share—will have a great impact on whether they continue with their relationship."

Using jargon shows your audience that you know the appropriate terminology. Including clear definitions and adding redundancy demonstrate two important points to audience members: (1) You recognize that they may not know all the special terms, and (2) you give them credit for being able to learn them quickly and easily.

Include Oral Footnotes

A second strategy for demonstrating competence to your audience is to include oral footnotes of the sources of evidence in your speech. The evidence you include in your speech supports and verifies your assertions; by referencing the sources of your evidence, you show the audience that other experts agree with your conclusions. Before long, the audience is likely to perceive you as one of those experts.

Providing personal testimony to support your point will also enhance the perception of your "expertness" with a number of co-cultural groups (see Chapter 3). When members of co-cultures that value this type of evidence see that you have had some real-life experiences with your subject, they will likely form the impression that you know what you are talking about.

Admit Your Ignorance

It is also very important to admit ignorance when you don't know something relating to your speech topic. If an audience member asks a question and you don't know the answer, admit it! Speakers often find such admissions difficult, but they are critical. Audiences are perceptive, and they quickly recognize evasion. The minute you try to side-step a question, stonewall, or make up an answer, the audience is likely to see right through you. If this happens, your entire presentation will be discredited, even though you may have been in complete control of the facts up to that point.

If you can't come up with the answer to a question right away because you're momentarily confused (or so anxious you can't think at all), you might try asking audience members for their opinion: "I don't know offhand. Can anyone help us out?" Turning to audience members for input and support communicates to them that you give them credit, too. At the same time, it gives you the chance to get your own thoughts together. More often than not, an audience member will volunteer an opinion; in turn, that response will trigger an appropriate answer from you. When admitting that you don't know the answer to a question, you can also boost your competency rating by adding, "I'll find out and get back to you as soon as I can."

Admitting that you don't know everything does more than just protect you from being discredited; in some instances, it can even boost the perception of your competence. When you have already shown audience members that you do know the facts fairly well, they are prepared to believe you *even more* after an admission of ignorance.

Look Competent

To make people believe that you are competent, you must also look the part! People tend to be more impressed by the box than by the product. That may sound cynical, but the reality is that packaging is important. Faced with rows of essentially equivalent soaps, soups, or sardines, consumers are more likely to buy the products in the most attractive packages. Audiences, too, are more likely to be impressed by a well-dressed and well-groomed speaker than by one who is not. What constitutes "well-dressed" and "well-groomed" may vary considerably from one audience to another, but the selection of the right combination that will signal competence to various kinds of audiences is an important aspect of your self-presentation.

Chapter 15 looks at the way clothing communicates status and power. For most formal presentations, power clothes generally consist of a suit or sport coat and tie for men and a suit or conservative dress for women—but not always. How might you alter your own "package" to appear confident and competent for each of the following speaking situations?

- Speaking before a group of overweight men about the benefits of looking and feeling fit
- Speaking to a group of dog owners about the benefits of obedience training
- Demonstrating to a group of homeowners how to frame a window

Arrange a Validating Introduction

Anybody who says, "This speaker needs no introduction," is dead wrong. Even the most prestigious speaker needs a well-organized introduction that testifies to his or her competence. Therefore, when appropriate, you should find someone to introduce you as a person who is competent to discuss the subject of your speech. When someone else describes how great you are, an audience tends to be impressed. But if you blow your own horn, some audiences may negatively conclude that you have a rather large ego. Most audiences are more likely to accept socially validated expertise than self-proclaimed credentials.

To illustrate the importance of an introduction, consider the case of Mary Fisher, who was asked to speak before the Republican National Convention in the summer of 1992 on the topic of AIDS. The audience may well have wondered why a white, affluent, heterosexual female and mother of two sons who did not do drugs would be chosen to speak on this issue. With the appropriate introduction, however, the audience quickly learned that this young woman, who hardly fit the stereotype of AIDS sufferers, had also contracted HIV. With that setup, an otherwise intolerant, even distracted audience listened intently to someone who knew what she was talking about.

Speakers are usually introduced formally by an emcee—a host or master of ceremonies. Never assume that your host will be familiar with your background or understand the importance of establishing your credibility. You must take it upon yourself to supply that person with information about yourself. You don't need to give a detailed life history. Rather, briefly summarize the most relevant features of your background that will help establish your competence concerning your topic. If you find you won't be given a formal introduction, work appropriate and relevant information about yourself into the text of your speech. But be careful not to give the appearance of bragging.

Generate Trust

Audiences appreciate speakers who exhibit **trustworthiness**—that is, speakers who come off as good, decent, honest people. After all, how can audience members perceive a speaker to be credible if they have little or no reason to believe the speaker is honest? This problem is illustrated by the stereotypical view of car sales representatives. National polls rank the job of selling cars near the bottom of a list of honest professions. So, when a potential customer enters the showroom, sales reps can expect the client to have serious misgivings about their trustworthiness. They must demonstrate a level of openness and sincerity to convince the client of their own personal trustworthiness or their sales pitch will not be deemed credible.

Perceptions of trust, like those of competence, are socially established and validated. In the process of social validation, it is the judgments of others that count, not the objective facts about a person whose qualities are not yet clear.[8] For example, in the case of a speaker who is a rabbi or a priest—occupations typically associated with honesty and decency—even the objective fact of the speaker's occupation may not be sufficient for all audience members to perceive the speaker as being trustworthy. Only when there seems to be a consensus among people whose judgment is respected that the individual is indeed trustworthy do most individuals believe that to be the case. Furthermore, there are often ample grounds for withholding trust on the basis of objective facts alone. Consider the case of former televangelist Jim Bakker, who lied, stole, and committed adultery before he was prosecuted, found guilty, and sent to prison.

Once trust is violated, it's very difficult to reestablish. Trust is often the bottom line for long-term interpersonal and professional relationships.[9] We require and expect our friends and family to be trustworthy—and when they are not, we feel violated. Within the public speaking context, we similarly demand that our speakers be honest with us. When we learn later that they lied to us, we often feel duped and misled. President Bill Clinton discovered the hard way the perils of misrepresenting the facts to the public. His misleading and evasive responses regarding his use of marijuana, the draft, Gennifer Flowers, Whitewater, Monica Lewinsky, and other issues have eroded his image as a principled, trustworthy leader.

How can you as a speaker generate perceptions of trust? The primary way to convince an audience you are trustworthy is to be consistently honest and sincere.

As mentioned previously, if you don't know the answer to a question, say so. If you try to fake an answer and are wrong (or the audience thinks you are wrong), audience members are likely to perceive you as being untrustworthy. If you are asked an embarrassing question and would rather not disclose the truth, it's better to state a reason for avoiding the question rather than evade it: "That is rather personal. I'd prefer not to say," or "My personal views are irrelevant in this case." Then proceed quickly to the next issue.

Exhibit Composure

A speaker who exhibits **composure** by appearing calm, cool, and collected before a large audience is easily admired. After all, every member of an audience can empathize with the perils of stage fright. Audiences often anticipate that speakers will be nervous. So, when a speaker demonstrates that he or she is perfectly capable of handling the situation, the audience will likely respond with appreciation and respect. This is especially true when the speaker is supposed to be under a lot of pressure. Responding to a crisis with apparent confidence and control increases speaker credibility. Conversely, if the speaker is unable to control her or his fears and anxieties, the audience is likely to disregard what the individual has to say.

The case of a news broadcaster who was on the air during an earthquake in Whittier, California, in the fall of 1987 provides a good illustration of how lack of composure can destroy credibility. While delivering his broadcast, the studio floor, cameras, and props all began to shake. Suspecting that this tremor was the forecasted "big one" that would destroy all of Southern California (and make Nevada beachfront property), the broadcaster ducked under his desk—and remained there while the cameras rolled! The poor man's nervousness and fear were ridiculed as one station after another replayed the scene during later broadcasts. Realistically, his response to the earthquake as an individual was entirely rational and appropriate. For a person in the role of a television newsperson, however, his reaction under pressure failed to instill a sense of security or to provide much needed assurance to an already frightened audience. Needless to say, the broadcaster's overall credibility suffered.

Maintaining composure can be very difficult for inexperienced speakers and even for people who regularly speak before an audience. Hecklers, people who walk out during a presentation, and people who ask difficult questions can all shake a speaker's confidence. Nevertheless, audiences want and expect speakers to maintain a sense of confidence and composure, even during difficult moments.

You can appear self-assured (even when you're not) by coming prepared. Know your material and rehearse your presentation! Rehearsal will help cut down on the number of "uhs," "ums," "you knows," and other such signs of nervousness. Distracting phrases can grate on an audience; some listeners even count a speaker's overuse of a particular word. Instead of filling pauses with such utterances, simply remain silent. Your pauses will probably seem longer to you than they do to the audience, and they can be used to good effect: A pregnant pause alerts the audience that something important will follow.

Nervous mannerisms can also detract from an audience's perception of your composure. If you realize that your hands are beginning to shake during a presentation, put them behind you for a moment; shift them to your side and then to your pockets; finally, place them on the podium or table. Also avoid **adaptors**—nervous gestures such as scratching your head, swinging your arms back and forth, picking lint off your clothes, twirling your hair, or fiddling with your glasses.

At the same time, little or no movement may indicate a lack of composure or suggest disinterest or apathy. Therefore, it is important that you plan and practice the use of purposeful but natural gestures. When you want to accentuate a point, do it the same way you would in an enthusiastic discussion with a friend, with a clenched fist or a dramatic sweep of your arm. Take care, though, to vary your gestures; punching the air the same way throughout an entire presentation is not likely to enhance your point and may bore the audience. Also, avoid pacing aimlessly. When you want to speak directly to one side of the audience, walk over there, stop, and do it. After a few moments, return to center stage. Then, after a bit, walk to the other side and do the same thing.

Composure does not just happen. A good speaker *practices* looking relaxed and confident. Make eye contact with audience members, and smile as though you are enjoying the experience. Slow down your speech rate from time to time, and speak deliberately and with conviction. The best way to be perceived as being confident is by your actions. Chapter 15 provides a variety of ways you can manage your nonverbal behaviors to maintain your composure and, at the same time, keep your audience attentive.

Highly congenial television talk show hosts like Ellen DeGeneres know how to communicate their sociability to their audiences.

Communicate Sociability

Most audiences prefer speakers who appear to be friendly. Perceptions of **sociability** are based on how congenial a person seems to be. When audience members find a speaker likable, they are more willing to listen and to give him or her the benefit of the doubt. Former president Ronald Reagan is a good example. Congressional leaders often quarreled bitterly over his policies on the floor of the House, but, socially, they appreciated and enjoyed his company. As for the public, they may not have always agreed with the president politically or even thought he was all that sharp, but almost everyone believed he was a very nice man who was sincere and doing the best he could. For that reason, they listened.

Sociability has the power to override or at least soften the blow of potentially alienating or unpleasant information. In other words, bad news is easier to take when the messenger seems well intentioned, likable, and sincere. The point is well illustrated by the converse: How likely would you be to work longer hours or willingly take a cut in pay from a boss who was decidedly unfriendly, cold, and unsympathetic? Wouldn't you be more likely to oblige if she were friendly and pleasant and seemed to care about you? Whether a source seems sociable can make a big difference.

As a public speaker, you must make every effort to appear sociable. Unfortunately, the stage often interferes with this goal. How friendly can a speaker appear to be under bright lights, tied to a stationary microphone, and partially hidden from the audience by a table or lectern? Even worse, how endearing or likable can a speaker be who appears to be suffering from stage fright, forgets major points, sweats, and begins to develop red blotches on his neck? In spite of these potential obstacles, you need to recognize that audiences prefer their speakers to be sociable; otherwise, speaker credibility may suffer.

Communicating sociability to a group requires that you rely heavily on nonverbal **immediacy** behaviors—nonverbal cues that communicate physical or psychological closeness. Nonverbal behaviors that contribute to the perception of liking or sociability include eye contact, smiles, nods, and physical closeness. Some of the same strategies outlined for demonstrating poise and confidence also help establish likability and friendliness: a relaxed, comfortable posture coupled with a genuine, warm smile and frequent eye contact. Recent research, including studies conducted by the text's authors, finds that these effects are maintained with audiences across a variety of co-cultures. Chapter 15 provides a more detailed explanation of the immediacy–likability relationship.

Referring to audience members in some familiar or intimate way may affect their perceptions of your sociability as well. People appreciate it when others remember and use their names; similarly, audiences are warm to speakers who make a point of saying something nice about their geographical location, history, or culture. In other words, an audience wants to be sure that a speaker recognizes its uniqueness as a particular group. Perhaps no one is more sociable than talk show personality Rosie O'Donnell. It's obvious to viewers of her show that Rosie gets a kick out of interviewing TV and movie stars. She seems genuinely excited to see her guests (particularly Tom Cruise and Barbra Streisand); she's interested in what they have to say; and she always finds something to laugh and joke about.

Display Extroversion

Extroversion is a speaker characteristic somewhat similar to sociability. It refers to the degree to which someone is outgoing—that is, people oriented, talkative, and gregarious. People who are low in communication apprehension are often perceived as being extroverted. Shy individuals, those who are highly apprehensive about communicating, are generally perceived as being introverted. As described in Chapter 4, positive qualities are often assigned to people who are low in communication apprehension, while certain negative attributes are often associated with people who are high in apprehension. Often incorrectly, introverts are thought to be purposefully withdrawn, detached, and disinterested in others. For many co-cultural groups, notably African Americans, Euroamericans, and Latinos, introverts are likely to be assigned low credibility simply because they are quiet and appear to be withholding information from others; their intelligence and even trustworthiness may be questioned. For other co-cultural groups, like Asian Americans and Native Americans, introversion may be perceived more positively. Rather than assume that an introverted speaker is ignorant or hiding something, members of these co-cultures may perceive the speaker as thoughtful, respectful, and deliberate.

Unlike introverts, extroverts talk a lot and reveal a great deal about themselves. They let people know how and what they think to a much greater degree than introverts. The same co-cultures that apparently disregard introverted speakers respond favorably to extroverts. For African Americans, Euroamericans, and Latinos, extroverted speakers have the advantage over introverts: Extroverts are likely to be judged by what they say as opposed to what they don't say.

We do not know whether these findings apply across all co-cultures. Although the available research suggests that extroversion is an overwhelmingly positive characteristic for public speakers in this society, that research has relied on predominantly Euroamerican subjects. No research has examined this characteristic for public speakers across co-cultures. Given the nature and demands of the public speaking context, however, we can only assume that extroverted speakers are more favorably received than introverted ones.

Even if you are inclined to be introverted, you can learn to act like an extrovert. Expand your gestures by extending your arms; this will seem to enlarge your whole being. Despite any fears you may have, you need to show enthusiasm, energy, and dynamism. You should smile, make eye contact with audience members, walk up to people in the audience, and, by all means, keep talking! Your audience will quickly relax and accept you, and you will begin to feel much more confident. When that happens, your credibility will be on the way up. (Refer to the box "Interview with a Professional: Dr. Patricia Ganer" for more on speaker credibility.)

SPEAKING OUT

Interview with a Professional

Dr. Patricia Ganer

Pat Ganer, 48, is a communication professor at Cypress Community College in California. She has been a rhetorical and media critic for a number of political campaign speakers, speeches, and debates.

How sensitive do you believe most contemporary audiences are to speaker attempts to create a favorable first impression?

I believe contemporary audiences are very sensitive to first impressions; we are a "channel-surfing" society that tends to make snap judgments. Unfortunately, I also think that those assessments are predicated far too often on judgments regarding delivery skills rather than content skills.

Do you agree that to some extent a speaker desiring to establish credibility needs to focus her or his efforts on being perceived as competent, trustworthy, composed, sociable, and extroverted?

I absolutely agree that these five dimensions are central to establishing credibility. My concern is that I think we tend to downplay competence in favor of the other dimensions; I believe that much too often this leads to superficial communication.

I am firmly convinced that competence is the most important of the dimensions. While I suspect that audiences tend to respond far more to composure and extroversion, I believe we do both students and society a disservice if we do not try to emphasize the importance of competence as the critical factor in communication. There is no question that a balance is necessary—but competence must remain at the forefront.

A Note of Caution

Just as there are pitfalls to being perceived as displaying too little competence, trustworthiness, composure, sociability, and extroversion, there is the danger of a speaker overdoing things and being perceived as showboating. Credibility can also suffer if a speaker is perceived as having too much of any of the five dimensions of credibility:

- *Competence.* A speaker who uses too much jargon, dresses too formally for the event, refers to a long list of books that she or he has written, and talks over the heads of audience members is likely to be perceived as being too competent. Acting pompous, arrogant, and superior does not make a good impression on the audience.

- *Trustworthiness.* Although it's difficult to say that someone can be too honest, a speaker who reveals too much personal information can embarrass an audience and make a negative impression. Confessing an indiscretion, a health condition, or the like may be ill advised. Unless the information is highly relevant to the topic or the strategy of the speech, such things are better left unsaid or, at the very least, disclosed tactfully and graciously.

- *Composure and sociability.* A speaker who sprawls across a table, plops down in front of an audience, leans against a backdrop, and never gets excited or rattled even when making an emotional statement or while being insulted will lose credibility. Being too friendly, smiling constantly and inappropriately, and agreeing too readily with patently unfair audience dissension may do more to damage credibility than being unsociable.

- *Extroversion.* A blabbermouthed speaker who demands center stage, draws constant attention to her- or himself, and jabbers on and on is more likely to be labeled a terrible bore than a great orator. Too much extroversion can be just as detrimental as too little.

With practice and experience, you will find the right mix of verbal and nonverbal messages to maximize your credibility with an audience. The key is to remember that credibility is not something that you inherently have or don't have—it is your audience that determines whether you are credible. And there are many practical things you can do to enhance your credibility with an audience and improve the overall impression you make.

BEING PERCEIVED AS AN ETHICAL PUBLIC SPEAKER

A second salient characteristic crucial to establishing a positive impression with the audience is speaker ethics. **Ethics** is the study of moral values—decisions people make about what is right and wrong. Being perceived as an **ethical public speaker** is closely related to establishing speaker credibility. Because perceptions of credibility often require that the audience trust what the speaker has to say, it's nearly impossible for a public speaker to be perceived as credible and unethical at the same time. Audience members need and want to believe that the speaker will operate from a moral code or set of rules that allows them to trust what the speaker has to say.

To understand the importance of being perceived as an ethical speaker, consider the characteristics that are typically associated with ethical and unethical people. (The box "Terms Commonly Associated with Being Ethical and Unethical" lists some of these characteristics.) Clearly, being ethical is a very positive characteristic that is associated with many other

---

A CLOSER LOOK

Terms Commonly Associated with Being Ethical and Unethical

Ethical	Unethical
Honest	Deceptive
Righteous	Pretentious
Sincere	Corrupt
Reputable	Devious
Decent	Immoral
Honorable	Indecent
Principled	Crooked
Truthful	Underhanded
Virtuous	Dishonorable
Genuine	Calculating
Moral	Deceitful
Humane	Circuitous
Forthright	Machiavellian

favorable traits. Being perceived as an ethical speaker is an important part of establishing an honest and trusting relationship with an audience.

The Ethical Obligations of Public Speakers

Modern thinking about the ethics of public speaking has been strongly influenced by the writings of Quintilian, a Roman rhetorician and orator who lived in the first century A.D. In his 12-volume work *Institutio Oratoria (Institutes of Oratory)*, Quintilian defined the effective public speaker as "a good man speaking well." In other words, a public speaker must, by definition, be a good person, someone who is virtuous and ethical. According to Quintilian, a person who is not good cannot be a good public speaker.

Quintilian's critics objected that his standards were impractical. There might be situations, they argued, in which a speaker would be forced to lie, such as when a lie would protect someone from needless hurt or divert an unjustified attack by an aggressor. Would such lying make the speaker unethical? Quintilian responded that in some situations, lying was an acceptable course of action. If the goal was worthy, lying could be employed because the end justified the means. He pointed out, however, that lying in these cases served a higher ethical value, such as protecting the innocent from harm. In such circumstances, lying is actually more ethical than telling the truth.

Quintilian made ethics fundamental to the notion of being an effective public speaker. Although his standards were both absolute and ideal, they have provided food for thought for generations of speakers and communication experts. Over time, certain standard practices have been identified as important to ethical speaking. The following discussion examines seven important guidelines for ethical public speaking.[10]

Present Evidence Truthfully
All public speakers incorporate evidence in one form or another into their speeches to substantiate, clarify, or elaborate on their points. Whether the speaker is the director of a special interest group attempting to persuade a group of teenagers not to smoke cigarettes, a manager informing a group of graphic designers about a new product, or a student demonstrating a camera to a class, all evidence should be assembled and presented to an audience as honestly as possible.

In most cases, speakers should present their evidence in an objective and unbiased form. This means

they should not alter evidence or present incomplete information to support a particular point or to mislead an audience in any way. For example, stating that Kansas City and Seattle have the same average rainfall is accurate—but incomplete. To avoid misleading the audience, a speaker would have to also note that it rains twice as often in Seattle. If evidence is either altered or subjective in nature, the speaker must inform the audience accordingly. Unless an audience is informed ahead of time, speakers must not play around with their statistics, quote out of context, or be dishonest by not telling their audience that their examples are invented rather than factual. All audiences assume and thus expect that the evidence presented will be accurate and communicated truthfully and fairly. Public speakers who communicate evidence truthfully and objectively increase their likelihood of being perceived as ethical.

Reveal Your Sources
Audiences also expect that the sources of information presented in a speech will be revealed in a responsible fashion. This means that speakers should be forthright about and give credit to the sources of their information. Presenting information without giving suitable credit to a source is **plagiarism**— an unethical and unacceptable speaker behavior. (The box "Avoiding Plagiarism" contains guidelines on giving proper credit to sources during a speech.) Revealing sources responsibly also means that a speaker should reveal any question about the credibility or the reputation of a particular source. Even when the only available sources of information are biased or of questionable character, speakers must let the audience know this fact.

For example, if evidence from the National Rifle Association is incorporated in a speech against gun control, it is the speaker's responsibility to point out that this association is distinctly anti–gun control. Indeed, it would be better to exclude the evidence altogether than to omit its source or to mislead the audience about the group's vested interest in laws against gun control.

Distinguish between Opinion and Fact
While preparing and delivering a presentation, enthusiastic public speakers frequently get carried away with the moment and become confused about distinctions between opinion and fact. Nevertheless, ethical public speakers must always make this distinction for their audiences. For example, a speaker may want to make the claim that the quality and reliability of domestic automobiles have improved in recent years and now match the quality and reliability of imported automobiles. Such a claim could be made as fact if it were

Avoiding Plagiarism

Plagiarism is using someone else's words or ideas without crediting the source. In publishing, plagiarism is illegal and can result in expensive lawsuits. In other contexts, it is, at the least, unethical; and even if no legal action results, plagiarism can have serious personal and professional costs. In 1987, Senator Joe Biden of New Jersey, a presidential hopeful, had his credibility and reputation severely damaged by the revelation that he had taken portions of some of his speeches from other sources without giving them appropriate credit. If a student is caught plagiarizing a speech, paper, or thesis, the result may be a failing grade, expulsion, or the revocation of an academic degree.

What constitutes plagiarism? Clearly, directly quoting someone else without crediting the source is plagiarism. For every quote used in your speech, you should provide oral footnotes—that is, tell the audience who said it. Paraphrasing or summarizing someone else's opinion, idea, theory, argument, or line of thinking without giving credit is also considered plagiarism. When you present someone else's ideas, you must give them credit in your presentation.

Is there anything that doesn't need to be footnoted? Factual information that is common knowledge does not need to be credited in a speech.

Tips for Avoiding Plagiarism

- Take careful notes while researching your topic. Keep track of all the sources of information you use, and indicate in your notes whether you are quoting or summarizing a source.

- Provide an oral footnote whenever you quote others or paraphrase their ideas, opinions, arguments, and so on. Include these oral footnotes in all stages of your speech outline—from the full-sentence outline to the abbreviated outline or notecards you use during your speech.

- Give credit whenever you are in any doubt whether to do so. It is much better to be too careful.

- List all the resources used in preparing your final speech text at the end of your outline.

---

supported by reports from reputable automobile magazines, consumer organizations, or safety experts. However, if the claim were supported only by the speaker's perceptions or by the personal experience of the speaker's next-door neighbor, it could be presented only as opinion. Moreover, if hypothetical examples are given, they should be identified as such. All audiences respond negatively to misrepresentations and distortions. To mix fact and opinion indiscriminately is to risk being branded an unethical speaker.

Respond to Questions Frankly
The question period that often follows a speech is extremely important to an audience's overall evaluation of a speaker's ethics. Many potentially effective presentations have been ruined when the speaker evaded a question. For example, suppose a teacher in a large mathematics class is asked a question by a student at the end of a lecture. Instead of valuing honesty and admitting that she doesn't know the answer and either asking someone in the class for the answer or indicating that she will find out and get back to the student, the teacher sarcastically replies that it is a stupid question that doesn't deserve an answer. Such a response would be interpreted by the students as dishonest, evasive, mean-spirited, and, thus, highly unethical. Needless to say, neither the student asking the question nor the rest of the class would respond favorably to the teacher's response, and her credibility would be diminished substantially.

All audiences expect frank and direct answers when they are given an opportunity to ask questions of a speaker. Evasive answers are judged negatively by audiences; they are interpreted as deceitful. Correspondingly, public speakers who answer questions evasively are judged to be unethical. It is far better for a speaker to admit that he or she does not know the answer to a question but will try to find out than to respond evasively or abusively and be perceived as unethical.

Respect Diversity of Argument and Opinion
Public speakers should value fairness and communicate respect for the diversity of argument and opinion that may exist concerning the topic of their presentation. Although there is some variation among co-cultures in what is valued as acceptable disagreement and dissent, democratic societies normally acknowledge and promote diversity of argument and opinion in the context of public presentations. Think of the many public

presentations that elected officials make in Congress. These presentations are typically followed by discussion, disagreement, and, ultimately, compromise—a process at the heart of our political system.

Failing to show respect for dissenting opinions is the same as saying, "I am closed to anything that opposes my position; I don't really care what you think about this issue!" Audiences do not respond well to dogmatic, narrow-minded public speakers. They feel they have not heard both sides or been allowed to decide for themselves what they should believe. Respecting dissent, then, is an important responsibility for an ethical public speaker. Speakers can demonstrate such respect by communicating a sincere interest in learning about alternative positions, by listening attentively when opposing opinions are discussed, and by illustrating through what they say that they have taken the time to research both sides of the topic.

Consider the Probable Effect of the Speech

Public speakers frequently face audiences that are overly sensitive to particular topics, issues, and arguments because of specific co-cultural orientations. Effective speakers always consider their audiences in their preparation and delivery. However, when a speaker intentionally disregards the unique orientation of an audience or knowingly presents information that will be harmful to someone in the audience, she or he is acting irresponsibly and unethically.

For example, a number of well-organized special interest groups take a strong position against abortion. Periodically, antiabortion presentations made by members of these groups have been shown to have dangerous consequences. Recall that radical members of some antiabortion groups have bombed clinics; in one well-known case, a physician who performed abortions was shot and killed. On highly sensitive issues, speakers must consider carefully the potential consequences of their presentations.

Act Responsibly When Appealing to People's Emotions and Values

A final obligation of ethical public speaking relates to the use of appeals to the emotions and values of audience members. Persuasive appeals can be employed responsibly or irresponsibly. An irresponsible appeal occurs when an unethical speaker evokes an irrational emotional response from the audience—at the expense of sound reasoning. Relying solely on an emotional audience response to support one's position and using false evidence to arouse the emotions of audience members are unethical persuasion strategies. For example, instead of running on key

platform issues, a political candidate might argue that his reelection is the only way to keep drunk drivers off the street because he supports harsher penalties for drunk driving. Imagine the emotional response this type of appeal would cause in an audience that included parents who had lost children to drunk drivers!

An irresponsible appeal to values follows a similar pattern: The speaker attempts to convince audience members of his or her position by evoking their deeply rooted values rather than using sound reasoning. Suppose a speaker wanted to argue that funding for AIDS should be cut. If the speaker knew the audience was intensely homophobic (fearful of homosexuals), he could argue that AIDS is God's way of punishing homosexuals for their sinful sexual behavior. Evoking an audience's deeply held values as the sole argument for a position is misleading, irresponsible, and unethical.

Speaking to evoke the emotions and values of audience members is not always unethical. Presenting such appeals in conjunction with other types of supporting materials is effective, ethical, and responsible. (The box "Guidelines for Ethical Public Speaking" summarizes the obligations of public speakers described in this section.)

The Important Decisions Public Speakers Make

Virtually every speaking situation carries some pressure—or even temptation—to act unethically to some degree. Many forces impinge on speakers as they make decisions about how to present themselves, what evidence to offer in support of their points, how to provide information about opposing views, what appeals to use to persuade their audience, how to answer questions, and so on. Speakers also have to make decisions about how culturally sensitive—or politically correct—they will be in their presentations, especially if they feel their ability to make their point is being compromised by such considerations. Finally, speakers are sometimes faced with the temptation to out-and-out lie.

Decisions about Ethical Dilemmas Public speakers are often faced with an **ethical dilemma**— a situation in which they have to choose among two or more alternative courses of action, each of which results in an ethical problem of some sort. Choosing one or another course means sacrificing, or at least compromising, an important value; thus, neither choice is entirely satisfactory.

For example, a person might have to choose between answering a grand jury's questions fully on the one hand and being somewhat evasive to protect

Guidelines for Ethical Public Speaking

- *Present evidence truthfully.* Assemble and distribute evidence accurately and objectively. Don't alter evidence to support a particular point or mislead the audience.

- *Reveal your sources.* Give proper credit to all sources of information. Make audience members aware of the sources of your evidence, and alert them if any source is potentially biased or may not be entirely credible.

- *Distinguish between opinion and fact.* Do not represent a personal opinion or belief as a universally established and accepted fact. Acknowledge your own opinions.

- *Respond to questions frankly.* Do not evade questions that are difficult or that you can't answer. If you don't know the answer, say that you will find out and get back with an answer at a later time.

- *Respect diversity of argument and opinion.* Do not be narrow-minded about the ideas and opinions of others.

- *Consider the probable effect of the speech.* Do not knowingly present information that will have injurious or harmful effects on your audience.

- *Act responsibly when appealing to people's emotion and values.* Avoid persuasive appeals that are used solely to incite an irrational, emotional response from your audience. And do not use appeals that are designed to provoke someone's deeply rooted values—at the expense of reason. To responsibly use persuasive appeals, present them in conjunction with other types of supporting material.

---

a friend on the other. Individuals who value truth above friendship might choose to testify fully, even if it means creating legal problems for a friend. Those who value friendship above truth might choose to testify less than fully if they can.

Similarly, a person might hold a particular position on an issue but discover after doing some research that there is little or no evidence to support that position. The person then has to decide whether to stick with the position—perhaps due to loyalty to a cause, the investment of time and energy in it, or even the desire to appear consistent—or to adopt a new position based on the facts.

As suggested by these examples, ethical dilemmas involve **values**—conceptions or beliefs about what is desirable. These dilemmas are hard to resolve because the individual sees the positive aspects of both values and is forced to choose which is *more* important. A person contemplating the abortion issue, for example, might feel strongly about the sanctity of life, the rights of the unborn child, and the responsibility of every human being to protect those rights. At the same time, the person might believe in women's rights to control their bodies and make decisions about their own lives. To actively support one side or the other, this individual must decide which values matter more. Take a few minutes to rank your values in the box "What Are Your Key Values?"

Most people in most cultures place a high value on ethical behavior, including telling the truth. When preparing a public presentation, most of us place

ethical behavior above other important values like friendship, wealth, status, achievement, and so on. However, there will be public speaking situations in which the demands of the context will test a speaker's inclination to be ethical. Suppose, for example, that a particular speaker values high social status above all else, including ethical behavior. If she found herself in a speaking situation in which the only way to maintain high status was to evade questions or be less than truthful, she might be sorely tempted to do so. She might adjust her normally ethical behavior to meet the demands of the value that was more important to her.

When aroused, then, our primary values, right or wrong, tend to dominate, eclipse, and supersede other important values. Therefore, they more directly influence our behavior as speakers. Everyone is susceptible to such influences at times. The important thing is to be aware of these influences and to have a strong sense of our personal values and priorities. Then, even under stress, we will not become confused and give in to the temptation to be evasive or untruthful. As speakers, we must be active in our efforts to behave ethically. Take a few minutes to complete the questionnaire in the box "How Do You Respond to Ethical Dilemmas?" to determine whether you might be forced to choose among your own personal values.

Decisions about Being Culturally Sensitive

Public speakers also have to make decisions about how to adapt their language and behavior to the

What Are Your Key Values?

Instructions

Below is a list of personal values common to most of us. Consider which values you find most important to you, and rank the top five, with 1 being the most important. Although many of the values listed below will be important to you, choose only the five you feel are *most* important to how you live your life.

—— Family	—— Friendship
—— Patriotism	—— Being ethical (truthfulness, trustworthiness)
—— Wealth	
—— Status	—— Forgiveness
—— Health	—— Humility
—— Cleanliness	—— Patience
—— Individuality	—— Tradition
—— Attractiveness	—— Obeying the law
—— Generosity	—— Hard work
—— Loyalty	—— Getting along with others
—— Religion (spirituality)	
—— Love	—— Saving face
—— Knowledge (education)	

Interpreting the Results

Once you've completed this very difficult task (it's tough to select only five), compare your answers with those of your classmates. How do your own priorities overlap with or differ from others' based on gender, race, religious background, ethnicity, and age? Why do you think this is so?

How frequently does the value of being ethical appear on others' lists? How prominent a value is being ethical to you? How important is this value to you when it comes to your perceptions of the following people?

President of the United States	Your advisor
Your best friend	Colleagues in your profession
Your boss	Your parents
Your spouse or significant other	Your instructor in this class

Notice how this list of values is common across most people. That is, each characteristic on the list is something we value, yet each of us ranks the values on the list somewhat differently. How might our different rankings influence how we communicate with or perceive one another?

---

expectations of co-culturally diverse audiences. In our society, speakers have to exercise judgment about the words they choose, the terms and labels they apply to various groups, and the way they discuss sensitive issues; at the same time, they must strive to be as candid, explicit, and honest as they can. Speakers who consider the co-cultural affiliations of their audiences minimize the chances that their message will be misconstrued or misunderstood.

Some people refer to such adaptation as being "politically correct," or "PC." The exact meaning of the term **political correctness** remains somewhat vague; people tend to use it differently and to give it different connotations depending on their own political agenda. Over the past decade or so, as many people in this society became aware of how words and actions could carry shades of meaning that demeaned or excluded various groups, interest grew in adapting language and behavior to the perceptions, perspectives, and interests of those groups. Being politically correct implied that a person was concerned about being fair and demonstrating respect for all diverse groups.

But some people—mostly on the far left of the political spectrum—have been charged with taking this trend to an extreme. They are accused by their critics (mostly on the far right of the political spectrum) of dictating a highly restrictive, confining, and oppressive set of rules that public speakers must follow when addressing diverse audiences. These critics have added a disparaging, derisive connotation to the term "politically correct": The politically correct speaker is either obsequious or cynical—someone who is intent on avoiding offense and looking good to an audience no matter what her or his real beliefs and attitudes are. The term "politically correct" thus becomes a weapon used to demean cultural diversity and those who attempt to adapt to it. Being politically correct in these terms means that a speaker can never say anything that might offend anyone in any audience. To deviate from these standards is to be a bigot.[11]

At the same time, some of the very critics who sneer at political correctness have adopted an equally counterproductive position, one totally opposed to cultural sensitivity and adaptation. They argue that speakers

How Do You Respond to Ethical Dilemmas?

Instructions

How would you respond to the following series of ethical dilemmas? You have only two options for resolving the dilemma—yes or no—and you must choose one. Record your first inclination in the space provided; don't worry about why you responded as you did.

_____ 1. Your best friend's spouse has been coming on to you for the past several months. Your friend is starting to get suspicious and confronts you. Knowing that your friend is deeply in love and that the truth will destroy their marriage, would you tell the truth?

_____ 2. Would you plagiarize important evidence to be included in your final speech if it meant you'd get an A in your speech class?

_____ 3. Suppose you knew your sister was abusing her child. Would you report her to the authorities, knowing that the child would be taken from her?

_____ 4. Your boss comes to work every day with terrible breath. Everyone in the office is talking about it. You like and respect your boss. Would you tell him about his bad breath?

_____ 5. Would you be willing to live in a shelter for the homeless for the next three years if you knew that you could earn fame and fortune by selling the movie rights about your experiences afterward?

_____ 6. If you or your partner were pregnant with a child with a devastating birth defect and the child would not survive beyond two years, would you or your partner have an abortion?

_____ 7. Would you distort the facts in a speech on smokers' rights in order to keep your job with the tobacco industry?

_____ 8. Would you ask a judge to be lenient in the sentencing of a man who had raped your child if you knew for a fact that this man was truly repentant and would never harm anyone again?

_____ 9. Would you be willing to cut ten years off your life to win the big state lottery today?

_____ 10. Would you rip off reference materials from the library to prevent other classmates from obtaining information that would help them get a better grade on their speech?

Interpreting Your Responses

After recording all your answers, share your responses with your classmates or with your family and friends. See how your responses compare with others'. Why do you think people's responses differ? What justifications do you and others give for the choices you made?

This questionnaire was designed to demonstrate how you and others make decisions based on personal value systems. For some individuals, the value of family supersedes other important values like wealth or health or obeying the law. For others, the values of friendship and loyalty may outweigh the value of telling the truth. Whose value system is correct? Why might it be inappropriate to evaluate another person's choices using your own value priorities?

After completing this test, you may want to return to the box "What Are Your Key Values?" to see if your top five values correspond with the choices you made for each of the ethical dilemmas here. For each ethical dilemma, did you find that your top five values consistently guided your choices? If not, why not?

should never have to adapt their language and behavior to the expectations or concerns of culturally diverse audiences. Having to do so threatens the speakers' constitutionally guaranteed right to freedom of speech. This view, which represents a position characteristic of those on the extreme right of the political spectrum, is just as unacceptable as that of the far left.

From a more moderate and constructive perspective, being politically correct means being concerned about fairness, equity, and respect for all the co-cultures represented in our society and being willing to adopt appropriate conduct when communicating with cultur-

ally diverse audiences. Adjusting to co-culturally diverse audiences is one of the responsibilities of an ethical speaker in a multicultural society. Successful public speakers demonstrate cultural sensitivity not only because it is fair and respectful—the "right" thing to do—but also because it maximizes the likelihood that their speech will be heard and understood by their audiences.

For example, speakers should refer to co-cultures in appropriate ways, such as African Americans, Asian Americans, gays and lesbians, and people living with AIDS (see Chapter 14 for more specific guidelines on bias-free language). If the topic of a presentation is potentially touchy for any co-culture represented in an audience (affirmative action, bilingualism in the public schools, and so on), the speaker must carefully monitor his or her language and approach. If a speaker suspects during a presentation that audience members are reacting negatively, she or he should assess the nature of the problem and make sensitive readjustments. This does not mean that speakers should misrepresent themselves by falsely claiming to hold opinions or attitudes similar to those the audience holds. Speakers should never compromise their convictions about what is right or wrong, moral or immoral, or honest or dishonest in order to please an audience. Doing so would be unethical. But if the speaker senses that his or her directness is a problem for audience members, the speaker should explain his or her position to minimize the problem. All of these efforts and adjustments are necessary to be an effective—and ethical—speaker in our society.

Decisions about Lying Finally, public speakers must sometimes decide whether to lie to an audience. **Lying** can be defined as deliberately concealing or falsifying information with the intent to deceive or mislead.[12] With this definition in mind, we can consider why some public speakers lie and how they justify it to themselves and others.

Public speakers who intentionally and frequently lie to audiences operate from one or more insidious assumptions that directly decrease their ethical behavior. Flagrant liars tend to be pathological liars; they lie virtually all the time and often end up believing that their lies are really true. They justify their behavior with one or more of the following claims: "Achieving all ends justifies any means"; "fairness is always beside the point"; "all rules and laws were made to be broken"; and "whenever in doubt or cornered, lie your way out."

Speakers who operate this way are highly unethical. To paraphrase Quintilian, they are definitely not "good people speaking well." They are self-centered and fraudulent in their presentations. Fortunately, public speakers who do not fall into this category (the honest people of the world) greatly outnumber those who do.

Public speakers who lie "only occasionally" to their audiences justify their behavior differently than those who lie on a regular and frequent basis. After all, occasional liars claim to lie in order to (1) help or protect others or (2) benefit themselves. Lying to help or protect others in some way would constitute what Quintilian described as lying for a noble end or ethical objective. Such objectives include lying to someone to protect him or her from harm or discomfort, lying in the name of national security, or lying in response to impending threat of injury or death. For instance, a speaker may overestimate the addictive power of marijuana in an effort to keep teenagers from smoking dope. Lies intended to help or benefit others are the easiest to justify—but they're still lies.

A second justification for the occasional liar is to benefit him- or herself. Self-interest lies occur when people try to get away with something, such as a driver telling a police officer that he wasn't really speeding, a student telling her teacher that she lost her public speaking book and couldn't study for the test, or a teacher who boosts his credibility by claiming to have done a lot of research on a topic. A speaker may lie about her background in order to get an audience to feel sympathetic: "When I was a child, I walked ten miles to school, through the snow and with no shoes." Apparently harmless, such lies have a way of backfiring, particularly when most of them can be easily detected.

People try all kinds of ways to justify the lying that they do. But ethical public speakers simply do not intentionally lie for these or any other reasons. Our advice is simple: Don't lie. Instead, go with the ethical alternative—tell the truth.

CHAPTER REVIEW

- The impression an audience forms about a speaker is critical to the success of the entire presentation. For you to achieve your speech goal, your audience must perceive you as being credible, knowledgeable, and worth listening to. Extensive research reveals that audiences form first impressions about a speaker quickly—often on the basis of very little information.

- Credibility is a salient characteristic that heavily influences how the audience responds to the speaker and the message. Contrary to what most people think, speaker credibility doesn't just happen; instead, it can be created and managed strategically. A number of strategies can be used to get your audience to perceive you as a competent, trustworthy, composed, sociable, and extroverted public speaker.

- Similar to establishing speaker credibility, part of being perceived as an ethical speaker is establishing an honest relationship with an audience. Audiences are more likely to trust a speaker who presents evidence truthfully, reveals sources responsibly, distinguishes between opinion and fact, responds to questions frankly, respects diversity of argument and opinion, considers the probable effect of the speech, and appeals to emotions and values in a responsible way.

- Public speakers must make a number of important ethical decisions during speech preparation and delivery. Speakers make such decisions when facing ethical dilemmas, when there is a need to be culturally sensitive, and when considering the advantages of lying over telling the truth.

- Unethical public speakers who engage in frequent and flagrant lying often assume that the ends justify the means, that fairness is beside the point, that rules are made to be broken, and that they should lie their way out whenever they are in doubt or cornered. Occasional liars attempt to justify their lies in order to help or protect others or, more directly, to benefit themselves. Ethical speakers don't lie; they tell the truth.

QUESTIONS FOR CRITICAL THINKING & REVIEW

1. Given what you now know about creating a positive first impression, what do you intend to do to make yourself appear highly credible in your next speech?

2. Are there any instances in which you would rather lie than tell the truth? Do you consider little white lies to be acceptable or unacceptable?

3. How important is being an ethical speaker to you? Do you expect your teachers to be ethical in their presentations to the class? Why or why not?

4. People today argue that politicians are less than truthful and can't be trusted. Do you think we demand too much from our politicians? Too little? How truthful and forthcoming do you think politicians should be about their personal lives?

5. Is plagiarizing someone's spoken words as unethical as plagiarizing someone's written work? Why or why not?

6. Are there circumstances in which you would consider being politically incorrect or would tolerate the cultural insensitivity of others? If so, when and why?

NOTES

1. Asch, S. E. (1946). Forming impressions of personalities. *Journal of Personality and Social Psychology, 41,* 258–290.
2. Eakins, B. W., & Eakins, R. G. (1978). *Sex differences in human communication.* Boston: Houghton Mifflin.
3. Pearson, J. C. (1982, February). *Gender, similarity, and source credibility.* Paper presented at the Western Speech Communication Association convention, Denver, CO.
4. Wells, W. O., & Siegel, B. (1961). Stereotyped somatypes. *Psychological Reports, 8,* 77–78.
5. Goffman, E. (1959). *The presentation of self in everyday life.* Garden City, NY: Doubleday Anchor.
6. McCroskey, J. C. (1986). *An introduction to rhetorical communication* (5th ed.). Englewood Cliffs, NJ: Prentice-Hall. McCroskey, J. C., & Richmond, V. P. (1996). *Fundamentals of human communication: An interpersonal perspective* (pp. 104–119). Englewood Cliffs, NJ: Prentice-Hall; Reardon, K. K. (1991). *Persuasion in practice* (2nd ed.). Newbury Park, CA: Sage.
7. McCroskey, 1986; McCroskey & Richmond, 1996, pp. 104–119; McCroskey, J. C., & Young, T. J. (1981). Ethos and credibility: The construct and its measurement after three decades. *Central States Speech Journal, 32,* 24–34.
8. McCroskey & Richmond, 1996, p. 107.
9. Burhans, D. T., Jr. (1973). The experimental study of interpersonal trust. *Western Journal of Speech Communication, 37,* 2–12; Rempel, J., Holmes, J., & Zanna, M. (1985). Trust in close relationships. *Journal of Personality and Social Psychology, 49,* 95–112.
10. See, for instance, Wallace, K. R. (1955). An ethical basis of communication. *Speech Teacher, 4,* 1–9.
11. Van De Wetering, J. E. (1991, December 1). Political correctness: The insult and the injury. *Vital Speeches of the Day,* 100–103.
12. Ekman, P. (1992). *Telling lies.* New York: Norton.

Chapter 6

ANALYZING AND ADAPTING TO DIVERSE AUDIENCES

A number of people in the audience were offended by Darlene's presentation. Committed to their own religious beliefs and organizations, how could they be expected to appreciate or support her plea that they switch faiths and become "born again"? Unaware of this potential reaction, Darlene had prepared a thoughtful persuasive speech advocating what she assumed would be an "easy sell." After all, she thought, who wouldn't want to follow the word of our Lord and Savior, Jesus Christ? Who wouldn't want to seek redemption in the ways that she was able to? Darlene had all the experiences and testimonials to back up her claims. She had spent the past five years working closely with her minister and congregation helping others find their way and, at the same time, soliciting members into the church. Convinced of her religious beliefs, Darlene was certain that she could reach out and connect with her classmates and peers in her public speaking class, too.

Darlene wasn't far into her speech before she realized that something was seriously wrong. She was genuinely shocked at the audience members' apparent unwillingness to listen and resistance to her message. Afterwards, Darlene remained stumped. "I just don't get it. I followed all the guidelines on how to prepare and deliver an effective presentation. But they still didn't seem to want to hear what I had to say."

So, what went wrong? Why was Darlene's speech, a speech that met all the objective criteria for a well-executed presentation, so poorly received? Unfortunately, Darlene failed to consider the religious convictions that members of her audience already held. As it turns out, a number of her classmates were Jewish, Muslim, or Catholic, and many held strong beliefs very different from Darlene's. They found her plea insensitive, her words carelessly chosen, and her attitude self-righteous. Perhaps if Darlene had more carefully analyzed this particular audience, she would have selected a different topic altogether—or at least modified the objectives of this one.

Clearly, speakers who alienate their audiences have a much harder time achieving their speech goals. Harry Jordan, a conservative Christian member of the South Carolina Board of Education, made derogatory comments about Buddhism and Islam during a public board meeting in which he advocated the posting of the Ten Commandments in public schools. His remarks were published widely, and his intolerant stance on non-Christian religions was held up as an argument in favor of the continued separation of church and state—and thus against his own position. Golfer Fuzzy Zoeller made ethnically insensitive comments about fellow golfer Tiger Woods during a CNN interview. Following a storm of criticism, Zoeller apologized publicly and stated that his comments were intended to be funny; however, he lost a lucrative sponsorship contract as a result of his remarks.

In each of these incidents, the speakers did not carefully consider their audiences. Without thoughtful consideration of the audience, speakers can easily say or do the wrong thing and, thus, make it more difficult for themselves to be effective and achieve their speech goals. Successful speakers take the time to learn about their audiences—who they are, why they're there, and what they're interested in—and adjust their message and communication style accordingly. This chapter examines how to analyze and adapt to diverse audiences. Remember that effective speakers give their audience first priority.

IDENTIFYING YOUR TARGET AUDIENCE

Identifying who your audience is may seem to be a simple task. For your speeches in the college classroom, your audience will be your classmates. And yet your peers are only one target group. You may find that your presentations in business, politics, the community, and elsewhere could be targeted to more than one audience. Many speeches are given to what we call the **contiguous audience** (or immediate audience), but often they are also carried to **media audiences**, including electronic and print audiences.

The Contiguous Audience

The contiguous audience comprises the people sitting or standing in front of you as you give your presentation. Although it is best to know the basic facts about your audience before you give your speech, you can learn useful information about your audience (age, gender, level of interest in your topic, and so on) merely by looking around during your speech. The feedback the contiguous audience provides during a speech can also guide you in tailoring your presentation.

The contiguous audience is made up of living, breathing, responding receivers; thus, you have someone to talk to. Whether you realize it or not, it's a lot easier giving a speech to a contiguous audience than to a media audience. If you've ever watched C-SPAN or some other congressional news show, you've seen one senator or representative at a time droning on and on into a microphone before a television monitor—with few or no receivers in sight. Of course, dull speaking goes on in Congress to ensure that the speeches become a matter of public record or to create filibusters to prevent key votes from being taken. Such

people look rather silly, and their speeches sound incredibly tedious.

Similarly, trying to "write" to someone by speaking into a video camera or tape recorder demonstrates how difficult it is to speak to an absent audience. Most of us sound (or look) stilted, awkward, and constrained. Even our attempts at humor seem hollow, and our laughter forced and artificial. The point is, we need an audience. Visible receivers help us make our presentations more closely resemble planned conversations by giving feedback (smiling, nodding, frowning, shrugging) to which we can respond. When audience members seem to like what we are saying, we become more animated and enthused. When they look confused, we try to help them understand. And when they seem tired or bored, we step up the pace by moving around, gesturing, and making eye contact with specific individuals. When we really pay attention to our audience, we discover that the audience can actually help us become better speakers.

The Media Audience

Speakers sometimes address a much larger audience than the contiguous one. Closed-circuit cable, live TV and radio broadcasts, newspapers and magazines—all allow speakers to communicate their messages far beyond the confines of a single room or auditorium. With the mass media, speakers can access homes and organizations across the country. However, not directly knowing the people in the media audience makes it very difficult for speakers to anticipate probable responses to their presentations. It is simply not possible to predict the reactions of every receiver. The most speakers can hope for is some vague idea of how audiences might interpret their messages.

In most media situations, the speaker must keep in mind both the contiguous audience and the media audience. Although some messages may be perfectly appropriate for a contiguous group, whose members may have a lot in common, the same messages may be totally inappropriate for other groups that represent a variety of attitudes, beliefs, and values. The bottom line is that mass media speeches are public—anyone has access to them. Because media audiences include almost everyone, their very size makes them difficult for speakers to identify and analyze. How can any speaker, then, reasonably adapt to a media audience? Any time a political or community leader speaks to the entire country, he or she will find in the audience some listeners who agree, others who disagree, and still others who just don't care.

ANALYZING YOUR AUDIENCE

Each audience member brings to the public speaking event her or his own attitudes, beliefs, and expectations—depending in large part on the person's own unique set of experiences and cultural background. Speakers who take the time to discover who their audience members are, what they generally believe in, and how they feel are in a good position to accommodate their audience. Recall from Chapter 2 that **audience analysis** is the systematic gathering of information about audience members in an effort to learn everything possible about them that is relevant to the topic. This section takes a closer look at some of the different characteristics of audience members that speakers should consider and some of the methods speakers can use to research their audience.

Audience Demographics

One practical way for making assumptions about audience members is to categorize them by their demographic makeup. Social categories you might consider in determining audience **demographics** include the following:

Gender	Regional affiliation
Religious affiliation	Ethnic or cultural background
Age	
Group membership	Place and type of residence
Income level	
Marital status	Occupation
Educational background	Political affiliation
Number of children	

Analysis by social categories such as these can reveal beliefs and orientations that audience members are likely to share and that are likely to affect

Contemporary audiences are almost always co-culturally diverse. Prior to making public presentations, speakers must do their homework by systematically gathering co-cultural and other relevant background information about their audience.

how they will respond to a particular topic and speaking style. To illustrate, imagine that you have been asked to give a speech to two separate audiences about raising the minimum wage. Your first audience is primarily Euroamerican, affluent, and childless; they have lived in California all their lives, are small-business owners, and vote Republican. Your second audience is primarily Latino (second or third generation), middle-income earners with three to five children; they have lived in Texas all their lives, work primarily in the computer industry, and typically vote Democrat. You might reasonably predict from these demographic profiles that one audience is likely to be more sympathetic to raising the minimum wage than the other one. Which one? Why do you think so? Why can't you give the same speech to both groups?

Audience Psychographics

Demographic audience analyses cannot reveal all you need to know about audiences. Knowing audience members' average age, income, and co-cultural affiliations does not tell you how they think and feel, nor does it tell you much about what they expect from you. Audience **psychographics** seek to determine what kinds of attitudes, beliefs, and opinions people share. A psychographic analysis of audience members might address these and other questions:

- *What are their motives for being part of the audience?* They may have some special interest in your topic, or they may have been required to attend for work or school purposes.
- *What topics are they interested in?* Choosing a topic that is relevant and interesting to your audience will certainly increase your effectiveness as a speaker.
- *How much do they already know about the topic?* If they know a great deal about the topic, you need to avoid talking down to them; if the topic is new to them, you need to take care not to talk over their heads.
- *How do they feel about the issue you plan to discuss?* If they already agree with your position, you can design a message that reinforces that position. If they are likely to disagree with your position, you have your work cut out for you; you must design your speech to make your position seem less extreme.

Sometimes you can infer psychographic information from a demographic profile, but these inferences can be wrong—and potentially ethnocentric. A psychographic analysis can help verify and elaborate these inferences. For example, suppose you want to give a speech on something you know a lot about, say, bodybuilding. Your audience consists primarily of classmates who are under 30, have moderate financial resources, and appear to be physically active. From this demographic information, you might infer that exercise is important to them and that most of them probably exercise already but can't afford to join an athletic club or hire a personal trainer. Thus, you might conclude that they would enjoy knowing about a home-training program.

Your inferences could be correct, but they also could be wrong. With a psychographic analysis, you would be in a better position to know for sure. What if you discovered that most members of your audience had never participated in any regular exercise regimen? What if you found that the majority of women in your audience equated bodybuilding with looking like a guy? In light of this psychographic information, it might be more appropriate to focus your talk on the basics of bodybuilding—its effects and health benefits.

Formal Methods of Analyzing Your Audience

Sometimes you can determine audience attitudes and beliefs by asking sample members what they think. You can also solicit information from the event's sponsor. Such informal questioning techniques work well when you are unable to conduct more formal interviews. (See the box "Informal Audience Analysis" for additional suggestions on how to gather information.)

Nevertheless, if you have the resources to conduct formal interviews, you will be able to acquire accurate, reliable, and detailed information that cannot possibly be obtained from less formal means. Formal interviews can take one of two forms: a **focus group interview** or a **questionnaire**. Both require some formal training in interviewing techniques, and both are susceptible to the same pitfalls: (1) The interviews are too long, and (2) the questions are often leading and misleading. People do not like to fill out lengthy questionnaires, and they do not want to spend hours answering questions. Keep the interview short (no longer than ten minutes) by asking essential questions only.

Be careful to word questions as objectively as possible. Try not to lead individuals to answer the

Informal Audience Analysis

If time or circumstances do not allow for formal audience analysis techniques, there are some quick and simple ways to gather basic information about an audience.

Observation

As Hall of Fame baseball player Yogi Berra put it, "You can observe a lot just by watching." In many of your public speaking situations, you will already be familiar with your audience; examples include company conferences, town council meetings, and classroom speeches. You can create an audience profile from your background knowledge of your audience members and your past observations of their behavior with different speakers: Who are these people? What kinds of speakers have they enjoyed in the past? What kinds of speeches did they like, and why? Their history with other speakers can help you make realistic assumptions about how best to present yourself and your topic.

Informal Research

One of the easiest and most useful strategies for researching an audience is to obtain information from the host or sponsor of the event—he or she is also very concerned with the success of your speech. Feel free to ask questions: Who will be in the audience? Why will they be attending my speech? What are they interested in? What do they already know about my topic? How do they feel about the issues? You can be very straightforward and ask: What exactly do they want or expect to hear? You can also solicit this kind of information by talking with several members of the audience or with others who share important characteristics with the audience.

Although formal interviews yield the most accurate and complete results, informal analysis techniques are useful when you cannot take a more structured, formal approach.

Focus Group Interviews Focus groups usually consist of a small group of people randomly selected from the audience itself or from a similar population. Group size ranges anywhere from 6 to 12 members. Smaller groups of 6 to 8 are optimal simply because members feel freer to talk more. For most audience analyses, one or two focus groups should be sufficient. Once the members agree to participate, they all meet to respond to a series of questions asked by a facilitator or moderator (you or a helper). To ensure that all the pertinent information is obtained, the primary questions are conceived beforehand. Besides asking the interview questions, the moderator is also responsible for encouraging every group member to talk. Successful focus groups generate a lively exchange of information.[1]

Focus group members often respond to questions that assess their attitudes, beliefs, and opinions about relevant issues. Suppose the general topic of your speech is birth control. You could use the focus group interview to help you narrow the topic. Should you talk about the latest birth control devices? How about abstinence or the practice of safe sex? Perhaps you should talk about AIDS. Or how about the controversial pill RU 486? A focus group will certainly tell you what they'd like to hear.

Often, focus group interviews are used to find out how sophisticated audience members are, that is, how much information they already have about birth control. Do they seem to be well informed?

Questionnaires Analyzing your audience with questionnaires is the second formal method of obtaining demographic and psychographic information. Questionnaires can be administered over the phone or in person. One of the best-known forms of questionnaire is the self-report, in which respondents are given a list of questions and asked to answer them in writing. Like focus group interviews, questionnaires require careful planning. Questions should be clear, specific, objective, and as straightforward as possible. Two general categories of questions can be used on a questionnaire: (1) **open questions**, which are broad and allow respondents a great deal of leeway in their answers, and (2) **closed questions**, which narrow respondents' answers by forcing them to choose among two or more possible responses. Open questions tend to generate in-depth answers and occasionally provide additional interesting, essential information. Unlike closed questions, open ones often reveal *why* respondents feel the way they do.[2] The down side of open questions is that they tend to generate lengthy answers

questions the way you want them to. **Leading questions** can sabotage the results of focus group interviews and questionnaires. Most people are likely to tell the interviewer what he or she wants to hear regardless of their personal opinion; still others deliberately state the opposite position. (See the box "What's Wrong with Leading Questions?" for some specific examples of how to recognize and avoid some common pitfalls.)

What's Wrong with Leading Questions?

To obtain accurate information from focus group interviews and questionnaires, be sure that your questions do not lead respondents to answer in a particular way. The wording of questions can have a huge impact on your survey results. For example, in the spring of 1993, Ross Perot and his United We Stand organization conducted a highly publicized nationwide survey. *Time* magazine and CNN then hired the Yankelovich Partners survey research firm to ask a split random sample of Americans two versions of the questions: Perot's original version and one rewritten by the Yankelovich firm. Consider the results for one of the questions:

Perot version: "Should laws be passed to eliminate all possibilities of special interests giving huge sums of money to candidates?"

Yankelovich version: "Should laws be passed to prohibit interest groups from contributing to campaigns, or do groups have a right to contribute to the candidate they support?"

Results Perot version: 80 percent yes; 17 percent no.

Results Yankelovich version: 40 percent for prohibition; 55 percent for right to contribute.

To help develop your skills in formulating good survey questions, review the following questions and the bracketed comments that demonstrate how each question sways the respondent's attitudes and beliefs. How might you change the following leading questions to make them more objective?

- Don't you think unborn babies should have the same rights as anyone else? [Pro-choice advocates would not necessarily label a fetus an "unborn baby." The negative wording— "Don't you think"—indicates that the interviewer expects a yes answer. Try restating the question more positively. How would that change the tone of the question?]

- Is saving an owl worth the loss of 20,000 jobs? [Is only one single owl at stake here?]

- Which is more important to you—a suntan or your life? [Given only those two choices, any reasonable person would choose the latter option. But do all people who get suntans die from skin cancer?]

Although those leading questions may be obvious, what follow are examples of more subtly loaded questions. Notice how a particular word or phrase cleverly attempts to conceal the interviewer's intent. An unwitting respondent can be misled easily with questions like these:

- Do you believe that mothers should or should not stay home to take care of their preschool children? [See how the question reads when the word "parents" is substituted for the word "mothers." Are "staying home" and "not staying home" the only possible options?]

- Do you think gays and lesbians should be given special privileges? [What does the interviewer mean by "special privileges"? Is the interviewer implying that gays and lesbians should be given the same rights as heterosexuals, or does the interviewer mean something more?]

- How much should cancer victims of second-hand smokers be able to sue for damages? Not more than $100,000? Not more than $500,000? Not more than $1,000,000? [What if the respondent feels that cancer victims should not be allowed to sue for damages at all? Or what if the respondent doesn't think that a million dollars is enough to pay for someone's life?]

- Do you think radical feminists are right when they advocate women in combat? [Why must these feminists be labeled as "radical"? What does that say about the interviewer's prejudices? Don't other people who do not consider themselves either radical or feminists also endorse women in combat?]

- Don't you think we ought to help our own before we attempt to help others? [Who is included in "our own"? And who are the "others"? The interviewer is pushing the respondent to agree with his or her position.]

- Working with senior citizens can be pretty frustrating, can't it? [What initially appears to be an empathic inquiry is, instead, the interviewer's attempt to put words into the respondent's mouth. If the respondent perceives working with seniors as being rewarding, she or he might find it difficult or awkward to overtly disagree.]

Sometimes a question can be worded objectively, but the interviewer's nonverbal behaviors tip off the respondent to the only "correct" answer. Consider the following:

- *Why* do you think Haitians have as much right as Cubans to immigrate to the United States? [The interviewer looks incredulous; her eyes are open wide—and so is her mouth!]

- Do you think that arriving at work on time is an essential employee attribute? [The interviewer raises his eyebrows and generally looks skeptical.]

- As a registered Democrat, do you support the president's health care bill? [As she says "health care bill," the interviewer rolls her eyes and smirks.]

Personal interviews provide an excellent source of information when gathering data about a particular audience. Interviews can be conducted by phone or in person. If approached properly, most people are willing to be interviewed about important issues.

A CLOSER LOOK

Open and Closed Questions

Sample Open Questions

- Why are you attending this meeting?
- How do you feel about physician-assisted suicide?
- What do you hope to learn from this presentation?
- What can you tell me about yourself?
- What do you think about the baseball strike?
- Why do you believe that Fidel Castro should be over-thrown?
- What exactly is meant by Rosh Hashanah?
- Why do you like living on the East Coast so much?
- What is there to do for fun in your hometown?

Sample Closed Questions

- What is your sex? —— Male —— Female
- What is your attitude toward physician-assisted suicide?
  - —— Extremely favorable
  - —— Favorable
  - —— Neutral
  - —— Unfavorable
  - —— Extremely unfavorable

- Which word in each of the following pairs best describes your feelings toward the legalized use of marijuana?

—— Good	—— Bad
—— Agree	—— Disagree
—— Moral	—— Immoral
—— Dangerous	—— Safe
—— Harmful	—— Harmless

- To what extent do you agree or disagree with each of the following statements? Circle the appropriate number.

Agree/Disagree

5 4 3 2 1   To fight the rising crime rate, we need to build more prisons.

5 4 3 2 1   Too many people purchase and carry guns in society today.

5 4 3 2 1   We need more police on the street.

- On a scale of 1 to 10, with 10 being the most physically attractive, how would you rate your boyfriend or girlfriend?

that can deviate from the main issue and make them more difficult to analyze. Closed questions may generate more superficial answers, but they tend to be on target and very easy to analyze. (See the box "Open and Closed Questions" for specific examples of these two basic categories of questions.)

A sample survey that assesses both demographic and psychographic information is shown in the box "Audience Analysis: Gathering and Interpreting Information." You can edit or add to this sample survey to create a tailor-made questionnaire for yourself, your speech topic, and your audience.

Audience Analysis

Gathering and Interpreting Information

Instructions

Use the following items to gather information about your audience in a systematic way. This questionnaire can be administered to a pilot sample of audience members or to a small group of individuals who resemble your actual audience. Because a questionnaire may not be feasible for every occasion, you could also ask and answer these questions about your projected audience yourself. When you make such guesses, however, try to be as informed as possible. Interview representative individuals who can validate or clarify your conclusions. Whichever data-gathering scheme you choose, the point of using a questionnaire of this type is to determine the demographic and psychographic makeup of your audience—information that may greatly affect your topic selection and purpose. After reviewing the following questions, consider what other characteristics of your audience may be relevant to your presentation. Add additional items as needed. Remember: Preparing and planning a speech is a strategic process.

So, with a particular audience in mind, have sample members complete the following items:

Demographic Information

1. What is your sex?
   a. Female
   b. Male

2. What is your approximate age?
   a. 18–21
   b. 22–29
   c. 30–39
   d. Over 40

3. What is your religious preference or background?
   a. Catholic
   b. Protestant

c. Jewish
d. Other _____
   (please indicate)
e. Not identified with any religious group

4. What is your primary co-cultural background?
   a. Euroamerican
   b. Latino, Hispanic, Mexican American
   c. Native American
   d. Asian American
   e. African American
   f. Middle Eastern American
   g. Other _____
      (please indicate)

5. What is your educational background? (Indicate the highest degree earned.)
   a. Doctorate
   b. Master's
   c. Bachelor's
   d. Associate degree
   e. High school diploma
   f. Other _____
      (please indicate)

6. What is your economic status or annual salary (or, if still a dependent, your parents' economic background)?
   a. Below $10,000
   b. $10,000–$19,000
   c. $20,000–$49,000
   d. $50,000–$100,000
   e. Over $100,000

7. What is your current marital status?
   a. Married
   b. Single
   c. Divorced

Audience Analysis   (Continued)

8. How many children do you have?

    a. None
    b. 1
    c. 2–3
    d. 4 or more

9. Where do you live?

    a. My parents' home
    b. My own apartment or house
    c. A dormitory
    d. A fraternity or sorority
    e. Other _____
        (please indicate)

Psychographic Information

____ 10. To what extent are you liberal or conservative in your political orientation? (Circle the number that most closely reflects your attitude.)

    Liberal   5   4   3   2   1   Conservative

____ 11. How involved are you on _____
    (insert the topic of your presentation)?

    Highly involved   5   4   3   2   1   Uninvolved

____ 12. How informed do you consider yourself to be on _____ (insert the topic of your presentation)?

    Highly informed   5   4   3   2   1   Uninformed

____ 13. How interested are you in _____
    (insert the topic of your presentation)?

    Very interested   5   4   3   2   1   Not interested

Calculating Overall Audience Scores

For items 1–9, calculate simple percentages. Percentages can be highly informative; for instance, comparing the percentages of males to females in your audience will give you more information than knowing only the total membership of the audience. For items 10–13, calculate the mean, or average, audience score by summing up the responses for each item and then dividing by the number in your sample. By obtaining mean scores or percentages for each item, you will have an idea of where your audience members are in terms of socioeconomic status, religious preference, degree of involvement in your topic, and so on.

Interpreting Audience Scores

Answers to these and other similar questions can give you valuable information to use in designing your own message. Consider the responses to demographic item 2. Suppose the average age of your audience is over 40; you would want the examples you select and the issues you address to be relevant and familiar to them. In a speech on music, for example, a reference to the rock group Spice Girls may not be as germane to this age group as, say, a reference to the Doors.

Similarly, responses to psychographic item 11 may be extremely important to your selection of specific persuasive appeals. Research on persuasion indicates that highly involved or committed audience members are extremely difficult to persuade. Consequently, you should be careful not to ask for too much change too quickly—particularly with highly involved audiences who disagree with your position. You want to avoid having your audience overreact and, instead, move your audience gradually toward your desired goal. (Chapter 12 discusses persuasive strategies in greater detail.)

Given the specific topic or issue you select for your presentation, you may want to ask additional questions regarding your audience members' demographic or psychographic characteristics. For example, you may wish to consider their college major, the geographic area in which they were reared, their source(s) of financial support, their grade point average, their career aspirations, their degree of religious or political convictions, or their attitudes toward gun control, AIDS research, the Palestinians, the wealthy, the homeless, and so on. With answers to these and other pertinent questions, you can begin to tailor your speech to meet your audience's specific needs and, at the same time, accomplish your own objectives.

Creating a Profile of Your Audience

The information that you gather from observation, informal questioning, focus group interviews, and questionnaires should put you in a good position to develop a fairly extensive audience profile. Figure 6-1 summarizes the potential features—both demographic and psychographic—of such a profile. What you don't know directly from analyzing the information at hand you can often surmise from your data (although it is a good idea to ask specifically about issues relating directly to your speech). For example, you may not have asked what your audience members watch regularly on television, but you could probably accurately hypothesize what general categories of shows they enjoy watching.

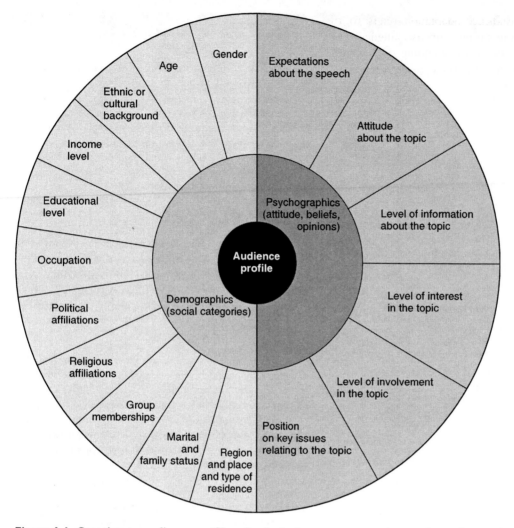

Figure 6-1 Creating an audience profile. To obtain the most accurate picture of an audience, it's important to look at both demographics and psychographics.

Suppose your audience analysis revealed the following demographic and psychographic information: The majority of audience members are over 40, middle- or upper-class, Euroamerican and African American, male, and married; they exercise regularly, consider themselves to be open-minded, read newspapers regularly, and enjoy drinking socially. Based on this information, which of the following types of television programs do you think they watch regularly?

Law-and-order shows

Sitcoms

Cartoons

Sports

Soap operas

Martial arts action shows

Cooking shows

News programs

Late-night talk shows

Romance movies

Even with a lot of information about your audience members, the resulting profile may not always lead you to accurately predict what they feel, what they believe, or how they behave. As with the profiles generated for each of the different co-cultures discussed in Chapter 3, no one individual may actually fit the composite you produce from your audience analysis. Nevertheless, you are more likely to be right than wrong. Your audience profile is an important tool for creating an effective speech.

ADAPTING TO YOUR AUDIENCE

Once you have identified your audience and gathered sufficient information to generate a sophisticated audience profile, you are ready to think about ways to adapt to your audience. **Audience adaptation** refers to the process of adjusting one's topic, purpose, language, and communication style to avoid offending or alienating members of the audience and to increase the likelihood of achieving speech goals. Consequently, audience adaptation does not involve becoming someone else simply to please the audience, but it does involve showing sensitive regard and respect for individual differences. Based on some of our own experiences and the experiences of other professional public speakers, we know that a number of challenging situations may call for a speaker to adjust his or her topic, purpose, language, or communication style. For each of those challenges, we suggest some guidelines to help speakers connect with, rather than alienate, difficult or demanding audiences.

Dealing with Co-Culturally Dissimilar Audiences

As indicated in Chapter 4, dealing with co-cultural dissimilarities is anxiety producing. If you, as the speaker, represent one co-culture and your audience members represent a distinctly different one, you are likely to feel apprehensive about communicating with them. Sometimes, when it's difficult to find common areas of interest and experiences, your anxieties may not be all that irrational. What is your purpose or goal? How should you approach your topic? These very real concerns can only be addressed when you know something about your audience's culture (and your own).

Consider for a moment a potential audience of second-generation Hmongs (pronounced Mongs). If you don't live in Minnesota or California, you may be unfamiliar with this co-cultural group, members of which migrated from China to the highlands of Laos and then to the United States in recent decades. The Hmongs had an oral culture—they had no written language until about 30 years ago. Isolated from other cultures, the Hmongs developed a system of codes and social customs quite different from those of many other U.S. co-cultures. For instance, a number of Hmongs living in the United States continue to practice early marriage. Girls often marry as young as 12 or 13; and many then drop out of school and begin to have children. Adolescence is absent from the Hmong culture; girls become women when they marry. Male children are particularly valued, and a male Hmong isn't considered a "real man" until he has a son. If a wife does not conceive a child or a couple has only female children, the man is likely to take a second wife.[3] Clearly, the Hmong culture has many distinguishing features, and a speaker from another co-culture may feel especially challenged having to adapt to such a distinctive audience.

However, no matter how great the cultural difference, speakers must consider the cultural beliefs and practices of their audiences and do their best to adapt to them.

How do you go about adapting to co-cultures different from your own? To begin, you must learn about that particular co-culture. Read everything you can about it. Talk to intercultural experts, and try to connect with members of that co-culture through focus groups or some other less formal interview format. Find out from them what topics might be most appropriate, what issues might be most relevant, and what attitudes they hold toward your subject area. Importantly, in your investigation of that co-culture, be sure to learn and understand why members of the co-culture hold particular practices and beliefs. In other words, create an audience profile.

Once you have learned all you can about your audience's co-cultural background, you should select a topic that you know will be interesting or relevant to audience members. If you were to address the Hmongs, for example, you might talk about the economic, social, or political costs associated with marrying young, or perhaps you could talk about the value of educating both women and men. You might even want to compare and contrast the marital or family practices of their co-culture with your own. Your topic selection, then, is dependent on your audience.

Next, you should carefully target your purpose to this particular co-cultural group. You would be foolish to think you could persuade an entire audience of Hmongs to hold off on marriage until their late twenties or early thirties or to practice birth control after having two children (particularly if both children were girls). Such far-reaching objectives would surely result in failure. (Chapter 12 discusses the problems associated with persuasion strategies that ask for too much change.) Instead, you would want to modify your purpose so that your audience of Hmongs would not be offended by or alienated from you. Keep in mind that you would need to demonstrate an understanding of and respect for what they believe and how they feel.

To begin, consider the topic of early marriage. By thoroughly investigating the Hmong culture, you would quickly understand how the Hmongs' marital and childbearing practices evolved. While living in war-torn Laos, many Hmong men died or were killed by the time they were 35; infant mortality was also very high. Thus, marrying young and bearing children were ways to preserve their culture.[4] Given that information, you might want to adjust your goal: Your new purpose might be to inform the audience that here in the United States, later marriages actually preserve and protect nuclear families. In your presentation, you might explain that because the normal life span is so much longer and infant survival rate is so much higher here than in Laos, people living in the United States have the luxury of obtaining an education and initiating a career before they marry and have children. Rather than deny the validity of the Hmongs' beliefs and values, your adjusted purpose would demonstrate some understanding of their priorities.

Finally, you need to be sensitive to the language you use and the communication style you exhibit. By familiarizing yourself with and using your audience's language codes, you communicate that you took the time to learn something about your audience. Although most audiences will appreciate such efforts, some may be suspicious of speakers who go too far. As discussed in Chapter 5, audiences don't take too kindly to liars and impostors.

Perhaps no other co-culture is more adept at code switching than African Americans. Many African Americans move easily from one code to another depending on the audience.[5] Speaking before their own ethnic co-culture, African Americans are likely to employ slang, lots of in-group gestures, laughter, and so-called Black English—a communication style sometimes referred to as "sounding black." With a predominantly Euroamerican audience, however, many African Americans have learned to switch their code to Standard American English and their style to one of restraint ("sounding white"). Such language or communication-style mobility is vital to communication within and among the various co-cultural groups living together in the United States. (See the box "Interview with a Student: Alanna Boatright" for more information about adapting to diverse co-cultural groups.)

Interview with a Student

Alanna Boatright

Alanna Boatright, 21, is a senior majoring in communication studies at California State University, Long Beach. She's a model for Vidal Sassoon's of Beverly Hills, and she's been in a number of commercials promoting products as diverse as pizzas and eyeglasses.

To what extent do you think your cultural background influences the way you communicate with a large group?

I'm African American, English, Irish, Russian, Jewish, and Cherokee. Because I'm so diverse ethnically myself, I think as a speaker I'm more geared to being inclusive in my speech. Even though we all hold stereotypes about groups of people, I am less likely to be accused of saying something that sounds prejudicial. I mean, we're all prejudiced, but when I say something that sounds stereotypical, people are more likely to accept it from someone who is as ethnically diverse as I am. Being part of so many groups allows me to categorize more than others. Because I come from all these diverse backgrounds, I feel like I have the floor to talk about more issues than most people; my voice becomes more acceptable to others. However, being multiracial does not mean that I am not capable of offending or excluding audience members. So, as a good speaker, I find it important to use inclusive language and understand that more than likely, the audience will contain ethnic groups other than those that I belong to.

Do you think that growing up and living in Southern California also might have influenced the way you communicate today?

I definitely think so. There are so many different ethnic groups living here. It's a real advantage in learning how to relate to others. We encounter so many different people on a daily basis. Living here helps us learn to relate and communicate with people from other cultures and countries with very little effort or work—particularly when you compare what it must be like for people who are not exposed to people of very diverse ethnic groups. By being in contact with large numbers of people of different ethnic and co-cultural backgrounds, you learn very quickly that adaptation is important. You must learn to be versatile and flexible with people who are unlike you. People who are raised around only one certain race or ethnic group probably aren't as open to, or don't have the experience of how to relate to, people who are dissimilar from you.

You began your college career as an engineering major. Why did you switch to communication?

Communication is fun and so much more of who I am and what I want to do with my life. It's more useful. Right now I'm pursuing an acting career, and communication studies has helped me more than anything else I've encountered. I'm learning how to deal with people, what makes people like (or dislike) others. I've learned to be more outgoing and friendly—all those qualities that people find interesting about you, qualities that make you stand out.

The Hmongs' communication profile is somewhat similar to that of Asian Americans (as discussed in Chapter 3). In general, Hmong Americans represent a collectivistic, high power-distance, high-context, and highly prescribed gender-role co-culture. Knowing these characteristics about Hmong audiences, you might want to show considerable restraint, be very polite, and demonstrate respect for members' opinions and points of view. You would also need to understand that the males, as opposed to the females, in the audience might be more likely to make decisions related to marital and family practices. Finally, you would need to recognize that although Hmong audiences might listen politely to everything you have to say, you should not mistake their apparent patience and tolerance for acquiescence. They might continue to disagree, but you would never know it.

Audience analysis only goes so far; it's what you do with that information that makes all the difference. To be an effective co-cultural public speaker, you must be able to adjust your purpose, topic, and language or style of communicating to meet the unique demands of audiences whose co-cultural affiliations may be different from your own. Adopting a perspective of cultural inclusion, not exclusion, is essential to your success. (The box "Audience Adaptation: Making Your Audience a Priority" summarizes the practical strategies presented in this chapter.)

Challenging Individuals and Situations

The same principles involved in adapting to a co-culturally dissimilar audience also apply to managing difficult individuals and situations. You may come across an audience member or a situation that makes it particularly difficult for you to communicate. Even so, managing these situations is no different from

---

BUILDING YOUR SKILLS

Audience Adaptation

Making Your Audience a Priority

Identify the Target Audience

- Consider whether the target audience is contiguous or extended (media).

  Contiguous audience: the people sitting or standing in front of you as you give your presentation.

  Extended audience: anyone who will be exposed to your speech through the media (newspapers, magazines, television, radio, and so on).

Analyze the Audience

- Consider audience demographics and psychographics.

  Demographics: the social categories—age, gender, ethnicity, occupation, education, and so on—into which audience members can be grouped.

  Psychographics: the audience's attitudes, beliefs, and opinions that are relevant to the topic: What are their motives for being in the audience? What topics are they interested in? What do they know about the topic? How do they feel about the topic?

- Use informal and formal methods to research the audience.

  Observation: Consider what you know about familiar audience members. What types of topics and speakers have they enjoyed in the past?

  Informal research: Talk with the sponsor of the event or a few audience members to obtain information about audience demographics and psychographics.

  Formal interviews: Put together a focus group interview or administer a questionnaire to representative audience members.

- Create an audience profile from your research.

Adapt to the Audience

- Select a topic of interest or relevance to your audience.

- Target your purpose to your audience. Set a reasonable goal for your speech.

- Use appropriate, bias-free language and an appropriate style of communication. Speak at the audience's level.

- Answer questions quickly, clearly, and thoughtfully.

- Adapt to your audience, but don't change who you are or what you think and feel in order to make a good impression.

handling any other kind of audience. What follow are some typical audience reactions you might have to handle sometime during your own speaking career and ways of dealing with each.

Hostile Audiences

Begin by finding out why your audience is hostile. The most fundamental reason audience members might be hostile is that they think they know what you are going to say and they don't like your message. Suppose you're a member of management in a large organization and you have to talk to a group of union employees about inevitable budget cuts and layoffs. Your audience members probably have a pretty good idea of what you're going to say—and they don't want to hear it. They suspect that because you represent management, you will argue in favor of freezing wages and downsizing the number of employees in the plant. Clearly, the audience has good reason to be less than responsive to your presentation.

Once you have discovered the basis for members' hostility, you will want to adapt your approach accordingly. You may want to forgo speaking directly to a large group of union employees on budget cuts and, instead, talk one-on-one with specific union representatives. Or you may decide to talk about the overwhelming economic problems facing the company. Rather than describing management's solution to those problems, you may want to solicit input from the workers themselves.

But if you do not have the freedom to change your tactics or to revise your speech topic, you can always adjust your purpose. Whereas your initial objective may have been to inform employees of layoffs and wage freezes, your purpose can be altered slightly to persuade them that making sacrifices now will preserve jobs for the future.

Finally, you will need to adapt your language and communication style to the audience. You might begin by emphasizing points on which management and employees agree: "We all want this company to survive." "We know times are hard, but we will emerge stronger in the end."

At all times throughout the speech, remain friendly and even-tempered. Whatever you do, avoid becoming defensive, and do not return their hostility. Realize that your audience members' concerns are real and possibly very frightening to them. What they need and want is some reassurance, some hope that everything will be okay. Show genuine respect for how they feel at all times.

Hecklers

A speaker's worst nightmare is a handful of **hecklers** in an audience who are determined to disrupt the speech and make the speaker look bad. In this situation, it is quite natural for you to lose composure and fight back, but the best advice is to simply ignore hecklers. By responding to their outcries and criticisms, you will end up giving their message substance.

When your patience wears thin, however, you may find yourself in an awkward position: You can't continue to talk and still be heard over their protests, yet to respond to their objections will give them credence they don't deserve. So what do you do? Begin by responding sincerely to the hecklers' concerns and then quickly return to your presentation. Audience members generally consider heckling to be rude, embarrassing, and disruptive. Your audience will want you to handle it. Consequently, you will need to rely on nonverbal behaviors of dismissal. That is, gradually walk in the direction of the hecklers while continuing to talk. If possible, put your hand on the back of one of their chairs. Standing that close gives them due recognition; however, do not make eye contact! (The minute you do so, the hecklers will seize the opportunity to interrupt again.) Instead, look away in the direction of your supportive audience and keep talking!

Questioners

Sometimes it is difficult to determine if questions from the audience are intended to heckle and disrupt or if they are truly legitimate and warrant a response. Receivers naturally tend to ask questions or offer comments. Even though feedback is restricted when receivers become part of a larger audience, the tendency to raise questions or make remarks still remains. For most audience members, remaining quiet within a large group is no difficult task, but for others, it's a real challenge to stay silent.

At first glance, there is no way of knowing whether the questioner's motives are good or bad. Consequently, you must treat each question as though it is legitimate. Respectfully, but briefly, respond to the question as best you can, and then return to your presentation. Should the questioner continue to interrupt, remind the individual that you have time constraints but that you would be glad to answer any questions following your presentation. If the individual persists, treat her or him as you would a heckler. Ignore the person; look away; and continue with your speech. Once again, you can generally count on audience support if you remain respectful and in control.

Interjectors Audience members who occasionally insert a brief comment during the presentation are known as **interjectors.** These interjections are also referred to as **cue- or call-response patterns.** Such response patterns are used by audience members to affirm what the speaker is saying. On cue or call from the speaker, audience members interject by saying "right on," "okay," "amen," "uh-huh," or some other brief affirming response. In this way, the audience joins in and becomes an active part of the speech transaction. For speakers from certain co-cultures, such as African Americans, interjections are both welcome and common. Without such feedback, an African American speaker may feel alienated and ineffective, but with cue responses, he or she is likely to feel connected with the audience and, thus, successful.

For speakers outside the African American co-culture, cue-response patterns from the audience may be both unexpected and unwanted. To Asian American or Euroamerican speakers, for instance, active audience responses may be interpreted as interruptions. For these co-cultural speakers, the optimal audience is polite, respectful, and mute. Can you imagine their dismay when confronted with an audience that shows similar respect and support by being outspoken and intense? Should this unexpected response happen to you, enjoy it. The audience is offering you high praise; after all, cue responding is designed to validate what you are saying. Consider it a rare opportunity for you to connect with your audience and inspire them at the same time.

Successful speaking means making your audience your top priority. By identifying who audience members are and developing profiles of them based on both psychographic and demographic information, you can begin to select an appropriate topic, define your purpose, and determine the most appropriate message and communication style. Careful, thoughtful consideration of your audience will help you understand how the members feel and what they might expect from you. Only then can you begin to meet their needs and expectations.

CHAPTER REVIEW

- Speakers often fail to successfully deliver their message by not considering their audience. Being able to connect with an audience requires that you identify who your target audience is and analyze audience characteristics that may make a difference in what you say and how you say it.

- Many speakers address more than one apparent audience. It is easier for speakers to relate to a contiguous audience. With larger media audiences, however, the same messages may be inappropriate.

- Because each audience may have different attitudes, beliefs, and expectations, you should learn as much as you can about your audience. Audience analysis requires that you ask and answer a number of questions: Who are these people? Why are they here? What are they interested in? What do they already know about this topic? How do they feel about the issues?

- It's important to analyze your audience systematically. Gather information about a prospective audience by observing audience reactions to other speakers, soliciting information from the sponsor of the speech event, and interacting with potential audience members. You can also use more formal methods, such as focus group interviews and questionnaires.

- Audience adaptation requires that you adjust your topic, purpose, language, and communication style. To successfully adapt, you may need to modify what you want to say so that audience members are neither alienated nor offended.

- Adapting to culturally dissimilar audiences is one of a speaker's biggest challenges. You must (1) learn as much as you can about audience members' co-cultural beliefs and practices, (2) select a topic that is relevant to them, (3) carefully target your purpose, and (4) adjust your own language and communication style. These guidelines also apply when managing hostile audiences, hecklers, questioners, and interjectors.

QUESTIONS FOR CRITICAL THINKING & REVIEW

1. Do you think politicians respond differently to an audience when they know a television camera is around? How might the presence of a TV crew affect a presentation by a local politician?

2. How does an audience profile help you prepare your presentation? How does someone's age, socioeconomic status, education, and co-cultural background influence the decisions you make as a public speaker?

3. To what extent should speakers adapt to the co-cultural needs, expectations, and concerns of their audiences? At what point does adaptation become misrepresentation? What are some examples of appropriate and excessive adaptation?

4. What would you do if an audience member fell asleep in the front row while you were giving a speech? Would you simply ignore him? What if he began to snore?

5. Someone in the audience has just interrupted your speech because she's angry at something you just said. What do you do?

NOTES

1. Plax, T. G., & Cecchi, L. F. (1989). Management decisions based on communication facilitated in focus groups. *Management Communication Quarterly, 2*, 511–535.
2. Stewart, C. J., & Cash, W. B., Jr. (1988). *Interviewing: Principles and practices* (pp. 59–62). Dubuque, IA: Brown.
3. Arax, M. (1993, May 4). The child brides of California. *Los Angeles Times* (Orange County ed.), pp. A1, A26–A27.
4. Hova Wa Yang, president of the National Hmong Council. Cited in Arax, 1993.
5. Hecht, M. L., Collier, M. J., & Ribeau, S. A. (1993). *African American communication*. Newbury Park, CA: Sage.

Chapter 7

LISTENING ACTIVELY

John glared at everyone in the group. He had just severely reprimanded one of his immediate subordinates. In fact, it was Mike, John's right-hand director, who was being publicly admonished for not bothering to listen to John's briefing.

All of the other directors, managers, and staffers at the meeting were stunned. Not only had they always felt that Mike was John's favorite, but they would never have expected such open hostility during a public briefing. Even more surprising was the fact that it was Mike's lack of attention that had aroused John's anger.

After calming down, John continued with his message, which was now targeted at his whole audience: "Every one of us is paid a large salary by this corporation. Whether you like it or not, *I* am the boss here. That means that I'm your *boss* and that I'm *in charge*. It is my butt that ends up in a sling when any one of you screws up! So, when I'm talking I expect you to listen *very carefully* to *each and every word!* That also means that I better be able to *tell* that you are listening to me! Do you all understand me?"

All heads nodded vigorously. John then turned his attention to Mike: "I don't know how many times I've had to tell you, Mike, that most of your mistakes around here follow directly from your not listening. You are officially on notice. If I sense again that you're not listening, I am going to put a letter of reprimand in your personnel file. And any subsequent failures to listen to me will bring even more severe disciplinary actions! Do you understand me, Mike?"

Mike was noticeably sweating. Everyone could see that his back was pressed tightly against his chair. "Yeah, John," Mike said shakily, "I understand—and I am truly sorry. It won't happen again. I promise that I will always listen to you."

At this point, John's briefing was over. After John had departed, Mike looked around at his coworkers and said apologetically: "Well, I feel pretty stupid. John was really mad, huh? I had no idea that it looked like I wasn't listening. The fact is, I wasn't and I didn't realize it. I'm really sorry to have put the rest of you in such a difficult situation. I need to concentrate on what people say. I just had no idea that it was such a problem."

Mike's failure to listen is by no means unusual. Very few of us are truly competent listeners. In a survey of Fortune 500 companies, over half of the respondents reported that they found it necessary to provide listening training to their employees.[1] Listening problems, however, are not restricted to the work environment. From time to time, we all fail to take note of what people are saying. And like Mike, some of us may even be chronically poor listeners.

Most people think that they already have the skills to be good listeners. However, research shows that no one should assume that his or her listening skills are well developed or that it is easy to be an effective listener.[2] **Listening** is a complex task that requires an individual's full focus and effort.

Sorting out what people really mean is an important skill for business, social encounters, and personal relationships. Good listeners are able to think critically about and evaluate what they hear; they get more from communication exchanges. By listening closely, good listeners can also help public speakers communicate more effectively and, at the same time, help themselves improve their own public speaking skills.

Learning Objectives

After reading this chapter, you should be able to do the following:

1. Differentiate between active and passive listening.

2. Identify the listening behaviors of audiences representing different co-cultures.

3. List the reciprocal responsibilities of speakers and audience members to ensure effective listening during public speaking situations.

4. Explain why the four common assumptions that people make about listening are inaccurate.

5. Give examples of the five barriers to effective listening.

Listening is an integral part of the public speaking process. Unlike everyday conversation, in which receivers can interrupt, ask for clarification, or pose questions, public speaking contexts offer limited opportunities for feedback. Because the speaker delivers the message only once, audience members must listen closely. Nevertheless, although audience members are the primary listeners in public speaking situations, the transactional nature of communication requires that speakers also have good listening skills. Good listening by both audience members and speakers enhances the experience of public speaking events.

Listening is a *skill* that can be *learned*. Competent listeners do not inherit the capacity; they learn to listen. This chapter takes a closer look at the listening process and some of the factors that can block effective listening. This chapter also provides concrete strategies for developing listening skills. (The box "Interview with a Professional: Charles Roberts" offers some advice on the importance of developing individual listening skills.)

UNDERSTANDING THE LISTENING PROCESS

The model of communication presented in Chapter 1 demonstrates that listening is a complex process.

Good listening requires attention to both verbal and nonverbal messages and is influenced by the context of the communication exchange. A clear understanding of the listening process is crucial to becoming an effective listener.

What Is Listening?

Many people inaccurately equate hearing with listening. Hearing is an automatic physiological process in which the ear receives sound. Listening is an active behavior that involves maximizing attention to and comprehension of what is being communicated by someone who is using words, actions, and other elements of the immediate environment. We all often hear things without actually listening to them. And although we may think of listening in terms of using our ears to hear, listening also involves monitoring the nonverbal and contextual aspects of public speaking. We listen with our ears, but we also "listen" with our senses of sight, touch, and even smell.

The context, or immediate environment, of a speech can convey many meanings and can influence our interpretation.[3] For example, we interpret speeches differently when we listen in familiar or

---

SPEAKING OUT

Interview with a Professional

Charles Roberts

Charles Roberts, 51, is a professor of communication studies at East Tennessee State University in Johnson City.

What general advice might you give students about improving their own listening skills?

There is no easy method for bettering listening. Listening effectively (listening at your optimal level) takes energy. One cannot listen at one's optimal level always. One must pick and choose when listening is important. You will not always be right in choosing to listen or not to listen at your optimal level. But you should take the responsibility for deciding when to listen. Don't believe that a speaker can or should make you listen. Don't believe that any speaker is inherently boring or interesting.

The listener determines what is interesting and what is boring. The listener determines what he or she will attend to, understand, and retain. To abdicate your right to decide for yourself

that which you will listen to almost assures that you will not be able to listen effectively when you wish to do so.

What do you think are the most dramatic barriers to effective listening?

Perhaps the greatest barrier that confronts us is the belief that there is some trick, some easy method, for listening more effectively. There is no pill, no secret short course that will make you a better listener. We all look for the "fountain of listening," but it just does not exist. There is no inoculation that will grant one effectiveness, nor is there an easy regimen that will grant us competence in this most important area. However, the greater effort that must be expended to achieve an elevated competence level is well worth expending. Listening is the most important verbal skill. Patient and prolonged practice of this basic skill pays dividends far greater than most that follow from effective reading, writing, or speaking. It is worth the effort to be able to listen habitually at your optimal level.

Effective listening means active listening. Audience members must try to get actively involved in what a speaker is attempting to communicate. Active listening takes a lot of effort.

unfamiliar places, in large- or small-group situations, or to speakers we know well or not at all. Members of the media audience (who listen to a speech through radio, TV, or other mass media) are exposed to a different context than are members of the contiguous audience; each speaking context has its own influence on the listening experience.[4] An audience actually attending the Democratic or Republican National Convention is likely to have a more intense reaction to the speeches than are the rest of us, who are watching the same presentations on TV. While those in attendance stand, cheer, and throw confetti, we lounge on our couches and reach for another slice of pizza. Same speech, different contexts—and so, different listener effects.

As described in Chapter 1, the interpretation of meaning is based on all the direct and indirect experiences an individual accumulates throughout life. Every individual has a set of personal and co-culturally based interpretations for the many words, symbols, gestures, and other elements that make up communication.

Only when the speaker and the audience have a sufficiently similar base of experiences can messages be sent and received in a parallel fashion, allowing individuals to share the same (or similar) interpretations. The level of comprehension, therefore, is directly dependent on the existence of parallel meanings, which can be produced accurately only by effective listening behavior.

The Importance of Effective Listening

Effective listening is no accident. Although some aspects of listening are habitual or reflexive, others certainly are not.[5] We cannot expect effective listening simply to happen naturally. Accurate communication requires that speakers and audience members actively and consciously attend to what is being communicated. Effective listening, therefore, is a key objective in public speaking situations. As speakers, we must intentionally watch and listen for audience feedback;

as audience members, we must deliberately focus on the speaker's messages.

To be done well, listening is something that we must consciously *manage*. We can successfully attend to what is being communicated only if we make deliberate listening a key objective. Listening deliberately, then, is not a part-time pursuit. Nevertheless, it is possible to listen too intently! We could not possibly give our total attention to what was being communicated to us in all speaking situations and via all media; none of us could cope with such a tidal wave of information. In any number of public situations, we wouldn't want to attend to and comprehend every bit of information.

Stated more simply, an important prerequisite to effective listening is discriminating between what we should give our attention to and what we can safely ignore.[6] We must be able to distinguish between those situations or cues that require our total involvement and those that do not. For example, we may want to ignore background messages from the TV while we are reading a book, or we may want to tune out hurtful gossip or irrelevant conversation. What are the behaviors, then, that will assist us in deliberately attending to those public speaking messages that we want and need to comprehend?

Active versus Passive Listening

Listening effectiveness is directly related to the amount of effort a listener exerts. **Active listening** occurs when substantial effort is exerted by the listener for the purpose of maximizing attention to and comprehension of what is being communicated by the speaker. When audience members actively listen, their efforts often enhance audience attention and comprehension and contribute greatly to the success of the public speaking situation. It is almost impossible to listen closely without being actively involved in what is being communicated. The feedback generated by active listening often motivates the speaker and makes the entire transaction successful.

Active listening is important even when the speaker and some audience members disagree over something. When audience members listen carefully, they can better understand the speaker's position, and they may find that their point of view does not differ from the speaker's as much as they initially thought.

Interesting speakers are easier to listen to. People have a tendency to disregard public speakers who appear to be dull; indeed, boring speakers are a serious obstacle to effective, active listening. Nevertheless, there are strategies for listening to a speaker who, at first, appears uninteresting. (See the box "Effective Active Listening" for some tips.)

By contrast, **passive listening** occurs when the listener exerts little or no effort in attending to what is being communicated. Passive listening can be due to boredom, hunger, disinterest, and apathy; of these four reasons, disinterest is probably the most common explanation for passive listening.

Some people take great pride in their ability to avoid listening. This is not to say that it is always bad to act as if we are listening when we are not. In fact, we sometimes need to appear as if we are not listening when we really are, or vice versa.

Some public speakers are convinced that what they have to say is critical to our survival. Thus, they expect us to at least *appear* as if we are highly attentive. Typically, as an audience, we give them what they want—we look and act as if we are listening, even though we are not. We look alert and perhaps nod wisely from time to time, but our minds may be miles away. In some cases, our inattention is totally justified; we don't need or want to listen to everything or everybody. The problem is that this listening mode can become habitual.

Co-Cultural Variations in Listening Behaviors

Recognizing the external actions, expressions, and other behavioral signs of a "good listener" is very important for understanding the relationship between speakers and audience members.[7] External listening cues tend to vary among individuals and among co-cultures. It is important to recognize the co-cultural differences in listening cues in order to properly interpret audience feedback. Picture a good listener in your mind. What is it about that person that makes him or her look like a good listener? What behavioral signs do you associate with active listening? Although it is not enough to say that good listeners "look and act like good listeners," they do stand out from poor listeners.[8] Nevertheless, not all good listeners look and act alike; consider the following co-cultural variations.

Among Euroamericans and African Americans, good listeners concentrate fully on a speaker, with their bodies subtly communicating receptivity to the speaker's message. They may lean forward slightly, with their eyes fixed on the speaker. They may nod in agreement from time to time. Their expressions are likely to be alert and amiable. More open and

Effective Active Listening

One of the greatest challenges in active listening is to stay focused and to concentrate on the content of the speech, particularly when you find the speaker or the topic boring or difficult to follow. The following strategies can help you listen more effectively:

- Take listening seriously. Set listening as your key objective.

- Before the speech starts, commit yourself to listen actively.

- Look for both the verbal and nonverbal messages.

- Isolate at least one interesting thing about the speaker. Redefine the speaker who initially appears to be boring and difficult to listen to as someone worthy of your attention.

- Look for the purpose, main points, and supporting material in the speech. Key into and remember the major ideas and essential points in the speech.

- Silently paraphrase or repeat important points to clarify your understanding. Ask yourself questions about the speaker's points to keep your attention focused.

- If your mind begins to wander, consciously focus on what the speaker is saying.

- Take notes to help you stay focused. Note taking is also a good strategy if the speech contains important information.

Remember: Listening is a skill that can be learned. Look for opportunities to practice and improve.

---

expressive listening behaviors, such as cue responding, are also common among African American audiences.

Compared to Euroamericans and African Americans, other co-cultures tend to have a more restrained listening style. Native Americans show deference and attentiveness by avoiding sustained and direct eye contact with speakers. Similarly, Asian Americans are likely to avoid eye contact with speakers and to exhibit little overt expression in their facial or bodily movements. These listening behaviors do not indicate boredom, disinterest, or fatigue; rather, they communicate respect for the speaker. (Some speakers misinterpret no expression or a positive expression as a sign of audience members' actual agreement with their position. Not so. Asian American and Native American audience members may simply be trying to communicate harmony in order to save the speaker from public embarrassment or humiliation.)

Latino and Middle Eastern American audience members are likely to show active listening behaviors similar to those exhibited by Euroamerican and African American audiences; they are likely to be overtly expressive in their nonverbal actions, nodding and smiling often. Like the Native American and Asian American audiences, however, they may make every effort to show pleasure and agreement—even when they may not like or agree with what they hear.

Male and female audience members also demonstrate active listening differently. Women's facial cues are normally more expressive than men's; women also initiate and reciprocate smiles more than do men. And women rely more on eye contact to show that they are interested and involved in what a speaker is saying. Compared to women, men may show more overt signs of displeasure and agitation when they disagree with a speaker, and they may be more willing to interrupt and challenge the speaker's arguments.

What about the listening cues of passive listeners? How do people usually act when they are bored by a speaker? Among co-cultures with expressive external listening cues, passive listeners often behave very differently than active listeners. They may stare off into the distance and lean back, with their eyes partially closed and arms crossed. They may fidget, look around the room, or check their watches. Passive listeners look bored or frown slightly. For co-cultures with more restrained active listening styles, passive listening behaviors are more difficult to detect. In an effort to be polite, audience members may display even more restrained facial expressions and body language.

In sum, the "look" of active and passive listeners varies from individual to individual and audience to audience. Correctly identifying different co-cultural listening cues can mean the difference between interpreting audience responses accurately and inaccurately.

The Benefits of Looking like a Good Listener

Looking like a good listener actually contributes to effective listening in two important ways. First, when an audience member is perceived to be a good listener, the speaker is likely to feel sympathetic toward that individual and to make more of an effort to ensure that his or her message will be understood clearly. Thus, mutual adaptation—by the speaker and the audience—contributes to the sharing of meaning. Second, looking like a good listener influences effectiveness by improving listening skills. To be perceived as a good listener, a person must exhibit a combination of behaviors that are easily identified and associated with high effort and motivation. Merely by *acting like* a good listener, a person can actually change her or his habitual listening behavior to become more effective.[9] Over time, engaging in the right external behavior can lead to internal changes.

Consider Mike, the poor listener described at the beginning of the chapter. For him, behaving like a good listener will be very difficult and will involve changing long-standing behavior patterns that have minimized his listening effectiveness. But if Mike makes the effort, he will eventually be perceived as a good listener. If he can learn to exhibit the right look, he not only will appear to be a good listener at work but will actually become one. In addition, if he can extend his efforts to speaking situations outside of work, he will transform himself into an effective listener in all facets of his life. The underlying principle for this transformation is simple: People who work hard to create a particular impression of themselves will become, over time, what others perceive them to be.

SPEAKER–AUDIENCE RECIPROCITY

In public speaking situations, the level of listening effectiveness is determined primarily by the audience. However, the transactional nature of a communication exchange means that the behaviors of both speakers and audience members are important. If accuracy is to be high, everyone participating in a public speaking situation must adapt to one another in ways that encourage active, effective listening.

Adaptation improves listening at all stages; it helps promote and maintain attention, which in turn improves message comprehension and communication accuracy. Adaptation can also help overcome potential barriers to accurate and easy message exchange, including language differences and other co-cultural variations. **Speaker–audience reciprocity** occurs when speakers and audience members engage in adaptation and feedback simultaneously, adjusting their behavior to one another. Reciprocity is similar to adaptation, but it involves both the adjusting activities and feedback cues and the consequent adaptations of each person involved in the public speaking situation. Reciprocity is the combined influence of these behaviors on both speaker and audience members as they adjust to each other.

How does reciprocity work? Imagine yourself as an audience member. When I begin to speak . . . you start to listen. If you cup your hand behind your ear . . . I talk louder . . . which causes you to lower your hand . . . which leads me to speak more softly. If I tell a joke . . . you grin . . . which makes me smile back. If I say something you like . . . you nod in agreement . . . which motivates me to provide more positive comments . . . which makes you blush or smile. Reciprocal adaptation can also occur at a more sophisticated level: When I present my argument, you mentally formulate a rebuttal, which leads me to anticipate just such a rebuttal. Therefore, I systematically incorporate counterarguments into my speech.

The need for reciprocity in a listening situation means that both speaker and audience members have certain listening responsibilities. If both parties meet their responsibilities, chances are good that the speaker will meet his or her goal of being understood and audience members will similarly meet their goal of understanding.

The Responsibilities of Speakers

What follow are the listening responsibilities that are unique to you as the speaker.

1. *You have a responsibility to fully grasp the content of your speech before presenting it.* You must make the effort to research your topic as thoroughly as possible. Become an expert in the area. It's your responsibility to know the material so

well that you can easily translate it to anyone willing to listen. You will want to organize and present your message in such a way that audience members can easily understand what you intend.

2. *You have a responsibility to carefully select the tone and style of presentation that are most appropriate for your message.* The manner in which you communicate your speech has a substantial effect on how it will be received. Should you present the message in a solemn, formal manner or a humorous, informal way? How you deliver your message will influence your audience's ability or willingness to listen. There is no single or universal tone or style; instead, the speech topic or purpose should give you some direction. Suppose you are accepting an award for your play as a member of the college volleyball team. The audience will want you to sound grateful and sincere when you receive your award.

If you sound boastful and unappreciative, the audience likely will tune you out.

3. *You have a responsibility to ensure that your presentation is appropriate for the context.* As you will recall, context refers to the actual physical setting for your presentation, including the room size and temperature, stage setting, audience seating, and time of day. Context also refers to the occasion—whether an award speech, an after-dinner presentation, or a political appeal. Clearly, public speaking contexts come in all shapes and sizes. The context can control how audience members interpret your speech and whether they listen actively. If you are delivering a eulogy, you don't want to make light of the occasion by telling tasteless jokes. Or, if the room is unbearably hot, you can't expect the audience to actively listen for any extended length of time. By adapting to these and other contextual

Audience members who get actively involved in the listening process often employ techniques to increase their listening effectiveness. For example, note taking can be a useful technique for increasing listening effectiveness.

constraints, you can make audience listening less effortful and more pleasurable.

4. *You have a responsibility to ensure that your message is tailored to your particular, targeted audience.* Remember: No two audiences are alike. To prepare and present a speech that fits all audiences, regardless of their makeup, would be a mistake. Although your particular speech text may be suitable for one audience, it might be entirely inappropriate for another. A particular audience may not understand certain words and phrases or, worse, be offended by specific words or labels. Some audiences may need more background information on your speech topic; others may already be aware of those issues and urge you to move on. Adapting your speech to each unique audience is essential for active listening.

5. *You have a responsibility to consider the consequences of what you say.* By considering all the possible consequences of what you say, you can avoid alienating audience members. Even if your message is controversial, you need to first acknowledge audience members' feelings and beliefs. For instance, suppose you want to persuade your college peers that tuition should be increased to pay for the cost of their education. It would not be a good idea to begin by telling them that they have been getting something for nothing at taxpayers' expense! Even if you followed that argument with less alienating ones, chances are slim that your audience would continue to listen to your speech.

The Responsibilities of Audience Members

Just as speakers have clear listening responsibilities, audience members are also obligated to ensure effective listening results.

1. *You have the responsibility to exert sufficient effort to listen well.* Some speakers and some topics require more or less effort than others. You will need to make more of an effort to listen to speakers whose dialect, accent, or pronunciations may differ from your own. Although some topics and issues may be difficult to comprehend, commit yourself to grasping the essential meaning of the message. That is, sort through, key into, and try to remember only the major points.

2. *You have the responsibility to seek out personally relevant information.* Assuming that all speakers have something relevant to say, it's up to you to discover just what that something is. Issues that may be personally relevant to one audience member may be irrelevant to another. Nevertheless, it's your responsibility, as well as every audience member's, to find something that has personal meaning. As a good listener, ask yourself what you can learn from this speech. That is, what points can you use or apply in your own life? What does all of this mean to you?

3. *You have the responsibility to give the speaker a fair hearing.* As discussed in Chapter 5, source credibility has a powerful influence on speaking effectiveness. You are more likely to pay attention to speakers you find believable, competent, trustworthy, warm, and friendly. Without question, it's much harder to give credence or listen actively to speakers who aren't particularly credible. Even so, you have the responsibility to sort through what the speaker has to say. Give the speaker a fair hearing before determining that he or she is not worth your attention; in short, suspend judgment. (You can and should, however, evaluate all speakers' messages carefully, especially when their credibility may be suspect. The box "Critical Listening" gives some tips on critically evaluating a speaker's message.)

4. *You have the responsibility not to overreact to what is being said or how it is being communicated.* Audiences often forget that a primary objective of all public presentations is to come as close as possible to sharing similar meanings. Failure to recognize this objective can arouse a variety of inappropriate responses that can decrease overall listening effectiveness. Suppose you are listening to a speaker who attempts to flatter the audience by indicating how grateful he is for the opportunity to speak before "this very special group." You might be tempted to conclude that he is trying too hard to please, and you might wonder what he is trying to gain. But the fact is, the speaker may have no veiled intentions at all.

Just as speakers are advised to avoid inappropriate words and phrases, as an audience member, you must also minimize the effects of

Critical Listening

Critical listeners get more from communication exchanges in business, social, and personal encounters, and they are less likely to be taken advantage of by unethical speakers. Critical listening involves both deciding when to listen and evaluating a speaker's message. Use the following guidelines and questions as a framework for critical listening.

- Discriminate between messages you should attend to and messages you can safely ignore.

    Is the topic of this speech important to you? Does the speaker or context of the speech make listening important?

    Does the speech contain information or arguments that are new, significant, or especially relevant to you?

- Try to discern the speaker's purpose or goal.

    Why is the speaker presenting this material?

    Is there any reason to suspect bias or a hidden agenda?

- Evaluate the evidence presented in a speech, especially when it is part of a key argument.

Is the speaker offering facts or opinions?

Does the evidence come from experts? (An expert is a person who, through education, training, experience, or observation, has special knowledge about a particular subject.)

Is there any reason to suspect bias in the information sources?

Does the evidence conflict with your personal knowledge or with evidence from other credible sources?

Does the evidence seem clear, precise, and unambiguous?

- Identify and evaluate the key arguments presented in the speech.

Are key arguments supported with compelling evidence?

Does the speaker use sound reasoning? Does she or he avoid the patterns of faulty reasoning?

Does the speaker provide sound and compelling arguments in addition to appeals to emotions and values?

---

inappropriate word choices. What emotionally laden words tend to turn you off? How about some of these:

Punk	Broken home
Pig	Old maid
Femi-nazi	Flesh-colored
Boy (instead of man)	Illegal aliens
Girl (instead of woman)	Handicapped
Ma'am, Miss, Little Lady	Stupid
Macho	Retard

Your first impulse may be to quit listening to any speaker who uses these or similarly offensive words and phrases—but don't do it. Try not to overreact to isolated words. Listen to the entire message first.

5. *You have the responsibility to help the speaker be successful by looking responsive and receptive.* No matter how good a speaker may be, an unwilling or passive audience can make the speaker's task extremely difficult. It's much easier for the speaker to address an audience that appears animated and eager to listen than one that looks half-asleep, bored silly, and anxious to leave. As an audience member, you must focus on that visual image. Become the audience member you would like to have when it's your turn to give a speech.

The box "Listening Responsibilities" provides an overview of the responsibilities that speakers and audience members must assume to ensure effective listening.

COMMON OBSTRUCTIONS TO EFFECTIVE LISTENING

Additional factors that can reduce our listening effectiveness include several common misconceptions that many people make about the listening process. These factors also include a variety of physical, co-cultural, and psychological barriers that need to be taken into account.

Listening Responsibilities

Listening well does not just happen. To ensure effective listening, both the speaker and the audience must assume some responsibilities.

Speaker Responsibilities

- Learn as much as you can about your topic before your presentation.
- Select the tone and style of delivery that are most appropriate for your message.
- Make sure your speech is appropriate for the context or occasion.
- Tailor your message to your particular, targeted audience.
- Consider the possible consequences of what you say.

Audience Responsibilities

- Exert sufficient effort to listen well; remember that some speakers and topics require more effort than others.
- Seek out personally relevant information.
- Give the speaker a fair hearing—even when she or he doesn't come across as being particularly credible.
- Don't overreact to what the speaker says or how he or she says it.
- Help the speaker be successful by looking responsive and receptive.

Common Misconceptions about Listening

Ineffective listening may result from making inaccurate assumptions about the listening process. Poor listeners hold at least four common misconceptions, as outlined here.

"Listening Is Easy" Although listening can be recreational at times, there is a problem with thinking about listening as a form of relaxation. Thinking of listening as a fun, easy activity changes how we attend to and understand what is being communicated. Most listening is definitely not easy, and effective listening is a complex activity that requires effort. Moreover, good listeners are not born; they are *made*—through hard work.

"It's Just a Matter of Intelligence" A second common misconception is that all smart people listen well. The conclusion that seems to follow from such an assumption is, "I am smart; therefore, I am already a good listener." Unfortunately, this is a non sequitur (an illogical conclusion). Recall the example of Mike in the chapter introduction. Mike is certainly smart, but he is not a good listener.

"Listening Requires No Planning" A popular belief is that because we engage in so much listening every day, we don't need to plan in order to listen more effectively. That is, the large amount of listening we do automatically makes us good listeners. Not true. Most of us neither practice good listening skills nor are able to assess the effectiveness of our own listening behavior. What do we actually learn, then, from most of our day-to-day listening? Almost nothing. Effective listening results from careful planning—not merely from the sheer frequency of doing it.

"If You Know How to Read, You Know How to Listen" A rather curious but misguided assumption is that by improving our reading ability we can also improve our listening ability. This idea is founded on the belief that what is acquired in learning one skill can be transferred to another, different skill. However, no educational research has shown that this transfer actually occurs. Just because someone can concentrate for long periods of time while reading does not also mean that she or he will be able to focus attentively while listening to a presentation. Unfortunately, listening and reading are not based on enough common skills to allow for the same kind of transfer.

Five Barriers to Effective Listening

In addition to the misconceptions just discussed, there are a number of barriers to effective listening. Here, "barrier" means any condition, either in the public speaking context or one that is personal to the audience member, that functions to reduce accuracy in listening.

Physical Conditions

One broad-based and important category of barriers is physical conditions that interfere with effective listening. For example, it is surprising how often actual noise in a public speaking situation can be problematic. Yet many people tend to ignore such obstacles and assume that they have no impact on the reception of a presentation.

Noise interference can come from any number of sources that may be beyond listeners' control. Printers, typewriters, lawn mowers, clattering dishes, traffic, aircraft—all can physically interfere with their ability to hear. Loud background voices can also distract listeners or limit their ability to receive messages. Thus, in noisy situations, listening effort and concentration must be especially high.

Personal Problems

Personal conditions can also pose barriers to effective listening. The most obvious are physical conditions—sickness, exhaustion, and discomfort caused by illness—that can influence the ability to listen effectively. Overindulgence in alcohol or even food can reduce listening capacity. Additionally, personal problems—money difficulties, a sick child, a stressful relationship—can distract listeners or even prevent them from concentrating effectively on other matters.

One additional personal condition that can decrease listening effectiveness is an individual's level of apprehension about listening to other people. Some people actually experience a high level of apprehension when they try to process information from others. Take a few moments to complete the test in the box "How Much Receiver Apprehension Do You Feel?" A comparison of scores from this test demonstrates that people have varying levels of receiver anxieties that can actually interfere with their ability to receive information and cause them to misinterpret the information they do receive.

Co-Cultural Differences

Many problems of ineffective listening are related to co-cultural differences between speakers and audience members. In normal, everyday living, women claim that men "just don't get it," and teenagers protest that their parents "just

don't understand." Each of these examples represents a classic case of a co-cultural barrier to effective listening.

Additional co-cultural barriers include disparate speaker–audience beliefs. For example, affluent audience members may have considerable trouble listening to a speaker advocate higher taxes for the rich; managers may not listen all that carefully to speeches by nonmanagers; and, more generally, individuals from a particular co-culture may not always listen willingly to what a speaker from another co-culture has to say—particularly if the message threatens their beliefs. In all of these situations, preexisting belief systems are shared within a particular co-cultural group—systems that may not be similarly shared by other co-cultural groups. So, when a speaker's version of reality conflicts with what audience members know or feel to be true, they are likely to dismiss the speaker and his or her views altogether. The only way to get around this barrier is to avoid taking an ethnocentric stand; instead, try to understand and respect why others think as they do.

Co-Cultural Prejudices

A fourth type of barrier to effective listening is prejudice—an unrealistic attitude toward an individual based on a stereotype of a particular category of people. Everyone holds stereotypes; they are a natural outgrowth of the process of perception. People and things are grouped and labeled by category to help make sense of the world. Stereotypes can be dangerous, however, because they typically represent oversimplifications and because they can form the basis of prejudice. In public speaking situations, if the audience prejudges a speaker based on the categories she or he belongs to, rather than on the speaker's individual characteristics, then the audience is listening to and evaluating the speaker in a prejudiced way.

Prejudices can be based on any social category, including ethnicity, age, socioeconomic status, religion, profession, and educational attainment. Some prejudices are obvious and well documented, such as those based on race or ethnicity. Other prejudices are more subtle and may even be unconscious. For example, audience members may tune out speakers who are not college educated or who are older or younger than they are.

Prejudices are a significant barrier to effective, accurate listening. They cause the audience to perceive

How Much Receiver Apprehension Do You Feel?

Instructions

This test, officially called the "Receiver Apprehension Test" (or RAT), is designed to examine how you feel about receiving information or listening to others. Enter the appropriate number in the space provided to indicate how each of the following statements generally applies to you: (5) strongly agree, (4) agree, (3) are neutral (undecided), (2) disagree, or (1) strongly disagree.

___ 1. For the most part, I feel comfortable when listening to others on the phone.

___ 2. It is often difficult for me to concentrate on what others are saying.

___ 3. When listening to members of the opposite sex, I find it easy to concentrate on what is being said.

___ 4. I have no fear of being a listener as a member of an audience.

___ 5. I feel relaxed when listening to new ideas.

___ 6. I would rather not have to listen to other people at all.

___ 7. I am generally overexcited and rattled when others are speaking to me.

___ 8. I often feel uncomfortable when listening to others.

___ 9. My thoughts become confused and jumbled when I am reading important information.

___ 10. I often have difficulty concentrating on what others are saying.

___ 11. Receiving new information makes me feel restless.

___ 12. Watching television makes me nervous.

___ 13. When on a date, I find myself tense and self-conscious when listening to my date.

___ 14. I enjoy being a good listener.

___ 15. I generally find it easy to concentrate on what is being said.

___ 16. I seek out the opportunity to listen to new ideas.

___ 17. I have difficulty concentrating on instructions others give me.

___ 18. It is hard to listen to or concentrate on what other people are saying unless I know them well.

___ 19. I feel tense when listening as a member of a social gathering.

___ 20. Television programs that attempt to change my mind about something make me nervous.

Calculating Your Score

1. Add together your responses to items 1, 3, 4, 5, 14, 15, and 16 = ___

2. Add together your responses to items 2, 6, 7, 8, 9, 10, 11, 12, 13, 17, 18, 19, and 20 = ___

3. Complete the following formula:

   42 − total from step 1 = ___

   + total from step 2 = ___

   Your total RAT score = ___

Interpreting Your Score

The possible scores for the RAT range from 20 to 100. (If your own final RAT score does not fall within that range, you have made a computational error.)

The average RAT score is 60. Higher scores reflect greater receiver apprehension. If you scored above 70, you are considered high in receiver apprehension. Because RAT levels are traitlike in nature, high RATs, as a rule, have trouble processing information from others; that is, they tend to miss out on crucial information while listening to others, and they often misinterpret the information they receive. Research indicates that individuals high in receiver apprehension experience more anxiety while listening to difficult or provocative material. Moreover, high RATs experience more anxiety while listening, and that anxiety interferes with their ability to concentrate or to process information.

If you scored low in RAT (below 50), you aren't as likely to experience the same kinds of listening problems that high RATs do. Low RATs are able to adjust to others and focus actively and attentively on what they are saying. Lacking the anxieties that high RATs experience, low RATs can comfortably process and accurately interpret large amounts of information.

How Much Receiver Apprehension Do You Feel?   (Continued)

Many people are more moderate in receiver apprehension (between 50 and 70). Such individuals are more situational in how they listen or process information. Sometimes they may have more difficulty listening than at other times; moreover, they may find it easier to listen to some individuals than to others. The truth is, moderate RATs may occasionally need some level of arousal when listening to others—to prevent them from becoming too comfortable and falling asleep on the speaker!

NOTE: The original RAT was developed by Buddy Wheeless and can be found in Wheeless, L. R. (1975). An investigation of receiver apprehension and social context dimensions of communication apprehension. *Speech Teacher, 24,* 261–268. For research supporting the validity of this scale, see Beatty, M. J. (1981). Receiver apprehension as a function of cognitive backlog. *Western Journal of Speech Communication, 45,* 277–281; and Beatty, M. J., Behnke, R. R., & Henderson, L. S. (1980). An empirical validation of the Receiver Apprehension Test as a measure of trait listening anxiety. *Western Journal of Speech Communication, 44,* 132–136.

a speaker and a speech within the framework of the stereotype, rather than focus on the actual characteristics, abilities, or intentions of the speaker. Like funhouse mirrors that distort images, prejudicial beliefs can cause listeners to misconstrue a speaker's message. Because the stereotypical view of the speaker's group becomes part of the speaker's message, prejudiced audience members are likely to construct meanings and interpretations that the speaker never intended. Listening effectiveness is reduced, and accuracy is eroded.

Imagine how some taxpayers in an audience might disregard the remarks of a welfare recipient who argues that he needs more money and more benefits for his family in order to survive. Rather than attending carefully to his arguments and concerns, prejudiced listeners may dismiss the message as the remarks of a habitual complainer or a welfare cheat or a societal sponge. By recognizing some of your own prejudices, you can begin to overcome this particular barrier to effective listening. If you hold stereotypical views about Democrats, the elderly, welfare recipients, or any other co-cultural group, understand that you are likely to engage in oversimplification. No person, issue, or policy is so easily understood; take the time to get the whole story. Active listening requires that you suspend judgment and consider thoughtfully the speaker's entire presentation.

Connotative Meanings A fifth barrier to effective listening is the **connotative meanings** associated with symbols used in speeches. Whereas denotative meanings generally refer to the dictionary definitions assigned to words, connotative meanings are the personal, subjective, and unshared interpretations people have for verbal and nonverbal symbols and signs. Suppose a public speaker refers to all the adult females in her audience as "girls" but consistently refers to the adult males as "men." Until recently, the term "girl" was commonly used to refer to a female from birth to age 92 (or so). But the parallel term "boy" has rarely been used to refer to a man unless it was meant to disparage or humiliate. Sensitive audience members might find the speaker's differential word choices offensive and demeaning to women. Unfortunately, the speaker probably did not mean to imply that women were somehow not afforded the same status as men. In other words, her connotation of the term "girls" was probably not the same as the audience's connotative meaning. Given this problem, just how receptive do you think her audience will be to the rest of her presentation?

Speakers and audience members often have different connotative meanings associated with the symbols used in a speech. The former unwittingly use them in encoding messages, the latter in decoding and interpreting the messages. The influence of connotative meanings is a vexing problem because it is hard to detect. A listener may come away from a speech feeling that he completely understood and totally agreed with the presenter only to find out later that another audience member recalled a completely different version of what the speaker said! Either person could conclude that the other had a faulty memory or deliberately misrepresented what was said. In fact, this type of situation demonstrates an erosion of accuracy in communication due to the very different connotative meanings produced in the encoding-decoding processes.

Unfortunately, little can be done about this barrier to listening. Usually, neither speakers nor audience members realize that they are failing to separate connotative and denotative meanings. However, as listeners, we can be aware of the problem. If we find ourselves recalling a speech differently than another person, we can then search for sources of connotative confusion.

CHAPTER REVIEW

- Effective listening is no accident. Listening must be deliberately and consciously managed. Effective listening is directly related to the amount of effort exerted. Active listening requires substantial effort, while passive listening requires little or no effort. Good listeners actually look like they're attentive. However, there are substantial co-cultural variations in audience listening behaviors, ranging from overt facial expressions, body movements, and cue responding to more restrained behaviors of eye contact avoidance and polite signs of "apparent" agreement (smiling, nodding).

- Speakers and audiences share reciprocal responsibilities to ensure that effective listening occurs. Speakers have the responsibility to know as much as they can about their topic before they talk about it, to select the appropriate tone and style of presentation, to make sure their presentation is appropriate for the context or occasion, to tailor their message to a particular audience, and to consider the consequences of what they are going to say.

- The audience has the responsibility to exert sufficient effort to listen, to seek out personally relevant information, to give the speaker a fair hearing, to avoid overreacting to the speaker, and to help the speaker succeed by being responsive and receptive.

- Listening effectiveness can be reduced when people assume that listening is easy, that it is simply a matter of intelligence, that it requires no planning, or that good listening is related to good reading skills. Listening can also be hampered by physical conditions, personal problems, co-cultural differences and prejudices, and connotative meanings.

QUESTIONS FOR CRITICAL THINKING & REVIEW

1. How does listening differ from hearing?

2. Why is it so hard to listen to some speakers but not to others? What do speakers do to make listening worthwhile and apparently effortless for the audience?

3. Suppose you are giving a speech and nobody is listening to you. What can you do? Suppose someone else is giving a speech and no one is listening. Do you have a responsibility to help out this speaker? What can you do?

4. Do you hold any stereotypes of or prejudices against people whose religious backgrounds differ from your own? Under what circumstances might those prejudices interfere with your ability to listen well? What can you do to prevent such interference?

5. Why is the ability to listen well essential to critical thinking?

NOTES

1. Wolvin, A. W., & Coakley, C. G. (1991). A survey of the status of listening training in some Fortune 500 corporations. *Communication Education, 40*, 152–164.

2. Kelly, C. (1967). Listening: Complex activities and a unitary skill. *Speech Monographs, 34*, 455–466.

3. Nichols, R. G. (1948). Factors in listening comprehension. *Communication Monographs, 15*, 154–163; Nichols, R. G., & Stevens, L. A. (1957). *Are you listening?* New York: McGraw-Hill.

4. DiGaetani, J. L. (1980). The business of listening. *Business Horizons, 57*, 40–46.

5. Goss, B. (1982). Listening as information processing. *Communication Quarterly, 30*, 304–307.

6. Barker, L. L. (1971). *Listening behavior*. Englewood Cliffs, NJ: Prentice-Hall; Meyer, J. L., & Williams, F. (1965). Teaching listening at the secondary level: Some evaluations. *Speech Teacher, 15*, 299–304.

7. Howell, W. S. (1982). The *empathic communicator*. Belmont, CA: Wadsworth.

8. Mehrabian, A. (1967). Orientation behaviors and nonverbal attitude communication. *Journal of Communication, 16*, 324–332.

9. Bandura, A. (1977). *Social learning theory*. Englewood Cliffs, NJ: Prentice-Hall.

Chapter 8

SELECTING AND RESEARCHING YOUR TOPIC

Learning Objectives

After reading this chapter, you should be able to do the following:

1. Demonstrate how topic selection depends on the occasion, time constraints, and the audience itself.

2. Select a topic and narrow it sufficiently for your speech.

3. Identify the general purpose of your presentation.

4. Gather information about your subject.

5. Determine what information you should use or not use based on its relevance, recency, and credibility.

Jim is desperate. Three weeks ago he was assigned to give an informative speech to his public speaking class. With only two days left, he still has not decided on a topic, and panic is setting in. For weeks, Jim discarded idea after idea—some as too boring, some as too complex, and some as just plain stupid. Jim's instructor had told him to select a topic that he already knew something about, a topic that he found personally interesting. Jim made a list of the things he liked and actually knew something about. There was car maintenance, but Jim figured a lot of his classmates would fall asleep. He liked to shoot baskets with his friends, but how can you make a speech from that? And for obvious reasons, he dismissed the topic of why public speaking should not be a required course for college graduation!

If you have had a similar experience, you can relate easily to Jim's frustration and fears. As the speech date looms near, you begin to panic. Selecting the topic should be easy; it's the researching, organizing, and practicing that are supposed to be a lot more difficult. And yet, like Jim, you may have despaired over the considerable time and energy you spent searching for a topic—but to no avail.

Finding a topic in a reasonable amount of time is important: The sooner you settle on a topic, the sooner you can begin building a speech around it. This chapter examines some strategies for choosing a topic so that you can start your speech preparation early. Once you select a topic, you will need to have something credible and substantive to say about it. Therefore, the chapter also explains how to research your topic and select the best supporting materials to use in your presentation.

SELECTING A TOPIC

Finding a suitable topic can be a difficult and frustrating experience, but there are many helpful strategies for generating and evaluating potential speech topics.

Getting Started

Although not any old topic will do in any given speech situation, there are a million things to talk about: the economy, religion, politics, dating, children, the American flag, profanity, the death penalty, evolution, Greenpeace, acid rain, computer software, jazz, health foods, vacation spots, foreign investments, defense spending, designer earrings, physical fitness, religious cults, and so on. Selecting an appropriate topic depends on three factors: the occasion, time constraints, and the audience itself.

Trying to figure out exactly what to talk about is no easy task. Selecting the right topic requires that you consider time constraints, speaking occasion, and any unique characteristics of your audience.

Determine the Occasion The occasion often narrows the range of potential topics. If you were giving a wedding toast, you wouldn't want to refer to the divorce rate or to any former boyfriends or girlfriends of the couple; instead, you might want to talk about commitment and sharing. In delivering a funeral eulogy, you would want to highlight the positive lifetime contributions of the deceased—not the fact that she or he still owed you money. These examples show how the occasion automatically restricts your topic selection options.

Importantly, your topic should be appropriate for the occasion. Will your speech be given on a particular religious or political holiday? Is the occasion an award ceremony or a fund-raising event? Clearly, the occasion will provide some clues as to the kind of speech topic you should select.

Specify Time Constraints For some public speaking occasions, you will have an hour to speak, and for others only five or ten minutes. Staying within your allotted time is very important in many speech situations. Interfering with audience members' schedules by talking too long can harm the impression you make and lessen the effectiveness of your speech. You might also cut into the time allotted to the next speaker. Nothing will hurt you as a speaker more than talking too much or too long. Even the best speakers make this mistake.

Likewise, finishing too quickly can also cause problems for the host, the sponsor, and the audience. The next speaker or event may not be ready; or audience members, given time away from the office to attend, may be disappointed by having to return to work early.

Some people take time guidelines literally, while others have a more flexible attitude toward time. These differences are based on individual and co-cultural attitudes toward time. (The box "Time Talks" examines these attitudes in more detail.) Take a few minutes to complete the quiz in the box "What Is Your Orientation toward Time?" Regardless of your individual attitude toward time, delivering a speech that is too long or too brief can cause problems.

Time Talks

Time affects communication and people's perceptions of one another. In other words, "time talks"—sometimes more plainly than words.[1] Unless you understand how time communicates, you may be misperceived and misinterpreted. Both cultural and personal factors influence how time talks to different people.

Co-Cultural Orientations toward Time

People who live in urban industrialized societies typically are consumed with time. This preoccupation certainly has infiltrated U.S. society: Just count the number of clocks in your school or office, or consider how many times a day you glance at a timepiece or ask someone for the time.

Other cultures that are much more flexible about time afford speakers almost unlimited time to present their ideas. Both Saddam Hussein and Fidel Castro, who are greatly admired in their respective societies for their rhetorical skills, often hold the stage uninterrupted for hours at a time. If a U.S. president were to do likewise, she or he could expect commercial breaks, media commentary, and a lot of channel surfing by audience members.

Time orientations vary among U.S. co-cultures. Euroamericans are extremely sensitive to time—more so than any other co-cultural group in the United States. Euroamericans are likely to be relatively rigid and inflexible regarding time. For this co-culture, punctuality is perceived as a positive trait, and habitual lateness a negative trait. Because Euroamericans are the largest U.S. ethnic co-culture, their time orientation has powerfully influenced that of mainstream U.S. society.

Other co-cultures have different attitudes about time. For example, Latinos are much less rigid about schedules, punctuality, and time. They feel that Euroamericans are "slaves to the clock and don't really know how to enjoy themselves." For many Latinos, "interruptions are routine, delays to be expected. Thus it is not so much that putting things off until *mañana* is valued, as some Mexican stereotypes would have it, but that human activities are not expected to proceed like clock-work."[2]

Individual Orientations toward Time

Some people are just naturally more punctual than others—regardless of their co-cultural affiliations. Some people take time literally, so that when they say a "minute" or an "hour," that's exactly what they mean. Others use time more flexibly, expanding a second, minute, or hour well beyond the norms of what some people will tolerate. For example, President Bill Clinton kept people waiting so frequently and for so long that aides began to refer to his schedule as "Clinton time."

Other personal differences toward time have to do with an individual's tolerance for early or late time schedules.[3] These differences seem to be related to an individual's biological clock. For example, some people are "night people"—they work best at night. They may plod lethargically through the morning hours, but they become more functional as the day wears on. Other people are "morning people"—they are sharp for their morning classes or business meetings, but they don't function as well in the late afternoon or evening. Morning people begin to fade just as night people begin to function at their best.

Cultural and personal factors influence an individual's time orientation. When people of different time orientations communicate, they need to be aware of the potential for misperception or miscommunication. For example, what difficulties might a Euroamerican and a Latino experience in a communication exchange that involved time? What can be done to help eliminate potential problems?

Notes

1. Hall, E. T. (1959). *The silent language* (p. 180). Garden City, NJ: Doubleday.
2. Condon, J. C. (1985). *Good neighbors: Communicating with the Mexicans* (pp. 66, 67). Yarmouth, ME: Intercultural Press.
3. Richmond, V. P., McCroskey, J. C., & Payne, S. K. (1987). *Nonverbal behavior in interpersonal relationships* (pp. 177–179). Englewood Cliffs, NJ: Prentice-Hall.

To avoid such problems, choose a topic that you can cover sufficiently in the time allotted.

Identify Your Audience The topic selection process depends, to a great extent, on audience analysis. Before selecting your topic, ask yourself at least four basic questions: (1) What will my audience like to hear? (2) What does this audience expect me to talk about? (3) What topics will be most appropriate for this audience? and (4) What topics should I avoid with this particular audience?

In response to the first question, you will want to determine what topics you think will interest audience members or make it worth their time to listen to you.

What Is Your Orientation toward Time?

Instructions

Below are a series of statements concerning how you might feel about time. Enter the appropriate number in the space provided to indicate how each statement applies to you: (1) strongly agree, (2) agree, (3) are neutral (undecided), (4) disagree, or (5) strongly disagree. Note that many of the statements are similar to one another. Note, too, that there are no right or wrong answers; simply record your first impression.

____ 1. I believe that when someone says to be there at "five o'clock," I should be there at exactly 5:00, not 5:30 or 6:00.

____ 2. People who are habitually late for social engagements care more about themselves than they do about me.

____ 3. I don't understand why some people make such a big deal about being on time for everything.

____ 4. When I suggest that I will be there "in a minute," I could mean anywhere from a minute to an hour or more.

____ 5. I am offended when invited guests arrive an hour late for dinner at my home with no really good excuse.

____ 6. I find it unforgivable when someone is more than 15 minutes late for a scheduled appointment with me.

____ 7. It's not unlike me to try to squeeze in just one more thing to do as I'm trying to go out the door. As a result, I tend to be 30 minutes or more late to a number of engagements.

____ 8. I don't understand why teachers get so upset when students turn in their work a day or two late.

____ 9. People who are always on time or who arrive early for business appointments are much too eager or ambitious for me.

____ 10. People who are always late for work (or who arrive late from lunch hour) are insubordinate and disrespectful to the organization.

____ 11. I think that people are much too preoccupied with being punctual.

____ 12. Anyone who shows up even a few minutes late for an interview isn't motivated enough to deserve the job.

____ 13. "Just a second" really refers to 15 or 30 seconds, but never longer than 1 minute.

____ 14. I appreciate it when people are late for engagements with me; it gives me enough time to be ready myself.

____ 15. You would not be my friend if you had a habit of showing up late all the time.

Calculating Your Score

1. Add together your responses to items 1, 2, 5, 6, 10, 12, 13, and 15 = ____

2. Add together your responses to items 3, 4, 7, 8, 9, 11, and 14 = ____

3. Complete the following formula:

$$42 - \text{total from step 1} = \underline{\quad}$$
$$+ \text{total from step 2} = \underline{\quad}$$

Your total time orientation score = ____

Interpreting Your Score

The possible scores range from 15 to 75. (If your own final time orientation score does not fall within that range, then you have made a computational error.)

The median score for this scale is 45. If your own score falls well above that midpoint, you are particularly sensitive toward time. Below that midpoint, you are much more flexible about time.

For instance, would your classmates enjoy hearing about the benefits of dietary protein supplements? Perhaps not. But if you could demonstrate that protein is "brain food" and, when taken appropriately, may result in greater academic performance, you might convince them that this topic is worthy of their time and attention.

In reference to the second question, many audiences will hold expectations of what you will be talking about, and it is important that you try to meet those expectations. Imagine your disappointment if you went to a concert by your favorite band and they refused to play their most popular songs. If your audience members expect you to talk about employment opportunities but you instead tell them why the Democrats are destroying the job market, your audience will likely feel shortchanged.

As for the third and fourth questions, the appropriateness of your topic will depend a lot on your audience's sensibilities. Some audiences may be offended by a speech on, say, Satanism, the use of condoms, breast or penile implants, prayer in schools, white supremacy, or black power. The point is, some topics are simply more appropriate for some audiences than for others. Show respect for your audience members by selecting a topic that does not offend their moral standards and values.

Selecting a General Area or Subject

Your search for just the right topic need not be haphazard. **Brainstorming** is one proven method of selecting a topic: You jot down a list of possible topics as quickly as you can—without stopping to evaluate each item. Allow ideas to flow freely through your mind, writing each one down as it comes to you; one idea often leads to another. You can work alone or with a group of friends. Some people brainstorm most effectively in a completely open manner. Others find it helpful to use a category system—letters of the alphabet or types of information, for example—to help generate a flow of ideas. For visual thinkers, a technique called **mapping** may be helpful. Picture your ideas linked or clustered in a pattern like a spider's web. Start with an idea or topic in the center; then, as related ideas occur to you, jot them down and link them with arrows and lines. (The box "Techniques for Brainstorming" illustrates the three approaches.)

Some of your ideas may seem foolish or absurd; others may appear vague and difficult to use as speech topics. But write them down anyway. The key to brainstorming—and the step most often forgotten—is avoiding the tendency to reject ideas. While brainstorming, refrain from evaluating any idea as good or bad, stupid or silly, appropriate or inappropriate. Wait until you have listed 50 or more topics; wait until you have exhausted your possibilities. Only then should you return to any one idea and begin to evaluate it.

To get you started with brainstorming, refer to the box "Topic Ideas," or turn back to the list of potential topics provided in Chapter 2. You'll note that the box of topic ideas in this chapter also contains a list of topics that instructors find "used and abused" by students.

Consider Yourself Relying on yourself as the major source for topic selection is the best approach. Only you know what you are interested in or what you already know something about. Don't assume the audience will find your interests boring, trivial, or silly. If your topic interests and excites you, chances are it will interest your audience as well. Soliciting advice from friends and family, looking through magazines, and scanning TV programs for possible topic areas can take up a lot of time and may fail to generate useful ideas. And, if you are an apprehensive communicator, resist the temptation to look elsewhere for your topic. Recall the discussion in Chapter 4 on communication apprehension and stage fright. Because highly apprehensive speakers rarely select a topic that is familiar to them, they are forced to spend considerable preparation time learning about their topic—at the expense of organizing and rehearsing the speech itself. Obviously, the less you know about a topic, the more reason you will have to worry about your speech.

Choosing a familiar subject speeds up topic selection and cuts down on the amount of research you'll need to do, leaving you more time to prepare and rehearse your speech text. In looking at yourself for possible topic ideas, consider the following:

- What are your hobbies, interests, and unusual skills?
- Where have you lived and traveled?
- What interesting experiences have you had?
- What are your most significant co-cultural affiliations? What would you like to share about them with others?
- What is your background? What about your background might be unique and interesting to your audience?
- What issues concern you most?
- What is your major? Where do you work? What are your goals at school and in the workplace?

The answers to these questions may suggest some topic areas for you to consider.

Consider Your Audience Thinking about your audience members and their interests can also generate ideas for speech topics, particularly when their interests overlap with yours. A topic that excites both you and your audience would be an excellent choice. Refer back to Chapter 6 for suggestions on how to generate a profile of your audience. Focusing on your audience may help you come up with some additional topic areas.

Techniques for Brainstorming

Brainstorming is an effective means of generating ideas for speech topics. Here are examples of brainstorming using the three most common methods. Some people prefer to brainstorm in a completely open manner. Others find it helpful to use some type of category system to guide their thinking. Mapping, a third brainstorming technique, is particularly useful for visual thinkers.

Brainstorming in an Open Manner

running	fitness testing	fire safety
racing	finding time to exercise	gun safety
10Ks and marathons	campus exercise facilities	gun control
training methods	outdoor exercise	campus policies
running shoes	campus safety	bike lanes
injury prevention	dorm safety	bike helmets
personal trainers	locks on doors	new safety laws
sports medicine	buddy system	speed limits
weight training	campus escorts	drinking and driving
exercise for health	smoke detectors	affordable cars

Brainstorming Using Categories

Hobbies/ interests	Places lived/ traveled	Major co-cultural affiliations	Special skills/ expertise
competitive running jewelry-making cooking volleyball	New Hampshire Indiana California trip to Alaska trip to India & Nepal	Indian/German woman college student athlete Democrat	10K races jewelry-making research project on gender roles Indian cooking

Family background/ interesting personal experiences	Issues of interest and concern	Career goals and areas of study
parents' immigration stories ran L.A. marathon serious fire in family home summer daycare volunteer at center for low-income families	child abuse adequate daycare fire safety pedestrian safety	psychology major goal: social work or family counseling part-time job at bead shop

Techniques for Brainstorming *(Continued)*

Brainstorming Using Mapping

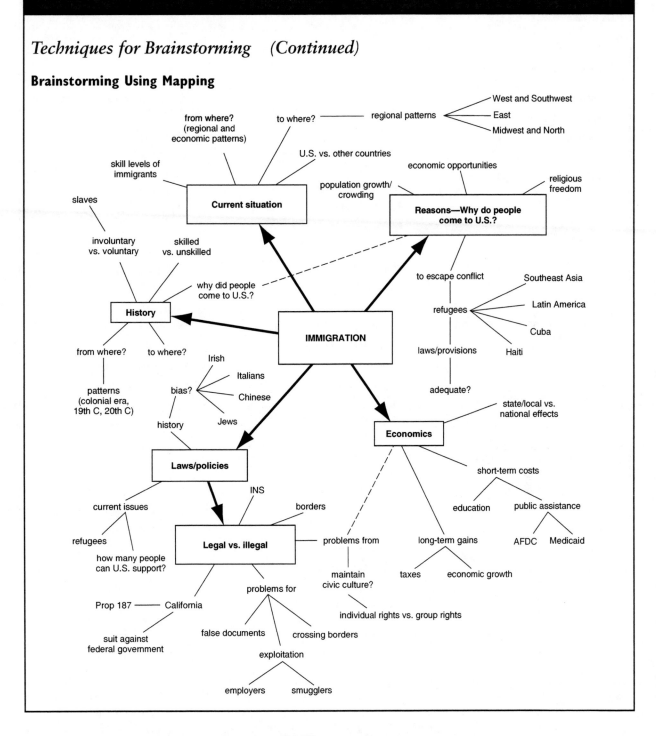

Consider Current Events Local and national newspapers and magazines can be good sources of topics. Look at the editorial pages for controversial topics to use in a persuasive presentation. For informative speech topics, examine both hard news on the front pages and soft news in subsequent sections. The Sunday edition of the newspaper may offer you the widest assortment of ideas. As you consider possible ideas from current events, ask yourself what issues interest you (and your

Topic Ideas

Novel Speech Topics

Face-lifts

Mystery novels

Child abuse

Superstitions

"Choosing" single parenthood

Religious cults

Women in combat

Gays in the military

Movie critics

Chlorofluorocarbons (CFCs)

Museum of Tolerance

Are we our brother's/sister's keeper?

Mondays

Fridays

No pain, no gain

Programming your VCR

Have we outgrown our need for labor unions?

Vegetarianism

Indian pottery (or Native American artists)

Petroglyphs

Rock collecting

Fencing

Growing your own herbs

Weight loss

Prenatal care

Writing a resume

Finding a job

Going to graduate school

Homophobia

The right to strike

TV talk shows

Tornado, hurricane, or earthquake readiness

Radio psychologists

Fashion fads

Teacher–student dating

Hosting a dinner party

Unfair employment practices

Sexual harassment

Skydiving

Health care benefits and illegal immigrants

Stock tips

Married couples in the military

Cheating at cards

Moving back home

Pet cemeteries

Family reunions

Used and Abused Speech Topics

Abortion

Gun control

The generation gap

The gender gap

Physician-assisted suicide

Legalizing marijuana

Drunk driving

How to bake a cake (or bread or cookies or whatever)

Bias in the media

The use of condoms

Seat belts

Recycling

The feminist movement

Motorcycle helmet laws

The ABCs of performing CPR

Antismoking (promoting a smoke-free environment)

"Just say no" to drugs

Prayer in the schools

Ride sharing

audience) the most and what issues you already know something about.

Boring Topics or Boring Speakers? Too often, speakers discard a topic on the basis of some arbitrary and self-imposed "dullness quotient." But before you do this, realize this little-known fact: Topics aren't boring; people are! Some speakers can make even the most mundane subject entertaining.

Consider NBC's *Tonight Show* host Jay Leno, who can make virtually any topic humorous and diverting. He is also extremely effective at interviewing his guests. His delivery pulls us in; we are narcotized into finding the life of even the most withdrawn guest worth our time.

On the flip side, there are speakers who can ruin almost any topic, no matter how potentially interesting. The important lesson here is that it is the speaker, not the topic, that has the ability to make the presentation fascinating, powerful, and gripping. So take care not to discard too many topics because you think they will bore the audience. Instead, look for ways to make each one of your topics interesting and exciting.

Narrowing the Topic

Once you have settled on a topic, you need to narrow it to something you can cover thoroughly in your allotted time. All of the topics listed previously are too broad. For example, take the topic of weight loss. How could you talk about weight loss in just ten minutes or even an hour? The point is, you couldn't. You would have only enough time to highlight information the audience probably already knows. Nevertheless, there are dozens of ways to narrow this topic. You could talk about the top five weight loss programs, whether diets actually work, society's preoccupation with thinness, prejudices against fat people, eating disorders, junk food addiction, exercise programs, social eating, and so on.

Even these topics can be restricted further. Consider the potential topics under the subheading "the top five weight loss programs": weight loss programs that work (or don't work), recidivism rates,

the costs and benefits of these programs, the way they generally operate, client profiles, and so on. As Figure 8-1 shows, the process of narrowing the topic provides an even broader selection of ideas from which to choose. But this time, the ideas are specific and easily managed. Narrowing your topic prevents you from wandering aimlessly and helps keep you focused on specific information to share with your audience. Once you have chosen a general subject area and narrowed your topic, you should evaluate your choice. (The box "Topic Checklist" lists some criteria by which to evaluate your choice.)

Specifying Your Purpose

The next step is to consider what effect you want to have on your audience members. Do you want to entertain them, inform them of particular issues, or perhaps persuade them? Regardless of your general speech goal, you need to specify from the beginning what you want to accomplish. Unless you know up front what you intend to do, the audience isn't likely to respond as you might like.

In a very general sense, then, you need to decide if you want to inform, persuade, or entertain. Write down your purpose statement using the words "I intend to inform (or persuade or entertain) the

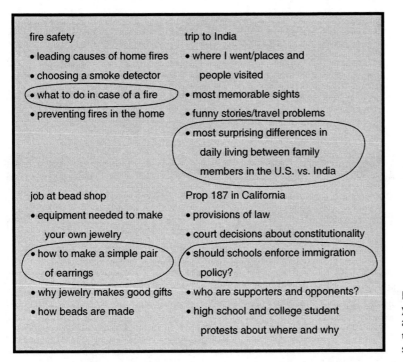

Figure 8-1 Narrowing a topic. Break up your general topic area and look at it from all sides. Find a topic that you can cover thoroughly in the time allotted for your speech.

Topic Checklist

Evaluate the topic you've chosen by answering the following questions. If you've chosen an appropriate topic, you should be able to answer yes to all of them.

—— Is this topic something that you are interested in or know about?

—— Is this topic something that you will enjoy and feel comfortable speaking about?

—— Will the audience be interested in hearing about this topic?

—— Is this a topic that the audience expects you to talk about?

—— Will the audience find this topic appropriate and inoffensive?

—— Can you cover this topic effectively in the time you've been allotted?

—— Is this topic appropriate for the occasion?

audience . . ." Complete the sentence and notice how your general purpose becomes specific and to the point. In other words, your general goal to inform becomes one that focuses more precisely on a specific purpose—what you want the audience to know, believe, or do after listening to your speech. Limit your purpose statement to one declarative sentence, keeping it simple and clear. Think back to the general topic of weight loss. Again, this topic could be narrowed to the top five weight loss programs and then, say, to client profiles or whether these programs actually work. Assume that the general purpose of your speech is to inform; to convert the general to the specific, you could state, "I intend to inform audience members that weight loss programs cater more to women than to men." Or, assume that the purpose of your speech is to persuade; again, to convert the general to the specific, you could state, "I intend to persuade audience members that they should avoid weight loss programs that promise too much." With a specific, simple, and clear purpose in mind, you can begin to develop the substance of your presentation.

Formulating a Thesis Statement

As described in Chapter 2, a thesis statement is a concise summary of the central message of your speech. It should contain the most essential points of your speech—what you plan to say to the audience to accomplish your specified speech goal. Like purpose statements, thesis statements should be specific, clear, and concrete. For example, a thesis statement for an informative speech on weight loss programs might be, "Weight loss programs cater more to women than to men in the setup of their programs and in the way their programs are advertised." A thesis statement for a persuasive speech might be, "You should avoid weight loss programs that promise too much because they are unethical and possibly unhealthy." (The box "Developing Specific Purpose and Thesis Statements" gives additional hints and examples.) Sometimes you

Developing Specific Purpose and Thesis Statements

General Guidelines

Your specific purpose statement should express what you want to accomplish—what the audience should know, believe, or do after listening to your speech. Your thesis statement should provide a concise summary of your central message—the most essential points of your speech. As you

formulate your specific purpose and thesis statements, keep the following guidelines in mind:

• Keep it simple—express a single, clear idea.

• Be specific and concrete.

• Use declarative sentences rather than questions.

Developing Specific Purpose and Thesis Statements (Continued)

Examples

Subject Area: Vegetarianism

General Purpose: To inform

Specific Purpose: To inform the audience of the benefits of being a vegetarian

Thesis Statement: Being a vegetarian is beneficial for three reasons: It is better for your health; it is better for the environment; and it respects the rights of animals.

Subject Area: Sleep

General Purpose: To inform

Specific Purpose: To inform the audience about the different stages of the sleep cycle.

Thesis Statement: Everyone goes through about five cycles of REM and non-REM sleep every night; there are different brain and body activities associated with each type of sleep.

Subject Area: Blood donation

General Purpose: To persuade

Specific Purpose: To persuade audience members to donate blood at an upcoming health fair

Thesis Statement: People should donate blood at the health fair next week because blood donation is safe and easy for the donor and it saves lives.

Subject Area: Gays and lesbians in the military

General Purpose: To persuade

Specific Purpose: To persuade the audience that gays and lesbians should be allowed to serve in the military without any restrictions

Thesis Statement: Gays and lesbians should be allowed to serve in the military without any special restrictions because it is their right as U.S. citizens and because so many gays and lesbians have served successfully in the past.

---

might find it easier to complete your research before finalizing your thesis statement.

RESEARCHING YOUR TOPIC

The purpose of topic research is to help you build a case so that both you and your argument come across as credible and believable. Facts or opinions attested to or endorsed by someone other than yourself are commonly referred to as **evidence.** Just as you would rely on your own personal knowledge of a topic, you should also gather evidence to prove or support your position. Using both personal knowledge and evidence equips you to inform and persuade. (See the box "Interview with a Professional: Sidonie Squier" for some examples of how evidence establishes credibility and creates compelling arguments.)

Gathering evidence or supporting material to use in a speech is like researching a term paper. You can draw heavily on what other people know by examining books, magazines, library references, and Web sites. You can also interview **experts**—over the phone or in person. (A true expert is a person who, through education, training, or experience, has special knowledge about a particular subject.) Even better, make effective use of your own personal knowledge about the subject. Of course, whether you depend on the experts or

yourself for information, you must critically evaluate the credibility and appropriateness of that evidence.

Types of Support

Just what should you look for when gathering information for your speech topic? You can begin by examining the most general aspects of your topic. Until you clarify the major outlines of your topic, you will find it hard to determine how more specific information fits in. For example, without understanding the role of animals in the development and testing of new medicines or the available alternatives, it would be difficult to develop a persuasive speech to convince people that animal experimentation should be stopped (or continued). You may have your own personal reasons for speaking on a specific issue, but you still need to consider the points and facts audience members will think about before they accept, or possibly reject, what you have to say. Consequently, you need to begin by reading as many general discussions of the subject as you can.

In addition, you should look for facts or data to use as evidence to back up your claims. (The box "Supporting Materials" gives some examples of basic types of supporting material.) Statistical data and physical evidence are very powerful. Euroamericans, and male Euroamericans in particular, appreciate

Interview with a Professional

Sidonie Squier

Sidonie Squier, 36, was the research director for the "Pete Wilson for Governor" committee in California. She was responsible for gathering and distributing the political and personal records of both Governor Wilson and his opponent, state treasurer Kathleen Brown.

How important would you say background research is to the effectiveness of a public presentation? What kinds of research support do you look for? What kinds of resources do you rely on when assembling your research? What actually makes for acceptable support materials?

Background research is a critical ingredient in determining the effectiveness of all public speeches! For example, everything I say when I make a presentation must be documented with hard copy. My audiences are very likely to ask me to provide my proof, so that they can show it to a group that they're speaking to, to coworkers, or to friends, family, and neighbors. During the campaign, my objective was to inform people about Kathleen Brown's record and persuade them to vote for Pete Wilson. As a result, I provided visuals depicting my research efforts in all my presentations.

When I was talking about Brown the taxer, I would whip out a letter that she wrote praising the 1991 tax increase. When I talked about Brown the wasteful manager, I would show a state treasurer's office that contained video reviews and David Letterman's top 10 list (all things that taxpayers provide for treasurer's office employees). When I talked about her lack of knowledge on the issues facing California, I would show an article that highlights Brown as saying, "I think the clouds are actually little rays of sunshine. Because they've been bringing a little rain—and isn't water what we want?" Unfortunately for Brown, the headline for that day read, "Storms batter crops: Growers assessing mounting losses."

By using tangible proof that the audience can see to make my points, I gain credibility right away. After that, I don't have to provide proof for each and every point. The audience just trusts that I know the facts. And I always do.

What kinds of issues do you consider when you begin to prepare for a public presentation—whether it is for your own speech or for someone else's?

Naturally, the audience is my first concern! As research director for Wilson's reelection campaign, I generally spoke to pro-Wilson groups. But that doesn't give me license to say whatever I want. Both the positive information that I impart about Pete Wilson and the negative (if appropriate) about Kathleen Brown depend on the type of audience. For example, even if both audiences are pro—Pete Wilson, my address to a group of health care workers would be very different from that to a group of manufacturers.

Gender is also a very important factor to consider when preparing for a public presentation. Females tend to be more sensitive to anything negative. I recall giving one speech in which I mentioned that the governor "gets angry" when he's told that Brown doesn't have a record on a particular issue (because he's not used to running against someone with no record). Later on, a woman from the audience telephoned to ask if I could speak to her group but asked if I could leave out the reference to the governor being angry.

Time, of course, is always an important issue during preparation. For example, the shorter the speaking time, the fewer subjects I could cover. I generally tried to cover the big five: crime, immigration, jobs/economy, education, and welfare.

data. They want and need to know how often a particular phenomenon occurs, in what location, and under what circumstances. They want and need the speaker to show them that it is true most of the time for most people. When you provide Euroamericans with statistical data from credible sources, they will be more disposed to accept your evidence as true and typical. Without the data, they may perceive your experience or example as representing only an unusual or abnormal case.

Do not be reluctant to rely on other types of support, including eyewitness accounts, stories, and quotable phrases. Besides adding credibility to your presentation, these types of support make your presentation more personal and sincere. Not all evidence must be grounded in hard, objective data to help prove your case. Take advantage of human interest stories, expert testimonials, and real-life examples to support and illustrate your main points. Although male Euroamericans rely heavily on facts and data to prove credibility, they still appreciate a well-told human interest story. In addition, female Euroamericans and other co-cultural audiences, including Latinos, African Americans, Asian Americans, and Native Americans, are likely to prefer personal examples and real-life experiences as predominant, meaningful sources of evidence.[1]

Supporting Materials

You can use many different categories of supporting materials in your speeches. Because individuals and cultures have different preferences for different types of evidence, you should use various types of supporting materials in every speech.

Type of Supporting Material	Examples
Facts Information that is verifiable	Paper products are the largest single component of household trash. The Hopi are a Pueblo tribe of the Southwest. They speak a Shoshonean dialect of the Uto-Aztecan linguistic family.
Statistics Numerical facts based on the systematic collection of quantitative data	Cardiovascular disease (CVD) kills about 930,000 Americans each year—accounting for one death every 34 seconds. CVD costs the nation over $110 billion per year for medical services and lost productivity.
Definitions Statements that explain what something is or what a word, phrase, or symbol means	A petroglyph is a drawing that has been carved into rock. The Arabic word *al-islam* means the act of committing oneself unreservedly to God.
Descriptions Verbal accounts that provide a mental image or picture of something	Intricately painted pottery portrays various aspects of Moche mythology, ritual, and everyday life. One well-preserved stirrup-spout jar shows a ruler sitting atop a high platform, wearing an elaborate headdress decorated with feathers and small pieces of metal. Messengers ascend a long series of steps to reach him.
Opinions Quotations or statements from experts or laypeople that express the views, judgments, or beliefs of someone else	According to British physicist Stephen Hawking, a black hole will disappear after all its mass is converted to radiation. My grandparents, who have been together for 55 years, say that the secret to a successful marriage is compromise and a good sense of humor.

Type of Supporting Material	Examples
Examples Specific cases—brief or extended, factual or hypothetical, or personal or from an expert source—that illustrate or develop a general concept or idea	The risk of a hurricane occurring in a particular place can depend on rainfall patterns in distant tropical areas. For example, when West Africa was wetter than average (1941–1965), 17 major hurricanes hit the East Coast of the United States; when West Africa was drier than average (1966–1990), only 2 major hurricanes hit the East Coast.
Explanations Statements that provide reasons or causes for something	Air pressure inside and outside the middle ear is normally equal. But as you go up in a fast elevator, the outside pressure decreases, leaving the pressure inside the middle ear higher. Your ears pop when air escapes from the middle ear into the throat, equalizing the pressure.
Analogies Comparisons or contrasts between unrelated objects or concepts typically used to clarify or emphasize differing or similar qualities of the two objects or concepts	My cat has the same amount of brain power as my car's hubcaps. "[Our religion] was too difficult to explain, like having six toes. You would rather keep your shoes on." [Garrison Keillor] "You are the children of Abraham Lincoln. We are at best only his stepchildren—children by adoption, children by force of circumstances and necessity." [Frederick Douglass]
Narratives First-person or third-person accounts of real or fictional events, typically told in a chronological sequence	"From infancy to my sixteenth year, I was reared according to the nineteenth-century ideas of Chinese womanhood. I was never alone, though it was not unusual for me to feel lonely." [Jade Snow Wong]

Consider, for example, the relative impact of statistical data when used with a concrete illustration. Not too long ago, Alex Pacheco, from the People for the Ethical Treatment of Animals (PETA), sent a letter announcing the results of PETA's campaign to save thousands of animals from being senselessly maimed (that is, tested) at Gillette Industries. Rather than belabor the statistical evidence, Pacheco enclosed a handwritten (copied) excerpt taken from a journal of a former Gillette employee, Leslie Fain. In the diary, Fain described how technicians in the animal testing labs callously heaped maimed and dying rabbits on the floor. The rabbits continued to crawl over one another, some convulsing, others bleeding from their mouths. Witnessing their needless suffering, Fain became ill and fled from the lab. Enclosed with the letter was a color photograph of a rabbit whose skin was being eaten away by chemical product testing. Who wouldn't be moved by this type of evidence? Would statistical data have had the same effect?

Gathering Information about Your Topic

Support for your speech can come from many sources. But where do you go to look for the support or evidence you will need in your speech? Before you answer, "the library" or "the World Wide Web," stop to consider another, more plausible, source of support—yourself.

Rely on Your Own Personal Knowledge and Experience

Selecting a topic that interests you and that you already know something about can eliminate a lot of headaches later on and save much time during the speech development process. Furthermore, audiences are more likely to enjoy a topic that you obviously understand and enjoy.

The failure to rely on oneself as a resource is demonstrated in a speech presented by Holly, a student speaker. The specific purpose of her speech was to persuade students to become more involved in the struggle against racial discrimination. She wanted

Interviewing a professional is an excellent way to gather important data and can increase your credibility as a speaker. When you conduct your interview, be sure to consider the time constraints of your interviewee and formulate your questions in advance.

Interviewing for Topic Research

Before the Interview

- Determine a specific objective for the interview, and identify the appropriate person to interview.

- Contact the person you want to interview, by letter or telephone or in person. Introduce yourself, and describe your project and the purpose of the interview. Set a specific time and time limit for the interview.

- Do some preliminary research to familiarize yourself with the topic. Don't waste time during the interview covering background information that you can look up in the library.

- Prepare your list of questions in advance. They should be specific, neutral, and nonleading (refer to Chapter 6 for guidelines for creating effective interview questions). In organizing your questions, you may want to begin with the easiest or least controversial issues.

During the Interview

- Dress appropriately and arrive on time.

- Restate your objectives for the interview, and begin by asking the first of your prepared questions.

- Listen carefully—the interviewee may bring up new issues and information that are directly relevant to your topic.

- Ask follow-up questions to clarify information or probe more deeply into particular issues.

- Be an active listener. Paraphrase responses to verify answers, and ask for further clarification if you are confused.

- If the interview gets off track, return to your list of prepared questions.

- Take brief notes that will jog your memory, but don't ask the interviewee to slow down so that you can take detailed notes. Alternatively, you can tape-record the interview, provided you obtain the interviewee's permission beforehand.

- Don't stay longer than the allotted time period, and thank your interviewee.

After the Interview

- Review your notes or your recording as soon as possible after the interview, while everything is fresh in your mind.

- Pull out the most useful ideas and examples for your speech.

- If you quote the interviewee in your speech, be sure your quotes are accurate and that you cite your source.

---

everyone to become more active in helping people understand and manage the problem. It was an excellent topic. In her presentation, Holly explained that with few exceptions, today's college students fail to understand the urgency of racial discrimination in the United States. No generation in recent history, she claimed, has been more apathetic toward this problem. She was armed with relevant statistics and credible sources, and her speech represented an impressive assembly of facts. But Holly failed to make use of her most interesting and most dramatic piece of evidence—herself. She could have told audience members that in her recent summer job, she had observed firsthand the consequences of discriminatory hiring practices. She could have explained how that experience changed her indifferent attitude and made her want to support the efforts of minority groups on campus. By alluding to her own experiences, Holly would have been far more persuasive. Audiences are more likely to empathize with, and eventually agree with, speakers who demonstrate some personal connection with their topic. In short, don't be afraid to rely on yourself as important reference material.

Ask the Experts Directly Not only can you use your own past experiences for developing speeches, you also can ask experts and professionals for their opinions, interpretations, and recommendations. Experts can be especially helpful in locating excellent sources of facts and findings. Colleges and universities are full of experts, most of whom will be glad to help you. Similarly, most business leaders do not mind a phone call—and may even prefer it to a more time-consuming personal interview. Others are willing to arrange a personal interview and will enjoy talking about subjects they know well.

Conducting an interview requires a lot of planning and direction. (See the box "Interviewing for Topic Research" for specific recommendations.) Besides setting up the meeting time and place and communicating a specific purpose to the person, you must ask the right questions. Refer to Chapter 6 to review how to word and frame both open and closed interview questions. Importantly, a good interviewing strategy requires that you prepare a list of clear questions ahead of time, pose the questions in a straightforward way, and be considerate of the time demands and needs of the interviewee.

Make Use of the Library Libraries are another key source of information for your topic. Most libraries provide pamphlets, displays, and orientation tours to teach patrons about their services. You can also obtain help from reference librarians, who can provide general information about the library or help steer you toward the best resources for your particular topic.

Libraries offer a variety of helpful materials, including the following:

- *Books* are good sources of general background information, especially for topics for which large amounts of material are available. You can locate books using the library's card catalog or computerized system.

- *General encyclopedias* can provide background information and historical perspectives. Some of the most widely used references include *Encyclopedia Americana, Encyclopaedia Britannica, and Collier's Encyclopedia*. Encyclopedias are generally not written by experts and, like books, quickly become dated. You should never limit your research to encyclopedias—supplement them with other sources.

- *Specialized encyclopedias* and dictionaries are available for a variety of fields, including music, economics, business, science, and philosophy. These sources provide more detailed technical overviews than general encyclopedias; many also include bibliographies that can direct you to other helpful resources.

- *Periodicals, or magazines*, are good sources for up-to-date and specific material on a variety of topics. You can locate periodicals by using the *Readers' Guide to Periodical Literature*; by referring to another, more specific, periodical index, such as the *Art Index or Social Sciences Index*; or by using an on-line search service. Libraries may carry periodicals published for particular U.S. co-cultures (for example, *Hispanic, Christianity Today, Modern Maturity, Working Woman, Vegetarian Times, and Audubon*) or published in

other countries; these can provide diverse viewpoints on issues.

- *Newspapers* are good sources of information and perspectives on current issues. Libraries typically carry a variety of newspapers, many of which have separate indexes or are indexed as part of an on-line search service.

- *Almanacs, yearbooks,* and other *statistical sources* can provide up-to-date information and recent developments on various topics. Some of the most widely used include *Facts on File*, a weekly summary of national and foreign news; the *Statistical Abstract of the United States*, a summary of social, political, and economic data published yearly by the U.S. Bureau of the Census;

A good place to gather information on your chosen speech topic is the library. Relevant books, periodicals, and other references are easily located with the help of computers. College and university libraries also offer computer-assisted access to sources of information located all over the world.

and *The World Almanac and Book of Facts*, which provides statistics and information about countries throughout the world.

- *Atlases* are best known as general sources of geographic information, but many specialized atlases are also available, presenting a wide variety of historical, economic, and cultural information.

- *Biographical dictionaries* and periodicals are good sources of background information on past and present newsworthy people. Some of the most widely used sources include biographical dictionaries—*Who's Who in America, Who's Who of American Women,* and *The International Who's Who.* The journal Current Biography includes longer essays about people who are currently in the news. The biographical material in many books and periodicals is indexed in the Biography Index.

- *Books of quotations,* including *Bartlett's Familiar Quotations, The Oxford Dictionary of Quotations, The Oxford Dictionary of Modern Quotations,* and *The Quotable Woman,* can help you track down catchy and pertinent quotations for your speeches.

- Government documents are good sources of information on current laws and actions by various government branches. The Congressional Record provides a daily account of the proceedings of Congress. The United States Reports publishes the opinions and decisions of the Supreme Court. For a complete listing of federal government publications, refer to the Monthly Catalog of U.S. Government Publications. Publications issued by the United Nations are listed in UNDOC: Current Index.

Libraries have many tools to help you locate appropriate materials. The card catalog is the best way to find books on your topic. You can search by author, title, or subject; the call number indicates where you can find a book in the library. Most libraries now have a computerized format for their card catalogs, which may indicate not only a book's call number but also whether it is currently on the shelf.

Other tools are available to help you search for other types of materials. The Readers' Guide to Periodical Literature is an index of articles found in more than 180 popular magazines and journals. To locate more technical information on a particular topic, more specialized indexes are available. For instance, if your subject is in the field of engineering, you might try the Engineering Index; for business or economics, the Business Periodicals Index; for education, the Education Index; and so on. Indexes are also available for newspapers. Most libraries have the New York Times Index and an index for the nearest major daily paper. Back issues of local and national newspapers are available on microfilm or microfiche in many libraries.

Many libraries also offer on-line computer search services such as InfoTrac, DIALOG, or ERIC (Education Resources Information Center). You can use these to create a tailor-made bibliography for your topic and to view abstracts or even complete articles. Figure 8-2 shows a sample InfoTrac entry. Some on-line services are free; others charge a fee to access a dial-up service. Ask the reference librarian what on-line services are available at your library and how best to use them.

Search the Internet You can also obtain supporting materials for your speech from the Internet. The Internet is a global network of computers that links together commercial on-line communication services, such as America Online and CompuServe, with tens of thousands of university, government, and corporate computers. The Internet is composed of many parts, including World Wide Web documents, e-mail, newsgroups, mailing lists, and chat rooms. With access to the Internet, you can obtain current, in-depth information about thousands of topics.

To reach the Internet, you need a computer and modem, access to the network through a provider, and browser software, which allows you to navigate the network. Internet access is often available to students at little or no cost through college computing centers. Commonly used browsers include Netscape Navigator and Microsoft Explorer. A browser sends requests for files across the Internet, and when these files are delivered, the information is displayed on your computer screen. Each browser works differently, and it may take a little practice for you to become familiar with how your particular browser operates.

Perhaps the most useful part of the Internet for researching speech topics is the World Wide Web. The Web is made up of computer files called Web pages or Web sites that have been created by individuals, companies, and organizations. The Web is considered a user-friendly part of the Internet because it offers easy access and navigation and has multimedia capabilities, such as audio, video, and animation. Each Web site is identified by an address or uniform resource locator (URL), such as http://www.census.gov (the Web site for the U.S. Bureau of the Census). To access a site, you can type the URL into the appropriate screen of your browser, or you can click on a hyperlink, a shortcut to another Web page or to a different part of the current page. When

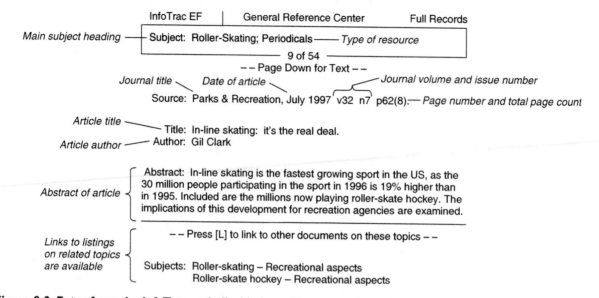

InfoTrac EF | General Reference Center | Full Records

Main subject heading —— Subject: Roller-Skating; Periodicals —— *Type of resource*

——— 9 of 54 ———
– – Page Down for Text – –

Journal title \ *Date of article* \ / *Journal volume and issue number*

Source: Parks & Recreation, July 1997 v32 n7 p62(8).— *Page number and total page count*

Article title —— Title: In-line skating: it's the real deal.

Article author —— Author: Gil Clark

Abstract of article { Abstract: In-line skating is the fastest growing sport in the US, as the 30 million people participating in the sport in 1996 is 19% higher than in 1995. Included are the millions now playing roller-skate hockey. The implications of this development for recreation agencies are examined.

Links to listings on related topics are available { – – Press [L] to link to other documents on these topics – –

Subjects: Roller-skating – Recreational aspects
Roller-skate hockey – Recreational aspects

Figure 8-2 Entry from the InfoTrac periodical index. Like many on-line indexes, InfoTrac provides article abstracts as well as bibliographical information.

you view a Web page, hyperlinks may appear as images or as text that is underlined and/or a different color. By clicking on links, you can jump quickly from one Web site to related sites, even if they are located on the other side of the world.

To search for information on a particular topic, you need to use a search engine such as AltaVista (http://www.altavista.digital.com), Excite (http://www.excite.com), or Yahoo! (http://www.yahoo.com). Figure 8-3 shows a sample Yahoo! directory. To use a search engine, you may need to enter key words or navigate through a series of increasingly more specific indexes or directories; some search engines offer both key word and index searches. Within seconds, the search engine will generate a list of sites, with hyperlinks, that match your search parameters, often with a brief description of each site.

For best results, make your key word searches as specific as possible. Refer to the search engine's help screen for advice and sample search entries. Different search engines have different rules for how best to enter key words. For example, you may need to enclose phrases in quotation marks or put plus or minus signs between words to obtain an appropriate result. Each search engine uses a different method of searching and will yield somewhat different results. If you don't find the information you are looking for using one search engine, try

another. As with print items, it is important to record complete source information for all of the Web resources you consult.

Direct experience is often the best way to master the use of your Web browser and become familiar with the various search engines. Your college library or computer center might offer useful information and introductory classes about the Internet; there are also many books that can help get you started.[2]

Whichever avenue you follow to research and access information for your speech, keep track of all of the sources you consult. If you take notes, be sure to write down when you are quoting or paraphrasing from a particular source. Careful note taking at this point will make it easy to cite your sources accurately and to create a complete reference list. The reference list you prepare for your speech outline should follow a standardized format. (The box "Documenting Sources" provides guidelines and samples from two widely used formats—APA and MLA.)

Selecting Only the Best Supporting Material

You will likely find innumerable sources to use in your speech. You might run across 10 different books, 12 magazine articles, 6 Internet documents, and 22 newspaper columns on your topic. Obviously, you can't read all 50 references and then take

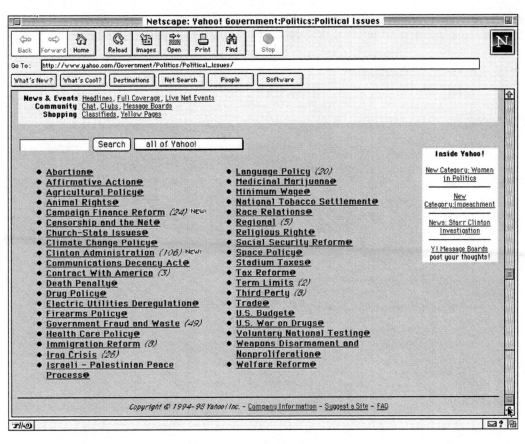

Figure 8-3 Sample Yahoo! directory. By clicking on one of the hypertext links on this page, the user will jump to a list of Web sites (with links) that focus on a particular political issue.

BUILDING YOUR SKILLS

Documenting Sources

Your references need to appear in a standardized bibliographic format at the end of your speech outline; your instructor will specify the format you should use. Two of the most widely used formats are those published by the American Psychological Association (APA) and the Modern Language Association (MLA). This text utilizes the APA format; examples of both formats are shown below.

American Psychological Association (APA) Format

Books

Book author(s) or editor(s). (Date of publication). Book title. City, ST: Publisher.

Kearney, P., & Plax, T. G. (1999). Public speaking in a culturally diverse society (2nd ed.). Mountain View, CA: Mayfield.

Periodicals

Article author(s). (Date of publication). Article title. Journal title, volume, pages.

Journal

Wagner, C., & Wagner, D. (1975). The relationship between the use of evidence and speaker credibility. Communication Monographs, 3, 235–241.

Magazine

O'Connor, B. (1992, September 1). Writing speeches for politicians. Newsweek, pp. 5, 10.

Continued

Documenting Sources *(Continued)*

Newspaper
Study finds speech anxiety "normal." (1989, July 1).
Sacramento Bee, p. A14.

Interviews

Person interviewed. (Date interviewed). Title, Company
Name. Type of interview.
Mays, C. A. (1998, May 12). President, Schopp Communication
Associates. Phone interview.

Internet Documents

To cite an Internet document, include the same information
that is provided for a print source—or as much of that
information as possible—followed by the Internet information.

Author. (Date). Page or document title [Type of document].
Location of publisher or producer: Name of publisher or
producer. Retrieval date and source: URL.
The Gallup Organization. (1997). Religious faith is widespread
but many skip church [Poll results posted on the World
Wide Web]. Princeton, NJ: Author. Retrieved March 25,
1998, from the World Wide Web: http://198.175.140.8/
POLL_ARCHIVES/970329.htm.
National Highway Traffic Safety Administration. (1997,
November 17). Air bags and on-off switches: Information
for an informed decision [Brochure]. Washington, DC:
Author. Retrieved February 18, 1998, from the World
Wide Web: http://www.nhtsa.dot.gov/airbags/brochure.

The APA style for citing Internet documents has been
evolving; for the most recent version, check their Web site
(http://www.apa.org).

Additional Guidelines

- List authors by last name and first initials.

- Capitalize the first word, proper nouns, and the first
  word after a colon in article, book, or pamphlet titles.
  For titles of journals and newspapers, capitalize major
  words.

- Use "&" instead of "and" for multiple authors.

- Omit the state if the city is very well known.

- Give the article title first if no author is listed.

- Journals do not use "p." or "pp."; simply include the page
  numbers following the volume number.

- Space once after every period.

- Indent the first line of every entry.

- Do not break words with a hyphen; start a new line.

- Double-space all entries.

- If the author is the publisher of the work, simply state
  "Author" following the publisher's location.

- Omit unnecessary publishing information such as
  "Publishers," "Company," or "Incorporated."

- Alphabetize all entries by author.

Modern Language Association (MLA) Format

Books

Book author(s) or editors. Book title. City: Publisher, Date
of publication.
Kearney, Patricia, and Timothy G. Plax. Public Speaking in a
Culturally Diverse Society. 2nd ed. Mountain View:
Mayfield, 1999.

Periodicals

Article author(s). "Article Title." Journal Title Volume and
issue numbers and/or date: page numbers.

Journal

Wagner, Chris, and David Wagner. "The Relationship between
the Use of Evidence and Speaker Credibility."
Communication Monographs 3 (1975): 235–241.

Magazine
O'Connor, Barbara. "Writing Speeches for Politicians."
Newsweek 1 Sep. 1992: 5+.

Newspaper
"Study Finds Speech Anxiety 'Normal.'" Sacramento Bee
1 July 1989: A14.

Interviews

Person interviewed. Type of interview. Date of interview.
Mays, Charles A. Telephone interview. 12 May 1998.

Internet Documents

To cite a source from the Internet, include as much of the
following information as possible and relevant.

Author of source. "Title of Article or Posting." Title of Book or
Document. Editor or translator of text. Publication information for print version. Version or volume and issue numbers.
Date of publication or latest update. Range of pages, sections, or paragraphs, if numbered. Retrieval date <URL>.

The Gallup Organization. "Religious Faith Is Widespread but Many Skip Church." Online posting. 29 Mar. 1997. 25 Mar. 1998 <http://198.175.140.8/POLL_ARCHIVES/970329.htm>.

National Highway Traffic Safety Administration. Air Bags and On-Off Switches: Information for an Informed Decision. 17 Nov. 1997. 18 Feb. 1998 <http://www.nhtsa.dot.gov/airbags/brochure>.

For the most recent version of MLA style for citing Internet documents, check the MLA Web site (http://www.mla.org).

Additional Guidelines

- Give the full author's name as it appears on the title page of the work being cited.

- For works with multiple authors, reverse only the name of the first author. If there are more than three authors, list them all or name only the first and add "et al." Spell out the word "and" between authors.

- Capitalize the first, last, and principal words of a title; do not capitalize articles, prepositions, and coordinating conjunctions if they fall in the middle of a title.

- If the location of the publisher is a city outside the United States that may be ambiguous or unfamiliar to people, add an abbreviation of the country (or of the province for cities in Canada).

- Shorten the names of publishers by omitting articles, including only surnames, and using abbreviations wherever possible.

- Abbreviate the names of months when citing publication dates.

- Give the article title first if no author is listed.

- For scholarly journals paginated continuously throughout each year, include the volume number, year, and page numbers for the article. For journals that paginate each issue separately, give both the volume and issue numbers in addition to the year and page numbers; for example, "11.2" would signify volume 11, issue 2.

- For articles printed on nonconsecutive pages, give the first page number followed by a plus sign (for example, "10+").

- Space once after every period.

- Double-space all entries.

- For each source, indent the second and subsequent lines.

SOURCE: Based on American Psychological Association. (1994). *Publication manual of the American Psychological Association* (4th ed.). Washington, DC: Author. American Psychological Association. (1997, October 16); *How to cite information from the Internet and the World Wide Web* [Document posted on the World Wide Web]. Washington, DC: Author. Retrieved March 25, 1998, from the World Wide Web: http://www.apa.org/journals/webref.html; Gibaldi, J. (1995). *MLA handbook for writers of research papers* (4th ed.). New York: MLA: Modern Language Association. (1997, December 19); MLA style [Document posted on the World Wide Web]. New York: Author. Retrieved April 10, 1998, from the World Wide Web: http://www.mla.org/main_stl.htm.

---

copious notes on each and every one of them! Instead, you will need to decide where to begin, what to skim or omit, and when to end your research. To selectively gather and absorb information for your presentation, choose evidence that is relevant, recent, and credible.

Is It Relevant? If the evidence isn't relevant to your topic, don't use it. **Relevant evidence** is information that is directly associated with your topic. Although you might run across an incredibly good quotation, a really funny story, or a fascinating statistic, use it in your speech only if it is directly relevant to the issue. The audience shouldn't have to spend time trying to figure out how something fits in with the content of the presentation; it should be obvious.

Take the case of Pilar, who gave an informative speech on the hazards of drunk driving (one of the topics on the "used and abused" list). She began her presentation with statistics on the number of deaths associated with car accidents in this country. She then compared those figures with data on deaths resulting from accidents involving airplanes, buses, and trains. The facts were impressive; the audience had no idea that automobiles were so dangerous. However, the audience was never really sure what she was trying to convey. Could Pilar really be suggesting that all or most of the fatal car accidents in this country were the result of drunk drivers? Could she be implying further that pilots, bus drivers, and conductors were exempt from this stigma? Can you figure it out? The point is, you shouldn't have to; the speaker should make sure the information is directly relevant to her or his purpose.

Rather than compare accidents across the different forms of transportation, Pilar might have focused on equivalent cases. That is, she could have compared the number of car accidents caused by drunk drivers to the number caused by sober drivers. And then she might have spoken about the number of deaths associated with car accidents from both types of drivers. And, appealing to the audience's emotions, Pilar could have revealed, in detail, what happened "on a lonely road one night to a family of four when they happened upon a drunk driver." Such information would have had more direct relevance to her purpose, and the audience would have readily perceived the linkage between drinking and driving that Pilar intended.

Is It Recent?

Audiences are more willing to find your evidence valid if the source is up-to-date. Given how rapidly information can change, **recent evidence** often is mandatory. But how "recent" is recent? It would be foolish to rely on a one-year-old newspaper or magazine article. In fact, yesterday's news can be outdated—particularly when it relates to, say, a political campaign or ongoing military operations during a war. For other kinds of information, however, recent information may include anything published within the last five or ten years. For instance, five- or ten-year-old scientific reports published in journals or periodicals are often still valid. Similarly, some age-old sources are perfectly legitimate; the writings of ancient philosophers and the teachings of Native American shamans are timeless.

Is It Credible?

Unless you use **credible evidence**, the audience will not accept the information you present. Evidence becomes credible when it remains fairly consistent with other known facts. Moreover, evidence becomes believable when the sources of that data are known to be credible themselves. For some co-cultural audiences, the Koran and the Bible are highly believable sources. For others, however, religious references may be inappropriate. Overall, your sources of evidence should be competent and well-known experts in their field. Sources of evidence should know what they are talking about and reflect a sense of impartiality and fairness in their reporting of the information. Credibility is a particularly important issue for Internet resources. (The box "Evaluating Information from the Internet" suggests additional strategies.)

To select only the best information to use in your speech, then, your evidence must be relevant, recent, and credible. Only then will your evidence do what it is supposed to do—make your presentation substantive and believable to your audience.

BUILDING YOUR SKILLS

Evaluating Information from the Internet

Anyone can post information on the Internet—true or false, good or bad. When evaluating information from the Internet, ask yourself the following questions:

- *What is the source of the information? Who is the author or sponsor of the Web page?* Web sites maintained by government agencies, professional organizations, or established news agencies are likely to present trustworthy information. Many other groups and individuals post accurate information, but it's important to stay alert and watch your sources carefully. If you can't identify the sponsor of a Web page or can't verify the author's credentials, don't use the information in your speech. Also pay attention to where you are. Even if you start out at a trustworthy site, the click of a button can catapult you into a completely different site. Learn how to read your current Web address so you know when you've left one site and entered another.

- *How often is the site updated?* Most Web sites will indicate the date of their most recent modification. Major organizations may update their Web pages on a daily or weekly basis. If the topic you are researching is time-sensitive, look for a site that is updated frequently.

- *Does the site promote a particular viewpoint or product? Are there obvious reasons for bias?* The same common sense you'd use to evaluate any claim applies to the Internet. Be wary of sites that appear to have an ax to grind or that advertise heavily.

- *What do other sources say about the topic?* To get a broad perspective on a piece of information, check out other sources—books, experts, other Web sites. Don't base an entire speech on information from a single Web page. You are more likely to obtain and recognize quality information if you use several different sources.

CHAPTER REVIEW

- The most difficult part of speech preparation is finding a suitable topic. Selecting an appropriate topic requires that you consider the speech occasion, time constraints, and the audience.

- Selecting a topic need not be a random activity. You can rely on a variety of sources in your search, starting with your own interests and expertise. Also, consider your audience's interests, and take advantage of current events. Don't be too quick to eliminate a topic idea; it's what you do with the topic that makes the difference.

- Once you have a general idea of a topic, narrow it considerably so that your subject is specific and easily managed. Next, determine your general purpose. Do you want to inform, entertain, or persuade? Then, specify exactly what you want to accomplish.

- Gathering information about your topic will help you build a case so that you and your argument are credible and convincing. Begin by reading a representative sample of general discussions of the subject. Look for facts or data to use along with eyewitness accounts, testimonies (or stories), and quotable phrases. Relying on personal knowledge and a variety of different types of evidence will make your speech more effective.

- Information for your speech should come from many sources, beginning with your own personal knowledge and experiences. Also, interview experts, and use the library. Three criteria should determine which materials to use in your speech: The evidence should be relevant, recent, and credible.

QUESTIONS FOR CRITICAL THINKING & REVIEW

1. Which type of supporting material is most important to you: statistical data or your own personal experiences? Why? Do you think your preference has anything to do with your co-cultural background?

2. Is a religious document, like the Bible or Koran, a credible source to use as evidence for a speech on family values? Do you think the perceived credibility of such a source would depend on the makeup of the audience? How?

3. The claim that "topics aren't boring, people are" is legitimate. And yet, some topics seem to be more dull than others. What strategies would you use to make seemingly dull topics engaging or fascinating for your audience? What about these topics: financing health care reform, filing your income taxes, forming good study habits, formatting a floppy disk, preventing heart disease, or leasing or buying a car?

NOTES

1. Sullivan, P. A. (1993). Women's discourse and political communication: A case study of Congressperson Patricia Schroeder. *Western Journal of Communication, 57*, 530–545.

2. Courtright, J. A., & Perse, E. (1998). *The Mayfield quick guide to the Internet for communication students.* Mountain View, CA: Mayfield; Kennedy, S. D. (1998). *Best bet Internet: Reference and research when you don't have time to mess around.* Chicago: American Library Association; Levine, J. R., Baroudi, C., & Young, M. L. (1998). The Internet for dummies (5th ed.). Indianapolis, IN: IDG Books; Whitely, S. (1997). American Library Association research handbook: An information age guide to researching facts and topics. New York: Random House.

Chapter 9

ORGANIZING AND OUTLINING YOUR SPEECH

Learning Objectives

After reading this chapter, you should be able to do the following:

1. Identify the dual purposes of organizing a speech.

2. Show how "making sense" of a presentation can be a function of a person's cultural background.

3. Identify and give examples of the five types of linear organizational patterns.

4. Identify and give examples of the four types of configural organizational patterns.

5. Demonstrate how to organize a speech either configurally or linearly.

6. Outline a speech (configurally or linearly) using the formal rules for outlining.

Dianne was invited to give a speech to a local group of National Rifle Association (NRA) members. She considered a variety of topics based on her own experiences as a gun owner and an expert marksperson. She obtained information about her audience by interviewing the host of the event and by telephoning several NRA members from a list of invitees provided by the host. What immediately struck her and disturbed her on viewing the list was the relatively small number of female NRA members. After all, Dianne reasoned, many women would enjoy the sport of target shooting just as she did, and women should become proficient at handling a gun for their own protection. She decided to give a persuasive speech to convince her audience that more women should be recruited into the association.

With her purpose set, Dianne began to research her topic. She considered her own experiences as a gun owner. She also interviewed a spokesperson from the national NRA office about membership statistics and recruitment policies and talked with several of her female friends who were active in the NRA. Finally, she compiled data from statistical abstracts, government publications, and periodicals that provided substantive arguments in support of her position.

With all that information, she should have been ready to go. But Dianne had a problem: She'd accumulated so much material—books, notecards, photocopied materials, and audiotapes from her interviews. How could she organize and condense all the information into a coherent format so that she could present her speech within the allotted time and still get her message across?

Dianne's problem is no different from the difficulties you may encounter when writing a lengthy term paper. After gathering a lot of information from the library, all of which relates to your thesis in some way, you still need to sift through the data, select the right materials, and organize them in some logical format. Only then can you begin to write your paper. Or, in the case of a speech, only then can you begin to talk through your presentation. This chapter provides you with concrete strategies for sorting through and organizing information for your speeches. So that you will be able to make sense of your presentations to both yourself and your audience, you will learn how to create outlines and notes to use during your speech preparation and delivery.

WHY ORGANIZE?

This "making sense" function of speech preparation is called "organizing." Organizing helps to put your thoughts and materials together in some logical manner. Begin to organize by discarding information that does not seem especially relevant to your position. The essential information you retain must then be arranged in some way that will allow you to understand what you're trying to say; you need to know where you're going and how you plan to get there. Also, the audience demands that you present your ideas in some organized way. Without organization, your ideas would be disseminated at random; audience members wouldn't be able to follow along; and everyone would conclude, ultimately, that you didn't know what you were talking about! Consequently, organization is important both to you as speaker and to your audience members as listeners.

Making Sense of the Speech for Yourself

Like Dianne, you may face a mountain of facts, testimonials, definitions, statistics, and examples. At some point, you must stop gathering information and quit reading. Don't let yourself be overwhelmed by the data. Instead, begin to make decisions about what information is truly relevant and what information you should discard. Strategically arrange your thoughts and ideas in some preliminary, systematic way. This initial arrangement of ideas is unlikely to be your final organizational scheme; it may be in rough, abbreviated form, but it will be a start. Organizing a speech may require two, three, or more attempts before you can arrange your thoughts and materials in a truly helpful way.

Once your speech is organized, begin to rehearse your actual presentation. (As you will see later in this chapter, an outline of your presentation has the advantage of doubling as notes for an extemporaneous delivery.) The personal benefits of making sense of your materials should now become obvious: Speakers who organize are able to stay on course. They should have little fear of losing their place, omitting important information, misquoting facts, repeating themselves, or wandering aimlessly from point to point.

Making Sense of the Speech for Your Audience

You, as speaker, aren't the only one who benefits from an organized presentation. Your audience will also appreciate a well-organized speech. Just as you expect your teachers to present their lectures and materials in some organized, logical fashion, audiences expect public speeches to be organized in some coherent way. Surprisingly, little research has been done on the effects of speech organization, but what does exist supports the claim that speakers need to arrange their ideas in some systematic way. For instance, research shows that audiences prefer organized speeches to disorganized ones.[1] That same research also shows that audiences tolerate some degree of minor disorganization. This is good news for speakers who may need to backtrack when they omit something or who may have to forgo a point when time runs out.

Besides documenting audience preferences for organized presentations, researchers have found that organized speeches result in greater audience comprehension.[2] The more disorganized a speech is, the more difficulty audience members will have understanding the speaker's argument. And yet, people vary widely in their conception of what "organized" means. Finally, organized speeches are associated with higher perceptions of speaker credibility.[3] What all this means for you as a public speaker, then, is that although there is no single best way to organize a speech, some type of organization is crucial for maximizing your overall effectiveness with an audience.

"MAKING SENSE" AS A FUNCTION OF CULTURE

"Making sense" doesn't always mean the same thing to everyone. What may seem very organized and coherent to one co-culture may appear disorganized to another. To help you appreciate how individuals make sense of information differently, the following section examines two general kinds of logic: linear and configural. First, to help you determine your personal logic preference, take a few minutes to complete the survey in the box "What Type of Logic System Do You Prefer?"

Linear Logic

Different cultures have distinct preferences for how they organize thoughts in formal written themes and in formal discourse, like public speaking. If you completed elementary and secondary school in the United States, you are probably familiar with **linear logic**—even if it is not the organizational pattern you prefer. U.S. schools have traditionally taught a step-by-step, linear method for organizing speeches

What Type of Logic System Do You Prefer?

Instructions

This survey examines the ways people reason or argue with one another. Listed below are ten pairs of statements. Read each pair of statements and check off the one that reflects your own preference for how you like to approach or be approached by others. In completing this survey, do the following: (1) Do not omit any item; (2) check only one item for each pair of statements; (3) do not refer back to items; (4) make each item a separate, independent judgment; and (5) record your first impression.

____ 1. I like to come right to the point when I have something to say.
    I prefer a more indirect route; I shouldn't have to spell it out for anyone.

____ 2. People who are blunt and outspoken are arrogant and rude.
    I like others to be frank and blunt with me.

____ 3. My motto is, "Why beat around the bush? Just say what's on your mind!"
    People will say what they have to say in their own time.

____ 4. I find it confusing and tiresome when people try to explain something by telling me some obscure story that's supposed to have some deeper, hidden meaning.
    People who use "one-step-at-a-time" logic on me insult my intelligence.

____ 5. I'm reluctant to make any decision based on an argument that relies solely on statistical facts.
    I'm reluctant to make any decision based on an argument that relies solely on emotional appeals.

____ 6. As long as a person is well known as an authority on the subject, I see no need for a lot of unnecessary evidence or proof.
    It doesn't matter so much if a person is an expert or not. If she or he can't show me or prove to me in some way that it's true, then I have trouble believing it.

____ 7. You can't trust old sayings or parables. They tend to be vague, old-fashioned, and wrong.
    A speaker who is able to recall and use famous ancient sayings shows that he or she is wise, respectful of tradition, and well schooled.

____ 8. The key to organizing a presentation is to clearly state your thesis at the beginning and then to provide the audience with an overview of your main points.
    An effective speaker would never insult audience members by telling them outright what she or he wants or intends. It's much better to approach an idea indirectly, only implying what you want or mean.

____ 9. When trying to convince someone of my position, I prefer to rely on facts, statistics, and testimony from objective, expert witnesses.
    When trying to convince someone of my position, I prefer to present my ideas in such a way that the audience feels moved by what I have to say.

____ 10. If I needed a favor, I might merely suggest to my friends that I could probably use their help.
    If I needed a favor, I would probably just come right out and ask my friends to help me.

Calculating Your Score

1. For each pair of statements, there are two possible responses. One response represents a linear logic orientation, the other, a configural logic orientation. Label the linear preferences "L" and the configural responses "C" according to the following key:

Item 1:	choice 1 = L	choice 2 = C
Item 2:	choice 1 = C	choice 2 = L
Item 3:	choice 1 = L	choice 2 = C
Item 4:	choice 1 = L	choice 2 = C
Item 5:	choice 1 = C	choice 2 = L
Item 6:	choice 1 = C	choice 2 = L
Item 7:	choice 1 = L	choice 2 = C
Item 8:	choice 1 = L	choice 2 = C
Item 9:	choice 1 = L	choice 2 = C
Item 10:	choice 1 = C	choice 2 = L

2. Next, score a 1 for each C, and a 0 for each L. In other words, you get no points for L responses, but one point for each C response.

3. Now add together your total points = ____

Interpreting Your Score

The possible range of scores is between 0 and 10. (If your own final score does not fall within that range, you have made a

Continued

153

What Type of Logic System Do You Prefer? *(Continued)*

computational error.) The higher your score, the more configural your own logic is likely to be. In particular, if your total score is 6 or better, your logic preference is more indirect than direct. That is, you are likely to prefer and use logic that requires the listener to interpret what it is you want or mean to say. You try not to insult people's intelligence by being too forthright and candid with them; instead, you prefer to imply or suggest your ideas or wishes to others. Thus, you might expect others to understand what you mean without having to tell them directly. You may like speakers who use parables and stories to make a point. You find it strange or insulting when someone explains something to you in detail, step-by-step—not unlike explaining something obvious to a child.

Lower scores, 4 or below, reflect more of a linear logic preference. If your own score reveals a linear propensity, you are like most Euroamericans, who prefer a direct approach toward organizing an argument or position. Euroamericans are taught that "logical" speakers are those who lay out a premise, provide relevant, supporting facts, and then draw out a very specific conclusion for others to buy into. Thus, you

probably become confused and disoriented with configural speakers who seem to wander around the point and never really tell you what they want or need. You may think that people who do not argue linearly tend to digress and include a lot of irrelevant information. You may have difficulty imagining how anyone could not be persuaded by your position when you go to the effort to lay out all the facts that lead "inevitably" to one conclusion. In your view, it is the speaker, not the listener, who is responsible for organizing all the information in a systematic, convincing way.

NOTE: A number of the items used in this scale were derived from discussions of the organizational patterns used by different cultures worldwide, including the Japanese, Euroamericans, English, and Arabs. See, for instance: Condon, J. C., & Yousef, F. (1975). *An introduction to intercultural communication* (pp. 240–245). New York: Macmillan; Hall, E. T., & Hall, M. R. (1987). *Hidden differences: Doing business with the Japanese* (pp. 120–125). New York: Doubleday; and Lustig, M. W., & Koester, J. (1993). *Intercultural competence: Interpersonal communication across cultures* (pp. 217–229). New York: HarperCollins.

and essays. A speech prepared according to linear logic follows a very straightforward pattern:

1. The speaker lays out the basic argument or thesis by providing a preview of each of the main points.

2. The speaker discusses the main points in detail, one at a time. These points are organized in some linear pattern—chronological, spatial, topical, problem-solution, or cause and effect. (These patterns are discussed later in this chapter.)

3. The speaker relies heavily on facts and data to clarify, illustrate, and support each main point.

4. The speaker uses phrases—called **transitions** and **signposts**—to connect each of the main points or supporting ideas. (See the box "Transitions and Signposts" for some examples of each.)

5. The speaker concludes with a summary of the main points and, if applicable, an explicit call for some kind of action or response on the part of audience members.

A speech organized in a linear fashion can be likened to a series of ordered steps that lead the audience in a straight line, point by point. Consider the

following speech excerpt to see how Donald relied on linear logic in this presentation:

There are three basic reasons why couples engage in conflict. The first and most common reason is because they spend too much time together. Trivial matters become exaggerated, and before you know it, some small thing becomes a major issue. The second most often cited reason why people fight is because they have to rely on limited resources, like money and time. Think about it: If you had enough time and money, you could make yourself and everyone around you feel pretty satisfied. It's when you don't have resources that everyone becomes unhappy. And third, couples fight because they like to argue. Have you ever known some couples or friends who argue just for the sheer thrill of it? Then afterwards, they get to make up and feel all good about each other again.

Donald lays out the three basic reasons couples fight. Notice how he previews his three major points and then ticks off each one of them by signaling with the words "first," "second," and "third." Step-by-step, he tells the audience the order of reasons (most common to least common) couples engage in conflict. By organizing his message in this progressive manner, Donald actively assists the audience in following along.

Transitions and Signposts

Transitions and signposts are hallmarks of linear speeches. Transitions are phrases that link together and establish relationships between what has been said and what will be said. They help unify a speech and clarify the relationship among points and ideas. Signposts are phrases that signal how a speech is organized and where the speaker is in the speech. Transitions and signposts provide a very clear and explicit road map that guides audience members through a speech.

Transitions

So	In truth	Comparatively	Nevertheless
Moreover	Unfortunately	And	Nonetheless
Therefore	Once we . . . , then	But	Although
In addition	In other words	Important to remember	To illustrate
The solution to the problem is	Along the same lines	Importantly	Take the case of
Accordingly	Specifically	Significantly	Visualize this
Consequently	For example	More to the point	Picture that
This all boils down to one thing	Consider the following	Or	Still
Thus	The point is	Afterwards	Yet
Hence	Another way of looking at this is	Well	Notwithstanding
What is the result of all this?	On the one hand	Alternatively	Closely related to . . . , is
What does all of this mean?	On the other hand	Instead	In fact
After completing that task, you need to	A good example of this is	Seriously now	That is
For instance	Similarly	On a lighter side	Remember
	In contrast	However	A far better way
	In a similar fashion	Regardless	Once again
		In spite of	

Signposts

First	Finally	Let me recap what I have said	Of secondary concern
Second	What follows is	But first let me begin by	The core of my argument is
Third	To begin with	Before we discuss that	My position is twofold
One	To preview	Subsequently	In review
Two	In overview	Starting with	To reiterate
Three	To summarize	Commencing with	To recapitulate
In conclusion	Three arguments support my position	Departing from my script	Moving to my first point
Let's turn our attention to	In closing	My primary concern	Lastly
Next			

In linear logic, the speaker is largely responsible for helping the audience understand the message.[4] The speaker goes to great lengths to ensure that the message is obvious to audience members and that they grasp it quickly and easily. By contrast, some individuals and cultures tend to find such direction and assistance unnecessary and even demeaning, preferring that the speaker give them

Speakers who present their speeches in a linear fashion introduce their points step-by-step, sequentially. This speaker is communicating to his audience that he plans to cover three main points, one at a time. In this way, he assists the audience in following the points covered in his speech.

credit for being able to figure out the message on their own.

Configural Logic

The term **configural logic** represents a wide variety of contrastive logic systems used by a number of Eastern, Native American, and Latino cultures. Whereas linear logic is direct and straightforward, configural logic is more indirect. Speakers using configural logic are not likely to provide a preview of the main points or spell out a specific conclusion. They explore issues from a variety of tangential views or examples. Links between main points are not made explicitly; direction is only implied.

Configural logic does not follow a linear pattern, but little research has been done on the precise kinds of patterns that do characterize configural logic. Although a number of recent intercultural writers acknowledge that configural logic patterns exist, there is little agreement about the nature of those patterns. Robert B. Kaplan is credited with alerting us to the idea that individuals

organize their ideas using different logics as a function of their language and cultural affiliations. Kaplan noticed that nonnative speakers of English—those proficient in English as their second language—wrote paragraphs and essays very differently than native English speakers. The ideas in the essays he examined were not organized according to the linear logic of the typical Euroamerican. Kaplan's observations led him to suggest a number of alternative organizational schemes represented in the essays.[5]

A speech organized with configural logic usually requires the audience to do more work than one organized with linear logic. As described in Chapter 3, people from high-context cultures rely more on the situation than the verbal message to convey meaning. It is not solely the speaker who is responsible for the message; the listener, too, must actively construct and interpret meaning.[6] A speaker using configural logic does not spell out her or his purpose and main points for audience members; instead, members must rely on what they already know about the speaker and the topic to interpret the speech.

The following speech excerpt is Donald's original speech (which was organized linearly) reorganized using an alternative configural structure:

> Have you ever known friends or couples who fight for the sheer thrill of it? Apparently, they like making up afterwards. Sometimes a lack of money and time can cause otherwise happy couples to fight with one another. We all need a certain amount of money to be happy. And we must find time to spend together. But, too much time can be our enemy, too. The last time I took a vacation for four days backpacking with my friend, we ended up fighting bitterly over the cooking. I thought we should take turns; he thought that I should do the cooking since he brought most of the food. Anyway, it was a trivial matter, but our time together almost cost us our friendship.

In this example, the audience must work much harder to figure out the purpose and understand the main points. Donald does not preview or list the main points. Instead, he assumes that audience members will be able to impose their own structure and meaning on the presentation. Notice how Donald approaches his topic from a variety of angles, using as evidence stories and personal testimony, such as the time he had an argument with a friend while on vacation. Main points are subtly implied or suggested rather than explicitly delineated as progressive steps.

Co-Cultural Logic Preferences

Robert Kaplan, who first recognized differences in cultural logics, later concluded that he had overstated both his case and the differences between logic patterns.[7] He now asserts that all of the various logic patterns he identified, linear and configural, are possible in any language. Kaplan acknowledges that ideas can be organized in many ways and that everyone has the ability to use any logic pattern. Culture and language do not restrict how an individual can organize ideas; rather, they act to create and maintain a preference for one type of logic over another.[8] Because we live in a multicultural, pluralistic society, we must be mindful of these preferences and try to respect them.

What cultural preferences for logics have been identified? Linear logic is most often associated with formal writing and public speaking among Euroamericans and with people working in the physical and social sciences. However, these associations are not rigid or clear-cut. During everyday speech, for example, Euroamericans regularly rely on nonlinear organizational schemes to communicate their thoughts and ideas. In addition, the association between the Euroamerican co-culture and linear logic may reflect a gender bias. Some writers have argued convincingly that linear logic relies on male rather than female logic preferences. Linguist Deborah Tannen maintains that whereas (Euroamerican) men value linear logic, women rely on emotion, intuition, and experience. That is, men follow an argument step-by-step in a linear progression until it is settled; women often change course midstream and seemingly digress with examples of personal experiences and observations.[9] Many feminist scholars would probably agree with Tannen's conclusions. They argue that traditional research in rhetoric has focused primarily on men's voices and experiences and then assumed that those voices applied universally to women as well. These scholars call for critics to analyze women's voices and experiences from the point of view of women, not men.[10]

For other co-cultures, there is even less agreement among scholars. Researchers looking at different languages agree that the rhetorical structure of each language differs, but they fail to agree on just how they differ.[11] More indirect, high-context co-cultures such as some Latino, Native American, and Asian American groups appear to prefer configural logic. However, more definitive generalizations will have to await additional research. Despite the recent recognition of male and Euroamerican bias in the literature, females and males of all U.S. co-cultures continue to be socialized to value and adopt linear logic. Females and non-Euroamericans are taught to devalue or denigrate nonlinear, or configural, types of logic, which they may actually prefer.

Until it is clear which co-cultures prefer which logic patterns, we can't offer precise advice about which pattern is most effective with a particular audience, but we can say with assurance that there is more than one way to make sense of ideas. It is important to remember that logic systems are not inherently good or bad, rational or irrational, organized or disorganized. Beware of the insidious, and often covert, nature of ethnocentrism. Everyone needs to understand, accept, and appreciate the logic systems employed by others—whether they be primarily linear or configural.

USING DIFFERENT LOGICS TO ORGANIZE YOUR SPEECH

You can organize your speech in a variety of ways. The particular organizational pattern you select need not depend entirely on the logic preferences of your audience. Selecting an appropriate organizational scheme depends on your topic and on your own logic preference. Fortunately, you can count on your audience members to make sense of your speech in their own way; research indicates that audience members can make sense out of a wide variety of organizational patterns, regardless of their cultural affiliations. Studies have shown that nonnative English speakers who prefer configural logic are able to recall the major points and thrust of linear passages at about the same frequency and rate as native speakers.[12] No comparable research has examined how accurately people who favor linear logic can recall information presented configurally. However, regardless of the organizational scheme employed, audience members are likely to reorder and prioritize the information in ways that make the message most meaningful to them while discarding or ignoring information they find redundant or meaningless.

So, although speech organization does affect message comprehension, audiences can decipher and make sense of unfamiliar and seemingly mildly disorganized speeches.[13] It is only when messages are highly disorganized, and apparently offered at random, that audiences are likely to have problems interpreting the message. What follows then, is an entire menu of different linear and configural logic patterns to help you and your audience make sense of your presentation.

Types of Linear Patterns

Various organizational patterns fall under the heading of linear logic. Each pattern follows a straightforward, step-by-step scheme.

Topical
If a subject breaks into natural categories or divisions, a topical organizational pattern may be appropriate. Many speech topics lend themselves easily to this pattern, which can be used for informative or persuasive speeches. Speeches arranged topically are divided into a number of headings or parts, such as advantages and disadvantages, specific types or categories, or lists of particular reasons. Here are two examples of speeches using topical organizational logic—one persuasive and the other informative.

Purpose: To persuade or convince my audience to vote in support of term limitations for U.S. senators and representatives

Thesis Statement: You should vote in support of term limitations because the current system causes three basic problems: representatives lose touch with the people, they focus too much on campaigning, and they do not share power equitably in Congress.

Main Points:
I. People who stay too long in Congress begin to lose touch with the American people.

II. Congresspersons spend too much time worrying about campaigning for their reelections and not enough time governing.

III. The current system in Congress gives all the power to senior members, oftentimes preventing newcomers from participating actively on key committees.

Purpose: To inform my audience of a variety of different exercises to strengthen arm muscles

Thesis Statement: You can do different types of exercises to strengthen different arm muscles.

Main Points:
I. Biceps
  A. Hammer curls
  B. Angled simultaneous dumbbell curls
  C. Alternating dumbbell curls

II. Triceps
  A. Tricep extensions
  B. Dumbbell kickbacks
  C. Pulley pushdowns

Each example divides topics into specific reasons or categories. The persuasive speech lists three distinct reasons for voting for congressional term limits. The informative speech breaks down the topic of strengthening arm muscles into two main categories—biceps and triceps—and then further subdivides into three distinct exercises for each muscle type.

Cause and Effect
Speeches arranged using a cause-and-effect **organizational pattern** demonstrate the relationship between certain things or events. Causal speeches have two main points: one focusing on causes, the other on effects. The speaker attempts to show how the causes bring about the effects. Sometimes speeches are arranged in reverse, with the effects stated first and the cause(s) explained later. In the two examples that follow, notice how both speech outlines reflect the same basic content—the first one demonstrating a cause-and-effect order and the second an effect-and-cause order.

Purpose: To inform my audience of the effects of following "the rules" for successful dating

Thesis Statement: Female daters who follow "the rules" will cause Mr. Right to eventually propose marriage.

Main Points:
I. Rules are prescriptive advice for women to follow in their efforts to make Mr. Right

obsessed with having you as his. Here's a sample of those rules: [14]

A. Rule 1: Don't call him; wait for him to call you.
B. Rule 2: Don't go Dutch treat on a date.
C. Rule 3: Don't accept a Saturday nite date after Wednesday.

II. These and similar rules for playing hard-to-get will make you a challenge to Mr. Right. Very soon he should find you to be the most irresistible and desirable woman he has ever known. The rules produce results: engagement!

Purpose: To inform my audience that following "the rules" for dating will cause Mr. Right to propose

Thesis Statement: Getting Mr. Right to marry you may very well be a function of following "the rules."

Main Points:

I. My friend Geri is dating the man of her dreams; Denise is happily married; and Siddalee keeps a book of all her male admirers. And yet, every day I see lots of young women, at least as attractive and as smart as my friends, who rarely date and complain that there just aren't any men!

II. To explain how my friends were able to capture the hearts of their men, I only need to review for you a few basic rules for dating. Here's a sample of those rules:

A. Rule 1: Don't call him; wait for him to call you.
B. Rule 2: Don't go Dutch treat on a date.
C. Rule 3: Don't accept a Saturday nite date after Wednesday.

Cause-and-effect logic, as demonstrated in these examples, is the basis for study in all physical and social sciences, including economics, communication, biology, psychology, physics, and mathematics. Scientists regularly hypothesize (reason) that one variable is likely to cause a change, or an effect, in a second variable. As common as this logic is for scientists, many people believe that things simply happen and that they are beyond any normal human control. Consequently, although cause-and-effect organizational schemes may seem particularly "logical" to some, others may find them difficult to understand or accept.

Problem-Solution Speakers who employ a **problem-solution organizational pattern** begin by stating the problem or need and then offering a viable solution to that problem. This type of organization is well suited for persuasive speeches that call for the audience to adopt a proposed solution. Chapter 12 provides a sophisticated

problem-solution format in Monroe's Motivated Sequence. In a simpler version of that format, the following example identifies the problem in the first main point and the solution in the second point.

Purpose: To persuade my audience that gays and lesbians should be allowed to legally marry in the United States.

Thesis Statement: The current federal policy toward gays and lesbians is discriminatory, so it should be changed to one that applies equally to everyone.

Main Points:

I. The current "Defense of Marriage" Act signed by the president in 1996 prevents same-sex marriages from becoming legal under federal law. This policy on homosexual and heterosexual conduct is inequitable and thus discriminates against gays and lesbians.

II. This problem should be resolved by allowing all couples to marry, regardless of their sexual orientation.

The first main point illustrates the seriousness of the problem. Of course, subpoints would further demonstrate the extent of the discrimination. The second main point proposes a solution. Again, subpoints would specify exactly what changes in the legal code would be required. This particular organizational format works best when the problem is strongly emphasized. Unless the audience actually perceives the seriousness or extent of the problem, no solution will seem worth the effort. In other words, "if it ain't broke, don't fix it." The speaker must show that the system really is in need of a change before the solution can be accepted.

Chronological Given the Euroamerican co-culture's preoccupation with time (see Chapter 8) and its general preference for linear logic, it should come as no surprise that a **chronological organizational pattern** is another frequently used form of linear logic. Chronological order follows a particular sequence: past, present, and future; first, second, and third; before and after. Consider the chronology of the speech outlined here:

Purpose: To inform my audience how a worm farm can be cultivated to keep garden soil aerated and alive

Thesis Statement: There are six easy steps for creating and maintaining a worm farm.

Main Points:

I. First, construct a shallow wooden container (1 × 2 × 3 feet; this size will produce about 10 gallons of worm castings a month).

II. Next, make a bedding of a combination of shredded newspaper or cardboard, peat moss, compost, and horse or rabbit manure.

III. Wet the mixture down for a week.

IV. Add 1,000 red worms to the bin.

V. Feed the worms soft mushy garbage and table scraps (but avoid dairy products and greasy foods).

VI. Keep the bin moist at all times, and place it in a shady location.

With chronological order, the sequence of steps is critical to the presentation. Reversing the order or mixing the sequence in any way would undermine the purpose of the speech. Many demonstration speeches, like the example here, demand a chronological organizational pattern. Consider these topics: making bread, tying nautical knots, performing a tracheotomy, conducting an interview, caring for African violets, planning a wedding, cutting a record, or wiring your own home. For these informative speech topics, the chronology is essential.

Spatial If the presentation of a topic requires the speaker to create a visual picture based on location or direction, a **spatial organizational pattern** may be most appropriate. Certain topics lend themselves easily to this pattern—for example, how to arrange your living room to make it more personal and interactive, how to design fast-food restaurants to encourage high customer turnover, how parts of an engine work, or what the private living quarters of the White House look like. Here is an example.

Purpose: To inform my audience that the relative consumption of apples and oranges depends on where you live in the United States

Thesis Statement: There is a clear geographical pattern in the consumption of apples and oranges in the United States.

Main Points:

I. North: Apple eaters

II. South: Orange eaters

III. East: Neither apple nor orange eaters

IV. West: Both apple and orange eaters

Speeches arranged spatially should be accompanied by pictures, charts, videos, or other visual aids that show the size, location, shape, or direction emphasized in the presentation. Clearly, a map of the United States would help demonstrate how and why apple and orange eaters live in different parts of the country.

The five basic linear patterns are summarized in the box "Linear Logic Patterns for Organizing Speeches." Additional examples of outlines and speeches based on linear patterns appear later in this chapter and in Chapters 11 and 12.

A CLOSER LOOK

Linear Logic Patterns for Organizing Speeches

Topical

This organizational pattern is based on natural categories or divisions of a topic.

Cause and Effect

This organizational pattern is based on a causal relationship between certain things or events. A cause-and-effect speech typically has two main points, one focusing on causes and one on effects. The speaker may discuss the causes first or begin instead with the effects.

Problem-Solution

This organizational pattern begins with the identification of a problem or need, followed by a description of possible solutions. A problem-solution pattern works best when the problem or need is strongly emphasized.

Chronological

This organizational pattern follows a linear sequence based on time, such as in a before-and-after comparison or a step-by-step how-to demonstration. A chronological organization is most appropriate when the order of steps is critical to the purpose and success of the speech.

Spatial

This organizational pattern is based on location or direction, such as top to bottom, north to south, near to far, or left to right. Charts, pictures, and other visual aids often are used to help the audience visualize the significance of the spatial arrangement.

Types of Configural Patterns

Little research has been done on this second major logic category. Even though some recent intercultural writers acknowledge that alternative logics (configural patterns) do, in fact, exist, there is little agreement about what those logics are. Most recently, feminist scholars have given us some insight into a variety of alternative organizational patterns that represent more configural thinking.[15] Recall that speeches organized configurally require the audience to participate actively in interpreting what is often only implied.

Rather than explicitly lay out the purpose or main points, configurally organized speeches provide subtle cues for the audience to interpret. Examples of patterns that reflect a more configural approach to speech organization include narrative, web, problem–no solution, and multiple perspective.[16]

Narrative In a **narrative organizational pattern**, the speech is told as a story, complete with characters, plot, and drama and a familiar introduction like "Once upon a time." The audience must figure out the moral of the story or the way the story relates to the speech topic and occasion. Here is a brief outline of a narrative:

Purpose: To persuade my audience to support guaranteed national health care

Thesis Statement: The story of Donita clearly illustrates the need for a system of guaranteed national health care.

Main Points:

I. Donita was young, smart, and ambitious, and she had a high-paying job at Newell-Howe's brokerage house. She was divorced, had three children, and owned a beautiful home.

II. One day, her daughter Monica was hit by a car and required extensive, long-term health care for her injuries.

III. The health care bills continued to pile up month after month. Soon thereafter, Donita's insurance carrier canceled her policy.

IV. To pay the bills, Donita had to sell her home, work extra jobs, and borrow money.

V. Today, Donita doesn't know how her family can continue to survive. How can something like this happen in America?

Notice that the story is only briefly outlined. The speaker could embellish the thesis by talking, for instance, about what an ideal life Donita had before her daughter's accident. The storyteller might elaborate the extent of Monica's injuries, her resulting pain and despair, and the family's fears about their future. Even though no central thesis or preview is provided, the story hints at a central problem: Donita and her family would benefit from guaranteed national health care.

Web In a web **organizational pattern**, speech ideas emanate from a core idea. Each specific idea, branching from the core, illuminates or extends the central point. The speaker begins with the central idea, examines a related idea, and then returns to the central point. The speaker repeats this pattern until all related ideas are explored. Consider the following example:

Purpose: To persuade my audience that photojournalists need to assume greater ethical responsibility when dealing with celebrities.

Thesis Statement: The unexpected consequences of recent paparazzi behavior illustrate the need for photojournalists to respect others' privacy.

Main Point:

I. Photojournalists should show more restraint in their coverage of celebrities, particularly those who don't seek such attention.

Subpoints:

A. Monica Lewinsky never wanted her name to become so sullied in the media. And she certainly never expected to have her face on the cover of every major magazine and newspaper in America as a result of her alleged affair with the president.

B. Whether at her father's home in Brentwood or at her mother's condo at the Watergate, media photographers hang out at all hours of the day and night, making it impossible for her to attend a movie, go out to dinner, or visit friends without a major media blitz.

Main Point:

II. Some tabloid photographers go too far in their attempts to get a story.

Subpoints:

A. Anxious to take pictures of Kim Basinger and Alec Baldwin's new baby, photojournalists ignored the couple's pleas for privacy. Photographers pushed and pulled their way through the crowd, snapping bulbs and shouting as the couple struggled to gain entrance to their home with their new baby in tow.

B. Annoyed with photographers and fearing for the safety of his defenseless wife and newborn baby, Baldwin fought back and was arrested for (and later acquitted of) for assault.

Main Point:

III. Disrespectful of others' needs and privacy, irresponsible photojournalists are likely one day to seriously hurt someone—or worse.

Subpoints:

A. Princess Diana was involved in a high-speed chase by the paparazzi, resulting in her death and the death of Dodi Fayed and their driver.

B. Tabloids all over the world were eager to purchase photos of the tragic auto accident.
C. Wouldn't the princess be alive today if the paparazzi hadn't hounded her?

With the web pattern, the speaker begins with the central idea (photojournalists should respect the privacy of others), moves to the first related idea (subpoint A), shows exactly how that point extends the central purpose (subpoint B), and brings it back to the central idea again (main point II). The speaker repeats this process until each subpoint is covered.

Problem–No Solution
With the **problem–no solution organizational pattern**, the problem is discussed at length, including its significance, but—unlike the linear problem-solution pattern discussed earlier—no solution is offered. A solution may be anticipated and welcomed, but the speaker encourages the audience to come up with one (or more). Consider this example:

Purpose: To inform my audience about teenage suicide and to enlist help in developing solutions to this serious problem

Thesis Statement: Teenagers at risk for suicide need our help.

Main Points:
I. Two thousand teenagers commit suicide every year—with up to 350 failed attempts.
II. Severe depression often triggers suicide.
III. Teenagers are unable to share the extent of their despair with people who can help them.
IV. Many families remain unaware of their child's suicidal tendencies.
V. What should we do to help prevent the rising rate of teenage suicide?

The speaker is anxious to resolve the problem and asks the audience to help generate some possible solutions. This approach is particularly suitable for problems requiring creative solutions.

Multiple Perspective
With the **multiple-perspective organizational pattern**, the speaker analyzes an idea or problem from a variety of viewpoints. Thus, the speaker exposes the audience to alternative ways of looking at an issue or determining the best solution to a problem. In the following example, the speaker explains how no one person is responsible for the problem of children committing serious crimes. To fully understand the problem, the speaker implores audience members to look at both parents

and various social, educational, and legal institutions as potentially culpable. In this way, the speaker encourages the audience to consider multiple solutions to a complex and growing problem. No quick fix can resolve a problem quite as profound as this one.

Purpose: To inform my audience about the forces that can turn children into serious criminals

Thesis Statement: Children who commit serious crimes (murder and assault) aren't born as criminals; they are created by everyone who knows them.

Main Points:
I. Parents fail the child.
II. Educators fail the child.
III. The social systems fail the child.
IV. The legal system fails the child.

The four configural organizational patterns are summarized in the box "Configural Logic Patterns for Organizing Speeches." For additional advice on choosing an organizational pattern for your speech, refer to the box "Interview with a Professional: Analisa Ridenour."

Sample Speech Logics
Sometimes it's difficult to visualize how to organize a given speech in completely different ways. This section focuses on one topic, with one purpose, but organizes it in two entirely different ways: linearly and configurally. For ease in distinguishing the two main logic types, the organizing logics are presented in outline form.

Linear Organization Let's assume for a moment that a speaker is preparing a persuasive speech about political (or co-cultural) correctness.[17] What follows is a brief outline of that speech—including the purpose, three main points, and supporting subpoints—following a linear logic.

Purpose: To persuade my audience that we should all relax a little about cultural or racial insensitivities

Thesis Statement: Hypersensitivity about cultural or racial insensitivity pulls people of different cultures apart and prevents them from communicating; we can alleviate these problems by relaxing a little about political correctness.

Main Point:
I. Hypersensitivity toward race, ethnicity, and gender does not bring people together; instead, it pulls people apart.

Configural Logic Patterns for Organizing Speeches

Narrative

This organizational pattern takes the form of an extended story, complete with characters, plots, and drama. The audience determines how the story relates to the speech topic, purpose, and occasion.

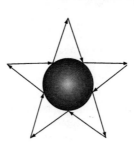

Web

This organizational pattern involves specific ideas that emanate from a central theme. Each specific idea illuminates or extends the central idea. The speaker returns to the central idea after discussing each specific idea.

Problem–No Solution

This organizational pattern is based on a specific problem. The speaker discusses the problem at length and encourages the audience to develop one or more solutions; however, the speaker does not offer an explicit solution.

Multiple Perspective

This organizational pattern examines a complex idea or problem from a variety of viewpoints. The speaker offers alternative ways of looking at a problem or explores different solutions.

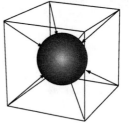

Subpoints:
- A. Charges of racism and chauvinism make it difficult for us to become friends.
- B. With everyone claiming to be victims of Eurocentrism, many of us have become "compassion fatigued."
- C. And when people are not playing victim to Eurocentrism, minority ethnocentrism raises its ugly head, making it nearly impossible for all of us to relate equitably and comfortably with one another.

Main Point:
II. The insistence on politically correct speech has had the perverse effect of closing off exchanges between people from diverse co-cultures.

Subpoints:
- A. People are so afraid they will say or do the wrong thing that they choose not to engage in dialog at all.
- B. When people are forced to interact, everyone is so busy editing what they say that they end up not saying anything important or controversial at all.

Main Point:
III. We can resolve these problems by not being so supersensitive and by not trying so hard to be politically correct.

Subpoints:
- A. By being patient and tolerant of others, we can begin to acknowledge similarities and eventually build unity among ourselves.
- B. We ought to welcome interaction with those who are different from us—even if we don't always know how to say what we mean—and be secure in knowing that others won't misinterpret or judge us as being racist, sexist, or classist.

The logic of this example follows a typical problem-solution pattern. The speaker begins by arguing that a problem exists in our multicultural society; in fact, the speaker offers at least two major reasons why we need to look for some kind of solution: (1) Hypersensitivity toward co-cultures alienates people, and (2) a preoccupation with how we talk and behave makes it too difficult to interact with diverse people. For each of those problems, the

163

Interview with a Professional

Analisa Ridenour

Analisa Ridenour teaches public speaking at California State University, Long Beach.

Is organizing a speech to make sense a function of someone's co-cultural affiliation? If so, how important is it for speakers to understand the difference between employing a linear versus a configural logic when organizing their speeches?

The notion of organizing or organization is subjective to some degree. What makes sense to me may appear as quite the contrary to someone else. Co-cultural orientations can certainly shape our organizational strategies. Understanding diverse types of logics is vital information for a speaker. From audience analysis, we can make some inferences about our potential audience's co-cultural orientation. If I was speaking to a co-culturally dissimilar group (say, high context), it would probably be to my advantage to adopt a configural structure.

When would you advise your students to employ each of the common types of linear logic?

Topical organizational patterns are great for their versatility in both informative and persuasive speeches. A topical approach allows the speaker to divide his or her speech into categories. If my topic was housing and college, three areas I could easily discuss are living in the dorms, living at home, and renting an apartment. I refer to cause-and-effect patterning as the "what and why scheme" because it attempts to answer or explain a phenomenon, such as why this is happening or what is going on here. For example, why is the AIDS epidemic increasing

among teenagers? Or, what is the relationship between secondhand smoke and the nonsmoker? Speakers must establish the linkage between the cause and the effect.

Problem-solution is best for a persuasive speech. The speaker must make the problem appear really pervasive in order for his or her solution to be adopted. Spatial is appropriate if your speech is based on a direction or location. If you were giving a speech on touring your campus or explaining an object like a tennis racquet, spatial would be appropriate. Take the tennis racquet as an illustration: I might begin with the grip (handle) of the racquet and talk about the different sizes and weights. Next, I could discuss the frames—wood, graphite, and aluminum. Then I could talk about the different sizes of the face (the netting). I've talked about the racquet in a systematic fashion, basically from bottom to top.

Because these patterns are linear, they would be most suitable for a low-context culture or an audience that expects explicit information and feels at ease with a step-by-step account.

Under what circumstances would you advise your students to use configural logic to organize a speech?

A configural pattern may be helpful when the speaker is dealing with a persuasive issue or even a hostile audience. If the audience is resistant to change, a configural approach allows the audience to make their own inferences, as opposed to a speaker who is telling them how they should respond. Moreover, co-cultures that are high context and indirect in their communication would be best suited for a configural approach.

speaker offers extended explanations in the form of subpoints. Notice how the information is objectively laid out, without a lot of qualification, interpretation, or emotional tone. The persuasive appeals are presented in a straightforward descriptive manner, with little in the way of personal experience or testimony.

Linear logic is necessarily explicit. The logic seems to march forward, step-by-step, not unlike a military parade.[18] Each successive point advances the argument yet another step, culminating in a call for change or a remedy to the problem. Main points I and II, followed by logical proofs, serve to document the fact that we have a pervasive problem that needs fixing. According to linear logic, these so called rational facts should be sufficient for the audience to accept the speaker's solution. The solution, spelled out in main point III, is not left up to the audience to

discover; instead, the speaker makes the solution explicit and carefully lays out the benefits for those willing to accept that solution.

Configural Organization Using the same topic and purpose, the linearly organized speech on political correctness can be restructured more configurally. As you read through the following outline, see if you can recognize the prominent features of this organizational pattern.

Purpose: To persuade my audience that we should all relax a little about cultural or racial insensitivities

Thesis Statement: Hypersensitivity about cultural or racial insensitivity pulls people of different cultures apart and prevents them from achieving true understanding; I think we could probably alleviate some of these problems by relaxing a little about political correctness.

Main Point:

I. *Hypersensitivity* toward race, ethnicity, and gender will not bring people together; instead, it may have the reverse effect of pulling people apart.

Subpoints:

A. Presidential candidate Ross Perot was charged with racism while speaking to an African American audience in California: He referred to them as "you people." Understandably, they were upset.

B. Ross Perot was greatly embarrassed by the audience's response. He did not mean to offend.

Main Point:

II. Ross Perot's unfortunate comments seriously undermined what he really meant to say. At the same time, being *overly sensitive* to these kinds of mistakes makes it harder for us to achieve true understanding.

Subpoints:

A. *Time* magazine offended Muslims by referring three times in one article to a particularly notorious area of prostitution as a "Mecca" for tourists and pedophiles.[19]

B. The editors of *Time* were greatly embarrassed by their readership's response. They did not mean to offend.

Main Point:

III. Once again, the editors' word choice was problematic and got in the way of understanding. At the same time, being *overly sensitive* to such mistakes makes it difficult for people to learn and accept new ways of thinking and communicating.

Subpoints:

A. A Latino group in Tampa, Florida, was outraged and called for a boycott of Taco Bell when the fast-food chain ran a commercial featuring Dinky, the talking Chihuahua, exclaiming, "Yo quiero Taco Bell!" ("I want Taco Bell!")

B. The call to boycott backfired. Those who disagreed accused the group of going too far. After all, they claimed, the dog was cute; the commercial was popular; and the food was good.

Main Point:

IV. I guess we can never be too politically correct in the words and labels we use. But can we sometimes be just a little *too sensitive* at the expense of achieving true understanding? With so many charges of racism, sexism, and classism, we could become "compassion fatigued." Perhaps we might try harder to build bridges, not walls, between people.

Can you figure out the organizational pattern of this particular outline? Sure, the web pattern. The configural logic of this example explores the issue of political correctness from a variety of tangential views but always returns to the same general theme (see the italicized words and phrases). The rationale for the problem or central thesis emerges indirectly from a pattern of stories, examples, and personal testimony that all come together to help the audience understand. The audience learns that the problem is real and widespread without the speaker having to lay out the thesis statement explicitly. In other words, with configural logic, the audience becomes actively involved and responsible for making sense of the message.

Common to both speeches is the use of argument. Both logics identify the speaker's opinion or point of view: The configural speech implies a central thesis; the linear one makes it more explicit. Both rely on a variety of supporting materials as evidence: The linear speech emphasizes facts and data; the configural speech features more personal examples and testimonials. Regardless of the organizational logic, then, both speeches demand sound arguments that make sense and appeal to the audience.

An important difference between the logics of the two examples is the degree of explicitness in each speech. For the linear speech, main points and subpoints are directly relevant to the argument—they are objectively and frankly exposed. By contrast, in the configural speech, the main points and subpoints are characterized by subtlety, implication, and suggestion. For example, rather than accuse the audiences for both Ross Perot and *Time* magazine of overreacting and charging them with being too sensitive about racial and ethnic issues, the speaker chose instead to focus on the need to understand problems that result when people, in general, become overly sensitive to others' unfortunate word choices.

Similarly, the configural speaker refrains from being too exact, forthright, and direct; instead, she or he merely suggests that the audience should consider the facts and arguments and then implies what the audience can do with the information. No explicit requests or demands are made. Qualifiers like "maybe," "perhaps," and "sometimes" are regularly used in configural speeches. Substituting "perhaps" for "it's a well-known fact," "you might consider" for "you ought to," or "you might try" for "you should" typically differentiates configural speeches from more linearly organized presentations.

Nowhere in the two speeches is the difference in logic more dramatic than in the conclusions. Whereas the linear speaker specifically and explicitly reveals a viable solution to the problem in main point III, the configural speaker allows audience members to connect the ideas and come up with their own solutions. The speaker merely suggests that audience members should try harder to build bridges, not walls, between people—without advocating a specific way to do that. Of course, the speaker hints at solutions, but only indirectly. No explicit connections are made; to do so might be considered intrusive and offensive by individuals who prefer more configural thinking. In fact, the speaker deliberately organizes the speech to avoid coming to one particular solution, encouraging audience members to construct their own course of action.[20]

OUTLINING

Regardless of the logic type you select for your own presentations, you will need to arrange your speech in some systematic way. Outlining a speech is an efficient, economical way to organize your material and provide you with the notes you will need to talk extemporaneously. An outline gives you the structure you need to present your ideas coherently; it also allows you the flexibility to talk about those ideas without being tied to a written script. Basically, there are two types of outlines that accomplish these goals: a **full-content (complete-sentence) outline** and an **abbreviated (short-phrase) outline**. Professional speakers use both types of outlines to assist them in their speech preparation and delivery.

Types of Outlines

A full-content outline consists of the entire introduction and conclusion written in full, all the main points and subpoints, examples and evidence, the purpose and thesis statements, and all the transitions that connect one idea to the next. As you might guess, a full-content outline forces you to develop your ideas fully and carefully. You should rely on this format during the early stages of putting your speech together so that you have a better idea of what you want to say—or don't want to say.

Later, in revised drafts of the full-content outline, you may want to substitute shorter phrases for lengthy sentences. You might also want to omit transitions and replace entire stories and examples with key words or simple phrases. In its final draft, this abbreviated outline can then be used as actual notes when you speak before the audience. If you relied on a full-content outline during your presentation, you might be tempted to read your sentences as written. Reducing the full-content outline to an abbreviated version allows you to merely glance at key words and phrases as you extemporaneously deliver your presentation in a conversational manner.

Simple Rules for Outlining Your Speech

Over the years, a number of rules have been developed that govern how outlines are supposed to be written. Even though your instructor probably has her or his own preferred method of constructing an outline, the rules are likely to be very similar to the following guidelines:

1. *Speech outlines generally begin with a title.* Because the title reflects the essence of your speech, you should make your title enticing to your audience. For some audiences, the title alone may be the single best motivator to attend a presentation. After all, alluring movie and book titles alone often attract moviegoers and readers. The same may be true for the audience that eventually attends your presentation. The title of the sample speech in the following section uses a familiar song title ("When I Fall in Love") followed by ellipses. The ellipses can be interpreted two ways: The rest of the verse will follow (". . . it will be forever"), or something else will. It's that "something else" that might pique the audience's curiosity about what the speaker has to say.

2. *Every speech outline begins with a specific purpose and thesis statement.* As discussed in Chapter 8, the specific purpose is a concise summary of the speaker's intent. The specific purpose should be clear and to the point. The thesis statement follows the purpose statement and lays out the central claim or message of the speech.

3. *Every outline consists of an introduction, a body, and a conclusion.* Following the specific purpose and central thesis statements are the introduction, body, and conclusion of your speech. Because you will want to track your speech quickly and easily as you speak from the outline before a group, you might want to type these major headings in capital letters.

4. *The introduction consists of two parts: an attention-getter and a preview.* Both parts should be carefully developed and written in paragraph form in a

This young man has outlined his speech on notecards so that he can communicate extemporaneously to his audience without restricting his speaking style to a written speech text. This gives him the freedom to talk more flexible about his speech topic.

full-content outline. The attention-getter should attract audience interest and make the topic relevant and personal to everyone. The preview comes next and provides an overview of what's to follow. Linearly organized speeches include an explicit preview. Configural speeches are more subtle, merely implying or hinting at what's to come. Regardless of the logic, your outline must include a preview.

5. *The body of the speech consists of at least two main points, indented and labeled with Roman numerals (I, II, III, and so on).* Two or three main points are probably sufficient for presentations ranging from five minutes to an hour.

6. *Main points are followed by subpoints, indented again and labeled with capital letters (A, B, C, and so on).* One of the conventions of outlining that has developed over the years is that any main point should have at least two subpoints. No main point can have only a single subpoint. The

reasoning for this rule is simple: One whole, when divided or partitioned, must consist of a minimum of two parts. Points can be divided into more than two parts, of course, but keep in mind that you have a limited amount of time to present your speech and that you want to avoid overloading your audience with information.

7. *If subpoints in the body are divided further, these additional subdivisions are indented again and labeled with Arabic numerals (1, 2, 3, and so on).* Once again, any time a subpoint is subdivided, a minimum of two halves, or two sub-subpoints, is required. These additional subdivisions are not included in the sample speech outline, but, when used, they generally refer to supporting materials, including further examples, stories, and facts. (Refer to the box "A Basic Framework for Outlining a Speech" for an overview of the conventional outline labeling system.)

A Basic Framework for Outlining a Speech

You can use the outlining framework shown below to build a complete outline for your speeches. It illustrates the conventional system of indenting letters and numbers used in formal outlines. The only key elements missing are transitions; these should be added in appropriate locations as you complete your outline.

Specific Purpose

Thesis Statement

INTRODUCTION

    Attention-getter

    Preview

BODY

I.   Main point

   A. Subpoint

   B. Subpoint

      1. Sub-subpoint

      2. Sub-subpoint

II. Main point

   A. Subpoint

      1. Sub-subpoint

      2. Sub-subpoint

   B. Subpoint

III. Main point

   A. Subpoint

   B. Subpoint

   C. Subpoint

CONCLUSION

    Summary

    Memorable closing statement

REFERENCES

8. *The conclusion follows the body of the speech and consists of two parts: a summary and a memorable closing statement.* Notice how this rule potentially violates some types of configural logic. After all,

some speakers may prefer to forgo a precise, specific conclusion, anticipating instead that audience members will want to supply their own. Even so, their speech outlines should specify a conclusion—even if it's stated implicitly rather than explicitly, even if it's suggested rather than advocated.

Like speech introductions, speech conclusions should be written in complete sentences. The summary reviews the main points discussed in the body of the presentation, and the memorable closing statement ends the presentation. The memorable closing statement (or paragraph) should tie in with the introductory comments (see how this is done in the sample speech that follows).

9. *Every outline ends with a reference list.* The reference list follows the conclusion and should include only those sources that you used in your speech as evidence or documentation. Do not include any other background materials that you might have read during the initial fact-finding stage of speech preparation. The format you use for references will be specified by your instructor; all the references used in each of our sample speech outlines follow the guidelines of the American Psychological Association (APA). (Refer to Chapter 8 for instructions on using APA reference style.)

Keep these basic rules in mind as you develop your outline. Once you've completed your outline, review it carefully for completeness and effectiveness. (See the box "Checklist for Full-Content Outlines" for some guidelines.) A well-developed full-content outline is a crucial precursor to a successful speech.

Sample Full-Content and Abbreviated Outlines

Following is a full-content outline that illustrates the organizational and outlining guidelines described in this chapter.

Some speakers are tempted to deliver their speeches using their full-content outlines. After all, everything is written out the way the speaker would like to say it. However, as described in Chapter 2, reading from a prepared manuscript is not the most effective way to deliver a speech. To have a conversational speaking style, a speaker needs to develop an abbreviated version that can be used to deliver the speech extemporaneously. Compare the partial abbreviated outline in Figure 9-1 with the full-content outline just shown to see how the full-content outline has been transformed into concise speaker notes.

Checklist for Full-Content Outlines

The following list of questions will help you evaluate the full-content outline you've created for your speech. Remember that your outline will probably go through several rounds of revision and polishing.

Overall

- Are all the basic elements in place?
    Title
    Specific purpose statement
    Thesis statement
    Introduction (attention-getter and preview)
    Body (main points and supporting material)
    Conclusion (summary and memorable closing statement)
    Reference list
- Is the outline written in complete sentences? Is the language clear, concise, and effective?
- Am I comfortable with the overall sequence and development of ideas? Is the outline consistent with the logic system and organizational pattern I've chosen?

Outline Framework

- Does my outline follow the rules presented in this chapter or those provided by my instructor?

- Does it utilize several levels of headings?
- Does each point have two subdivisions, if any?
- Are less important ideas subordinated under more important ones? Do different levels of headings clearly reflect different levels of importance?
- At each level of the outline, are the ideas of approximately equal importance?

Main Points

- Do the main headings represent the most important points of the speech? Are they essential for achieving my purpose?
- Are the main points distinct from one another?
- Are they balanced with respect to time? That is, will each one require about the same time to cover?

Supporting Material and Transitions

- Does each piece of supporting material relate directly to the point it supports?
- Is there any unnecessary repetition of supporting material?
- Would any point benefit from additional supporting material?
- Are transitions and signposts in place where needed?

SAMPLE SPEECH OUTLINE

When I Fall in Love . . .

Specific Purpose: To inform my audience that couples often commit to one another for reasons other than love

Thesis Statement: Couples stay together for one of three general reasons: (1) because they want to, (2) because they have to, or (3) because they feel they ought to.

The title of the speech reflects the essence of the speaker's message and entices the audience to listen.

The speaker's purpose statement tells exactly what he wants to accomplish—what he wants the audience to learn from his informative speech. The thesis statement summarizes the main points of the speech—the basic reasons couples stay together. Placing these on top of the outline helps the speaker keep his

Continued

INTRODUCTION

Attention-Getter: The childhood fantasy and promise of "living happily ever after" depends on our falling in love and getting married. So we all spend a lot of time, energy, and money searching for that special someone. Once we have a partner, we discover that the search was the easy part. The hard part is sustaining that relationship over the years. Shouldn't love be sufficient to make a relationship work? When I fall in love, shouldn't it be forever?

Preview: Even though many of us may have been raised with these expectations about our own future (or current) love relationship, it's important to learn that not all couples continue to stay together simply because they love each other. Couples stay together for one of three basic reasons: (1) because they want to, (2) because they have to, or (3) because they ought to. Today I will describe each type of relationship in more detail.

BODY

I. The first reason couples may commit to one another and stay together is because they want to. This is the type of relationship most of us want to have.

   A. The commitment of this type of couple is based on attraction and positive regard. The attraction and regard remain constant over time, even as the relationship develops and changes.

   B. Couples who commit to each other because they want to are likely to report greater relational satisfaction than the other two categories of couples I will be describing.

Transition: Just what is a relationship like for couples who stay together because they want to?

   C. Take the example of Rich and Wesley. They have been together for 14 years. Both report a great deal of warmth and affection. "If we had to do it over again, I would still choose Wes and he would choose me." Although their relationship has changed over time, Rich and Wesley say that they have remained very satisfied.

Transition: Rich and Wesley are a good example of a relationship based on mutual satisfaction. But wanting to stay together is not the only reason couples give for staying in a relationship.

---

goal and central message in mind as he builds his speech.

Labeling the introduction helps to set it off as a distinct and critical part of the speech.

The attention-getter attracts the audience to the topic by making it relevant and personal. The last line refers to the song title used as the title of the speech.

The preview statement provides an overview of the main points of the speech.

The body of the speech is labeled to set it off as a distinct section and to make the outline easier to follow.

The body of the speech is divided into three main points, indented and labeled with Roman numerals I, II, and III.

Subpoints within each main point are indented and labeled with capital letters A, B, C, and so on. Any time a point is divided to provide greater detail, there must be a minimum of two subpoints. If subpoint A were divided further, the sub-subpoints would be indented and labeled with Arabic numerals 1, 2, 3, and so on.

Including transitions in the full-content outline ensures that the speaker has worked out ways to get from one idea to the next.

Specific examples provide concrete and memorable illustrations of the abstract categories of relationships the speaker describes.

The speaker includes transitions between main points and between subpoints.

II. Some couples stay in relationships for a second reason—because they have to.

   A. Such couples have decided individually that there is no other viable alternative to staying in the relationship.

   B. They decide that it is easier to stay together than to face disapproval from family and friends or some other kind of hardship.

   C. Couples that stay together because they feel they have to are likely to report low relational satisfaction.

Transition: Can you imagine some specific reasons why a couple might feel they had to stay in a relationship?

   D. Consider the case of Emir and Gahlit, who have been married 23 years. They both own a lot of property and have invested well over the years. Terminating their relationship is unthinkable to them, even though they seem to live separate lives. "We can't afford to split up. Neither of us would end up with anything. It's just not worth the trouble or the money."

Transition: We've looked at couples that remain together because they want to or because they feel they have to. There is one more reason couples stay together.

III. Some couples stay together because they feel they ought to.

   A. Couples in this type of situation have a relationship based on obligation.

   B. They may feel they should stay together for the sake of their children, the institution of marriage, or because they somehow owe it to their partner.

   C. Azana and Bill illustrate this type of relationship. Azana became pregnant, so she and Bill got married. That was five years ago. Bill has never been very happy with their marriage, but they do have a beautiful and intelligent little girl. Divorcing Azana would mean destroying his daughter's happy home. "Azana and I owe it to our little girl to stay together and make her home stable and her life secure." The obligation they feel toward their daughter keeps them in the relationship.

Transition: What should you learn from the examples of Rich and Wesley, Emir and Gahlit, and Azana and Bill?

This speech divides naturally into three sections—one for each type of relationship—so the speaker uses a topical organization. He follows the same framework for each of the three main points: a general description followed by a specific example.

CONCLUSION

Summary: When you find yourself falling in love and committing yourself to someone very special, recognize that commitment can take many forms during the life of your relationship. Ideally, you and your partner will always commit to each other because you both want to, yet you may end up staying together because you have to or because you believe that's what you ought to do.

Memorable Closing Statement: Falling in love may be forever; it may even be completely. But commitment to forever may require that you adapt to changing times, situations, and circumstances.

This transition refers to the three main points of the speech and cues the audience that the conclusion is next.

The conclusion is labeled to set it off as a key part of the speech.

The speech summary provides a review of the main points discussed in the body of the speech.

A memorable closing statement concludes the presentation. The speaker ties the speech together by referring back to the words of the song mentioned in his introduction.

REFERENCES

Johnson, M. P. (1973). Commitment: A conceptual structure and empirical application. *The Sociological Quarterly, 14,* 395–406.

Knapp, M. L., & Vangelisti, A. L. (1992). *Interpersonal communication and human relationships.* Boston: Allyn & Bacon.

The outline concludes with a list of the sources the speaker used in his speech. The sources are formatted according to the APA reference style.

```
INTRO                    [LOOK at them;  SMILE!]              #1

"Living happily ever after"
Falling in love and getting married
Spend energy finding that "special someone"
    – – BUT the search was the easy part.
When I fall in love, shouldn't it be forever?

                    [PAUSE]

3 reasons couples stay together:
   I.  Want to
   II.  Have to
   III. Ought to
```

```
BODY                                                         #2

    I. Want to

       A. Attraction & positive regard
       B. Greater relational satisfaction
       C. Rich & Wesley

    But wanting to stay together is not the only reason . . .

    II. Have to

       A. No viable alternative
       B. Face disapproval
       C. Low relational satisfaction
       D. Emir & Gahlit
```

Figure 9-1 Sample abbreviated outline on notecards. An abbreviated outline includes key phrases and main points to help jog a speaker's memory and stay on track. Notecards should not contain the entire text of the speech written out in complete sentences, although statistical information and direct quotes can be noted in full. Notecards can also be used to cue the speaker's nonverbal behavior.

CHAPTER REVIEW

- Organizing enables you to make sense of your speech both for yourself, as speaker, and for your audience, as receivers. It helps you determine what information is truly relevant and what is not. The relevant information should be arranged in some logical manner that makes sense. But "making sense" doesn't always mean the same thing to everyone. Culture influences people's preferences for how they organize information, either linearly or configurally.

- With linear logic, the speaker assumes responsibility for laying out the message in an orderly, step-by-step progression. The speaker previews what she or he is going to say, lists and discusses each main point, offers detailed supporting evidence for each main point, and provides an explicit conclusion. Linear logic is often used in organizing formal speeches, including topical, cause-and-effect, problem-solution, chronological, and spatial presentations.

- Configural logic assumes that the audience will take equal responsibility for comprehending the message. Thus, the speaker need not use explicit previews, transitional phrases, or specific conclusions; the speaker explores issues from a variety of viewpoints. Such speeches are organized using narrative, web, problem– no solution, and multiple-perspective patterns.

- Regardless of the logic type you prefer or intend to use, you must present that logic in some systematic way. Outlining—either full-content or abbreviated—is a means of doing just that.

QUESTIONS FOR CRITICAL THINKING & REVIEW

1. What type of logic—configural or linear—is easier for you to comprehend? Do you think your gender or ethnic co-cultural background has anything to do with your ability to understand one type of thinking more than the other?

2. How might the formality of a speaking situation influence the type of logic you use? For example, what type of logic might you choose for a business presentation? For talking with a good friend?

3. How might you use a narrative organizational pattern to present a speech on the importance of prenatal health care? Now, try organizing the same speech topic using a cause-and-effect pattern. Which organizational pattern do you think works better for this topic? Why?

4. When speaking to a group of children, which type of logic—configural or linear—do you think you should use to help the audience clearly understand your message? Do you think age has anything to do with logic preferences? Why or why not?

NOTES

1. Smith, R. G. (1951). Effects of speech organization upon attitudes of college students. *Speech Monographs, 18,* 292–301.

2. Darnell, D. K. (1963). The relation between sentence-order and comprehension. *Speech Monographs, 30,* 97–100; Thompson, E. (1967). Some effects of message structure on listening comprehension. *Speech Monographs, 34,* 51–57.

3. McCroskey, J. C., & Mehrley, R. S. (1969). The effects of disorganization and nonfluency on attitude change and source credibility. *Speech Monographs, 36,* 13–21; Sharp, H., Jr., & McClung, T. (1966). Effects of organizations on the speaker's ethos. *Speech Monographs, 33,* 182.

4. Lustig, M. W., & Koester, J. (1993). *Intercultural competence: Interpersonal communication across cultures* (pp. 220–221). New York: HarperCollins.

5. Kaplan, R. B. (1966). Cultural thought patterns in intercultural education. *Language Learning, 16,* 1–20.

6. Lustig & Koester, 1993.

7. Kaplan, R. B. (1987). Cultural thought patterns revisited. In U. Connor & R. B. Kaplan (Eds.), *Writing across languages: Analysis of L₂ text* (pp. 9–21). Reading, MA: Addison-Wesley.

8. Kaplan, 1987; Lieberman, D. A. (1991). Ethnocognitivism and problem solving. In L. A. Samovar & R. E. Porter (Eds.), *Intercultural communication: A reader* (pp. 229–234). Belmont, CA: Wadsworth.

9. Tannen, D. T. (1990). *You just don't understand: Women and men in conversation.* New York: Morrow.

10. Foss, S. K. (1989). *Rhetorical criticism: Exploration and practice.* Prospect Heights, IL: Waveland Press.

11. Kaplan, 1987.

12. Connor, U., & McCagg, P. (1987). A contrastive study of English expository prose paraphrases. In U. Connor & R. B. Kaplan (Eds.), *Writing across languages: Analysis of L₂ text* (pp. 73–86). Reading, MA: Addison-Wesley.

13. Smith, 1951.

14. Fein, E., & Schneider, S. (1995). *The rules: Time-tested secrets for capturing the heart of Mr. Right.* New York: Warner Books; Fein, E., & Schneider, S. (1997). *The rules II: More rules to live and love by.* New York: Warner Books.

15. Foss, S. K., & Foss, K. A. (1994). *Inviting transformation: Presentational speaking for a changing world.* Prospect Heights, IL: Waveland Press.

16. Foss & Foss, 1994.

17. Detlefson, R. R. (1989, April 10). White like me. *The New Republic,* 18–21.

18. Anderson, J. W. (1991). A comparison of Arab and American conceptions of "effective" persuasion. In L. A. Samovar & R. E. Porter (Eds.), *Intercultural communication: A reader* (pp. 96–106). Belmont, CA: Wadsworth.

19. In a letter to the editors of *Time* magazine (July 12, 1993, p. 7), Erum Fatima Naqvi asked whether *Time* had deliberately intended to offend Muslims by using the term "Mecca" in a pejorative sense in its special report "Sex for Sale" (June 21, 1993).

20. Condon, J. C., & Yousef, F. S. (1975). An introduction to intercultural communication (pp. 240–244). New York: Macmillan.

Chapter 10

INTRODUCTIONS AND CONCLUSIONS

Professor Luis Martinez was the keynote speaker for a conference on cultural diversity. The purpose of his speech was to persuade his predominantly Euroamerican audience to accept and embrace cultural differences in the United States. During the host's elaborate introduction of her guest, Dr. Martinez suddenly interrupted her to correct her Anglo pronunciation of "Santa Barbara, California." He then began his own presentation by accusing Euroamericans of condoning and promoting racial bias, prejudice, and exclusion. "Racism," continued Dr. Martinez, "is rampant among Anglos. Even the most well intentioned white American harbors negative views about blacks, Latinos, and Asians." He went on to cite research that documented the number of hate crimes committed by white Americans (most notably the Ku Klux Klan). He described how whites attribute positive characteristics to their own kind but impose negative traits on "people of color." Dr. Martinez even pointed out the disproportionate number of whites (to the exclusion of others) in the room. *And that was only his introduction*!

The purpose of Dr. Martinez's speech was to convince his predominantly Euroamerican audience members that they ought to tolerate and embrace cultural diversity. Given such an introduction, what do you think his chances were of achieving that goal? Not good at all. In fact, the very people he was trying to persuade felt put off by his speech. Most of the audience members felt alienated as soon as they heard his introduction. Although audience members waited politely for Dr. Martinez to finish his presentation, they did not "listen" past his opening remarks. If they had, they might have learned something; after all, he had several good points to make. But because they were so offended by his opening comments, they chose to tune out everything else he had to say.

As this example illustrates, a speech introduction must be carefully planned. It should never alienate or estrange an audience; rather, it should entice and invite. How speakers begin and end their speeches is critical to gaining audience interest and attention. This doesn't mean that speakers should stay away from anything politically sensitive or controversial. But they should make every effort to encourage the audience to actively listen. Unless the audience is willing to listen, even the most articulate speakers will go unheard and be misunderstood.

An effective conclusion for a speech is as important as an effective introduction. The conclusion is the speaker's last chance to convey information or seek the audience's agreement. If the conclusion is effective, the audience will go away remembering the speech—and wanting to hear more. The beginning and ending of a speech share similar content and serve similar purposes. The introduction previews what is going to be said, and the conclusion summarizes what was just said. Both are intended to stimulate audience enthusiasm and generate interest in the content of the speech. Given these similar functions, it makes sense that some of the same techniques work for both introductions and conclusions. This chapter demonstrates just that.

BEGINNING YOUR SPEECH

What you say and do during the first few minutes of a presentation has a major impact on audience members' perceptions of your credibility and on their willingness to listen. Audience members begin to form first impressions of you as soon as the host introduces you. If the host informs them that you are an expert in the subject area and in high demand as a professional speaker, they will form an initial impression of you as a credible, worthwhile speaker. As soon as they see you, they will extend or modify that impression. If you are dressed professionally and appear calm, cool, and collected, they may sit up straight and take extra notice. But before their first impressions really gel, they must hear your opening remarks. It's those opening remarks, the introduction to your speech, that seem to make all the difference.

With all the pressure to ensure a positive first impression of both you and your speech, be assured that you can plan ahead to maximize your success. A good speech introduction accomplishes three main objectives: (1) It establishes your credibility in relation to your topic; (2) it compels your audience to listen; and (3) it previews the remainder of your speech. This section examines each of those objectives and recommends ways for you to accomplish them all.

Establish Your Credibility

In most formal speaking situations, you will be introduced by a host. (Chapter 5 discussed the importance of having someone else set the stage for the speaker.) The audience needs to hear about your credentials from a reliable source. (They could hear it all from you, but they might think you were a little carried away with yourself!) Effective speeches of introduction help validate your credibility, especially in the area of competence.

From that point on, building and maintaining credibility depends entirely on you. The audience needs to hear from you exactly what qualifies you (instead of somebody else) to speak on this particular topic. Perhaps the single best strategy to establish credibility is to rely on your own personal testimony. Ask yourself, "Why or how am I an expert on this topic?" Perhaps your expertise derives from your professional background, educational credentials, or personal experiences with the subject. Denise Brown became a powerful spokesperson for victims of spousal abuse shortly after O. J. Simpson

Part of effectively introducing your speech is establishing yourself as someone who is worth listening to. The first impression you give your audience often depends on how you look. This speaker commands audience attention by his dress, grooming, and demeanor.

was alleged to have brutally slain her sister Nicole. Actor and now director/producer Christopher Reeve became the director of the American Paralysis Association after a fall from his horse left him paralyzed. Sally Quinn, political reporter for the *Washington Post*, reinvented the "Washington hostess," becoming the leading authority in "how to give the best party for any occasion."[1] In these examples, each speaker's expertise is related in some way to his or her own life experiences.

The "package" in which you present yourself also has a significant impact on your audience's first impression of you. Audience members can see you as a physical object as soon as you walk to center stage. All eyes are on you, and audience members are assessing what they see. It is a dramatic moment! What you communicate nonverbally during those first few seconds onstage can have a major impact on the audience's collective perception of your credibility.

Following is an illustration of what should *not* happen during this brief period. One of the authors of this text, Pat Kearney, gave a presentation before a professional group in Portland, Oregon, many years ago. She was seated at the front table with four other persons, waiting for her turn to speak and making every effort to suppress any sign of her very real stage fright. Finally, when it was her turn to speak, she carefully stacked her notecards, pushed her chair away from the table, stood up, and approached the podium. All of a sudden, there was a loud crash behind her. The folding metal chair she had been sitting on had collapsed.

Confusion reigned! Everyone scrambled to be helpful and to right the chair. Eventually—after what seemed like hours to Pat—the commotion ceased. Now at the podium, she could get on with her presentation. However, before she could speak her first line, she was told to adjust the microphone. Unfortunately, the microphone had a life of its own and refused to stay attached to the podium. It fell to the table and, after bouncing several times, came to rest on the floor. Needless to say, those first few agonizing moments did little to make a positive initial impression.

Ideally, those first few seconds should—and most often do—go something like this: The speaker's name is announced, and she nods and smiles at the audience while gathering her materials inconspicuously and getting up gracefully. Dressed immaculately in subdued professional attire, she walks confidently to the podium, looking at the entire audience and smiling calmly. Setting her materials down, she backs away from the podium, waits briefly to build a little suspense, and then begins her presentation. From the beginning, her audience is with her.

As suggested in Chapter 5, your credibility depends, in part, on what you wear. Clothing sends powerful messages. Even if you feel that physical appearance has little to do with who you really are, it is a fact that first impressions are often based almost exclusively on personal appearance. For instance, dressing neatly in a professional style connotes credibility. Being well groomed shows that you made an effort to look good for the occasion. Even without thinking about it consciously, members of an audience sense the time and trouble you took to present the best possible you.

There are other ways to look and act credible. Chapter 5 discussed the importance of appearing composed and poised. Audience members will be looking for signs of apprehension, but don't let them see any. They need and want to feel comfortable and to know that you can handle the situation easily and confidently. Looking composed, then, is critical to appearing credible. The more apparent signs of looking relaxed include smiling, nodding, making prolonged eye contact, and using slow, deliberate movements. Concentrate on those behaviors before getting up to give your presentation. And once you are onstage and in place to deliver your opening line, pause momentarily. Sweep your eyes across your audience, but be sure to take notice of actual faces. See audience members as individuals. Smile, nod, and say hello. Then, and only then, are you ready to proceed.

Compel Your Audience to Listen

To be an effective speaker you must acknowledge the fact that your audience needs a reason to listen. The typical audience is likely to ask, "What's in it for us to sit here and listen to this speaker today?" If you can't give a good answer to that question, your audience will hardly feel motivated to pay attention. It's up to you, then, to determine why audience members should listen and then to tell them that reason.

Even though you know your own personal reasons for speaking, you have to tell your audience members why they ought to listen. You must compel them to listen by furnishing them with audience-centered reasons for listening. The more personal the reasons are, the more likely the audience will listen. For example, illegal immigration may be an attention-grabber for Californians, Floridians, and Texans, but how would you make the issue personally relevant to folks living in Iowa or Missouri? You might want to acknowledge the problem of relevance directly: "I'll bet you're wondering why we, living in the Midwest, need to be concerned about illegal immigration when most illegals settle in the border states." You could then offer personally relevant reasons by suggesting that illegal immigrants become a problem for everyone when their children, born here in the United States, automatically become eligible for legal, welfare, medical, and educational benefits: "And who pays for those benefits? Not just citizens living in those border states; *we all do!*" You might make the point even more personally relevant by specifying how much money the average taxpayer contributes each year to finance services related to illegal immigration. When social or political issues extend to the wallet, they become personally relevant.

You can also motivate your audience by using a dramatic device, such as a humorous story, a startling statement, or a little-known fact in your introduction. Take a few minutes to assess your own communication style by completing the survey in the box "How Open and Dramatic a Speaker Are You?" Later in this chapter, you'll find specific strategies that will help you be more dramatic as a speaker—particularly when you want to create an introduction (or conclusion) that is extraordinary, impassioned, and arousing.

Preview Your Speech: Tell Them What You're Going to Tell Them

An introduction to a speech should provide a brief preview of what will follow. As indicated in Chapter 2, you need to "tell them what you're going to tell them." The whole point of previewing the speech is to help your audience organize what's to follow in some systematic way. Like a preview of an upcoming movie, a speech preview lets the audience know the highlights or main points. A very simple statement that lists those main points is sufficient.

Let's assume for a moment that you have been asked to give a speech on facials. For your purpose, you have decided to demonstrate how audience members can give themselves a facial. In your introduction, you need to establish your own expertise on the topic by stating your credentials and your personal experience with facials:

I'm a licensed skin consultant. For the past three years, I have given myself a facial every two weeks. The results are phenomenal. My skin is now healthy and blemish free and feels good to the touch. My wife and kids tell me I look younger. And I feel younger, too.

Next, you want to compel audience members to listen by making the topic personally relevant to them:

All day long we expose our faces to the ravaging effects of air pollution, harsh chemicals, the burning sun, and the drying wind. We give little or no thought to the devastation that accumulates day after day, month after month, year after year. And then, one day, we pass by the mirror; startled, we stop and look again: "Have I really aged that much?"

How Open and Dramatic a Speaker Are You?

Instructions

Public speakers vary greatly in how they begin and end a speech. In this survey, consider how you present yourself when speaking before a large group. Enter the appropriate number in the space provided to indicate how each of the following statements reflects how you *generally* communicate when you begin and end your speeches in formal public speaking situations: (1) strongly agree, (2) agree, (3) are undecided, (4) disagree, or (5) strongly disagree. Record your first impressions only.

—— 1. I am good at telling a dramatic story to open or close my speech.

—— 2. I like being theatrical or melodramatic when I give a presentation.

—— 3. I think of my speaking style as being pretty ordinary.

—— 4. When I give a presentation, I strive to create some kind of intense relationship with my audience right away.

—— 5. My speaking style tends to be subdued and passive.

—— 6. I would characterize my public speaking style as lively and animated.

—— 7. I do not tend to be a very dramatic speaker.

—— 8. When I tell a story to open my speech, I am good at building suspense.

—— 9. I am good at performing in front of a group.

—— 10. I know how to get the audience excited about my ideas.

—— 11. I am good at getting an audience involved right away in what I have to say.

—— 12. It's hard for me to open up or act out in front of a group.

—— 13. When I'm onstage, I become self-conscious and reserved.

—— 14. Most audiences wouldn't find me particularly stimulating or inspiring.

—— 15. I like to exaggerate a personal experience or story to get a response from my audience.

—— 16. I tend to be pretty understated as a speaker.

—— 17. I am not very outgoing in front of a large group.

—— 18. I'm not very entertaining as a speaker.

—— 19. I often try to conclude my speeches with some story or little-known fact that will startle or astonish my audience.

—— 20. I have to admit that I'm not a very exciting speaker.

Calculating Your Score

1. Add together your responses to items 1, 2, 4, 6, 8, 9, 10, 11, 15, and 19 = ——

2. Add together your responses to items 3, 5, 7, 12, 13, 14, 16, 17, 18, and 20 = ——

3. Complete the following formula:

    60 − total from step 1 = ——

    + total from step 2 = ——

    Your total dramatic style score = ——

Interpreting Your Score

The possible scores range between 20 and 100. (If your own score does not fall within this range, you have made a computational error.) The median score for this scale is 60. If your score falls well above that midpoint, you have a highly dramatic speaking style. If your score falls below that midpoint, you are more reserved in your speaker orientation.

For the most part, audiences prefer speakers who are more open and dramatic in their overall presentational style. This preference is particularly true for Latino, Middle Eastern American, African American, and Euroamerican audiences. However, other audiences also indicate a very positive response toward speakers who exhibit a dramatic style. Speakers who are highly dramatic are more likely to elicit audience attention and maintain audience interest throughout the entire speech. Dramatic speakers enjoy telling a good story, and they like to exaggerate and embellish a tale just to get a reaction from the audience. They tend to be animated, humorous, and lively when they talk. In short, they seem to enjoy performing in front of a group.

For the most part, audiences find it hard to pay attention to speakers who come across as too reserved or too monotonous. Most audiences expect to be entertained, aroused, or stimulated in some way, and unless the speaker makes an effort to do that, members are likely to fall asleep. Moreover, speakers who lack drama in their presentations come across as bored with their topic and reluctant to address the audience—even when that may not be the case. When this happens, the audience may wonder, "If the speaker doesn't care about us or the subject, then why should we?"

Obviously, there's a much greater payoff to being a dramatic speaker. Dramatic speakers aren't born; anyone can learn to be a dramatic speaker. Because being dramatic is most important for effectively opening and closing your speech, many of the strategies that are suggested in this chapter will help you achieve that effect.

And finally, you want to give the audience a preview of what's to come:

> Today I want to share with you some very simple things you can do to prevent the aging and deterioration process that shows so readily on your face. I'm going to show you how to give yourself a facial that will replenish the natural oils of your skin and return your skin to the healthy glow that you want and deserve.
>
> First, I'll show you the essential, basic skin care products that you will need. Second, I will demonstrate how to apply each of those products. And third, I will explain how each step in the facial protects your skin and replenishes its natural oils.

Often, speakers use signposts (see Chapter 9) in their previews, such as "first," "second," and "third." The preview always comes at the end of the introduction. Then the speaker is ready to leave the introduction and proceed with the body of the speech.

ENDING YOUR SPEECH

Some wonderful speeches, delivered by truly gifted speakers, have been destroyed by endings that left audiences perplexed, troubled, and annoyed. No doubt you have heard some of these or similar endings: "Well, I guess that's it"; "That's all I have to say"; or "My time's up." Perhaps you've seen a speaker who kept the audience's attention throughout the introduction and the body of the speech but, with nothing left to say, abruptly stopped talking and sat down. Or perhaps you've seen a speaker who concluded her or his speech by slowing the pace, looking down at the floor (or up at the ceiling), and lowering his or her voice. Talk about leaving the audience flat! Like the introduction, the conclusion should review the main points of the speech and then provide some kind of memorable statement that leaves the audience thoughtful, interested, and aroused.

Summarize Your Speech: Tell Them What You Just Told Them

The sole purpose of the summary is to provide your audience with a quick review of all the major points. The summary, which immediately follows the discussion of the final main point, looks a lot like the preview. Whereas your preview forewarned audience members of what was to come, your summary will tell them what you just told them. Like the preview, your summary should be brief and to the point. Any time you use the phrase "In conclusion," your audience will expect you to wrap up the presentation momentarily. You should not add new information at this point. If you were to mistakenly use a concluding phrase as a transition into more topics or ideas, your audience might get the wrong idea and start packing up to leave. Thus, you should save the following list of transitions for concluding remarks only:

In conclusion	To review
In overview	In sum
Taking a look at the major points	In summary
	And so
In short	
In brief	

Leave Them Wanting to Hear More

Besides summarizing the main points of your speech, your conclusion should sign off and leave the audience wanting more. You want to leave audience members thinking, "Gee whiz! I didn't know that!" Jolt them if possible. In other words, you want your speech to be memorable and your final scene to be as dramatic as possible, especially when other speakers are to follow. You want your ending to stand out from all the others. Even after your audience members have gone home, you want them to remember you and your message. To do this, use closing lines that hook up with your opening remarks in a clever way, rely on a famous and relevant quotation, or relate a dramatic story.

Consider the following example: Several years ago, a student delivered a rather dramatic conclusion that remains memorable even today. Julia's speech was about the state lottery system. She talked about lottery winners—how much money they generally won and sometimes lost, and how a number of winners squandered their money and eventually lost even their cars and homes. Julia explained how family, friends, neighbors, and even strangers came to the winners begging for and demanding handouts. After reviewing a number of actual cases supporting her contention that lottery winners suffer a great deal of unexpected sorrow and grief from jealous and greedy family, friends, and neighbors, Julia concluded with this startling disclosure: "Two and a half months ago, my husband and I became lottery winners ourselves. After much thought, we decided to keep it secret from our family and friends. We hate the deception, but we love our friends and relatives more." It was an astonishing admission that drove her point home.

Julia's closing remarks are a wonderful illustration of how to end a speech. She made very effective use of pause time. She also lowered her voice and spoke so softly that audience members had to lean forward to hear each and every word. And they weren't disappointed. As soon as Julia announced that she was a lottery winner, the audience began to buzz: "When was that?" "How much did she say she won?" "She doesn't look like a millionaire!" And so she waited. She waited until they became silent and attentive again. Just when they thought she was wrapping up, she astonished them once more with her second revelation—that she and her husband were hiding this information from relatives and friends. Anticipating another audience buzz, she paused again, looked around the room, and finally delivered her exit line: "We hate the deception, but we love our friends and relatives more." Seemingly unperturbed by the audience's reaction, she calmly walked away from the podium. Julia's message, both verbal and nonverbal, gave her audience much to think about.

Whatever device you choose to end your speech with, consider carefully *how* you present your conclusion. As soon as you finish reviewing your main points, abandon your notes. If you must, memorize your final remarks. Once again, to elicit maximum audience attention, stop and pause for a few seconds—and look carefully around the room. Then slow down your talking rate and deliver your final story, joke, quotation, or illustration, which should be crafted in such a way that it clearly signals the end of your presentation. You need not tell your audience members that you have finished—they should understand it fully. Save everyone from cute gestures and trite endings like Porky Pig's "That's all, folks!" Instead, slowly and deliberately pick up your materials and walk casually back to your chair or offstage. However, be prepared to acknowledge applause! If it comes, smile broadly, nod, thank the audience, and leave.

The box "Effective Introductions and Conclusions" summarizes the general characteristics of effective speech openings and endings. Refer to the box "Interview with a Professional: Victoria Orrego" for additional advice. The next section looks at a number of strategies to motivate your audience in your opening remarks or to grab them in your conclusion.

STRATEGIES TO GRAB AND MOTIVATE YOUR AUDIENCE

You would think that coming up with a relevant introduction and conclusion should be no problem—especially when compared to all the work involved in finding a topic, researching it, organizing the materials, and outlining the speech content. Nevertheless, capturing audience members' attention in your introduction and ensuring that they will remember your remarks for a long time takes considerable thought and creativity. Fortunately, a variety of strategies can help you to do both. (By the same token, numerous techniques are overused and abused by many speakers; these techniques will be discussed later in the chapter.) The following section examines excerpts from famous speeches to show you how the "experts" do it.

Personal Stories

Audience members like to get to know the speaker beyond the professional resume. They are likely to ask themselves, "Who is this speaker really? Is this speaker like me? How do I know that she or he will really understand how I feel?" Consequently, when a speaker relies on a personal story to begin a speech, the audience can feel a sense of shared background, experience, and history. Take a look at how Janice Payan, vice president of U.S. West Communications, used a personal story to begin her speech. After a highly credible introduction was given by her host, Payan cast aside her rather impressive credentials to relate directly to her audience of working Hispanic women:

> Thank you. I felt as if you were introducing someone else because my mind was racing back 10 years, when I was sitting out there in the audience at the Adelante Mujer [Onward Women] conference. Anonymous. Comfortable. Trying hard to relate to our "successful" speaker, but mostly feeling like Janice Payan, working mother, glad for a chance to sit down.

A CLOSER LOOK

Effective Introductions and Conclusions

An effective speech introduction accomplishes three main objectives:

- Establishes a speaker's credibility on the topic. Credibility can be conveyed through personal and professional qualifications, appropriate "packaging," and poise and composure.

- Gives audience members a reason to listen by making the topic personally relevant to them and by using dramatic speaking devices.

- Provides a preview of the speech by giving the audience an idea of what to expect.

An effective speech conclusion accomplishes two main objectives:

- Summarizes the main points of the speech.
- Leaves the audience interested and wanting to hear more.

> I'll let you in on a little secret. I still am Janice Payan, working mother. The only difference is that I have a longer job title, and that I've made a few discoveries these past 10 years that I'm eager to share with you.[2]

Similarly, Joanne Belknap, an assistant professor of criminal justice at the University of Cincinnati, disclosed her own personal and private concerns and anxieties about speaking on the topic "Racism on Campus":

> It's with some apprehension that I am speaking with you today about racism at UC. In fact, after hanging up the phone and agreeing to speak, I seriously questioned whether I had done "the right thing." I asked myself, "Shouldn't there be a woman of color on this panel?" "Shouldn't there be a person of color from UC on the panel?" But I decided to speak because I do agree . . . that racism is not simply a Black person's issue. Racism is an issue for people of all races, and I believe it is important to have white faculty taking a stand.[3]

Personal stories can also help bring home a point in a conclusion. Todd Buchholz, when acting as the associate director of the Economic Policy Council for the Bush White House, spoke out against some school representatives' refusal to commemorate controversial

Interview with a Professional

Victoria Orrego

Victoria Orrego, formerly a student at California State University, Long Beach, is now completing her doctorate in communication at Michigan State University. She teaches introductory courses in public speaking.

What do you feel are the primary concerns that need to be addressed when beginning a public presentation?

In designing introductions, students should concentrate on maintaining composure and demonstrating enthusiasm. These can be accomplished through the three factors that make up a great intro- duction: Establish credibility, compel the audience to listen, and pre- view the speech. I believe that these three steps are essential to an effective introduction. I have found that students have the most prob- lems with establishing credibility and compelling an audience to listen. First impressions are crucial in every situation. So I tell my students that they should start creating these impressions the minute they take center stage, even before they say anything.

The first thing they need to be aware of in making a good first impression is their nonverbal behavior: eye contact, smiling, facial expressions, gestures, body movement, and general appearance. So I tell them to smile and to look like they are happy to enlighten us with their speech. Moreover, I tell them to practice, practice, practice; work hard on feeling and looking confident. A good introduction takes time and hard work.

How about ending a public presentation?

Similar to the beginning of a speech, the conclusion is an often- times overlooked area of preparation. Students frequently want to finish their speech, losing steam as they head into their concluding remarks. Most conclusions are too brief and uneventful. Students must realize that conclusions contain the final thoughts of their speech. They must be impressive and memorable! Audiences must be left with something to think about—an impact or implication of what was just said in the body of the speech. Students should first summarize their points and then close by leaving the audience wanting more. To leave the audience wanting more, students need to be creative and dramatic. I always tell my students to be creative and express themselves.

I tell my students that their closing lines should be powerful and memorable. To link their ending with their introduction— demonstrate unity and flow and progression of thought—is espe- cially effective. Specifically, I tell them, "Finish your story, illustration, or personal anecdote that you used to begin your speech." I also recommend using a quotation. Whatever strategy a student decides to use is completely a personal and unique choice. All I suggest is to make an impact, because this is the last and strongest impres- sion that a speaker leaves an audience with.

---

figures or events, like Columbus Day. According to Buchholz, celebrating traditional heroes and holidays helps pass on values and teaches children virtue. His personal tale was designed to help the audience conclude, as he does, that teachers should focus not on ethnic issues, but on the lessons those heroes teach us:

> Today's "multiculturalists" are walking children down a treacherous path. Instead of learning com- mon stories and sharing a common heritage, they are told to find role models that match their eth- nic makeup. Blacks should not dream of becoming Albert Einstein. And whites should not strive to follow Martin Luther King.
>
> This trend splinters our communities and clouds our children's dreams. When I was a child, my hero was not a white, blue-eyed male from New Jersey. My hero was a black man from Westfield, Alabama. His name was Willie Mays. When I received my Little League uniform, I asked my mother to sew number "24" on the back. I'm glad my teacher didn't force me to change my number so that my complexion matched my hero's.[4]

Emotional Appeals

Appealing to feelings and emotions is another way to connect with an audience. Depending on the topic and purpose of the presentation, the speaker may want to incite fear, guilt, anger, passion, pity, love, or other emotional responses. Importantly, the desired emotion should not alienate the audience from the speaker, but instead should foster empathy or shared feelings between the audience and the speaker. Rosalyn Wiggins Berne, of the University of Virginia Darden School, helped create that bond when she spoke before a women's group about a dilemma fac- ing women today: choosing to work or to stay at home with the children. The potentially divisive debate between those in the audience who chose to work and those who chose to stay home (and work) was immediately disarmed by these opening remarks:

> I happened to mention to our new baby sitter that I would be speaking to you this evening. After explaining the topic she looked puzzled, and so

I turned the discussion and asked if her own mother worked outside of the home while they were growing up. She paused, and replied, "Well, I guess so. In those days, we didn't have no running water so she was hulling water from down at the well. And we heated it in the stove, so she was carrying wood to the house. She had all the washing, and tending to the chickens and garden and all, so I guess you could say she always worked." Our baby sitter is 40 years old. "Those days" for her were not so long ago. I realized after listening to her that my words to you this evening will not apply to all women. The subject addresses the lives of women who have a choice. And while in theory we all have choice, some of us have virtually none.[5]

Berne reminded the audience that having the privilege of choice superseded all the inherent difficulties associated with those choices. With that simple but emotional reminder, the audience was ready to openly and willingly listen to the choices she had confronted.

Emotional appeals are also useful for conclusions. Following is another excerpt from the speech by Janice Payan, in which she effectively used an emotionally charged appeal in her final remarks. After deploring the barriers resulting from racism and sexism, she challenged the Hispanic women in her audience to make their own opportunities:

Hispanic women in America have been victims of racism, sexism and poverty for a long, long time.

I know, because I was one of them. I also know that when you stop being a victim is largely up to you.

I don't mean you should run out of here, quit your job, divorce your husband, farm out your kids or run for President of the United States.

But I do mean that "whatever" you can dream, you can become.

A couple of years ago, I came across a poem by an Augsburg College student, Devoney K. Looser, which I want to share with you now.

I wish someone had taught me long ago
How to touch mountains
Instead of watching them from breath-takingly safe distances.
I wish someone had told me sooner
. . . .
I wish I had realized before today
That I can touch mountains
But now that I know, my fingers will never cease the climb.

Please, my sisters, never, ever, cease the climb. Adelante Mujer![6]

Humor

Humor is another excellent way to begin or end a speech. Of course, the material must be genuinely funny, and it must have something to do with the topic. Often known for his rather "wooden" appearances in front of a crowd, Vice President Al Gore faced the formidable role of opening speaker for the 1996 Democratic National Convention. Exaggerating the impression that he typically comes across as stiff and awkward, Gore deflected potential criticism from the media and the audience. After thanking the party delegates and television audience for the opportunity to serve alongside the president over the past four years, he began his speech this way:

Tradition holds that this speech be delivered tomorrow night. But President Clinton asked me to speak tonight. And you can probably guess the reason: My reputation for excitement.

The audience laughed and clapped in delight. He waited until the floor was almost quiet, and then he began again:

I've been watching the convention. I've seen you do the macarena. And if I could have your silence, I'd like to do the Al Gore version of the macarena.

In anticipation, the audience waited and then waited some more to see him perform. Nothing happened. Al Gore simply stood there. After what seemed an interminable pause, he continued:

Want to see me do it again?[7]

For the crowd of Democrats gathered together, Gore's humor worked: His self-deprecation was a welcome relief for those who feared a rather long, dry presentation. Notice how he waited to let the audience enjoy a good laugh before proceeding. That's good delivery!

Again, the humor must be relevant to the speech topic or purpose. Even though Gore's opening remarks had no relevance to the remainder of his speech, they set positive expectations for what was to follow. Following his humorous opening, Gore moved right into the accomplishments of the Clinton/Gore administration over the previous four years.

Using humor to both gain audience attention and provide a lead-in to his speech topic, Clyde Prestowitz, Jr., president of the Economic Strategy Institute, told this story in his introductory remarks before the Economic Club of Detroit. Notice how he preluded the tale by hinting at his topic in the very first line:

Some of the major problems underlying the U.S. economy are well illustrated by a recent story about the hiker in California who ate a condor, a protected species of bird. It seems the hiker was apprehended and taken before a judge, who sentenced him to life at hard labor. Before leaving the courtroom, however, the defendant asked the judge to listen to his side of the story because he felt there were exonerating circumstances. The hiker explained that he had been lost in the wilderness and had been hiking for three days and three nights without food or water, and just by chance had spotted this bird sitting on a rock, had thrown a rock at it, killed it and ate it, and then walked for three more days and three more nights before getting to civilization. Said the hiker, "If I hadn't eaten that bird, I wouldn't be alive to be here today." The judge responded by saying that those certainly were unusual circumstances and in view of the fact that the hiker's life had been in danger, he, the judge, would suspend the sentence. The defendant thanked him and began to leave the courtroom, but as he did the judge asked, "Oh, by the way, what did that condor taste like?" The hiker paused for a moment and then responded, "Well, it was kind of between a bald eagle and a spotted owl."[8]

Now that's a funny story! In the next few lines that immediately followed this story, Prestowitz led the audience right into his topic on economic policies in the United States:

The point is, you see, that the judge was operating on the basis of a false premise. He was assuming that he and the hiker adhered to similar premises and views about protected species. In the same way, the United States has been operating on a basis of three false premises for most of the past forty-five years with regard to economic policies.

The first false premise is . . .[9]

Similarly, take a look at the humorous story that Carl Hensley, a professor of speech communication at Bethel College, used when he spoke before a Kiwanis Club:

A woman went to an attorney and said, "I want to divorce my husband." Lawyer: Do you have any grounds? Woman: About 10 acres. Lawyer: Do you have a grudge? Woman: No, just a carport. Lawyer: Does your husband beat you up? Woman: No, I get up about an hour before he does every morning. Lawyer: Why do you want a divorce? Woman: We just can't seem to communicate.[10]

That story received a well-deserved belly laugh. But also notice how Hensley used his tale to address the purpose of his speech in the lines that immediately follow:

This woman's problem is not unique. Many husbands and wives, many parents and children, many managers and employees, many professionals and clients can't seem to communicate.

Why is this?

Why do so many intelligent, well-meaning people have trouble communicating?

Perhaps it's because they have a wrong idea of what communication is. Perhaps they base their communication on inadequate assumptions.[11]

So, not only are these stories funny, but each story has a point—a point that is directly relevant to the speech. And, just in case the audience fails to see that point, the speaker also tells the audience exactly how the tale relates to the topic.

Repetition

Repetition of a phrase adds rhythm to a speech and draws attention to the subject. Here's how First Lady Hillary Clinton relied on this strategy in her introductory remarks to celebrate International Women's Day:

. . . [W]hy should I or any American care about women in developing countries around the world? Why should women . . . be a concern of ours and our foreign policy here in the United States? Well, . . . if half of the world's citizens are undervalued, underpaid, undereducated, underrepresented, fed less, fed worse, not heard, put down, we cannot sustain the democratic values and the way of life we have come to cherish.[12]

Count the number of times Clinton used the word "under." Count the number of words or phrases that imply inequity. How effective would she have been in convincing audience members that they should extend their concern for women beyond the borders of the United States without this device? Consider this alternate version: "American women aren't the only ones who suffer from inequities. In the interest of a democratic society, women all over the world need our help." The message is essentially the same, but without repetition, without the rhythm of repetition, the audience would hear only unimaginative speech. As a result, audience reaction would be lacking. With repetition, the speaker invites the audience to focus on and become engaged in the speech.

Repetition was effectively employed by Farah Walters, president and CEO of University Hospitals of Cleveland, in the conclusion to her speech advocating national health care reform. She finished her presentation with these remarks:

Will it [health care reform plan] work?
  It will, if we allow it to.

> It will, if we are willing to listen to the voices of reason.
>
> It will, if we can accept a challenge.

She then asked:

> But do we have the national will and the national character to see it enacted?
>
> I hope so.
>
> I hope so, because it is the smart thing to do.
>
> I hope so, because it is the right thing to do.[13]

Once again, the repetitious phrases "it will" and "I hope so" evoke a powerful message. Without the cadence of repetition, the message would simply be, "I hope the plan will work." Clearly, something gets lost in the translation!

Famous Quotations

Relying on famous quotations and familiar sayings or borrowing phrases from famous speakers, politicians, and entertainers is another effective way to begin or end a presentation. Occasionally, a particular thought or phrase will capture a message precisely. Attorney General Janet Reno concluded a commencement address with a call for students to stand for what is right and good in this world with this quote:

> In another springtime, 33 years ago, the Reverend Martin Luther King, Jr. sat in a Birmingham jail, exhausted from years of seeking justice for all. He was dispirited, and now even some of his fellow ministers were saying he should back off and wait for progress to happen on its own. He must have struggled to keep cynicism out of his every thought, and sitting in that jail cell day after day, with progress coming slowly or not at all, he had to wonder why any man had a right to hope.
>
> But Reverend King made his choice. He began writing until his words filled the margins of a secondhand newspaper. The power of his choice flowed out of the pen, and into the conscience of America.
>
> Today, as you prepare to make your choices in life, I would like to close with a few of those words from Dr. King's letter from that Birmingham jail:
>
> "We must come to see that human progress never rolls in on wheels of inevitability. It comes through the tireless efforts and persistent work of men, willing to be co-workers with God, and without this hard work, time itself becomes an ally of the forces of social stagnation. We must use time creatively, and forever realize that the time is always right to do right."
>
> I hope and pray that you will make your choice the choice of standing for what is right and good in this world.[14]

Notice how Reno gave credit not to herself, but to the original source of that quote. It is important that speakers cite the sources for their quotes. Sometimes the source is unknown; notice how Douglas Leatherdale, chair and CEO for the St. Paul Companies, likewise made sure that credit was given not to him, but to some generalized "other" for the quote used in his speech on workers' compensation:

> As you study workers' compensation, three things become clear: The picture isn't pretty. The issues aren't simple. The answers aren't easy. But they merit our attention, understanding and action.
>
> As an old American proverb states, "The surest way to mishandle a problem is to avoid it."[15]

Sometimes direct quotes are paraphrased. Even then, credit should be given to the source of the paraphrased remarks. Consider how Joseph Nolan gave credit to David Brinkley in his introduction. Nolan, a visiting instructor at Flagler College, began his speech on the presidency and public opinion this way:

> Let me say at the outset how much I admire both your tolerance and stamina. For the past six months of the Presidential campaign, the air has been filled with speeches—and vice versa. Yet you are still game for another one.
>
> David Brinkley was saying recently he's worried that we may be approaching the point where we have more people willing to make speeches than we have people willing to listen to them. I earnestly pray that we will not reach that fateful point this morning.[16]

Startling Facts and Statistics

Facts and statistics that amaze, rather than bore, can entice an audience to respond, "Gee, whiz!" Julia Hughes Jones, state auditor of Arkansas, used the following little-known facts to highlight the significance of her speech delivered on the anniversary of women's suffrage in the United States:

> Many of you realize that suffrage means the right to vote, but it also implies the responsibility to vote.
>
> Why is a vote important? Many times, a single vote has changed the course of history. . . .
> - In 1776, one vote gave America the English language instead of German.
> - In 1845, one vote brought Texas and California into the Union.
> - In 1868 one vote saved President Andrew Johnson from impeachment.
> - In 1923 one vote determined the leader of a new political party in Munich. His name was Adolf Hitler.
> - In 1960, one vote changed in each precinct in Illinois would have defeated John F. Kennedy.[17]

Each of those amazing facts underscored her thesis that responsibility comes with the right to vote. Consider the startling statistic regarding audience attention spans that F. Robert Reilly, professor of sociology at Juniata College, used to begin his address:

> While doing some research for today's address, I stumbled onto . . . an article entitled, "Audience Reaction to Commencement Addresses and Similar Speeches: A Meta-analysis." The findings of this research suggest unequivocally that at any point during these kinds of presentations, only about 18 percent of the audience is actually paying attention to what is being said and that this 18 percent only really listens for about forty-five seconds at a time. Even more revealing is the expectation that fewer than 1 percent of the audience will remember any details about the address six months from the time of its delivery. On the one hand, I find some refuge in this state of affairs as it implies that no one will listen to me closely enough to hold me accountable for whatever I say. . . . The down side of this situation is that I have given considerable thought to the address I am about to give and I think it is well worth a good listen.[18]

Of course, no research statistics on human behavior are as "unequivocal" as Reilly suggests. And yet, these numbers might compel even the most reluctant members of the audience (hopefully more than 18 percent) to pay attention longer than 45 seconds!

Dramatic Illustrations

Beginning or concluding a presentation with a dramatic illustration or a story that paints a picture of the emotions a speaker wants to express and elicit from an audience is another effective rhetorical strategy. The more visual the experience, the more likely the audience will respond and remember the illustration. Faye Wattleton, president of Planned Parenthood, delivered this opening story:

> As I was preparing my remarks for today, I was reminded of a story about the great Renaissance artist Michelangelo, a famous statue, and a boy named Giovanni. Every day after school, Giovanni would rush to Michelangelo's studio to watch the famous sculptor chip away at a 14-foot-high block of marble. Week after week, the boy came and watched, as the magnificent form of David began to take shape. Finally, it was done. The boy was absolutely amazed by the transformation of a piece of stone into the beautiful David, and, in all innocence, he said to Michelangelo, "How did you know he was in there?"[19]

Wattleton went on to say that Michelangelo knew because he had a vision and he worked hard to make that vision a reality. Similarly, she recounted,

> seventy-five years ago, Margaret Sanger also had a vision—of a world in which women could enjoy their sexuality, control their reproduction, and take charge of their destinies.[20]

Thus, Wattleton helped her audience "see" Sanger's vision by comparing it to the vision and labors of the artist Michelangelo.

Jesse Jackson is another speaker who relies extensively on illustrations—along with personal stories, repetition, and the other attention-getting devices discussed in this section. Consider the illustrations Jackson used to visualize a rather abstract but important concept—caring for others:

> On a small Southern college campus, I once observed a lesson never to be forgotten. I saw a dwarf and a giant walking together—they were an odd couple. He was six feet three, she was three feet tall. When they reached the parting paths, they embraced. He handed her her books and she skipped down the path. It looked to be romantic. I asked the president—what is this I am seeing? He said, I thought you would ask. You see, that is his sister, in fact his twin sister. By a twist of fate he came out a giant, she a dwarf. All the big schools offered him athletic scholarships. The pros offered him money. But he said I can only go where my sister can go. And so he ended up here with us.
>
> Somewhere that young man learned ethics, caring for others. Few of us are driven by a tailwind. Most of us struggle with headwinds. Not all of us can be born tall; some are born short, motherless, abandoned, hungry, orphaned. Somebody has to care. It must be us. And if we do, we will win, and deserve to win. Keep hope alive.[21]

Not so incidentally, Jackson's speech, delivered at the Democratic National Convention, was received with wild applause. The image he evoked with his tale of the dwarf and the giant reminded audience members that like the giant, they needed to reach out and help others less fortunate. Once again, he could have simply said, "We can win this election if we just show that we care." But his illustration helped the audience visualize the problem, feel the need, and want to do something about it.

The preceding speech excerpts demonstrate a number of effective ways to begin and end a speech. (See the box "Strategies to Begin and End Your Speeches" for a summary.) In each example, the speaker was careful to entice and invite the audience to listen and to leave the audience believing in some cause or feeling

Strategies to Begin and End Your Speeches

Strategies That Work

- *Personal stories* help establish shared backgrounds and beliefs between speaker and audience.

- *Emotional appeals* help create empathy between speaker and audience.

- *Humor*, in the form of funny stories that are directly relevant to the speech topic, captures audience members' attention and puts them at ease.

- *Repetition* of phrases adds rhythm to the speech and draws attention to the subject.

- *Famous quotations* can capture the message a speaker wants to convey.

- *Startling facts* and statistics can amaze and entice the audience and underscore the speaker's main points.

- *Dramatic illustrations* visualize the emotions a speaker wants to elicit from the audience.

Strategies to Avoid

- *Overused clichés* detract from a speech because they are tiresome and trite.

- *Disclaimers and apologies* create a negative impression and make a speech seem less worthwhile.

- *Rhetorical questions*, when overused or used ineffectively, make a speaker appear tentative and lacking in conviction.

---

some emotion. Provoking thought, attention, and feeling requires that a speaker strategically plan both the opening and the closing of the speech.

STRATEGIES TO AVOID

Sometimes knowing what you should not do is just as important as knowing what you should do. This section examines briefly those techniques that seldom work in the introduction and conclusion of a speech. Unfortunately, you will recognize many of them—simply because they are so frequently used.

Overused Clichés

Clichés are trite phrases or expressions that are so common and overused that people cringe when they hear them. At one time, many "clichés" were probably effective as openers or closers. But because speakers relied on them so often, audiences began to view them as tiresome, unoriginal, and even annoying. Anything that's overused can also be perceived as being insincere or superficial. For each of the clichés listed here, a parenthetical translation has been provided to suggest what the audience might think the speaker *really* means. In the meantime, see if you can add to this list of overused clichés. The following clichés are commonly used to open a speech:

- "It's a pleasure to be here today." (Translation: "I don't want to be here.") Do audiences really believe that—particularly if the speaker seems

anxious or nervous? And, if they have reason to believe it, isn't that opening just a little unoriginal?

- "Good evening, ladies and gentlemen." (Translation: "Hi. I'm formal," or, "I don't know how else to begin.") This greeting may be appropriate for some very formal occasions, but it's also pretty dull. Hopefully, this opening isn't a sign of what's to come.

Or consider the following lines commonly used to close a speech:

- "Thank you for listening." (Translation: "I know I bored you; I'm just grateful you were so polite and patient with me.") Effective speakers won't need to thank the audience; instead, the audience will thank the speaker for a delightful, interesting, and profound presentation.

- "Well, that's it. Any questions?" (Translation: "I'm done. Can I go home now?") On the surface, asking the audience for feedback may seem to be a good idea. A closer look, however, reveals that the speaker is really hoping there won't be any questions after all. Immediately following this question, the speaker is likely to leave the stage—quickly, before the audience has a chance to respond.

Disclaimers and Apologies

Disclaimers are used to deny any responsibility for a faulty presentation. Up front, the speaker warns audience members that they should not expect too much. And later on, the speaker reminds them that this is all they're going to get. With apologies, the speaker assumes total responsibility (and much regret) for doing a bad job or for having nothing further to contribute. Both apologies and disclaimers are used to set up the audience for a failed presentation. Consider these commonly used disclaimers and apologies:

- "I'm not much of a speaker." (Translation: "This speech won't be worth your time and attention.") What audience is willing to sit still after hearing that opening? The speaker who begins with this confession probably won't need to tell the audience how awful he or she is as a performer—the audience will discover it soon enough.

- "Can I start over? I'm so nervous." (Translation: "Don't expect much.") A speaker who announces to the audience that she or he is nervous assigns blame for the potential failure to some psychological cause that everyone will identify with. In other words, with this disclaimer, the speaker expects the audience to be kind and sympathetic. After all, it could happen to anyone. While a sympathetic response may, in fact, result, the audience is also likely to perceive the speaker as being less credible and less competent overall.

- "That's all I have to say." (Translation: "That's all I know about the subject.") This line fails to leave the audience with much of a gee-whiz response. It is an apology for not being more capable and competent, and it can make an audience wonder how or why that particular speaker was selected to talk at all.

Rhetorical Questions

Rhetorical questions are those questions a speaker asks an audience without expecting an actual response. Instead, the speaker answers the question for the audience and presumes that the audience will agree. Consider these rhetorical questions:

"What are we going to do about crime in America?"

"Is God dead?"

"Who will help the hungry and the sick?"

In each example, the audience is not expected to answer the question; instead, the speaker will. Indeed, rhetorical questions can be very effective at motivating the audience to listen or to feel, but when overused or trite, they make the speaker appear to be tentative and to lack conviction. Consider these questions:

"Nice day, isn't it?" (Does the speaker really expect the audience to disagree or agree in unison aloud?)

"How many of you think we need to do something about the deficit?" (Does the speaker really expect a show of hands?)

"Doesn't equal opportunity apply to *all* people?" (It would be un-American for anyone to answer in the negative.)

Fortunately, rhetorical questions can be reframed easily as assertive, declarative statements. Consider the powerful impact of these six reframed rhetorical questions:

"We must do something about crime in America. We can no longer wait."

"God is not dead. God is alive and living among us today."

"We will help the hungry. We will help the sick."

"What a glorious day for a college graduation!"

"Either we pay now or our children will pay later!"

"Equal opportunity is a constitutional right for all people living in America today."

Compared to rhetorical questions, assertions have greater power to drive a point home. Assertions also suggest that a speaker is confident and determined.

Obviously, some rhetorical questions, some overused clichés, and even some disclaimers can be effective in opening or closing a speech. For the most part, however, you should try another approach. Examine carefully the effective strategies suggested earlier. Try using humor, revealing a personal story, relying on a famous quotation, or startling your audience with a little-known fact or statistic. You may be surprised at the effect!

CHAPTER REVIEW

- How you begin and end your speech is critical to gaining audience interest and attention. Your speech introduction should (1) establish your credibility, (2) give your audience a reason to listen, and (3) provide a preview of what will follow. Your conclusion should (1) briefly summarize your major points and (2) leave the audience interested and wanting to hear more.

- You can use a number of tried-and-true strategies to begin and conclude your speech. Those that help motivate the audience include personal stories, emotional appeals, humor that is relevant to your subject, repetition, famous quotations, startling facts or statistics, and dramatic illustrations.

- Just as some strategies work, other strategies do not. Avoid used and abused clichés that come across as tiresome or insincere. Disclaimers and apologies do nothing to motivate an audience. And, finally, remove excessive rhetorical questions from your presentation or reword them as forceful assertions.

QUESTIONS FOR CRITICAL THINKING & REVIEW

1. Speech outlines always include an attention-getter and a preview in the introduction. In this chapter, you are reminded that another introduction objective is to establish credibility. Why, then, isn't credibility included on your speech outline? Provide a rationale.

2. To compel your audience members to listen, you want to give them a reason for listening. Assuming your audience is made up of 18- to 23-year-olds, what list of audience-centered reasons can you generate for the speech topic of retirement?

3. Why are signposts important to use in a speech preview?

4. Previews, as a rule, tend to be direct and explicit (that is, low context). How can a high-context speaker use a preview in a way that is consistent with his or her more indirect and implicit style?

5. This chapter claims that rhetorical questions are often overused and far too predictable; however, that doesn't mean they should never be used. When are rhetorical questions particularly useful or appropriate in a speech?

NOTES

1. Quinn, S. (1997). *The party: A guide to adventurous entertaining*. New York: Simon & Schuster.
2. Payan, J. (1990, September 1). Opportunities for Hispanic women: It's up to us. *Vital Speeches of the Day*, 697.
3. Belknap, J. (1991, March 1). Racism on campus: Prejudice plus power. *Vital Speeches of the Day*, 308.
4. Buchholz, T. G. (1992, April 15). Teaching virtue: The grim attack on American tales. *Vital Speeches of the Day*, 397.
5. Berne, R. W. (1990, November 1). Keeping our balance in the 90's: Women at work, women at home. *Vital Speeches of the Day*, 55.
6. Payan, 1990, p. 700.
7. Gore, A. (1996, August 28). Remarks at the 1996 Democratic National Convention. Online. Text Transcript. Available: http://www.dncc96.org/day3/gore0828.html.
8. Prestowitz, C., Jr. (1992, September 1). In search of survival: Why haven't we done anything? *Vital Speeches of the Day*, 698.
9. Prestowitz, 1992, p. 698.
10. Hensley, C. W. (1992, December 1). What you share is what you get: Tips for effective communication. *Vital Speeches of the Day*, 115.
11. Hensley, 1992, p. 115.
12. Clinton, H. (1997, March 12). Remarks by the First Lady: International Women's Day. Online. General Speeches. Available: http://www.whitehouse.gov/WH/EOP/First Lady/html/general speeches/1997/africa.htm.
13. Walters, F. M. (1993, September 1). "If it's broke, fix it": The significance of health care reform in America. *Vital Speeches of the Day*, 691.
14. Reno, J. (1996, May 3). Keynote address: University of South Carolina spring commencement. Online. Gifts of Speech. Available: http://gos.sbc.edu/r/reno/html.
15. Leatherdale, D. W. (1992, December 15). The workers' compensation dilemma: An insurer's perspective. *Vital Speeches of the Day*, 151.
16. Nolan, J. (1993, January 15). The presidency and public opinion: Communicate to the American people. *Vital Speeches of the Day*, 218.
17. Jones, J. H. (1992, December 1). A greater voice in action: Women and equality. *Vital Speeches of the Day*, 109.
18. Reilly, F. R. (1992, September 1). The erosion of trust: Better days. *Vital Speeches of the Day*, 696.
19. Wattleton, F. (1992, June 15). Planned parenthood and pro choice: Sexual and reproductive freedom. *Vital Speeches of the Day*, 524.
20. Wattleton, 1992, p. 525.
21. Jackson, J. L. (1992, August 15). Democratic National Convention: The moral center. *Vital Speeches of the Day*, 654.

Chapter 11

SPEAKING TO INFORM

As president of the Republic of Ireland, Mary Bourke Robinson provided the keynote address to the International Conference on Hunger.[1] Although the agenda of the conference was very diverse, Robinson wanted to inform (if not remind) participants of a single overriding issue: "the growing gap—not simply between rich and poor—but between the idea of hunger and the fact of it."

Her basic format for informing her audience included an introduction, a body, and a conclusion. The actual structuring and polishing of the final speech was heavily influenced not only by her general knowledge about world hunger but also by the historical fact that famine had devastated her homeland 150 years ago. Speaking before a rather sophisticated international audience, Robinson nevertheless packaged her thesis in clear, specific, and concrete terms. "Let me give you, right away," she explained, "an example of the fact of hunger and its companion circumstance which is poverty. And let me put that against the idea of it." She began with this fact: "In 1993, we are informed, more than 12 million children under the age of five died in the developing world. This is in itself a terrible fact." She went on to lament that $11\frac{1}{2}$ million of them could have been spared "if those children had the same access to health care and nutrition as the modern Irish child does." The idea of hunger must become a reality to all of us, she claimed, if we are truly going to do something about it.

Robinson struggled to make her audience narrow their gap of understanding between some abstract, remote idea of hunger and the horrible, unnecessary reality of it. She relied on a variety of techniques to drive her point home and to ensure understanding. For instance, she used the tactics of repetition and redundancy, frequently reminding the audience of the idea/reality gap. Although she cited statistics for support, she kept them brief and simple so as not to overwhelm or distract her audience. Referring to historical examples from the Irish famine, she provided concrete illustrations of otherwise abstract, theoretical points and themes.

Successful in her presentation, Robinson was confident that everyone in the audience would begin the conference with a clearer understanding of the single issue that brought them all together. What the participants would do to resolve that issue, however, remained.

Although you may never have to formally present information to an international audience, you will probably have to give informative speeches in class, at work, and perhaps within your community. This chapter gives you the strategies to inform a large group effectively.

Learning Objectives

After reading this chapter, you should be able to do the following:

1. Differentiate among the three goals of informative speaking.

2. List and give examples of the four types of informative speeches.

3. Organize and outline an informative speech.

4. Identify and incorporate strategies to make your speech easily understood by your audience.

GOALS AND TYPES OF INFORMATIVE SPEECHES

Informative speaking is often equated with teaching an audience to think about something in a new or different way. For such thinking to result, some kind of learning must also occur. The learning process, then, must involve changes in the audience's *factual* beliefs about some topic or issue. Accordingly, as defined in Chapter 2, an informative speech is a public presentation designed to change audience members' factual beliefs (the way they think) about a topic or an issue.

An informative speech provides new information or helps the audience view an issue in a different way. Often, however, a persuasive speech does the same thing; that is, speakers try to persuade their audiences by providing more information. What, then, is the difference between informing and persuading? In a nutshell, informing teaches; persuading advocates. Mary Bourke Robinson intended to inform or remind her audience that children continue to die every day from hunger—not to persuade them to give money or consume fewer resources or provide agricultural technology. Similarly, a speaker urging his audience to practice safe sex or abstinence intends to persuade. The same speaker describing various ways to practice safe sex intends to inform.

Sometimes the distinction is subtle, but the speaker's overriding intent should be clear. Notice in the preceding examples that the speaker determines that intent. When you prepare your own speeches, specify your intent in your purpose statement. Determine first and foremost if your motive is to persuade or to inform your audience.

Goals of Informative Speaking
Speaking to inform emphasizes one of three goals: (1) to communicate new and unfamiliar information to an uninformed audience, (2) to extend what the audience already knows, or (3) to update old information about a topic or issue. Figure 11-1 gives examples of each of these goals.

Communicating New and Unfamiliar Information We are constantly exposed to new and unfamiliar information. There are so many things to comprehend and learn about new topics. Consider the following situations: being diagnosed with a previously unknown bacterial infection, finding a new vegetable at the grocery store, or having to take a car in for its first engine overhaul. These kinds of situations require us to think differently—to learn—about the topic or issue. The information we receive from the doctor, the grocer, or the mechanic will be the basis of our new knowledge and, thus, of our new set of factual beliefs.

The doctor, grocer, and mechanic are similar to the public speaker who presents new information to an uninformed audience. For example, consumer advocates inform the public about the harmful effects of pesticides, the dangers of prescription drugs, and the nutritional content of certain foods; TV news reporters make nightly informative presentations about political corruption, corporate takeovers, and international affairs. The point is, many kinds of public speakers communicate new information to audiences all the time.

Extending What the Audience Already Knows Public speakers also inform by communicating information that extends what an audience already knows about some topic or issue. For example, many professional public speakers make presentations about such topics as traveling, sports, politics, and cooking. In their initial presentations, they may communicate new information for audience members who are unfamiliar with the subject matter, but in subsequent presentations, they provide information that adds to what the interested audience already knows. A good example is political commentators who follow elected officials from speech

COMMUNICATING NEW OR UNFAMILIAR INFORMATION	EXTENDING WHAT THE AUDIENCE ALREADY KNOWS	UPDATING OLD INFORMATION
Alcohol consumption is bad for your health.	Even minimal amounts of alcohol can impair your senses.	New research indicates that alcohol can be good for your health: Moderate amounts can protect against heart attacks.
Human beings evolved over time from apelike ancestors.	Humans have walked the earth for over 3 million years.	Recent discoveries reveal that humanlike creatures walked the earth some 4.4 million years ago.
Illegal immigration is a big problem for California, Texas, and Florida.	Denying schooling to children of illegal immigrants is unconstitutional (U.S. Supreme Court, 1982).	We used to say, "Give us your tired, your poor, and your hungry." Today, a majority of Americans want to seriously restrict immigration.

Figure 11-1 Three general goals of informative speaking. Most informative speeches are designed to change audience members' factual beliefs about a topic or issue.

to speech and give their follow-up evaluations in the form of mediated public presentations.

Updating Old Information

Public speakers can also bring a new perspective to a topic by reinterpreting or updating what an audience already knows or believes. Correcting misconceptions or revealing the latest research that alters what the audience might already believe or know is an important part of effective informative speaking. Most of us can't keep up with the information explosion. What we think we know and what we believe about many topics may be outdated according to more recent information. Informative speakers help us update the way we think about a variety of important issues.

For example, the medical community has informed us for decades that most stomach ulcers are stress related and that drinking milk can ease the associated pain when other prescribed medication is unavailable. Based on current research and thinking, however, the medical community now tells us that stomach ulcers are caused by a particular stomach bacteria and that milk worsens the discomfort by increasing the level of acidity. Another good example of updating old information is the current thinking on weight lifting. Historically, bodybuilders focused on working out with weights and placed only secondary importance on diet as it related to muscle development. Contemporary research suggests that lifting weights is important but that a high-protein, low-fat diet is also instrumental in building lean muscle mass. Fitness experts inform today's audiences about building muscle by updating such old information.

Types of Informative Speeches

As Figure 11-2 shows, informative presentations typically fall into one of four categories: briefings (reports), lectures, demonstrations, and training presentations. Each speech type emphasizes one informative goal over the others. Informative presentations occur daily in various settings—in the classroom, at work, in the community. The types of informative presentations often overlap, but recognizing the unique characteristics of each type can help you speak more effectively.

Briefings and Reports

A **briefing**, or **report**, is an informative speech designed to provide recently available information to an audience with a general understanding of the topic. Briefings are delivered frequently and in every public and private sector of

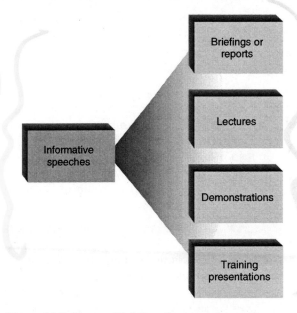

Figure 11-2 Types of informative speeches. Most informative speeches fall into one of four categories. The primary goal of all informative speeches is to teach audiences something.

society—between and within groups and also across organizations. Briefings can be short or long, but they typically run 10 to 15 minutes. Formal briefings often use a visual aid known as a "briefing chart," in which the points and subpoints of the speech are organized and listed in sequence. (Briefing charts and other visual aids are described in detail in Chapter 17.) Examples of briefings include the following:

- A business planner presents a strategic plan to corporate executives.
- A marketing manager briefs a CEO on an advertising campaign.
- A group of supervisors brief their manager on worker productivity during a monthly status meeting.
- An employee informally updates her boss about a particular project.

Lectures

A **lecture** is an instructional presentation that typically provides new or additional information about a subject. Lectures can be straightforward informative speeches, but they can also entertain. Good teachers recognize that their lectures are a type of informative speech, and they use public speaking skills to make their teaching more effective. Lecturers, however, are not always professional teachers, and lectures can be found beyond the confines of the traditional

Skip

classroom. President Mary Bourke Robinson's keynote address to the International Conference on Hunger is an example of a lecture outside the classroom. Other examples include the following:

- A lobbyist talks with a group of students about what it is like to work in politics.
- A police officer talks about home safety at a condominium association meeting.
- A nutritionist discusses family nutritional needs at a PTA meeting in a school gymnasium.
- An accountant gives a presentation on local TV about budgeting for retirement.

Lectures are normally longer than briefings. Depending on the topic and the time available, a lecture can last several hours, although one hour is the average duration. Lectures are often more flexible than other types of informative speeches. Many lecturers invite questions and comments from the audience, so lectures must be open to change.

Demonstrations A **demonstration** is a how-to speech that provides information about doing a particular activity or using a specific object. Demonstration speeches typically last a few minutes; any longer than that and the demonstration may appear too complicated or overwhelming. Examples of informative demonstrations include how to train a cat, how to make chocolate chip cookies, and how to use a crescent wrench. Demonstration speeches can take place in a variety of settings:

- A student demonstrates card tricks in the classroom.
- An employee demonstrates how to use an electric pasta maker in a cooking equipment store.
- A sales representative demonstrates the features of a new athletic shoe at a sports equipment trade show.

Training Presentations A **training presentation** teaches a concept or instructs listeners how to complete a task with an acceptable degree of accuracy.

A briefing is an informative speech designed to provide recently available information to an audience with a general understanding of the topic. Leaders, managers, and administrators in industry, education, and politics all use the briefing format to inform their audiences.

194

Training presentations are similar to lectures in that instruction is the primary goal—new or additional information is provided to help the audience learn. But training presentations differ from lectures because they almost always involve adult learners in industrial or organizational environments. Moreover, the audience for a training presentation (that is, employees) is typically required to attend—and to learn.

Training presentations can be technical or nontechnical. In a nontechnical training presentation, the speaker presents information to employees in a conference room or other meeting area. These presentations can last a few minutes or be broken into several sessions over a week. Nearly every conceivable topic of importance in the workplace can be presented as a nontechnical training presentation. Consider the following examples:

- A personnel director describes payroll and benefits procedures to a group of new employees.
- A finance director describes a new retirement plan to all eligible employees.

Technical training presentations are designed to teach employees how to perform a particular task with a given level of competence (evaluated in terms of quality or speed of performance). Technical training presentations are highly structured around specific content in order to increase training success. In fact, people who run technical training sessions usually receive rigorous instruction before they train others. Topics of technical training sessions include the following:

- How to solder, weld, and wire a transformer
- How to repair a vending machine
- How to sew collars and sleeves into dress shirts
- How to program a computer

ORGANIZING AND OUTLINING AN INFORMATIVE SPEECH

You might think that informing people in any of the ways just described can't be all that difficult. After all, it's merely a matter of telling them what they need to know—and once they hear it, they will know it. Unfortunately, it's not that simple. Because an informative speaker often has only one chance to explain and the audience has only one chance to comprehend, it is critical that an informative speech be constructed in a way that maximizes its effectiveness.

A Basic Format for Informing

Virtually every informative speech—from a classroom lecture to a televised public service announcement—relies on the same basic plan. All organized informative speeches, whether structured linearly or configurally, have some kind of identifiable introduction, body, and conclusion (see Chapter 9). In this sense, they are not much different from term papers or written reports. With this approach to organizing an informative speech, you always begin with opening and introductory statements, followed by main points and supporting materials, and you always reach a conclusion that includes a summary. In other words, every speech designed to inform follows an ancient pedagogical formula: First, tell them what you're going to tell them; then tell them; and, finally, tell them what you've just told them!

Introduction As described in Chapter 10, the introduction should compel your audience to listen by including some kind of attention-getter and by previewing what's to come. Gaining and holding attention is obviously important. How will your audience members learn or comprehend what you have to offer if they don't pay attention or, worse, are bored and disinterested?

There are many ways to capture audience attention; some work better than others. You might open your speech with a dramatic story, a humorous anecdote, or some other effective motivating strategy, as described in Chapter 10. But remember that your attention-getting opener should be relevant to the topic. For example, one student, Yanmin, used a knock-knock joke to begin her classroom presentation. The previous speakers had all chosen the same topic—abortion. So, Yanmin began by saying, "Knock! Knock!" The audience played along by asking in chorus, "Who's there?" "Orange," Yanmin replied. "Orange who?" the audience countered. "Orange you glad I'm *not* going to talk about abortion?" Audience members laughed, and when they quieted down, they were ready to listen. Yanmin had obtained her initial goal of getting their attention. Unfortunately, the effect did not last. When she switched gears and began talking about her main theme—the different ways that color communicates meanings—her audience tuned out. Yanmin would have been better off using an attention-getter more directly related to her topic. A revised version of Yanmin's speech outline appears later in this chapter; in it, you'll find a more effective attention-getter for her speech, one that would arouse audience members' curiosity about the topic and make them eager to hear her speech.

Once you have the audience's attention, you should provide a brief preview of your speech. The preview usually includes the thesis statement and an overview of the main points. After completing your preview, you're ready to move on to the body of your speech.

Body Because most informative classroom speeches are allotted five to ten minutes, you must restrict the main points covered in the body of your presentation. Most short speeches focus on no more than two or three main points. The same is true for longer speeches; too much information organized around too many points usually results in information overload, which, for the audience, translates into confusion, incoherence, and, ultimately, boredom. Therefore, you need to be very selective when you consider the major points to be addressed.

The main points in an informative speech need to be arranged in a meaningful order. You should choose a linear or configural organizational scheme (see Chapter 9) that suits your topic, purpose, and audience. Don't be overly concerned about creating a rigid organizational pattern; research on informative speeches organized in different ways demonstrates that unless a speech is wildly disorganized, listeners can interpret and understand the information just fine.[2] Keep in mind one important rule: The organizational scheme you select should help your audience make sense of your message.

Once your main points and organizational pattern are set, you need to flesh out your skeleton with facts, explanations, and examples. The supporting materials you gathered earlier can now be put to good use. Identify which main point each piece of supporting material fits, and locate each accordingly as subpoints. Your main points are set forth in the preview as assertions; your evidence and personal experiences document your assertions and help maintain your credibility. Keep in mind that choosing a variety of evidence can help you appeal to audience members of different co-cultures.

Conclusion Your informative speech should include a carefully crafted conclusion. Once you've covered all the relevant facts, you need to wrap things up. At this point in the speech, you do not want to add any new information. As described in Chapter 10, in your conclusion, you should provide a succinct review of your main points and then sign off.

Keep your concluding remarks brief. A typical conclusion for a five-minute informative speech should only take about 30 to 40 seconds; for an hour-long speech, four or five minutes. If the conclusion drags on, people may start looking at their watches, fidgeting, putting on their coats, and so on.

Be dramatic in your conclusion. You may want to use a clever quotation or a brief but relevant story. Or you may want to hook up with your opening remarks in some creative way. To be effective, your conclusion should jolt your audience and leave them wanting to hear more. (In the box "Interview with a Student: Kristi Toma," one student describes how she put together her informative speech.)

 SPEAKING OUT

Interview with a Student

Kristi Toma

Kristi Toma, 18, is a first-year student at California State University, Long Beach, majoring in business administration.

For your first assigned informative speech, we asked you to select one of your co-cultures and tell us about it. Describe how you selected and then narrowed your topic.

I began by making a list of all the co-cultures that I belong to. From there, I selected one, Japanese American. Then I made another list of all the things about that co-culture that I thought would be relevant. I picked three major points from that list that would be both entertaining for my audience and something in

which I could use myself as a source. When preparing a speech, you are your own best source.

What was your purpose statement?

On the outline, my purpose statement read: "The purpose of my speech is to inform the audience of the similarities, differences, and lifestyles of members in my co-culture." Thinking about it later, however, my purpose was to show the audience that they shouldn't rely solely on stereotypes to describe people who represent one culture or another. The title of my speech was "My Life as a Japanese American." I wanted to show them that I was a lot

Interview with a Student   (Continued)

like the stereotype of a Japanese American girl, but I was also a lot different from that stereotype.

What attention-gaining device did you use? If you had to do it over again, what device would you use now?

Asking questions at the beginning of my speech was my attention-getter. I asked the audience if being a part of a certain co-culture means that you necessarily share all of the same characteristics of that culture. I tried to get people thinking about what I would be talking about later on. After listening to other speeches over the semester, though, I think I would instead use a personal story to get people interested in my topic and get them to relate.

How did you go about selecting your major points?

I started by brainstorming and making clusters of ideas. When I finished brainstorming, I picked the main points I could talk most about. I only selected three because I knew that any more would make the speech too long.

What examples and illustrations did you use to make your speech familiar and relevant to your audience?

To show how I was similar to other Japanese Americans, I told them that as a child, I was always taught to respect my elders because they are wiser than me. To show how I was different from

the stereotypes, I told the audience that some students in Japan commit suicide because they didn't get into the college that their parents wanted them to. I was always told to try my best in school, and even though I never got straight A's, my parents were always proud. My parents never pushed me to study. They didn't make me stay home and study every night.

For that same speech, what memorable conclusion did you use?

After summarizing my main points, I ended my speech with a statement that would get my audience thinking about my speech even when I wasn't around. I concluded by saying, "I hope I did not give you the idea that I am not proud of my co-culture. The truth is, I am proud to be a Japanese American, and I hope all of you can honestly say that you are proud of all your co-cultures as well."

What kind of response did you receive from your audience? Do you think they liked your presentation? Why?

I think they did because they thought about their own co-culture and the stereotypes they had to live with. I left my audience comparing themselves to the stereotypes of their co-cultures. In my speech, I told them that not everyone in a co-culture is exactly alike.

SAMPLE SPEECH OUTLINE

Color Me Blue

Specific Purpose: To inform my audience about some intriguing, little-known facts about how and what color communicates about us

Yanmin's clever speech title captures the essence of what she will say. Although she is unlikely to announce the title of her speech, it may be needed by the person introducing her or for a printed announcement of her presentation.

Placing her purpose statement at the top of the outline helps Yanmin clearly identify her goal and keep it in mind as she organizes the rest of her speech.

Continued

Thesis Statement: Color tells a lot about who we are, our personalities, where we're from, our educational and socioeconomic background, and even how we feel on a given day.

Yanmin's thesis statement provides a concise summary of the central message of her speech.

INTRODUCTION

Attention-Getter: Show two different shades of red, and ask audience members to indicate their preference for each. Then tell them that according to color research experts, most men will choose the red with a yellow tone while most women will choose the blue-based red.

Yanmin's attention-getting strategy gets audience members personally involved in her topic and piques their curiosity.

Preview: We know that color can tell a lot about us, including our gender, where we live, even our personality type. Today I want to share with you some little-known but important facts about *how* and *what* color communicates. We all use colors every day, but we may not realize what they communicate. So, let's take a closer look at how color influences our lives. First, we'll look at how each of the primary colors communicates different moods and feelings. Next, we'll examine what our favorite colors say about who we are.

Yanmin's preview lets her audience know what she plans to talk about and introduces her two main points.

BODY

I. Each primary color communicates a different mood or feeling.

   A. We know that people are affected a great deal by color.
      1. A color researcher, Birren, discovered that human beings react 12 percent faster when they see red traffic lights, and they react much slower when they see green traffic lights.
      2. Another researcher, Knapp, reports that a city jail in Oregon was painted soft colors, pastel pinks and blues, in order to have a calming effect on the inmates. It seemed to work.

   B. Studies show that people are able to identify certain moods with individual colors.
      1. Red = Arousing, stimulating
      2. Blue = Secure, comfortable
      3. Black = Powerful, strong
      4. Orange = Distressed, upset
      5. Purple = Dignified, stately
      6. Green and Blue = Calm, peaceful
      7. Yellow = Cheerful, joyful

II. Our favorite colors say a lot about who we are.

   A. Geographic region
      1. Southern, warm climates = White or bright colors
      2. Temperate climates = Grayed or neutral colors
      3. West or Midwest U.S. = Warm and neutral colors
      4. Green or flat areas = Cool and neutral tones

The body of Yanmin's speech is divided into two main points; these are labeled with Roman numerals I and II. She utilizes a linear topical organizational pattern for her speech.

Yanmin enhances her credibility by supporting her points with relevant research findings. She lets the audience know that these ideas are all based on research studies.

Specific examples help make Yanmin's speech more concrete and compelling for her audience. She could use visual aids to show audience members each color as she describes it.

Again, visual aids could help Yanmin's audience see and feel the connections between color and geography, personality, and demography.

B. Personality type: Look at the predominant colors in your wardrobe.
 1. Red = Extroverted, impulsive, sensual
 2. Blue = Highly educated, cultured, introverted
 3. Yellow = Philosophical, compulsive, intellectual, confident
 4. Orange = Friendly, extroverted, athletic
 5. Green = Fair, respectable, frank, wants to impress
 6. Black = Vain, sophisticated, worldly
 7. Brown = Earthy, conscientious, shrewd, dependable
 8. White = Simple, decent, flirtatious
C. Demographic characteristics
 1. Loud color preferences with a lot of variety = Low educational attainment, younger, lower socioeconomic status
 2. Subtle, delicate colors with little contrast = High educational attainment, older, higher socioeconomic status

CONCLUSION

Summary: Color communicates a variety of different moods and feelings, ranging from the calming effects of pastels, blue, and green to distress signals associated with the color orange. Our favorite colors, the colors we wear most often, the colors we use to decorate our homes, can tell a lot about us—including where we're from, our personality types, and how much money we make!

Memorable Closing Statement: Go home; take a look in your closet. What's the predominant color? What does that say about you? Take a look at your living room or bedroom. What do the colors in each room communicate about you to others? Do the colors communicate a secure, comfortable environment? Or do the colors in your home seem to communicate a sense of strength, dignity, or, perhaps, peace? If you had to pick a color for yourself, what color would you want it to be?

The conclusion begins with a summary and finishes with a gee-whiz ending. In her summary, Yanmin reinforces the central idea of her speech. Her closing questions are designed to involve audience members in her topic and make it personally relevant to them.

REFERENCES

Birren, R. (1965). *Color psychology and color therapy*. New York: University Books.
 Compton, N. H. (1962). Personal attributes of color and design preferences in clothing fabrics. *Journal of Psychology, 54,* 191–195.
 Knapp, M. L. (1978). *Nonverbal communication.* New York: Holt, Rinehart & Winston.
 Richmond, V. P., & McCroskey, J. C. (1995). *Nonverbal behavior in interpersonal relations* (pp. 165–166). Boston: Allyn & Bacon.
 Wexner, L. B. (1954). The degree to which colors (hues) are associated with mood-tones. *Journal of Applied Psychology, 38,* 432–435.

The reference list includes sources that Yanmin used in her speech. Although she used others in the earlier stage of gathering material, she lists only those sources that are included as evidence in her speech text. Sources are written in APA style.

Outlining the Informative Speech

A detailed outline for your speech is mandatory. Although legend has it that President Abraham Lincoln jotted only a few notes on the back of an envelope for his Gettysburg Address, like most great speakers, he actually relied on a carefully drafted set of notes. Your outline should follow the format described in Chapter 9. The sample outline that follows includes all the appropriate elements and illustrates many of the important principles of informative speaking.

SIX STRATEGIES FOR INFORMING

Some of the findings of instructional communication and education research have been condensed to provide six practical strategies that you can use to inform your audiences efficiently and successfully.[3] Whenever possible, this section also provides some perspective regarding the influence of co-culture as it applies to each strategy.

Keep It Simple

The fewer points your speech presents, the more likely your audience will learn them. Similarly, excessive statistical details, long lists, and too many subpoints turn people off. Thus, every aspect of your presentation—your reasoning, illustrations, explanations, and definitions—should be brief and easy to understand. Keep in mind that an audience rarely gets the opportunity to ask a speaker to back up. The keep-it-simple strategy applies to audiences of all types, sizes, and co-cultures and is especially important when presenting information that is new or totally different from what the audience knows.

Keep It Concrete

The more abstract your issues are and the more theoretical your explanations, the less likely your audience will comprehend the message. Thus, avoid abstract explanations. For instance, suppose you were going to talk about reliability in measurement. You could say that reliability refers to the "test-retest consistency of a measure" and that "reliability is essential to validity," and so on, just the way actual researchers discuss the term. Such an approach is not wrong, but it might put your audience to sleep.

A much better approach would be to explain the idea using everyday, concrete illustrations. For example, you might demonstrate the concept by asking your audience, "When you step on a brand new scale to weigh yourself, aren't you tempted to step on it again a second or even a third time?" By suggesting that wanting to make sure that a scale provides a "reliable" estimate of weight—that it consistently yields the same results every time—is a common consideration, you illustrate your idea with a concrete example. This need for concrete examples applies to all audiences.

Be Repetitive and Redundant

Repetition and redundancy are two different techniques. **Repetition** involves referring to something the same way over and over again. **Redundancy** involves explaining something more than once

but in a slightly different way each time. Notice the repeated phrases (italicized) in the following example. Even the word ending "ism" is a repetitive device.

> When *prejudice* is based on *gender, it's called "sexism."* When it's based on *age, it's called "ageism."* When it's based on *race, it's called "racism."* When it's based on *an attitude of superiority, it's called "ethnocentrism."*

Using the same idea, notice how redundancy can be substituted for repetition:

> All kinds of prejudices exist, including sexism, ageism, racism, and homophobia. For each type, the prejudice relies on some kind of characteristic about the individual. Prejudices against specific races, women, the elderly, and gays and lesbians all thrive in society today.

The first and last sentences of this example are not repetitive; instead, they phrase the various types of prejudices in slightly different ways.

Both repetition and redundancy are extremely important strategies to ensure that an audience remembers certain points. Each is used for different purposes. Repetition is essential for remembering lists of simple but important concepts. For example, many adults mentally rehearse their ABCs in the exact order when they look up a word in a dictionary or a name in the telephone book. Redundancy helps audiences remember more complex ideas and arguments. Because an audience hears a speech only once, it is important to build in some degree of redundancy with the old formula: Tell audience members what you're going to tell them (introduction); then tell them (body); and, finally, tell them what you told them (conclusion). The same general ideas are expressed in each part but in a slightly different way.

You can also provide additional examples to support or explain your topic. Repeat key definitions, extend explanations, or review main points and connect them to subsequent points. Without repetition and redundancy, your audience may fail to understand or simply miss key issues and explanations.

Repetition and redundancy are especially important for audiences made up of nonnative English speakers. Such audiences may have difficulty perceiving or interpreting your message. Similarly, if you employ a dialect or an accent different from that of your audience, you may want to capitalize on this strategy to prevent audience members from having trouble deciphering your message. You will minimize potential misinterpretations by repeating key words and phrases and by varying the way you explain your ideas. Both techniques will help you increase listener comprehension.

Elicit Active Responses

One way to increase understanding and retention is to stimulate your audience to do something in an open and public way. This ancient technique was used by church leaders and educators for centuries in the form of "responsive reading": The teacher or church official would read aloud one passage from some book or from scriptures, and the students or congregation would read aloud the next passage in unison.

You can use a number of techniques for eliciting **active responses** during your informative speech. Merely asking the audience a question is insufficient; in most circumstances, the audience will assume that the question is rhetorical and wait politely for you to supply the answer. Instead, you might begin by asking for a show of hands in response to some question. At a more interactive level, you might say, "Teen pregnancy is a problem in Salt Lake City. Isn't that right?" Such a question would encourage the audience to respond "Yes" in unison. You could continue: "Teen pregnancy is a problem in the State of Utah. Isn't that right?" By this time your audience would have the idea and say, "Yes!" Finally: "Teen pregnancy is a problem throughout the United States!" At this point, you might open your arms wide in a clear invitation for them to give another emphatic "Yes!" You might also invite your audience to become involved in other ways: "We demand *more* from our government; we need *more*; and we deserve *more*. OK now, what is it that we want?" And with that, you encourage your audience to respond all together with a rousing "More!"

You will be far more effective at eliciting such enthusiastic responses if you use dramatic nonverbal gestures as well. When you ask for a show of hands, hold your own hand high. When you want to draw a response from your audience (such as "More"), point dramatically at your audience. Because most audiences are accustomed to remaining seated and silent, some may be surprised by such tactics. But even if that is initially the case, your audience members will probably get into playing their part.

Recall one type of active audience response that was defined in Chapter 6: Cue- or call-response patterns are an open and actively expressive form of positive audience feedback. Because these response patterns are unique to the African American communication style, they might be more effective with African American audience members than with other co-cultures. Because collectivistic co-cultures value more restrained communication behavior, it might be more difficult to obtain or elicit observably active responses from audience members who are Asian American and Native American.

Use Familiar and Relevant Examples

Everyone needs some kind of cognitive framework to learn and recall information efficiently and effectively. You store information in your memory, which you tap to help yourself recall experiences. These recollections of past experiences serve as frameworks to help you understand new and unfamiliar experiences. For your audience members to understand an unfamiliar idea, you can help them mentally frame the information by providing them with familiar and relevant examples that stimulate their memories of past experiences.

To illustrate, suppose you had to explain the concept of statistical correlation—a relatively sophisticated procedure used widely in scientific studies. For an audience unfamiliar with the concept, you wouldn't want to define it as "the ratio between the covariance between two arrays of numbers and the geometric mean of their variances." Although this definition is technically correct, it might cause your audience to drift off into inattention.

It would be better to explain correlation by using two familiar ideas that every audience member would understand and be able to recover easily from memory: (1) the average daily temperature in a typical American city and (2) the daily crime rate in that city. To explain correlation, you could show that as the average temperature goes up or down in the city, the crime rate does the same thing. In other words, they rise and fall together.

Using familiar and relevant examples and illustrations will enhance your audience's ability to store and recall new ideas. Without linking the new ideas to an established set of familiar ideas, however, your information might be ignored, misunderstood, or forgotten. Because human memory works the same

Helping the Audience Understand and Remember What You Have to Say

- *Keep it simple.* Don't overwhelm your audience. Stick to your main points. Avoid long lists, lots of complex statistics, and too many points and subpoints. Keep explanations and examples brief and to the point.

- *Keep it concrete.* Explain abstract ideas and concepts with solid, concrete examples and illustrations. Don't rely solely on textbook definitions of terms; try to explain things plainly by using ordinary terms and examples.

- *Be repetitive and redundant.* Repeat main points and important ideas. Use redundancy as well; rephrase any ideas or main points that might be important for the audience to remember.

- *Elicit active responses.* Audiences understand and remember more when they are actively involved in

the communication exchange. Get them to participate by asking them questions (not rhetorical ones). Elicit their responses by signaling to them verbally and nonverbally that you really want them to respond.

- *Use familiar and relevant examples.* Present new or unfamiliar information with examples or illustrations that make sense to your audience. Be sure your audience can relate to the examples you use to explain your points.

- *Use transitions and signposts.* Give frequent warnings to audience members. Let them know what comes first, second, and third. In other words, use signposts. Also, help your audience understand how one point relates to the next by using transitions.

---

way for everyone, this informational strategy should produce equally positive results with audiences of diverse co-cultural backgrounds. Nevertheless, if you come from a co-culture that is dramatically different from that of your audience, your challenge will be to find examples that are familiar and meaningful to your audience.

Use Transitions and Signposts

Let your audience know when you're leaving an old point and moving on to a new one. Recall that transitions are phrases that link one main point to another, while signposts are phrases that signal organization. Both alert your audience to change or movement in your presentation. (For examples, refer back to the box "Transitions and Signposts" in Chapter 9.)

For example, consider a transition that can be used to link up a first main point with a discussion of the second: (wind up the first main point) ". . . So, a color may depress us or it may cheer us up"; (next use a transition) "But color can do more than that"; (and then introduce the next main point) "Color can reveal a lot about who we are." Use signposts as well, such as counting off numbers verbally and nonverbally (using your fingers): "First, we will consider . . ." or "The second reason

we need to be concerned is . . ." Transitions and signposts help your audience visualize your speech outline, follow your presentation, and retain information. Once again, this strategy functions well for all audiences.

The strategies described in this section are summarized in the box "Helping the Audience Understand and Remember What You Have to Say." These are by no means the only techniques available to induce audience learning and retention; however, they will give you a good start. To check how well you've absorbed these strategies, take a few moments to complete the quiz in the box "How Familiar Are You with Informative Speaking Strategies?"

Now that you are familiar with the basic guidelines for preparing and delivering your own informative speech, read the following section, which contains the full text of student Sean Dunlap's speech on criticizing others. Notice how he incorporated many of the strategies listed in this chapter for developing an organized and engaging informative presentation.

SEE WHAT YOU THINK: A STUDENT'S INFORMATIVE SPEECH

Sean Dunlap, a new major in communication, delivered this six-minute speech in an introductory public speaking class at Santa Barbara City College.

How Familiar Are You with Informative Speaking Strategies?

Instructions

Read each of the following pairs of statements and place a check mark in the space provided to indicate which statement is part of successfully preparing and delivering an informative speech. In completing this survey: (1) Do not omit any item; (2) check only one item for each pair of statements; (3) do not refer back to items; (4) make each item a separate, independent judgment; and (5) record your first impression.

_____ 1. Because there is only one opportunity to inform the audience, the speaker should include as many points in the speech as possible.
The fewer points presented in the speech, the more likely the audience will learn them.

_____ 2. A speaker should include only concrete illustrations in the speech.
Both abstract and concrete explanations should be included in the speech.

_____ 3. No one likes a speaker to repeat the same points.
Audiences generally appreciate repetition and redundancy in a speech.

_____ 4. Audiences are "trained" to be silent during a speech; consequently, members don't appreciate speakers who try to get them to join in.
Any time the speaker can get audience members to react during the speech by openly responding, the speaker is more likely to get them to commit to what she or he has to say.

_____ 5. The speaker should only use examples that the audience will find humorous and enjoyable.
The speaker should only use examples that the audience can relate to.

_____ 6. The speaker should warn the audience when he or she is moving on to a new point.
For most audiences, warnings (or signposts) only make the speech sound too structured and far too organized.

Calculating Your Score

For each pair of statements, there is only one correct response. Using the following key, give yourself 1 point for each correct response:

Item 1: choice 2	Item 4: choice 2
Item 2: choice 1	Item 5: choice 2
Item 3: choice 2	Item 6: choice 1

The total of your correct responses = _____

Interpreting Your Score

The possible scores range from 0 to 6. The higher your score, the more clearly you understand the six strategies discussed in this chapter for increasing your effectiveness in preparing and delivering an informative speech. If your total score is 5 or 6, you have a good grasp of the six rules and should be able to apply them when preparing your informative speech. Scores of 4 or less suggest that you do not understand all six of the rules and that you will have difficulty preparing an effective informative speech. You need to review the rules again before moving on to the next chapter.

Although he had already successfully delivered a series of brief one-minute presentations, this speech was Sean's first major presentation in college. His teacher awarded Sean an A for this speech. Notice how Sean relied extensively on outside sources to lend credibility to and, in some cases, stimulate interest in his speech. Following Sean's speech, his teacher recommended that he make greater eye contact with the entire audience (not just his friends), add drama to his speech with pause time, and specify on his outline all the references he used. As you will discover, Sean's speech is well organized, with an identifiable introduction, body, and conclusion. He relies on a variety of different kinds of supporting material for each main point. His preview is clear, and his main points are signposted along the way. And, even though his introduction and conclusion could have been more memorable or dramatic, Sean strategically links the two together. What follows is an annotated text of his speech.

Criticizing to Perfection

Sean Dunlap, Santa Barbara City College

When was the last time someone criticized you for doing (or not doing) something? [Wait for audience response.] Now then, when you were criticized, just exactly *how* did that make you feel? And, more to the point, did you end up changing your behavior as a result of that unwanted criticism? According to the psychological research on criticism, if you're like most people, your feelings were hurt, you became somewhat defensive or felt inadequate, and it sure didn't cause you to change!

Interestingly, the concept of criticism wasn't intended to be negative or to make people feel bad. Instead, criticism is intended to motivate, to teach, and to encourage self-improvement. When it's given in the spirit of these intentions, criticism allows a person to take a good look at her or his actions, and points the way toward improvement and, ultimately, success. Unfortunately, all too often, people lose sight of the real goals of criticism. Too often, criticism comes off as negative, destructive and hurtful. In an effort to encourage more people to use constructive criticism (instead of the destructive kind), today I will point out three dangers or problems associated with the use of destructive criticism and then I will provide you with some advice or solutions that may change the way you think about criticizing others. Let's begin by looking at some of the dangers of criticism.

The first danger has to do with where you target the criticism. Sometimes the critical comment focuses not on the person's actions, but targets instead the person's self-worth. When this happens, you can expect the target of your criticism to feel angry and defensive. Let me tell you a story that shows you exactly what I mean. One day a husband came home from work with an anniversary present for his wife—a necklace. Made out of diamonds?? No, nothing so elegant. The necklace was made of 300 buttons she'd forgotten to sew on his shirts in their 27 years of marriage! Incidentally, *she* had the last laugh. She used the necklace as evidence of mental cruelty in her lucrative divorce suit later that same year. Obviously, a person can't go around missing buttons; but how this man registered his complaint with his wife only made a bad situation worse. We might also wonder why this guy couldn't learn to use a needle and thread himself. But, nevertheless, criticism can be dangerous when it's used to attack a person, rather than the person's actions.

Second, criticism often becomes dangerous when we're critical of things or people we really don't know or don't understand. In Eugene O'Neill's play *Long Day's Journey into Night*, the character Marie says, "Jamie always looks for the worst weakness in everyone, when he doesn't know a thing about them." Criticism is problematic when we are too quick to be too harsh on people or things we aren't well acquainted with. Abraham Lincoln, noted for his diplomacy, once observed that "only a little man will criticize something which he knows nothing about, but an effective motivator will be understanding, forgiving, and silent." Both O'Neill

---

Title: The title arouses interest and curiosity. Taken together, the two main words seem almost oxymoronic.

Introduction: The question-asking technique that Sean employs in his introduction encourages active audience responses. This device, appropriate for a lecture-style informative speech, invites audience members to participate and lets them know that the topic will be relevant personally to each of them. He concludes the introduction with an explicit preview of the organizational format of his speech (problem-solution). In this way, he helps the audience make sense of what he's going to say next. Sean leads into the body of his speech with a transition that helps the audience focus on the problem phase of his speech.

Body: Sean employs signposts throughout the problem phase of his speech to signal the first, second, and third problems or dangers associated with the use of criticism, helping the audience to track. To illustrate his first problem, he relies on a humorous story that easily conveys his point.

For each main point, Sean uses repetition and redundancy to draw attention to his contention that "criticism can be dangerous." Each problem begins and ends with similar kinds of statements.

and Lincoln foreshadowed Ann Landers's famous line: "MYOB," or "mind your own business." Criticism can be dangerous if we're unfamiliar with the situation.

There is a third and last major problem associated with our use of criticism. Criticism is usually worthless! No matter what people are told, they seldom see themselves at fault anyway. Dale Carnegie said in his book *How to Win Friends and Influence People*, "When criticizing, we aren't dealing with creatures of logic, but creatures of emotion, driven by pride and vanity." The notorious Al Capone supported this contention when he said, "I've spent the best years of my life giving people pleasure, and helping them have a good time, and all I get is abuse: I'm a hunted man." See what I mean? After being called America's most notorious public enemy by his critics, Capone didn't see himself as a menace to society, but as an unappreciated and misunderstood public *benefactor*. Criticism can be dangerous if the target is unwilling or unable to see the problem.

Sean uses quotations from well-known sources to support his theme.

Now that we've seen some of the dangers of destructive criticism, we need to recognize that in some cases, constructive criticism is necessary. For instance, our purpose as students would be defeated if we never received any feedback from our teachers. But how do we avoid the risk of hurting, instead of *helping*, people with our criticism?

Notice the transition Sean employs to leave the problem phase of his speech and move on to the solution phase.

The solution, first of all, is to realize that as humans, we all have faults! Don't be so quick to criticize something that could only be corrected if the person were perfect. After all, when describing the human race in the play *Hamlet* as "Noble in reason, infinite in faculty, and godlike," Shakespeare was exaggerating! We all know of politicians who are hardly noble, children who are less than infinite in their faculties, and as close as some of us come, none of us is godlike! No criticism can change that. So next time you feel like correcting someone, ask yourself if his or her flaw is really big enough to worry about.

Second, avoid criticizing people or things you don't know well. President Franklin D. Roosevelt said, "Any fool can criticize, and most fools do." But the harsh words of unknowledgeable critics drove the rather sensitive British writer Thomas Hardy to give up writing forever. Ironically, today, Hardy's works are considered by the "critics" as some of the greatest pieces of English literature in existence. Get the background details on the person, the situation, and the person's actions before being critical. Seek other people's opinions to help decide whether your opinions are on target or out of line. Going the distance to preserve the target's feelings may, in the long run, preserve your relationship with that person.

Again, Sean signals his organizational plan or logic with signposts throughout his three-part solution.

Third, when criticism is necessary, employ the art of positive reinforcement. Noted psychologist Ashley Montagu explains that criticism is pointing out faults, while at the same time praising successes. Always couch your criticism with acknowledgments of a person's positive attributes. Find something nice to say about the person or his or her actions before and after your criticism to soften the blow. Dr. Henrie Wiesinger, an expert on criticism and human relationships, suggests that when you can, make some suggestions on how the person may improve. This lets people know that your criticism isn't an attack, but an effort to help them.

Sean provides listeners with concrete behaviors (not abstract, theoretical ideas) they can use to solve the problem.

Continued

In the end, criticism is still a big risk, no matter how certain we are that it's justified. The smallest amount of misunderstood criticism can result in a lifetime of bitter resentment toward the very people who may have been the only ones who cared enough about us to try to change us in the first place.

So, recalling the three dangers of criticism and some advice on how to offer it more constructively, hopefully you'll think twice the next time you prepare to jump down someone else's throat! Think twice about who and what you criticize, the words you choose, and whether it's really necessary to say anything at all.

Conclusion: Sean attempts to hook up his conclusion with the introduction by cautioning his audience about jumping down someone else's throat. And even though he compels the audience to recall both the problems and solutions associated with the use of criticism, he should have used redundancy—that is, briefly reviewed each of the problems and each of the solutions.

Finally, Sean could have disclosed one or more personal examples or stories that reveal his personal connection with the topic.

CHAPTER REVIEW

- Informative speeches intend to teach, to change the way an audience thinks about an issue or topic; in contrast, persuasive speeches intend to advocate or advance a cause, product, or idea. When you design an informative speech, your goal is to communicate new information to your audience members, extend what they already know, or update old information about a topic or issue.

- Informative presentations typically fall into one of four different categories: briefings (or reports), lectures, demonstrations, or training presentations.

- All organized informative speeches have three main parts—an introduction, a body, and a conclusion. The introduction gets the audience's attention and previews the substance of the speech. The body of the speech is usually limited to two or three main points and can be organized linearly or configurally. The conclusion summarizes the main points and signs off with a memorable statement or story that jolts audience members and leaves them wanting to hear more.

- An outline of an informative speech provides the road map or plan that helps you systematically organize and deliver the presentation.

- To be effective, as an informative speaker, you should keep the message simple and concrete; use repetition and redundancy throughout; involve your audience in active responses as much as possible; make examples and illustrations familiar and relevant to your audience; and use transitions and signposts to help keep your audience organized and alert.

QUESTIONS FOR CRITICAL THINKING & REVIEW

1. When do informative speeches become persuasive? What examples can you provide of college lectures that you think were actually persuasive? How do you know they were persuasive?

2. A college professor is presenting a lecture on a rather difficult concept to the class: probability theory. What advice might you offer this instructor to ensure that everyone understands (learns) the presentation?

3. Eliciting active audience responses is one way to increase your effectiveness as an informative speaker, yet some people are reluctant to respond openly in large groups. What personality traits or co-cultural characteristics might influence that reluctance? What can or should you expect from an audience made up of reluctant communicators?

4. Is it ever possible to make a presentation appear too simple or too concrete? How do you know where to draw the line?

NOTES

1. Robinson, M. (1995, May 19–20). Keynote address: International Conference on Hunger. Online. Gifts of Speech. Available: http://gos.sbc.edu/r/robinson.html

2. Darnell, D. (1963). The relation between sentence order and comprehension. *Speech Monographs, 30*, 97–100; Kissler, G., & Lloyd, K. (1973). Effect of sentence interrelation and scrambling on the recall of factual information. *Journal of Educational Psychology, 63*, 187–190.

3. For an overview of the research findings pertinent to these strategies, see Eggen, P. D., Kavchak, D. P., & Harder, R. J. (1979). *Strategies for teachers: Information processing models in the classroom.* Englewood Cliffs, NJ: Prentice-Hall; Higbee, K. L. (1977). *Your memory: How it works and how to improve it.* Englewood Cliffs, NJ: Prentice-Hall; Woolfolk, A. E. (1987). *Educational psychology.* Englewood Cliffs, NJ: Prentice-Hall.

Chapter 12

SPEAKING TO PERSUADE

Take a moment to consider some great speakers in U.S. history, speakers who have "made a difference" because of their ability to influence audiences. Examine the list below, and ask yourself, "What impact has each of these great American speakers had on U.S. history?"

Martin Luther King, Jr.	Billy Graham
Jesse Jackson	Ronald Reagan
John F. Kennedy	Cesar Chavez
Malcolm X	Maya Angelou
Sarah Weddington	Hillary Clinton
Barbara Jordan	Peter MacDonald

Your familiarity with each of these speakers depends, to a large extent, on media coverage, as well as your own personal stake in the issues each speaker represents. Common to all these speakers are their unique abilities to motivate and activate an audience. Although you may not agree with a particular individual's politics, religion, or social cause, each of these speakers' influence on U.S. society is indisputable. Malcolm X encouraged African Americans to internalize the attitude "black is beautiful." The Reverend Billy Graham has stirred the hearts and souls of people in their worship of the Lord. Attorney Sarah Weddington convinced enough Supreme Court justices to make Roe v. Wade the law of the land. Peter MacDonald, chair of the Navajo Nation, has been a vigorous leader in the struggle for Native Americans' fundamental human rights. And Cesar Chavez did more to improve the lives of migrant laborers than any other individual in America.

How have these great leaders been able to articulate their visions and persuade others to follow? They have done so with words forged into messages that have stimulated and motivated people into action. This chapter examines the techniques and strategies persuasive speakers employ in their efforts to change the way people think, feel, and behave.

GOALS AND TYPES OF PERSUASIVE SPEECHES

The primary difference between a persuasive speech and all other types of speeches is the speaker's goal. As discussed in Chapter 11, the goal of an informative speech is to teach. In speaking to persuade, however, the goal is to advocate. In order to advocate some cause or convince an audience to engage in some new or alternative behavior, a speaker must influence the audience's attitudes and beliefs. For example, a speaker might want audience members to change their opinions about a congressional gun control bill, to change their beliefs about seat belts, or to behave more tolerantly toward gay and lesbian co-cultures. In each case, the goal is to advocate some kind of change. A persuasive speech aims to change the way the audience feels, thinks, or behaves. (Refer to the box "Sample Topics for Persuasive Speeches" for examples of presentations whose goals are to change the way an audience feels, thinks, or behaves.)

Learning Objectives

After reading this chapter, you should be able to do the following:

1. Differentiate among the three goals of persuasive speaking.

2. List and give examples of the five types of persuasive speeches.

3. Determine ways to adapt to audiences that agree or disagree with or remain neutral to your position.

4. Organize and outline a persuasive speech using Monroe's Motivated Sequence.

5. Employ strategies that will prevent or at least manage potential audience resistance to your persuasive intent.

Sample Topics for Persuasive Speeches

The death penalty should be administered more often.

Having children should be a privilege, not a right.

People should use ecologically safe cleaning products.

Don't use drugs of any kind.

Home schooling has benefits.

There is no such thing as "safe sex."

Workers should always have the right to strike.

College isn't for everyone.

Teachers shouldn't date their students.

Moving back home is hazardous to your mental health.

Learn to appreciate poetry readings.

Reduce fat in your diet.

Respect the environment.

Honor your parents.

Condemn cheating of any kind.

Be ready to accept an apology.

Cooking can be fun.

Eat at home.

Take responsibility for what you do.

Television violence has become far too explicit.

Tattoos are sexy.

Grades are important.

Attorneys are honest and trustworthy.

An all-vegetarian diet is not necessarily healthy.

Using credit cards can be disastrous.

There should be a dress code for college students.

Working your way through college is a valuable experience.

People should not engage in premarital sex.

Women belong in our armed forces.

Animals should have rights, too.

Children should have rights, too.

Our beaches are being destroyed by pollution.

The sun is hazardous to your health.

Guns don't kill; people do.

Everyone deserves basic food and shelter.

Health care should be a right, not a privilege.

Don't try to talk a police officer out of a ticket.

Term limitations should be imposed on all publicly elected officials.

We need more student parking on campus.

Donate $2 a week to a charity of your choice.

Register to vote.

Go to the dentist twice a year.

Save money by shopping with coupons.

Women: It's your turn to ask a man out for a date.

Buy weekly lottery tickets.

Take a class in stand-up comedy.

Quit smoking.

Carpool to work.

Give blood.

Donate money to Save the Children.

Join a volunteer group.

Buy life insurance.

Join the military.

Change your major to speech communication.

Attend worship services regularly.

Join an exercise club.

Visit Mexico.

Sign up as an organ donor.

Join a club.

Recycle your trash.

Buy "American."

Read the newspaper every day.

Try out for a game show.

Save a pet from a shelter.

Seek out a mentor at work.

Changing Attitudes

To change attitudes, the speaker must influence audience members to feel more positive or negative about an issue. The speaker may want to persuade the audience to feel sad, glad, pain, pity, disgust, or triumph. The speaker's predetermined goal is to change the audience's feelings or emotions. Consider the following attitude-based topics from the list of persuasive speech topics:

- Cooking can be fun.
- Respect the environment.
- Learn to appreciate poetry.
- Tattoos are sexy.

Suppose you want to persuade your audience members that contrary to what others might believe, tattoos are sexy. Even though you are not advocating that they all run out and get tattoos themselves (changing behavior), you want them to feel more positively about tattoos and, perhaps, about people who wear them. To accomplish this objective, you might associate tattoos with a variety of positive images by listing politicians, military leaders, actors, poets, and rock stars who have worn tattoos, or you might assert that tattoos communicate individuality. The point is, your goal is to advocate a change in attitudes, to convince your audience to feel more positively about tattoos.

Changing Beliefs

Speakers can also persuade by changing audience members' beliefs. Beliefs refer to the truth or falsity of a given proposition. A quick look at the list of sample speech topics reveals a number that emphasize beliefs:

- Attorneys are honest and trustworthy.
- Our beaches are being destroyed by pollution.
- The sun is hazardous to your health.
- Television violence has become far too explicit.

Speaking to persuade audience members to change their beliefs about an issue can be similar to informative speaking. Adding new information can often provoke people to reexamine what they thought they knew to be true (or false). Persuasion involves the reversal of an individual's true or false conviction. Once again, the difference between informing and persuading is the speaker's primary intent. A speaker who intends to inform does not necessarily advocate that audience members believe differently; a speaker who intends to persuade advocates that they should or must.

Suppose you are an attorney representing the American Bar Association and your intent is to persuade an audience of laypeople to change the way they think about your profession. According to one source, lawyer bashing has become a popular pastime.[1] Many people believe attorneys have become too powerful and too rich. Fully 73 percent of Americans today believe there are too many lawyers, and as few as 5 percent would recommend that their children go into law.

So, your purpose is to persuade audience members that their beliefs about attorneys are false. To accomplish this goal, you will need to persuade your audience that attorneys, as a rule, care more about their clients and the law than they do about power and money. Moreover, you will need to convince them that most attorneys do not, in fact, make six-figure salaries. You could change their beliefs about attorney power and greed by citing all the pro bono (free) work that attorneys do for needy clients and the fact that lawyers donate more of their time and services than do members of any other profession, including doctors, teachers, engineers, and police

officers. You might also note that mocking lawyers has become a sanctioned prejudice that can be hurtful to an individual's morale or professional pride. You could add that a number of so-called successful lawyers suffer from social isolation and alienation—alienation from the very people they are dedicated to serving.

Throughout your speech, your goal is to alter audience members' beliefs and to advocate that they reconsider some of their misperceptions about lawyers in general. To accomplish this goal, you must inform audience members (add new information that conflicts with what they thought was true) and then persuade them to accept a new set of beliefs (attorneys are caring, hard-working people). Changing beliefs, therefore, automatically involves both informing and persuading.

Changing Behavior

To change behavior, the speaker must motivate the audience to take some kind of action, or at least commit to some action. Ultimately, the goal of all persuasive speaking is to change audience behavior. But a speaker cannot really know how persuasive the presentation has been—that is, whether she or he has effectively altered audience attitudes or beliefs—until the audience somehow *shows* it.

How would you know, for example, that you persuaded audience members to actually change their attitudes toward tattoos? You could not know unless you observed some actual behavioral change. Some behaviors are easily observed: Some members of your audience might actually run out and get tattooed! Other behavioral evidence is more subtle: Your audience might merely admire your tattoos. As another example, how would you know if audience members actually changed their beliefs about lawyers? Perhaps your audience will sign a petition calling for a cease-fire on all lawyer jokes. Or audience members might simply avoid telling lawyer jokes themselves and remind others that such jokes are truly tasteless. In both cases, whether your goal is to change an attitude or to change a belief, the desired result is some sort of change in behavior.

Sometimes the speaker's primary purpose is not to change attitudes and beliefs, but to motivate the audience to do something. Persuasive speeches that emphasize some kind of behavioral change focus more on explicit behavioral outcomes than do persuasive speeches that emphasize either attitude or belief changes. An examination of the list of sample persuasive speech topics reveals several topics that emphasize some kind of observable behavioral change:

- Buy "American."
- Join an exercise club.
- Quit smoking.
- Register to vote.

In each of these examples, the speaker's primary goal is to persuade audience members to behave differently than they did before the speech. To accomplish this objective, the speaker might have to first address audience members' attitudes and beliefs and then lay out the specific observable actions they should engage in.

The common denominator in all persuasive speeches is advocacy. The speaker's primary purpose is to advocate some sort of change in attitude, belief, or behavior. (The box "Goals of Persuasive Speeches" summarizes these goals.)

Types of Persuasive Speeches

The separate but related goals of changing attitudes, beliefs, and behaviors often are determined by the occasion. Sometimes a speaker may want to stress behavior change; other times a speaker may want to emphasize attitude or belief changes. There are many different kinds of persuasive speeches that tend to underscore one or more of these goals. Figure 12-1 shows some familiar types, and this section discusses them briefly.

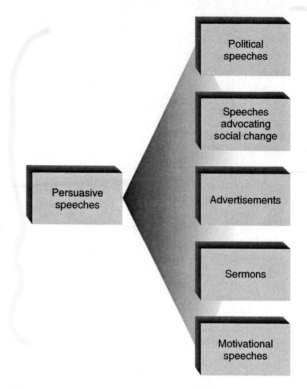

Figure 12-1 Types of persuasive speeches. Most persuasive speeches fall into one of five categories. The primary goal of all persuasive speeches is advocacy—to change the audience's attitudes, beliefs, or behavior.

Political Speeches The overriding goals of a political speech are to change or reinforce audience beliefs and to secure votes. Professional political campaign strategists write campaign speeches, handle the press, interpret opinion poll and focus group data, prioritize the issues, schedule meetings and presentations, and carry out other important tasks. Political speeches are highly crafted, thoroughly tested, and well rehearsed. No single phrase, look, or gesture goes unnoticed under the close scrutiny of the press and the American people. It is no wonder, then, that politicians rely on these experts to successfully "package" them as candidates.

Speeches Advocating Social Change Many televised speeches emphasize social change. These speeches might advocate that condoms be made available to high school students, that Americans return to core family values, that basic health care be made available to all Americans, or that deadbeat parents be forced to pay child support. Advocates of social change tell us how we *should* feel, think, or behave. Persuasive speeches advocating social change provide an open market for introducing new ideas and challenging old ones.

Advertisements Advertising speeches promise to change your life—using everything from exercise equipment and special diets to cosmetic makeovers and car wax. These so-called infomercials pitch a consumable product that the media audience is supposed to dash out and purchase. Obviously, the overriding goal of advertising speeches is behavioral change—here's the product, now purchase it.

Sermons Most sermons or religious presentations attempt to change or reinforce an audience's attitudes toward God or some other supreme being. The sermon is designed to share a vision of eternal life, to give meaning to our existence, and to help us lead a good and moral life. Some well-known religious leaders who also happen to be effective public speakers are Billy Graham, Jesse Jackson, and televangelists Jerry Falwell and Oral Roberts.

Motivational Speeches These speeches are designed to persuade audience members to feel better about themselves. They are also designed to incite people to do something about their lives. Their primary goal is attitude change—and, hopefully, behavior change. The motivational speaker typically begins by acknowledging the sorry state we are all in. Perhaps we all hate how we look: Our bodies are too fat, too thin, too flabby, too short, too tall. After that gloomy introduction, the speaker then helps us rethink our lives. We are told that we need not remain in this awful condition and that we can and must change. The speaker may want us to change how we view ourselves (fat is beautiful) or how we behave (we can lose fat).

CONSIDERING THE AUDIENCE

This text stresses the importance of audience analysis. It is of particular importance for speeches to persuade. A speaker must consider how an audience feels, believes, or behaves in relation to a speech topic in order to appear credible and achieve the goal of his or her presentation. This section examines how and why audiences can be so difficult to persuade.

The Human Tendency to Resist Change

When people in an audience discover that the speaker's intent is to change how they feel or what they think or do, they typically resist the proposed change. Psychologist Jack Brehm's theory of **psychological reactance** provides insight into why people react this way.[2] All people expect and enjoy the freedom to choose and control how they think, feel, and behave. Openly persuasive attempts tend to threaten people's personal freedoms. After all, they don't want to be talked into doing something they might not want to do. To reassert or regain their freedom, then, people are strongly motivated to resist any persuasive attempt.

Consider Coca-Cola's 1985 attempt to replace Coke with "New Coke." The company conducted in-depth marketing studies that showed that consumers really liked New Coke. However, when Coca-Cola tried to retire the old formula and replace it with New Coke, consumers saw it as a threat to their freedom to choose and reacted by buying large amounts of the old Coke.

The universal tendency to resist change has been widely researched. The authors of this text, for instance, studied the reasons college students tend to resist teacher demands.[3] We identified strategies students use to resist teacher attempts to change their behaviors. Take a few moments to complete the questionnaire in the box "How Do You Resist Persuasion?" to see what type of resister you tend to be.

How can you as a persuasive speaker counteract the universal human inclination to resist change? Rather than wait for audience resistance to occur, you can use several preventive techniques. Perhaps the most useful strategy is to focus your persuasive speech on the reasons for changing. You must convince audience members that there's something wrong with the status quo; otherwise, they probably won't be persuaded to think or act differently.

Adapting to Your Audience

You can deal with psychological reactance more easily when you identify what attitudes your audience members already hold toward your speech topic. Are they likely to agree or disagree with or remain neutral toward your position?

If the Audience Agrees with Your Position If your audience members already agree with your position, they are ready to agree some more. Therefore, you can adjust your purpose to intensify their attitudes, beliefs, and behaviors. You may want them to contribute more money, to be more deeply committed to their beliefs, or to feel more passionate about the issue. Because your audience members already support your position, you don't need to go over well-known background information; instead, remind them why they hold these shared attitudes and beliefs toward the issue to help them remain committed to their position.

Next, you can provide some motivation to strengthen their attitudes and beliefs. By relying

213

How Do You Resist Persuasion?

Instructions

According to the theory of psychological reactance, people are naturally resistant to others' attempts to influence them. A speaker who tries to persuade members of an audience to think, feel, or do something differently can expect them to resist or react negatively. The purpose of this questionnaire is to determine how you, as a potential audience member, might resist a speaker's attempts to influence you.

Imagine for a moment that you are a member of an audience listening to a speech on the dangers of alcohol consumption. The speaker argues that drinking alcohol is dangerous to your health and is one of the leading causes of vehicular manslaughter. Moreover, the speaker claims that teenagers and young adults are most susceptible to alcohol abuse. With these arguments in mind, the speaker advocates that the national drinking age be raised to 25.

You oppose this speaker's proposed solution. Below is a list of strategies you might use to resist this speaker's persuasive attempts. Enter the appropriate number in the space provided that indicates how likely you would be to use each strategy in response to this speaker: (5) extremely likely, (4) likely, (3) maybe (undecided), (2) unlikely, or (1) extremely unlikely.

____ 1. I would get up and leave the room.

____ 2. I would raise my hand, wait to be recognized, and then argue against the speaker's position.

____ 3. I would interrupt and tell the speaker that he or she is wrong.

____ 4. I would wait until the speaker was finished and then challenge her or his facts and assumptions.

____ 5. I would ignore the whole situation and not do anything.

____ 6. I would disagree openly and try to get others in the audience to agree with me.

____ 7. I would show my disapproval nonverbally by shaking my head at critical points during the speech.

____ 8. I would keep my opinion to myself, realizing that not everyone thinks the same way.

____ 9. Even though I disagreed with the speaker, I would continue to smile and nod my head politely.

____ 10. I wouldn't do anything until after the presentation was over. Then I would discuss my feelings with others from the audience just to make sure I'm right.

____ 11. I would make an effort to find areas of agreement even though I disagreed with the speaker's solution.

____ 12. I would simply disregard the speaker's solution as deviant or eccentric.

____ 13. Rather than continue listening to the speech, I would open a book or turn my attention to other things.

____ 14. I would raise my hand and accuse the speaker of being out of touch with young adults today.

____ 15. I would protest by publicly inviting members of the audience to join me for a beer afterwards.

Calculating Your Score

1. Add together your responses to items 5, 8, 9, 10, 11, 12, and 13 = ____

2. Add together your responses to items 1, 2, 3, 4, 6, 7, 14, and 15 = ____

3. Complete the following formula:

    42 − total from step 1 = ____

        + total from step 2 = ____

    Your total audience resistance score = ____

Interpreting Your Score

The possible scores range from 15 to 75. (If your own score does not fall within that range, you have made a computational error.) The median score is 45. Higher scores reflect greater active audience resistance. If you scored above 60 (or even above the median of 45), you are considered a highly active resister. Individuals who actively resist persuasion let the speaker and others in the audience know that they disagree. Although they don't intend to be impolite, active resisters are forthright in the way they express their views. They place a high priority on standing up for what they believe in.

If you scored below 30 (or even below the median of 45), you are considered a highly passive resister. Individuals who passively resist are concerned with saving face for the speaker—or perhaps for themselves. They may disagree, but they will do so in more private ways. They tend to be diplomatic in their approach to disagreement and to value politeness over frankness. Rather than make an issue or create a scene to make their point known, they would rather just leave well enough alone.

Continued

primarily on emotional appeals, you can energize or motivate audience members to change even further.

Finally, you can afford to be more direct with supportive audience members when it's time to call for change. Tell them exactly what you want or need.

To see how these strategies can be put into action, imagine that you are preparing a presentation advocating support for the timber industry in the Northwest. Your audience is made up of second- and third-generation timber workers. This means your audience probably doesn't favor the concerns of environmentalists (such as for the spotted owl or the snail darter) over those of the timber industry. Consequently, your task is fairly simple: Remind your audience how the timber industry supports the livelihood of the community. List all the contributions the industry makes to families, education, and the economy. Detail how life would be different without the timber industry; describe a hypothetical neighborhood family out of work, poor, and hungry. Ask audience members, "What can we do to keep that from happening to us?" And then tell them exactly what you want them to do.

If the Audience Is Neutral or Undecided

Sometimes audience members have no opinion on the topic. They may not know enough about the issue to have an opinion, or they may be so confused by the facts that they can't make up their minds. With neutral or undecided audience members, you must first get their attention before you can persuade them. After you get their attention, you want to help them develop a reasonable attitude. To do this, you need to give them some background information, reveal your own attitudes and beliefs about the issue, and then support your position with evidence.

Suppose your audience members know nothing about the struggle between environmental groups and the timber industry. You might begin by alerting them to the dangers of giving particular animals or ecosystems priority over human beings: "How is it that environmentalists and government regulators value the life of an owl over the lives and well-being of thousands of women, men, and children?" Explain the controversy by briefly relating the concerns first of environmental groups and then of the timber industry. (Audience members are more likely to side with you if they think you've given some thought to both sides of the issue.) Next, tell them how you feel and think: "We need jobs a lot more than we need to save the spotted owl." And, finally, back up your attitudes and beliefs with facts, illustrations, and testimonials.

If the Audience Disagrees with Your Position

Resistance is more likely with an audience that is unfavorable toward your position. In this case, the first thing you must do is modify your objective. Rather than advocating a large amount of change, you should try to get audience members to shift their attitudes slightly. That is, rather than pushing them to change from complete disagreement to complete agreement, plan instead on moving their attitudes from more disagreement to less disagreement. Second, you should establish some common ground with your audience members. Show them that you understand and respect their position. Where there are points of agreement, say so. Third, tell them where you disagree. Be careful: The more disagreement you reveal, the more they'll resist. Try not to sound disagreeable; set aside areas of disagreement that you need not deal with on this particular occasion. And, finally, back up your position with lots of evidence.

To see how this strategy works, imagine that you're going to give your speech advocating support for the timber industry to an audience of environmentalists. Knowing how they feel, you cannot expect them to abandon their beliefs solely as a result of your speech. Your modified goal, then, is to persuade them to feel some compassion for workers in the timber industry—without sacrificing their concern for the spotted owl or larger environmental issues. If you can do that, then you can begin to build a suitable compromise over time.

You can show some empathy with the audience's feelings by sharing your own concerns for the preservation of all species, including the controversial spotted owl: "No animal should suffer. We should all strive to live together in harmony." Then, after demonstrating overlapping areas of agreement, you can introduce some moderate amount of disagreement with their position: "No man, woman, or child should suffer, either." At this point, you will need to show how real people are affected by an extreme pro-environment position. Demonstrate the economic plight of a local family that has relied on the timber industry for generations—out of work and forced to live on welfare. (Be sure to describe a real family going through real hardships.) Then cite relevant statistics showing that this family is not an anomalous case: "Thousands of workers' livelihoods are jeopardized by conservation efforts." At the conclusion of your speech, you are finally ready to ask for change—but remember to keep your request to a minimum: "There must be a solution to this very real problem. Let us together explore alternative ways to preserve the sanctuary of the spotted owl and, at the same time, lend a hand to humanity."

Knowing your audience's position on the topic of your speech is critical to developing an effective persuasive strategy. The box "Adapting Your Persuasive Speech to Your Audience" summarizes the advice presented in this section.

ORGANIZING AND OUTLINING A PERSUASIVE SPEECH

This universal inclination to resist change can be a real problem. If audience members are reluctant to change, then the speaker must give them sufficient reason to change. Here's where the organizational pattern plays a central role: The organizational logic must establish why audience members must change, why they should feel, think, or behave differently. Unless audience members feel there's something wrong with the status

---

BUILDING YOUR SKILLS

Adapting Your Persuasive Speech to Your Audience

Choosing the most effective persuasive strategies depends in part on your audience's attitude toward your topic.

If the audience agrees with your position:

- Remind audience members why they hold shared attitudes and beliefs on the issue.
- Use emotional appeals to energize and motivate them.
- Be direct and explicit in your calls for change.

If the audience is neutral or undecided:

- Get audience members' attention and make the topic relevant for them.
- Provide background information about the issue.

- Tell them your own beliefs and attitudes—how you think and feel about the issue—and then back up your position with facts, illustrations, and testimonials. Help them develop a reasonable attitude.

If the audience disagrees with your position:

- Modify your purpose so that you ask for only a small amount of change from audience members.
- Establish common ground by showing that you understand and respect their position. Note any points of agreement.
- Carefully reveal areas of disagreement, but deal with a limited number of points.
- Give your position and back it up with lots of evidence.

quo, they are unlikely to go along with some new way of thinking or behaving.

Chapter 9 provides a variety of linear and configural organizational patterns. To preempt psychological reactance and induce persuasion, the cause-and-effect, problem-solution, narrative, web, and multiple-perspective organizational patterns are all effective. But the most widely used organizational pattern for persuasive speaking is one developed by Alan Monroe.[4] With this organizational pattern, both linear and configural logics merge to produce a rather unusual but extremely effective approach.

Monroe's Motivated Sequence

The format for **Monroe's Motivated Sequence** is based on philosopher John Dewey's work and on Monroe's own early experiences training sales personnel. It is a working scheme for motivating people to accept and even welcome change.

Monroe's Motivated Sequence most closely resembles the problem-solution organizational pattern described in Chapter 9. It can be used for any persuasive speech, whether the goal is to convince audience members to floss their teeth regularly or to vote for a proposal to provide adequate housing and health care to Native Americans. Monroe's Motivated Sequence consists of five steps (rather than the typical three-part organizational framework of introduction, body, and conclusion).

Step 1: Gain the Audience's Attention
As with all speeches, the first step is to grab the audience's attention. (Use one of the techniques described in Chapter 10.) Make the audience curious about what you're going to say. To help avoid the effects of psychological reactance, do not include a preview statement.

Consider the example of Eric, a speaker who hopes to persuade his audience to purchase more baking soda. He grabs his audience's attention by complaining about all the different household cleaning products that seem to fill up his shopping cart every time he goes to the store. He exclaims in an exasperated tone, "By the time I get through with the cleaning aisles, I have no room and no money for food. Isn't there one simple, inexpensive product that can do it all?" The audience can relate to his complaint, so they are interested in his speech.

Step 2: Identify Unfulfilled Needs
The success of Monroe's Motivated Sequence relies heavily on this step. The importance of this second step cannot be emphasized enough. It is critical that you establish in the minds of the audience needs that are clear and urgent and yet unfulfilled. You must show audience members why your topic should concern them and why change is necessary. Don't identify the solution at this stage; focus on identifying and clarifying the audience's needs. If the solution is identified too early, it may stimulate resistance.

In his speech on baking soda, Eric discusses all the problems that he and the audience encounter—problems, he will later show, that can be eliminated by his solution. He identifies embarrassing smells that everyone experiences—smells emitted from the refrigerator every time he stores onions, fish, or liver. He explains that guests can quickly detect pet odors. And, he laments, "Have you ever noticed how your garbage disposal seems to take on a life of its own and breathe spoiled smells throughout the kitchen?" Eric's examples focus attention on the problems he and his audience share and on the need for change. Audience members come to share Eric's concern, and they begin to anticipate that Eric will offer a solution.

Step 3: Propose a Solution That Satisfies Those Needs
Once you have established a problem or need, it is time to present your solution. Describe how your plan will work and how it will satisfy unfulfilled needs. Relate the solution back to each of the needs or problems you've described. In this step, it's also important to identify and address possible objections to your proposed solution. Listeners may be concerned about cost, effort, time, or other issues related to the solution. Good speakers are able to empathize with audience members and to anticipate and address their objections.

To accomplish his speech goal, Eric must show how baking soda will satisfy the audience's needs. He holds up a box of baking soda and declares, "What we need, folks, is baking soda! It will solve the problem and satisfy our need for a universal cleaning and odor-control product." He goes on to explain how it works: "Baking soda can be used in dry form by sprinkling it directly on spots or down the drain or by leaving an open box in the refrigerator. Baking soda can be used in liquid form by mixing half a cup with a gallon of water." Eric relates his solution back to each of the needs and problems he identified in step 2: "A little baking soda scattered in the cat's litter box or on a pet-stained carpet will conceal pet odors. Sprinkle baking soda in the garbage disposal and, by morning, no unfortunate reminders of last night's dinner will remain."

Eric also identifies and eliminates possible objections that audience members might raise to his solution: "I know what you're thinking: A product that does so much good in so many ways must cost a lot. Well, you're wrong. The largest container of baking soda costs less than $2! Or, maybe you're thinking this product promises more than it can deliver! At one time I might have agreed with you, but that was before I tried it. It does what it promises. You have my word on that!"

Step 4: Visualize What Satisfaction Will Mean

Once you propose a solution, you can intensify audience members' desire for the solution by getting them to visualize what their lives will be like once they've adopted it. Use vivid images to illustrate the benefits of your solution; describe what will happen if the audience rejects your solution or adopts an alternative one; or present both the undesirable and desirable outcomes to heighten the contrast.

Eric paints a clear picture of what life will be like if audience members adopt his solution: "Suppose you went home today with a single box of baking soda. In no time, you'd be living in an odor-free environment. No longer will your children's friends complain about the smell from the litter box. No longer will your mother-in-law or father-in-law be able to guess what you had for dinner the night before."

Step 5: Identify Specific Actions

In the final step, tell audience members how they can obtain or implement the solution and reap the benefits you've described. Keep this step brief and to the point—if the solution appears complicated or difficult to obtain, your audience may not want to exert the effort. Finish with a quick and memorable conclusion.

Eric spells out exactly where his audience can buy baking soda (the local supermarket) and where it's located (in the baking goods aisle next to the flour and cake mixes). He concludes with a catchy and memorable finish: "The next time you go to the grocery store, pick up a box of baking soda. Pick up several. Baking soda doesn't just bake anymore!"

Making the Most of Monroe's Motivated Sequence

Monroe's Motivated Sequence is a highly effective tool for persuading others to change their attitudes, beliefs, or behaviors. But it is important to go through the steps systematically and in sequence. (The basic format is summarized in the box "Monroe's Motivated Sequence: A Five-Step Plan to Persuade.") Monroe himself advised that the pattern be viewed as a flexible arrangement. Sometimes speakers will be more effective by describing only a positive vision of the future with the solution, omitting any reference to a less rosy future without the product, idea, or policy. Some solutions, such as the baking soda example, require only

cursory explanations. Other, more complex, solutions, such as a water purification system, may require more lengthy descriptions or demonstrations. The kind and amount of supporting information may also vary greatly from speech to speech.

Even though Monroe's Motivated Sequence most closely resembles a problem-solution organizational format, the plan digresses from linearity in several important ways. Like a number of more configurally oriented logic patterns, step 1 omits an explicit purpose statement and preview; instead, it merely seeks to pique curiosity and interest—leaving the audience to fill in the blanks as to how the remainder of the speech will be structured. Later on, during step 3, notice how the structure tends to deviate from linearity by addressing objections the audience might have concerning the solution. And, finally, step 4 is inserted in an otherwise predominantly linear sequence: Visualize what satisfaction will mean. Whereas the initial steps lay out an objective analysis of what the problem is and how the solution deals with the problem, step 4 seems to digress by helping the audience "appreciate" the solution. Not until step 5 does the sequence return to linearity.

Regardless of the logical structure of this speech pattern, Monroe's Motivated Sequence contains one fundamental principle: To persuade, the speaker must focus more and spend more time on the audience's needs than on the proposed solution. (The box "Interview with a Student: Sylvia Morales" explores this idea in more detail.) Monroe found that anxious salespeople often begin a sales pitch with a lengthy monolog about the features of a product without first identifying consumers' needs—a highly ineffective sales technique. Like salespeople, public speakers need to assess what needs are pertinent to their audience and then respond to those needs. If audience members do not have readily identifiable needs related to the speech topic, the speaker may need to create needs and wants for them. This is a common strategy for advertisers, who first convince potential consumers that they have a need or problem and then provide a solution. For example, advertisers of carpet-odor-control products create a need by claiming that all carpets smell after prolonged use, and then they provide a product to control these odors.

Outlining a Persuasive Speech

In the speech outlined here, Carmen uses Monroe's Motivated Sequence to convince her audience members to change their language behavior by eliminating sexist implications. Each of the five steps is represented by a Roman numeral. Main points and subpoints follow the notation style described in Chapter 9.

Monroe's Motivated Sequence: A Five-Step Plan to Persuade

Steps

1. *Gain the audience's attention.* As recommended for other types of speeches, begin with some clever attention-getting device. However, do not include a specific preview, which might trigger psychological reactance.

2. *Identify unfulfilled needs.* To persuade your audience, establish that there are clear and urgent needs to be fulfilled.

3. *Propose a solution that satisfies those needs.* Introduce your solution at this point. Show how only your solution can satisfy those needs. Explain how it works, and anticipate and address any potential objections.

4. *Visualize what satisfaction will mean.* Intensify audience members' desire for your solution by having them visualize what their lives will be like with (or without) your solution.

5. *Identify specific actions.* Don't assume that your audience members will know how to obtain or implement your solution. Close the deal by telling them exactly what they need to do to adopt your solution. Keep it brief and simple.

Example

1. *Attention.* Last year, while riding her bike home from calculus class, my roommate crashed. We don't know exactly how it happened because she can't remember. She suffered a serious concussion and broke her foot, several ribs, and a cheekbone. She spent over a week in the hospital.

2. *Need.* Nearly 50,000 bicyclists suffer serious head injuries each year. Three out of four cyclists killed in a crash die as a result of head injuries. On a concrete surface, a fall from less than one foot can cause a concussion. Cyclists clearly need to protect themselves from head injury.

3. *Satisfaction or solution.* Cyclists can protect themselves by wearing helmets. A helmet reduces the risk of serious head injury by almost 90 percent. I used to think that helmets looked stupid and were unnecessary. But there are many attractive helmets, and after what happened to my roommate, I do the smart, safe thing now by always wearing a helmet.

4. *Visualization.* If everyone wore a helmet, the number of fatal bicycle injuries would be reduced by 75 percent. With a helmet on, you can feel confident that you're doing what you can to keep yourself safe.

5. *Action.* There are three places within a mile of campus that sell helmets. Look for a brand that is certified by the American National Standards Institute.

Interview with a Student

Sylvia Morales

Sylvia Morales, 24, is a senior majoring in communication studies at California State University, Long Beach.

Now that you have taken several courses in persuasion theory and persuasive speaking, how difficult is it for you to persuade others?

It's difficult for anyone to persuade others simply because people, by nature, are typically grounded into their beliefs. After all, people want to believe what they already believe. They want to believe what they were taught to believe and what they think is correct. And none of us wants to admit that we are ever wrong. To be persuaded means that we must change, and sometimes admit that we must have been wrong. People can be persuaded, but it's not so easily accomplished.

Recognizing that psychological reactance exists, what advice would you give to students who are just learning how to construct persuasive messages?

Important to being a successful persuader, you must know who you're trying to persuade, know who members of your audience are, know your target. Find out as much as you can about them—their beliefs, their values, and their attitudes. Find out where they are coming from. Even discovering audience members' ethnic background, age, or sex can help you determine how they're going to react to this argument or that one. Whatever you do, don't go in there blind and try persuading them with some generic message or appeal. It won't work.

Continued

Interview with a Student   (Continued)

Sylvia Morales

How does "knowing your audience" fit into Monroe's Motivated Sequence?

Monroe's Motivated Sequence offers a simple outline, a formula to follow in trying to persuade. But critical to that formula is the problem or need step—and it's the most difficult one to learn how to do well. You have to begin by knowing your audience. Unless you know your audience, you can't know what problem or need to target. What you might consider a problem might not be a problem for your audience, or for certain members of your audience. How are you *going to make them see that there is a problem in the first place? And how are you going to make the problem relevant to them? That is the issue. Keep in mind that as the persuader, you're already convinced. Now you need to convince them. It doesn't do any good to try and provide the audience with a solution when they don't see a problem or a need to change. That's why you need to know your audience. Once you understand where they're coming from, then you can build on the problem as they see it and try to meet their unfulfilled needs. Only then can you convince them of your solution.*

SAMPLE SPEECH OUTLINE

Neutralizing Our Language

A speech title is useful when a host introduces the speaker or for printed announcements.

Specific Purpose: To persuade audience members to neutralize their language in an effort to eliminate sexist implications in speech

Thesis Statement: Because sexist language is exclusionary and potentially harmful, we should use alternative words and phrases that include both women and men in our daily speech.

The purpose and thesis statements keep the speech on track by sharply defining the speaker's intent and clearly laying out the problem and solution she will discuss. Notice how Carmen modifies her purpose to fit her audience by choosing a more modest and reasonable goal.

I. Attention
   A. What do the words "chairman," "salesman," "workman," and "mailman" have in common? They all include the word "man," but, more importantly, they all exclude women.
   B. We've all been guilty of using these so-called generic words. After all, they seem harmless enough. But they are not harmless!

Carmen's attention step contains two main points, each designed to grab her audience's attention. Unlike in the introduction of an informative speech, here Carmen does not provide a preview of her central thesis or her main points.

II. Needs
   A. Research has shown that how we view the world is closely tied to how we use language. In turn, language helps to shape how we perceive and understand the world. The way we understand something shapes our actions toward it. Therefore, how we use language influences how we act toward one another.

In the needs step, Carmen demonstrates clearly that a problem exists and that it is time for a change. She provides

Continued

B. Women are excluded or viewed as afterthoughts when we use masculine pronouns and "man"-linked words as generic terms. Such phrases place women in a secondary, subordinate position.

C. Studies have shown that masculine generic phrases are not, in fact, associated equally with men and women. Instead, people are more likely to perceive "he" and other masculine generics as referring only to males.
   1. When job descriptions contain masculine generics, women do not view the jobs as either suitable or appropriate for women.
   2. Students who read textbooks that contain masculine generic pronouns and "man"-linked words were 40 percent more likely to assume that the passages referred to men only rather than to both women and men.
   3. In research studies, both children and adults exposed to masculine generic words assume that only males are being referenced.

D. In other words, what we once thought of as harmless speech turns out to be potentially harmful. Clearly, we have a problem. We can't assume that masculine generic pronouns and "man"-linked words are viewed as referring to both sexes. And we can no longer assume that it makes no difference. Exclusionary language promotes sexist attitudes and actions.

III. Satisfaction

A. To address the problem of biased language, we need to use alternatives to masculine generics and "man"-linked words.
   1. Rather than using third-person singular pronouns ("he," "him," or "his"), switch to the second person ("you") or the first- or third-person plural ("we," "they," "us," or "them").
   2. Alternate between masculine and feminine pronouns, or pair them ("she" or "he," "him" or "her") if appropriate.
   3. Replace "man"-linked words with gender-neutral ones ("flight attendant" instead of "airline steward" or "stewardess"; "mail carrier" instead of "mailman").

B. These kinds of changes are already being implemented.
   1. The new edition of Roget's Thesaurus doesn't contain sexist categories (for example, it includes the heading "human-kind" instead of "mankind").
   2. English teachers are beginning to accept alternatives to the use of masculine generic pronouns.

C. Neutralizing our language may seem difficult or unnecessary, but it's not so.
   1. We might agree that switching pronouns to include "she" and "her" is a hassle and awkward to do. But it's surprising how quickly we can get used to it. It was hard for me at first, too. Now it has become a habit.
   2. Others might believe that we're making much ado about nothing. But the research findings tell us something quite different. Children and college students alike are affected. Put simply, sexist language encourages sexism.

IV. Visualization

A. If gender-biased language were eliminated from our vocabulary, we would be well on our way to establishing a world free of sexual bias. After all, language helps shape how we view our world and one another.

evidence and research findings to support her claims and increase her credibility. After listening to her points, her audience should be sympathetic to the problem and ready to accept a solution.

In the satisfaction step, Carmen immediately and explicitly reveals her solution to the problem she has outlined. Prior to this point, her speech has been primarily an informative one, in which she describes problems with the status quo. Now she provides specific examples of her solutions and backs them up by showing that they've been used in respected publications and professions.

During the satisfaction stage of her speech, Carmen also deals with the audience's potential objections to her plan. She states these objections and shows her understanding of them—but then she argues against them. She shows why she no longer shares those objections and why the audience shouldn't either.

In the visualization step, Carmen ties her proposed solution to the audience's need by having members imagine a world free of

Continued

B. But if we continue to insist that masculine generic pronouns and "man"-linked words are harmless, then we can expect to go on as before, condoning and encouraging inequality and alienation between the sexes.

biased language. She offers a vivid contrast between the positive vision of a world that adopts her solution and the negative vision of a world that remains biased and discriminatory.

V. Action
   A. Practice eliminating gender-biased language in your everyday speech, in your conversations, and in your letters.
   B. Give gentle reminders to others when they use these so-called harmless words and phrases. Suggest alternatives they can use.
   C. We don't want to reverse sexism; we want to eliminate it. Let's begin now with ourselves, in our everyday speech. Neutralize!

Carmen finishes her speech with a call to action that is brief and to the point. Before she leaves the stage, however, she adds a dramatic appeal and a final positive command. A dramatic ending helps ensure that her audience remembers her speech and her message.

REFERENCES

Bem, S. L., & Bem, D. J. (1973). Does sex-biased job advertising "aid and abet" sex discrimination? *Journal of Applied Social Psychology, 3,* 6–28.

Pearson, J. C., Turner, L. H., & Todd-Mancillas, W. (1991). *Gender and communication* (2nd ed., pp. 76–103). Dubuque, IA: Wm. C. Brown.

Todd-Mancillas, W. (1981). Masculine generics-sexist language: A review of literature and implications for speech communication professionals. *Communication Quarterly, 29,* 107–115.

Carmen's outline concludes with a list of the references she used in her speech.

NINE STRATEGIES FOR PERSUADING

The theory of psychological reactance was presented earlier in this chapter to show how and why people are naturally reluctant to change the way they think, feel, and behave. From the start, then, persuasive speakers have their work cut out for them. To successfully influence others, speakers must be sensitive to the dynamics of persuasion and resistance. What follow are nine practical strategies that have been derived from a large body of theory and research on persuasion. These strategies consider how speakers attempt to influence and how audiences resist that influence.

Conceal the Intent to Persuade

By now, it should be clear why you want to mask your objective to influence others. In general, people are repelled when someone tries to pitch them a line or hustle a product. Their first response is to resist persuasion and to say no. Don't give your audience the opportunity to say no too quickly. Instead, identify the need; spend sufficient time developing that need; and then, and only then, provide your audience with the solution.

Don't Ask for Too Much

Your message should not be overly demanding—that is, it should not be too far from what you can realistically ask your audience in the way of change. A whole body of research on message discrepancy indicates that speakers who deliver a message that is too far afield from what their audience is willing to accept are doomed to failure. This does not mean that you should deliver only messages that appeal to your audience; however, you should only ask for gradual, minor progress toward the changes you want. This advice would be especially important if you were to face an audience that disagreed with your point of view. If your message varied greatly from the audience's point of view, psychological reactance would set in, and the boomerang effect would result. The idea of the boomerang effect can be illustrated by a simple example.

Bob wants to convince Nadia that they should get married. If Bob had his way, they'd be married now, but Nadia has resisted the whole idea. So, ignoring the caution against asking for too much, he decides to try and persuade Nadia to marry him within the next two weeks. If she says no, he will threaten to leave her. Sure enough, Nadia resists. But she does more than engage in psychological reactance. She becomes so put off by his attempt that she tells him that not only will she refuse to marry him within the next two weeks, but she has no intention of ever marrying him—the relationship is over!

With the boomerang effect, the outcome is the opposite of what the persuader wanted to achieve. Now imagine the same situation; this time, however, Bob chooses another strategy and avoids asking for too much. He already knows that Nadia isn't particularly thrilled about the idea of marriage. So, forcing a decision in two weeks is out of the question. He avoids a lengthy discussion about marriage altogether and instead suggests an informal engagement. She agrees. Later in the relationship, he asks her to formalize the engagement with a ring. She says okay and agrees to wear his ring. Still later, he suggests a possible wedding date. Nadia rejects that appeal, but she is warming up to the idea. By reducing the amount of change requested at each stage, Bob avoids getting hit by the boomerang and stands a much greater chance of achieving his goal.

Avoid Inflammatory Phrases

Unfortunate word choices can also backfire. There are probably certain words that make you angry or phrases that you find disgusting or that push your emotional buttons. For example, Carmen's speech on neutralizing gender-based language could boomerang easily if she employed explosive terms during her arguments. Because the issue is a sensitive one for many people, Carmen has been careful to select phrases that will not arouse negative feelings toward her. Rather than use phrases like "feminist," and "chauvinist," Carmen has chosen substitutes that are relatively innocuous or even positive but that have the same basic meanings, like "gender-neutral" and "gender-biased." By doing so, Carmen will not alienate large segments of her audience to the point that they will resist listening, learning, or changing.

Use a Two-Sided Message with Refutation

Message sidedness refers to how arguments are presented. There are three basic ways to present an argument: (1) One-sided messages give only the speaker's side of an argument while ignoring the opponent's argument; (2) two-sided messages attempt to give both sides a fair hearing (or at least appear to do so); and (3) two-sided messages with refutation present both sides and refute the validity of the opposing side. Of the three message-sided options, audiences are most influenced when the speaker discusses both sides *and* takes the time to argue against the opposing view. Such a presentation demonstrates that the speaker is credible, intelligent, and objective and that he or she is aware of all the issues at stake and is forthright about presenting them. Consequently, the speaker fulfills the ethical obligation to be fair and responsible and, at the same time, presents her or his point of view in the best light. By spelling out audience objections and sensitively counterarguing the issues on both sides, the speaker either refutes or denies the legitimacy of the opposing position.

To explain how this strategy works, consider Carmen's speech outline on gender-based language one more time. She will indicate a connection with audience members who might object to her topic by using the words "our" and "we." She will go on to state that "we might agree that switching pronouns . . . is a hassle," but she will not agree that it is too much trouble. Next, she will tell the audience that switching pronouns "was hard for me at first, too. Now it has become a habit." Thus, she will further empathize with the audience's position but will demonstrate as well how she was able to change without great difficulty. Carmen's plan is carefully designed to avoid alienating her audience with a one-sided presentation—stating only her perspective. She will take care not to denigrate other positions. She will state her side and then touch on opposing viewpoints. However, she won't leave it at that. If she recognizes that her audience's position is counter to her own, she will be sympathetic but will downplay and then refute those objections. Throughout the speech, Carmen plans to create a we–they mentality. She and the audience will become one team, and "they" (the less politically sensitive) will make up the other.

For many years, researchers and teachers have argued that on occasion, a one-sided message is more appropriate than a two-sided refutational approach, especially when the audience already agrees with the speaker's position. More recent research demonstrates that regardless of the audience's attitudes toward the topic, a two-sided refutational message is still the best bet.[5] The next-best approach, however, is the one-sided message—with the two-sided message without refutation being a poor third choice.

Inoculate against Counterarguments

You may be tempted to forgo using a two-sided message with refutation when you know that your audience already agrees with your position. However, you might want to take the opportunity to "inoculate" the audience against a possible counterargument. If you are to be preceded or followed by a speaker who advocates a contrary position, then **inoculation** by a two-sided message with refutation becomes essential. Even if you know your audience members already agree with you, this strategy helps to ensure that they won't be swayed by the other speaker. The use of evidence is key to the inoculation process.[6]

Suppose, for instance, you are giving a speech advocating the importance of getting good grades in school. Assume that your audience of teenagers already agrees with you; they know that good grades please their parents and will help them get into college. Assuming that they have already been exposed to counterarguments from their peers ("Only geeks and nerds study that hard"), you may want to inoculate your audience. Briefly explain what those counterarguments might be and then refute each one with further argument and evidence. In this way, you arm your audience to resist future counterarguments.

Keep Objections to a Minimum

In step 3 of Monroe's Motivated Sequence, the speaker is supposed to identify and counter potential audience objections to the proposed solution. But keep in mind that this step can be carried too far. At most, a speaker should raise only a couple of objections and, in a five- to ten-minute speech, spend no more than 30 to 60 seconds to recognize and refute these objections.

The purpose of the speech is to persuade the audience not to counter any possible objections to the solution. Thus, if the speaker spends too much time on the objections, at the expense of the advantages of the proposed solution, the audience will probably be more influenced by the objections. Moreover, the speaker risks exposing audience members to objections they may never have thought of before. And once raised, those new objections may sound pretty convincing!

Combine Reason with Emotion

Arguments that persuade are generally rooted in sound reasoning (see Chapter 13). The power to persuade is often based on evidence—facts, statistics, physical data, expert testimony, and eyewitness accounts. As discussed in previous chapters, Euroamericans, particularly male Euroamericans, appreciate objective data. Other co-cultures, including Latinos, African Americans, Asian Americans, and Native Americans, prefer personal testimony and real-life experiences as meaningful sources of evidence. But co-cultural preferences notwithstanding, all groups respond to **emotional appeals**. Aristotle referred to such appeals as *pathos*. Emotional appeals often evoke feelings of disgust, anger, outrage, sorrow, pity, sadness, joy, guilt, and so on. Whatever the targeted emotion, such appeals motivate audience members to do something, to take some action inspired by their new feelings.

Some topics lend themselves more easily to emotional appeals. Obviously, persuasive speeches that center on the homeless, pollution, nuclear war, starving children, victims of rape or abuse, violent crime, or the AIDS epidemic arouse emotions that can be channeled in the direction of change. With the power to manipulate people's emotions, however, comes the responsibility to use it wisely. For example, emotional appeals that incite violence, reinforce hateful prejudices, promote greed or jealousy or selfishness, or capitalize on grief and despair are both unethical and destructive.

Use Fear Appeals—When Appropriate

The use of **fear appeals** is another communication strategy to influence change. High fear appeals, based on threats to one's life, are designed to arouse a high level of anxiety. Low fear appeals are designed to arouse only a low level of anxiety. The original research examining the effectiveness of this strategy indicated that moderate fear appeals produced more change than high or low fear appeals.[7] More recent studies, however, suggest that high fear appeals have more influence than moderate or low fear appeals.[8] Today, it seems clear that within reason, using high fear appeals is an effective way to persuade.

Some speeches lend themselves to fear appeals, such as speeches that advocate stiffer penalties for people who drive drunk, consume illegal drugs, or fail to respect others' property. Spokespersons for automobile safety have been known to rely heavily on fear appeals to persuade people to buckle up or to influence Congress to pass a variety of auto safety bills. Some of these speakers show devastating films of the mangled bodies of auto accident victims; others cite catastrophic statistics or provide personal testimonials to the destruction that occurs when seat belts are not used or when air bags are unavailable. Other media messages that employ strong fear appeals include campaigns that warn consumers against smoking or eating foods high in fat or cholesterol. Ethical speakers must weigh the benefits of using high fear appeals against the disadvantages.

Repeat Your Message

Chapter 10 discussed the importance of previewing and reviewing the main points of a speech—to increase audience attention to what's really important and to increase audience retention. That is, what's repeated gets remembered. Even though Monroe's Motivated Sequence is not set up to either preview or review the major points of a speech, it does require the speaker to discuss the solution at length and to have audience members visualize the adopted solution in their own lives—strategies designed to obtain the same or similar learning effects. And, of course, the problem-solution, web, and other organizational patterns lend themselves easily to repetition.

Another way to optimize your effectiveness as a persuader is to repeat your entire message or relevant portions of it two or three times. When audience members are exposed to a message again (and again), they are more likely to recall the arguments more accurately, understand the message more thoroughly, and believe in the proposed solution more fully. Nevertheless, avoid repeating your message too frequently to prevent psychological reactance, irritation, or boredom. Repeating a message three times seems to be optimal, with one time being too infrequent and five times too frequent.[9]

Although this strategy may be unsuitable for some speech performances, it can be very effective for recorded speech events. The media often highlight speech segments during political campaigns; major newspapers often reprint the entire text of an important speech delivered the previous day; and news networks provide extensive coverage or highlights of policy speeches presented in Congress or at national conferences. In effect, these repeated messages help the media audience digest the information and warm up to the speakers' proposals.

This picture was used as a visual aid in a speech that argued vigorously against drinking alcohol and driving. The speaker employed high fear appeals to support her position. Although the appropriate use of high fear appeals raises an ethical question, using them to persuade an audience produces more change than using either low or moderate fear appeals.

Strategies for Persuading

- *Conceal the intent to persuade.* Because people are repelled when someone tries to pitch them a line or hustle a product, you're better off being more indirect. Begin by identifying and developing a need before introducing your product or idea.

- *Don't ask for too much.* When it comes to persuasion, expect only small, gradual changes from your audience. If you ask for too much change, the boomerang effect likely will occur.

- *Avoid inflammatory phrases.* Because some issues can be particularly sensitive, avoid offensive or provocative words that can turn off your audience. Instead, use phrases that are more neutral.

- *Use a two-sided message with refutation.* Two-sided messages with refutation are designed to give both sides a fair hearing and, at the same time, argue against your opponent's view. Use this type of argument to demonstrate to your audience that you are a credible, responsible speaker.

- *Inoculate against counterarguments.* Inoculation is important when audience members already agree with you and you want to prevent them from being swayed by another

speaker. Inoculate them against counterarguments by systematically refuting what others are likely to say or have already said.

- *Keep objections to a minimum.* Even though you should identify potential objections the audience might have to your persuasive message, you want to be careful not to spend too much time on them—at the expense of your own appeal. Your discussion of objections should be limited to two or three items.

- *Combine reason with emotion.* Logic and reason are vital to persuasive speeches, but don't forget to use emotional appeals as well. Emotional appeals motivate audiences to think, feel, and behave differently.

- *Use fear appeals—when appropriate.* Whenever you use fear appeals to persuade your audience, remember that high fear appeals are more effective than moderate or low fear appeals. Use fear appeals responsibly. Ask yourself, "Does the end justify the means?"

- *Repeat your message.* Be sure to repeat your main points to increase audience attention and retention. What's repeated gets remembered!

The nine persuasive strategies described in this section are based on only some of the more relevant and interesting research findings that can be translated to practical use; many other strategies are available to speakers. (The box "Strategies for Persuading" summarizes the nine strategies.) Clearly, the art and science of persuasive speaking are very complex. The following annotated text of a sample speech is provided to show you how the strategies for organizing and delivering a persuasive speech were effectively employed by one student, Lauren Perez.

SEE WHAT YOU THINK: A STUDENT'S PERSUASIVE SPEECH

Lauren Perez delivered the following five-minute speech in a public speaking class. For this particular persuasive presentation, she received an A. Her delivery was excellent: She was intense, sincere, and earnest; her nonverbal gestures, posture, and facial expressions helped

emphasize important points in her presentation; and she made eye contact with the audience and rarely relied on her notes. The content of her speech was also substantive. She used expert opinions to support her argument, offered interesting and relevant examples, and followed Monroe's Motivated Sequence as she progressed through her speech. By observing the general principles of persuasion, Lauren was careful not to stimulate psychological reactance in her audience. What follows is an annotated text of her speech.

Can you derive the purpose and thesis statement for this speech? Lauren indicated on her outline the following:

Specific Purpose: To persuade my audience to wait until age 30 to get married

Thesis Statement: Because there are too many divorces, too many people living in unsatisfactory marriages, and too many young parents bringing babies into unhappy, broken homes, people should wait to get married until they are at least 30.

SAMPLE SPEECH

It's Worth the Wait

Lauren Perez, Santa Barbara City College

All of us probably know someone who got married early, gave up their education, and are now emotionally and financially destitute because their marriage dissolved. And what's more, I can't go out to a restaurant or the mall without seeing at least one really young couple, barely 20 years old, struggling to get their kid or kids to keep up with them—clearly frustrated with their not-so-small burden.

Sound familiar? Yes, there are a lot of extremely young married couples out there, many of whom have many huge prices to pay for their premature—and immature—unions. In today's complex society, early marriage is a recipe for economic hardship and emotional distress for many couples. In fact, a nationally known radio talk show host, Dr. Laura Schlessinger, has written several books that discuss this issue in detail. Doesn't it say a lot that these books are titled *Ten Stupid Things Women Do to Mess Up Their Lives*, and not to be gender exclusive, Ten Stupid *Things Men Do to Mess Up Their Lives* . . . and another, *How Could You DO That?*

What are some reasons that people marry so young? And what happens as a result? For one thing, a number of people get married barely out of high school because the woman is pregnant. These young people barely know how to take care of their own needs, let alone those of a baby. Most of them have never lived on their own, been responsible for paying rent, the cost of food, clothing, or travel—and some have never even done a load of laundry by themselves!

It's been said that "choices should be made out of courage, not force." Being forced into a marriage that you are too young to handle because of a baby is unfair to the couple and to the child. Let's be frank: failing to use birth control or getting pregnant on purpose when you're young and unmarried are irresponsible behaviors that lead to unhappy homes.

A second problem that results in young, troubled marriages occurs when people get married right out of high school and one or the other gives up the chance to go to college. Or, others get married right out of college before starting careers, and one or the other sacrifices career opportunities. The odds of divorce are stacked against people who get married right out of college—and are worse yet for those who have just graduated from high school. Can you imagine sacrificing college or launching your career only to be swiftly divorced with no way to support yourself?

My own sister married her husband as soon as they graduated from college. He was a Marine officer, so they moved frequently. Consequently, my sister never developed the career she'd prepared so diligently for in college. Later, in her mid-forties, when they divorced, my sister had not had a full-time job in close to 20 years. She'd be glad to tell you how difficult it is for a middle-aged woman with a college degree she's never used to find a job to support herself and two children. See, it's nice to have companionship—and sex can be nice, too—but as Dr. Laura says, "To be truly manly, or womanly, needs must supersede wants." An education and a way to make a living are two of our most basic needs.

Finally, no matter what reason they give for marrying, most very young people, under the age of 30, haven't had enough experience with relationships to decide if they

---

Title: *The title is attention-catching and prevents psychological reactance to the speaker's topic. The audience, instead, will wonder, "What's worth the wait?"*

Attention: *Lauren mentions several ideas that her audience is likely to relate to. She builds common ground with her example of seeing young couples with children at the mall—a scene that's familiar to many. She ends the introduction on a humorous note by naming two books with the phrase "ten stupid things" in the titles.*

Needs: *Lauren clearly establishes three basic needs or problems: (1) young women who marry because they are pregnant, (2) marriages that involve one or the other partner giving up his or her education or career track, and (3) the lack of experience with relationships and dating that people under thirty have. Lauren does an excellent job supporting each need with a relevant quote or, in the case of point number two, a personal example.*

Continued

are willing to fulfill the many obligations that come with a lifelong commitment. It's a simple fact that the younger we are, the less time we've had in relationships. The fewer people we've dated, the less we know about our likes and dislikes. I can't even get along with a roommate who's a good friend for very long! What would I do with a *lifelong* roommate whom I couldn't possibly know very well? And, the fewer people we've dated and known intimately, the less we know about what other people like about US. It's important to know which of our behaviors, eccentricities, and positive attributes affect people who are close to us.

Fortunately, there is a way that we can increase our chances of happiness and lifelong satisfaction. It's a solution that allows us to learn more about ourselves, relationships, and other people, to pursue an education, and establish our independence. It's a solution that guarantees we'll relate to our partner on a mature level, because we haven't had to sacrifice things like education and experience. Since the statistics show that odds of divorce decrease as the age of the partners increases, *wait until you're at least 30 to marry!*

Waiting until you're 30 gives you time to finish school, start a career, and save some money to build a financial base. While many say that money is the root of all evil, it's also the basis for stability and independence. When we have an education, a career, and some money, we have choices.

It's hard to know now how much "better" you'll be at relationships and intimacy in just ten or fewer years (if you're under 30). But others have convinced me just how much more well equipped I will be for a long-term commitment if I wait just a few years. Think about it—you'll have the chance to date more people, finish school, establish financial independence, spend more time by yourself, and decide where you want to live. All of these factors will allow you to be more confident and satisfied with yourself. Then you'll be more confident and satisfied with your relationship. If the chance of divorce decreases the longer you wait, waiting until you're at least 30 INCREASES your chance of a lifelong, satisfying companionship than if you were to marry now or right after college.

So, I'd like you to think twice before you enter into a lifelong commitment, especially if you are under 30. Take time to get your own life on the right track by finishing college, developing your career, and establishing your independence before you marry. Date or spend time alone, but please wait until you're at least 30 to get married! It will be worth the wait.

Satisfaction and Visualization: After establishing the need, Lauren offers a solution: Wait until you're at least 30 to get married. She helps her audience visualize why this is a satisfactory decision by naming a number of advantages, including finishing school, establishing a career and independence, and building a savings account.

She mentions a divorce statistic that might be more credible if she were to indicate the exact figure and who reported it.

Action: Lauren clearly states her solution for the problems she has described. Her call to action may have been strengthened if she had encouraged her audience to discuss this issue with their friends as well.

CHAPTER REVIEW

- Whereas the goal of informative speaking is to teach, the overriding goal of persuasive speaking is to advocate. Persuasive speakers want the audience to feel, think, or behave differently as a consequence of their speech. Different kinds of persuasive speeches include political speeches, speeches advocating social change, advertisements, sermons, and motivational speeches.

- Persuading others to change how they think, feel, or behave is no easy task. According to the theory of psychological reactance, people are naturally resistant to others' attempts to influence them. When exposed to persuasive messages, some audiences, feeling that their freedom of choice is being threatened, may resist or react negatively. Different persuasive techniques should be used with three different types of audiences: an audience that already agrees with the speaker's position, a neutral or undecided audience, and an audience that disagrees with the speaker's point of view.

- Because people tend to resist persuasion, the simple three-step format used to organize an informative speech is not necessarily the best way to organize a persuasive speech. Instead, Monroe's Motivated Sequence provides an effective five-step way of organizing a persuasive message that appeals to audiences. Combining both linear and configural organizational patterns, the sequence begins by gaining the audience's attention and identifying (or creating) unfulfilled needs. Only after the needs are established does the speaker present the solution, explain how the solution works, and eliminate potential objections to that solution. Next, the speaker helps audience members visualize what their lives will be like with (or without) the solution. Finally, the speaker specifies how to obtain the solution, be it a product, a proposal, or some kind of practice.

- Numerous research studies have demonstrated how complex and sophisticated the process of persuasion can be. Nine particularly effective strategies derived from some of these studies range from rather simple advice, such as conceal the intent to persuade, to more complicated recommendations, such as use a two-sided message with refutation.

QUESTIONS FOR CRITICAL THINKING & REVIEW

1. Does anyone have the right to try to persuade others to do something they may not want to do—or to change their attitudes and beliefs? From an ethical point of view, when is persuasion good?

2. This chapter recommends that you use a two-sided message with refutation in a persuasive speech. Do you think a one-sided message would ever be appropriate? If so, when?

3. Are some speaking situations not suited to the use of emotional appeals? Can an audience be motivated to respond with too much emotion? When?

4. Knowing that humans have a natural tendency to resist persuasive attempts, can you identify a situation in which an audience may actually welcome persuasion?

NOTES

1. Sachs, A. (1993, August 16). First, kiss all the lawyers. *Time, 39.*
2. Brehm, J. W. (1966). *A theory of psychological reactance.* New York: Academic Press.
3. Burroughs, N. F., Kearney, P., & Plax, T. G. (1989). Compliance-resistance in the college classroom. *Communication Education, 38,* 214–229; Kearney, P., Plax, T. G., & Burroughs, N. F. (1991). An attributional analysis of college students' resistance decisions. *Communication Education, 40,* 325–342.
4. Monroe, A. H. (1935). *Principles and types of speech.* Chicago: Scott, Foresman.
5. Allen, M., Hale, J., Mongeau, P., Berkowitz-Stafford, S., Stafford, S., Shanahan, W., Agee, P., Dillon, K., Jackson, R., & Ray, C. (1990). Testing a model of message sidedness: Three replications. *Communication Monographs, 37,* 275–291.
6. McCroskey, J. C. (1970). The effects of evidence as an inhibitor of counterpersuasion. *Speech Monographs, 37,* 188–194.
7. Janis, I., & Feshbach, S. (1953). Effects of fear arousing communications. *Journal of Abnormal and Social Psychology, 48,* 78–92.
8. Boster, F., & Mongeau, P. (1984). Fear-arousing persuasive messages. In R. Bostrom (Ed.), *Communication yearbook 8* (pp. 330–377). Beverly Hills, CA: Sage.
9. Cacioppo, J. T., & Petty, R. E. (1979). Effects of message repetition and position on cognitive response, recall, and persuasion. *Journal of Personality and Social Psychology, 37,* 97–109.

Chapter 13

GENERATING ARGUMENTS

Linda sat down at her desk and began to outline the central argument for her upcoming persuasive speech. She had just returned from the library, where she had spent many hours gathering facts, statistics, and other types of evidence on her topic. Linda knew that how effective she was at persuading her audience would depend on her ability to present reasons and evidence for accepting what she was arguing in her speech. As she began to organize her thoughts, she reminded herself that a good persuasive speech is always constructed around at least one strong argument. She knew that an argument always includes a series of related reasons for accepting what is being advocated in a speech.

The intent of Linda's speech is to convince her audience that the federal government should pass a law prohibiting the smoking of cigarettes, pipes, and cigars in all public places. In her argument, she asserts that such a law is needed at this time because of certain well-documented facts. First, a large amount of scientific research demonstrates that smoking is clearly linked to a variety of fatal diseases. Second, a large amount of scientific research indicates that indirect exposure to tobacco smoke is also clearly linked to a wide variety of fatal diseases. Third, the costs of health care associated with smoking and exposure to second-hand smoke are estimated to be in the billions of dollars. Finally, a majority of Americans favor a ban on smoking in public places. Linda brings her argument to a close by concluding that based on this evidence, the federal government should pass a law prohibiting the smoking of cigarettes, pipes, and cigars in all public places.

Linda's approach to crafting her speech represents one of the many different forms of argument that are available to you as you prepare a persuasive speech. This chapter focuses on how to construct sound arguments to include in persuasive speeches. Specifically, it describes the two general ways arguments can be formulated, examines common forms or patterns of reasoning, and discusses some of the more compelling errors in reasoning.

Learning Objectives

After reading this chapter, you should be able to do the following:

1. Differentiate between inductive and deductive reasoning and formulate clear and convincing arguments of each type.

2. Describe the elements in Toulmin's model of argument and diagram an argument according to the model.

3. Describe and use each of the five common patterns of reasoning.

4. Identify and avoid common patterns of unsound reasoning.

THE BASICS OF THE REASONING PROCESS

Whenever we publicly take a position and argue it with facts, observations, and other supporting evidence, we are engaging in the **reasoning process**. Most of us engage in this process all the time. In fact, virtually all serious communication exchanges include the reasoning process in one form or another. We employ reasoning when we deliberate with our spouse or significant other over where to go on vacation; we utilize it when we argue with our friends over where to go to dinner on Friday night; we use it when we debate the merits of alternative approaches to completing a project with our coworkers; and we use it in our speech class when, like Linda, we argue our position in a persuasive speech. In this section, we'll look at basic types of arguments and basic strategies for constructing sound argument.

Inductive and Deductive Reasoning

Whether you are constructing a highly subjective argument to employ with a friend or are generating an argument based on well-documented scientific research to present to an audience, the pattern of reasoning you use typically falls into one of two general categories—inductive or deductive. In **inductive reasoning**, specific examples or observations are presented to support a general conclusion; in **deductive reasoning**, a general statement or principle is applied to a specific case. Inductive and deductive arguments can be developed within a speech or can underlie a speech as a whole. Let's take a closer look at these two general types of reasoning.

Inductive Reasoning Inductive reasoning involves drawing, formulating, or inferring a reasonable general conclusion from specific supporting evidence, examples, or data. It is a common pattern of reasoning in persuasive speeches. Linda's argument described in the opening of the chapter is an example of the inductive reasoning process. She provides specific evidence to support the claim (conclusion) she makes in her speech:

Supporting Evidence

- A large amount of scientific research demonstrates that smoking is clearly linked to a wide variety of fatal diseases.
- A large amount of scientific research indicates that indirect exposure to tobacco smoke is clearly linked to a wide variety of fatal diseases.
- The costs of health care associated with smoking and indirect exposure to smoke are estimated to be in the billions of dollars.
- A majority of Americans favor a ban on smoking in public places.

Conclusion

- Therefore, Congress should pass a law prohibiting the smoking of cigarettes, pipes, and cigars in all public places.

Notice that Linda's **conclusion** can be inferred from the supporting evidence she presents. When we reason inductively, we argue that a general conclusion is or will be true because of one or more particular instances or specific pieces of evidence.

When you construct an inductive argument for a speech, consider the following guidelines for creating an effective **argument**:

1. Provide a sufficient number of examples or pieces of evidence to support your conclusion. The more

sweeping or general your conclusion, the more evidence you will need.

2. Choose evidence that is relevant, representative, and reliable. Back evidence with statistics and expert testimony. (See the discussion of evidence in Chapter 8 for more information.)

3. Qualify or limit your conclusion if your evidence doesn't support a sweeping generalization. For example, Linda concluded that Congress should ban smoking in public places; she didn't argue for criminalizing all tobacco use. The latter conclusion is not supported by the evidence she presented in her speech.

To evaluate the inductive reasoning used by another speaker, ask yourself if she or he has followed these guidelines.

Deductive Reasoning Deductive reasoning typically involves moving from a general category to a specific case or instance. When we reason deductively, we argue that a particular instance is true because it follows from a general proposition. Deductive arguments include three basic elements: a major **premise**, a minor premise, and a conclusion. The major premise is a general statement about a class or category of things—people, events, objects, and so on. The minor premise links a specific thing or case with the general group described in the major premise. The conclusion of a deductive argument states that what is true of the general group in the major premise is also true of the specific case in the minor premise. If formulated correctly, the logic of a deductive argument is inescapable. Consider the following examples:

Major Premise: People who don't have a college ID card can't borrow books from the college library.

Minor Premise: Richard doesn't have an ID card.

Conclusion: Therefore, Richard can't borrow books from the college library.

Major Premise: Members of Congress who run for reelection won't vote for tax increases.

Minor Premise: Pat Simmons is a senator from California who is running for reelection.

Conclusion: Therefore, Pat Simmons will vote against raising taxes.

Deductive reasoning doesn't yield new information or knowledge in the same way that inductive reasoning does. Rather, it involves extracting conclusions that are hidden but implicit in information we already have. Inductive and deductive reasoning are not opposites, however. A conclusion from an inductive argument may establish or verify a principle that can be used as the major premise of a deductive argument.

Strategies for putting together a sound deductive argument include the following:

1. Make certain that your major and minor premises are accurate. If one of the premises is false, the conclusion of the argument cannot be accepted.

2. Determine whether your major and minor premises will be accepted by your audience. If your audience is unfamiliar with one or both of your premises, you may need to explain them and use inductive reasoning to support them.

3. Clearly state the relationship between the general category in the major premise and the specific case in the minor premise.

4. Qualify your premises or conclusion as needed. If audience members can think of exceptions to something that you have stated in absolute terms, they may reject your argument if you do not qualify it in some way. Consider the qualifiers in the following deductive argument: The *vast majority* of smokers want to quit smoking; Will is a smoker; therefore, it is *very likely* that Will wants to quit smoking.

The Toulmin Model of Argument

Whether you employ inductive or deductive reasoning in your speech, your argument must be convincing if you are to persuade your audience. Philosopher Stephen Toulmin developed a method of diagramming or mapping key portions of an argument to help assess its soundness or defensibility.[1] His method uncovers elements of an argument that might otherwise be hidden. Applying Toulmin's method can help you create and strengthen your own arguments, as well as evaluate the arguments used by other speakers.

According to the **Toulmin model of argument**, arguments must contain three basic parts:

- **Claim**—the conclusion or generalization supported in an argument
- **Grounds**—the facts, information, or evidence used to support the claim
- **Warrant**—the explanation, justification, or underlying assumption that connects the grounds and the claim

As Figure 13-1 shows, any argument can be divided into these three component parts, diagrammed, and carefully examined. Many arguments used in persuasive speeches jump from grounds to claim without spelling

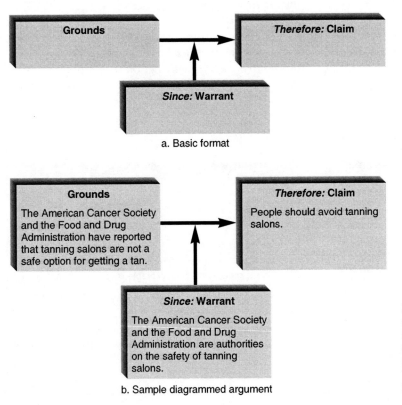

a. Basic format

b. Sample diagrammed argument

Figure 13-1 Basic format for diagramming arguments using the Toulmin model. Every argument includes a claim, grounds for accepting the claim, and a warrant that links the grounds and the claim. The terms "since" and "therefore" help illustrate the reasoning process.

out the warrant, so warrants are often implied rather than actually stated. However, examining a warrant is a key part of evaluating an argument. Consider the following argument: The American Cancer Society and the Food and Drug Administration have reported that tanning salons are not a safe option for getting a tan; therefore, people should avoid tanning salons. What is the warrant in this case? The underlying, implicit assumption in this argument is that the American Cancer Society and the Food and Drug Administration are authoritative sources on the safety of tanning salons (see Figure 13-1).

In addition to claim, grounds, and warrant, arguments may include other elements. As described earlier, *qualifying statements* are sometimes needed to limit or narrow the scope of a claim. If the grounds for an argument do not support a sweeping conclusion, the claim should be qualified appropriately. In the tanning salon example, if the evidence against the safety of tanning salons applied only to certain types of tanning salons or only to certain groups of people, then the claim would need to be qualified. In addition, if the warrant for an argument might not be generally agreed upon, additional *backing* may be required. Although most people would agree that the American Cancer Society and the Food and Drug Administration are authoritative sources, a speaker might want to provide evidence of their expertise—for example, citing the number of studies these organizations have carried out on tanning salons—to back up the warrant. Finally, some arguments may include *rebuttals*, responses to expected disagreements with the claim. If a speaker can anticipate possible audience disagreements, she or he can rebut

these, thereby creating a more convincing argument. (See the discussion of inoculation against counterarguments in Chapter 12.)

Once an argument has been diagrammed, it is easier to examine and evaluate its parts. The box "Strategies for Evaluating Arguments" provides a list of questions that you can use to evaluate arguments you create for your persuasive speeches and arguments used by other speakers.

COMMON PATTERNS OF REASONING

Arguments used in persuasive speeches commonly fall into five general categories: reasoning by example, reasoning by analogy, reasoning by cause, reasoning by sign, and reasoning by authority. In this section, we'll examine each of these patterns of reasoning using the Toulmin model of argument and the method of diagramming described previously.

Reasoning by Example

Reasoning by example involves drawing a conclusion or asserting a generalization based on one or more events, instances, or supporting cases.[2] For instance, a speaker may reason that there is a definite need for more student parking on campus because she has talked to many students (examples) who have been unable to find a parking space on a regular basis. Or a speaker might argue that it is a waste of time to try to talk a police officer out of a speeding ticket because a number of his friends (examples) have tried and failed. Or a speaker may reason that prolonged exposure to the sun is a health hazard because he has met

---

BUILDING YOUR SKILLS

Strategies for Evaluating Arguments

To evaluate an argument, ask the following questions:

- Is the claim stated clearly? Is it specific and detailed?

- Does the claim need to be qualified in any way? Would qualifying the claim make the argument more convincing?

- Is all the evidence presented as grounds true?

- Do the grounds clearly and sufficiently support the claim? Would the inclusion of more evidence strengthen the argument?

- Is the warrant clear and generally agreed upon by the audience? Would additional backing or support for the warrant make it more acceptable to the audience?

- Should the warrant be explicitly stated in the argument, or is it so obvious that it need not be stated?

- Is the audience likely to object to the claim for some reason? Should rebuttals of these likely objections be included to strengthen the argument?

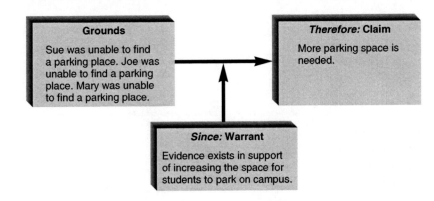

Grounds

Sue was unable to find a parking place. Joe was unable to find a parking place. Mary was unable to find a parking place.

Therefore: Claim

More parking space is needed.

Since: Warrant

Evidence exists in support of increasing the space for students to park on campus.

Figure 13-2 Reasoning by example.
This pattern involves drawing a conclusion or asserting a generalization based on one or more events, instances, or supporting cases.

several people (examples) who sunbathed regularly for years and who now have skin cancer. In each of these cases, the speaker shows how the conclusion or generalization follows from the examples provided.

A diagram of a sample argument involving reasoning by example is shown in Figure 13-2. The diagram clearly illustrates the elements of this argument. However, the soundness of this line of reasoning still needs to be established. The following questions can provide a good test of the quality of reasoning by example:[3]

- *Is each example presented truthfully and accurately?* As described in Chapter 5, ethical speakers present evidence in an objective, unbiased form. Hypothetical examples can clarify points and add interest to a speech, but they should not be used as evidence in an argument. In the sample line of reasoning diagrammed in Figure 13-2, we would ask whether Sue, Joe, and Mary are actual students who truly had trouble finding parking on campus.

- *Is each example relevant to the matter under consideration?* Is each of the student examples used to support the claim shown in Figure 13-2 truly applicable to the issue of the availability of parking on campus?

- *Are a reasonable number of examples provided?* Do the three students in the example represent a large enough sample to support the claim? Exactly how large a representative sample would be in this case depends on the size of the student body at the college in question.

- *Do the examples cover a critical time period, or are they restricted in some fashion?* In the sample case, were the limitations on parking space common throughout the semester or quarter or the entire academic year?

- *Are the examples typical or representative of the problem in question? Are there other examples that do not support the conclusion?* For our sample argument, we would need to ask if there were more examples of students who indicated they did *not* have problems finding places to park.

If the answer to each of these questions is an unqualified yes, then the soundness of the argument is clear. If not, then additional work should be done to strengthen the argument before including it in a speech.

Reasoning by Analogy

An analogy is an inference that if two or more things are alike in some respects, they will probably be similar in other respects as well. **Reasoning by analogy** consists of making a comparison between similar cases and inferring that what is or will be true in one case is or will be true in the others.[4] For example, consider John and Sherri, two teenagers of the same age and socioeconomic background who attend the same high school. If John goes to the dentist twice a year to get his teeth cleaned and hasn't had a cavity in years, we can infer that if Sherri went to the dentist at least twice a year, she would have similar dental health. Or consider Ed, a college student who needed to save money to pay for car insurance. Ed was able to save $200 for his insurance in one year simply by using food coupons at the grocery store. Philip is a student at the same college and is similar to Ed in a number of important ways; he also needs to save money for his car insurance. Based on Ed's experience and the many ways in which Ed and Philip are similar, we can infer that Philip can save the money he needs to pay his car insurance by using coupons at the grocery store.

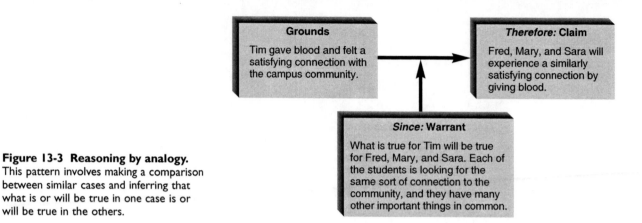

Grounds
Tim gave blood and felt a satisfying connection with the campus community.

Therefore: **Claim**
Fred, Mary, and Sara will experience a similarly satisfying connection by giving blood.

Since: **Warrant**
What is true for Tim will be true for Fred, Mary, and Sara. Each of the students is looking for the same sort of connection to the community, and they have many other important things in common.

Figure 13-3 Reasoning by analogy.
This pattern involves making a comparison between similar cases and inferring that what is or will be true in one case is or will be true in the others.

A third analogous argument is diagrammed in Figure 13-3. Tim, a college senior, gave blood during a recent Red Cross blood drive on campus and felt very satisfied for having done so. He had been looking for a way to connect more to the campus community, and giving blood gave him that feeling of connection. Fred, Mary, and Sara, three other seniors from the same town as Tim, have also been looking for ways to connect with the campus community. We can conclude that giving blood will provide Fred, Mary, and Sara with that satisfying sense of attachment to the campus community, just as it did for Tim.

The following questions can be used to assess the quality of arguments by analogy:

- *Are the cases presented in the argument the same or similar in all the relevant respects?* Are Tim, Fred, Mary, and Sara really similar in all the ways that are important to supporting the claim?

- *Are there any key differences among the cases being compared that are relevant? Do the differences outweigh the similarities and thus negate the analogy?* In the sample argument, for example, would the fact that Fred and Sara are from Middle Eastern backgrounds and Tim and Mary are Euroamerican in their co-cultural orientation nullify the strength of comparison? What if Fred has never given blood before but Mary and Sara have donated blood many times in the past?

Reasoning by Cause

When we infer that one event is the direct result of another event, we are reasoning by cause. Causal arguments can be presented in a cause-to-effect format or in a reversed effect-to-cause format.[5] The essential difference between the two formats is one of chronology. In **reasoning from cause to effect**, a speaker moves from a known fact or event to a predicted result that occurs later in time. For example, if interest rates are raised (cause), a speaker may predict that the stock market will go down (effect). In **reasoning from effect to cause**, a speaker moves from a known fact or event (effect) backward in time to the predicted cause. Medical diagnosis is an example of effect-to-cause reasoning: An individual comes down with symptoms of food poisoning (effect), and a doctor looks back at the foods the individual has eaten to pinpoint the source of the illness (cause).

Speakers often employ causal reasoning in persuasive speeches. For example, a speaker might argue that if we would simply outlaw all guns, then the murder rate would drop substantially. Another speaker might reason that if people who are serious about losing weight would reduce the amount of fat in their diets, they would lose pounds. Finally, as shown in Figure 13-4, a speaker might argue that the burning of fossil fuels such as gasoline will cause the world's temperature to rise. Obviously, in each of these examples, the result (effect) in question could be attributed to a variety of potential causes. To help determine whether a causal argument is sound, consider the following questions:

- *Does the effect clearly follow as a result of the cause, or do the events simply occur together in time?* For a causal argument to be sound, the connection between the two events must be real. (Reasoning by sign, which is discussed in the next section, uses events that occur together in time but that are not causally related.) In the argument diagrammed in Figure 13-4, we would need to ask if the studies on the effects of carbon

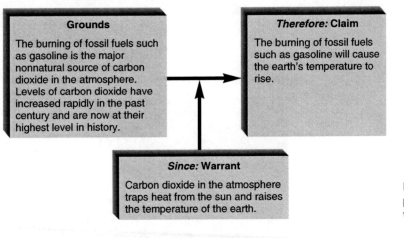

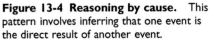

Figure 13-4 Reasoning by cause. This pattern involves inferring that one event is the direct result of another event.

dioxide were appropriate in type and magnitude to realistically be applied to the question of global temperature.

- *Is the cause in question the sole or primary factor influencing the effect? Are there other causes of equal or greater importance?* To evaluate the strength of a causal argument, other possible causes must be carefully considered. In the example of fossil fuel burning, there may in fact be other facts that influence global temperature. For example, long-term fluctuations in weather patterns that have nothing to do with human activity could have a greater impact on global temperature. A convincing causal argument must show that the cause in question is a substantial contributor to the effect—that without the cause, the effect would have been much smaller or would not have occurred at all.

- *Is the cause strong or large enough to produce the predicted effect?* Is the increase in carbon dioxide from the burning of fossil fuels significant enough to cause global changes in temperature?

Reasoning by Sign

Reasoning by sign is sometimes misinterpreted as reasoning by cause. However, rather than reasoning from either cause to effect or effect to cause, **reasoning by sign** involves reasoning from *effect to effect*.[6] If we argue that one effect is a meaningful indicator of one or more other effects, we are employing sign reasoning. A main distinction between sign and causal arguments is that when we reason by sign, we make no assumption that a given sign is the cause of any effect.[7] For example, if we argue that because the

sky is clear and there are no rain clouds in sight, it is not going to rain, we are reasoning by sign. In this case, the clear sky is a sign that it will not rain (the effect). Obviously, whether it rains on any particular occasion is the result of many possible *causes*. We are not arguing that a clear sky causes dry weather; we are simply inferring that the clear sky is a reliable *sign*, or indicator, that it will not rain.

Another example of reasoning by sign is diagrammed in Figure 13-5. In this example, we infer based on several signs that John doesn't respect the environment: (1) He doesn't recycle; (2) he drops trash around the park when he goes on picnics; and (3) he refuses to participate in community cleanup projects. We do not infer the causes of John's disrespect for the environment; rather, we simply conclude that the evidence indicates that he is disrespectful of the environment.

Use the following questions to assess the quality of arguments by sign:

- *Are the signs reliable indicators of the effect under consideration?* In the example of John, does his behavior truly substantiate his disregard for the environment?

- *Are there conflicting signs?* Are there other things John does that provide evidence of his respect for the environment?

- *Is any sign employed in the argument an accidental or chance occurrence?* Are any of the indicators of John's lack of respect fluke occurrences? If any or all of the signs used to construct the argument are chance events, then the argument will not hold up to scrutiny.

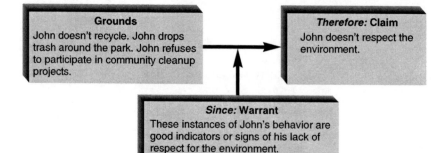

Figure 13-5 Reasoning by sign.
This pattern involves reasoning from effect to effect.

Reasoning by Authority

The final type of argument we'll consider in this chapter is reasoning by authority. In **reasoning by authority**, we argue that our claim or conclusion is warranted because there are one or more trusted experts who stand behind it.[8] Public speakers reason by authority all the time. For example, if a speaker argues that students should begin saving money for retirement right out of college and states that this idea is strongly supported by the presidents of Bank of America, Wells Fargo Bank, and American Savings and Loan (three credible financial institutions), she is reasoning from authority. Another example of reasoning by authority, as shown in Figure 13-6, is a speaker arguing that according to the American Medical Association, to avoid problems with high blood pressure in middle age, we should exercise vigorously for at least 20 minutes, four or more times a week.

The following questions can be used to assess arguments by authority:

- *Is the authority referenced in the argument truly a credible authority on the topic in question? Is there any reason to suspect bias?* Is the AMA really a credible authority on approaches to prevent high blood pressure? (See Chapter 8 for more on evaluating sources of information.)

- *Is the claim supported by other credible authorities?* If, for example, the American Cancer Society, another highly credible organization, also endorses this exercise recommendation, the support for the claim is even stronger. But if some similarly credible organization like the American Lung Association cautioned people about the potentially adverse effects of excessive exercise, the claim could be weakened.

Combining Different Types of Reasoning in Your Speech

As you become more skillful at generating different types of arguments, you may choose to include more than one type of reasoning in a single speech. Incorporating two or more patterns of reasoning into your speech can add to the overall persuasiveness of your presentation. Consider the following example of a speaker who wants to persuade her audience that women in the armed forces are just as capable as men of engaging in combat. She might employ the following arguments:

- *Reasoning by example:* Cite representative cases in which women have successfully operated in combat situations.

- *Reasoning by analogy:* Describe how women in the military in this country are virtually the same in

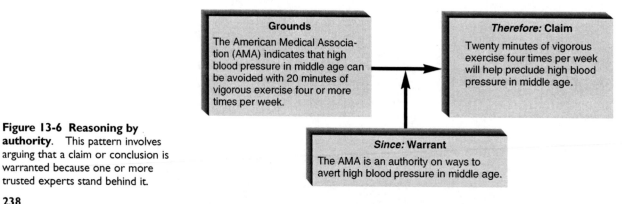

Figure 13-6 Reasoning by authority. This pattern involves arguing that a claim or conclusion is warranted because one or more trusted experts stand behind it.

all pertinent ways as women in the military in countries like Israel, where women are authorized to engage in combat.

- *Reasoning by cause:* Explain the highly specialized training (the cause) that would produce a female soldier who would be more than capable of meeting the demands faced in combat (the effect).

- *Reasoning by sign:* Explain that during military training, a number of important indicators of success in combat can be indexed to ensure that only women who appear ready will be sent into combat situations.

- *Reasoning by authority:* Note the many highly credible military leaders and strategists who support the use of properly trained women in combat situations.

In preparing a speech, then, you can employ many patterns of reasoning to increase the overall impact of your presentation on your audience. The box "Common Patterns of Sound Reasoning" briefly summarizes these patterns.

A CLOSER LOOK

Common Patterns of Sound Reasoning

- *Reasoning by example:* Drawing a conclusion or asserting a generalization based on one or more events, instances, or supporting cases.

- *Reasoning by analogy:* Making a comparison between similar cases and inferring that what is or will be true in one case is or will be true in the others.

- *Reasoning by cause:* Inferring that one event is the direct result of another event. In cause-and-effect reasoning, one moves from a known fact or event to a predicted future result. In effect-to-cause reasoning, one moves from a known fact or event backward in time to the predicted cause.

- *Reasoning by sign:* Inferring from the occurrence of one event or sign that another event will occur.

- *Reasoning by authority:* Arguing that a claim is accurate because it is supported by one or more trusted experts.

EVALUATING THE SOUNDNESS OF ARGUMENTS

Whether you rely on one type of argument or many, the soundness of the reasoning in your speech is critical to your ability to influence your audience. Audience members are often highly sensitive to errors in reasoning, and they react adversely to speakers who treat them like they are stupid by incorporating either inaccurate evidence or faulty reasoning into a speech. Once one or more audience members identify a serious flaw in a speaker's reasoning, there is no chance for persuasion to occur. It is like being caught in a lie—whatever credibility you had is gone! So what can you do to make sure that you make **sound arguments** in your speeches?

As mentioned previously, diagramming each of your arguments using the Toulmin method helps to uncover any weak points or unsound reasoning. Answering the questions associated with each type of reasoning also gives you an opportunity to strengthen your arguments and correct any points of evidence or reasoning that are inaccurate, misleading, or false. Unfortunately, diagramming arguments and answering pertinent questions aren't always enough. Even though we may have the best of intentions in constructing our arguments, we can still fall prey to any number of inherently faulty patterns of reasoning. Interestingly, a primary reason speakers sometimes employ faulty arguments in their speeches is that at first glance, they can be highly compelling. As public speakers, however, we are ethically bound to identify and correct errors in logic and to present arguments that are sound and reasonable. Speakers may fall into these unsound practices of reasoning unintentionally; however, unethical and manipulative speakers employ them to fool or mislead their audiences. Ethical speakers prepare their arguments carefully and rework them to ensure that they are accurate and sound. (See the box "Interview with a Professional: Jennifer Waldeck" for more on the importance of using sound reasoning practices when speaking persuasively.)

What follow are some common reasoning errors for you to keep in mind when developing and refining your own speech arguments.[9]

Proposing a False Dilemma

A speaker gives only two alternatives when there are actually more. For example, a speaker could claim that either audience members support the idea of prayer in the public schools or they are atheists. Or a speaker could claim that if audience members haven't

Interview with a Professional

Jennifer Waldeck

Jennifer Waldeck, 26, is an experienced teacher in the field of communication and has special expertise in public speaking.

How important is it for a speaker to ensure that all of the arguments included in a speech are carefully crafted and soundly reasoned?

When people argue controversial issues, there are always others just waiting for an opportunity to target something— and an unsound argument is easy prey for the opposition. In fact, an unreasonable argument is the first thing your opposi- tion should attack. Once they have pointed out inaccuracies, falla- cies, or gaps in your logic, you're done! Remember that there are always two sides to every issue, and a carefully researched and worded argument can help you win support for your side.

How large a part does the soundness and defensibility of arguments in a persuasive speech play in reaching the overall objective of a presentation?

A well-organized argument that is supported by credible evidence is the foundation of a persuasive presentation. In other words, the most polished, attractive, or educated speaker may not necessarily be able to meet his or her objectives if the argu- ments in the presentation are not well reasoned and supported by facts. However, delivery style and verbal and nonverbal immediacy are important factors in the persuasive process as well. For instance, I once worked with a candidate for state office who is extremely well educated—a superb researcher who was always well prepared with the facts to support his arguments. However, his candidate appearances weren't always successful because he appeared too "bookish"—the voters couldn't relate to him. So, I helped him to incorporate more personal examples and stories into his arguments as means of support. His popularity increased dramatically over time, and people really began to hear and understand his views, rather be put off by his analytic, intellectual articulation of the issues.

Which of the more common types of faulty reasoning are the most compelling to inexperienced speakers (and why?) and thus the most likely to be employed?

Inexperienced students of public speaking often don't have the ability to consume information wisely; consequently, many are

likely to rely on false experts. Speakers should read all evidence skeptically and submit it to tests of credibility before using it in a persuasive argument. How recent is the information? Who is the source, and what expertise (including education, experience, and record of accuracy) does the individual have to speak to this issue? Second, in politics, we often see even experienced speakers criticizing the source of an argument rather than the issue being discussed. For instance, currently, many conservative and liberal pundits are quick to judge Monica Lewinsky as an overweight, attention-seeking bimbo, and independent counsel Kenneth Starr as an anxious zealot. In both cases, the critics are ignoring the basic issue of whether something illegal has taken place and instead are focusing on the personal attributes of key players in this real-life political drama. Students should avoid this easy, yet unethical, method of argument. When the opposition's reason- ing seems indefensible, persuasive speakers should take the high ground by criticizing evidence and logic rather than using personal attacks.

What guidelines should speakers follow in their efforts to remain ethical when they construct their arguments for a persuasive speech?

First, speakers should avoid unsound reasoning. Speakers who knowingly employ such methods with an unsus- pecting audience are, in a way, victimizing their listeners. Often, an uninformed audience, or one that is untrained to detect fallacious reasoning, trusts that a speaker will argue an issue reasonably. Then, the speaker has an ethical obligation to do so. Second, persuasive speakers are obligated to thoroughly research the issue and provide appropriate oral and written citations for the sources of their information. Third, and related to the second point, speakers should never, ever distort the facts to suit their needs. Finally, speakers should avoid overuse of the emotional appeal. Emotional appeals sometimes have an important place in persuasive arguments; ideally, though, speakers should rely primarily on the facts and data that support their contentions.

subscribed to a particular magazine, it means they don't like to read. In each case, the alternatives offered do not exhaust all the possible positions or reasons. Since there are definitely other options, the reasoning is faulty.

Criticizing the Source Rather Than the Issue

A speaker attempts to refute an argument by criticizing the source rather than focusing on the argument itself. Consider this argument, for example: "Darla's explanation of why people need to shower after working out at the gym cannot be accurate because Darla is an unstable person and can't be trusted." In this argument, Darla's instability has absolutely nothing to do with the accuracy of her explanation. In other words, the soundness of an argument does not necessarily depend on characteristics of the person who proposes it.

Relying on False Experts

A speaker argues that a position on an issue is true because an authority on a subject unrelated to the issue says so. For example, a speaker might argue that you should vote for a particular Democratic candidate simply because Barbra Streisand supports the candidate. Here, Streisand's expertise as a singer, actor, and director has nothing to do with her expertise in political matters (or lack thereof). In other words, for a person to be an authority, he or she needs to be an expert in the field in question.

Claiming That "Everybody Does It"

A speaker claims that something must be true because everybody does it or believes it to be the case. For example, a speaker might claim, "Smoking cigarettes can't be harmful to your health. After all, look at how many people smoke!" Remember, approval or popularity of "anything" is not a reliable index of the truth about "anything."

Arguing That "That's the Way It Has Always Been Done"

A speaker argues that something is true because that's the way it has always been done. For example, many managers persist in the traditional belief that their employees should work only at the office, not in their homes. This tradition, like many others, has been proven wrong: In today's complex work world, many employees demonstrate greater productivity working from home than from the office. The fact that people have always done something in a particular way does not mean either that it is correct or that we should continue to do it that way. Tradition alone is not a sufficient reason for accepting a conclusion.

Using Threats

A speaker uses the threat of harm to support a claim. For example, in a speech to a group of insurance company CEOs, a speaker might argue that women are as qualified as men to be managers in insurance firms. As evidence, the speaker states that women have as much education and experience as men and that insurance firms and their CEOs are likely to be sued for discrimination if they don't promote women to management positions. Although certainly compelling to the CEOs, the speaker's final reason does not provide additional evidence for women's qualifications for management positions; instead, it threatens harm if the speaker's claim is not acted on. Threatening an audience might coerce them into doing something, but it does not offer a sound argument for doing it.

Jumping to Conclusions

A speaker argues to a sweeping conclusion based on very few facts or experiences. For example, a speaker might conclude, "All Euroamericans are unethical because every Euroamerican I have met is unethical." To generalize to a large group based on limited data is wrong—and unethical. Sound reasoning doesn't involve using a highly limited amount of supporting evidence to draw a false claim about an entire class or category of anything.

Arguing a False Cause

A speaker argues that two things are causally connected when they aren't. For example, a speaker might reason, "Illegal immigration is on the rise—and so is crime. Thus, crime is a result of illegal immigration." The fact is, a lot of factors can lead to an increase in crime. Just because crime happens to increase during a period of increased illegal immigration does not connect the two causally. Only if all of the alternative potential causes have been eliminated from consideration can a causal link be substantiated.

Common Patterns of Unsound Reasoning

- *Proposing a false dilemma:* Proposing only two alternatives when there are actually more.

- *Criticizing the source rather than the issue:* Refuting an argument by criticizing the source rather than focusing on the argument itself.

- *Relying on false experts:* Arguing that a position on an issue is true because an authority on a subject unrelated to the issue says so.

- *Claiming that "everybody does it":* Claiming that something must be true because everybody believes it to be the case.

- *Arguing that "that's the way it has always been done":* Arguing that something is true because that's the way it has always been done.

- *Using threats:* Threatening harm to support a claim.

- *Jumping to conclusions:* Arguing to a sweeping conclusion based on very few facts or experiences.

- *Arguing a false cause:* Reasoning that two things are causally connected when they aren't.

- *Arguing in circles:* Including the conclusion of the argument in one of the premises; also known as "begging the question."

Arguing in Circles

A speaker includes the conclusion of his or her argument in one of the premises. For example, a speaker might argue that an individual is telling the truth about his qualifications for a job because he's an honest person and wouldn't lie about something like that. Also referred to as "begging the question," this pattern of unsound reasoning does not provide any justification for accepting a claim other than the claim itself.

The box "Common Patterns of Unsound Reasoning" summarizes these errors in reasoning. Test your ability to recognize faulty patterns of reasoning by taking the quiz in the box "Can You Spot the Flaws in Reasoning?"

Can You Spot the Flaws in Reasoning?

Each of the following arguments contains one or more of the errors in reasoning described in the text and summarized in the box "Common Patterns of Unsound Reasoning." Can you identify the error in each one? Answers are given at the end of the box.

1. We have had to put up with a lot of charges about campaign contributions during this debate. But let's look at the context in which these charges are being made. The election is only three weeks away, and our opponents are still trying to find an issue with which they can connect to the public.

2. Use of steroids is rampant among college athletes. I know that all five guys from my high school who are playing football at State are using them.

3. If we don't vote more money for California schools, you can count on seeing more and more foreign workers taking high-paying technical jobs away from Americans.

4. I believe what Senator Jackson has said about the charges of influence peddling. I have known him for 20 years, and he just would not lie about that sort of thing.

5. We have to make a distinction between free speech and hate speech. The First Amendment does not give people the right to shout ethnic slanders or to engage in anti-Semitic, antiblack, or antigay baiting. If we don't take steps to curb these hate-mongers in our midst, we are going to see our society degenerate into armed camps.

6. What do you mean, you don't want me to copy that program from Margie's computer? Where do you think all our coworkers got their copies?

Can You Spot the Flaws in Reasoning? *(Continued)*

7. The new restrictions on getting a driver's license are so unfair! What do a bunch of middle-aged guys in Albany know about being a teenager?

8. Can you believe I was pulled over last night for merging onto Central Expressway? The police officer said it was illegal to merge across the double white line and that I shouldn't have merged until I got to the dotted line. But I see cars doing that all the time. In fact, two cars did the same thing right behind me! I'm going to plead not guilty to the ticket!

9. My parents have stopped contributing to the city's AIDS support network. They say that medical advances have transformed AIDS from a fatal disease into a manageable chronic condition, like asthma. That's why I'm contributing to the battered women's shelter instead.

10. Some spokespeople for ethnic groups want their native languages to have the same currency as English. Extensive bilingual education programs have been put in place in our schools, and we now even have bilingual ballots and voting instructions. But immigrants coming to the United States have always had to learn English to survive and succeed, and historically, English has served our nation well. If English continues to be threatened by proponents of language segregation, we should pass a law making it the official language of the United States.

11. Statistics show that the incidence of violent crime is down across the nation. For that we can thank our criminal justice system, which has not shrunk from carrying out the death penalty where it has been applied by juries.

12. The great books of Western civilization must not be superseded by works selected to match population shifts in gender and ethnicity. Certainly we can read works by members of other groups, but first we must master our own culture. The Western tradition has produced generations of American leaders, in education, politics, and business, and it continues to nurture future leaders.

13. I believe in God because I just don't think a supreme being would put the idea of God in our minds if it weren't true.

14. We can easily reduce the federal budget deficit and get our national budget balanced, but the voters aren't willing to accept cuts in Social Security or Medicare to pay for it!

15. Alcoholics need help to overcome their illness, because people can't overcome alcoholism on their own.

Answers

1. Criticizing the source rather than the issue. The speaker avoids the issue of campaign contributions by attacking the opposing candidate.

2. Jumping to conclusions. Even though all the athletes the speaker knows are using steroids, it doesn't necessarily follow that all or many college athletes do the same.

3. Using threats and proposing a false dilemma. Rather than offer reasons for giving the schools more money, the speaker states that negative consequences will occur if such money isn't provided. The speaker also sets up a false dilemma by suggesting that either money be given to the schools or jobs will be lost.

4. Arguing in circles. The speaker says he believes Senator Jackson would not lie because he believes Senator Jackson would not lie.

5. Using threats and proposing a false dilemma. The speaker threatens us with the degeneration of our society if we don't curb hate speech. The speaker also suggests that these are our only two alternatives.

6. Claiming that "everybody does it." The speaker implies that because others are using pirated software, it's acceptable for her to do it, too.

7. Criticizing the source rather than the issue. Whether the new restrictions are legitimate is unrelated to the age of the lawmakers.

8. Claiming that "everybody does it." No matter how many other drivers cross the double white line, it's still a traffic violation.

9. Relying on false experts. The speaker's parents may be authorities on some subjects, but that doesn't make them experts on the medical or societal implications of the new AIDS treatments.

10. Arguing that "that's the way it has always been done." No argument is put forth in support of making English the official language except tradition.

11. Arguing a false cause. Although the incidence of violent crime may be down and the incidence of executions up, there is no evidence that one is caused by the other.

Continued

Can You Spot the Flaws in Reasoning? *(Continued)*

12. Arguing that "that's the way it has always been done." As in item 10, no argument is made for the Western canon other than tradition.

13. Arguing in circles. The speaker uses her belief in a supreme being to support her belief in God.

14. Proposing a false dilemma. The speaker suggests that the only way to reduce the deficit is to cut Social Security and Medicare payments.

15. Arguing in circles. The "reason" is a reiteration of the statement.

How many errors in reasoning did you identify correctly? If you had difficulty spotting the flaws in these examples, review the section in the chapter about evaluating the soundness of arguments.

CHAPTER REVIEW

- Virtually all serious communication exchanges include the reasoning process in one form or another. Whether we are constructing a subjective argument or a highly objective one, our reasoning represents one or the other of the two general approaches to reasoning an argument—inductive or deductive.

- The Toulmin model for diagramming the important parts of an argument can assist in evaluating the soundness or defensibility of the entire argument. The model looks at three basic elements of an argument: a claim (conclusion), grounds (data or evidence), and a warrant (the explanation that connects the grounds and the claim).

- Common types or patterns of reasoning are reasoning by example, by analogy, by cause, by sign, and by authority. A number of criteria can be used to test the quality of the reasoning in each type of argument.

- Skilled public speakers frequently incorporate two or more different patterns of reasoning into their speeches to add to the overall persuasiveness of their presentations.

- The soundness of a speaker's reasoning is critical to his or her ability to influence an audience. Speakers are ethically bound to identify and correct errors in logic and to present sound arguments. To ensure soundness, a number of common reasoning errors—from proposing a false dilemma to arguing in circles—need to be kept in mind when developing and refining an argument.

QUESTIONS FOR CRITICAL THINKING & REVIEW

1. Why is the reasoning process so central to all of our serious communication exchanges? Are there specific exchanges in which our personal opinion is more important than how we formulate an argument? What are those specific communication exchanges?

2. This chapter recommends that specific questions be asked in order to test the soundness of an argument. Why is it important that soundness or defensibility be substantiated?

3. Audiences react negatively to speakers who employ faulty reasoning in their speeches. Why do you think audiences respond so emotionally to speakers who incorporate either faulty reasoning or inaccurate evidence into a speech?

4. Ethical speakers work hard to ensure the accuracy and soundness of their arguments. How is the issue of being an ethical speaker linked to guaranteeing the accuracy and soundness of the arguments included in a persuasive speech?

NOTES

1. Toulmin, S. E. (1958). *The uses of argument.* Cambridge: Cambridge University Press.
2. Reinard, J. C. (1991). *Foundations of argument: Effective communication for critical thinking* (p. 195). Dubuque, IA: Brown.
3. Adapted from Freely, A. J. (1966). *Argumentation and debate* (2nd ed.) (pp. 114–115). Belmont, CA: Wadsworth.
4. Reinard, 1991, pp. 195–197.
5. Reinard, 1991, p. 197.
6. Reinard, 1991, pp. 198–201; Freely, 1966, pp. 123–124.
7. Reinard, 1991, p. 198.
8. Reinard, 1991, p. 175; Kruger, A. N. (1960). *Modern debate: Its logic and strategy.* New York: McGraw-Hill.
9. Adapted from Schick, T., Jr., & Vaughn, L. (1995). *How to think about weird things*: Critical thinking for a new age (pp. 285–291). Mountain View, CA: Mayfield.

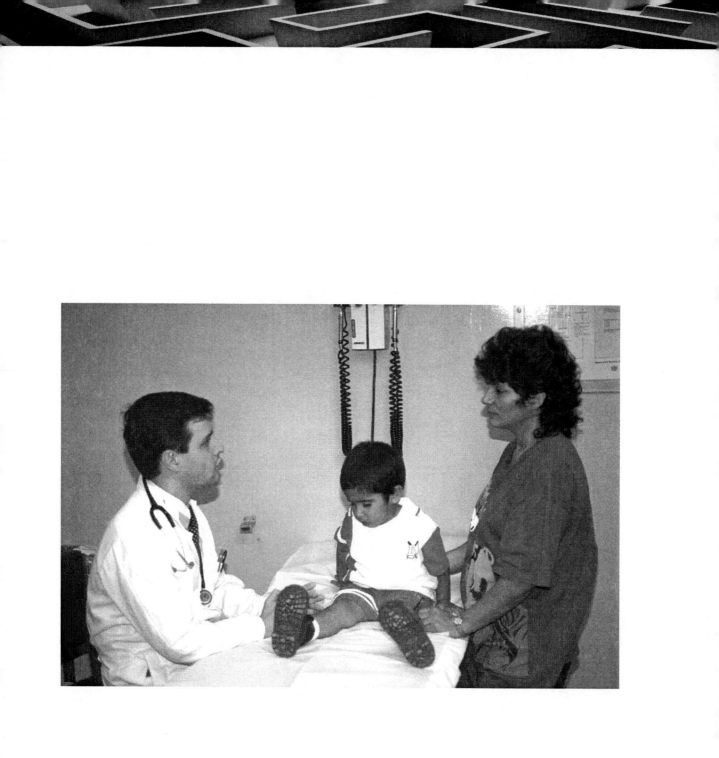

Chapter 14

VERBAL COMMUNICATION: MAKING EVERY WORD COUNT

Every speech requires polishing and fine-tuning to convert it from a form that is basic and mechanically correct to one that communicates with force, passion, and panache. Communication professor Carl Wayne Hensley had much to say about that in an unusually powerful presentation to students at the Graduate School of Business at the University of St. Thomas in Minneapolis. In his research on professional speakers and speeches, he explored what made some speakers superior to others. He discovered that good speakers used language with precision and power—that is, "they had style." In the following excerpts taken from Hensley's speech, notice not only what he says and means but also how he says it with *style*.[1]

Dressing ideas in carefully chosen language—this is the original meaning of the word "style." In the long march across public speaking history, style has walked a road which rises and falls between high peaks of precision and deep valleys of neglect. Unfortunately, in contemporary American speaking, style has been forced to build her home in the valley—ignored, if not forgotten. When it comes to style in American speaking—political, religious, reform, corporate—most speeches are about as exciting as a made-for-TV movie.

If speakers (and speech writers as well) want to lift a speech to a higher level of interest and influence, let them work on improving their style. Frederick Buechner, a scintillating speaker and writer, expresses the value of style when he says: "Words have color, depth, texture of their own, and power to evoke vastly more than they mean; words can be used to make things clear, make things vivid, make things interesting, and make things happen inside the one who reads them or hears them." Thus, my claim, quite simply, is: Style provides increased impact to a speech. In order to help you improve your style, I want to give you four suggestions. Follow these suggestions and watch your speeches increase in impact.

The first suggestion is: Guard against language homicide. Many speakers murder the English language by what Edwin Newman called "bloating"—adding unnecessary, redundant words to express an idea. Have you heard someone refer to "foreign imports," "imports into this country" and "exports out of this country?" How about "few in number" as if few were not number related?

. . . While some speakers murder the language by bloating it, others murder it by suffocating it with jargon. . . . Consider some stifling jargon of the last few years: synergy (I think it means that we work together), proactive (we anticipate), wellness (what happened to the dependable "healthy"?), interface (computers interface, but people talk to each other). In a cartoon, a professor sits at his computer, looking puzzled. Another character asks, "What's the problem?" The professor replies, "It's a simple case of power source input interface inversion." Then, after a pause, he adds, "It's not plugged in."

. . . Not only do we murder our language by bloating it and suffocating it with jargon, but we also "age" and "ize" it to death. A few months ago, Tama Starr, president of the Artcraft Strauss Sign Corp., tackled (or should I say "tackleized") this felon in a letter to the magazine Signs of the Time: *"We always thought we built signs. But lately, we keep finding ourselves invited to bid on signage. What is signage? Is the simple, old, four-letter word 'sign' too straightforward for this state-of-the-art day and age? Like rummage, tonnage, baggage, luggage, roughage, garbage and the Biblical 'mess or pottage,' signage sounds like something heavy, lifeless and full of lumps."*

Learning Objectives

After reading this chapter, you should be able to do the following:

1. Employ strategies that will help your audience better understand your message.

2. Use language in such a way that your message will come across as powerful and strong.

3. Use bias-free language that will include, rather than alienate, your audience.

4. Employ strategies that will help your audience notice and remember what you have to say.

. . . No less deadly to our diction than "aging," is our propensity to "ize" words: politicize, unpoliticize, utilize, calendarize, spiritualize, finalize, synergize, athleticize, problemize, and by all means, prioritize. One quickly concluizes *that we have a* surplussage *of "ize-itis."*

Another method of murder relies on clichés such as back to the drawing board, track record, bottom line, touch base later, scenario (worst case/best case, of course), for all practical purposes, and flagship (I've yet to find a business type who knows the origin of this metaphor). Without a doubt, the corporate world (and the academic world and political world and athletic world) speaks in wonderful ways, and communication becomes the casualty.

. . . All of these lethal lesions on our language have drained its stamina and led to a steady decline in its health. Therefore, speakers and speech writers must guard against the widespread efforts to commit stylistic murder. . . .

Rescue style from her exile in the valley of neglect. Elevate style to her peak of precision. Honor style as a staunch ally. Because, beyond a doubt, style provides increased impact to a speech.

Transforming bland phrases into inspirational words involves the use of **rhetorical devices**. Your own communication style—including how you use language and humor—contributes to the overall packaging and success of your speech. That is not to say that packaging alone can motivate an audience, embrace disparate groups, or persuade individuals to endorse a cause. But polishing and packaging can help you disarm hostilities with laughter, confront controversy without alienation, maintain listener interest, and enhance your credibility. Choosing to use just the right words and phrases makes all the difference between a superior speech and one that is merely adequate. Quoting Mark Twain, Dr. Hensley concludes:

> *"The difference between the right word and the almost right word is the difference between lightning and the lightning bug."*

This chapter focuses on verbal communication strategies that can help you transform your speech from one that is merely good to one that can be great. With your speech objective in mind, your outline prepared, your evidence at hand, and your speech well organized, you must take one more important prepresentational step—polish your speech text. Even though most of your speeches will be extemporaneous, plan on using certain phrases that will affect how your message is received. Employing only a few of the following

strategies will help make your presentation unique, rhetorically exciting, and worth listening to.

SPEAKING TO BE UNDERSTOOD

Perhaps the most obvious speech goal—speaking to be understood by all members of the audience—is also the most important goal. Remember: The audience is hearing your words for the first and, perhaps, only time. Once your speech is over, you will have few, if any, opportunities for instant replays of salient points that may be missed or issues that may be misperceived. What follow, then, are strategies for making your oral presentation easily received and readily understood by your audience.

Keep It Simple

Sometimes simple phrases have the most impact on an audience. When complex thoughts are expressed using uncomplicated language, the audience is more likely to grasp the idea quickly. Consider Nancy Reagan's "Just say no!" or James Carville's "It's the economy, stupid!" In other words, clear, straightforward language can communicate forceful, powerful thought. Recall Ann Richards's speech at the 1988 Democratic National Convention: Five times she told her audience that the Republican administration was "wrong." She preceded each of these claims with a story—about farmers going under, working mothers struggling to keep their families together, domestic industries being threatened by foreign markets and unfair trade laws, and air and water being polluted. She followed each story with the phrase, "Well, that's wrong!" Richards then did a turnabout by telling the crowd that there's nothing "wrong with you—nothing wrong with you that you can't fix in November!"[2]

Cartoonist Garry Trudeau also used the principle of simplicity in his 1997 commencement address to students at Colorado College.[3] However, he heightens the value of plain speaking by relying first on language that is elaborate, complex, and metaphorical: "So what is it that makes you so uniquely qualified to storm the citadel of conventionality? The same things that made me qualified when I graduated from college: *You're young, you're clueless, and you have nothing to lose.*" Similarly, Trudeau accentuates a rather simple phrase by prefacing it with words that are highly abstract: "Innocence, which is the absence of dispiriting experience, is almost a precondition for real innovation. Protected and nurtured by the academy for four years, you have not yet been overwhelmed by the collective insight of your 30-something predecessors that *life may, in fact, suck.*"

By using simple, clear, concise language, you help audiences focus on the core issues of your presentation. The juxtaposition of relatively uncomplicated, straightforward talk with sophisticated, complex thoughts communicates to audiences how they should feel about an issue, how they ought to vote or behave, or how they should evaluate a policy. Thus, simple words can replace or complement big, bulging words and phrases that often confuse and lose an audience. Short, lean (even redundant) phrases help prevent information overload, reduce ambiguity, and facilitate comprehension. (Nevertheless, be careful not to oversimplify to the extent that complex issues become distorted or your message lacks substance.)

Limit Your Use of Jargon and Acronyms

The occasional use of **jargon**—technical terms unique to a particular group or profession—can help convey to your audience your competence in your topic. Use technical terms to show that you know what you're talking about, but use them only when you must. You might also use **acronyms**—words formed from the first letters of each word in a name or phrase. It makes sense, for instance, to use the acronym NAFTA to refer to the North American Free Trade Agreement—particularly if you use the term repeatedly in your speech. Be sure to define the acronym quickly (do not assume the audience already knows what it means), and then go on. Keep in mind, however, that excessive use of jargon or acronyms can tire audiences, prevent them from understanding the message of the speech, and make the speaker appear pompous or affected.

Consider these acronyms that are commonly used by professionals in the field of speech communication: CA (communication apprehension), PRCA-24 (a 24-item scale called the Personal Report of Communication Apprehension), NCA (National Communication Association), and QJS (*Quarterly Journal of Speech*). And then there is the highly technical jargon of speech communication:

Dyad = two people interacting

The Pollyanna principle = the common tendency to hold an optimistic bias; an inclination to see the good and positive in people and events

Reciprocal listening = listening to others only because we want them to listen to us when it's our turn to talk

All special interest or professional groups have their own jargon. Feel free to use jargon and acronyms with members of your in-group, but use them sparingly with audiences who may be unfamiliar with a particular acronym or phrase.

Avoid Phrases That Don't Say Anything

Avoid using bloated speech—practically content-free speech that is intended to be ambiguous or act as filler. All too often, politicians are coached to use bloated speech to avoid answering potentially difficult or embarrassing questions. Consider the language Hillary Rodham Clinton used to deal with interviewers' questions about allegations of her husband's infidelity. Without specifically denying the rumors, she called the accounts "sad and unfortunate" and "terrible" and went on to say, "I think my husband has proven that he's a man who really cares about this country deeply . . . and, when it's all said and done, that's how most fair-minded Americans will judge my husband."[4] So, what exactly did she say?

Occasionally, it's a good idea to be vague and ambiguous. For instance, department store Santas are instructed to be evasive when children request specific gifts or miracles for Christmas: "I'll consider what you have asked for"; "I'll think it over"; or "Let's see what old Santa can do."[5]

In other, more serious public speaking contexts, evasions can be problematic. Comments that contribute nothing to the meaning of the speech can reduce speaker credibility and, of course, confuse the audience. In public speaking, you should adhere to a very wise old line: "Say what you mean and mean what you say."

Pronounce Your Words Accurately

A mispronounced word has the same effect on an audience as a misspelled word on an English teacher. Warranted or not, the audience will likely perceive the speaker as lacking credibility, or worse. You should learn how to pronounce difficult words by consulting a dictionary or an expert. Moreover, make an effort to learn how to pronounce the names of pertinent sources or of particular individuals in the audience whom you may need to refer to during your presentation. Whenever possible, ask the individual directly for the correct pronunciation. Otherwise, you may have to rely on media sources to supply you with the correct pronunciation of a city, country, or person. Consider how you were able to learn the correct pronunciation for some or all of the following names and places:

Aleksandr Solzhenitsyn	Sarajevo
Mohamed Farah Aidid	Albuquerque
Gloria Estefan	Des Moines

Heidi Fleiss	Puerto Rico
Ross Perot	Mobile, Alabama
Maya Angelou	Seoul

Remember: Audience members may become annoyed or defensive if they suspect a speaker hasn't taken the time to learn how to pronounce their names or where they come from; moreover, speaker credibility can suffer.

Adapt to Audience Responses to Your Accent or Dialect

Everyone speaks with some type of accent or dialect. An **accent** is a distinctive way of pronouncing words and is usually determined by the speaker's regional or cultural background or native language. The twangy drawl of the Texan and the clipped speech of the New Englander are two examples. A native of New Orleans is likely to pronounce her hometown "Nawlins"; outsiders might refer to the same location as "New Orleeeens" or "New Or-luhns." Is the name "Leroy" supposed to be pronounced with the emphasis on the first or the second syllable? Should the common Vietnamese American name of "Nguyen" be pronounced phonetically, or should it rhyme with "when"? Clearly, co-cultural affiliation plays an important role in how words are pronounced. The correct pronunciation cannot always be determined by referring to the dictionary; most often, it is the actual people who carry the name or occupy the place who determine the preferred pronunciation.

Like accents, **dialects** are also based on an individual's regional or cultural background; however, a dialect reflects a unique vocabulary and syntax as well as a distinctive accent. Consider the following examples of dialectic variations in vocabulary: Southerners might refer to hot cereal made of cornmeal as "grits"; Midwesterners might call the same thing "mush." Depending on where you are from, a soft drink could be called a "Coke," "soda," "cola," or "pop."

Regional and ethnic accents and dialects often are associated with positive and negative attributions about a speaker's level of intelligence, social status, credibility, and power. Of course, such judgments are unfair: Dialect and accent have nothing to do with these characteristics. Some researchers have found that teachers discriminate against students with so-called foreign accents by rating them as disadvantaged or as having lower social status. Other studies suggest a negative relationship between a speaker's accent and others' perceptions of his or her intelligence, social abilities, and chances for success.[6]

Importantly, audiences and speakers alike should show tolerance and respect for other people's unique ways of communicating. Everyone grows up with his or

her own curious ways of talking. In your role as a public speaker, you want to make sure that you are understood, that your audience knows what you mean. Does this mean you have to give up your own dialect and accent and adopt the speaking style of your audience? No. Your accent and dialect are an important part of who you are as a speaker. (See the box "Interview with a Professional: Vandye Forrester" for more discussion of this issue.)

At the same time, try to counter any negative audience perceptions your speaking style might cause by doing the following:

1. Be sure audience members understand the particular phrases you use by regularly looking for nonverbal cues (Do they seem puzzled and confused?) and actively eliciting their feedback ("Am I making myself clear?").

2. Clarify the meanings of the words you use. Spell out any words that the audience may have trouble recognizing. And define dialect-specific words that may be confusing ("Grits are hot cornmeal mush or cereal").

3. To demonstrate recognition of and respect for your audience members' unique dialect and accent, occasionally use a phrase unique to their region or co-culture.

Appreciate Your Efforts to Speak English as a Second Language

As teachers of public speaking, we often encounter nonnative-English-speaking students who apologize for their lack of fluency. If the truth be told, these same students generally speak formal English better than native speakers! And, yet, English-as-a-second-language (ESL) students typically regard their speaking abilities as limited and report a certain amount of reluctance and anxiety about speaking before a group. ESL speakers are likely to experience more public speaking anxiety than others. Switching to English is no easy feat! Anyone who has tried to learn or communicate in a foreign language can fully appreciate the difficulty nonnative English speakers face.

So, if you are an ESL speaker yourself, try some of the following strategies to enhance listener comprehension:

1. Speak a little more slowly so that audience members can adjust to your accent, word choices, and phrasing.

2. Use gestures and facial expressions to reinforce your speech.

Interview with a Professional

Vandye Forrester

Vandye Forrester, 52, has been a communication consultant for 25 years. He teaches courses in public presentation at both the college and university level.

What kind of experiences have you had with students regarding accents?

An African American student from south Alabama asked me how he could reduce or lose his Alabama accent. He said his high school teacher had told him that a Southern accent was viewed by others as a sign of stupidity. I told him, instead, that he should be proud of his accent. His accent was like a fingerprint and identified him as unique. Not only did it make him unique among all other humans on earth, but his accent was something that no one should or could take away from him.

I reminded him that people often seemed fascinated with those who have a Southern accent. As a result, he could use his accent to his advantage. "Stand tall," I told him. "Walk proud and speak naturally." This student turned into one of the finest and most powerful speakers I have had in my classes over the years!

What do you tell your students about the importance of making every word count when giving a presentation?

I tell my students that a speech is for the ear. The audience must get the message the very first time since they cannot go back

and reread the text. The speech must be simply worded with short, crisp sentences. No sentence should be more than 12 words, and normal rules of written grammar are out the window. Sentences don't have to be complete; sentence fragments are fine and in some cases preferable to long, complex sentences. I tell my students that short, easy words are to be used. If an audience has to stop and figure out what some 64-dollar word means, the speaker has lost them. Plus, the audience becomes angry at the speaker for making them feel stupid for not understanding a strange word.

A speaker should paint the listener into the action with vivid word images that cause the listener to become emotionally involved. I advise my students to use strong, emotionally charged words and a vivid, dramatic delivery style including strong, passionate hand, arm, facial, and body language and gestures.

What do you advise your students about using humor in their speeches?

I tell them that humor is one of life's shock absorbers. I advise the reasonable use of humor in a speech to make points more memorable. If a humorous story or imagery will help clarify a point or help an audience see a situation from another, more interesting perspective, then by all means use humor.

---

3. Most importantly, do not apologize for your speech efforts; speaking multiple languages is often perceived as a sign of intelligence, status, and educational attainment.

4. Don't be reluctant to rely on phrases native to your own language, but be sure to translate for your audience. Introducing your audience to your own language and culture can only lead to greater mutual understanding and appreciation.

SPEAKING TO SHOW STRENGTH

Besides speaking to be understood, good public speakers know that they must also communicate power and strength. Incorporating a few of the following suggestions into the text of your speech will help you command your audience's attention, enthusiasm, and respect.

Use Imaginative Imagery

Imagery involves the use of carefully chosen words that appeal to the senses of touch, taste, sound, sight, and smell to create concrete, realistic impressions about what you are saying.

Concrete Images A big city is easier to visualize when you make it concrete: Chicago. The abstract image of an outstanding athlete becomes more perceptible when you evoke a specific name: Michael Jordan. Vivid images are most easily aroused with the use of concrete language. For example, consider Oprah Winfrey's attempt to persuade audience members to learn to be more fully who they are and not try to be somebody else:

I was born in 1954. On TV there was only Buckwheat, and I was ten years old before I saw Diana Ross on "The Ed Sullivan Show" with the Supremes and said I want to be like that. It took me a long time to realize I was never going to have Diana Ross' thighs, no matter how many diets I went on, and I was not going to have her hair neither unless I bought some.[7]

By using concrete language embedded within a specific example, Winfrey created a vivid sensory image for her audience members to experience and, perhaps, spurred them to reexamine their own goals and dreams.

The use of concrete language to arouse imagery can help your audience attend to and perceive your message with greater sensitivity and urgency than might more abstract messages. For example, consider how Jesse Jackson made concrete the problems of poverty and crime in America:

As we gather here tonight:

- *one-fifth of all American children will go to bed in poverty;*
- *one-half of all African American children grow up amidst broken sidewalks, broken families, broken cities, broken dreams;*
- *the No. 1 growth industry in urban America—jails;*
- *one-half of all the public housing built in this nation during the last decade—jails;*
- *the top 1 percent wealthiest Americans own as much as the bottom 95 percent—the greatest inequality since the 1920s.*[8]

Emphasizing the economic disparity between the privileged few and the neglected majority, Jackson spelled out for the audience in tangible, specific ways the direction he perceived our country had taken.

Similes and Metaphors
Two literary devices are often used to create images in speeches: simile and metaphor. Both rely on comparisons between two seemingly dissimilar things. But whereas **similes** create images through the use of a direct, expressed analogy, **metaphors** develop a picture through an implied analogy.

Similes are easy to recognize because they show a direct comparison by using the word "like" or "as." Some of the more mundane and banal similes include "slept like a baby," "hungry as a bear," "sly as a fox," "light as a feather," "silly as a goose," "poor as a churchmouse," and "dumb as a board." Rather than trotting out used and abused similes, which can detract from your presentation, use your imagination to create unique similes. For example, Eugene Dorsey, president of the Gannett Foundation, employed a number of similes in a speech to characterize (and criticize) the

rampant consumerism and materialism of the 1980s: "VCR's and compact disc players became as necessary as a can opener to a gold miner. . . . Rolexes sprouted on wrists like crocuses announcing spring."[9] Or, consider the similes used by Ann Richards (then state treasurer for Texas) when she charged Republicans with making America a debtor nation by spending money it didn't have: "It's kind of like that brother-in-law who drives a flashy new car but he's always borrowing money from you to make the payments."[10]

Many times, similes can be converted into metaphors by omitting the comparative "like" or "as" and, instead, labeling the object or event with another, apparently dissimilar label to imply an image. However, metaphors, like similes, are often overworked. Such expressions as "dog tired," "late bloomer," and "can't see the forest for the trees" are trite.

Metaphors can be rich, imaginative, and powerful. For example, the Reverend Jesse Jackson, who is well known for his use of imagery, employed a strong metaphor to arouse images of the poor and unfortunate children of the Watts neighborhood of Los Angeles: "Their grapes of hope have become raisins of despair."[11] He might have been tempted to employ a simile, such as, "Their hope has turned to despair, like the grape into a raisin." But note how Jackson's metaphor is infinitely more powerful than the comparable simile. It's easy to imagine hope *becoming* a plump round grape, and despair a dried, shriveled raisin. In that same speech, Jackson tried to relate to working people everywhere through this metaphor: "I was not born with a silver spoon in my mouth. I had a shovel programmed for my hand."[12]

Consider the metaphor of the "cancerous individualism" of the "Me Generation," members of which John Silber, president of Boston University, blames for overlooking and neglecting the welfare of society "on which every individual is dependent."[13] In ridiculing syndicated talk shows, Don Hewitt, executive news director of CBS, referred to them as "cesspools overflowing into America's living rooms."[14] And in her acceptance speech for Michigan's Teacher of the Year award, Cynthia Ann Broad used a metaphor in the title of her presentation, "I Touch the Future: I Teach."[15] All of these speakers relied heavily on metaphor to communicate an attitude, an idea, a policy, or a dream expressively and definitively to their audiences.

Use Intense, Animated Language
Often, the difference between a dull (albeit mechanically correct) speech and an exciting listening experience is the

speaker's use of intense, animated language. Moreover, vivid language contributes a great deal to attitude and behavior change. To illustrate, imagine your friend wants to convince you to see a movie with her: "I read in the paper that a new movie has just come out and it's playing in the neighborhood. I heard it was good—a lot of action and all that. Wanna go?"

Now imagine the same pitch but with some intense, animated language, and see how the persuasive appeal changes: "Steven Seagal's new film shows him piercing the villain's lungs with a simple poke of his finger—he even reaches inside this guy's eye socket, pulls out the eyeball, and then lobs it on the table. Let's go!" Even though the violence may not appeal to you, notice how dramatic the contrast is between the two presentations. The use of intense, animated language offers an effective way to move others. Try substituting dramatic words for drab ones; use action words; employ unusual metaphors and similes; and offer more descriptive detail.

Consider a speech presented by Martin Luther King, Jr. In August 1963, he spoke to thousands in front of the Lincoln Memorial in Washington, DC, and to millions on television and radio, when he delivered his classic, historical speech entitled "I Have a Dream." With intense, vivid language that few have been able to duplicate, King moved people—he touched the emotions of people of all races and creeds. A century after the end of the Civil War and the emancipation of all Americans, his impassioned speech stirred the dream of equality and freedom from oppression for every citizen:

> But one hundred years later, the Negro is still not free. One hundred years later, the life of the Negro is still sadly crippled by the manacles of segregation and the chains of discrimination. One hundred years later, the Negro lives on a lonely island of poverty in the midst of a vast ocean of material prosperity. One hundred years later, the Negro is still languished in the corners of American society and finds himself an exile in his own land. And so we've come here today to dramatize a shameful condition.
>
> In a sense we've come to our nation's Capitol to cash a check. When the architects of our republic wrote the magnificent words of the Constitution and the Declaration of Independence, they were signing a promissory note to which every American was to fall heir. This note was a promise that all men—yes, black men as well as white men—would be guaranteed the unalienable rights of life, liberty and the pursuit of happiness.
>
> It is obvious today that America has defaulted on this promissory note insofar as her citizens of color are concerned. Instead of honoring this sacred obligation, America has given the Negro people a bad check; a check which has come back marked "insufficient funds."[16]

The language of this speech is vivid. According to King, the life of African Americans was still "crippled," not just hurt. These citizens, he said, weren't simply poor; they lived "on a lonely island of poverty in the midst of a vast ocean of material prosperity." They "languished" and became "exiled" in their own country. King characterized the writers of our Constitution as more than simply authors; he called them "architects." King further described Americans as "heirs" to the promises of life, liberty, and the pursuit of happiness. Overall, this classic speech relies heavily on intense, animated language that evokes especially vivid imagery. It also makes use of concrete language, metaphors, and similes.

Choose the Active Voice

Grammatical voice refers to the relationship between the subject of a sentence and the action of the verb. In the **passive voice**, the subject receives the action; in the **active voice**, the subject performs the action. Consider the following:

Passive: The speech was written by Edna.

Active: Edna wrote the speech.

Passive: The homeless were saved from the bitter cold by people who cared.

Active: Caring people saved the homeless from the bitter cold.

Passive: Her remarks were interrupted by hecklers.

Active: Hecklers interrupted her remarks.

Which of the sentences in each pair expresses the idea more strongly? By definition, active voice is stronger than passive voice. Switching from passive to active voice makes your language more concise, more exciting, and more inviting. See how changing the following sentence makes the subject actually perform in some vivid, imaginative way:

Passive: The entire plate of food was eaten by the child.

Active: The child ate the entire plate of food.

The revised sentence may still seem a bit lifeless, but by combining the active voice with intense language and vivid imagery, you can make this statement more powerful:

Active: The child devoured every last bit of food on her plate.

Active: The child savored every last morsel of food on her plate.

Active: The child feasted on prime rib, mashed potatoes, and gravy.

Use Power Words and Avoid Unnecessary Qualifiers

Some expressions weaken and undermine a speaker's position and arguments. Consider these simple statements:

"I'm not sure, but he looks sick to me."

"This may not be right, but we need to turn left at the next corner."

"You probably know more about this than I do, so think about what criteria we need to use to evaluate this speech."

Or consider these seemingly innocent expressions:

"I think we should go to the movies."

"I feel we should donate money to Emily's List."

"She's very smart, *don't you agree?"*

Notice how the italicized phrases sap the strength from these statements. By eliminating these qualifiers from your speech, you (and your position) will come across as stronger, more assertive, and more factual. In other words, if you employ power language, people will assume that you know what you are talking about and that you have the courage of your convictions.

It is especially important to eliminate qualifiers when speaking to Euroamerican and African American audiences. But for other co-cultures, particularly high-context, feminine cultures, the occasional use of qualifiers may be appropriate. Communicating indirectly—relying on implication and suggestion—is often preferred by women, Native Americans, Asian Americans, and Latinos.

SPEAKING TO INCLUDE, NOT ALIENATE

From the first chapter, this text has stressed the importance of being inclusive, rather than exclusive, in your communication behavior. There are some additional, concrete ways to modify your verbal messages to show respect for and acceptance of people of different co-cultures.

Use Bias-Free Language

To be an effective speaker in a culturally diverse society, it is critical that you avoid reinforcing questionable attitudes and assumptions about people's ethnicity, gender, or other co-cultural affiliations. The use of biased language reduces your credibility and can seriously damage the effectiveness of your speech. This section presents some general guidelines for speaking free from bias.[17]

Apply the Principle of Self-Definition One of the most important guidelines for speaking inclusively is to use names or labels that individuals or groups choose for themselves. For example, during the opening ceremonies of the 1994 Winter Olympics, commentators pointed out that members of the group usually called "Lapps," a name given to them by their Scandinavian neighbors, prefer to be called "Samis," their name in their own language. Here in the United States, an individual of Latin American or Spanish ancestry may prefer to be called Hispanic, Chicano or Chicana, Mexican American, or Latina or Latino.

See if you can identify culturally sensitive alternatives to the following labels:

Old people	Poor
Drunk	Handicapped
Dope addict	Pro-abortion
Fat people	Homosexual

Some people use words and phrases like these in their everyday speech. Members of such groups, however, are likely to find such labels offensive, demeaning, or hurtful. As a public speaker, you should select labels that show your respect for and sensitivity to every individual or group. Keep in mind, however, that this strategy can be taken too far. (The box "Politically Correct Phrases" illustrates what can happen when overly euphemistic phrases are used.)

Don't Mention Group Membership Unnecessarily When group membership is relevant to what you are speaking about, there is nothing wrong with including it: "Thurgood Marshall was the first African American justice on the United States Supreme Court." Unfortunately, many speakers, assuming that the "average" person is a white male, make a point of mentioning the gender, race, or ethnic background of anyone

Politically Correct Phrases

The term "politically correct" is often batted about in the media in a derisive way. Humorists Henry Beard and Christopher Cerf had some fun developing an official handbook and dictionary for both perpetrators and victims of political correctness. What follows is a sampling from that handbook. But keep in mind that these so-called politically correct terms are intended as humor and should not be misconstrued as valid substitutions!

Incorrect	Correct
Failure	Incomplete success
Fail	Achieve a deficiency
Old	Chronologically gifted
Significant other	Spouse equivalent
Slum	Substandard housing
Elderly	The longer-living
Bald	Hair disadvantaged
Patient	Guest
Inmate	Guest
Wild	Free-roaming
Dishonest	Ethically disoriented
Janitor	Environmental hygienist
Spacey	Differently focused
Boring	Differently interesting

SOURCE: Beard, H., & Cerf, C. (1993). *The officially politically correct dictionary and handbook.* New York: Villard Books.

who is not a white male: a female prosecutor, an Asian first-grade teacher, a Middle Eastern American grocer. If co-cultural affiliation is irrelevant to your point, don't bring it up.

Give Parallel Treatment

Parallel treatment requires that the speaker provide similar labels for comparable groups. "Man" and "woman" are parallel labels, and so are "husband" and "wife." "Man" and "wife," however, are not parallel. If you refer to a man by his professional title (Professor O'Brien), you should refer to a woman in the same speech by her professional title (Dr. Lee). But watch out for false parallels. For example, "white" is specific while "nonwhite" lumps everyone else together. When using paired gender phrases, such as "boys and girls" or "Latinas and Latinos," alternate the order of the terms.

People often use the term "girls" inappropriately to refer to women of all ages but reserve "boys" for preadolescent males. Don't use the term "girls" if males

of a similar age would find the term "boys" inappropriate or demeaning.

Be Inclusive and Avoid Making Unwarranted Assumptions

Don't use wording that excludes individuals or groups or that treats them as unequals. The statement "All law school graduates and their wives are invited to the picnic" assumes that all law school grads are male. Likewise, to say "America is a nation of recent immigrants" completely ignores Native Americans.

Don't Use Masculine Terms as Generics

Masculine pronouns should not be used as generic terms to refer to both women and men. Research has shown that statements like "As a speaker gains experience, *he'll* become more adept at audience analysis" are not perceived as referring to people of both sexes. There are a variety of remedies for this bias:

1. *Use the plural:* "As speakers gain experience, they . . ."
2. *Use the second person:* "As you gain experience, you will . . ."
3. *Omit the pronoun:* "With experience, a speaker will . . ."
4. *Pair the pronouns:* "As a speaker gains experience, she or he will . . ."
5. *Rephrase the statement:* "Experience leads to greater skill in audience analysis."

Similarly, don't use "man," "men," or "mankind" if you mean "people," "men and women," or "human beings." Table 14-1 lists common, generic man-linked terms that should be avoided.

Don't Use Feminine Endings

Feminine endings such as "esse" and "ette" specify gender when it's irrelevant, imply that maleness is the norm, and convey a sense of smallness or cuteness (as in "launderette" or "luncheonette"). Terms such as "actor," "author," and "usher" encompass both sexes (see Table 14-1). If the gender of the person is important to your speech, use adjectives ("male actor") or pronouns ("the author read from her work") to indicate gender.

Remember That People Are People First

Describing people as "AIDS victims," "the deaf," or "the disabled" may inappropriately define them by a particular characteristic. Mention the person before giving any qualifiers: "people living with AIDS," "people who are deaf," and "people with disabilities."

TABLE 14-1 USING NONSEXIST LANGUAGE

INSTEAD OF	USE	INSTEAD OF	USE
Man-Linked Terms Used as Generics		**Terms with Feminine Endings**	
ADMAN	Advertising executive, copywriter, ad agent	ACTRESS	Actor
		AUTHORESS	Author
CAMERAMAN	Photographer, camera operator	COMEDIENNE	Comedian
CHAIRMAN	Chair, chairperson, director, head	HEIRESS	Heir
CONGRESSMAN	Member of Congress, congressional representative, legislator	HOSTESS	Host
		POETESS	Poet
FIREMAN	Firefighter	SEAMSTRESS	Sewer, tailor, alterer
FOREMAN	Head juror, jury leader, foreperson	STARLET	Young or aspiring actor, future star
FRESHMAN	First-year student, class of, entering student	STEWARDESS	Flight attendant, flight crewmember
		WAITRESS	Server, waiter
MAILMAN	Mail carrier	**Other Gender-Linked Terms**	
MAN (NOUN), MANKIND	Human beings, people, humanity, humankind		
		BELLBOY	Bellhop
MAN (VERB)	Operate, serve, work, staff	BEST MAN,	Attendant bridesmaid
MANMADE	Artificial, synthetic, manufactured	BOYISH, GIRLISH	Naive, childlike, innocent
POLICEMAN	Police officer	CLEANING WOMAN	Housekeeper, household worker
REPAIRMAN	Repairer, technician, service representative	FATHERLAND,	Homeland, native land, home motherland
		MANHANDLE	Abuse, mistreat, damage, beat up
SALESMAN	Sales representative, sales clerk, agent	MATERNITY LEAVE	Family leave, parental leave
		PAPERBOY	Paper carrier, news deliverer, news carrier
SPOKESMAN	Speaker, publicist, agent, mediator, representative, spokesperson	UNWED MOTHER	Unwed parent, single parent, head of household, mother, woman
WEATHERMAN	Weather reporter, meteorologist		

And don't mention the qualifiers unless they are relevant to your speech. Also, avoid the negative, patronizing language of victimization. For example, use "wheelchair user" or "person who uses a wheelchair" instead of "wheelchair-bound."

Watch for Hidden Bias

You can send a biased message even when you avoid the use of biased terms. Depending on the context, how you say something can reflect a biased point of view, as these examples show:

Biased: More unmarried women than ever before are having babies.

Bias-free alternative: More unmarried couples than ever before are having babies.

Biased: Not all of the AIDS cases diagnosed so far in the United States have been transmitted via the activities of gay men.

Bias-free alternative: In approximately 60 to 65 percent of AIDS cases diagnosed so far in the United States, the AIDS virus was transmitted via sexual contact between men.

Using language that is free from bias is a crucial part of being a successful speaker in a culturally diverse society. The strategies presented in this chapter are summarized in the box "Using Bias-Free Language."

Practice Being Verbally Immediate

In one language strategy, speakers employ certain words to reduce the physical or psychological distance, or **immediacy**, between themselves and their audience. Normally, people associate immediacy with nonverbal behaviors, such as standing physically close to someone or maintaining prolonged eye contact.

However, immediacy can also be developed through verbal communication, including the use of specific

Using Bias-Free Language

- Apply the principle of self-definition. Use only names and labels that individuals or groups choose for themselves.

- Don't mention group membership unless it's relevant.

- Use parallel treatment when discussing different but comparable groups.

- Be inclusive, and avoid making unwarranted assumptions.

- Don't use masculine terms to refer to both women and men.

- Don't use feminine endings.

- Remember that people are people first. Relevant qualifiers should describe people, not categorize them.

- Watch for hidden bias in the way you word statements or present facts.

labels (such as using first names rather than formal titles) and communication strategies (such as using humor, complimenting or praising others, and encouraging people to talk).[18] Through the use of specific **verbal immediacy** behaviors, a speaker can interact with audience members and simultaneously trigger feelings of positive affect or liking and perceptions of closeness and inclusion. Take a few minutes to complete the questionnaire in the box "How Verbally Immediate Are You?" to assess your own verbal immediacy as a public speaker.

The research on verbal immediacy is unequivocal. Whether speaking one-on-one with a significant other or lecturing to a classroom of students, the more immediate you are, the more your listeners will find you an attractive, friendly, likeable communicator. Interestingly, this finding has been obtained across U.S. co-cultures for verbally immediate teachers and their multicultural students in the college classroom.[19] And, especially for ESL students, verbally immediate teachers are associated with greater speaking clarity and ease in understanding.[20] People generally perceive immediate speakers to be warm and accepting; they find them easy to talk to and easy to understand, and they prefer spending time listening to them.

One of the more useful verbal immediacy strategies is to use first-person pronouns such as "we" and avoid second- or third-person pronouns like "you" or "they." Think about it: The word "we" is inclusionary; "they" (and in some cases "you") is exclusionary. *We* are in this together. *We* think alike. *We* would enjoy similar experiences. On the other hand, *they* probably would not. And neither would *you*.

Verbally immediate speakers are likely to refer to audience members and their beliefs and opinions as "we" and "ours" rather than "they" and "theirs."

Thus, they are likely to refer to themselves and audience members as somehow belonging to the same group or co-culture (for example, we are all Americans, or law-abiding citizens, or God-fearing people, or whatever we all happen to have in common). And they are likely to relate personal experiences, respond to audience questions and concerns (even if they are seemingly unrelated), use humor, solicit feedback, and take the time to converse one-on-one with individual audience members before and after their presentation.

Avoid Profanity

Speakers occasionally make the mistake of inserting a swear word, telling a dirty or ethnic or sexist joke, or using an obscene gesture. Even if the words or gestures are intended as humor, some members of your audience may not be amused. Being profane is more than using coarse language; it's showing irreverence or contempt for something that others find sacred or meaningful. Whoopi Goldberg and Ted Danson found that out the hard way: Danson put on blackface paint and made racial jokes at a Friars' Club roast for Goldberg. Several audience members found the act offensive, although Goldberg didn't. Even common exclamatory phrases such as "Good Lord!" or "Oh my God!" might be interpreted by some people as sacrilegious.

SPEAKING TO BE NOTICED AND QUOTED

All speakers enjoy hearing themselves quoted and having audiences show their appreciation by laughing aloud. Sometimes speakers even get satisfaction from having media commentators evaluate their speeches

How Verbally Immediate Are you?

Instructions

The following statements describe verbal immediacy behaviors a public speaker might use during a presentation. Enter the appropriate number in the space provided to indicate how likely you might be to say or do each of the following when presenting your own speech before a large group: (5) extremely likely, (4) likely, (3) maybe (unsure), (2) unlikely, or (1) extremely unlikely.

—— 1. I would use personal examples and talk about experiences I've had while giving my speech.

—— 2. I would encourage audience members to ask questions both during and after my speech.

—— 3. I would use humorous examples in my speeches.

—— 4. I would address members in the audience by name whenever possible.

—— 5. I would encourage audience members to address me by my first name.

—— 6. I would get into conversations with audience members before and after my speech.

—— 7. I would use the words "our group" and "we" to refer to my audience.

—— 8. I would respond to individuals' questions or concerns even if they were apparently unrelated or pointless.

—— 9. I would ask audience members for feedback both during and after my presentation.

—— 10. I would ask questions during my speech that solicited viewpoints and opinions from my audience.

—— 11. I would find ways to praise the audience or individuals in the audience.

—— 12. If individuals from the audience asked me questions unrelated to my speech, I would take the time to respond.

Calculating Your Score

Add together your responses to all 12 items. Your total verbal immediacy score = ——

Interpreting Your Score

The possible scores for this scale range from 12 to 60. (If your own score does not fall within that range, you have made a computational error.) The median score for this scale is 36. Higher scores reflect greater verbal immediacy. If you scored well above the median of 36, you are on your way to becoming a verbally immediate speaker. High verbally immediate speakers tend to be inclusive, rather than exclusive. Immediate speakers make every effort to appear psychologically close to audience members. Audiences perceive them to be warm, friendly, approachable, and responsive. Immediate speakers show warmth and friendliness by referring to audience members by name and by encouraging them to reciprocate. They also encourage audience members to participate by asking questions or airing their opinions. They never try to embarrass anyone in the audience and treat everyone as if they were personal friends.

If you scored below the median, you have your work cut out for you. Low verbally immediate speakers are actually perceived as nonimmediate; that is, audiences are likely to find them distant, aloof, and indifferent to members' concerns and opinions. Nonimmediate speakers come across as very formal and closed; they are unlikely to use humor or reveal much personal information about themselves. To avoid such negative audience perceptions, nonimmediate speakers need to relax a little, relate to audience members on a more personal basis, and encourage them to ask questions. They should make an effort to get to know individual members of the audience and then, during their presentation, emphasize those things they have in common with the audience.

NOTE: For this text's purposes, the items were modified to reflect public speaker, as opposed to teacher, immediacy. Adapted from Gorham, J. (1988). The relationship between verbal teacher immediacy behaviors and student learning. *Communication Education, 37,* 40–53.

---

negatively—at least they were noticed. When speakers are noticed and quoted, they know that what they had to say must have been sufficiently significant (or controversial) and that people remembered their message long enough to talk about it. How can you ensure that your own words will be noticed, quoted, and remembered?

Maintain Rhythm and Momentum

Truly great speeches have a rhythm and a momentum all their own. The recurrence of specific sounds or phrases meets the audience's need for regularity, predictability, and familiarity. Rhythm enhances the audience's pleasure and heightens the sense of emotion toward the speaker and her or his message. A favorite device of skilled orators is the repetition of key phrases, which often become memorable slogans. The following excerpt from Martin Luther King's speech illustrates the use of repetition:

> I say to you today, my friends, so even though we face the difficulties of today and tomorrow, I still have a dream. It is a dream deeply rooted in the American dream.
>
> I have a dream that one day this nation will rise up and live out the true meaning of its creed, "We hold these truths to be self-evident, that all men are created equal."
>
> I have a dream that one day on the red hills of Georgia the sons of former slaves and the sons of former slaveowners will be able to sit down together at the table of brotherhood.
>
> I have a dream that one day even the state of Mississippi, a state sweltering with the heat of injustice, sweltering with the heat of oppression, will be transformed into an oasis of freedom and justice.
>
> I have a dream that my four little children will one day live in a nation where they will not be judged by the color of their skin but by the content of their character. I have a dream today.
>
> I have a dream that one day, down in Alabama, with its vicious racists, with its governor having his lips dripping with the words of interposition and nullification, one day right there in Alabama little black boys and black girls will be able to join hands with little white boys and white girls as sisters and brothers. I have a dream today.
>
> I have a dream that one day every valley shall be exalted, every hill and mountain shall be made low, the rough places will be made plane and the crooked places will be made straight, and the glory of the Lord shall be revealed, and all flesh shall see it together.
>
> This is our hope. This is the faith that I go back to the South with."[21]

King relied on repetition. Recall the final words of that famous speech:

> Free at last! Free at last! Thank God Almighty, we are free at last![22]

Why does repetition make this speech so memorable? Notice how the use of rhythm establishes a pattern of expectation for the audience. It only takes a single restatement for the audience to develop the expectancy that more, and perhaps more important, points will be made. When the expectation is fulfilled—that is, when the second or subsequent restatement is spoken—audience members feel gratified that their prediction was warranted.

Moreover, repetition almost always ensures retention. People remember the special phrases they hear frequently. For instance, many people still remember Senator Ted Kennedy's humorous refrain in his speech at the 1988 Democratic National Convention in Atlanta:

> The Vice President says he wasn't there—or can't recall—or never heard—as the Administration secretly plotted to sell arms to Iran. So when that monumental mistake was being made, I think it is fair to ask—where was George?
>
> The Vice President says he never saw—or can't remember—or didn't comprehend—the intelligence report on General Noriega's involvement in the cocaine cartel. So when that report was being prepared and discussed, I think it is fair to ask—where was George?
>
> The Vice President claims he cares about the elderly—but evidently he didn't know, or wasn't there, when the Administration tried repeatedly to slash Social Security and Medicare. So when those decisions were being made, I think it is fair to ask—where was George?
>
> And the Vice President, who now speaks fervently of civil rights, apparently wasn't around or didn't quite hear when the Administration was planning to weaken voting rights, give tax breaks to segregated schools, and veto the Civil Rights Restoration Act of 1988. So when all those assaults were being mounted, I think it is fair to ask—where was George?[23]

Kennedy continued his assault and finally concluded with yet another repetition:

> On too many tough issues, George Bush's only defense is that he was a hear-nothing, see-nothing, do-nothing Vice President.[24]

What these passages illustrate is that restating simple phrases or even entire lines adds rhythm to a speech. In addition, rephrasing with similar, redundant words or word series can add pulse, or cadence, to an otherwise ordinary presentation. Marian Wright Edelman, president of the Children's Defense Fund, used rhythm in this passage from her 1994 commencement address at Harvard Medical School:

> Violence romps through our children's playgrounds, invades their bedroom slumber parties, terrorizes their Head Start centers and schools, frolics down the streets they walk to and from school, dances

through their school buses, waits at the stop light and bus stop, lurks at McDonald's, runs them down on the corner, shoots them through their bedroom windows, attacks their front porches and neighborhoods, strikes them or their parents at home, and tantalizes them across the television screen every six minutes.[25]

Over and over, Edelman forces us to confront the pervasiveness of violence—on the streets, in our schools, and even in our own homes. Redundancy adds emphasis and force to her point that violence is endemic to our society, that the "morally unthinkable has become normal."

Generally, then, rephrasing and restating key phrases help to build the rhythm of a speech. Rhythm triggers anticipation, generates suspense, and compels attention. Besides eliciting attention, rhythmic speech also subtly stimulates the audience to focus, to learn, and to remember central ideas in a presentation.

Use Humor

Have you ever noticed how often humorous lines from political speeches are picked up by the media and repeated for the larger audience? Media analysts know that humor entertains; laughter makes people feel better about themselves and more responsive to others. And laughter is what Gray Panther leader Maggie Kuhn triggered during her keynote address at the Conference on Conscious Aging. She began her speech by reflecting on the joys of "being old":

> There are three things that I like about being old. First, I can speak my mind, and I do, and I'm always surprised at what I can get away with . . . . the second thing I like about being old is that I have outlived much of my opposition. The people who said to me, "Maggie, that will never work; it's just a crazy idea," they're gone. But the third thing in my life in my old age is the honor and the privilege and the sheer joy of reaching out to people like you and being a part of your future.[26]

A funny story can warm up an audience and, when used appropriately, can even disarm the most hostile audiences, making them more receptive to a speaker's message. When used wisely, humor can help you establish rapport with your audience.

Create Your Own Sound Bites

Good speakers know ahead of time which of their lines or phrases stand a good chance of being noticed, remembered, reprinted, or taped for later media use. You should plan for what the news industry calls **sound bites**, whether or not your speech is likely to be reported by the media. The expression "sound bite" is really a metaphor for a brief passage, such as a sentence or two, taken from a press release or presentation that is reprinted or taped for later news reports. Because time and space considerations usually preclude showcasing an entire speech text, reporters carefully select brief passages that best capture an emotion or a major idea stressed by a speaker.

Consider the famous sound bite from the motion picture *Sudden Impact*. Clint Eastwood, as Dirty Harry, points a loaded gun at the villain and challenges him, "Go ahead—make my day!" See if you can identify the origins of the following common sound bites:

"Ask not what your country can do for you, but what you can do for your country."

"If it looks like a duck, walks like a duck, and quacks like a duck, it must be a duck."

"Men and women can't be friends because the sex part always gets in the way."

"Ginger Rogers did everything that Fred Astaire did. She just did it backwards and in high heels."

"Hello, Newman!"

"Just say no!"

"Just the facts, ma'am."

Not all sound bites become widely recognized. In fact, most are disseminated and then quickly forgotten. Sometimes unfavorable sound bites are picked up by the media—much to the chagrin and embarrassment of the speaker. The point is, sound bites can hurt or help speakers. Planning for those that will help (and avoiding those that will hurt) is an important step in polishing any speech. Your goal is to select the right kinds of phrases that will be repeated by others and possibly picked up by the media. Try to encapsulate major ideas in your speech into one or two memorable phrases—and then repeat those phrases so your listeners will notice, recall, and maybe even quote them later.

There are many rhetorical devices you can employ to enrich your speech and make it more effective. Try to incorporate some of these strategies as you polish and rehearse your speech text. The box "Strategies for Effective Verbal Communication" summarizes these rhetorical devices.

Strategies for Effective Verbal Communication

Speak to Be Understood

- *Keep it simple.* Audiences are more likely to understand complex ideas when they are presented in uncomplicated, unsophisticated language.

- *Limit your use of jargon and acronyms.* Use appropriate technical terms and acronyms, but use them sparingly.

- *Avoid phrases that don't say anything.* Audiences quickly tune out when bloated or content-free speech is used to evade an issue or question.

- *Pronounce your words accurately.* It is particularly important to correctly pronounce the names of people, places, and objects that are a critical part of your presentation.

- *Adapt to audience responses to your dialect or accent.* Even though you need not switch your dialect or accent to match your audience's, you should (1) ensure that your audience understands you, (2) clarify or translate meanings of unusual words, and (3) occasionally employ a particular phrase that audience members may use themselves.

- *Appreciate your own efforts to speak English as a second language.* Anyone who has tried to learn or communicate in a foreign language can fully appreciate the efforts of nonnative English speakers. Relax. Your audience will be patient with you.

Speak to Show Strength

- *Use imaginative imagery.* Employ concrete images, similes, and metaphors to paint vivid pictures for your audience. If you can involve the senses, you'll make a stronger and more lasting impression.

- *Use intense, animated language.* Vivid language touches and moves people and makes a presentation more gripping and appealing.

- *Choose the active voice.* The active voice expresses ideas more strongly than the passive voice. Combine the active voice with vivid imagery to inject vitality into your speech.

- *Use power words and avoid unnecessary qualifiers.* Don't use qualifiers that sap strength and vigor from a speech.

Speak to Include, Not Alienate

- *Use bias-free language.* Choose words that show respect for and acceptance of culturally diverse members in your audience.

- *Practice being verbally immediate.* If you can build rapport with your audience, they will be more likely to perceive you as friendly and worth listening to.

- *Avoid profanity.* Swear words, slurs, and dirty, racist, sexist, or ethnic jokes can offend and alienate an audience.

Speak to Be Noticed and Quoted

- *Maintain rhythm and momentum.* Audiences respond positively to predictable and familiar elements in a speech. Repetition helps them remember key ideas.

- *Use humor.* A funny story helps establish rapport with an audience and can help overcome hostility.

- *Create your own sound bites.* Emphasize a brief statement that captures a key emotion or idea from your speech. Clever, memorable sound bites can help the audience remember your message.

CHAPTER REVIEW

- Polishing your speech requires that you plan ahead to use certain phrases that will make your speech worth listening to. A variety of language strategies will help you to (1) be better understood by your audience, (2) come across as a strong and powerful speaker, (3) include, rather than alienate, your audience, (4) make yourself noticed, and (5) cause your message to be quoted.

- To be understood, you must keep your language simple, limit your use of jargon, avoid bloated speech, and pronounce key words correctly. Effective speakers adapt to how others respond to their unique dialects and accents and recognize that audience members appreciate the efforts made by ESL speakers.

- Strong speakers create imagery through the use of concrete images, similes, and metaphors. Employing intense, animated language will also contribute to your audience's perceptions of your strength as a speaker. Relying on active (as opposed to passive) voice and selecting power phrases are other effective strategies.

- Speaking to include (rather than exclude) audience members requires that you be sensitive to the labels and words when communicating with different co-cultures. By being verbally immediate, you can trigger feelings of closeness to and inclusion with your audience. To avoid alienating audience members, refrain from telling offensive jokes or using profanity.

- Speaking to be noticed and quoted can be accomplished through the rhythmic use of repetition and rephrasing, the telling of humorous stories, and the strategic use of sound bites.

QUESTIONS FOR CRITICAL THINKING & REVIEW

1. What accents and dialects do you evaluate more positively (or negatively) than others? How do you think you developed these biases?

2. Which co-cultural groups are more likely to prefer that you use more (or fewer) metaphors and similes in your speech?

3. Which co-cultural groups are more likely to employ intense, animated language not only in their speeches but also in their normal conversations with others?

4. Do you think that people make too much out of using bias-free language? Which co-cultural groups may be most sensitive to this issue? Why?

5. Which of your instructors tend to be verbally immediate? Does it make a difference in how you evaluate them? Why?

NOTES

1. Hensley, C. W. (1995, September 1). Speak with style and watch the impact. *Vital Speeches of the Day*, 701–704.

2. Richards, A. (1988, August 15). Keynote address. *Vital Speeches of the Day*, 647.

3. Trudeau, G. (1997, May 19). Colorado College commencement address. Online. Available: http://www.colorado.edu/NewsAndPublications/Speeches/Garry Trudeau.html.

4. Broder, J. M. (1993, December 22). First lady assails charges of her husband's infidelity. *Los Angeles Times* (Orange County ed.), pp. A1, A26.

5. Yes, Virginia, there is a how-to manual. (1993, December 27). *Time*, 18.

6. For a review of that research, see Richmond, V. P., McCroskey, J. C., & Payne, S. K. (1991). *Nonverbal behavior in interpersonal relations* (2nd ed.). Englewood Cliffs, NJ: Prentice-Hall.

7. Winfrey, O. (1997, May 30). Wellesley College commencement address. Online. Available: http://www.wellesley.edu/Public Affairs/PAhomepage/winfrey.html.

8. Jackson, J. (1996, August 27). Address at the Democratic National Convention. Online. Available: http://www.pbs.org/newshour/convention96/floor_spee ches/jackson.html.

9. Dorsey, E. C. (1988, July 15). Giving yourself away: The demise of greed. *Vital Speeches of the Day*, 594.

10. Richards, 1988, p. 648.

11. Jackson, J. (1988, August 15). Common ground and common sense. *Vital Speeches of the Day*, 652.

12. Jackson, 1988, p. 653.

13. Silber, J. (1988, January 15). Education and national survival: The cycle of poverty. *Vital Speeches of the Day*, 217.

14. Hewitt, D. (1997, December 1). Let's not compete with the sitcom: What's become of broadcast journalism? *Vital Speeches of the Day*, 48.

15. Broad, C. A. (1994). I touch the future: I teach. In V. L. DeFrancisco & M. D. Jensen (Eds.), *Women's voices in our time: Statements by American leaders* (pp. 61–67). Prospect Heights, IL: Waveland Press.

16. King, M. L., Jr. (1992). I have a dream. In R. L Johannesen, R. R. Allen, & W. A. Linkugel (Eds.), *Contemporary American speeches* (7th ed.) (pp. 366–367). Dubuque, IA: Kendall/Hunt.

17. For a more comprehensive look at bias-free and nonsexist language usage, see Maggio, R. (1997). *Talking about people: A guide to fair and accurate language*. Phoenix, AZ: Oryx Press; Miller, C., & Swift, K. (1988).

The handbook of nonsexist writing: For writers, editors, and speakers (2nd ed.). New York: Harper & Row.

18. Gorham, J. (1988). The relationship between verbal teacher immediacy behaviors and student learning. *Communication Education, 37,* 40–53.

19. Sanders, J. A., & Wiseman, R. L. (1990). The effects of verbal and nonverbal teacher immediacy on perceived cognitive, affective, and behavioral learning in the multicultural classroom. *Communication Education, 39,* 341–353.

20. Powell, R. G., & Harville, B. (1990). The effects of teacher immediacy and clarity on instructional outcomes: An intercultural assessment. *Communication Education, 39,* 369–379.

21. King, M. L., Jr. (1992). I have a dream. In R. L. Johannesen, R. R. Allen, & W. A. Linkugel (Eds.), *Contemporary American speeches* (7th ed.) (p. 368). Dubuque, IA: Kendall/Hunt.

22. King, M. L., Jr. (1992). I have a dream. In R. L. Johannesen, R. R. Allen, & W. A. Linkugel (Eds.), *Contemporary American speeches* (7th ed.) (p. 369). Dubuque, IA: Kendall/Hunt.

23. Kennedy, E. M. (1988, August 15). Where was George? *Vital Speeches of the Day,* 654–655.

24. Kennedy, 1988, p. 656.

25. Edelman, M. W. (1996). Harvard Medical School commencement address. In D. G. Straub (Ed.), *Voices of multicultural America: Notable speeches delivered by African, Asian, Hispanic, and Native Americans, 1790–1995* (p. 348). Detroit, MI: Gale Research.

26. Kuhn, M. (1994). Keynote address at the Conference on Conscious Aging. In V. L. DeFrancisco & M. D. Jensen (Eds.), *Women's voices in our time: Statements by American leaders* (p. 233). Prospect Heights, IL: Waveland Press.

Chapter 15

NONVERBAL COMMUNICATION: MAKING EVERY GESTURE COUNT

Which speaker would you rather hear, Heather or Rachel?

Our first speaker, Heather, begins her presentation by standing at the podium and shuffling her notes to get them in order. Her clothing is decidedly casual and a bit rumpled. Even though she's practiced her speech several times, Heather stares at her notes, making little eye contact with her audience. She seldom smiles and gestures only infrequently. She twists and knots the gold chain that hangs from her neck, and she speaks with hesitation. When she's finished speaking, she looks relieved and hurries back to her seat.

Our second speaker, Rachel, begins her presentation by taking a deep breath and looking out at her audience. She smiles, and then, as she delivers her introductory remarks, she purposely moves away from the podium and into the audience. Her clothes are professional-looking and neat. Even though she has notes in her hand, she doesn't seem to need them; instead, her delivery is smooth, polished, and extemporaneous. Rachel is animated, her gestures are broad and purposeful, and she varies the mood and rhythm of her speech. When she's finished, she stops speaking with reluctance; Rachel seemed to enjoy interacting with her audience.

Rachel is obviously going to receive a more favorable reception than Heather. Rachel shows every sign of being a well-seasoned public speaker. Experienced speakers devote time and attention to such seemingly extraneous details as clothing, body movement, and voice sound and quality. They recognize that these details are central to the impression that they will make on an audience. How people communicate can be as important as what they actually say. To be effective, speakers need to present themselves in such a way that the audience perceives them as credible, interesting, and, sometimes, entertaining. Some researchers maintain that nonverbal messages are more important than the verbal content of the speech, making up as much as 90 percent of what is communicated. This is a considerable exaggeration, but the way a speaker communicates does make a substantial impression on the audience.

What makes up the nonverbal portion of a speech? **Nonverbal communication** is the deliberate or unintentional use of objects, actions, sounds, time, and space to arouse meanings in others. For example, a speaker's use of postures, gestures, eye contact, facial expressions, clothing, tone of voice, and even odors can communicate meanings to the audience. Nonverbal behaviors typically complement or reinforce a verbal message rather than communicate on their own. For instance, a speaker may jab the air with a fist for emphasis or tick off key points by touching the tips of the fingers one after the other. Most verbal messages are accompanied by nonverbal behaviors that reinforce their meanings. This reinforcement helps convey a message more accurately—a particularly important factor in public speaking contexts, in which the speaker has only one chance to convey her or his message.

Learning Objectives

After reading this chapter, you should be able to do the following:

1. Choose and wear clothing that makes you look like a credible public speaker.

2. Use gestures that will help your presentation and eliminate those that can hurt it.

3. Maintain eye contact with your audience.

4. Employ strategies that will help you keep the audience interested in what you have to say.

5. Vary your voice (volume, pitch, and rate) to emphasize important points in your speech and to increase audience attention.

6. Employ nonverbal immediacy behaviors that initiate and maintain psychological closeness and warmth with your audience.

In the late nineteenth and early twentieth centuries, teachers of elocution (as the art of oratory was called) emphasized a speaker's nonverbal behavior. In 1893, the popular text *Practical Elements of Elocution* described the "law of the pauses," which recommended 17 separate pause rules for students to follow in their delivery.[1] Even a speaker's elbows were said to be important in expressing meaning. One authority of the time set forth this remarkable "law of the feet":

> *The most natural position is for the weight of the body to rest mainly on one foot, the feet nearly at right angles and not wide apart nor touching each other. This gives the body such poise that the arm may be used with freedom of gesture, unity being preserved by employing the right hand in gesture when the weight of the body is on the right foot and changing the weight to the left foot when necessary to use the left arm.[2]*

These types of recommendations were designed to minimize the distracting gestures or body movements that speakers often exhibit when they are tense. All such advice was accompanied by the (impossible) caution that gestures, body movements, and voice should be "natural, not contrived"!

Today, communication experts advise a more conversational approach to public speaking. Although certain behaviors are recommended, they are designed to make speakers appear as if they are interacting one-on-one with audience members. This less prescriptive approach does not mean that speakers can overlook their nonverbal behavior, however. Nonverbal body language is often unintentional, and without special attention, speakers may unknowingly alienate or offend an audience or unconsciously communicate fear, anxiety, and insecurity. For example, a speaker may unintentionally frown during a portion of her speech, which tells the audience that she disagrees or is uncomfortable with this section of her presentation. Unintentional nonverbal behaviors can have a devastating effect on how an audience evaluates a speaker or speech.

In this chapter, you'll learn how to consciously plan and use nonverbal communication behavior to complement your verbal message so that audiences will be more likely to listen, understand, enjoy, and be moved by your speeches.

LOOK LIKE A PUBLIC SPEAKER
Audiences begin to form their impression of you by examining what you wear. Even if you believe that clothing has little or nothing to do with who you really are, you must accept that first impressions often are based almost exclusively on personal appearance. Dressing neatly and professionally communicates credibility. Being well groomed shows the audience that you are a professional, that you are someone to be respected, and, most importantly, that you made an effort to look good for the occasion. Unconsciously, audience members acknowledge and appreciate the time and trouble you took to present the best possible you.

Clothing Communicates Power and Status
Power and status are commonly associated with clothing. Historically, clothing often distinguished individuals of higher social status from those of lower social status.

What are the rules of appropriate attire for public speakers? Co-cultures that value power, rank, and status may prefer and expect formal dress. Conversely, co-cultures that place a higher premium on equality may prefer informal dress in some circumstances. Nevertheless, because public speaking situations typically are formal, you will want to look credible and professional. For women, that generally means wearing a dark, plain business suit, conservative blouse, and plain pumps; for men, it means a dark suit, solid-colored shirt (blue or white), and a conservative tie. Gaudy, informal, or casual clothes are likely to result in lowered perceptions of competence and overall credibility.

Of course, less formal occasions or particular speech topics may require a different kind of attire. What clothing is likely to communicate power and status for the following speaking situations?

- Persuading an audience to take tae kwon do lessons
- Informing homeowners how to make their homes secure from intruders
- Demonstrating how to hang wallpaper

For your own classroom presentation, you might wear clothes that are somewhat casual and yet one notch above what your audience is likely to wear. Women might wear a casual dress, skirt, or dress pants and a blouse or sweater. Men might wear casual pants (not jeans) and a shirt and tie (coat is optional) or sweater. Remember: Your goal is to look credible.

Clothing Communicates How We Feel
Clothing often communicates how we feel—or how we want others to think we feel. For example,

a speaker at a funeral would normally wear dark-colored, formal clothes to communicate grief and respect for the deceased. An elementary school teacher meeting his or her class for the first time might wear bright colors and patterns to communicate friendliness, warmth, and enthusiasm. On their famous campaign bus trip through the Midwest in 1992, candidates Bill Clinton and Al Gore frequently donned work shirts, denim jackets, and local feed company caps to relate to, identify with, and show respect for their rural audiences. Whether you think such clothing codes are important, trivial, or even silly, many people in our society continue to judge the credibility and personal characteristics of speakers on the basis of what they wear.

USE YOUR BODY EFFECTIVELY

Chapter 5 discussed the importance of appearing cool, calm, and collected, especially in a tension-producing public speaking situation. Your audience wants to know that you can handle the situation easily and confidently. Looking composed, then, is critical to impression formation. The gestures you use can either contribute to or undermine the impression of being relaxed and in control.

Nonverbal Emblems

Even though speakers generally use nonverbal communication to reinforce verbal messages, they occasionally substitute actions for words. For example, speakers might use nonverbal gestures or facial expressions rather than words to communicate dismay, disgust, frustration, hostility, or love. In everyday life, some nonverbal gestures have relatively straightforward meanings, such as raising a thumb to hitchhike, rotating the first finger around one's ear, sticking out one's tongue, or blowing a kiss. These nonverbal gestures that have direct verbal translations that are widely understood are known as **emblems**. (Additional examples of emblems are listed in the box "Common Nonverbal Emblems Used in the United States.")

Nevertheless, although certain emblems may seem reasonably clear to you and to others, you should avoid using them in your presentations unless you are sure everyone in your audience shares the same meanings for the emblems you use. Some emblems may seem vague or difficult for audience members to understand, especially when you and your audience members do not share the same co-cultural background.

Nonverbal Adaptors

Another category of potentially problematic gestures is **adaptors**—unintentional hand, arm, leg, or other body movements used to reduce stress or relieve boredom (such as tapping a pencil, biting one's nails, smoothing a jacket sleeve, or repeatedly adjusting eyeglasses). For the most part, speakers are unaware of their adaptors, yet audiences are quick to respond to these gestures. The uncontrolled use of adaptors can communicate that the speaker is nervous, insecure, uptight, or unprepared—messages no speaker wants to convey. Rehearsal and experience will help

Rehearsing Your Speech

- Practice first from the complete outline of your speech. Based on your first rehearsals, decide what key phrases you'll need to include in your speaking notes to prompt yourself. Your abbreviated outline should contain just enough information to keep your extemporaneous speech on track.

- Time your rehearsals. If your speech is too long, trim material that is not crucial; if it's too short, flesh out your supporting material.

- Rehearse in the approximate physical conditions in which you will deliver the speech: standing or sitting (behind a podium or table), using notecards, using visual aids, and so on.

- As you rehearse, imagine that you are speaking before an audience.

- Don't be discouraged if your first few rehearsals don't go as smoothly as you'd like. There's a big difference between thinking through a speech and

actually delivering it. Your delivery will improve as you rehearse.

- As you become more comfortable with delivering your speech and using your notecards, incorporate some of the nonverbal strategies described in this chapter. Practice in front of a mirror so you can see your gestures and movements.

- If possible, tape-record or videotape one of your rehearsals. Evaluate your speech and your delivery constructively, and make needed improvements.

- When you are ready, deliver your speech for friends or family members. Watch for and adapt to their feedback. Ask them to comment on your speech text and delivery.

- Rehearse until you feel comfortable and confident. If you are still feeling anxious, try some of the strategies presented in Chapter 4 for managing public speaking anxiety.

you minimize the use of nonverbal adaptors. (See the box "Rehearsing Your Speech" for additional tips on how to use practice sessions to improve your speech.)

Nonverbal Illustrators

Another category of gestures is **illustrators**—hand and arm movements used to demonstrate and reinforce the meanings intended by verbal messages. For example, pointing to a chart on a board behind you while saying "this one over here" is an illustrator. Others include looking at your watch to show that it's time to wrap things up, slapping your hand against your forehead to show that you just remembered something, punching the air with your fist to accentuate a word or phrase, and spreading your hands out to show length (such as the fish that got away).

Whereas emblems and adaptors can be problematic, illustrators can be helpful in communicating to your audience that you are composed and in control. Whenever you use illustrators, you are using multiple means to get your message across to the audience. Illustrators restate the verbal message

by communicating in another way what it is you are trying to say. To demonstrate how effective these gestures are, imagine giving directions to someone without using illustrators!

Audiences interpret illustrators quite differently than they do adaptors, which often communicate nervousness and anxiety. Speakers who want to appear dynamic, decisive, and committed might hold up fingers to count aloud or pound on the podium to make a point. To make your illustrators effective, you need to exaggerate them. At first, you may find exaggerated illustrators awkward and unnatural, but unless you swing your arms wide, raise your hand high, and then emphatically pump your fist in the air, your gestures might be missed by audience members in the fifth, tenth, or hundredth row.

Exaggerated illustrators also may seem awkward and unnatural to speakers from high-context co-cultures, like Asian Americans or Middle Eastern Americans, for whom verbal messages tend to be subtle. Nevertheless, the communicative demands of public speaking require some norm violations to ensure message accuracy and audience comprehension. Because some audiences may be unable to

Interview with a Professional

Mari Iizuka Harris

Mari Harris, 35, teaches public speaking at several different community colleges in Southern California.

What do you feel are the primary concerns that students need to understand when it comes to making nonverbal cues count in a public presentation?

Before talking about appropriate nonverbal behaviors in my classes, I always teach my students to stay away from inappropriate ones such as certain adaptive behaviors, irrelevant movements, and forced gestures. Basically, I advise my students to move naturally and purposefully. Some students are naturally dynamic, while others are more reserved; they should take their personalities into consideration and adopt appropriate nonverbal behaviors accordingly. Regardless of the personality traits, however, unwanted nonverbal behaviors are annoying and distracting.

As for dress, I suggest that my students dress up for their speeches whenever possible. Listeners generally form their first impression of the speaker from the way he or she dresses; accurately or inaccurately, the first impression tends to be carried over to a personality judgment. The speaker should never underestimate the communicative power that dress creates.

What do you tell students about the proper use of their hands and arms during a speech?

My motto is to teach my students to gesture as gestures come naturally to them. I happen to be a very expressive speaker who gestures dynamically, but I refuse to make already self-conscious students feel extra nervous by forcing them to gesture the way I do unless that is what they normally do comfortably. One time, a rather reserved male student told me that he just didn't know what to do with his arms while speaking. I told him to simply let his arms hang by his sides. I also advised him to give himself some opportunities to gesture by using visual aids, pointing to a graph or a picture, for example.

What do you tell students to do nonverbally to keep an audience interested in what they are saying?

Eye contact is probably one of the most important factors in nonverbal communication. A speaker who reads his or her speech rather than delivering it will lose the audience's attention for sure. Paralanguage is another factor. A monotonous speaker will put his or her audience to sleep quickly. The speaker should vary the rate, pitch, volume, and tone of his or her voice to add accent to a speech. Regarding volume, it is sometimes a good strategy for a speaker to lower his or her volume when he or she wants to get the audience's attention. In addition, pauses can be used to create a feeling of anticipation among the audience.

interpret subtle nonverbal cues and because the message is delivered only once, speakers must be more explicit than they normally would be in more relational, interactive contexts. (For additional advice on the effective use of gestures, refer to the box "Interview with a Professional: Mari Iizuka Harris.")

LOOK AT YOUR AUDIENCE

Look at your audience! This point may seem obvious and logical, yet it is often the hardest to drive home to novice speakers. Novice speakers almost always avoid looking directly at anyone in the audience; instead, they look up, down, around, and away—anywhere but at their audience.

As soon as you reach the podium, pause momentarily and let your gaze sweep across your audience. Be sure to take notice of actual individuals—what are they wearing, who is in the back row, and what response are you getting from the center? Then, acknowledge them. Try to show every person that you recognize him or her—smile, nod, hold eye contact a moment, and say hello. Then, and only then, are you ready to proceed.

Eye contact commands an audience's attention. Imagine how hard it would be to doze off during a lecture with the professor looking right at you. Eye contact elicits audience involvement. Consequently, the more you look at your audience, the more likely your audience will stay interested and attentive. It is very difficult for audience members to avoid a speaker who seems to be looking directly at them. In most cases, eye contact obligates a person to reciprocate.

Making eye contact is a good strategy even if your audience includes members of co-cultures that may refrain from direct eye contact in some communication situations. Research indicates that college students representing a variety of U.S. co-cultures reported a consistent preference for teachers who looked at them as opposed to teachers who didn't.[3]

KEEP YOUR AUDIENCE INTERESTED

To generate interest in your audience, you must show interest yourself. There are lots of ways to show the audience that you're excited about being there and anxious to speak about your topic. In addition to nonverbal illustrators and eye contact, overall body movements are an effective way to communicate confidence and enthusiasm. A speaker who strides confidently toward the podium to begin a speech is likely to come across as more committed and enthusiastic than one who shuffles timidly along. A speaker who walks purposefully around the room to directly address different groups will be perceived as friendlier and more open than one who paces nervously or wanders aimlessly.

Posture can also signal your interest and involvement in your message. Leaning toward the audience can communicate intensity and concern for the more meaningful issues of your presentation. Direct, face-to-face posture also suggests active interaction and a sense of belonging to the group.

Use Your Voice to Your Advantage

The most certain way to lose an audience is to deliver a speech in a **monotone**—a voice that never varies in rate, volume, or **pitch** (how high or low a voice sounds). Perhaps you've been subjected to speakers who seemed bored with their own presentations; they droned on without any variation in their vocal quality. As a number of studies demonstrate, a monotonous delivery interferes with audience comprehension and later recall of the information.[4]

Vary Vocal Volume and Pitch

You need to vary the way you use your voice by changing the volume. Speak softly when you want audience members to quiet down—they will if they want to listen. Speak loudly, but build to a crescendo—that is, gradually increase your volume for effect. You might want to dramatize a story by culminating in a loud, booming voice, or you might want to gradually decrease your volume to show the seriousness of your message.

The same can be said for vocal pitch. It matters more that you frequently change your pitch than whether you talk too high or too low. As Figure 15-1 illustrates, variation in volume and pitch within a sentence can also help convey meaning.

Vary Speech Rate

Audiences also prefer speakers who vary their speech rate. Although you may have been told to slow down when talking before a large group, sometimes it is advisable to alternately speed up and slow down your rate of speech. Listeners can process information much more quickly than people can speak; in fact, research indicates that faster rates of speech tend to increase listener comprehension and recall.[5] When listening to a consistently slow or normal speech rate, audience members tend to tune in and out. Varying your speech rate will keep them alert and help them retain your message.

Practice using slower rates during your introductory and closing remarks. You might also reduce your speech rate when you want to emphasize a sound bite or reinforce a central point. And, of course, if you

You can help.	Today is my birthday.	I can do that.
YOU can help.	TODAY is my birthday.	I can do that.
You CAN help.	Today IS my birthday.	I CAN do that.
You can HELP.	Today is MY birthday.	I can DO that.
YOU CAN HELP.	Today is my BIRTHDAY.	I can do THAT.

Figure 15-1 Varying pitch and volume can heighten interest and convey meaning. Placing the emphasis on different words in a sentence can convey different messages.

suspect audience members may have trouble adjusting to your accent or dialect, slow your speech down, at least initially, until they get used to the way you talk. Otherwise, you should resume a normal speed or shift to an even faster speech rate to keep your audience attentive and to promote recall.

Use Silence Strategically

Pause time—the strategic use of silence—is another strategy that can affect audience attention. A pregnant pause before or after a phrase can add emphasis to your message. Many novice speakers find pause time very awkward and often fill gaps with "uhs," "ers," and "you-knows," which only detract from their presentation. Rehearsal and experience can help you eliminate these filled pauses. Learn to be comfortable with silence and to use it strategically to your advantage. Use a lengthy pause right before you begin your speech and again at the conclusion, right before you deliver your final memorable story or statement. Stop and pause. Put down your notes. Take off your glasses. Lean forward, and scan your audience. Then proceed with your introductory or closing remarks. Pause time captures audience attention and builds suspense and drama.

PRACTICE BEING NONVERBALLY IMMEDIATE

Chapter 14 examined verbal immediacy behaviors that reduce the distance between speakers and audiences. Similarly, speakers can use various **nonverbal immediacy** behaviors to establish a sense of closeness with the audience. In addition to smiling, making eye contact, using illustrators, using purposeful body movements, and changing vocal quality, other nonverbal immediacy behaviors include nodding, using open gestures, and standing close to and even touching audience members.[6] Collectively, these nonverbal behaviors contribute to positive perceptions of closeness.

Curiously, these same nonverbal behaviors have been shown to be effective in interpersonal relationships as well.[7] Here's how it works: Immediacy behaviors communicate warmth, friendliness, and liking. When someone smiles at you, makes lots of eye contact, uses open gestures, is facially expressive, and sits or stands close to you, you might assume that he or she likes you. And, when you see that someone apparently likes you, approves of you, and enjoys being

with you, you feel like returning those feelings. In other words, people like people who apparently like them.

Immediacy also happens to beget immediacy. If, as a speaker, you engage in behaviors that communicate immediacy, your audience will likely mirror similar behaviors. Thus, if you make eye contact and smile at audience members, they will likely look back at you and return your smile. Because immediacy connotes liking, both you and your audience members will believe the feeling to be mutual.

Apparently, this immediacy phenomenon holds for all kinds of people. Research on teacher immediacy found that college students, regardless of ethnic affiliation, evaluated their instructors and their courses more positively when the instructors were verbally and nonverbally immediate. Students also reported that they learned more from these professors. These findings held true for Euroamerican, Asian American, Latino, and African American students.[8] If immediacy is such a powerful predictor of how students respond to teachers, imagine the similar effect it can have on audiences in other public speaking contexts.

In the context of formal speaking events, however, it's not easy to engage in immediacy behaviors that transmit messages of closeness; it's seldom appropriate or even physically possible to touch members of your audience. Nevertheless, research on teacher immediacy reveals some techniques that will help reduce the psychological distance between you and members of your audience.[9] Before reading further, take a few minutes to complete the questionnaire in the box "How Nonverbally Immediate Are You?" to assess your own style.

To be nonverbally immediate, avoid standing behind a podium, table, or desk while communicating. These props often act as barriers between you and the audience, and you will find it is much easier to talk without some obstruction in your way. If you need to use a microphone, request a handheld one or, better yet, use a lavaliere or clip-on mike.

Move toward your audience—and then away again. Use broad, open gestures to reinforce what you have to say, but be sure that your body movements are purposeful and meaningful and that your posture makes you look relaxed, comfortable, and confident. As you look at individual audience members, give them a warm, friendly smile and lean forward. If there are aisles between audience members, move up and down and within the group

How Nonverbally Immediate Are You?

Instructions

The following statements describe some nonverbal immediacy behaviors a public speaker might use during a presentation. Enter the appropriate number in the space provided to indicate how likely you might be to engage in each of the following behaviors when presenting your own speech before a large group: (5) extremely likely, (4) likely, (3) maybe (unsure), (2) unlikely, or (1) extremely unlikely.

____ 1. I would sit behind a table or desk while speaking.

____ 2. I would use a lot of purposeful gestures while talking to the group.

____ 3. I would use a monotonous, dull voice when talking to an audience.

____ 4. I would look directly at my audience.

____ 5. I would smile at the group while talking.

____ 6. I would feel tense and rigid while giving my speech.

____ 7. I would approach or stand beside individual audience members.

____ 8. I would move purposefully around the room while speaking.

____ 9. I would avoid looking at individual audience members during my speech.

____ 10. I would look at my notes frequently during my presentation.

____ 11. I would stand behind a podium or desk while giving my speech.

____ 12. I would assume a very relaxed posture while talking to the group.

____ 13. I would smile at individual members in the audience.

____ 14. I would use a variety of vocal expressions while talking.

____ 15. I would engage in a lot of nervous gestures or body movements, such as wrinkling my notecards or shifting from one foot to the other.

Calculating Your Score

1. Add together your responses to items 1, 3, 6, 9, 10, 11, and 15 = ____

2. Add together your responses to items 2, 4, 5, 7, 8, 12, 13, and 14 = ____

3. Complete the following formula:

   42 − total from step 1 = ____

   + total from step 2 = ____

   Your total nonverbal immediacy score = ____

Interpreting Your Score

The possible scores range from 15 to 75. (If your own score does not fall within that range, you have made a computational error.) The median score is around 45. If your own score falls above 50 (or above the median of 45), you are a public speaker high in nonverbal immediacy. Speakers who practice immediacy behaviors are perceived as being more credible and attractive, as sharing similar attitudes with the audience, and, overall, as being more approachable and likable. Audience members enjoy immediate speakers and are more likely to be attentive to what they have to say. In addition, audience members are likely to find immediate speakers highly motivating.

If your score falls below 40 (or below the median of 45), you might want to learn and practice the specific immediacy behaviors suggested in this chapter. Without engaging in immediacy behaviors (that is, being low in nonverbal immediacy), you can expect your audience to take less interest in your presentation and to become less involved in what you have to say. Nonimmediate speakers are often perceived as less likable and less willing to communicate. Taken to the extreme, nonimmediate speakers appear nervous, anxious, and disinterested. To turn those negative perceptions around, then, practice nonverbal immediacy skills and incorporate them into your overall presentational style.

NOTE: This scale was originally designed to assess teachers' nonverbal immediacy in the classroom. For purposes of this chapter, however, this scale has been revised to assess how you, as a public speaker, might use nonverbal immediacy while giving a presentation before a large group. An easily obtainable source for this scale is: Christophel, D. (1990). The relationships among teacher immediacy behaviors, student motivation, and learning. *Communication Education, 39,* 323–340. The original source for this scale is: Richmond, V. P., Gorham, J., & McCroskey, J. C. (1987). The relationship between selected immediacy behaviors and cognitive learning. In M. L. McLaughlin (Ed.), *Communication yearbook 10* (pp. 574–590). Beverly Hills, CA: Sage.

Nonverbal Immediacy

- Stand close to the audience, and, if possible, move around among them.

- Don't use a podium or stand behind a table; both act as barriers between you and the audience.

- Assume a comfortable posture, and try to appear somewhat relaxed (even if you're not).

- Use purposeful body movements: Walk purposefully, gesture purposefully, and gaze purposefully.

- Lean toward your audience to signal closeness—and interest.

- Use open, broad gestures. Avoid adaptors and emblems; instead, stick to nonverbal illustrators that reinforce your message.

- Know your speech well enough not to have to look at your notes all the time. Save your eyes for the audience.

- Look at your audience. Establish and maintain eye contact.

- Smile at your audience. Nod your head.

- Use vocal variety. Vary the volume, pitch, and rate of your speech.

---

while talking. Notice how professional interviewers like Oprah Winfrey and Sally Jesse Raphael move within the group while interacting one-on-one with audience members. (See the box "Nonverbal Immediacy" for a summary of strategies for developing nonverbal immediacy.)

Initiating and maintaining immediacy with your audience will help establish a cooperative communication exchange. When you show that you like your audience by employing nonverbal (and verbal) immediacy behaviors, members will respond in kind. They will mirror many of your own immediacy behaviors by leaning forward themselves, smiling broadly, and looking back at you. With a responsive, enthusiastic audience like that, you're bound to be a success. For a summary of these techniques, see the box "Effective Nonverbal Communication."

Effective Nonverbal Communication

- *Look like a public speaker.* Choose clothing that communicates power, status, and credibility. Your clothing should be appropriate for the occasion and speech topic—it should communicate a particular mood.

- *Use your body effectively.* Use exaggerated nonverbal illustrators to reinforce meanings in your verbal message. Avoid nonverbal adaptors that communicate anxiety, and do not use nonverbal emblems that may confuse your audience.

- *Look at your audience.* Maintain direct eye contact with audience members in order to command their attention. Take note of individual faces in the audience—smile, nod, and make eye contact.

- *Keep your audience interested.* Move confidently and purposefully. Stand close to or lean toward your audience, using a face-to-face posture to maintain interest and attention.

- *Use your voice to your advantage.* Vary the quality of your voice—volume, pitch, and rate—to emphasize particular points and to keep the audience listening. Use silent (as opposed to filled) pauses to build suspense and drama.

- *Practice being nonverbally immediate.* Establish a sense of closeness with and positive regard for your audience by engaging in nonverbal immediate behaviors.

CHAPTER REVIEW

- How a speaker communicates is often as important as (if not more important than) what a speaker says. Speakers should rely on posture, gestures, clothing, distance, eye contact, facial expressions, and vocal quality to help communicate their message. Speakers should practice minimizing unintentional body language that can alienate audiences or undermine presentations by leaking nonverbal messages that say something quite different from what was intended.

- Audiences begin forming their impressions of you as a public speaker the minute they set eyes on you. Your overall appearance, then, is critical to making a good first impression. The right kind of clothing can communicate power, status, and emotion and is a key to how the audience will respond to you.

- Of the different gestures you can use, illustrators are the most effective for reinforcing your message.

Exaggerate illustrators so that your audience members will perceive them as purposeful.

- It's important to view your audience members as individuals. Eye contact and purposeful body movements signal interest and involvement with your audience.

- You are more likely to gain and maintain audience interest and enthusiasm in your presentations by varying your vocal volume, pitch, and rate. Use intentional pauses strategically to build suspense and drama.

- Collectively, these different nonverbal behaviors communicate immediacy between you and your audience. Engaging in nonverbal immediacy behaviors, such as smiling, nodding, making eye contact, leaning forward, and using open gestures, can help your audience warm up to you. Immediacy also encourages audience members to respond in kind.

QUESTIONS FOR CRITICAL THINKING & REVIEW

1. What public speaking situations require formal dress? What about informal? To what extent do you think clothing affects your audience's perception of you?

2. This chapter stresses the importance of maintaining eye contact with the audience. And yet, Chapter 3 described some co-cultures (Asian American and Native American) that do not engage in a lot of eye contact in normal conversations. Why, then, do you suppose eye contact remains an important public speaking cue—for all co-cultures?

3. What do adaptors communicate about a speaker to an audience? What adaptors do you tend to use? What do you think they communicate to your audience?

4. What does silence convey to an audience? Why is it important to use pause time during a public presentation? Which co-cultures do you think might be more comfortable with intentional pauses? Which might be less comfortable?

NOTES

1. Fulton, R. I., & Trueblood, T. C. (1893). *Practical elements of elocution* (pp. 53–54). Boston: Ginn.
2. Fenno, F. H. (1912). *Fenno's science of speech* (p. 139). Chicago: Emerson W. Fenno.
3. Powell, R. G., & Harville, B. (1990). The effects of teacher immediacy and clarity on instructional outcomes: An intercultural assessment. *Communication Education,*

39, 369–379; Sanders, J. A., & Wiseman, R. L. (1990). The effects of verbal and nonverbal teacher immediacy on perceived cognitive, affective, and behavioral learning in the multicultural classroom. *Communication Education, 39,* 341–353.
4. Glasgow, G. M. (1952). A semantic index of vocal pitch. *Speech Monographs, 19,* 64–68; Richmond, V. P.,

McCroskey, J. C., & Payne, S. K. (1987). *Nonverbal behavior in interpersonal relations* (p. 102). Englewood Cliffs, NJ: Prentice-Hall.

5. Richmond, McCroskey, & Payne, 1987, p. 102.

6. Mehrabian, A. (1971). *Silent messages*. Belmont, CA: Wadsworth; Mehrabian, A. (1981). *Silent messages: Implicit communication of emotions and attitudes* (2nd ed.). Belmont, CA: Wadsworth; Andersen, J. F., Andersen, P. A., & Jensen, A. D. (1979). The measurement of nonverbal immediacy. *Journal of Applied Communication Research*, 7, 153–180.

7. Bell, R. A., & Daly, J. A. (1984). The affinity-seeking function of communication. *Communication Monographs*, *51*, 91–115.

8. Powell & Harville, 1990, 369–379; Sanders & Wiseman, 1990, 341–353.

9. Christophel, D. (1990). The relationships among teacher immediacy behaviors, student motivation, and learning. *Communication Education*, *39*, 323–340; Richmond, V. P., Gorham, J., & McCroskey, J. C. (1987). The relationship between selected immediacy behaviors and cognitive learning. In M. L. McLaughlin (Ed.), *Communication yearbook 10* (pp. 574–590). Beverly Hills, CA: Sage.

Chapter 16

DEWELOPING YOUR OWN RHETORICAL STYLE

Learning Objectives

After reading this chapter, you should be able to do the following:

1. Identify and develop your own personal style of communicating with your audience.

2. Understand three cautions associated with developing a rhetorical style.

3. Identify and characterize the four personal communication styles particularly suited for public speaking.

4. Differentiate between feminine and masculine styles of communicating.

What do the following pairs of well-known celebrities have in common?

Marcia Clark and Vernon Jordan
Celine Dion and Melissa Etheridge
Jerry Seinfeld and Roseanne
Jay Leno and David Letterman
Madonna and Meg Ryan
Jimmy Smits and Dennis Franz
Matt Lauer and Al Roker
Barbara Walters and Jenny Jones
Helen Hunt and Michael Richards

Besides sharing a common profession, the members of each pair couldn't be more different. Whereas Jay Leno comes across as warm, affectionate, and likable, David Letterman seems to work at being cynical, distant, and insolent. Same job, different people. Compare a Celine Dion concert with one by Melissa Etheridge; or contrast LeAnn Rhimes with Alanis Morissette. The same exceptional talent, but different styles of singing. And can you imagine Roseanne trying out a Jerry Seinfeld monolog? Outrageously funny people, but very different approaches. Of course, what all these people do have in common is their own unique way of relating to an audience. Each style is very different but seems to fit each person. In fact, it's those very styles that make each person special and unique.

Like celebrities and politicians, all great speakers carve out their own unique style of communicating with their audience. **Rhetorical style** (or **communication style**) is the overall qualitative way a speaker communicates, using verbal and non-verbal messages. Everyone, then, has a style of communicating. But not everyone knows what that style is or how to use it to his or her advantage. Sometimes style is enhanced by accents or regional dialects: Actors Rosie Perez, Fran Drescher, Sean Connery, and Emma Thompson display unique cultural and regional accents. Other styles are distinguished by a predictable look or smile: film star Denzel Washington and TV star Calista Flockhart (*Ally McBeal*) are both known for smiles that could warm a cold meat locker!

If you are a novice speaker, you must identify a rhetorical style that works well for you. Once you have isolated a personal style, you can showcase that style to your own advantage. (The box "Interview with a Student: Marveina Peters" focuses on one student's rhetorical style.) This chapter should help you recognize and capitalize on your own personal strengths as a communicator that audiences will find compelling, entertaining, and engaging.

DISCOVERING YOUR OWN RHETORICAL STYLE

Before reviewing the characteristics of some well-known rhetorical styles, take a closer look at your own personal style of communicating. There are three key considerations to keep in mind when determining exactly what style suits you and how to use it to be an effective public speaker.

Choose a Style That Fits You

First, don't try to adopt a style that doesn't fit who you really are. Don't try to be like someone else unless that someone is like you. It's a lot like buying new clothes: Unless you feel comfortable wearing the outfit, it's not a good idea to buy it. Of course, you may not yet know which style is likely to fit. Therefore, you may have to "try on" several different styles to see which one style or combination of two or more styles "wears" best.

Build on Your Own Strengths as a Communicator

Second, when selecting your rhetorical style, examine your own special strengths as a communicator. Instead of trying to emulate someone else's rhetorical style, try to discover your own unique style. Ask yourself,

Part of becoming an effective speaker is figuring out what rhetorical style best suits you. Consider the nonverbal strengths that characterizes the styles of late night talk show hosts Jay Leno. What are your own personal strengths as a speaker? Once you discover your own unique way of communicating, you can relate more effectively to your audience.

SPEAKING OUT

Interview with a Student

Marveina Peters

Marveina Peters, 18, is a first-year student at California State University, Long Beach.

What are your special strengths as a speaker? What makes you so good at what you do?

My special strengths in public speaking are giving the audience eye contact, speaking loud enough to be heard, and creating for the audience some kind of visual image in their minds so that the audience not only hears what I am saying, but they can also visualize it.

What makes me good at this is practice. It doesn't just happen. Practice makes perfect. I practice my own speeches in front of my mother, my father, my brother, and my two sisters

over and over. One of the things I learned from them was that I was memorizing my speeches. I didn't know I was, but they knew I was. I guess I kept looking up in the air trying to remember every word, every line. They'd say, "What's up there?" I learned to try to look at them and talk to them. With practice, you can fix your mistakes.

Everyone has his or her own unique way of communicating. What is it about the way you communicate in front of a large group that makes you unique?

The fact that I give the audience what it is they want. They want, first of all, to hear the speaker. I'm loud; they can hear me. Next, they want to visualize what the speaker is saying, and I give

Interview with a Student *(Continued)*

them some kind of visual image. I try to use a lot of specific, concrete examples. I tell personal stories that will help them relate. They also want a speaker who speaks in conversational form, and I always speak to my audience as if they are all personal friends of mine. That way, no one in the audience feels isolated or alienated.

How important is rhetorical style to you? To what extent do you think your own co-culture (African American) influenced how you developed your own unique rhetorical style?

Rhetorical style refers to each individual's own unique way of speaking. I believe that rhetorical style is very important. Rhetorical style is what really makes the individual; it sets

a speaker apart from the rest. I think my own co-culture influenced how I developed my own unique style a lot. For one thing, in my culture, I learned that style is very important. My culture also helped me to be more distinctive, more open, and more expressive than other speakers. In my culture, I've learned how important it is to be heard. We like to be heard. We're taught not to be embarrassed or intimidated by anyone or anything. If we have something to say, we're taught to say it, to speak out.

It showed in this class. African American speakers stood out from the rest. We were all a lot more outgoing. We used a lot more gestures and hand movements. And our words and phrases were more vivid. We all participated more in class, and our speeches were more expressive and powerful.

"What is it about the way *I* communicate that makes me unique?" The box "Identifying Your Own Communication Style" provides a list of questions to help you determine the characteristics that reflect your own typical way of communicating.

Don't Stress Style over Substance

Third, do not place more emphasis on the way you communicate than you do on the content of your presentations. Style is no substitute for substance. Being able to deliver a speech with style and eloquence is not

---

Identifying Your Own Communication Style

The following questions are designed to help you identify your own strengths as a communicator. Answering yes to any of these questions will help you determine your own unique way of relating to people. Check off the appropriate questions to help you begin developing and capitalizing on an overall style of communication.

- Do others find me a particularly good listener?
- Do people think I'm amusing, sarcastic, or entertaining?
- Do I come across as patient and kind?
- Am I especially open or self-disclosing when I communicate?
- Can I tell a good story?
- Do I enjoy being dramatic?
- Do I use a lot of energy when I communicate?
- Do I enjoy acting or playing a role for others?

- Am I a particularly sympathetic communicator?
- Can I tell a joke?
- Am I an unusually animated speaker?
- Do I come across as confident and in control?
- Am I generally a relaxed communicator?
- Do I use a lot of gestures and make eye contact when I relate?
- Do I tend to use metaphors or anecdotes when I speak?
- Am I good at explaining complex ideas to others?
- Do others tend to listen attentively to me when I speak?
- Do people think I'm friendly and pleasant to be around?
- Am I good at making others feel comfortable?

Developing a Personal Rhetorical Style

- *Choose a style that fits you.* Try out different styles or combinations of styles—both as you rehearse and as you give different speeches. See which style seems natural and comfortable.

- *Build on your own strengths as a communicator.* Pay attention to how you normally communicate. Isolate and capitalize on those communication behaviors that you like the most about yourself and that make you a unique and effective communicator.

- *Don't stress style over substance.* Remember that to give an effective speech, you must first have something substantial to say. Spend time developing a well-researched, well-organized presentation before you consider what communication style to use in front of a particular audience.

enough—you must have something to say! This statement may seem obvious, but it is critical to effective public speaking. This chapter on style is intentionally placed toward the end of this book, after you've had a chance to learn about putting together the content of your speech. Attention to style can help you communicate your ideas more effectively to an audience, but style without substance has the potential to misrepresent messages, mislead listeners, or even undermine the purpose of public speaking.

The three key considerations for developing a personal style are summarized in the box "Developing a Personal Rhetorical Style." With these considerations in mind, you are ready to look at four personal styles of communicating that have proven especially useful and effective for public speaking situations.

PERSONAL COMMUNICATION STYLES WELL SUITED TO PUBLIC SPEAKING

In recent years, the research on communication styles has identified a number of easily recognizable ways in which people habitually communicate.[1] Among them are the friendly style, contentious style, relaxed style, dominant style, precise style, and impression-leaving style. There are also four rhetorical styles that are most effective in the public speaking context: the dramatic, animated, open, and humorous styles.[2] With these in mind, you should be able to see exactly how you can develop or refine your own rhetorical style.

Dramatic Style

Some people tell stories so dramatically that they literally command the audience's attention. Speakers who use a **dramatic style** are generally humorous, but

they need not be funny to be dramatic. Dramatic speakers approach the public speaking event as if they were performers on center stage. They know how to build tension when telling a story, use colorful words or metaphors to create a mood or paint a picture, exaggerate for emphasis, and joke and play with the audience. Dramatic speakers often use magnified gestures to illustrate their point, hold eye contact with individuals in the audience just a little longer than is comfortable, and vary their vocal quality (volume, rate, and pitch) to hold attention and create certain effects. Dramatic speakers typically work their audiences so well that people respond with sympathy, laughter, interest, or surprise.[3]

In the movie *Primary Colors*, the character Jack Stanton (played by John Travolta) epitomized the dramatic style when he told a group of adults enrolled in a literacy/reading program how courageous they were for going back to school. As he listened intently to each student's tale of personal struggle, tears rolled down his face. Finally, he took out a handkerchief, blew his nose, shook his head, and stood. Then he began to tell an incredible tale about his uncle, a war hero who had won the Congressional Medal of Honor. All his friends and family were so proud of him. They wanted to know what he was going to do with his life now that he was home: Was he going to take a job at the bank, or maybe open his own business? The world was waiting for him to continue to do great things, but Jack's uncle just lay on the couch, day after day, doing nothing. And then Jack asked his listeners if they knew why? Jack paused, looked around the room at everyone, and finally confessed, "Because he couldn't read." Jack admitted that his uncle didn't have *their* courage, the courage to go back to school and learn to read. Then he walked over, shook their hands, and hugged them as he told them how proud he was to meet each and every one of them!

In addition to using vocal variations, rhythmic repetition, gestures, movement, and pause time, Jack Stanton communicated dramatically by reversing himself. Recall that he began by telling the group what courage his uncle possessed—but then concluded by revealing the courage his uncle lacked. Even though we discover later in the movie that no such uncle existed, the story was a dramatic way for Jack to commend the group for their own courage.

Two other ways to add emphasis are overstatement and understatement, such as exaggerating a story to make it seem more than it is or delivering lines with dry wit. Comedians Ellen DeGeneres and Bill Maher are both known for their dramatic use of under- and over-statement. But comedians aren't the only ones who use dramatic devices in their speech. Former Texas governor Ann Richards is well known for her dramatic rhetorical style. In her speech condemning the U.S. defense budget, she argued: "But when we pay billions for planes that won't fly, billions for tanks that won't fire, and billions for systems that won't work, that old dog won't hunt."[4] Notice how she exaggerated the quality of defense equipment and then followed with the down-home phrase "that old dog won't hunt."

Stories often provide another avenue of drama to a public speaking event. Good storytellers like Bill Cosby, Vanessa Redgrave, Maya Angelou, Bette Midler, and James Earl Jones are known for their dramatic style. Some storytellers take too long and bore their listeners, but good ones use pacing effectively to build tension and anticipation. Beginning or ending a presentation with a story is a dramatic way to make a point. Tracy Bohannon, a biology major, began her informative speech with this amazing story:

> One cold winter night not too long ago, a tall young man brought in a five-month-old kitten; she was black, female, and quivering with fright. As the receptionist took down the animal's history, the man explained that the cat had gotten stuck in the fan belt of his car. Since then, the cat hadn't been able to use its back left leg. The vet came in, examined the kitten, and noted that its leg had been severely fractured, almost completely severed, and that it needed to be treated for infection with several antibiotics. Immediate surgery was also required—or the cat would have to survive on three legs. An expensive proposal, the owner left to think it over.
>
> Four days later, the cat owner returned and began to cry as he revealed the fact that he was the one who had fractured the kitten's leg by throwing it against the wall. Then he told me that he could not afford the surgery nor could he incur the expense of extensive treatment with antibiotics. He gave us permission to put the kitten down. This story is typical of many of the clients that come into the animal clinic. I couldn't put that kitten down; I took her home with me. But I can't save all the animals.

Without question, this dramatic opening compelled the audience to listen thoughtfully to the remainder of the presentation. Audiences find it hard to remain detached or to develop resistant arguments when a speaker exposes her or his emotional attachment to the issue. By dramatizing a personal commitment to the topic, the speaker stands a good chance of involving the audience.

Animated Style

Dramatic speakers are often animated and use a lot of energy when they communicate. Energy, enthusiasm, and excitement are the central characteristics of the **animated style**. Animated speakers show every emotion they are feeling by exaggerating their nonverbal behaviors—gesturing broadly, smiling frequently, walking purposefully, nodding knowingly, and raising or lowering their eyebrows.[5] Audiences know exactly what an animated speaker thinks and feels by watching his or her face, eyes, gestures, and body movements.

Some animated speakers gesture wildly with their arms. These speakers, who seem unable to think or talk without moving their hands and arms, stand out clearly from more restrained speakers. Consider, for example, the contrasting styles of these well-known personalities:

Charles Grodin and Kathie Lee Gifford

Janet Reno and Katie Couric

Oprah Winfrey and Spike Lee

Cuba Gooding, Jr., and Christopher Darden

Disregarding their particular biases, to which type of speaker would you rather listen? For how long? Most people would rather listen to speakers whom they find emotionally arousing and enthusiastic about what they have to say. Enthusiasm is contagious; the more aroused and excited a speaker appears, the more stimulated and tuned in the audience will become. By smiling, nodding, and gesturing expressively, you can direct your audience members to listen and solicit their support of your message.

Open Style

Speakers using an **open style** of communicating often invite audience involvement by coming across as affable, sincere, trusting, and self-disclosing. Open speakers take a conversational approach to public speaking. They rely on their own personal histories, experiences, and feelings to relate to their audience one-on-one. Like animated speakers, open communicators are unafraid to show how they feel. When they are angry, they show their outrage; when they are joyful, they show their elation. Open speakers often are frank—they do not hesitate to express satisfaction or disappointment, agreement or disagreement.

Open speakers outwardly display feelings and attitudes and invite others to do the same. They convey to audience members that it is safe to say what they think and to show what they feel. The most obvious way open speakers invite audience involvement is by revealing information about themselves. Such self-disclosures are often positive, but sometimes they reveal negative or personal information that potentially puts the speaker at risk. After all, to what extent can the speaker trust the audience to handle the information with some degree of sensitivity and understanding?

It turns out that audiences appreciate forthright, honest, and open speakers. If the speaker risks disclosing personal information, then audience members feel that he or she can be trusted to handle any information they disclose in return. Of course, an audience may tire of a speaker who seems too intent on talking about him- or herself: "my accomplishments," "my dreams and goals," "my fears and anxieties," and on and on. Moreover, some kinds of disclosure are totally inappropriate for a public presentation; revealing a deep, dark secret might lead an audience to conclude that the speaker is more than a little bit peculiar. Unlike talk show hosts who invite guests to let it all hang out, credible public speakers should proceed with caution!

One well-known open communicator, Kathie Lee Gifford, has been moved to tears, laughter, anger, and frustration on national television, and the public seems to know a lot about her opinions, children, and marital life. Rosie O'Donnell is another celebrated open communicator. Almost everyone knows that she has adopted two kids, recalls every childhood advertising slogan and jingle on TV, considers Madonna one of her best friends, and is absolutely "ga-ga" over Tom Cruise. Poet and Wake Forest University professor Maya Angelou epitomizes the open (and dramatic) speaker. Reciting her own poetry aloud for the nation at the Clinton inaugural in January 1993, Angelou drew us all closer together, uniting us to common causes, concerns, and responsibilities. And, either because or in spite of his spinal injury, actor/producer Christopher Reeve reaches out to millions, revealing his unrelenting efforts to recover and his optimism that he will, in fact, walk again one day. Simultaneously, he discloses his frustrations with the lack of funding for research on spinal injuries. Even though you may not know Reeve personally, doesn't he seem like the kind of person you could talk with for hours? Isn't he the kind of person you would like as your friend and confidant?

Contrast those communicators who convey images of warmth, sincerity, and openness with those who appear unavailable, unapproachable, or closed, like *Nightline*'s Ted Koppel, attorney Vernon Jordan, figure skater Nancy Kerrigan, and Judge Judy. Of course, all most people really know about each of these communicators is how they are presented via the media. Beyond the TV cameras, these same individuals may, in fact, be highly open and responsive individuals. These contrasting examples are presented only to show you the relative impact an open versus a closed style can have on an audience. Overall, speakers who appear sensitive, warm, sympathetic, and understanding are more likely to be accepted and trusted by audiences.

Humorous Style

A **humorous style** relies primarily on humor to engage audiences. If you suspect that your most effective means of communicating is using a humorous style, you will need plenty of feedback from others to validate your perception—and not just from your mother! For instance, when you tell a joke, do people laugh politely? When you volunteer to tell a funny story, do your friends quickly interrupt and change the subject? Or, do people tell you that you have a good sense of humor? Do they ask you if you have heard any good jokes lately?

How can you decide if humor is for you? Take a few minutes to complete the questionnaire in the box "What Is Your Humor Orientation?" to determine how regularly or effectively you use humor when you communicate with others.

Whatever your score on the humor orientation questionnaire, being humorous in front of a large group of people can be difficult if you don't carefully plan your strategy. First, most speakers don't feel particularly humorous when they are about to deliver a 20-minute presentation to a large audience. Second, most speakers feel so anxious that any attempts at humor are likely to be bungled. Third, most speakers know that humor is in the eye (or is it ear?) of the beholder—it is the response of the audience that counts.

The important point is that if you think your speaking style leans toward the humorous, you should capitalize on that quality by planning to be humorous. Even if you are low in humor orientation, you can still

What Is Your Humor Orientation?

Instructions

The following statements describe how various people use humor when relating to others. Enter the appropriate number in the space provided to indicate the degree to which each of these statements applies to you: (5) strongly agree, (4) agree, (3) are neutral or undecided, (2) disagree, or (1) strongly disagree.

_____ 1. I regularly tell jokes and funny stories when I am with a group.

_____ 2. People usually laugh when I tell a joke or story.

_____ 3. I have no memory for jokes or funny stories.

_____ 4. I can be funny without having to rehearse a joke.

_____ 5. Being funny is a natural communication style for me.

_____ 6. I cannot tell a joke well.

_____ 7. People seldom ask me to tell stories.

_____ 8. My friends would say that I am a funny person.

_____ 9. People don't seem to pay close attention when I tell a joke.

_____ 10. Even funny jokes seem flat when I tell them.

_____ 11. I can easily remember jokes and stories.

_____ 12. People often ask me to tell jokes and stories.

_____ 13. My friends would not say that I am a funny person.

_____ 14. I don't tell jokes or stories even when asked to.

_____ 15. I tell stories and jokes very well.

_____ 16. Of all the people I know, I'm one of the funniest.

_____ 17. I use humor to communicate in a variety of situations.

Calculating Your Score

1. Add together your responses to items 3, 6, 7, 9, 10, 13, and 14 = _____

2. Add together your responses to items 1, 2, 4, 5, 8, 11, 12, 15, 16, and 17 = _____

3. Complete the following formula:

$$42 - \text{total from step I} = \underline{\hspace{2cm}}$$
$$+ \text{total from step 2} = \underline{\hspace{2cm}}$$

Your total humor orientation score = _____

Interpreting Your Score

The possible scores range from 17 to 85. (If your own score does not fall within that range, you have made a computational error.) The average or mean score for this scale is typically 59 or 60. If your score falls well below that mean, you are low in humor orientation (not frequently funny and not particularly adept at telling jokes). If your score falls well above the mean, you are high in humor orientation. People high in humor orientation use humor frequently and consider themselves to be adept at telling jokes. They tend to be spontaneous in their encoding of humorous things to say and do, whereas people low in humor orientation are more likely to plan their humor. Apparently, anybody can be funny, assuming there is sufficient opportunity to prepare for using humor. This means that when appropriate, any speaker can inject at least some preplanned humor into her or his speeches.

SOURCE: Adapted from Booth-Butterfield, S., & Booth-Butterfield, M. (1991). Individual differences in the communication of humorous messages. _The Southern Communication Journal, 56,_ 205–218.

use humor if you prepare well ahead of time. Locate interesting quotes or anecdotes. Joke-telling reference books are available, such as Fuller's _2500 Anecdotes for All Occasions_. For memorable quotes, use Bartlett's _Familiar Quotations_. _Reader's Digest_ contains humorous anecdotes, and you can often find offbeat stories in newspapers and national news magazines. Almost anything by Mark Twain contains quotable stories. Television is another useful source for humor, particularly late-night talk shows like the _Late Show with David Letterman_ or sitcoms like _Frasier_.

Perhaps the best source for humor is to recall some of your own personal experiences and rework them

into humorous narratives. You can even transform an everyday scenario into a humorous story. _Seinfeld_ remained popular for years by relying on simple, everyday situations, like waiting in a restaurant for a table or losing a car in a large parking garage. Using your own experiences as a source of humor not only makes audiences laugh but also makes you, as the speaker, appear more human.

To be truly humorous, however, you must practice. Add animation and drama to your presentation. Rehearse in front of a mirror and again in front of your friends. Vary the rate, volume, and pitch of your voice, or even try adding an accent or drawl to borrowed or regional phrases and one-liners: "I'm busier than a cat covered up!"; "Yessiree-bob!"; or "Like, totally!"

Borrowing expressions from well-known media sources works best when you repeat their lines using their voice and animation. Imagine saying, "Show me the money!" (à la Rod Tidwell and Jerry Maguire) without also increasing your speech volume, adding just the right rhythm to the phrase, and swinging your body back and forth. Don't be afraid to use gestures, make eye contact, lean forward, cross your arms, or shrug—use your body to communicate a sense of the ridiculous as well.

You must also be willing to take some risks. Don't be afraid to look (and feel) foolish. Exaggerate your expressions: Roll your eyes, raise your eyebrows, lower your eyeglasses (a great prop!), walk slowly and deliberately, gaze thoughtfully upward, put your hands on your hips—or use whatever exaggerated movement helps to reinforce your tale. Nonverbal behaviors are key to effectively presenting a humorous story by emphasizing simple, innocuous phrases. Take, for instance, George Costanza's "Yadda yadda yadda" or Bart Simpson's "Don't have a cow, man!" or Andrew Dice Clay's "Unbelievable!"

There are several cautions to keep in mind when using humor. First, there is a humor threshold for every joke, story, or anecdote; worn-out sayings will evoke groans, not laughter, from your audience. Likewise, there's a story threshold for every presentation; telling too many stories can tire an audience.[6]

Second, speakers can try to be too funny. Research on humor in the classroom, for instance, reveals that award-winning teachers use humor frequently, but not as often as other non-award-winning teachers.[7] Similarly, informative or persuasive speakers who use more humor than their audience wants to hear might be dismissed as jokers or lightweights. Thus, anything they have to say will not be taken all that seriously. Remember: Use humor in moderation.

Third, your decision to use humor must depend, in part, on the topic and the occasion. Topics such as drunk driving, the death penalty, senility, racism, drug abuse, and gay bashing are not inherently funny. Even if you found something humorous to say about these or related topics, your audience might consider you and your joke to be inappropriate. Speaking at a funeral or some other solemn occasion calls for compassion and sensitivity. Although humor is sometimes used to alleviate tension, speakers who are normally humorous table their clever wit on such occasions.

Despite its potential pitfalls, humor affects people in a number of positive ways. Research on humor indicates that audiences like speakers who use humor when appropriate more than speakers who do not. Audiences perceive humorous speakers as being friendly, and they generally feel closer to speakers who use humor. As it turns out, humor is actually a component of verbal and nonverbal immediacy (see Chapters 14 and 15) because it enhances closeness between people.[8]

BUILDING YOUR SKILLS

Using Rhetorical Styles Well Suited to Public Speaking

Dramatic Style

- Use colorful words and metaphors.
- Exaggerate for emphasis; overstate or understate your point.
- Tell stories.
- Use humor.
- Use rhythmic repetition.
- Joke and play with your audience.
- Use strong, magnified gestures.
- Maintain eye contact with your audience—just a little longer than is comfortable.

- Vary your vocal quality (rate, volume, and pitch).
- Use pause time strategically: Set up dramatic statements or conclusions by building tension.

Animated Style

- Show your emotions.
- Show energy, enthusiasm, and excitement.
- Use exaggerated nonverbal behaviors: Gesture broadly and walk purposefully.
- Smile, nod, and raise or lower your eyebrows to show how you feel.
- Be facially expressive. Look alive!

Within limits, humorous speakers are also perceived as being more competent and intelligent than nonhumorous speakers.[9] Perhaps people admire speakers who can be witty under tense and conspicuous circumstances. Research findings are mixed on whether humor helps audiences understand and remember what they hear.[10] Some studies suggest that humor helps; other research indicates that there is no relationship whatsoever. Fortunately, no study finds humor to retard comprehension or retention. Even so, too much humor or humor that is unrelated to the point may actually interfere with audience comprehension and recall of the message.

The main characteristics of each of the four rhetorical styles presented in this section are summarized in the box "Using Rhetorical Styles Well Suited to Public Speaking." Whatever rhetorical style you select and develop, you will find that it overlaps with others. After all, dramatic speakers are often both animated and humorous; animated speakers may also be dramatic and open; and humorous speakers may employ both dramatic and animated behaviors to be funny.

GENDER-BASED COMMUNICATION STYLES

Categorizing communication style according to gender is problematic, especially when one gender-based style is afforded more status or credibility than the other. For our purposes here, we would prefer simply to lay out how men and women have been socialized to communicate differently. At the same time, we want to acknowledge up front that by examining these differences, we may, in fact, be obscuring the similarities.[11] After all, women and men talk more alike than they talk differently. They share common goals and objectives when giving a speech, and they typically rely on the same verbal and nonverbal rhetorical strategies to inform and persuade others.

Nevertheless, the *way* men and women communicate differs sufficiently to make it difficult sometimes for the sexes to relate to each other. According to linguist Deborah Tannen, men and women often talk past each other.[12] By failing to acknowledge their different conversational or rhetorical styles, men and women cannot begin to understand what the other sex truly means or intends to mean. Before describing the different gender-based communication styles, it is important to acknowledge that there is great variability among women and men and how they communicate. For instance, although men tend to dominate talk and to interrupt others more than women do, there are some women who do that, too, and some men who do not do that at all. The point is, gender-based communication styles are often attributed to biological sex simply because most adult females today are socialized to be feminine and most males are socialized to be masculine. When individuals are able to escape such gender-role stereotyping, they can transgress the boundaries of style and flexibly interact as either masculine or feminine communicators. Style, then, is not necessarily sex-linked, but it is based on learned gender-role behaviors.

Feminine Communication Style

Chapter 3 provided an overview of the different communication styles of women and men. To review, feminine communicators are more likely than masculine communicators to insert intensifiers into their speech ("I'm *extremely* upset"), use qualifiers like "maybe" and "perhaps," rely on verbal fillers during silent, awkward pauses, and employ tag questions ("The color of this room is awful, *don't you agree?*"). Feminine talk is also characterized by more apologies ("I'm sorry that I can't make you feel better about that") and more indirect (rather than direct) requests ("My coffee could sure use a warm-up"). Nonverbally, feminine communicators smile more than masculine communicators, use more gestures, and make more eye contact.

A close examination of these communication behaviors suggests that the more **feminine style** of communicating emphasizes one important, recurring value: interpersonal connection. Psychologist Carol Gilligan argues that feminine communicators (mostly women), seek human connection—more so than they do winning, status, or power.[13] Applying that value to the context of public speaking, feminine communicators are likely to make every effort to relate to audience members as individuals and to come across as inclusive rather than exclusive. They strive to be attentive, responsive, and open to the audience. Knowing that verbal and nonverbal immediacy behaviors are a good way to initiate and generate a sense of closeness with the audience, feminine communicators are likely to be especially immediate in their style of speaking.

Deborah Tannen further asserts that conflict is a threat to connection.[14] Thus, in an effort to avoid conflict in public speaking, feminine speakers are more likely to acknowledge and emphasize areas of agreement between themselves and the audience. They try to value and show respect for how others might view the same situation or problem differently. This is not to say that feminine speakers don't offer alternative solutions, but when they do, they are careful not to deny the validity of others' viewpoints.

After examining the rhetoric of women orators in general, and famous African American women orators in particular, rhetorical scholar Karlyn Campbell argued that the feminine style of communication is primarily inductive or associative in logic[15] (that is, configural). Feminine speakers tend to draw conclusions or associations from their own observations, and they derive most examples from personal experience. In an effort to connect with the audience and seek audience assent, feminine orators rely heavily on rhetorical questions, attempt to build empathy, and appeal to the feelings and personal experiences of audience members.

Speakers who demonstrate a predominantly feminine style of communicating are easy to find. One well-known female orator who happens to model a feminine style is Supreme Court Justice Ruth Bader Ginsburg. Only the second woman ever to be appointed to the Supreme Court, she is one of the most powerful women in our country today. Known for her vigorous opposition to institutionalized discrimination against women, Ginsburg first attracted attention for arguing six cases on behalf of women's rights before the Supreme Court—and winning five of them! In addition to focusing on women's issues, Ginsburg emphasizes the importance of talking with people, of maintaining direct human contact. In keeping with a feminine style, Ginsburg often gives equal weight to her own personal experiences and the personal experiences of others to defend her position on equal rights. She is quick to disclose the fact that despite graduating from Columbia at the top of her class, she had trouble obtaining a job in her chosen "male" profession as an attorney and began her career as a teacher instead.

In her formal role as jurist, Ginsburg elevates understanding and connection above the more traditional communication modes of informing, convincing, and persuading. In an after-dinner speech before the American Law Institute, Justice Ginsburg redefined the role of conventional argument. Notice how she justifies the need for dialog and the importance of asking questions:

> [Oral argument] is an occasion for an exchange of views about the case, a dialogue or a discussion. . . . Some lawyers, I have been told, resent interruptions in an oral argument that they have carefully planned as a lecture and some judges ask few questions. My colleague, Justice Blackmun, for example, often tells of the advice that he was given by Justice Hugo Black in the 1970s. Justice Black cautioned, "Never ask many questions from the bench, because if you don't ask many questions, you won't ask many foolish ones." But it seems to me, a waste of a lawyer's precious opportunity to use oral argument or attempt to use it just to recapitulate the briefing instead of trying to uncover what is in the decision maker's mind.[16]

Ginsburg elaborated further by discussing the importance of "conversation, accommodating clarifications, interjections, even interruptions" during oral arguments before the bench in efforts to understand—rather than simply to win. Not wishing to sound too distant or powerful, Justice Ginsburg often attempts to build bridges with the public. For example, she began her speech by claiming to have some prepared remarks but stated that she hoped her remarks would "stimulate some questions because I would like to spend most of the time we have together in conversation with you." Other females who prefer a feminine communication style include Leeza Gibbons, Sandra Bullock, Janet Jackson, and Susan Molinari.

Males who exhibit a predominantly feminine style of communicating include former President Jimmy Carter, John Travolta, and the character Bobby Simone on *NYPD Blue*. Consider also Jerry Seinfeld and Paul Reiser, whose sitcoms contemplate people's lives and dissect relationships—including their own. In addition, most talk show hosts, like Jerry Springer, Charles Grodin, and Geraldo Rivera, tend to be more feminine in their communication style in order to engage the audience.

President Bill Clinton's rhetorical style is decidedly more feminine than those of other U.S. presidents. In a written critique of Clinton's feminine style of communicating, Steven Stark of National Public Radio concluded that "the Clinton style is really a textbook example of a leader who communicates in ways often more characteristic of women than men."[17] In support of that claim, Stark asserted the following:

> If other Presidents tended to speak by lecturing us ... Clinton often communicates by listening ("I feel your pain"). Whereas other Presidents tended to address the country most effectively from above at a rostrum or alone at a desk, Clinton is at his best in level conversation, when he can look at the people with whom he is talking. ... the maternal hug and the "all ears" attentive body language are the characteristics of this President.[18]

As a public speaker, Clinton stresses connection above all else. He makes every effort to relate one-on-one with people. He is unafraid to disclose his own personal experiences and history—including the fact that his brother and stepfather were substance abusers. Consistent with the feminine style of communicating, Clinton likes to meet new people, to talk (and listen) for hours at a time (often at the expense of those waiting for his next appointment), to collaborate rather than oppose, and to reach consensus rather than assume control. As you can see, then, the feminine style of communicating need not be owned solely by women; men, too, can adopt successfully a feminine way of relating to the audience.

Masculine Communication Style

As Chapter 3 discussed, in contrast to feminine communicators, masculine communicators (mostly men) tend to dominate conversations by talking more, interrupting others, and controlling the discussion. Compared to feminine communicators, masculine speakers are more likely to dominate or make their presence known nonverbally as well. Although they may use fewer gestures than women, men's gestures are more noticeable; they are broader and more intense. Recall that the feminine style of communicating emphasizes interpersonal connections. In contrast, because males are socialized to dominate or control, the **masculine style** is characterized by assertions of status and power. Important to masculine communicators, then, is demonstrating strength and independence. Obviously, connecting with others is not *un*important to them, but asserting control or authority is a value that often dominates the masculine style.

Probably no communication event is more amenable to the masculine style of relating than is the context of public speaking. Consider the typical roles defined for speaker and audience: The speaker is supposed to do most of the talking; the audience is supposed to listen. The speaker commands attention; the audience complies. The speaker controls what is said and how it is said; the audience concedes. The speaker demands a certain amount of credibility and authority to speak on the subject; the audience accedes. Such role definitions underscore the status differential between speaker and audience. This inequality makes public speaking particularly conducive to the masculine style of communicating.

Consistent with that interpretation, Deborah Tannen argues that many men are more comfortable than most women with using talk to draw attention to themselves.[19] Public speaking, according to Tannen, is an opportunity for the masculine communicator to become the focus of everyone's respect and admiration. Rather than trying to connect with the audience, masculine communicators tend to demonstrate distance and authority by claiming expertise in the subject matter. Typically, masculine speakers show the audience that they are in a position to know better, to give advice, and to influence others. As a result, masculine speakers emphasize differences to appear more credible, more powerful, and more successful than others. In an effort to impress, masculine communicators may convey how important they are by mentioning famous people they know or revealing some of their own more meaningful accomplishments.[20] These and similar strategies may be interpreted as self-serving boast-and-swagger by feminine communicators, but to masculine speakers, such techniques are important means of establishing status and power.

Given what is known about the masculine style of relating, it stands to reason that masculine speakers are forceful, direct, and aggressive in their speech style. Tentative statements or provisional comments are infrequently used or omitted altogether—even when there may be reasons or data to suggest that a remark should be qualified. Rather than rely on personal accounts to demonstrate an idea or support an argument, masculine speakers prefer objective facts, hard data, and expert testimony. To add credence to a point, masculine speakers give long, detailed explanations—typically in a loud, declamatory voice.[21] In these ways, masculine speakers leave little doubt that they know what they are saying and intend for the audience to know it, too! (See the box "Characteristics of Feminine and Masculine Communication Styles" for a summary of the verbal and nonverbal behaviors associated with these styles.)

Examples of well-known masculine speakers can be readily found among famous men in U.S. society. Like most (if not all) military leaders, General Colin L. Powell, retired chairman of the Joint Chiefs of Staff, models a predictably masculine style of communicating. Besides focusing on so-called men's issues, like foreign policy, U.S. military involvement around the world, and gays in the military, Powell emphasizes

---

A   C L O S E R   L O O K

Characteristics of Feminine and Masculine Communication Styles

Feminine Communication Style

- Feminine speakers try to connect with their audience through direct human contact and demonstrations of equality. For them, people and relationships are most important.

- Feminine speakers relate to the audience as individuals and respect other points of view.

- Feminine speakers stress collaboration over conflict. They emphasize areas of agreement between themselves and the audience.

- Feminine speakers are inclusive and build bridges between themselves and the audience.

- Feminine speakers are attentive, responsive, and open to the audience.

- Feminine speakers tend to use inductive, associative (configural) logic to frame their arguments.

- Feminine speakers appeal to the feelings and personal experiences of audience members. They use personal stories and their own observations to support their position.

- Feminine speakers have a less formal speaking style and often use everyday phrases. Qualifiers, intensifiers, tag questions, rhetorical questions, and apologies are also common.

- Feminine speakers use nonverbal immediacy behaviors to communicate closeness with, attention to, and interest in the audience. Typical immediacy behaviors include leaning toward the audience, smiling and nodding, gesturing, and making lots of eye contact.

Masculine Communication Style

- Masculine speakers try to show superior strength and independence. For them, control and authority are most important.

- Masculine speakers stress status differences (not equality) between themselves and the audience. Masculine speakers establish their expertise and credentials clearly to place themselves in a position to advise and influence the audience.

- Masculine speakers occupy center stage—the focus of the audience's respect, attention, and admiration.

- Masculine speakers use objective facts, hard data, and expert testimony to support their position.

- Masculine speakers favor long, detailed explanations and stories.

- Masculine speakers are forceful, direct, assertive, and aggressive. Tentative statements or qualifiers do not characterize their speech.

- Masculine speakers commonly use a loud, declamatory voice and power words.

- Masculine speakers use gestures and body movements to stress power and status. Gestures are few in number but are large and intense.

- Immediacy behaviors are not typical of masculine communicators.

the importance of his own status and power, as well as that of the military. By virtue of his position in the military, he assumes the power and the authority to argue convincingly for his military agenda. He is also physically impressive: He is handsome, stands tall, and dresses in full decorated uniform. He is articulate, friendly (but reserved), intelligent, and composed, and his message is always forceful. Speaking before a town hall meeting in Southern California, General Powell advocated that despite the end of the Cold War, the United States should not abandon its superpower status, but should continue to sustain military strength and supremacy throughout the world. After all, Powell exclaimed,

> the proper safeguards are the same safeguards that have secured the Free World's liberties for over four decades—our strong values, our resilient democracies, our vibrant market economics, our strong alliances, and yes, our proud and ready armed forces.
>
> All of these things constitute our great systemic strength. That strength sustains the Free World, just as in America it sustains our great Union. . . . No one is better fitted for these tasks than America and her allies. If we stay strong and lead, the world will follow. Of that, I am sure.[22]

Notice all the power words (and the lack of qualifiers) Powell used ("strong," "resilient," "vibrant," "proud and ready," and "great systemic strength") to create deliberate images of strength and status. Notice further how Powell closed his speech with his personal guarantee that the world would follow America's lead: "Of that," he claims, "I am sure."

In this same speech, Powell told his audience several times just how qualified he was to propose the military policy he advocated. He began his presentation by telling the assembled group that he came to California frequently in his "last job as Commander in Chief of the U.S. Army Forces Command";[23] later on, he told a military story about the time he was a "Corps Commander in Europe" and how he and his volunteers "were poised to stop a Soviet invasion into West Germany."[24] He also told his audience that he began his career "in that same corps as a second lieutenant 28 years earlier"[25] and that he had just returned from a meeting with East European and Soviet military leaders. Consistent with the masculine style of communicating, Powell was not at all reluctant to assert his credentials and accomplishments to speak credibly on this topic.

The masculine style of speaking is not solely defined by men. Bay Buchanan, Stephanie Miller, and Laura Schlessinger represent a more masculine communication style. Known for her aggressive (some might even say contentious) style of communicating, Dr. Laura Schlessinger—syndicated radio talk show host, licensed psychotherapist, author, and lecturer—offers counseling to callers and listeners on a variety of interpersonal problems. In no uncertain terms, she tells callers when they're wrong, stupid, or shameless. She gasps when they break marriage vows, neglect their children, or in other ways abdicate character, courage, and conscience.[26] She argues, interrupts, attacks, condemns, advocates, and concludes with the strength and conviction of a moral, rational leader. At other times, she congratulates, sympathizes, laughs, teases, and supports—but again, with that same level of passion and frankness of opinion. Besides being widely criticized for her frequent use of the label "stupid" (*Ten Stupid Things Women/Men Do to Mess Up Their Lives*), she often startles listeners and readers when she challenges their assumptions and self-indulgences. She is often known to say, "Oh puhleeze!" Consider her response to men's complaints that women fail to appreciate truly nice guys: "I've heard this pathetic whining quite often in my life. . . . It's just garbage. The real problem is you!" And then she goes on to give them "the real scoop" on what nice guys fail to do.[27] With similar directness, she tells women that they "knowingly do stupid things—like using complaining, whining, anger, depression, anxiety, food, and chemicals to avoid taking active steps to improve their lot. They 'cop out.' They get 'chicken.' *They act stupid.*"[28]

Consistent with the masculine style of communicating, Dr. Laura demonstrates strength and commitment in her spirited appeals for people to take personal responsibility for what they say and do. Forthright and direct, she eliminates any hint of hesitancy, qualification, or tentativeness in her message; she communicates with confidence and assertiveness. But unlike the typical masculine-style speaker, Dr. Laura does not give long, detailed explanations; instead, she gets to the point quickly and forcefully. Her sentences are short and clipped; her examples, while numerous, are brief, not the protracted explanations more characteristic of masculine communicators.

You now should be familiar with the various communication styles available to you as a public speaker. One of these styles, a combination of two or more styles, or perhaps other styles not mentioned in this chapter will be most appropriate for you. Keep in mind that whatever style you choose to develop, your overriding goal should be to help the audience decipher the literal meaning of your message. For some audiences, it may be more suitable to employ an open style of communicating; for others, a more reserved style may be justified. Some topics may require a more masculine style of communicating, others, a more feminine style. Importantly, whatever communication style you develop, be sure it is one with which you feel competent and comfortable. When you use rhetorical style to your advantage, audiences will not only enjoy and appreciate your presentations but also better understand what you have to say.

CHAPTER REVIEW

- Good speakers develop their own unique rhetorical style. In selecting a style, (1) try on several to see which style best fits you, (2) focus on your own special strengths as a communicator, and (3) never substitute style for substance.

- Four different rhetorical styles are well suited to the public speaking context: dramatic, open, animated, and humorous. Dramatic speakers are good story-tellers; they command audience attention through the use of dramatic verbal and nonverbal effects. Animated speakers are highly emotive and use a lot of energy when they communicate. Open communicators are honest, forthright, self-disclosing, and warmly receptive to their audiences. Finally, humorous speakers engage their audiences with well-planned, appropriate anecdotes, quotes, jokes, and so on.

- Even though women and men talk more similarly than differently, the *way* women and men have been socialized to communicate differs sufficiently to make it sometimes difficult for the sexes to relate. Because the feminine style of communicating emphasizes interpersonal connections between people, feminine speakers (whether male or female) strive to be attentive, responsive, and open to their audience. They are more likely to emphasize areas of agreement between themselves and their audience and to rely heavily on personal experience in their speech texts. Because the masculine style of communicating emphasizes status and power, masculine speakers (whether female or male) strive to control the public speaking event by being forceful, direct, and assertive in their speech style. They tend to emphasize their credibility, to prefer objective facts and expert testimony, and to deliver long, detailed explanations that underscore their expertise.

QUESTIONS FOR CRITICAL THINKING & REVIEW

1. How would you label and describe your own personal rhetorical style?

2. Do you prefer the feminine or the masculine communication style? Why? Are there situations in which one or the other style might be more appropriate or effective?

3. This chapter stresses the importance of *what* you say over *how* you say it (that is, substance over style). Are there any public speaking situations in which the American public has come to expect style over substance? If so, is this a problem? What solutions might there be?

4. Considering the ethnic and gender co-cultural communication styles described in Chapter 3, which co-cultures do you think would feel most comfortable with each of the four personal communication styles outlined in this chapter (dramatic, animated, open, and humorous)?

5. Can speakers come across as too dramatic, too animated, too open, or too humorous? If so, what advice might you give to these individuals?

NOTES

1. Norton, R. (1983). *Communicator style: Theory, applications, and measures.* Beverly Hills, CA: Sage.
2. Norton, 1983.
3. Norton, 1983, pp. 129–153.
4. Richards, A. (1988, August 15). Keynote address. *Vital Speeches of the Day, 54,* 648.
5. Norton, 1983, pp. 67–68.
6. Gorham, J., & Christophel, D. M. (1990). The relationship of teachers' use of humor in the classroom to immediacy and student learning. *Communication Education, 39,* 46–62.
7. Downs, V., Javidi, M., & Nussbaum, J. (1988). An analysis of teachers' verbal communication within the college classroom: Use of humor, self-disclosure, and narratives. *Communication Education, 37,* 127–141.
8. Gorham, J. (1988). The relationship between verbal teacher immediacy behaviors and student learning. *Communication Education, 37,* 40–53; Gorham & Christophel, 1990.
9. Bryant, J., & Zillman, D. (1979). Teachers' humor in the college classroom. *Communication Education, 28,* 110–118; Gruner, C. R. (1966). A further experimental study of satire as persuasion. *Speech Monographs, 33,* 184–185.
10. See, for instance, Gorham & Christophel, 1990; Kaplan, R., & Pascoe, G. (1977). Humorous lectures and humorous examples: Some effects on comprehension and retention. *Journal of Educational Psychology, 69,* 61–65; Weaver, J., Zillman, D., & Bryant, J. (1988). Effects of humorous distortions on children's learning from educational television: Further evidence. *Communication Education, 37,* 181–187.
11. Wood, J. T. (1993). Gender and moral voice: Moving from woman's nature to standpoint episte- mology. *Women's Studies in Communication, 16,* 1–24.
12. Tannen, D. (1990). *You just don't understand: Women and men in conversation.* New York: Morrow.
13. Gilligan, C. (1982). *In a different voice: Psychological theory and women's development.* Cambridge, MA: Harvard University Press.
14. Tannen, 1990.
15. Campbell, K. K. (1986). Style and content in the rhetoric of early Afro-American feminists. *Quarterly Journal of Speech, 72,* 434–445.
16. Ginsburg, R. B. (1994, May 19). Speech at the annual dinner of the American Law Institute. Online. Gifts of Speech. Available: http://gos.sbc.edu/g/ginsburg.html.
17. Stark, S. D. (1993, March 14). Practicing inclusion, consensus: Clinton's feminization of politics. *Los Angeles Times,* p. M6.
18. Stark, 1993, p. M6.
19. Tannen, 1990, p. 88.
20. Tannen, 1990, p. 219.
21. Tannen, 1990, p. 239.
22. Powell, C. L. (1992). U.S. foreign policy in a changing world. In R. L. Johannesen, R. R. Allen, & W. A. Linkugel (Eds.), *Contemporary American speeches* (p. 313). Dubuque, IA: Kendall/Hunt.
23. Powell, 1992, p. 305.
24. Powell, 1992, p. 306.
25. Powell, 1992, p. 306.
26. Schlessinger, L. (1996). *How could you do that?!* New York: HarperCollins.
27. Schlessinger, L. (1997). *Ten stupid things men do to mess up their lives* (p. 8). New York: HarperCollins.
28. Schlessinger, L. (1997). *Ten stupid things women do to mess up their lives* (p. xviii). New York: HarperCollins.

Chapter 17

USING VISUAL AIDS

Tim Sutton was extremely effective at preparing briefings and other types of public presentations for executives at International Aerospace Corporation. He was good at matching the content and the visual parts of their presentations to suit the unique characteristics of a particular audience. Developing effective visual aids to enhance a presentation or briefing was the most fascinating and satisfying part of Tim's job.

Tim often created high-quality visual aids on his computer; he also worked with the graphic design department when constructing a special chart, graphic, photo layout, or some other type of visual display. One thing he had learned was that in most cases, presentations can be made more appealing to audiences by incorporating one or more professional-looking visual aids. In fact, in the briefing he had just finished, he incorporated a colorful organizational chart of the company, a world map to show where business was being conducted, and a diagram of the commercial satellite that International was currently marketing.

As Tim watched the vice president of marketing present his briefing to the other corporate executives, he could see their positive reaction to his carefully designed visual devices. His visual aids clearly added to the credibility of the speaker and made the presentation more interesting.

As this example shows, the appropriate use of visual devices is important to practically every aspect of public speaking. In this chapter, you will learn how to develop and use these materials for all types of public presentations.

Learning Objectives

After reading this chapter, you should be able to do the following:

1. Define visual aids and determine their role in public speaking.

2. Evaluate whether to include particular visual aids in your own speech.

3. Differentiate among the standard types of visual aids commonly used in public speaking.

4. Differentiate among the various ways visual aids can be projected and displayed during a speech.

5. Identify methods for using a computer to enhance the creation and presentation of your visual aids.

6. Identify and apply to your own presentation nine guidelines for using visual aids effectively.

VISUAL AIDS IN PUBLIC SPEAKING

Virtually every public speech can benefit from the use of one or more **visual aids** to highlight the content of the presentation. Public speakers have used visual devices to enhance their presentations since the beginning of recorded history. No well-seasoned public speaker would deny their importance. Using them effectively, knowing when to use them, and knowing which ones to use in a particular public speaking situation are some of the decisions facing experienced speakers as they plan their presentations.

What Are Visual Aids?

Anyone who has ever tried to give directions to someone understands the advantages of having a map to actually show how to get to a specific location. It is so much easier to understand directions if you can see the way to go. A visual aid is any supplemental visible device a speaker can employ to help clarify for the audience the message of a speech. The range of possible visual aids is virtually unlimited. The more commonly used visual aids are discussed later in this chapter. But first, it is important to consider when it is appropriate or inappropriate to use visual aids in a public speech.

Deciding Whether to Use Visual Aids

Although visual aids often are used to enhance the message of a speech, their use may be inappropriate for some public speaking situations. Before deciding to use a visual aid, ask yourself five questions. If you answer yes to any of these questions, then a visual aid should contribute positively to your presentation.

Will Visual Aids Clarify Something Important?

Under the proper circumstances, a visual aid can clarify an important point in a speech by providing valuable information. For example, suppose you wanted to explain the advantages of buying a new car. Although most people get really excited by the idea of owning and driving a brand-new car, your audience might have difficulty imagining features like soft leather seats, a padded steering wheel, and a flashy paint job without actually seeing large color photos of a new car. The old saying "A picture is worth a thousand words" applies here. By including the appropriate visual aids, you would increase your audience's understanding of and appreciation for the new car.

Will Visual Aids Make the Speech More Interesting?

The right visual aid can heighten your audience's interest by emphasizing an important point in a visually striking manner. Suppose you were preparing a speech on choosing a high-paying occupation. Everyone wants to earn a good salary. In fact, people go to college in large part so they can get a good job and make a good salary; many students even compare the potential money-making capabilities of different jobs when choosing their major in school. A student audience, then, would probably be attentive to a speech on the potential for making money in, say, the health care industry. You could heighten their interest substantially by showing a graph comparing the earnings of medical occupations with those of other professions to demonstrate the greater earnings potential in the health care industry.

Will Visual Aids Increase Audience Retention?

Visual aids can increase an audience's retention of information by highlighting important points. Consider how you would give a demonstration speech on changing a flat tire. The problem with learning how to actually change a tire is not being able to remember what to do step-by-step when the time comes. If you included high-quality drawings highlighting each step in the process, however, you would significantly increase your audience's recall of how to complete the task.

Will Visual Aids Save Time?

Many speech topics require a great deal of explanation. For such speeches, visual aids can be helpful. For example, speeches on calculating the rate of inflation or repairing an electrical circuit involve complicated processes and thus require thorough explanations. When extended explanation is required, other important parts of a presentation—like introductions, transitions, and conclusions—often are slighted. Using the right visual aid as a kind of "word picture" for one or more parts of the presentation can help you explain a topic or idea without having to go into an elaborate discussion.

Will Visual Aids Help Explain the Topic?

The right visual aid can emphasize the organization of a speech by delineating logically the points being covered. For audience members to follow a linearly or configurally organized presentation, they may need to see the organization laid out visually. Imagine, for example, that you want to explain how your company is organized internally. You could easily display an organizational chart at the appropriate point during your briefing. Such a visual aid would help you explain your topic and, at the same time, help your audience follow your logic.

TYPES OF VISUAL AIDS

Visual aids come in an almost infinite number of forms. The selection of an appropriate visual aid depends on the speaker, the topic, and the context of the speech. Common types of visual aids include graphs, tables, maps, charts, photographs, drawings, physical objects, scaled models, and even people, who can serve to illustrate a point or demonstrate an activity. Whichever types of visual aids you choose to employ, be careful. Don't get too carried away with graphic possibilities. Keep in mind that your visual aids need to be easily understood by an audience. Simplicity and clarity should never be sacrificed for the sake of artistic quality.

This section briefly describes some of the most popular types of visual aids. In the next section, you'll learn the best ways to display or project your visual aids.

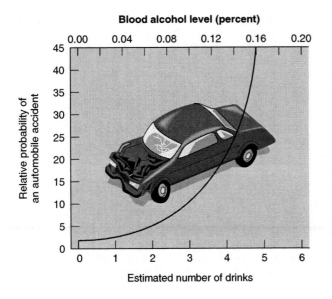

Blood alcohol level (percent)

Relative probability of an automobile accident (y-axis: 0 to 45)

Estimated number of drinks (x-axis: 0 to 6)

Relationship between Alcohol Consumption and Automobile Accidents

Figure 17-1 A line graph shows the quantitative relationship between two variables. Like all visual aids, line graphs can be enhanced by colorful and striking graphic designs. SOURCE: *Insel, P., & Roth, W. (1996). Core Concepts in Health (updated 7th ed.) (p. 256). Mountain View, CA: Mayfield.*

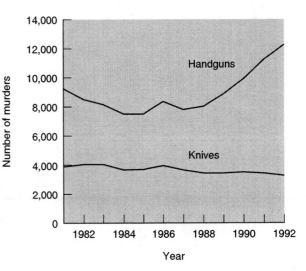

Annual Murders with Handguns and Knives

Number of murders (y-axis: 0 to 14,000)
Handguns
Knives
Year (x-axis: 1982 to 1992)

Figure 17-2 Sample fever graph. A fever graph is an effective way to show how the numerical value of something changes over time. SOURCE: *FBI*, Crime in the United States, 1993.

Graphs

A **graph** is a pictorial device used to illustrate quantitative relationships. Graphics can be produced in many different formats and can be two- or three-dimensional in design. They are among the most versatile and powerful types of visual aids. There are three primary types of graphs.

Line Graphs A **line graph** is a diagram that shows the relationship between two quantitative variables—how one variable changes with respect to the other. For example, a line graph could illustrate how the risk of being involved in a car accident relates to the number of alcoholic beverages consumed in the previous hour (see Figure 17-1). **Fever graphs** are a particularly popular type of line graph. They show visually how the numerical value of something—home sales, cable TV costs, or interest rates, for example—changes over time (see Figure 17-2). The rising and falling line in the graph is referred to as a "fever line." If you want to show how statistics applicable to your topic change over time, a fever graph is a good choice.

Bar Graphs A **bar graph** displays quantities or values of data in a series of bars that correspond in height or

length to the quantities represented (see Figure 17-3). Unlike fever graphs, bar graphs are not well suited for illustrating change over a long period of time; they are more appropriate for showing differences in sets of data at one time or over a short time span. For example, bar graphs could be used effectively to show the amount of money spent on lunches and dinners in the United States during each of the four quarters of a particular year or the numbers of American-made and Japanese-made cars purchased in each year during the 1990s.

Pie Graphs Pie graphs, also called "circle graphs" or "divided circles," are used to show the division of something into component parts—percentages or proportions of the whole. Pie graphs are in the form of a circle divided into wedges that are proportional in angle and area to the relative size of the quantities represented (see Figure 17-4). Pie graphs are most useful for displaying data that can be divided into a small number of categories or parts; after about five or so divisions, it is difficult to discriminate between different slices of the pie. Possible topics for pie graphs include the federal budget, commercial markets, job categories, television viewing preferences, and family spending patterns.

Tables

A **table** is an orderly arrangement of numbers, words, or symbols in rows and columns. A tabular

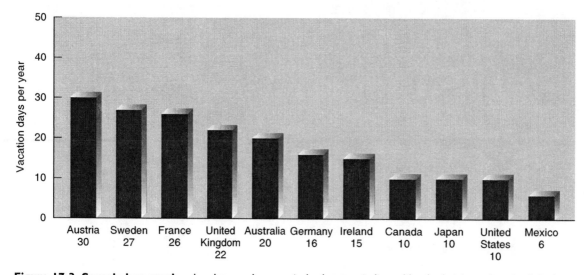

Legally Mandated or Customary Vacation Days for Selected Countries

| Country | Austria 30 | Sweden 27 | France 26 | United Kingdom 22 | Australia 20 | Germany 16 | Ireland 15 | Canada 10 | Japan 10 | United States 10 | Mexico 6 |

Figure 17-3 Sample bar graph. In a bar graph, numerical values are indicated by the height or length of the bars. Bar graphs help audiences make quick comparisons. SOURCE: Data from Rand McNally, *Almanac of World Facts,* 1995.

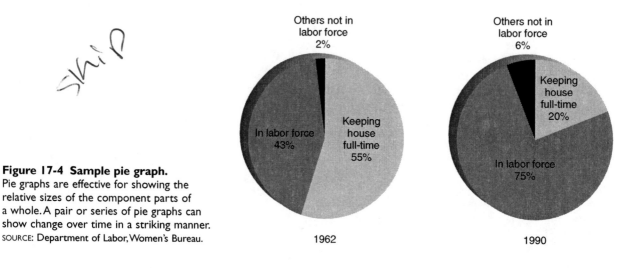

Labor Force Status of Women 25–54 Years of Age

1962: Others not in labor force 2%, In labor force 43%, Keeping house full-time 55%

1990: Others not in labor force 6%, Keeping house full-time 20%, In labor force 75%

Figure 17-4 Sample pie graph.
Pie graphs are effective for showing the relative sizes of the component parts of a whole. A pair or series of pie graphs can show change over time in a striking manner. SOURCE: Department of Labor, Women's Bureau.

arrangement of information allows for the easy viewing and comparison of large numbers of similar facts (see Figure 17-5). Like graphs, tables are often used to display statistics, but tables use a straightforward arrangement of columns and rows rather than a graphic format. Tables most often present quantitative data (numerical statistics), but a table consisting of words or phrases can be used to present qualitative comparisons.

Charts

Several different types of charts are commonly used as visual aids. In general terms, a **chart** is a pictorial representation of the relationship between parts of a group or object or of the sequence of steps in a process (see Figure 17-6). Many charts are in the form of boxes connected with lines or arrows. An organizational chart like the one shown in Figure 17-6 is an effective way to illustrate the internal organization of

Attitudes of First-Year College Students	Those who agree strongly or somewhat with these issues, statements, or positions	
	Female	Male
Political views		
Liberal or far left	26%	23%
Middle of the road	57	52
Conservative or far right	17	26
Social issues		
Abortion should be legal	73	68
Abolish death penalty	28	22
Federal government should do more to control handguns	92	76
Racial discrimination is no longer a problem	8	3
Interpersonal issues		
Sex okay if people like each other	33	59
Married women best at home	15	25
Prohibit homosexual relations	18	36
Man not entitled to sex on date	96	87

Figure 17-5 Sample table. Tables typically allow for easy comparisons by displaying data in an orderly pattern of rows and columns. SOURCE: Dey, E. L., Astin, A. W., & Korn, W. S. (1992). *The American freshman: Twenty-five year trends.* Los Angeles: The Higher Education Research Institute, University of California.

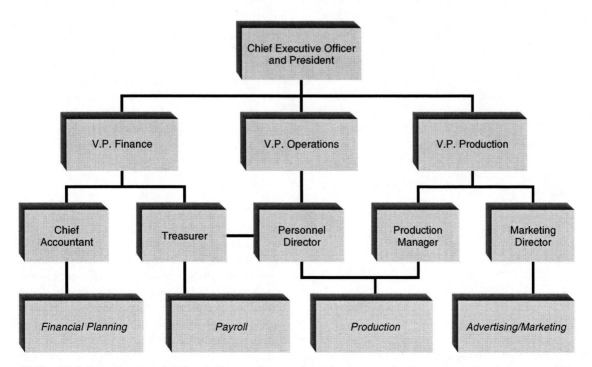

Figure 17-6 Sample organizational chart. Commonly used in business briefings, organizational charts provide a clear picture of the internal structure of a company.

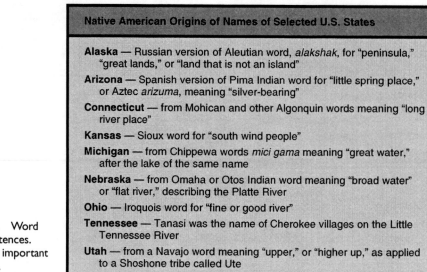

Native American Origins of Names of Selected U.S. States

Alaska — Russian version of Aleutian word, *alakshak*, for "peninsula," "great lands," or "land that is not an island"

Arizona — Spanish version of Pima Indian word for "little spring place," or Aztec *arizuma*, meaning "silver-bearing"

Connecticut — from Mohican and other Algonquin words meaning "long river place"

Kansas — Sioux word for "south wind people"

Michigan — from Chippewa words *mici gama* meaning "great water," after the lake of the same name

Nebraska — from Omaha or Otos Indian word meaning "broad water" or "flat river," describing the Platte River

Ohio — Iroquois word for "fine or good river"

Tennessee — Tanasi was the name of Cherokee villages on the Little Tennessee River

Utah — from a Navajo word meaning "upper," or "higher up," as applied to a Shoshone tribe called Ute

Figure 17-7 Sample word chart. Word charts consist of words or short sentences. They are typically used to emphasize important points or examples in a presentation. SOURCE: World Almanac and Book of Facts, 1995.

a company and is used in many types of business presentations. A flow chart, illustrating the steps in a process, is another effective type of visual aid.

Word Charts

Text alone, in the form of words or short sentences, can also serve as an effective visual aid. A text-only visual aid is often referred to as a **word chart** (see Figure 17-7). A typical word chart might highlight the key issues or examples in a presentation or the steps being carried out in a demonstration speech. Word charts are probably the most popular type of visual aid used by public speakers.

Word charts are commonly used in many business presentations. **Briefing charts** typically contain the main points and subpoints from a speech outline. These textual visual aids are introduced sequentially to highlight key points and to help the audience follow the organization of the presentation.

You might consider using two other categories of visual aids in your presentations. Physical representations (objects, models, people) and visual representations (photographs, maps, hand drawings) can be used to increase your audience's interest in and understanding of your topic and to illustrate important points.

Physical Representations

Objects For certain speech topics, introducing a physical object during the speech can enhance audience understanding and interest. For example, if you were giving an

informative speech on rock collecting, you could hold up a large, colorful piece of petrified wood so that your audience could experience the "real thing" while listening to your speech. Other physical objects that might be employed in speeches include rock-climbing ropes, scuba gear, fishing poles, and various types of food. When displaying objects, be sure that they can be seen clearly by your entire audience.

Models Often, scaled-down models are used as visual aids, especially when the original article is large and unmanageable or simply not available. For example, you could display a small model of the space shuttle in a speech on the U.S. space program to give your audience a deeper understanding of the vehicle's design. Other commonly used models include model airplanes, cars, and boats; models of entire towns; and dolls. Be sure that your model truly represents the original article and that it is large enough for the entire audience to see.

People Sometimes *people* can serve as convenient, effective visual aids. For example, asking a friend to assist you in demonstrating the Heimlich maneuver would be more effective than presenting a series of graphic charts. People are commonly employed as visual aids in presentations on sporting activities, clothing design, and hair styling. Note, however, that trying to manage more than one person at a time during a speech is difficult. Therefore, limit the number of people in your presentation, and, above all, be sure they are well rehearsed beforehand.

Visual Representations

Photographs Photographs are commonly used as visual representations to illustrate important aspects of a speech. For example, in a speech on nineteenth-century French painting, you could display a large photograph of an impressionist painting to illustrate more clearly than with a mere verbal description the use of color in this genre. Photographs can enhance speaker effectiveness in many other topics, such as bird watching, star gazing, international travel, and archaeology, to name just a few.

Be cautious when using photographs in public presentations, however. The photographs must be large enough, high quality, and pertinent to your topic, and they must be introduced in a way that does not detract from the rest of your speech. As for all visual aids, spend the necessary time practicing your speech with the photograph prior to the actual presentation.

Maps Maps are another type of visual representation frequently included in speeches. They are extremely effective for illustrating a large geographic area or a specific route from one location to another (see Figure 17-8). For example, you could strategically display a map of the western United States to show an audience the sites of the heaviest rainfall during the El Niño storms of 1998. For your presentation, your map must be large, high quality, and truly pertinent to the region you're describing, and it must be introduced and removed at appropriate points in your speech.

Hand Drawings Another commonly used visual representation is a hand drawing. For certain speech topics and for particular audiences, hand drawings are inexpensive, effective aids for visually representing an important idea or concept. For example, a hand drawing of a clock face is an effective tool for teaching schoolchildren how to tell time. Hand drawings must be prepared carefully to ensure the proper quality and clarity. Quickly sketching a concept on a pad of paper will not enhance a speaker's credibility. Because audiences

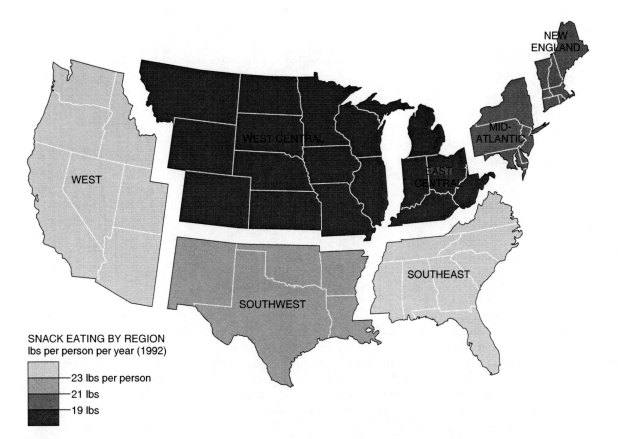

Figure 17-8 Sample map. Maps are effective visual representations for geographical patterns, travel routes, or specific locations that may be unfamiliar to an audience. SOURCE: Snack Food Association, 1992.

Types of Visual Aids

Bar graphs	Objects
Charts	People
Hand drawings	Photographs
Line graphs	Pie graphs
Maps	Tables
Models	Word charts

expect speakers to be professional in the presentation of all material, their hand drawings must also look professional.

These standard types of visual aids are but a few of the many ways to visually enhance your public presentation. (The box "Types of Visual Aids" gives a brief summary.) When planning your speeches, be sure to consider the large variety of visual aids you can employ.

PRESENTING YOUR VISUAL (AND AUDIO) AIDS

You can present visual aids to your audience in a number of ways. Choosing the appropriate approach to presenting your visual aid is a separate and important part of the process of planning for an effective public presentation. There are two general categories for the presentation of visual aids: projection techniques and display techniques. A third category—audio techniques—represents a different medium of presentation. Although not visual, audio techniques offer an important presentation alternative for increasing your speech's effectiveness.

Projection Techniques

Visual aids can be projected in two different ways. One type of projection—the immobile, or fixed, approach—is referred to as "still projection." This method of projection is accomplished with transparencies, slides, opaque projectors, and filmstrips. Of the visual aids described in this chapter, word charts, graphs, photographs, maps, and hand drawings are normally presented using still-projection techniques; however, it is possible to project them using another technique, known as "moving projec-

tion." This second technique typically employs films and videotapes. (Techniques for projecting computer-based images are described later in the chapter.)

With the exception of videotapes, all of the following projection techniques require a darkened room, which can be distracting to you as the speaker and, thus, can detract from the effectiveness of your speech. Moreover, all of these techniques rely on electrical equipment that can malfunction unexpectedly. To ensure that the equipment is in good working order and that you are comfortable with the presentation technique, you should always practice before your actual presentation.

Transparencies Charts, photographs, drawings, and maps can be copied or drawn by hand on clear sheets of acetate plastic called **transparencies**, which can then be shown to an audience using an overhead projector system. Overhead projectors cast the transparency onto a screen so that it can be seen by an entire audience. Although it is possible to actually draw on a transparency during a presentation, it's best to prepare your transparencies beforehand to avoid unexpected problems.

Slides Using slides is another method of projecting visual aids. **Slides** are small mounted transparencies that are used to project charts, diagrams, tables, and other images onto a screen. Because slides are small, they are easy to transport.

Opaque Projectors Certain types of visual aids can be shown to an audience with an **opaque projector**, which casts a still image from some opaque material (like paper) directly onto a screen. Anything that will fit on the lit surface of an opaque projector will be projected onto the screen. With this projection method, a speaker can present and enlarge either black-and-white or color visual aids without having to work with slides or transparencies.

Filmstrips A **filmstrip** is a continuous series of images copied onto a strip of 35-mm film and projected by means of a still-frame projector. Filmstrips employ the same size film as slides, but the images on filmstrips are smaller than those on slides. Certain types of visual aids, such as charts, photographs, and hand drawings, can be transferred to a filmstrip. However, most instructional media centers stock a variety of filmstrips, so be sure to investigate what's already available.

Films and Videotapes Speakers often use films and videotapes to augment their presentation on a particular topic or step-by-step process. Moving projection has advantages and disadvantages. Unlike most other types of visual aids, films project large images that are easily seen by an audience. Nevertheless, most films are too long and are not normally designed to directly support the material in a speech. Videotapes are projected by means of a videocassette recorder. The advantage of videotapes is that they allow for instant replays and freeze-frame images. Like films, however, they can detract from the material of a speech. Also, if they are not carefully edited, videotapes may be too long to include in a presentation.

Display Techniques

The second general way to present visual aids is to display them. Flip charts, demonstration boards, and handouts are display techniques that appear simple to administer; however, they all require practice to be used skillfully.

Flip Charts Certain types of visual aids (such as word charts, graphs, and tables) can be displayed for an audience on a flip chart. A **flip chart** is a large, simple, and highly visible tablet of paper (normally placed on an easel) that reveals, point by point, the major issues of a presentation. The material on each page in the flip chart sequence should be as uncomplicated and concrete as possible; each page typically contains no more than one or two of the points covered in a presentation. As the speaker completes a particular chart, she or he flips the page to uncover the next point in the presentation. (Some speakers find it helpful to strategically place a blank page in the sequence of charts to allow for a break between points.) The last page of the flip chart typically summarizes all of the points discussed during the presentation.

Demonstration Boards **Demonstration boards** encompass a variety of techniques for displaying information in a presentation. These techniques often are used to present material in the same way as with transparencies, slides, and opaque projection. The most common demonstration boards are chalkboards, porcelain boards, felt boards, and magnetic boards. Chalkboards are a widely used means of displaying materials, but they can be messy. Porcelain boards are less messy than chalk-

boards, but they require special markers for writing on the white porcelain surface. Felt boards have a flat display surface made of either flannel or burlap on which a presenter can stick presentation materials made of the same substance as the board surface. Magnetic boards feature a metal display surface on which materials with magnetic backings are displayed. Felt boards and magnetic boards are less messy to use than either blackboards or porcelain boards.

Handouts The handout is another important display technique for presenting visual aids. Word charts, graphs, photographs, maps, and other visuals can be transferred to handouts to be distributed to the audience. If you plan to use handouts, avoid distributing them before or during your speech. Audience members who have materials to look at while your presentation is in progress will be distracted from both you and your speech. There are only two reasons for ever using handouts. First, handouts are appropriate if your material cannot be displayed or projected in any other way. If you must hand out materials before or during your speech, closely monitor audience members so that their attention does not stray too far from your presentation. Second, handouts are useful when your audience needs the material for study or reference after the speech. In this case, however, it is best to distribute your handouts after your presentation, as the audience is leaving.

Audio Techniques

Audiocassettes, compact discs, and records can be effectively incorporated into a presentation if either the topic or the objective of a speech invites audio support. For example, audio techniques can be employed in speeches to present music, interviews of famous people, excerpts from speeches, and various background support for filmstrips, films, and videotapes. When using audio techniques, however, you must be careful that they do not interfere with your speech. Moreover, you need to make sure that the sound is loud and clear enough and that the audio equipment is in working order prior to your presentation.

As you can see, there are many options for presenting your visual and audio aids. To choose the appropriate technique, consider the options and questions in the box "Choosing a Method to Present Your Visual and Audio Aids."

Choosing a Method to Present Your Visual and Audio Aids

Visual and Audio Aids

Demonstration boards   Opaque projectors

Films and videotapes   Slides

Filmstrips   Transparencies

Flip charts   Audiocassettes, compact
                                        discs, and records

Handouts

Key Questions

- What visual or audio techniques are available at the location of your speech?

- What visual or audio techniques are most suited to your presentation? How can your visual aids best be displayed?

- What visual or audio techniques do you feel most comfortable using?

USING A COMPUTER TO ENHANCE YOUR PRESENTATIONS

Most visual aids—graphs, tables, charts, word charts, maps, diagrams, and drawings—can now be created on the computer with graphics, spreadsheet, and word-processing software. Computer-generated visual aids can add a level of professionalism, sophistication, and flash to your speech that surpasses what you usually can attain with hand-rendered graphics.

Probably the most common way of presenting computer-generated graphics, especially in the classroom, is by means of overhead transparencies. You begin by creating your graphic on the computer and printing it out on an 8½-by-11-inch sheet of paper. You then copy the image onto an acetate transparency (or have a copy shop do it) and project the image on a screen using an overhead projector. If an overhead projector is not available in the room where you will give your speech, you can have your paper version enlarged and/or mounted at a copy shop for display on an easel. Alternatively, your copy shop may be able to enlarge and print the graphic directly from your disk.

If you have access to a scanner, you can scan pictures from books or magazines into your computer and then include them in your presentation as well. Some software allows you to adapt scanned images for your own use, such as by cutting certain parts and enlarging others.

You can also create your own slides (to summarize your points, for example), using "presentation software." Among the better known of these programs are Microsoft PowerPoint, Adobe Persuasion, Corel Presentations, Lotus Freelance, and Harvard Graphics. Most of these programs provide many options for the design and appearance of your slides. PowerPoint,

for example, offers a variety of slide templates, with different designs, colors, type styles, and background patterns, and a choice of hundreds of ready-made drawings and clip art items. You can also choose how one slide will transition to the next, such as by fading, dissolving, uncovering, or wiping. Some presentation software allows you to jump from one image to another in your set of slides, instead of following a predetermined order, in response to audience feedback, shifting time constraints, and so on.

To present electronic slides, you will need special equipment in the room where you give your speech, including a computer, an overhead projector, and a liquid crystal display (LCD) projection panel, which is placed on top of the overhead projector and connected by a cable to the computer. When this equipment is set up, the slide that appears on the computer screen is projected onto a screen for the audience to view. You change slides simply by touching a key or clicking the mouse. If there is an Internet connection available in the room where you give your speech, you can also connect to the World Wide Web and show Web pages as part of your presentation.

Other software can be used to create multimedia presentations, allowing you to combine graphics, sound, photographs, video clips, and even animation for your presentation. Although such presentations require elaborate equipment and the expertise to use it, they are already standard in business settings and are becoming increasingly common in college classrooms.

Undoubtedly, computer-generated graphics and computer-assisted presentation can enhance a speech. However, these new technologies have several drawbacks. First, they require some rather expensive equipment, including the computer, the software, and the projection equipment. Second, it takes time to learn and master the programs used to generate the graphics or run the slide show or multimedia presentation. If you have a limited amount of time to prepare a speech, you may not want to spend it learning how to generate graphics or creating flashy PowerPoint slides. There is also the danger that you will spend *all* your time creating the visual aids at the expense of preparing the speech itself! A related danger is that you will "overdesign" your graphics or slides; as with any visual aid, electronic presentation aids work best when they are clear and simple. Similarly, remember that the visual aids are meant to support your speech, not dominate it. Create your speech first, and then design the graphics around it, not the reverse.

Using electronic aids during your presentation raises additional hazards, since it increases the number of things that can go wrong. If you are using a computer in your speech, you must familiarize yourself with all the equipment ahead of time, know the room you will be speaking in, and practice your speech using the electronic aids. Try to know enough about the equipment that you can handle any basic technical problems that arise. Always make a backup copy of your slides as transparency acetates in case the worst—a computer crash—occurs.

Another disadvantage of using electronic aids is that your visuals may take the focus away from you, the speaker. If the room is darkened, then the brightly lit screen is especially likely to become the center of attention, and you will be marginalized during your own speech. The darkened room may also make it difficult for you to see your notes.

All of these difficulties can be overcome with planning and practice. Because computer-aided presentations offer so many opportunities for enhancing your speech, it is worth the investment of time and energy to master these challenging new technologies.

GUIDELINES FOR EFFECTIVELY USING VISUAL AIDS

What follow are several guidelines to consider before you construct and employ visual aids in your speech. (The box "Interview with a Professional: Ted Ross" contains additional advice on constructing and using effective visual aids.)

Use Visual Aids That Serve a Definite Purpose

During the early stages of speech preparation, carefully consider which of your points can be enhanced by a visual aid. Ask yourself whether a specific point can be better communicated visually than verbally.

For example, including a beautiful photograph of the ocean in a speech on sailing would serve no purpose; however, incorporating a professional-looking drawing of a sailboat would help your audience better visualize the topic. Visual aids should never be used solely for their artistic or aesthetic merits. They must always serve a specific purpose.

Use Visual Aids That Are Appropriate for the Topic, Audience, and Occasion

When selecting a visual aid, carefully consider what you are talking about, whom you are talking to, and what the nature of the speaking situation is. For example, it would be inappropriate to display a series of cartoons while speaking on gun control to a group of police officers at their annual convention. It would be more suitable to incorporate professional-looking graphs and high-quality photographs to illustrate the seriousness of your presentation.

Don't Overuse Visual Aids

Too often, speakers include too many visual aids in their presentations. Remember that the primary objectives of employing visual aids are to clarify, add interest, increase information retention, save time, and help explain the topic more effectively. You could not achieve any of these objectives if you included so many visual aids that your audience attended more to the visual aids than to you and your speech.

Use Visual Aids That Require Little or No Explanation

Visual aids must be simple. They must not contain a lot of complex material or too much information! This may seem obvious, but many visual aids are ineffective because they are too complicated, too crowded, and too cluttered. For a visual aid to contribute positively to a presentation, it must be simple enough to speak for itself. Audiences should not need an interpreter to understand the material in a graph, word chart, or other type of visual aid.

Use Visual Aids That Catch and Hold Your Audience's Attention

Be sure to create visual aids that will really catch and hold your audience's attention. Your visual aids must be distinctive and professional looking, and they should never be obtained or constructed at the last minute. Like the rest of your presentation, your visual aids should look as if they required a lot of time and work to construct.

Interview with a Professional

Ted Ross

Ted Ross, 36, is the founder, president, and CEO of Ross-Campbell, Inc.—a Sacramento, CA, company that specializes in environmentally related advertising and public relations.

How important are visual aids to the effectiveness of a presentation?

There are two main reasons I advocate the use of visual aids in speaking presentations. First, good visual aids help promote viewer interest. They help to engage the audience and break the monotony that is all too common in speeches delivered by nonprofessionals. Second, visual aids ensure that accurate information is consistently provided. Let's face it, presenters can misspeak or inadvertently skip important material that is critical to a presentation. Assuming that a presenter has taken the time to prepare accurate, attractive visual aids, the audience will receive the information provided by the visual aids with little chance of error.

What determines whether a speaker should use a visual aid?

The bottom line here is: Will visual aids add to or detract from the presentation? I've made presentations with and without visual aids. In those instances where visual aids were not used, it was because I was able to best deliver the message via succinct and powerful words, and visual aids would have actually distracted the audience.

I find that people often use visual aids as a crutch. They are not confident in their ability to deliver a presentation without the assistance of some additional tool. There are a lot of good reasons to use visual aids, but this is not one of them.

In terms of the overall effectiveness of a presentation, how important is it that a visual aid be of high professional quality?

In a word, the visual must be good. The quality of the visual aid directly impacts the perceived quality of your general presentation,

you the presenter, and your product and/or service. If you can't afford the time, energy, or resources to produce a good-quality visual aid, forget it. A poor-quality visual aid will be a liability to your presentation.

What guidelines do you follow for effectively using visual aids?

As I indicated previously, visual aids should truly enhance a presentation. My rule of thumb is that visual aids are there to assist the presenter in making the presentation—not the other way around. Again, as mentioned earlier, too many people rely on visual aids as a crutch. They hope that the visual aid will do the majority of the work with a little help from the presenter. In most cases, this equation is not only unrealistic but usually results in an ineffective presentation.

In a nutshell, the guidelines for the effective use of visual aids are as follows: First, determine if the use of visual aids will add to your presentation. If the answer is yes, next prepare your presentation so that at key points during your speech you can rely on a visual aid to assist you in driving home your message. Once you've determined what needs to be communicated with your visual aids, then plan, design, and produce high-quality aids. And, finally, prepare the presentation of your visual aids well in advance of your speech. Make sure that your slides are in order, that there is equipment and/or power available if necessary, that all in the audience will be able to reasonably view your materials, and that you are able to smoothly transition back and forth between speaking and presenting visual aids.

Use Visual Aids That Are Easy to See

Your visual aids must be large enough that people in the last row of your audience can see them easily. This means that both the visual aid and its elements (like the words, graphs, diagrams, and numbers) must be sized appropriately for the room and your audience. Visual aids must also be projected or displayed so that every person in an audience can see them without any difficulty. You need to make sure that the environment where you will be presenting your speech is conducive to achieving these objectives. If it is not, make the appropriate adjustments before your presentation.

Keep Your Visual Aids in Your Possession during Your Presentation

In the discussion on handouts, you were cautioned against giving out materials before and during your presentation except in unusual circumstances. This guideline applies to all types of aids that are potentially handleable. Audience members will want to touch or hold an interesting object like a detailed model airplane, an attractive piece of Native American pottery, or a large chunk of quartz crystal. Or they may demand a copy of a chart to follow along. Do not be swayed by either their enthusiasm or their demands. Losing your visual aids to the hands and

When employing visual aids in your speech, make sure that your audience can clearly see them. Being able to see a visual aid refers not only to actual size but to the readability of any words or numbers. This visual aid doesn't meet these conditions because it is not easy for everyone in the audience to see or comprehend.

eyes of audience members is a sure way to divert their attention from you and your speech.

Remove Your Visual Aids from Sight When You Are through with Them

If your visuals aids are truly professional in quality, they will be hard not to look at. In fact, audience members tend to stare at and even fixate on all visual aids. If the visual aids are on display during your entire presentation, they can detract from your main objective—having your audience listen to your speech. Thus, you should present each visual aid at the appropriate time; when its usefulness to your speech is over, remove it from view.

Thoroughly Rehearse Using Your Visual Aids before Your Presentation

It is difficult to say that any one of the preceding guidelines is more important than the other. This one, however, is perhaps the most important guideline. Practice and rehearsal have been emphasized throughout this book. Practicing with visual aids is no exception. Even the best-researched speech and the highest-quality visual aids would be wasted if you did not devote time to rehearsing the inclusion of each visual aid in your presentation. Effectively rehearsing with your visual aids means not only practicing your presentation with the aids to achieve correct timing but also rehearsing your speech to become comfortable with the equipment you will be using to project or display your aids.

The box "Guidelines for Effectively Using Visual Aids" summarizes the strategies described in this chapter. You should now be able to decide whether to include visual aids in your speech and how to choose just the right one(s). As a final means of evaluating your choices, answer the questions in the box "Evaluating Your Visual Aids."

Guidelines for Effectively Using Visual Aids

- Use visual aids that serve a definite purpose.
- Use visual aids that are appropriate for your topic, audience, and occasion.
- Don't overuse visual aids.
- Use visual aids that require little or no explanation.
- Use visual aids that catch and hold your audience's attention.
- Use visual aids that are easy to see.
- Keep your visual aids in your possession during your presentation.
- Remove your visual aids from sight when you are through with them.
- Thoroughly rehearse using your visual aids before your presentation.

Evaluating Your Visual Aids

The following questions cover all of the points you should consider when evaluating the use of a particular visual aid in your public presentation. Although it would be difficult for any one visual aid to satisfy all of the following criteria, if you can answer yes to a number of these items, you should feel comfortable about including that particular visual aid in your speech.

- Does this visual aid clarify something important for my audience?
- Will including this visual aid make my speech more interesting for my audience?
- Will including this visual aid increase my audience's retention of my speech?
- Will including this visual aid save me valuable time?

- Will including this visual aid help my audience follow the organization of my speech?
- Does this visual aid serve a definite purpose in my speech?
- Is this visual aid appropriate for my speech topic?
- Is this visual aid appropriate for my audience?
- Is this visual aid appropriate for this speaking occasion?
- Does this visual aid require minimum explanation?
- Will this visual aid catch and hold the attention of my audience?
- Will this visual aid be easy for my entire audience to see?

CHAPTER REVIEW

- Speeches can be enhanced by the inclusion of one or more visual devices to highlight the content and delivery. To use visual aids strategically and effectively, you must know when to use them and which ones to use in a particular public speaking situation.

- You must answer a number of questions before deciding whether to employ a visual aid in your speech. Will visual aids add new information and thus clarify something for your audience? Will they make your speech more interesting for your audience? Will they help your audience remember important points and

ideas? Will they save you valuable time? Will they help you explain your topic more effectively?

- Visual aids come in an almost infinite number of forms. A graph is a pictorial device that illustrates quantitative relationships. The three primary types of graphs are line graphs, bar graphs, and pie graphs. Tables arrange numbers, words, and symbols in an orderly format using rows and columns. Charts represent the relationship between parts of a group or object or the sequence of steps in a process. A word chart, which contains text only, is probably the most popular type of visual aid. Speakers also commonly employ physical representations (objects, models, and people) and visual representations (photographs, maps, and hand drawings) in their presentations.

- Visual aids can be presented to an audience using projection techniques and display techniques. Audio techniques can also be employed to enhance the effectiveness of a presentation. Choosing the appropriate presentation technique of a visual aid is a separate and important part of planning for an effective public presentation.

- Most types of visual aids can be created on a computer and displayed as transparencies, flip charts, or slides. Both slides created with presentation software and materials from the Internet can be projected directly from a computer with the right equipment. A successful computer-assisted presentation requires careful planning and rehearsal.

- Guidelines for constructing and employing visual aids in your presentation range from using visual aids that serve a definite purpose to thoroughly rehearsing with the visual aids.

QUESTIONS FOR CRITICAL THINKING & REVIEW

1. Why is it often the case that a picture is worth a thousand words? Under what circumstances can a picture say too much?

2. TV news rarely tells a story without using a still or action picture. Watch the news tonight. Which visual aids are particularly helpful to your understanding of the story? Which do nothing to enhance the story or possibly even interfere with it?

3. When reading a magazine, what type of graphs do you tend to examine? Which do you tend to ignore? Why do you think some graphs are more, or less, appealing to you?

4. Why do audiences prefer colorful graphs and charts as opposed to black and white? How does color help an audience understand a point? Could color ever interfere with an audience's understanding? When and how?

Chapter 18

SPECIAL OCCASION SPEECHES AND GROUP PRESENTATIONS

What do each of the following have in common?

- Rose Piotrowski is introducing the keynote speaker at the next city council meeting.
- Audrey Hauth is welcoming the Japanese runners to the annual Long Beach Marathon.
- John Thome is presenting the Citizen of the Year award at the annual city banquet.
- Victoria Luna is retiring after 40 years and will be accepting a gold watch for her service at the spring retirement dinner.
- James Sparks is running for city planner, and Roberta Vega will publicly nominate him at the next political rally.
- George Scott will be giving the eulogy for Tom Hernandez at the site of Tom's burial services on Saturday.
- Andrew Resendez will be making a short presentation in a small group symposium being sponsored by the Los Angeles chapter of Mothers Against Drunk Driving (MADD).

All of these events require the speaker to give a short speech that celebrates or acknowledges the significance of a particular person, event, or occasion. These kinds of specialized presentations, frequently called **ceremonial speeches**, play major roles in our lives.

CEREMONIAL SPEECHES

Learning Objectives

After reading this chapter, you should be able to do the following:

1. Differentiate among the various kinds of speeches used for special occasions.

2. Understand which guidelines to follow when preparing for each of these different types of specialized speeches.

3. Handle questions from the audience effectively—even loaded and negative questions.

Most people's lives are filled with social, political, and professional occasions that require some type of ceremonial presentation: political rallies, holidays, birthdays, christenings, memorials of passing, weddings, anniversaries, hirings, promotions, retirements, award banquets, and many more. Because there are so many special occasions in our lives, you likely will be asked to deliver a specialized speech at one time or another.

This final chapter examines the process of preparing and delivering the more common types of special occasion speeches. The speeches discussed in this chapter are ones that individuals either experience as a participant at some special occasion or that people routinely observe.

Speakers must follow a few simple rules regarding content and delivery of specialized speeches. One universal rule is that with rare exception, a specialized speech should last no more than a few minutes. It is true that some ceremonial speeches observed in the media are considerably longer; the particular setting or occasion often demands that a speaker be given more time. For example, a speech nominating a presidential candidate at a national political convention normally runs much longer than a nominating speech for a student body president at a university political rally.

For the most part, audiences dislike specialized speeches that go on interminably. After all, they aren't assembled to listen to a speech per se but to witness or participate in some event, whether it be a funeral, a wedding, or an award ceremony. During those occasions, a lengthy speech can detract from the purpose of the event.

Another rule to keep in mind when preparing specialized speeches is to direct most of your time and attention to the targeted individual or the occasion itself. Too often, presenters of awards, eulogies, tributes, and nominations take the opportunity to talk about themselves or to advance some political or social cause—at the expense of the honoree. Also, for speeches that focus on a specific individual, it is important to know how to correctly pronounce the person's name. Other general rules focus specifically on the delivery of specialized speeches. That is, speakers should be enthusiastic and communicate sincere regard for the person or event targeted in the speech. They should make eye contact with and smile warmly at the entire audience, avoid nervous mannerisms, be verbally expressive, employ a conversational style, and maintain appropriate decorum and self-control.

These strategies are summarized in the box "General Guidelines for Special Occasion Speaking." Other important rules to keep in mind are explained in conjunction with the specific specialized speeches discussed in this chapter.

Introductions

In many public contexts, speakers are introduced to the audience by the host or emcee of the event. An effective **introduction speech**—one that helps a speaker and topic be perceived as credible, entertaining, and worthy of the audience's attention—can help create a successful public speaking event. In an introduction

speech, the host provides the audience with sufficient reasons for actively listening to a particular speaker. The following guidelines are designed to help you give an effective introduction. (Refer back to Chapter 5 for advice about how to introduce yourself successfully on occasions when you, as speaker, will not be given a formal introduction.)

Perhaps the best-known introduction speech is, "Ladies and gentlemen, the president of the United States." This is also probably the shortest introduction on record! The reason it's so brief is that virtually every audience has enough information about the president of the United States to fill in the normal details of the introduction. Although your speech of introduction should not be a single line, this example illustrates the important rule mentioned earlier: Be brief.

Because an introduction is so crucial to establishing speaker credibility and audience interest in the topic, consider the following guidelines when preparing your speech:

1. Spend some time with the speaker to get personal information to include in your introduction. You will be much more effective at introducing a speaker if you know something about her or him firsthand. This step will help with a number of recommendations that follow.

2. Mention the speaker's name several times during the introduction, and be sure to pronounce his or her name correctly. Doing so will ensure that most audience members will know the speaker's name— and be able to pronounce it—by the time the speaker begins to talk.

3. Establish the speaker's credibility. Clearly describe the speaker's qualifications to talk about the speech topic. If it's relevant to the speech topic, mention the speaker's educational background, business

BUILDING YOUR SKILLS

General Guidelines for Special Occasion Speaking

- Unless the occasion demands otherwise, be brief—no more than three minutes.

- Focus your attention on the individual or occasion that is the subject of the event.

- Pronounce names correctly.

- Communicate regard and enthusiasm for the person or event targeted by the speech.

- Use verbal and nonverbal behavior appropriate for the audience and occasion.

experience, or other important credentials. You may need to interview the speaker ahead of time and ask for relevant background information that she or he might want the audience to know.

4. Explain why the audience should listen to the speaker. That is, sell the audience on the speaker and the speech. However, be careful not to overstate the speaker's credentials or to promise the audience too much in the way of fun or solutions. You may end up setting unrealistic expectations for the speaker.

5. Initiate a good relationship between the speaker and the audience. Tell audience members how much you like the speaker and why they should share the same feelings.

6. Set the tone for the particular speaker and the topic. Let the audience know if the speech will be entertaining, informative, reinforcing, or potentially disturbing.

7. Express your sincere pleasure for the privilege of being able to introduce the speaker.

8. If provided, tell the audience the title of the speech. Many times, a title lends additional information and, perhaps, a bit of intrigue to the upcoming speech.

9. Avoid trite or distracting expressions. For example, never use any of the following:

   "This speaker needs no introduction."

   "We are truly honored to have with us today . . ."

   "Without further ado . . ."

   "It is indeed a high privilege . . ."

   "On this most memorable and ceremonial occasion . . ."

   "Ladies and gentlemen, heeeere's . . ."

   "We are a lucky audience because we have none other than . . ."[1]

10. Finally, try to capture your audience's attention. Set the stage for the speaker, give up your position quickly, and let the speaker assume the key role. After all, your primary purpose is to quickly do everything you can to help the speaker move effectively into his or her presentation.

The following speech might be delivered by an undergraduate to satisfy these criteria in a beginning public speaking class.

It is my sincere pleasure to introduce your keynote speaker, John Martin Bruner, who will be speaking to you today on working in the aerospace industry during a period of impending layoff. John is the manager of the technical support team at the McDonnell Douglas Corporation in St. Louis, Missouri. John has worked in the aerospace industry for more than ten years. He has survived numerous workforce reductions. John has worked both in human resources and in a number of technical areas. He is an excellent speaker! In these and other ways, he has extensive qualifications to speak in an informative fashion on this topic. I spent some quality time with John earlier this evening. I like him; you will too. I find him very informative, and I am looking forward to his presentation. I encourage you to listen carefully to John Bruner.

Another example of a brief introduction speech was delivered by California governor Pete Wilson in his preliminary remarks at the opening of the Ronald Reagan Memorial Library in November 1991. Governor Wilson gave a series of introductions for the former U.S. presidents and first ladies and other dignitaries visiting on this occasion. He did an exceptionally good job of introducing former President Jimmy Carter:

Our next speaker brought to the Oval Office an abiding faith in right over might, a deep compassion for the oppressed, a determination to make human rights America's hallmark around the world.

And recent events in Madrid bring to mind perhaps the greatest achievement of President Jimmy Carter, the Camp David Accord. Earlier, when I recognized Mrs. Sadat, I couldn't help but think that this must be a day of poignant pride for her. Anwar Sadat had the courage to face his former enemies; and to extend to them the open hand of friendship and of peace.

At different times, Mrs. Sadat, each of our five special guests worked with your great husband to forge and sustain that enduring peace.

No one had a higher regard for him, or a deeper appreciation for the challenge of bringing that peace to the Middle East, than our next speaker.

It is my honor to introduce President Jimmy Carter.[2]

Welcomes

Welcoming individuals to a special occasion can be an extremely important part of ensuring that their experience is satisfying and successful. In circumstances such as hosting a professional convention, organizing an athletic event, dedicating a new city building, or emceeing a banquet, there are always special visitors who need to be welcomed publicly. **Welcoming speeches** provide a formal, public greeting to visiting persons or groups, making them feel comfortable and appreciated.

A welcoming speech must be gracious, thoughtful, simple, and brief. In giving a welcoming speech, you should extend warm greetings and make your guests feel at home. You should also help your visitors feel comfortable by providing them with information about the occasion, about those in attendance, and about their new environment. The following two welcoming speeches meet these criteria:

> It is with a great deal of pleasure that I welcome our visitors from the state of New York to the annual California Humane Society banquet. You are the first visitors from New York that we have had in attendance at this very special yearly event. It is reassuring to know that other areas of the country share in our concern for the protection of all living creatures. We sincerely appreciate your coming such a long distance. We want to make sure that you feel completely at home while you are here.

> I want to formally welcome the distinguished senior senator from New Mexico to the monthly dinner meeting of the Clovis City Council. We represent a small community in the middle of California and, thus, we are especially honored to have such an important visitor come such a long way. We hope that you will feel at home with us during your stay and that you will feel comfortable participating in our question-and-answer session following dinner. To ensure that your visit is an informative one, we have compiled a packet for you containing maps and relevant information about this area.

Nominations

Many formal nominations are made at public gatherings. The typical **nomination speech** should be brief and to the point. A formal or public nomination consists of a brief persuasive speech in which an individual is publicly put forward as a candidate. Your primary goal in putting together a nominating speech is to lay out in two or three minutes all the qualities that make your candidate the most suitable person for the award, honor, or position. As the nominator, you should (1) describe the generic qualities required for the award, office, or honor, (2) list your candidate's personal and/or professional qualifications that meet those criteria, and (3) end the speech by designating your nominee by name. What follows is a sample speech a student might use to nominate a candidate for student body president:

> This is a very important day for the students at Bradley University. For it is on this day that we nominate the candidates for the office of student body president. This activity must be taken seriously, for the individual who is eventually elected to this office must possess a number of special qualifications. Most importantly, she must understand the difficulties of managing a student body this large. Next, she must be able to represent and interact with a highly diverse student population. She needs to be able to develop a good working relationship with the central administration—she must be an effective communicator. Accordingly, she must serve as a role model for new and continuing students.

> It is with these and many other pertinent qualities in mind that I nominate an individual who was born and raised here in Peoria. A person who has spent the last three years working in student government and who has a proven record of successfully working with the president and other administrators at this university. This individual's academic record is outstanding. She has maintained a 4.0 average every semester since her arrival. Majoring in communication, she has a long history of supporting the development of opportunities for the many underrepresented student groups on this campus. It is with great pleasure that I nominate Melanie Ray as a candidate for next year's student body president.

Award Speeches

On many occasions, one speaker presents an award of some kind to a particular person or group, and another speaker graciously accepts that award. People present and receive awards at the Academy Awards, the Grammys, the Tonys, and so on. Awards are also presented and accepted at such events as social and civic banquets, employee recognition ceremonies, and high school, college, and university graduations.

Presenting an Award In an **award presentation speech,** the speaker recognizes the notable accomplishments of an individual or a group. Award presentation speeches should be brief. When giving an award, you should focus on the particular award itself by mentioning both the organization bestowing the recognition and the values represented by the award. You should also describe the selection process, summarize the qualifications of the award recipient, and reference how she or he is similar to previous honorees. Finally, you should relate to the audience precisely what makes the recipient's achievements worthy of such an honor. The following example shows how a student might present an award at a university banquet:

> Every year, the student body honors a graduating senior for service to the university that is truly outstanding. This very special recognition is

bestowed on students who have been nominated by a peer and then evaluated by a panel of students, faculty, and administrators. The evaluation process is extremely demanding, and only one student can receive this honor each year.

This year, the student body honors James Lim. As an economics major with a 4.0 record, James has distinguished himself as an outstanding student and as an individual who has devoted himself to opening opportunities for Asian American students at this university. During his four years as an undergraduate student, he served every term as a math and economics tutor for students in the department of Asian American studies. He has worked regularly with the offices of student and academic affairs to recruit capable Asian American students from high schools all over the country. He is personally responsible for the sizable increase in the number of Asian American students majoring in economics. James deserves a great deal of recognition for all of his efforts. It is with a great deal of admiration that I present this service award to James Lim.

Accepting an Award In an **award acceptance speech**, the recipient graciously acknowledges the award and communicates appreciation for having his or her accomplishments recognized. Brevity is also important when delivering an acceptance speech. Frank Sinatra learned this rule the hard way: Accepting the Grammy Legend Award in 1994, Sinatra's rambling oration was rudely interrupted when CBS cut away to give another announcement!

In addition to being brief, an acceptance speech should be gracious. Television viewers of that same Grammy program will remember U2's Bono, who came on stage smoking a cigarette and then accepted his award for the album *Zooropa* by declaring that "we shall continue to abuse our position and f——— up the mainstream."[3] This is not the way to graciously accept an award!

Rather than offend your audience, your acceptance speech should sincerely express your appreciation for being honored and recognized. Your speech should be humble, but unless the award was unexpected, don't feign surprise. Doing so will only make you look insincere. Be sure to thank the group giving the award. Within reason, thank all of the people who made your accomplishment possible— possibly even acknowledging your family and friends for their support—but realize that it's virtually impossible to list everyone who contributed to your success.

The following excerpt from an acceptance speech was given by Branko Lustig, coproducer of the Oscar-winning movie *Schindler's List*, a movie depicting the Holocaust. In his speech, Lustig recognized the contributions of untold others whose deaths he witnessed:

My number was A3317. I'm a Holocaust survivor. It's a long way from Auschwitz to this stage. People died in front of me. The last words they said were, "Be a witness to my murder. Tell the world how I died. Remember."[4]

Notice how Lustig tells the audience just how important the award was to him personally. When accepting an award yourself, you should do the same. And, when appropriate, compliment the competition for making the selection process so difficult. In an acceptance speech, it is appropriate to be generous toward those who did not receive the award; however, you must never apologize for receiving an award. Finally, do not use the opportunity to advance some social or political cause unless the award is relevant to such an issue.

The following is a typical acceptance speech for an academic award given at a graduation ceremony:

I want to express my sincere appreciation for being honored by the college for my undergraduate academic achievements. I am thrilled to be receiving this award—it means a great deal to me! I feel that I have profited greatly from the education here. Knowing that there are other meritorious students here today who have also been successful makes receiving this honor that much more meaningful. Under a different set of circumstances, one of them might be receiving this award. I want to thank the dean of the college, my department, and the faculty who recommended me for this honor. I also want to thank my family for all their support and encouragement over the last four years. I wouldn't be standing here today without their support.

Tributes

A **tribute** is a speech that publicly acknowledges the major or long-term accomplishments of an individual or a group. Tribute speeches are intended to honor far-reaching and highly symbolic accomplishments. For example, in 1994, Diana Ross received a tribute at the annual American Music Awards for her accomplishments as an entertainer in music, film, and live performance. Tributes are also given on special holidays that celebrate the notable accomplishments of individuals and groups, such as Memorial Day, which pays tribute to U.S. soldiers who fought and died serving their country. Tributes often are presented to individuals when they retire or to community groups that raise large amounts of money for special causes.

Although the content of a tribute speech is similar in some ways to an award speech, a physical award may not be presented at the end of a tribute. The spoken tribute itself is often the award. Moreover, tribute speeches always include the word "tribute" or "celebration" to show respect for the individual or group. When delivering a speech of tribute, you should express your strong appreciation for the honoree(s) and stimulate the audience to feel the same sense of admiration and gratitude. The most common types of tribute speeches you are likely to encounter are eulogies and simple toasts.

Eulogies

A **eulogy** is a special type of tribute that praises or honors the accomplishments of an individual, usually someone who has recently died. Eulogies normally are presented at the grave site or at the memorial service. Some eulogies are published in the local newspaper or handed out in printed form to attendees following a memorial service. A eulogy is often as short as one minute, but it should be long enough to set a respectable tone for the occasion. Importantly, when eulogizing a person's life, you must be genuine and sincere. You should also maintain appropriate decorum and self-control during your presentation. Remember: Your overriding task is to pay tribute, not to show others how grief-stricken you are.

A good eulogy typically relates a personal story or a vivid anecdote about the person being honored. You should point out what was significant and good about the person and praise his or her lifetime contributions. Finally, express your own personal sorrow, and attempt to console family and friends of the loved one by offering your solace.

The following is an excerpt of the eulogy that Earl Spencer, Princess Diana's brother, delivered on the somber occasion of her sudden and unexpected death:

I stand before you today the representative of a family in grief in a country in mourning before a world in shock. We are united not only in our desire to pay our respects to Diana but rather in our need to do so.

. . . Diana was the very essence of compassion, of duty, of style, of beauty. All over the world she was a symbol of selfless humanity, a standard-bearer

for the rights of the truly downtrodden, a truly British girl who transcended nationality, someone with a natural nobility who was classless, who proved in the last year that she needed no royal title to continue to generate her particular brand of magic.

Today is our chance to say "thank you" for the way you brightened our lives, even though God granted you but half a life. We will all feel cheated that you were taken from us so young and yet we must learn to be grateful that you came along at all. Only now you are gone do we truly appreciate what we are now without and we want you to know that life without you is very, very difficult.[5]

As another example, consider this excerpt from the eulogy for Richard Nixon given by Henry A. Kissinger, who was secretary of state for and longtime devoted friend of the late president:

During the final week of Richard Nixon's life, I often imagined how he would have reacted to the tide of concern, respect, admiration, and affection evoked by his last great battle.

His gruff pose of never paying attention to media comment would have been contradicted by a warm glow and the ever-so-subtle hint that another recital of the commentary would not be unwelcome.

And without quite saying so, he would have conveyed that it would mean a lot to him if Julie and Tricia, David and Ed were told of his friends' pride in this culmination to an astonishing life.

When I learned the final news, by then so expected yet so hard to accept, I felt a profound void. In the words of Shakespeare: "He was a man. Take him, for all in all, I shall not look upon his like again."[6]

Toasts

A **toast** is a short speech of tribute. At virtually every special occasion, someone volunteers or is asked to make a toast—at holiday dinners, at wedding receptions, at luncheons celebrating a promotion, or at any other formal or informal occasion on which someone's achievements or accomplishments are being celebrated.

A toast should be brief and to the point, and it should set a tone of good cheer. The following toast might be given by a parent to celebrate his daughter's college graduation:

I am very proud of Kerry! She has worked long and hard to complete her college education. I can remember her first week in college. She seemed so insecure. She even indicated that she didn't think she could make it. As her years of success at school went on, however, I watched her confidence

Impromptu Speaking

Imagine that you find yourself in one of these situations:

- In a monthly business meeting, you are suddenly called on to describe your department's current project.

- During a memorial service, friends and family are invited to stand and say a few words about the deceased.

- While attending a local school board meeting, an issue of concern is raised and you feel compelled to rebut the position put forward by another speaker.

Although this text stresses the benefits of the extemporaneous mode of delivery, some circumstances, like the ones just described, may require you to give a brief impromptu speech. Lack of preparation time can make an impromptu speech a particularly challenging and anxiety-producing experience. Here are some strategies to help you give more effective impromptu speeches:

- Be aware that you will probably have a few seconds or minutes between the time you realize you will be speaking and the time you actually begin to speak. Thus, plan what you want to say by quickly running through the following basic speech preparation steps:

  Consider your audience and the occasion. What does the audience expect you to talk about? What do they know about the topic?

Identify the major purpose and message of what you will say, and select an overall organizational framework. If time allows, sketch out a brief key-word outline.

Review what you know about the topic—chances are you will have prior knowledge and personal experiences to draw on.

Work out how you will begin and end your speech.

- Take cues from other speakers who have gone before you. Did they speak for too long or too short a time? Did they stand in front of the group or remain seated? Can you respond to their statements? Do you disagree with a previous speaker's position, or can you add to what another speaker has already said?

- Be brief. If you don't have anything else to say, don't keep talking.

- Maintain your composure. Speak slowly and confidently.

- Don't demand too much from yourself. The audience likely will know that your response is impromptu and so will not expect you to give a perfectly polished presentation.

Remember, you use impromptu speech all the time in casual conversations—and you *can* do it in more formal circumstances.

---

grow. She made the dean's list every quarter of her last year. Here's to Kerry Ritter; I knew you could do it!

The next example is a toast a sister might give to her younger brother at a private awards banquet:

I want to toast my brother for earning a letter for playing varsity football this season. I am so proud of his athletic accomplishments. I must admit that only three years ago I wasn't sure he was big enough to play varsity football. Since that time, he has made a serious and successful commitment to bodybuilding and weight gain. He just isn't the same person he was three years ago. Great job, Donald! I love you and respect what you have accomplished. Keep up the good work.

Toasts should focus on some positive attribute or characteristic of the honoree. To give a toast, you might begin by telling a personal story or a humorous anecdote that demonstrates something positive about the person. (Be careful, however, not to tell stories that make the individual feel unduly embarrassed or ashamed.) Try to create a vivid, memorable image of the person being honored. In terms of delivery, present your toast in a conversational, yet eloquent speaking style. Be sure to end your presentation with a dramatic gesture that acknowledges the honoree by name.

Although toasts are often planned in advance, you may be called on at some time to deliver a toast on the spot. See the box "Impromptu Speaking" for some strategies for giving a successful impromptu presentation.

Commencement Speeches

People who complete a formal educational degree program or some specialized on-the-job training or certification program generally take part in some type of commencement exercise. **Commencement speeches**, which are part of virtually all graduation ceremonies, are delivered by all sorts of people—school principals, college or university presidents, deans and faculty, notable people in the community, and distinguished alumni. Perhaps you will be asked one day to deliver a commencement speech. Similar to awards and tributes, commencement speeches are presentations delivered at graduation exercises in which a speaker praises and congratulates individuals who have formally completed a prescribed set of educational requirements. Commencement speeches also challenge those who are graduating to consider carefully the important future roles they can play in society.

Because graduation ceremonies are attended primarily by parents, relatives, and people who are truly proud of those graduating, these speeches must be highly complimentary. Moreover, they should be relatively brief because audience members are anxious to experience the ritual of seeing their graduate receive either a diploma or a certificate. Although commencement speeches typically last a little longer than the other ceremonial speeches discussed so far, it's a good idea to ask your host just how much time is ideal. In a commencement speech, you should begin by describing, recognizing, and celebrating the significance of the special occasion. Next, you should praise those graduating. Be sure to acknowledge audience members for their support as well. Finally, you should challenge those graduating to achieve some significant social, political, or personal goal.

The following excerpts are from a commencement speech delivered by actor/comedian/educator Bill Cosby to graduates of the University of Pennsylvania:

> ... First of all, those of you who took a "C" in a couple of courses here, I'd like you to write the professors a letter and apologize. Because you could have done better, you just didn't want to. And I've spoken to these professors, they're crying. And they're not too thrilled because they think they failed.
>
> Number two: You're in debt. That's why your folks want to talk to you. You got a degree now they expect you to work your way out of it. Those people are back there not to receive you but to shake your hand and let you know you don't live there anymore. It's a wonderful example of how to get rid of your kids finally.
>
> The third thing is, I want you to pay off your student loans. Now this is super important because there are people coming behind you. Or else just

> write a note and tell the people you're not going to pay the loan off because you don't want anybody coming behind you. ...
>
> In terms of your life from this point on, it's no big deal. You've got a lot of time now. Not to stay at home, not to sponge off of anybody, but just to develop yourself and get going.[7]

Cosby continued by challenging the graduates to make the best of the opportunities they'd earned and been given. He told them to be self-reliant, to set goals, and to move forward. In his 15-minute speech, Cosby entertained, motivated, and congratulated the graduating class and their parents.

Dedications

Dedications are ceremonies that celebrate the beginning of something totally new, such as a building, road, bridge, ship or plane, or some other commodity. A dedication marks the date when a particular commodity is available for operation. **Dedication speeches** commit the new commodity to an ideal or value, like improved community relations, good service, or community development. Dedications should be short, acknowledging the contributions of those involved and describing how the commodity being dedicated symbolizes a certain ideal or value.

On April 12, 1994, California governor Pete Wilson dedicated the reopened Interstate 10, which had suffered major damage during the Northridge earthquake in January of that same year. The following excerpted speech is somewhat lengthy due to the political nature of this occasion, yet it provides a good example of an effective dedication:

> Good morning. It's a pleasure to be here today to celebrate with the people of Los Angeles the reopening of the Santa Monica Freeway.
>
> This, the busiest freeway in the world, was turned into a ruin by the Northridge Earthquake last January.
>
> At the time, it was one of the most stirring symbols of devastation in the Southland. Today, less than three months later and 74 days ahead of schedule, I-10's reopening makes it the most stirring symbol yet of California's endurance—and the spirit that drives the California Comeback.
>
> We accomplished this marvel by doing what government should always do—slash bureaucracy and get out of the way.
>
> In the private sector, construction jobs completed early are followed by a bonus for the contractors—because an early completion means money saved. This is a simple economic principle that worked well here on the Santa Monica Freeway.

C. C. Meyers Construction worked around the clock and got the job done well—high-quality and speedy work. . . .

This project was an enormous success, and everyone who worked on it deserves praise and congratulations. Because of them, Los Angeles is moving again . . . in the fast lane for recovery. . . .

I'd also like to thank those here from Washington, Vice President Gore, Secretary Pena, and the California congressional delegation, as well as congressional leaders, for their involvement in making sure this project is funded. . . .

Finally, I want to recognize the people of Los Angeles who pulled together after the earthquake hit and are still working together, still making the sacrifices that'll make this city greater than it was.

Many of us have to live . . . and work . . . and commute in terrible circumstances. But you've shown the spirit that made this state what it is today. You never gave up. You pitched in. You worked side by side with strangers. You've proven what I've always believed . . . that they can shake us, but they can't break us. Thank you, and drive safely.[8]

Farewells

Saying good-bye in a formal setting normally requires a brief **farewell speech**. There are two types of farewell speeches: (1) a short presentation in which a person who is leaving ceremonializes her or his good-bye, and (2) a brief ceremonial in which a presenter communicates a good-bye to a departing person. Both types of farewell speeches can occur on the same special occasion. Farewell speeches are given when a person retires, relocates for a new job, is promoted to a different company, takes a leave of absence, and so on.

In the case of your own departure, your farewell speech should express your pleasure, gratitude, and fondness for such things as long-term associations with colleagues and friends, the opportunity to serve the group or organization, and the tribute of celebrating your departure. It is important that your farewell speech allow your audience to share as vividly as possible this important ceremonial moment with you. To do that, include metaphors, similes, and intense, animated language in your speech. Tell your audience how you feel about your ties to the area, community, or organization. Your speech of farewell should help others understand how you would like to be remembered—what impression or accomplishment you would like them to remember. Also, if you are given

a farewell gift, thank your audience sincerely for the gift and explain what the memento means to you.

If you are going to give a send-off speech for someone else's departure, you should acknowledge the person's contributions by giving a sincere and enthusiastic thank-you. Be sure to praise the person for specific past achievements and accomplishments, and perhaps recall some unique experience that you shared. A sincere farewell should create a familial feeling; that is, the person should leave feeling emotionally tied to the community, group, or organization. Finally, your formal farewell speech should conclude on a positive note by wishing the individual good luck. President Bill Clinton's farewell speech to Regina Montoya, director of the Office of Intergovernmental Affairs, is a good example of an effective good-bye speech:

I appreciate the outstanding work Regina Montoya has done as the director of the Office of Intergovernmental Affairs.

When I asked Regina to join my administration, I knew she was sacrificing a great deal to leave a successful legal career and her family in Dallas. When she informed me she was contemplating returning to Dallas because of the difficulty the commute has placed on her family, I was supportive of her decision to reunite her family.

I applaud her decision and thank her for the hard work and dedicated service she gave her country and wish her happiness and success in the future. And I look forward to calling on her for her insight in the future.[9]

OTHER TYPES OF SPECIALIZED PUBLIC PRESENTATIONS

Several types of public presentations do not fall under the category of ceremonial speeches. Although some of the following specialized presentations could be given in a ceremonial context, they frequently occur in a variety of other business, academic, and social situations.

Oral Performances of Literature

Another important form of public presentation is the **oral performance of literature**. This activity, also called the "oral interpretation of literature," refers to the presentation of some type of literature through the medium of oral performance. There are a variety of special occasions when an individual orally interprets or performs for an audience her or his own original poem or prose or someone else's material. For instance, students orally perform different types of literature in the classroom;

The oral performance of literature is a distinct form of public speaking that can be used in the classroom or in celebrating a special occasion or event. It can also be very effective when you are presenting personal narratives that help explore the lives of people different from ourselves.

poets introduce their material at poetry readings and other social and professional gatherings; speakers interpret literary material at weddings and funerals; and authors are commissioned to write and present poems at political inauguration ceremonies.

Maya Angelou, the well-known African American poet and Wake Forest University professor, presented her original inaugural poem *On the Pulse of Morning* at the inauguration of President Bill Clinton on January 20, 1993. Angelou's presentation illustrates how the oral performance of literature helps set the stage for celebrating a special occasion and for making a statement about the agenda of the individual being honored. Both the poem and its message made a powerful impact on Clinton's inauguration ceremony. Although it was the entire poem that produced this forceful effect, the last few lines of *On the Pulse of Morning* best illustrate its strength:

> *Here on the pulse of this new day*
> *You may have the grace to look up and out*

> *And into your sister's eyes,*
> *And into your brother's face,*
> *Your country,*
> *And say simply*
> *With hope—*
> *Good morning.*[10]

Although the nature of the material being presented dictates in part the organization and design of the oral performance of literature, certain rules govern this activity in all situations. For example, the length of the presentation depends on the length of the material; however, (again!) brevity and succinctness are important. In terms of other, more generic rules, introductions to these presentations should include the title of the selection, the author's name, and the overall theme of the written work. As the person presenting the material, you should set the appropriate tone by explaining any background material relevant to the characters and setting. The body of the presentation (the actual literature) should be consistent with the theme of the occasion and be appropriate for your particular audience.

When you deliver your oral performance of the literature, you need to be highly expressive both verbally and nonverbally. Use your face, your voice, and your body to show emotion. Rehearse your presentation often enough to commit most of it to memory. How you physically handle the manuscript during your presentation is important, too. Treat the manuscript as a prop, and use it to remind the audience that the presentation is a literary performance. In your conclusion, be sure to leave your audience with a memorable or gee-whiz experience. Practice being dramatic and emotive. (For more on the oral performance of literature, see the box "Interview with a Professional: Steve Mortenson.")

Entertaining Speeches

Sometimes an occasion will call for a speech that will entertain an audience. **Entertaining speeches** attempt to get an audience to enjoy an interesting presentation in a relaxing, lighthearted, and enjoyable atmosphere—often through the creative use of humor. Although speeches to entertain frequently are called "after-dinner speeches," they can occur around any meal and at any time of day—at breakfast meetings, luncheons, dinners, or any get-together where people can sit back and enjoy a lively, cheerful presentation. Speeches to entertain are more like persuasive and informative speeches in the completeness of organization and design than most special occasion speeches. They also normally run longer than other specialized

SPEAKING OUT

Interview with a Professional

Steve Mortenson

Steve Mortenson, 28, is a doctoral candidate in the department of communication at Purdue University. He also writes and orally performs literature to groups around the country.

How would you describe the place of the oral performance of literature in the speech communication discipline?

I believe we can use the performance of literature to explore the experiences and lives of people different from ourselves. I have seen the performance of narratives taken from survivors of incest that threw a whole new light on the topic for me. I have also seen personal narratives performed from Alcoholics Anonymous that illuminated the experiences of being an addict. I have heard and performed the literature of people from different co-cultures and found that such performances can serve to give a voice to the different perspectives that people possess. Performance can be a very powerful medium for conveying the perspective and experiences of others.

How can this kind of speaking influence someone's overall effectiveness as a public speaker?

I feel that an oral performance is an ideal exercise for improving delivery in public speaking. Oral performance emphasizes the awareness of voice, emotion, gesture, movement, and facial expression. I believe it helps students free up and bring out their emotions in a public speaking environment. After students do an oral performance, I generally see a marked improvement in their delivery skills.

How should someone go about selecting material for an oral performance?

I would try to find literature that has a voice, something active and dynamic as opposed to instructive and abstract. I always try to find pieces that move me emotionally. Literature that builds emotion in us upon reading it will be better suited to our performance. I also try to stay away from things with more than two characters— it is just too difficult to differentiate among too many voices and personas. Finally, I look for language that conveys imagery. The action of a performance occurs in the heads of the audience members. They imagine what the performer speaks. With this in mind, I always look for (or attempt to write) literature that paints a picture inside the minds of the audience.

What would you say to a student who asked for advice on preparing and presenting this specialized type of public presentation?

To me, performance is about recalling your emotions and experiences and "fleshing" the written words with them. Consequently, I would ask the student, "What do you sound like, what do you do when you feel the emotions you think are in this piece of literature?" Try doing it this way: First, identify what the piece is about, and identify the specific words and phrases that best convey that meaning to you personally. Next, explore the emotional underpinnings of the piece so that you have an idea what the piece feels like. And then, explore your own emotional responses and incorporate them into the piece.

Speakers who give presentations on a regular basis will be called on to answer questions from members of the audience. How you respond to a question from a single audience member can influence the impression you have on an entire audience. President Bill Clinton must think carefully about his answers before he responds to questions. At all times, he must keep his cool in order to be perceived as credible.

speeches, ranging from six to eight minutes or more, given the demands of the particular social event.

If you are asked to give a speech to entertain, you can choose practically any topic that is suitable for your particular audience, the setting, and the occasion; virtually all speech topics can be developed into an entertaining presentation. Your choice of humor must be based on a thorough understanding of your audience members and their co-cultural affiliations; humor can just as easily offend as entertain. Make your humor relevant to the topic and material being presented. Rather than rely on stale jokes and worn-out clichés, use fresh, original material. Effective speeches to entertain often contain witty illustrations, humorous anecdotes, and recollections of unique and amusing experiences.

More than any other speech type, speeches to entertain rely heavily on how something is said and thus require a great deal of practice to be delivered effectively. Your style of delivery should be animated and dramatic to keep your audience keenly attuned to what you have to say. Plan exactly how you want to say your lines and how you want to look. Don't assume that your lines must be funny simply because you think they are; instead, strategically plan your delivery so that your audience will find your material entertaining. Rehearse your delivery thoroughly, and make every effort to appear affable, genial, and good-natured.

Finally, plan to use pause time. Your entertaining speech should result in periodic laughter from your audience; when they laugh, wait before delivering your next line. When they clap to show their appreciation, wait again. If you rush ahead, the audience will learn not to laugh so loudly or clap too long so they don't miss anything.

Question-and-Answer Sessions

Speakers often are asked to participate in question-and-answer sessions immediately following their presentations. Audience members typically want to raise questions about issues discussed during the presentation or about the speaker more directly. The question-and-answer session is a format of public presentation that demands special consideration. On the surface, asking and answering questions seems simple and harmless enough. Yet many speakers fail to handle questions effectively by becoming defensive, evasive, apprehensive, long-winded, or even hostile. How a speaker responds to questions can affect how audience members finalize their impression of the speaker and the overall presentation. For these important reasons, answering questions from an audience can be tricky! Take a few minutes to complete the questionnaire in the box "Responding to Questions: How Defensive Are You?" to assess your likely reaction to questions from an audience.

As with all of the stages of the public speaking process, you should be as strategic as possible when answering questions from an audience. Most importantly, you should always be careful about what you say (and, thus, are held accountable for). Once you

Responding to Questions: How Defensive Are You?

Instructions

The following statements reflect how various speakers feel about responding to questions or comments from an audience. Enter the appropriate number in the space provided to indicate the extent to which each of these statements applies to you when speaking before a large group: (5) strongly agree, (4) agree, (3) are neutral (undecided), (2) disagree, or (1) strongly disagree.

—— 1. For the most part, I appreciate comments from the audience.

—— 2. It makes me nervous to have to handle questions from the audience.

—— 3. I don't like it when someone from the audience asks me a probing question about something I said.

—— 4. It's easy for me to remain pleasant when people from the audience ask me questions about my speech.

—— 5. I like it when individuals from the audience ask me difficult or challenging questions.

—— 6. I would rather not have to answer any questions or deal with any comments from the audience at all.

—— 7. I get visibly rattled or upset when someone from the audience asks me a loaded or difficult question.

—— 8. When someone from the audience tries to make me look bad, I find it a real problem to handle.

—— 9. I often become confused and tongue-tied when responding to questions from the audience.

—— 10. It doesn't bother me to tell the audience that I don't happen to know the answer to a particular question.

—— 11. I like it when audience members contribute to my speech by asking questions or making comments.

—— 12. When members of my audience don't ask questions, I worry that they got bored and quit listening.

—— 13. Questions or comments from the audience make me defensive.

—— 14. I enjoy the challenge of facing questions from the audience.

—— 15. I encourage members of my audience to ask questions or give feedback.

—— 16. No matter what kind of question someone from the audience asks, I remain polite and considerate toward the questioner.

—— 17. If I don't happen to have all the facts, I have trouble admitting to the audience that I just don't know the answer.

—— 18. I look forward to questions from the audience.

—— 19. If possible, I try to avoid follow-up question-and-answer sessions with the audience.

—— 20. In my opinion, when someone from the audience tries to intentionally make me look bad, she or he deserves a rude response.

Calculating Your Score

1. Add together your responses to items 1, 4, 5, 10, 11, 12, 14, 15, 16, and 18 = ——

2. Add together your responses to items 2, 3, 6, 7, 8, 9, 13, 17, 19, and 20 = ——

3. Complete the following formula:

$$60 - \text{total from step 1} = \text{——}$$

$$+ \text{total from step 2} = \text{——}$$

Your total speaker defensiveness score = ——

Interpreting Your Score

The possible scores range from 20 to 100. (If your own score does not fall within that range, you have made a computational error.) The median score for this test is 60. Higher scores reflect greater speaker defensiveness. If you scored above 70 (or even above the median of 60), you are considered highly defensive in your role as a public speaker. Your tendency is to avoid questions from the audience and to become nervous and upset when asked difficult questions. You may even evade or dodge questions that you are unable to answer. For highly defensive speakers, this chapter presents seven well-proven rules that will help you with your approach. Importantly, you do not want to come across as being defensive when answering questions from the audience. If you do become defensive, you risk losing any credibility and goodwill that you may have gained during your presentation.

If you scored low in speaker defensiveness (below 50 or the median of 60), you aren't as likely to experience the same kinds of problems as highly defensive speakers. Nondefensive or low-defensive speakers are able to easily and openly respond to questions from the audience. They remain pleasant and polite—even when the questioner appears to have a hidden agenda, like trying to make

Continued

Responding to Questions: How Defensive Are You? *(Continued)*

the speaker look bad. When nondefensive speakers are asked a loaded or negatively worded question, they rephrase the question in more positive or neutral terms before attempting to answer it. If you are a nondefensive speaker, you are likely to find question-and-answer sessions enjoyable and stimulating and to approach them as opportunities to heighten your credibility and strengthen your position on the topic of your presentation.

If you are more moderately defensive (a score between 50 and 70), you tend to be more situational in how you respond to questions from the audience. Sometimes you may have more difficulty handling an audience than at other times; moreover, you may find it easier to respond to some audience members than to others. Depending on how much you know about the topic, you may feel more or less comfortable with questions from the audience. Regardless of the situation or topic, however, you should practice the seven rules given in this chapter.

---

say it, you can't take it back. Following from this principle, there are seven time-proven rules to help you strategically deal with even the most difficult question-and-answer session:

1. *Solicit questions from all sections of your audience.* Each audience member wants to believe that he or she has an equal opportunity to ask questions. Be sure to respond to questions originating from all segments of the audience to create the impression that every questioner has equal status.

2. *Listen carefully to each question before responding.* Many a speaker has fallen prey to what appeared on the surface to be a safe question to answer. There really aren't any totally safe questions—only safe answers! To avoid the pitfalls of a question with a hidden agenda, listen actively and critically to what an audience member is asking before responding to any question.

3. *Repeat aloud all positive questions, and when possible, rephrase any negative or loaded questions.* It is always safest to restate a question before answering it. In the case of an apparently positive question, repeating it back to the questioner (1) gives you an opportunity to make sure you really understand the question before responding and (2) compliments the questioner in front of the rest of the audience. Audiences like to be recognized and reinforced by the speaker.

In the case of a negative or a loaded question, paraphrasing (and thus clarifying) the question aloud gives you the opportunity to recast it in a more positive form before responding. Consider the following loaded question: "Do you believe abortion is the murdering of helpless unborn children?" By paraphrasing the question in a more neutral or positive way ("If you are asking me what policy I would endorse about legalized abortions . . ."), you could potentially answer the question without offending either the obviously pro-life questioner or others who may be pro-choice on the issue. Rewording negative or loaded questions is the first strategic step toward minimizing an adverse reaction to your answer.

4. *When responding to negative or loaded questions, make eye contact with the general audience rather than the questioner.* Audience members who ask loaded or negative questions often do it intentionally to make a speaker look bad. Even when a speaker rephrases a loaded question in a more positive form, the questioner might try other ways to hurt the speaker's credibility. By avoiding direct eye contact with a questioner and looking at the entire audience, you can diffuse other intentional, person-specific efforts to make you look bad. Not being able to make direct eye contact with you will make it difficult for the questioner to gain the floor.

5. *Always admit when you do not know an answer.* Audiences are smart. They can easily distinguish a direct, honest answer from an evasive answer. Believable answers illustrate clearly that a speaker knows the topic thoroughly. Such answers are brief and to the point and, where appropriate, include relevant facts or examples to support what is said. If you cannot credibly answer a particular question, it is better (and much safer) to say so. Because most audiences interpret such honesty as a strength rather than a weakness, they are likely to respond favorably.

6. *Give answers, not lengthy sermons or lectures.* Keep your answers brief and to the point. Do not extend or overstate an answer.

7. *Be pleasant and polite at all times.* No matter how rattled, angry, irritated, or impatient you get, keep your cool. When you maintain composure under tense or stressful circumstances, audiences will perceive you to be credible and believable.

SPEAKING IN GROUPS

Although this is primarily a how-to book about getting up in front of an audience to make an effective presentation, you need to consider briefly those public speaking occasions that occur when you are part of a small group. Speaking as a member of a small group is different in some respects from speaking as an individual. In the broadest sense, **small group discussions** involve three to eight people who engage in face-to-face interaction around some common purpose or objective. Small groups sometimes exceed eight people; however, the number should be determined by a group's ability to allow for effective interaction among its members. Because of their membership in a group, participants normally experience a sense of belonging, which alters in some fashion the way they communicate. Group members also have and consciously sense some mutual influence on how they communicate both as individuals and as participants.

Working as a member of a small group has inherent advantages and disadvantages. The more obvious disadvantage is the pressure to conform to the norms of the group. All too often, one member may dominate the group interaction and, thus, cause other participants to rely too much on her or his attitudes and beliefs. If that member lacks essential expertise, he or she can be an obstacle to reaching the most effective solution to a problem. Another disadvantage is that groups typically take a lot more time than a single person to deal with certain topics or tasks.

Even with their inherent disadvantages, small groups can be very effective in problem-solving situations. The most obvious advantage of working in groups is that the members can provide for a greater exchange of knowledge and information about a topic than one person working independently. The more complex the task, the more input is needed. For the same reason, groups are typically more creative in solving problems; with group interaction, members generate more and better solutions and learn from one another. Correspondingly, satisfaction when working on a task tends to be greater for groups than for individuals working on the same task alone.

Group Presentation Formats

You will probably be involved in group work frequently throughout your academic, social, and professional life. As part of your group membership, you may have to speak publicly before an audience. Four well-used formats govern the type of public speaking that can occur in your group.

Public Discussions A **public discussion** involves a predesignated group of individuals interacting and exchanging ideas about a particular topic while seated in front of an audience. Although the members of the audience are not allowed to take part in the group discussion, they gain information about the topic by observing and listening to the group interact among themselves. Public discussions are appropriate for city, county, and state planning meetings, which are open for public view but not for public participation. They also occur at condominium association meetings, at which elected officers openly discuss issues while residents observe.

Symposiums A **symposium** is a public presentation in which a series of short, preplanned (and thoroughly practiced) speeches about some topic are delivered to an audience. Each member of the group presents a separate speech; each speech is likely to represent a slightly different perspective on the overriding topic of the symposium. Little (if any) interaction occurs among the members of this type of group presentation. Symposiums are intended to give group members a high degree of autonomy while offering audiences the maximum diversity of thought on a particular topic. The symposium format is common at academic, business, and professional meetings and conferences, where experts are brought together in front of an interested audience to present their research and thinking on a particular topic.

Forums A **forum** is a public presentation in which audience members advance questions to the entire group; individual group members (often authorities on the topic) then provide answers. Forums, which are typically much less structured than other forms of group presentations, often take place after the completion of either a public discussion or a symposium. That is, when the public discussion or symposium portion of a meeting is completed, the structure changes to a forum format, during which the audience is invited to ask questions and to participate in follow-up conversations. Forums are appropriate for and can occur at virtually all types of public meetings.

Panel Discussions

A panel discussion involves an organized and moderated group presentation to an audience. These discussions differ from public discussions and symposiums in that a designated moderator or chairperson formally leads the discussion. In panel discussions, the moderator first organizes and then facilitates or verbally manages the members of the group to inform the audience about a particular problem or topic; no preplanned speeches are given. Much like all good leaders, moderators are crucially important to panel discussions. They organize work, help get tasks accomplished, and help maintain the social and task climates throughout the group presentation. Panel discussions can occur in the classroom and at all types of public and professional meetings in which issues and topics are being debated. Like public discussions and symposiums, panel discussions often open up into forums for audience participation.

Guidelines for Group Participation

Whatever the format—public discussion, symposium, forum, or panel discussion—effective group participants share several characteristics. When you participate in a group, follow these guidelines:

1. Be prepared.
2. Don't recommend solutions before adequately analyzing the problem.
3. Examine available evidence adequately.
4. Help the chairperson summarize the group's progress.
5. Listen and respond courteously to others.
6. When necessary, help to manage conflict in the group.

Whether a presentation is being delivered by an individual standing alone before an audience or within the context of a group, the basics of speech preparation remain the same. The presenter needs to formulate a clear objective, identify the key points to be covered, research and organize the points and information into an outline, choose an appropriate method of delivery, weigh the pros and cons of using visual aids, and practice the presentation. The fact that the speaker is a part of a group doesn't significantly alter what needs to be considered during preparation. A few minor issues need to be considered, however. For example, when speaking in a group, presenters often deliver their message seated around a table. Before actually giving the speech, the speaker should practice being seated at a table while presenting. Furthermore, with more than one presenter in the group, time becomes more of an issue. Thus, the presenter needs to manage his or her time allocation carefully. Moreover, trying to use visual aids within a group can be difficult. Presenters who choose to employ visual aids during their speech must consider the presence of other members of the group in their preparation.

The bottom line on successfully adapting a public presentation to the group context: Consider carefully those contingencies that affect the presentation speeches within a group and practice the speech so as to adapt to those unique contextual demands.

CHAPTER REVIEW

- On many occasions, some type of specialized presentation is needed. Speeches associated with special occasions play major roles in your life and in society more generally.

- The most common types of presentations for special occasions are speeches of introduction, welcome, and nomination, award speeches (both presenting and accepting an award), tributes (including eulogies and toasts), commencement speeches, dedications, and farewells.

- There are a number of rules governing specialized presentations. Brevity is the most universal requirement of virtually all specialized speeches.

- A speech to entertain is another type of specialized public presentation. The topic and humor should be appropriate for the audience and setting, and the delivery must be well planned and rehearsed to be effective.

- Members of an audience typically expect to ask questions at the conclusion of a presentation. How a speaker responds to questions can determine how audience members finalize their impression of the speaker and the overall presentation.
- Speaking as a member of a small group is different in some respects from speaking as an individual.

Group participants normally experience a sense of belonging because of their membership, which alters in some fashion the way they communicate. They also sense some mutual influence on how they communicate both as individuals and a participants.

- The four identifiable formats for making group presentations to audiences are public discussions, symposiums, forums, and panels.

QUESTIONS FOR CRITICAL THINKING & REVIEW

1. Why do you suppose it is so difficult for people to accept an award? What public speaking advice might you give someone who is about to accept an award?

2. As a society, we seem to be predisposed to give a speech to celebrate a lot of different occasions. Why? How do think this type of specialized speaking emerged and, ultimately, became a tradition?

3. Why do some speakers orally perform literature that was written to be read, not spoken aloud?

How do you think an oral performance of literature changes the nature of the medium?

4. Why do some speakers find it so hard to handle questions from the audience? Why are questions from the audience often interpreted as challenges or attacks? What can you do as a speaker and audience member to improve question-and-answer sessions?

NOTES

1. Detz, J. (1992). *How to write and give a speech* (p. 92). New York: St. Martin's Press.
2. Wilson, P. (1991, November 4). Introductory remarks: Reagan library, Yorba Linda, CA. Unpublished speech.
3. Bellafante, G. (1994, March 14). People. *Time*, 109.
4. Lustig, B. (1994, March 21). *The 66th Annual Academy Awards*. Los Angeles: American Broadcasting Company.
5. Spencer, E. (1998, March 11). A tribute to Princess Diana. Online. Available: http://rampage.ml.org/users/jka/diana/earlspeech.html.
6. Kissinger, H. A. (1994, April 28). Excerpts from eulogies: "A great man," yet "one of us." *Los Angeles Times* (Orange County ed.), p. A18.
7. Cosby, B. (1997). Commencement address, University of Pennsylvania. Online. Available: http://www.upenn.edu/almanac/v43/n35/commence.html.
8. Wilson, 1991.
9. Clinton, W. J. (1993, August 7). Statement on White House staff changes. *Weekly Compilation of Presidential Documents, 29*, 1591.
10. Angelou, M. (1993). *On the pulse of morning*. New York: Random House.

Appendix

SAMPLE SPEECHES

These three sample speeches were presented by public speaking students at Santa Barbara City College. The first two speeches are informative; the third is persuasive. You can use these speeches for analysis and discussion and as a source of ideas for your own classroom presentations.

THE POWER OF NONVERBAL COMMUNICATION

Bonnie Arnold

How many times have you just looked at someone, and based on what you see, decided you'd like to date that person? Or *not* date that person? Do you size up your professors on the first day of class and decide if they are cool, strange, approachable, or unapproachable—just based on what they're wearing or what their mannerisms are? And for those of you who may be going out on job interviews, are you able to walk into a company, and based on what and whom you see *before you even meet* your interviewer, decide what kind of working environment it would be? The answer for many of you will be "yes," because that guy or woman in the bar, your professors, and all the people working for that company you interviewed for all give off nonverbal cues. Nonverbal communication is an important aspect of how we present ourselves: Do you know that *more* meaning is conveyed via nonverbal cues than verbal ones? Prepare to learn more about this fascinating, important topic—because through nonverbal communication, we send powerful messages about ourselves without even saying a word.

Just as we judge people based on how they look, other people are doing the same thing to us. The person at the bar, the professor, and the job interviewer were sizing up, making snap judgments about you—based on the nonverbal communication signals you were sending. Today, I'd like to talk about types of nonverbal cues which communicate volumes about us. I'd also like to talk about how we can better manage the impressions we send off by our nonverbal behavior, and finally, consider the nonverbal behavior that works best in different situations—like the dating scene, the classroom, and at work—so we can all become more successful in those situations.

First, what are the nonverbal cues that people recognize when communicating with potential friends, dates, and colleagues? You've heard that expression, "Beauty is in the eye of the beholder"? Well, believe it or not, our beauty, as others see it, is a dimension of our nonverbal communication.

An attractive person is one whom we perceive as a potential associate: someone we'd like to spend time with. According to the text *Fundamentals of Human Communication*, there are three types of attractiveness. When we think of someone as *physically* attractive, we perceive them as someone we'd like to date, or become intimately involved with. The second type, *social* attraction, occurs when we decide a person is someone we'd like to be friends with. They are funny, seem to have things in common with us, or have things to offer us socially. People to whom we relate on a *task* basis are referred to as "task attractive." These "task-attractive" people are ones we'd like to work with. That guy in your history class who tapes the lectures, takes copious notes, and visits the teacher often probably sends messages nonverbally to you that say "This guy would be a good partner for a group project!" How attractive we make ourselves in each setting—a social setting (with the goal of finding a date or just a friend), or a task setting—will be one of the deciding factors of whether we'll be successful.

How do we communicate our attractiveness? (You might say, well, some people are just born ugly. I'd like to suggest to you one way even "marginally attractive" people can create more attractive impressions.) One way we can strategically "flaunt" our approachability and attractiveness is by selecting appropriate clothing. In a study of how an individual's style of dress is related to their success in different settings, Hendricks and her colleagues found that what we wear greatly influences what others think of us. For example, conforming to fads and trends reflects an individual's desire to be accepted and liked. In another study, a group of women were asked to describe the most popular and attractive women they knew, and they listed clothing more often to describe these popularity princesses.

Elsewhere, research on nonverbal communication tells us that people who are typically conservative and traditional in their style of dress are viewed as more restrained, submissive, and even boring. People who wear brightly colored clothing, on the other hand, are frequently viewed by others as sophisticated, fun, attractive, and according to one study, *really* fun—immoral.

We need to look at the situation we're in, and what type of attraction signals we're trying to send (physical, social, or task) and wear the appropriate clothing. For example, conservative suits are appropriate for job interviews, while jeans would be off limits. On the other hand, a formal dress wouldn't be right for a first date—movies and a sandwich.

You may think that worrying about this type of nonverbal communication seems very shallow, that you know lots of very extroverted people who wear dark, boring clothes—but beware overlooking it. I interviewed two of my friends regarding what they thought about attractiveness, and here's what they said.

> (Male) "I tend to judge a book by its cover and person by his or her looks. When I see someone is unattractive, I tend to lose interest in wanting to meet them. Sometimes I even try to avoid them. It seems like ugly people who are sloppy, dirty, or dressed inappropriately don't care what others think of them. I wonder sometimes how they think they are going to get by in the world."

> (Female) "The way a person looks says a lot about them. I find myself being more interested in people (especially guys) I think are attractive. They seem more sure of themselves and confident. They don't get as nervous around other people because they don't have to be self-conscious about their looks. Since they have more experience around lots of other people, they know how to act. They're a lot smoother, and I'm never embarrassed to be around them."

So, the point of all this is that we must all carefully monitor how we dress and how we look in order to give off the right nonverbal cues. Some specific strategies: (1) Be clean and neat, (2) be appropriate for the setting, (3) learn how to manipulate your appearance in order to be seen by a variety of people in a positive way. Tom Masson once said, "'Be yourself' is the worst advice you can give some people."

A second important nonverbal cue which lends to others' impressions of us is our *body movements and facial expressions*. I often see tall women—whom I envy greatly given my short stature—walking or sitting with their shoulders slumped or in unflattering flat shoes, simply to make themselves appear shorter. What this tells me is that they lack self-confidence! Other people never seem to smile or make eye contact when they're talking. These people seem unfriendly, avoidant, or unwilling to communicate. Do you have teachers who never leave their lectern? Or who never come close to their students? They seem *connected* to their chalkboard and the front of the room.

Body posture, facial expression, and movement within a space is referred to as *kinesics*. Once again, in order to make the most favorable impression on others, we need to be tuned in to our level of eye contact with them, our relative positioning to them, and our body posture. Poor posture looks sloppy and illustrates low self-confidence, and standing or sitting far away from a person while failing to smile or look at them tells them "this person is avoiding me, doesn't like me, or is socially inadroit."

Albert Mehrabian investigated the impressions others form of us based on our posture, movement, and facial expression. He discovered that people make judgments about how much we like them, how powerful we are, and how responsive we may be, based on our body language. We can show someone that we like them by leaning forward, facing them, getting physically closer to them, touching them appropriately, appearing relaxed, and by using a lot of eye contact. Victor Borge said, "A smile is the shortest distance between two people," and the research shows that smiling and other such behaviors definitely let others know we like them.

A final important nonverbal communication behavior to monitor is our use of personal space. Maintain appropriate space at all time. Intimate distance includes touch to about 18 inches away. Usually done in private, intimate distance signals that something more is going on than just a social conversation. Personal space includes eighteen inches to about four feet, and encourages intimate, personal conversation. We can appropriately use personal distance when telling someone a secret, when we need to talk quietly, or at crowded parties or bars. Social distance is used by standing four to twelve feet from our communication partner. Social distance is usually used by people doing business. Finally, public space exceeds twelve feet.

Different people have different expectations about how nonverbally close others should be—and if we violate those expectations, they will view us in a negative light! So how are we supposed to know what others' expectations are? What is appropriate depends on the situation, the cultural background of both people, and their size and gender. For instance, women tend to be more comfortable than men communicating at a close distance. Also, we tend to stand closer to smaller people—we may be less threatened or intimidated. Furthermore, we can often take our cues regarding nonverbal space from others—if they appear open and close to us, they will probably appreciate our efforts to be open and close as well.

The nonverbal messages we send truly are powerful—and critical predictors of whether we'll be liked, accepted, and successful. As children, sometimes we would say inappropriate things and everyone would think it was really cute or funny—and as we grew up, we learned how to monitor what we said, what secrets we revealed because we knew that after we reached a certain age, people wouldn't view us as cute or funny anymore. Instead, they'd view us as just weird. I hope I've demonstrated to you today the need for learning to monitor our nonverbal communication in the same way. Because in the real world, interviewers and bosses don't look favorably on people who don't dress appropriately. Potential friends or significant others are not often attracted to someone who doesn't smile, or look at them when they speak. These same people take violations of personal space very seriously—even as grounds for not liking a person. And professors probably don't like students who don't show, at least nonverbally, if not verbally, some interest or liking for their class. So start with a smile, take a look in the mirror, stand up straight, and be confident—because you've mastered the basics of making a good nonverbal impression.

A BEGINNER'S GUIDE TO APPRECIATING AND SERVING WINE

Sarah Copeland

Do you know the difference between a "Cabernet" and a "Merlot"? Do you know the best glass for tasting white wine—and that a different shaped glass is the right one for red wine? Do you know how to detect a wine's bouquet? Or in your mind, is bouquet nothing more than a flower arrangement? And Cabernet, a fancy French word for "cabinet"? If you answered "no" to the first three questions, and "yes" to the last two, then allow me to introduce you to the world of wine!

In this informative speech, I would like to explain some of the different types of grapes that are used to make the wines that we are used to drinking or hearing about on a regular basis, and review what foods are most often served with certain wines. Then I will walk you through the serving of wine so that you can do so without hesitation at your next dinner party or social gathering.

The names of most wines refer to the grapes used to make them. Interestingly, the grape color is not what determines the color of the wine; a particular process called maceration is what accounts for the difference in color. Red wines are fermented with their skins, and sometimes stems, and white wines are not. Some popular white wines include Chardonnay, Sauvignon Blanc, Riesling, Chenin Blanc, and Gewurztraminer. The most common, Chardonnay, is a "dry" white wine that is not a favorite with those who prefer a sweeter drink. The Chardonnay grape is most commonly produced in France, California, Australia, and New Zealand. California Chardonnay grapes, according to wine expert Michael Schuster, have improved a great deal in the last twenty years. Chenin and Sauvignon Blanc can both be moderately dry white wines, and experts note that the highest quality grapes of these varieties are grown in France. Riesling and Gewurztraminer are sweeter, lighter white wines than Chardonnay and Sauvignon Blanc, but the best "Gevertzes" are dry and crisp. Most commonly, white wines are served with "white foods" like poultry, pork, or seafood. Riesling and Gewurztraminer are better suited for spicy foods due to their semi-sweet flavor; the others are more mellow.

The most popular varieties of red wine include Cabernet Sauvignon, Merlot, and Syrah. According to *The Beginner's Guide to Understanding Wine*, Cabernet is the "Chanel No. 5 of red wine; you probably know the name even if you don't know the product." The Cabernet grape is also used to produce claret and Bordeaux blends. Cabernet grapes are grown in a number of countries, including France, northeast Italy, eastern Europe, South America, and South Africa. California produces a number of "cabs," as well. Cabernet can be described as a hearty wine, very flavorful, and somewhat heavy for some wine drinkers who prefer the lighter, fruitier white wines.

A second type of red wine, Merlot, is produced from grapes produced primarily in the Bordeaux region of France. The taste of a Merlot is smoother, softer, and less "peppery" than a Cabernet Sauvignon. All of the red wines are usually enjoyed with red meat, such as steak or filet mignon.

How should you serve wine so as not to be embarrassed?! You can do several things that will make you seem like a wine "aficionado" even if, before this experience, you thought Merlot (pronounced "merlow") was pronounced "Mer-lot," as a friend of mine's beer-loving father recently gaffed. First, remember which wines are best suited to which types of food. When serving different varieties of wine with a multicourse meal, remember the following order: dry wines before sweet ones, white before red, and light before heavy. However, wine experts agree that wine lovers should exercise personal preference here and not be bound by rules. For first-timers, though, try the guidelines I've offered. When serving multiple types of wine, offer guests water or wine biscuits (available in most grocery stores) to "cleanse their palettes" between courses.

Temperature is another important thing to observe when serving wine to guests. White wine tastes best quite cold, while red is served at room temperature. Do not serve white wine over ice; ice will dilute the flavors of the wine. If you've forgotten to chill your white wine, a few minutes in the freezer will do the trick (but don't forget the bottle there!).

Finally, if you really feel like showing your guests that you know what you are doing, invest in at least two shapes of wine glasses. Wide, very rounded goblets are best for red wines, while narrower, taller glasses (described as "tulip" shaped) should be used for white. Many wine lovers report that wine tastes "better" in heavy (expensive!) glass or crystal.

People who love wine describe it as one of life's greatest pleasures. No one should be intimidated by the science of wine making and tasting so that you fail to experiment with different varieties of wine. The next time you have friends in for dinner or have a party, follow some of the guidelines I've presented today, and taste away until you find a repertoire of wines that you enjoy. Then you, too, can discover one of life's greatest pleasures—and no longer confuse the *Cabernet* with the *cabinet*!!

Oppose Private School Vouchers

Patricia Anderson

Did you know that there are numerous programs that provide FREE private education to hundreds of thousands of schoolchildren in the United States? And did you know that the funds to provide that FREE education, if the U.S. Congress decides to approve the plan, will come from YOUR pockets? When was the last time you looked at the stub of your paycheck and noticed the astronomical federal and state taxes taken from your check? That money may soon be funding other people's educations—when you are most likely struggling to pay for your own!!

There is a movement afoot to allow parents' tax money—or tax credits—to choose between public and private schools for their children. These are most often referred to as "private school vouchers." Ostensibly, supporters say that these vouchers would allow low-income, inner-city children to attend private schools which are supposedly better than the available public education. However, experts agree that the plan for vouchers is flawed and will damage our education system more than help it.

As more and more students leave public schools to attend private ones, the important public education infrastructure that this country was built upon will fall apart. In a recent speech at the National Press Club in Washington, D.C., U.S. Secretary of Education Richard Riley was adamant in his and President Clinton's belief that tax dollars should be used to renovate and build new public schools rather than abandon the public system. The secretary said that the use of private school vouchers "undermines the American commitment to the 'common' school."

Furthermore, vouchers, which supporters claim would "empower" poor families, may only make their situation worse. Vouchers are only designed to pay for about half of private school tuition. Vouchers would be made available to both poor and rich families. As a result, the wealthy, who can afford to pay the other half, will benefit the most!! Low- and middle-income families with a lot of children won't be able to afford the difference between the tuition and the voucher amount. Disadvantaged children, under the voucher program, will remain disadvantaged.

Under the *$7 million* plan, the constitutional line separating church and state would be obliterated. Vouchers would support private religious schools. According to Americans United for Separation of Church and State, religious-oriented schools account for 85 percent of the total private school enrollment in the United States. These schools base their curriculum in religious doctrine, and indoctrinate their students in strict, narrow views on controversial subjects such as abortion, creationism, and the role of women in society. *The U.S. Constitution prohibits the government from subsidizing religious education.* Americans voluntarily support a wide variety of religious institutions and schools. They should not be forced to pay taxes for schools that teach religious views they disagree with! This flies in the face of the law of the land, the U.S. Constitution.

Voters should not support the move toward private school vouchers. Only by directing our attention and tax dollars to the public education system will we be able to improve it; finding ways to get kids out of public schools is only like putting a band-aid on a shotgun wound—and it will create a new wound that may be worse. The important constitutional provision for separation of church and state will be trounced on, public schools will become more decrepit, and the large number of kids who have to remain in public schools will suffer even more than they presently do.

You may argue that as things are now, private schools provide a better education than public ones and that the trend will only continue if vouchers are okayed. Yet the notion that private schools far outrank public schools is a myth! According to *Money* magazine, overall, private schools rank no better than comparable public schools. The best private schools are no better than the best public schools, and the average private school is no better than the average public school. Also, recent studies, according to *Money*, show that participation in public/private school choice programs does not result in significant educational gains for kids.

If tax dollars were spent to improve our public education system, focusing on the *worst* public schools first, rather than abandoning our sacred public school system, we would see the benefits. Reading and math would improve. The skills of America's public school teachers would improve, computers would be in every classroom, old schools would be renovated and new schools with "smart" classrooms built. As Secretary Riley said in his speech, if vouchers are rejected and the focus put back on public schools, "diplomas will mean something again and the next ten years will be the golden era of American education."

Write to your representatives, to Congress, and to your state legislators. Encourage them not to support the voucher plan. If a ballot initiative comes up on this issue, vote NO and encourage your friends to do the same. Send a message that you believe in public education and separation of church and state. Let others know that the plan for private school vouchers is flawed, and do not let yourselves be persuaded otherwise!!

GLOSSARY

abbreviated (short-phrase) outline An outline containing all elements of a speech written as short phrases or key words. An abbreviated outline is used during the final stages of speech preparation and as speaker notes during the actual presentation.

accent A distinctive and characteristic manner of pronunciation usually determined by the regional or cultural background of the speaker or the phonetic patterns of the speaker's native language.

acronym A word formed from the first letters of each word of a name or phrase.

active listening Listening that is characterized by substantial effort on the part of the listener in attending to and comprehending the message.

active response A response by the audience—such as a show of hands, clapping, saying yes or no in unison—that is elicited by a request or suggestion from the speaker.

active voice A grammatical construction in which the subject performs the action described by the verb.

adaptation The process by which speakers and audience members modify their thinking and behavior independently of each other as they transmit and receive messages.

adaptors Unintentional hand, arm, leg, or other body movements used to reduce stress or relieve boredom.

animated style A rhetorical style in which the speaker relies on energy, enthusiasm, excitement, and expressive nonverbal behavior to communicate.

APA format A standardized method of recording references that is endorsed by the American Psychological Association (APA) and used in most research journals in the field of speech communication.

argument A line of reasoning offered in support or refutation of a position or viewpoint, consisting of one or more premises and conclusions.

assimilation The process of being absorbed into the culture of a population or adopting that culture voluntarily.

audience adaptation The process of adjusting one's speech topic, purpose, language, and communication style to avoid offending or alienating audience members and to increase the likelihood of achieving speech goals.

audience analysis The first step of speech preparation in which the speaker gathers information about his or her intended audience in order to learn everything about them that is relevant to a particular speech topic.

award acceptance speech A specialized speech in which a recipient graciously acknowledges an award and communicates appreciation for having her or his accomplishments recognized.

award presentation speech A speech that recognizes a notable accomplishment of an individual or group.

bar graph A graph that displays quantities or values of something as a series of bars that correspond in height or length to the quantities represented.

boomerang effect A phenomenon in which the outcome of a persuasive attempt is the opposite of what the speaker intended; in public speaking situations, it typically occurs when the speaker asks for too much change from the audience.

brainstorming A method of generating topic ideas in which individuals write down whatever occurs to them, no matter how strange or irrelevant it may seem. Ideas are not evaluated until the brainstorming session is complete.

briefing (or report) A type of informative speech designed to impart recently available information to an audience that already has a general understanding of the topic.

briefing chart A word chart used during a business presentation (briefing) that typically contains the main points and subpoints from the speech outline.

cause-and-effect organizational pattern A linear pattern based on a causal relationship between specific things or events.

ceremonial speech A specialized speech that acknowledges or celebrates the significance of a particular person, event, or occasion.

channels The means by which communicators transmit messages back and forth, including the physical senses and mass media.

chart A pictorial representation of the relationship between parts of a group or object or of the sequence of steps in a process.

chauvinism A boastful, exaggerated, and sometimes belligerent attitude about the superiority of one's own group to all other groups; excessive ethnocentrism.

chronological organizational pattern A linear pattern based on time or sequence.

claim A conclusion or generalization supported in an argument.

clichés Phrases or expressions that are so common and overused they have become trite.

closed questions Questions used in interviews that narrow the respondents' options by asking them to choose among a finite group of possible answers.

co-culture A specialized or unique culture that characterizes a particular group within a society; such groups are distinguished from each other by such factors as race or ethnicity, gender, age, and profession.

cognitive restructuring A method of treating apprehension in which a person's interpretations of anxiety-producing situations are brought to awareness, challenged, and changed. The person identifies negative self-statements and replaces them with positive ones.

collectivism A cultural pattern or orientation in which the group is emphasized and group interests are valued over individual interests.

commencement speech A presentation delivered at graduation exercises in which a speaker praises and congratulates individuals who have formally completed a prescribed set of educational requirements.

communication A process by which sources use verbal and nonverbal symbols to transmit messages to receivers in such a way that similar meanings are constructed and understood by all.

communication apprehension Fear or anxiety associated with either real or anticipated oral communication encounters.

competence (of a speaker) As a dimension of speaker credibility, a judgment on the part of audience members about the amount and validity of a speaker's knowledge of his or her subject.

composure (of a speaker) As a dimension of speaker credibility, a judgment on the part of audience members about how calm, confident, and in control a speaker is.

conclusion The position that is being supported by the premise(s) of an argument.

configural logic A way of organizing thoughts and ideas in which points are made in an indirect way and linkages and conclusions are implied.

connotative meanings Meanings associated with verbal and nonverbal symbols in addition to their literal meanings. Typically personal and subjective, connotative meanings are not necessarily shared by different individuals or co-cultural groups.

context The time, place, or occasion that frames the communication exchange. *See also* high context, low context.

contiguous audience The audience that sits or stands immediately before a speaker and engages in face-to-face communication with the speaker.

credibility (of a speaker) A judgment on the part of audience members about the believability of a speaker, based on their opinions of (1) the speaker's competence, trustworthiness, extroversion, composure, and sociability and (2) the truth of the speaker's message.

credible evidence Evidence that is consistent with other known facts or data and comes from a source known to be credible. Credibility is one of three criteria used to determine the appropriateness of a particular piece of evidence.

critical thinking The careful, deliberate process to determine whether a particular conclusion or claim should be accepted or rejected.

cue- or call-response patterns Patterns of response in which audience members, following a cue from the speaker, affirm what the speaker is saying with brief responses such as "right on," "okay," "uh-huh," or "amen."

cultural exclusion An attitude or behavior pattern based on the belief that one's own way of thinking and acting is the only right way and that those who think or act differently are wrong.

cultural inclusion An attitude or behavior pattern based on the belief that those who think or act differently from oneself deserve respect; a commitment to acknowledge, respect, and, when possible, adapt to those different from oneself.

cultural pluralism A social condition or policy in which members of diverse groups maintain their co-cultural affiliations and identities within the larger framework of a common, shared culture.

cultural relativity A viewpoint based on the belief that values and practices may legitimately differ from one culture to another and that there is no single, absolute standard for how people should think and act.

culture The customs, ideas, institutions, and patterns of behavior that people acquire as members of a society; a way of life.

decoding The transformation of verbal and nonverbal symbols into symbolic thoughts and ideas.

dedication speech A brief speech dedicating some new commodity (like a building, road, or ship) to an ideal or value (like improved community relations, good service, or community development).

deductive reasoning Inferring that a particular instance is true because it follows from a general proposition.

demographics The social categories into which people can be grouped, including gender, age, ethnic or cultural background, educational background, religious preference, marital and family status, place and type of residence, political affiliation, and profession.

demonstration   A type of informative speech designed to explain to an audience how to do a particular activity or use a specific object; a how-to speech.

demonstration board   A surface, frame, or device such as a chalkboard, porcelain board, felt board, or magnetic board that is used to display information.

dialect   A variety of language shared by a particular group or regional population based on a unique accent, vocabulary, and syntax.

disclaimers   Statements that speakers make to deny any responsibility for problems associated with their presentations.

dramatic style   A rhetorical style in which the speaker commands the audience's attention by building tension through stories; by using metaphors, exaggeration, and humor; and by magnifying and varying nonverbal gestures, body movements, eye contact, and vocal quality.

emblems   Nonverbal gestures that have direct verbal translations that are widely understood.

emotional appeals   Appeals designed to evoke anger, fear, hatred, pity, guilt, or other emotions from audience members.

encoding   The transformation of meanings into verbal and nonverbal symbols in order to transmit them.

entertaining speech   A speech whose primary purpose is to get an audience to enjoy an interesting presentation in a relaxing, lighthearted, and enjoyable atmosphere, often through the creative use of humor.

ESL   An acronym for "English as a second language."

ethical dilemma   A situation in which a person must choose between two or more alternative courses of action, each of which results in an ethical problem of some sort, usually involving a compromise or sacrifice of a key value.

ethical public speakers   Speakers who operate from a moral code or set of rules that guide their presentational behavior.

ethics   The study of moral values—decisions people make about right and wrong.

ethnicity   The shared identity of a social group whose members have a common national, linguistic, religious, or cultural background.

ethnocentrism   A belief that one's own group and way of life are superior to all others.

eulogy   A special type of tribute that praises or honors the accomplishments of an individual, usually someone who has recently died.

evidence   Facts or opinions used as supporting materials that are attested to or endorsed by someone other than the speaker.

expert   A person who, through education, training, or experience, has special knowledge about a particular subject.

extemporaneous delivery   A presentation mode in which the speaker gives a speech from a well-organized, well-rehearsed speech outline.

extroversion (of a speaker)   As a dimension of speaker credibility, a judgment on the part of audience members about how outgoing—that is, people-oriented, talkative, and gregarious—a speaker is.

farewell speech   A short speech in which (1) a person who is leaving ceremonializes his or her good-bye or (2) a speaker provides a brief ceremonial good-bye to a departing person.

fear appeals   Appeals designed to arouse fear or anxiety from audience members; a type of emotional appeal.

feedback   Verbal and nonverbal messages that receivers send back to a source that convey how the message is being received.

feminine style   A communication style, rooted in gender-role socialization, that emphasizes interpersonal connection and is characterized by sensitivity, responsiveness, and the sharing of personal experiences.

femininity   A cultural pattern or orientation that emphasizes a traditionally female gender orientation in which nurturance, cooperation, empathy, and collaboration are valued and gender roles are flexible.

fever graph   A line graph that illustrates how the numerical value of something changes over time.

filmstrip   A strip of 35-mm film containing a continuous series of images that can be projected onto a screen using a still-frame projector.

flip chart   A large tablet of paper that is hinged at the top and can be placed on an easel so that the sheets can be flipped over to present information sequentially.

focus group interview   A formal audience-analysis method in which a moderator interviews a small group of people and encourages them to exchange in-depth information and views about a particular topic. Typically involving 5 to 15 people randomly selected from a target population, focus group interviews are often used in public speaking to research audience psychographics.

forum   A session in which audience members advance questions to participants in a group discussion and particular group members, often authorities on the topic, provide answers; a forum typically follows a group presentation in which audience members were not allowed to participate.

full-content (complete-sentence) outline   An outline, written in complete sentences, that contains the title, the purpose statement, the thesis statement, all elements of the speech itself (introduction, main points, supporting materials, transitions), and the list of references. Full-content outlines are used during the early stages of speech preparation.

grammatical voice   The relationship between the subject of a sentence and the action of the verb.

graph A pictorial device used to illustrate quantitative relationships.

grounds Facts, information, or evidence used to support a claim.

hecklers Audience members who intentionally disrupt a speech event and try to make the speaker look bad by breaking in with unsolicited comments and criticisms.

high context As a cultural communication factor, the amount of information implied by the setting or conditions of a communication exchange. In high-context communication, much of the message is inherent in the setting and simply understood by the people involved. *See also* low context.

humorous style A rhetorical style in which the speaker uses humor to engage audience attention and build a positive reaction; jokes or funny stories and exaggerated nonverbal behaviors used for contrast or emphasis are common among speakers using this style.

illustrators Purposeful nonverbal gestures used to demonstrate and reinforce the meanings intended by verbal messages.

imagery The use of words and phrases that appeal to one or more of the senses.

immediacy Physical or psychological closeness conveyed through verbal behaviors such as using first names and inclusive language and nonverbal behaviors such as making eye contact, smiling, and nodding.

impression management The process of transmitting verbal and nonverbal messages that are deliberately designed to create a particular set of impressions on others.

impromptu delivery A presentation mode in which the speaker presents a speech on the spot, with little or no lead time or formal preparation.

individualism A cultural pattern or orientation in which the individual is emphasized and autonomy, independence, and individual success are valued.

inductive reasoning Drawing, formulating, or inferring a reasonable general conclusion from supporting evidence, examples, or data.

informative speech A speech whose primary purpose is to teach, impart knowledge, or change the audience's factual beliefs.

inoculation A persuasive strategy in which a speaker argues against an opposing position in front of an audience that already agrees with the speaker's position in order to ensure that the audience will not be swayed by counterarguments.

intercultural communication An exchange of messages between people of different co-cultures under conditions in which their co-cultural backgrounds influence or change the process in some way.

interjectors Audience members who engage in cue responding during a speaker's presentation.

introduction speech A brief speech in which a host or emcee provides an audience with sufficient reasons for actively listening to a particular speaker and speech topic.

jargon Technical or specialized terminology used by members of a particular group or profession.

leading questions Questions that prompt an interviewee to respond a particular way; questions can be leading because of how they are worded or because of verbal and nonverbal cues provided by the interviewer.

lecture A type of informative speech designed to provide new or additional information about a subject to audience members.

linear logic A way of organizing thoughts and ideas in which points are made in an ordered, sequential way and linkages and conclusions are explicitly stated.

line graph A diagram that shows the relationship between two quantitative variables—how one varies with respect to the other.

listening An active behavior involving the attention to and comprehension of a message communicated through words, actions, and other elements of the immediate environment.

low context As a cultural communication factor, the amount of information implied by the setting or conditions of a communication exchange. In low-context communication, the bulk of information is communicated overtly and explicitly through the spoken word. *See also* high context.

lying Deliberately concealing or falsifying information with the intent to deceive or mislead.

mainstream culture The basic culture of a society, consisting of the most common language, the basic social institutions, the material artifacts and technologies in use, and the basic values to which most people in the society subscribe.

manuscript delivery A presentation mode in which the speaker reads a speech word for word from a prepared text.

mapping A method of brainstorming in which individuals jot down ideas and note the relationships between them by visually linking ideas in a pattern resembling a spider's web.

masculine style A communication style, rooted in gender-role socialization, that emphasizes status and power and is characterized by control or aggression and the establishment of authority (or credibility) and status differences.

masculinity A cultural pattern or orientation that emphasizes a traditionally male gender orientation in which achievement, success, ambition, assertiveness, and competitiveness are valued and gender roles are clearly differentiated.

meanings Thoughts, perceptions, and feelings that people experience or create in response to cues from the outside world. Meanings are the subjective understandings that sources attempt to convey to receivers during the communication process.

media audience The large, extended audience that may be exposed to a speaker's message via television, radio, magazines, newspapers, and other electronic or print media.

melting pot policy A nineteenth- and twentieth-century U.S. policy geared toward eradicating cultural differences among people and promoting the rapid assimilation of immigrants into mainstream American culture.

memorized delivery A presentation mode in which the speaker recites a speech from memory without using notes or an outline.

message discrepancy The degree of disagreement between the audience's position on an issue and the speaker's position. High message discrepancy can result in the boomerang effect.

messages The verbal and nonverbal symbols that, when taken together, are supposed to reflect the meanings transmitted by the source. In other words, the message is what the speaker communicates in words and gestures to the audience.

message sidedness The method of presenting different positions on an issue. The three basic types include the one-sided message, in which the speaker presents his or her position only; the two-sided message, in which the speaker presents both sides; and the two-sided message with refutation, in which the speaker presents both sides but also refutes the opposing position.

metaphor A rhetorical device that creates images through the use of an implied comparison between two unlike things.

minority A social group that is regarded as distinct from the larger group of which it is a part and that is sometimes subjected to differential treatment.

minority majorities Populations of ethnic minority groups that, when combined, outnumber the Euroamerican population within a given city or region in the United States.

monotone A manner of speech delivery with unvaried pitch, rate, and volume.

Monroe's Motivated Sequence An organizational pattern for persuasive speeches developed by Alan Monroe. It includes five steps: (1) attention, (2) need, (3) satisfaction or solution, (4) visualization, and (5) action.

multiple-perspective organizational pattern A configural pattern in which an idea or problem is analyzed from a variety of different viewpoints.

narrative organizational pattern A configural pattern in which information is presented as a story, complete with characters, plots, and drama.

nomination speech A brief persuasive speech in which an individual is publicly put forward as a candidate.

nonverbal communication The deliberate or unintentional use of objects, actions, sounds, time, and space to arouse meanings in others. Nonverbal behaviors and characteristics that have the potential to communicate include posture, gestures, eye contact, facial expression, clothing, tone of voice, physical distance, and even body odors.

nonverbal immediacy Closeness that develops from the use of nonverbal behaviors such as eye contact, smiling, leaning forward, nodding, illustrators, open body movements, touch, vocal variety, and reduced distance.

nonverbal symbols Gestures, actions, objects, and sounds used to transmit meanings. Aspects of time and space may also be used as nonverbal symbols.

norm A trait or pattern of behavior regarded as typical of a particular social or cultural group; an unwritten social or cultural rule that results in such behavior.

opaque projector A projection system that casts a still image from some opaque material (like paper) onto a screen.

open questions Questions used in interviews that are open-ended and allow respondents to express themselves freely in their answers.

open style A rhetorical style in which the speaker invites audience involvement and participation through responsiveness, self-disclosure, sincerity, and affability.

oral performance of literature The presentation of some type of literature through the medium of oral performance.

panel discussion An organized, publicly moderated group discussion of a topic or problem with the goal of informing an audience.

passive listening Listening that is characterized by little or no effort on the part of the listener in attending to and comprehending the message.

passive voice A grammatical construction in which the subject of a verb is acted upon.

pause time The strategic use of silence to command audience attention.

perception The process by which individuals make sense of some aspect of reality that they have apprehended with their senses.

persuasive speech A speech whose primary purpose is to change audience opinions, attitudes, beliefs, or behaviors.

pie graph A circle divided into wedges that correspond in angle and area to the relative size of the quantities represented; also called a "circle graph" or "divided circle."

pitch How high or low a voice sounds.

plagiarism The use of someone else's words or ideas without crediting the source.

political correctness Concern for fairness and equity and respect for all U.S. co-cultures; it entails a willingness to adopt appropriate conduct when communicating with culturally diverse audiences. The phrase is sometimes given a disparaging connotation.

power distance As a cultural communication factor, the relative importance a group places on power, rank, and status. High power-distance cultures place a high value on social status, birth order, and occupational or political status. Low power-distance cultures value equality and minimize the importance of power and status differences among members.

prejudice   A biased, often negative attitude toward a group of people.

premise   A claim or statement, either true or false, that provides a reason for believing the conclusion of an argument.

presentation of self   The process by which an individual formulates and transmits verbal and nonverbal messages to others about what kind of person he or she is.

problem–no solution organizational pattern   A configural pattern in which a problem or need is identified and discussed at length and then the audience is encouraged to develop solutions.

problem–solution organizational pattern   A linear pattern in which a problem or need is identified and then one or more possible solutions are described.

process   A series of stages in which something undergoes transformation at each stage.

psychographics   Categories into which people can be grouped on the basis of their attitudes, beliefs, opinions, and level of information about a particular subject.

psychological reactance   A theory that proposes that people resist persuasive attempts when they believe their freedom of choice is being threatened.

public discussion   A public presentation in which a pre-designated group of individuals interact and exchange ideas about a particular topic while seated in front of an audience; public discussions typically take place without interruption.

public speaking   A formal, planned, and organized communication exchange in which a speaker acts as the principal source and audience members act as the principal receivers.

questionnaire   A formal audience-analysis method in which an interviewee responds to a list of prepared questions either verbally or in writing; the questions may relate to demographics, psychographics, or both.

race   A socially constructed way of grouping people on the basis of physical characteristics, such as skin color or facial features. Although there is little biological basis for conventional racial groupings, race as a social construct can be a factor in co-cultural identity.

reasoning by analogy   Making a comparison between similar cases and inferring that what is true in one case is true in the others.

reasoning by authority   Arguing that a claim is accurate because it is supported by one or more trusted experts.

reasoning by example   Drawing a conclusion or asserting a generalization based on one or more events, instances, or supporting cases.

reasoning by sign   Inferring from the occurrence of one event or sign that another event will occur.

reasoning from cause and effect   Inferring that a known fact or event (cause) will lead to a particular future result.

reasoning from effect to cause   Inferring that a known fact or event (effect) was the result of a particular fact or event (cause) that occurred earlier.

reasoning process   The process of taking a position on a topic or issue and arguing it with facts, observations, and other supporting evidence.

receiver   An individual who receives, interprets, and decodes a message transmitted by a source.

recent evidence   Evidence that is contemporary and up-to-date. Recency is one of three criteria used to determine the appropriateness of a particular piece of evidence.

redundancy   Expressing a message or idea more than once using slightly different words or a slightly different form of speech each time.

relevant evidence   Evidence that is directly associated with the topic of a speech. Relevancy is the first and most important of the three criteria used to determine the appropriateness of a particular piece of evidence.

repetition   Expressing a message or idea more than once using the same words or form of speech.

rhetorical (communication) style   The overall qualitative way a speaker communicates, using verbal and nonverbal messages.

rhetorical devices   Verbal communication strategies designed to transform an otherwise bland presentation into one that is unique and inspirational.

rhetorical questions   Questions asked for effect with no answer expected; in public speaking situations, the answer may be assumed or supplied by the speaker.

salient characteristic   A notable feature or quality of an individual that others use to construct first impressions.

selective perception   The process by which individuals choose and interpret messages in ways that conform to what they know, expect, or want.

self   The pattern of beliefs, meanings, and understandings each person has developed through communicating with others concerning her or his own nature and worth as a human being.

shyness   A general reluctance to interact socially with others, or an avoidance of such interactions, due either to fear (communication apprehension), poor communication skills, or an overall unwillingness to communicate.

signposts   Phrases that signal how a speech is organized and where a speaker is in a speech.

simile   A rhetorical device that creates images through the use of an expressed, direct comparison between two unlike things.

skills training   A method of treating communication apprehension in which a person receives training in skills through systematic coursework in public speaking.

slide   A small mounted transparency that can be used to project images onto a screen through the use of a slide projector.

small group discussion   An assembly of three to eight people who engage in face-to-face interaction around some common purpose or objective.

sociability (of a speaker)   As a dimension of speaker credibility, a judgment on the part of audience members about how friendly, warm, and congenial a speaker is.

sound argument   An argument containing premises that are accurate and that provide sufficient reasons for accepting the conclusion.

sound bite   A brief passage taken from a speech that is reprinted or taped for later news reports; when created effectively, sound bites encapsulate a speaker's key message.

source   An individual who formulates, encodes, and transmits a message to a receiver.

spatial organizational pattern   A linear pattern based on location or direction.

speaker–audience reciprocity   Successful, simultaneous adaptation and feedback by speakers and audience members.

specialized speech   A speech whose primary purpose is to meet a goal determined by an occasion or situation and which is not easily categorized as entertaining, informative, or persuasive (such as a eulogy, an award acceptance, or an introduction) and that is not easily categorized as entertaining, informative, or persuasive.

specific purpose   A concise expression of what a speaker wants to accomplish with a speech, stated in terms of what the audience should know, believe, or do after listening to the speech.

stage fright   Communication apprehension associated with a public performance or speech before a group.

stereotype   A set of fixed, oversimplified beliefs, positive or negative, about a particular group.

symposium   A public group presentation in which a series of short, preplanned, and independent speeches about some topic are delivered to an audience without interruption.

systematic desensitization (SD)   A method of treating apprehension in which a person is gradually exposed to a sequence of increasingly stressful situations and taught to associate muscle relaxation rather than tension with each one.

table   An arrangement of numbers, words, or symbols in rows and columns for the purpose of easy comparison.

thesis statement   A concise summary of the central idea, message, or argument of a speech.

toast   A special type of short tribute made at any formal or informal occasion where someone's achievement or accomplishment is being celebrated.

topical organizational pattern   A linear pattern based on natural categories or divisions in a topic.

Toulmin model of argument   Format for diagramming arguments that includes a claim, grounds for accepting the claim, and a warrant that links the grounds and the claim.

training presentation   A type of informative speech designed to teach an idea or concept or explain how to complete a task with an acceptable degree of competence. Although training presentations are similar to lectures, the term "training presentation" is normally reserved for speeches that occur in industrial or organizational environments.

trait   A relatively stable, predictable pattern of behavior that has become part of an individual's personality.

traitlike communication apprehension   A generalized avoidance of most communication situations most of the time.

transaction   A process in which two parties reciprocally influence each other; in communication, simultaneous encoding and decoding by communicators who thus act as both sources and receivers.

transitions   Phrases that link together and establish relationships between what has been said and what will be said.

transmission   The passage of messages between sources and receivers through space and time.

transparency   A clear sheet of acetate plastic used to project charts, photographs, maps, and drawings onto a screen through the use of an overhead projector.

tribute   A specialized speech that publicly acknowledges the major or long-term accomplishments of an individual or a group.

trustworthiness (of a speaker)   As a dimension of speaker credibility, a judgment on the part of audience members about a speaker's level of honesty, goodness, and decency.

value   A principle or quality that an individual deeply believes is desirable and that serves as a guideline or standard for behavior.

verbal immediacy   Closeness that results from verbal behaviors such as praise, humor, solicitation of questions and feedback, and the use of first names and first-person pronouns.

verbal symbols   Words and phrases used to transmit meanings.

visual aid   A supplemental visible device employed by a speaker to help clarify for audience members what is being communicated in a speech.

visualization A technique used to reduce anxiety and improve performance in which individuals imagine, or "see," themselves performing successfully.

warrant The explanation, justification, or underlying assumption that connects the grounds and the claim in an argument.

web organizational pattern A configural pattern in which specific ideas that extend or illuminate a core idea are examined; the focus returns to the core idea between each specific idea.

welcoming speech A brief speech to publicly greet visiting persons or groups and make them feel welcome in their new and unfamiliar environment.

word chart A visual aid consisting of text alone—words or short sentences—without any graphs or other pictorial material.

The Name/Subject Index can be found
on the textbook website at
http://custom.thomsonlearning.com/OLC/0759349398.

NAME INDEX

SUBJECT INDEX

symposiums, 323–5
systematic desensitization (SD), 62, 63, 64, 70, 336

tables, 295
tag questions, 48, 286
thesis statement, 27, 28, 136, 137, 158, 159, 161, 162, 164, 165, 166, 196, 226
threats, 13, 224, 241
time, 128, 129, 294
title, 144
toasts, 314, 315, 324
topical organizational pattern, 158
topic selection
  and audience analysis, 129, 131
  brainstorming
  and communication apprehension, 129, 131
  and cultural diversity, 103
  narrowing, 135
  purpose, 100
  sample topics, 209
  thesis statement, 27, 28, 136
  and time constraints, 128, 140
Toulmin model of argument, 233, 234, 244
training presentations, 193, 194, 195
traitlike communication apprehension, 55
traits, 55, 62, 74, 75, 84, 175, 207
transaction model of communication, 5
transitions, 154, 155, 166, 169, 180, 202, 206, 294

transmission, 5
transparencies, 300–2, 307
tributes, 21, 310, 313, 314, 316, 324
trustworthiness, 76, 79, 82, 83, 88

values, 86, 87, 88. *See also* emotions/ values
verbal communication
  accent/dialect, 75, 261, 262, 271, 277
  and audience adaptation, 103, 105, 107
  bias-free language, 90, 247, 254, 256, 257
  bloated speech, 249
  connotative meanings, 123, 124
  and English as a second language, 53, 61, 70, 156, 250, 261
  grammatical voice, 253
  humor, 260–2
  imagery, 251–4
  immediacy, 256–8, 271
  inappropriate language, 94, 118, 119, 294
  jargon, 249, 261
  profanity, 127, 257, 261, 262,
  pronunciation, 118
  rhythm, 261, 262
  simplicity, 13, 200, 261
  sound bites, 260–2
  vivid language, 253, 261
  See also communication style
verbal fillers, 48, 286

verbal immediacy, 77, 257, 258, 271, 272
verbal symbols, 5, 336
videotapes, 300, 301, 302
visual aids
  audio techniques, 300–2, 307
  charts, 294, 296–8, 300, 302
  computer-generated, 302
  display techniques, 300, 301, 307
  evaluation, 70, 75, 118, 262, 271
  graphs, 294, 295
  guidelines for, 303, 305, 307
  importance of, 293
  physical representations, 298, 307
  projection techniques, 300, 307
  tables, 294, 295–7, 300
  visual representations, 298, 299
  word charts, 298, 300, 301, 302
visualization, 68, 219, 221, 228
visual representations, 298, 299
vivid language, 253, 261
voice (grammatical), 253
voice (vocalics), 270, 272
volume, 270, 272

warrant, 57, 106, 233, 235–8, 244, 337
web organizational pattern, 161
welcoming speeches, 311, 312, 337
word charts, 298, 300, 301, 302
World Wide Web, 140, 143, 302

Yahoo!, 144, 145
Yearbooks, 142